Independent Groups *t* Test (*Continued*)

[10.5] $\quad \hat{s}_{\overline{X}_1 - \overline{X}_2} = \sqrt{\left[\dfrac{(n_1 - 1)\hat{s}_1^2 + (n_2 - 1)\hat{s}_2^2}{n_1 + n_2 - 2}\right]\left(\dfrac{1}{n_1} + \dfrac{1}{n_2}\right)}$

[10.6] $\quad \hat{s}_{\overline{X}_1 - \overline{X}_2} = \sqrt{\left(\dfrac{SS_1 + SS_2}{n_1 + n_2 - 2}\right)\left(\dfrac{1}{n_1} + \dfrac{1}{n_2}\right)}$

[10.8] $\quad t = \dfrac{(\overline{X}_1 - \overline{X}_2) - (\mu_1 - \mu_2)}{\hat{s}_{\overline{X}_1 - \overline{X}_2}}$ [10.11] $\quad \text{eta}^2 = \dfrac{SS_{\text{EXPLAINED}}}{SS_{\text{TOTAL}}}$ [10.12] $\quad \text{eta}^2 = \dfrac{t^2}{t^2 + df}$

Correlated Groups *t* Test

[11.2] $\quad \hat{s}_{\overline{D}} = \dfrac{\hat{s}_D}{\sqrt{N}}$ [11.3] $\quad t = \dfrac{\overline{D} - \mu_D}{\hat{s}_{\overline{D}}}$ [11.6] $\quad \text{eta}^2 = \dfrac{t^2}{t^2 + df}$

One-Way Between-Subjects Analysis of Variance

[12.10] $\quad F = \dfrac{MS_{\text{BETWEEN}}}{MS_{\text{WITHIN}}}$ [12.15] $\quad \text{eta}^2 = \dfrac{SS_{\text{BETWEEN}}}{SS_{\text{TOTAL}}}$

[12.16] $\quad \text{eta}^2 = \dfrac{(df_{\text{BETWEEN}})F}{(df_{\text{BETWEEN}})F + df_{\text{WITHIN}}}$ [12.17] $\quad CD = q\sqrt{\dfrac{MS_{\text{WITHIN}}}{n}}$

One-Way Repeated Measures Analysis of Variance

[13.13] $\quad F = \dfrac{MS_{\text{IV}}}{MS_{\text{ERROR}}}$ [13.14] $\quad \text{eta}^2 = \dfrac{SS_{\text{IV}}}{SS_{\text{IV}} + SS_{\text{ERROR}}}$

[13.15] $\quad \text{eta}^2 = \dfrac{(df_{\text{IV}})F}{(df_{\text{IV}})F + df_{\text{ERROR}}}$ [13.16] $\quad CD = q\sqrt{\dfrac{MS_{\text{ERROR}}}{N}}$

Chi-Square Test

[15.1] $\quad E_j = \left(\dfrac{CMF_j}{N}\right)(RMF_j)$ [15.2] $\quad \chi^2 = \sum \dfrac{(O_j - E_j)^2}{E_j}$ [15.5] $\quad V = \sqrt{\dfrac{\chi^2}{N(L - 1)}}$

Two-Way Between-Subjects Analysis of Variance

[17.19] $\quad F_A = \dfrac{MS_A}{MS_{\text{WITHIN}}}$ [17.20] $\quad F_B = \dfrac{MS_B}{MS_{\text{WITHIN}}}$ [17.21] $\quad F_{A \times B} = \dfrac{MS_{A \times B}}{MS_{\text{WITHIN}}}$

[17.22] $\quad \text{eta}_A^2 = \dfrac{SS_A}{SS_{\text{TOTAL}}}$ [17.23] $\quad \text{eta}_B^2 = \dfrac{SS_B}{SS_{\text{TOTAL}}}$ [17.24] $\quad \text{eta}_{A \times B}^2 = \dfrac{SS_{A \times B}}{SS_{\text{TOTAL}}}$

[17.25] $\quad CD = q\sqrt{\dfrac{MS_{\text{WITHIN}}}{nb}}$ [17.26] $\quad CD = q\sqrt{\dfrac{MS_{\text{WITHIN}}}{na}}$

[17.27] $\quad SS_{A \times B(k)} = \dfrac{n(\overline{X}_a + \overline{X}_d - \overline{X}_b - \overline{X}_c)^2}{4}$ [17.28] $\quad F_{A \times B(k)} = \dfrac{MS_{A \times B(k)}}{MS_{\text{WITHIN}}}$

Statistics for the Behavioral Sciences

Applications of Statistics, PSYC 214

Fifth Edition

James Jaccard | Michael A. Becker

CENGAGE
Learning™

Australia • Brazil • Japan • Korea • Mexico • Singapore • Spain • United Kingdom • United States

Statistics for the Behavioral Sciences: Applications of Statistics, PSYC 214, Fifth Edition

Statistics for the Behavioral Sciences, 5th Edition
James Jaccard | Michael A. Becker

© 2010 Cengage Learning. All rights reserved.

Executive Editors:
Maureen Staudt
Michael Stranz

Senior Project Development Manager:
Linda deStefano

Marketing Specialist:
Courtney Sheldon

Senior Production/Manufacturing Manager:
Donna M. Brown

PreMedia Manager:
Joel Brennecke

Sr. Rights Acquisition Account Manager:
Todd Osborne

Cover Image:
Getty Images*

*Unless otherwise noted, all cover images used by Custom Solutions, a part of Cengage Learning, have been supplied courtesy of Getty Images with the exception of the Earthview cover image, which has been supplied by the National Aeronautics and Space Administration (NASA).

For product information and technology assistance, contact us at
Cengage Learning Customer & Sales Support, 1-800-354-9706
For permission to use material from this text or product,
submit all requests online at cengage.com/permissions
Further permissions questions can be emailed to
permissionrequest@cengage.com

This book contains select works from existing Cengage Learning resources and was produced by Cengage Learning Custom Solutions for collegiate use. As such, those adopting and/or contributing to this work are responsible for editorial content accuracy, continuity and completeness.

Compilation © 2011 Cengage Learning

ISBN-13: 978-1-133-35842-8

ISBN-10: 1-133-35842-X

Cengage Learning
5191 Natorp Boulevard
Mason, Ohio 45040
USA

Cengage Learning is a leading provider of customized learning solutions with office locations around the globe, including Singapore, the United Kingdom, Australia, Mexico, Brazil, and Japan. Locate your local office at:
international.cengage.com/region.

Cengage Learning products are represented in Canada by Nelson Education, Ltd. For your lifelong learning solutions, visit **www.cengage.com /custom.**
Visit our corporate website at **www.cengage.com.**

Printed in the United States of America

BRIEF CONTENTS

PART 1

STATISTICAL PRELIMINARIES

CHAPTER 1

Introduction and Mathematical Preliminaries

1.1   The Study of Statistics

Behavioral science research has revealed many fascinating pieces of information about our society and everyday life. Consider the following examples:

> A majority of children born in the United States today will not grow up in the traditional nuclear family environment. Over 50% of white children and over 80% of black children will spend some time in a single-parent family before they reach the age of 18.
>
> Drunk driving is responsible for 10,000 to 15,000 deaths per year, a rate that over the period of two years roughly equals the number of Americans killed throughout a decade of fighting in Vietnam.
>
> In the context of dating and friendships, do opposites attract? Research suggests not. In general, the more similar your beliefs are to another individual's, the more you will tend to like that individual.
>
> Some theorists have suggested that exposure to violence in the media may increase aggression in children and adults, whereas others suggest that it may actually reduce aggression. Research tends to support the former position: The more media violence individuals watch as children, the more aggressive they tend to be as adults, other things being equal.
>
> Infertility in the United States is more widespread than people believe. Estimates are that as many as 20% of American couples who want to have (additional) children have difficulty doing so.
>
> Many people believe that social problems such as crime, alcoholism, suicide, and divorce are more likely to occur in large cities. However, research suggests otherwise. For example, one analysis found that an individual is more likely to become a victim of crime in the parking lot of a suburban shopping mall than in the central section of a large city. Another analysis found that cities like New York, Chicago, Houston, Detroit, and Atlanta are not among the metropolitan areas with the highest overall rates of these problems, but that Odessa (Texas), Reno (Nevada), and Lakeland (Florida) are among the 15 areas with the highest such rates in the nation.

These findings come from studies in different disciplines, but all have at least one thing in common: They all used statistics to help reach their conclusions. In fact, the conclusions would have been impossible to make with any degree of scientific validity without the benefit of statistics. The behavioral scientists who conducted the research were not statisticians. Rather, they were trained as psychologists, sociologists, health professionals, anthropologists, and economists. Nevertheless, they needed to use statistics as a tool to help them gain perspective on the particular social problems of interest to them.

It has become common for courses in statistics to be required of students who major in the behavioral sciences. Many students question why statistical training is necessary. One reason is that, consistent with the examples just mentioned, statistics is an integral part of research activity. Important questions and issues are addressed in behavioral science research, and statistics can be a valuable tool in developing answers to these questions. For the student who makes a career of conducting research, statistical analysis will prove to be a useful aid in the acquisition of knowledge.

But, in fact, many students who take statistics courses will not end up in careers that require them to play an active role in research. For example, many psychology students want to counsel others or conduct psychotherapy. They are uninterested in conducting formal psychological research. Although these students may not actually conduct research, they may still be required to read, interpret, and use research reports. These reports will usually rely on statistical analyses to draw conclusions and suggest courses of action. Knowledge of statistics is therefore important to help one understand and interpret these reports.

Research that uses statistical analysis clearly has an impact on society, both in our everyday lives and elsewhere. On television we see commercials that report research "demonstrating" that one product is more effective than another. In national magazines and newspapers, we read the results of surveys of public opinion and attitudes toward politicians. Many magazines include special sections designed to disseminate to the public at large the results of research in the physical and behavioral sciences. As our society becomes more technologically complex, greater demands are being placed on professionals to understand and use the results of research designed to solve applied problems. This generally requires a working understanding of statistical methods.

A knowledge of statistical analysis also helps to foster new and creative ways of thinking about problems. Several of our colleagues have remarked on the new insights they developed when they approached a problem from the perspective of statistical analysis. Statistical "thinking" can be a useful aid in suggesting alternative answers to questions and posing new ones. In addition, statistics helps to develop one's skills in critical thinking, both in terms of inductive and deductive inference. These skills can be applied to any area of inquiry and, hence, are extremely useful.

1.2   Research in the Behavioral Sciences

The major concern with statistics in this book is how they are used in behavioral science research. As such, it will be useful to consider briefly the research process as it is commonly used in the behavioral sciences.

Most people do not view scientific research as a process but rather as a product: Reference is made to a "body of facts" that is known about some phenomenon. However, scientific research is better characterized as an ongoing process that consists of five general steps. The first step is the formulation of a question about some phenomenon: Why do people smoke marijuana? Why do some children do better in school than others? Why do some people fail to help another person who is in need of aid? The second step is forming a **hypothesis**—a statement proposing that something is true—that addresses the question about the phenomenon. For instance, one might hypothesize that people smoke marijuana because of pressure from their peers to do so. Or one might hypothesize that children's school performance is influenced by the value placed on education in the home. The third step is conducting an investigation to test the validity of the hypothesis. In such an investigation, one makes systematic observations of individuals or groups of individuals in settings that are conducive to testing the hypothesis. The fourth step is analyzing the data collected in the investigation in order to help the researcher draw the appropriate conclusions. This is generally done with the aid of statistics. The final step is drawing these conclusions and thinking about the implications of the investigation for future research.

This characterization of the research process is somewhat oversimplified and does not do justice to the diverse ways in which scientific knowledge is gained. For example, sometimes theories and hypotheses are formed after empirical observations have been made, and then these theories are subjected to further evaluation in subsequent studies. Many investigations focus on a complex set of hypotheses rather than a simple, single hypothesis. Indeed, some of the most prominent behavioral theories have evolved from a process that is different from that just described. For example, much of the theoretical work of Sigmund Freud was based on intensive case studies that were not subject to rigorous scientific testing and feedback. Science is best characterized as an interplay between theory and data, and the exact manner in which theory and data interact to advance our information base is complex. However, it is safe to say that statistics serves as a bridge between theory and data and, as such, it is an important tool for the behavioral scientist.

Although it may seem surprising, the most exciting aspect of research for many scientists is statistical analysis. This is because it is during the act of statistical analysis that the results of one's investigative efforts first become apparent and the researcher gets a first insight into what the data are suggesting. On numerous occasions, we have had colleagues burst excitedly into our offices with a computer printout in hand, ready to discuss a fascinating result that has emerged from a statistical analysis.

The remainder of this chapter is designed to introduce you to some basic concepts that are central to statistical analysis. With this as a foundation, we turn to formal aspects of data analysis in future chapters.

1.3 Variables

Most behavioral science research is concerned with **variables.** A variable is a characteristic that takes on different values, or *levels.* For example, gender is a variable that takes on two values: male and female. The number of hours per week that someone watches violent television programs is a variable that takes on values of 1 hour, 2 hours, and so on. In contrast, a **constant** does not vary within given constraints. For instance, the value to four decimal places for the mathematical quantity π (pi) is always 3.1416. Because it takes on only one value that never changes, π is a constant. If an investigation is conducted with only women, then in the context of that investigation, gender is a constant because it takes on one and only one value (female).

Variables can differ on several dimensions. One important distinction is between *independent variables* and *dependent variables.* Suppose that an investigator who is interested in the relationship between the gender of job applicants and hiring decisions conducts an experiment in which 50 personnel managers are provided with a description of a job applicant and asked whether they would hire that applicant. The applicant is described to all 50 managers in the same way on several pertinent dimensions. The only difference is that 25 of the managers are told that the applicant is a woman and the other 25 managers are told that the applicant is a man. Each manager then indicates a hiring decision. In this experiment, the hiring decision is the **dependent variable** because it is thought to "depend on" the information about the gender of the applicant. The gender of the applicant is the **independent variable** because it is assumed to influence the dependent variable and does not "depend" on the other variable (that is, the hiring decision).

A useful tool for identifying independent and dependent variables is the phrase "the effect of _____ on _____." The variable name that fits into the first blank identifies the independent variable, and the variable name that fits into the second blank identifies the dependent variable. For example, in a study of the effect of psychological stress on blood pressure, the independent variable is the amount of psychological stress that an individual is experiencing and the dependent variable is the individual's blood pressure. Similarly, if the effect of child-rearing practices on intelligence is studied, the independent variable is the type of child-rearing practice and the dependent variable is the child's intelligence.

The term *independent variable* has assumed different meanings in various areas of the behavioral sciences. Some investigators restrict the definition of an independent variable to a variable that is explicitly manipulated in the context of an experiment (such as the information about the gender of the applicant in the hiring example). We adopt the more general definition of an independent variable as any variable that is presumed to influence a second variable (the dependent variable). According to this definition, it is not necessary for a variable to be experimentally manipulated in order for it to be an independent variable. Note that just because a researcher presumes that one variable influences another does not necessarily mean that it does. This is only a presumption made for the purpose of the investigation.

The distinction between independent and dependent variables parallels cause-and-effect thinking, with the independent variable being the cause and the dependent variable being the effect. The distinction is central to theorizing in the behavioral sciences because so many of our theories are based on cause-and-effect reasoning.

When reading research reports or evaluating statistical results, it is important to distinguish between the presumed cause and the presumed effect. Sometimes this will not be entirely clear. In fact, there will be situations in which it may be possible to logically reverse the order of the cause-and-effect relationship. For example, some theorists argue that the more violent television that people watch, the greater their aggressive tendencies will be. Could it be that the reverse is true: that aggressive tendencies lead someone to watch more violent television programs? As it turns out, statistics and clever experimental design can help us tease out these competing explanations of an association between television-viewing habits and aggression.

1.4 Measurement

A major feature of behavioral science research is **measurement**. Most empirical research involves measurement of some kind. For example, behavioral scientists who study intelligence have developed tests to measure intelligence. Organizational psychologists who study how happy people are at work have developed a variety of measures of job satisfaction. Some psychologists have even tried to measure such difficult concepts as love.

Developing valid measures of concepts can be difficult. Entire subdisciplines within psychology and sociology (called *psychometrics* and *sociometrics*, respectively) have evolved that specialize in identifying procedures for developing good measures. It is not surprising that there is some controversy about the best way to conceptualize the measurement process and the best way to develop measures. The issues are important not only because measurement is so central to scientific investigations but also because measurement increasingly underlies major decisions that affect our lives. For example, a substantial number of elementary school districts in the United States use scores on aptitude tests to place children into programs for advanced study. But are these aptitude tests really sufficiently valid that we can justify using them as a basis for providing different educational experiences to children? Some behavioral scientists argue "yes" and others argue "no."

Measurement involves translating empirical relationships between phenomena into numerical relationships. In the behavioral sciences, this usually takes the form of assigning numbers to individuals in such a way that the numbers have meaning and convey information about differences among people. For example, suppose that we measure the intelligence of 20 people using a standard IQ test. If two people are of equal intelligence, we would expect them to have identical scores (that is, numbers) on our measure of intelligence. If one person is smarter than another, then we would expect the former individual to have a higher score (that is, a higher number) on our measure.

Four Types of Measurement

Obviously, there are many ways in which differences among people can be mapped onto a number system. Therefore, there are many different types (or levels) of measurement. We now discuss the four types of measurement that are typically used in the behavioral sciences: nominal, ordinal, interval, and ratio.

Nominal measurement involves using numbers merely as labels. For example, an investigator might classify a group of people according to their religion—Catholic, Protestant, Jewish, and all others—and use the numbers 1, 2, 3, and 4 for these categories. In this case, the numbers have no special meaning; they are used merely as labels. If we wished, we could have used any other set of numbers instead (for instance, 13, 48, 7, and 101). In behavioral science research, the basic statistics of interest for variables that involve nominal measurement are frequencies (for example, how many people are Democrats, how many are Republicans, and so forth), proportions, and percentages.

A second level of measurement is **ordinal measurement**. A variable is said to be measured on an ordinal level when the categories can be *ordered* on some continuum. Suppose that a developmental psychologist is studying the effects of psychological stress during pregnancy on the growth of the fetus and uses the height of the newborn as one index of physical growth. The psychologist takes four newborns who differ in height and assigns the number 1 to the shortest infant, the number 2 to the next-shortest infant, the number 3 to the next-shortest infant, and the number 4 to the tallest infant. In this case, height is measured on an ordinal level, which allows the infants to be ordered from shortest to tallest. Thus, with ordinal measurement, the researcher classifies individuals into categories that are ordered along a dimension of interest.

Note that in the preceding example height was *not* measured in terms of feet or inches. The shortest infant had a score of 1 on the measurement scale, the next-shortest infant had a score of 2, and so on. This set of measures (that is, the rank order from shortest to tallest) exhibits ordinal characteristics. As we illustrate shortly, height can also be measured in ways where the measures have more than just ordinal characteristics.

A third level of measurement is **interval measurement**. Interval measures have all of the properties of ordinal measures but allow us to do more than order people on a dimension. They also provide information about the *magnitude* of the differences between the individuals. For example, interval measures not only tell us that one infant is taller than another but also convey a sense of how much taller one infant is than another. Stated somewhat more technically, interval measures have the property that numerically equal distances on the scale represent equal distances on the dimension that is being measured.

For example, a psychologist might study the effect of temperature on aggression. When temperature is measured in degrees Fahrenheit, the difference in room temperature between 68° and 70° is the same as the difference in room temperature between 101° and 103°. In both instances, the difference of 2° corresponds to the same absolute amount of heat in the air. If we were to add each of these 2° to the air temperature, the level of heat would increase by the identical amount on each occasion because any 2° represents the same amount of heat as any other 2°. Note that this was not true with the ordinal measure of height. It was not necessarily true that the difference in height between infants 3 and 4 was the same as the difference in height between infants 1 and 2. It was only true that infant 4 was taller than infant 3, who, in turn, was taller than infant 2, who, in turn, was taller than infant 1. It is because of this property that interval measures provide information about the magnitude of differences.

A fourth level of measurement is **ratio measurement**. Ratio measures have all of the properties of interval measures (and, hence, ordinal measures as well) but provide even more information. Specifically, ratio measures map onto the underlying dimension in such a way that ratios between the numbers represent ratios on the dimension that is being measured. For example, if we use inches to measure the underlying dimension of height, a child who is 50 inches tall is twice the height of a child who is 25 inches tall. Similarly, a child who is 60 inches tall is twice the height of a child who is 30 inches tall. Inches are a ratio-level measure of height. In contrast, a temperature of 80°F is not twice as hot as a temperature of 40°F in the sense that the amount of heat in the air at the former temperature is not twice that at the latter temperature.

We can provide an informal, intuitive appreciation of the differences between ordinal, interval, and ratio levels of measurement by examining three different ways of measuring the height of buildings. Suppose that an environmental psychologist who is interested in how people perceive the height of buildings that are taller than 100 feet measures the exact heights of all such buildings in a particular section of a city. Figure 1.1a depicts the heights of four such buildings and indicates how tall each one is. The first way of measuring the height of these buildings is to assign the number 1 to the shortest building, the number 2 to the next-shortest building, the number 3 to the next-shortest building, and the number 4 to the tallest building (see Figure 1.1b). This assignment represents ordinal measurement.

It allows us to order the buildings on the dimension of height, but it does not tell us anything about the magnitude of the heights.

A second method is to measure by how many feet each building exceeds the 100-feet criterion. In this case, we find that building D is 2 feet taller than the criterion, building B is 4 feet taller than the criterion, building C is 80 feet taller than the criterion, and building A is 104 feet taller than the criterion (see Figure 1.1c). In

FIGURE 1.1 Three Different Ways of Measuring Four Buildings

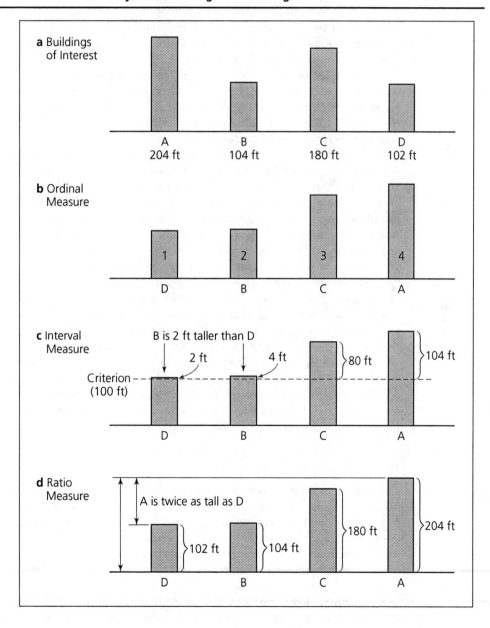

contrast to the previous (ordinal) measurement, now not only can we order the build-ings on the dimension of height but also we have information about the relative mag-nitudes of the heights: Building B is $4 - 2 = 2$ feet taller than building D, building C is $80 - 4 = 76$ feet taller than building B, and so on. We have measured height on an interval scale. Note that on this scale, even though building B has a score of 4 (that is, it is 4 feet above the criterion) and building D has a score of 2 (it is 2 feet above the criterion), it is not the case that building B is twice as tall as building D. We cannot make a ratio statement because all measurements were taken relative to an arbitrary criterion (100 feet).

Finally, we can measure each building from the ground, which is a true zero point, rather than an arbitrary criterion. Building D is 102 feet high, building B is 104 feet, building C is 180 feet, and building A is 204 feet (see Figure 1.1d). We can now state with confidence that building A is twice as tall as building D.

Care must be taken not to interpret this example too literally. For example, it is *not* the case that ordinal, interval, and ratio measures must occur on scales that are restricted to positive integers. On the contrary, all of the scale types can be used with integers that take on positive or negative values. For instance, consider the ordinal measure of building height, where the four buildings have the scores (from shortest to tallest) of 1, 2, 3, and 4. Suppose that we perform a simple transforma-tion on these scores by subtracting 3 from each one. The new scores are $-2, -1, 0,$ and 1. Notice that these four scores still preserve the ordinal characteristics of the measure: The higher the score, the taller the building. Also, although the new scores include a value of 0, this does not mean that there is a true zero point for the scores. A complete discussion of measurement properties is beyond the scope of this book, and interested readers are referred to Krantz, Luce, Suppes, and Tversky (1971).

Knowing whether a set of measures has nominal, ordinal, interval, or ratio properties is important because the level of measurement affects the way that scores can be interpreted. For example, suppose that we measure the math aptitude of a group of children on a scale that ranges from 0 to 100. One child obtains a score of 50, and another child gets a score of 90. If the measures have only ordinal properties, then we know that the second child has more math aptitude than the first child, but we do not know how much more. Maybe the true difference in math aptitudes between the two children is trivial, or maybe it is substantial. Unless the measures possess or at least approximate interval or ratio-level characteristics, their interpre-tation is restricted. Most measures in behavioral science research are nominal, ordi-nal, or interval in nature, with few being ratio level.

The Measurement Hierarchy

The four types of measurement can be thought of as a hierarchy. At the lowest level, nominal measurement allows us only to classify individuals into categories. The sec-ond level, ordinal measurement, not only allows us to classify individuals into cate-gories but also indicates the relative ordering of the categories on a dimension of interest. Interval measurement, the next level, possesses the same properties as ordinal measurement but, in addition, is sensitive to the magnitude of differences along the dimension. However, ratio statements are not possible at this level. It is only at the final level, ratio measurement, that such statements are possible. Ratio measures have all of the properties of interval measures and also permit ratio statements to be made.

Quantitative and Qualitative Measures

An important distinction can be made between nominal measurement, on the one hand, and ordinal, interval, and ratio measurements, on the other. A variable measured at one of the latter levels takes on an ordered set of values along some dimension. Scores can thus be ordered on the dimension in question depending on their values. In contrast, scores on a nominal level cannot be ordered. Rather, they merely distinguish among categories.

Variables that are measured on an ordinal, interval, or ratio level are known as **quantitative variables,** whereas variables that are measured on a nominal level are known as **qualitative variables.** Any variable can be classified as either quantitative or qualitative. As we will see later, the distinction between quantitative and qualitative variables is crucial in statistics.

Determining the Level of Measurement

Determining whether a variable is measured on a nominal level is usually straightforward in the behavioral sciences. This is not necessarily true for the other levels of measurement, however. For example, there is disagreement as to whether intelligence test scores (such as those on the Wechsler Adult Intelligence Scale) represent only an ordinal measure of intelligence or whether they represent an interval measure of intelligence. The critical question is whether test score differences of a given magnitude *always* represent equivalent differences in intellectual ability—for instance, is the difference in *intelligence* between individuals who have intelligence test scores of 110 and 120 the same as the difference in intelligence between individuals who have test scores of 90 and 100? If so, scores on the Wechsler Adult Intelligence Scale represent an interval measure. If not, they represent an ordinal measure. What is clear is that intelligence test scores do not reflect a ratio measure; there is no evidence that intelligence tests have a true zero point.

The majority of the statistical techniques that we consider in this book assume that the dependent variable is measured on a level that at least approximates interval characteristics.* This means that these variables must be measured on an ordinal level that approximates interval characteristics, on an interval level, or on a ratio level.

STUDY EXERCISE 1.1

For each of the following experiments, specify the independent and the dependent variables, indicate the level of measurement for each, and indicate whether each is quantitative or qualitative in nature. Also, identify any variables that are explicitly held constant by the experimenter.

Experiment I

Goldberg (1968) investigated gender bias among women. One hundred female college students were asked to rate an article on education in terms of its persuasiveness.

---

* See Anderson (1970) for a discussion of techniques for testing the assumptions of various measures.

Participants were assigned to one of two groups. One group of 50 women read the article and were told that it was authored by a woman named Joan McKay. The other group of 50 women read the same article but were told that it was authored by a man named John McKay. After reading the article, each woman rated it on this 7-point scale:

1	2	3	4	5	6	7
Not at all persuasive						Very persuasive

The average rating score was compared for the group that was told that author was male and the group that was told that the author was female. The results indicated that the average persuasiveness rating was higher when the article was attributed to a male rather than to a female author.

Answer   The independent variable is the gender of the author of the article. It is a nominal measure and, hence, a qualitative variable. The dependent variable is the persuasiveness rating. This constitutes at least an ordinal measure because the higher the rating, the more persuasive the article was perceived to be. Because the dependent measure has at least ordinal characteristics, it is a quantitative variable. Numerous variables have been held constant. One of the most obvious ones is that the study was conducted with only women. Also, the content of the article was held constant.

Experiment II

Research on extrasensory perception (ESP) has focused on many different topics. Recently, attention has been given to the possibility that hypnosis may be helpful in fostering ESP. One standard ESP task involves the use of special cards, known as Zener cards, that depict the following five symbols:

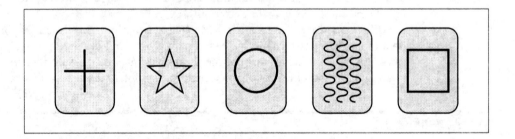

After shuffling a deck of 200 cards, a "sender" looks at the first card and thinks of the denomination of that card while the person who is being tested tries to determine what symbol the card depicts. This process is repeated for the entire deck. ESP ability is measured by the number of correct answers given by the "receiver."

Casler (1964) used this task with 100 female college students. In the first of the two conditions, 50 women were hypnotized and then given the task just described. In the second condition, a different 50 women completed the task without being hypnotized. The average number of correct answers was computed for the two groups. These averages turned out to be roughly equivalent, and it was concluded that this result was not consistent with the possibility that hypnosis affects ESP.

Answer The independent variable is whether or not the participant was hypnotized. This can be conceptualized as either a qualitative variable (the presence or absence of hypnosis) or a quantitative variable (the degree of hypnosis: none versus some). As this example illustrates, the distinction between the two types of measures is sometimes arbitrary.

The dependent variable is the number of correct answers on the 200 trials. This represents at least an ordinal measure of ESP ability and, thus, it is a quantitative variable. You might be inclined to view this measure as having ratio characteristics because it appears that there is a true zero point (that is, no correct answers) and that ratio-type statements are therefore possible (for instance, 10 correct is twice as many as 5 correct). Actually, it is unclear whether this is the case. One can conceptualize the number of correct trials as an *index* of ESP ability. However, this does not necessarily mean that 10 correct trials relative to 5 correct trials reflects *twice* as much ESP ability.

Numerous variables have been held constant. Again, one of the most obvious ones is that all of the participants were women. Try to identify some others.

This example illustrates some of the complexities involved in identifying the properties of variables and their measurement. It also underscores the fact that conceptualizations and definitions of variables are imposed by researchers, and sometimes these may differ from one person to the next.

Measures Versus Scales

Technically, the use of the word *scale* to represent the way that a variable is measured is somewhat misleading. Nominal, ordinal, interval, and ratio properties are characteristics of a set of measures, not just the scales used to generate those measures. A measure has as its referent not only a particular scale (for example, inches) but also an individual on whom the measure is taken, a time at which the measure is taken, and a setting in which the measure is taken. All of these factors must be considered when evaluating the properties of a set of measures.

We can illustrate this idea using height as an example. Consider four individuals whose heights are 54, 53, 52, and 51 inches. We can rank order these individuals from shortest to tallest. The two sets of scores are listed below, where X is used to represent height in inches and Y is used to represent the rank order:

Individual	Height, in inches (X)	Rank order of height (Y)
1	54	4
2	53	3
3	52	2
4	51	1

We typically think of rank-order measures, such as Y, as having ordinal but not interval properties. However, for this particular set of measures (that is, for these four individuals at this time and in this setting), the measures on Y have interval-level properties. More specifically, a difference of 1 unit between the Y scores of any two individuals (for example, individuals 1 and 2) corresponds to the same amount of underlying height difference as for any other two individuals who have a difference of 1 unit on Y. For this particular set of measures, Y has interval properties, even though it is measured on a scale that is traditionally thought of as yielding only ordinal-level properties (that is, a rank-order scale).

Now suppose that we add to this set a 58-inch-tall individual who receives a rank of 5:

Individual	Height, in inches (X)	Rank order of height (Y)
1	54	4
2	53	3
3	52	2
4	51	1
5	58	5

Now Y no longer exhibits interval properties. It instead represents a set of measures with only ordinal properties. This is because it is no longer true that a 1-unit difference in Y always corresponds to the same underlying height difference. When we compare individuals 1 and 2, a 1-unit difference on Y ($4 - 3 = 1$) corresponds to a $54 - 53 = 1$-inch difference on the underlying height dimension, whereas when we compare individuals 5 and 1, a 1-unit difference on Y ($5 - 4 = 1$) corresponds to a $58 - 54 = 4$-inch difference on the underlying height dimension. The point is that the concepts of nominal, ordinal, interval, and ratio properties are inherent in all facets of measurement.

Suppose that instead of adding an individual who is 58 inches tall, we add an individual who is 55.1 inches tall to the initial four individuals. This individual receives a rank score of 5, just as the 58-inch-tall individual did:

Individual	Height, in inches (X)	Rank order of height (Y)
1	54	4
2	53	3
3	52	2
4	51	1
5	55.1	5

Strictly speaking, the rank-order measure Y no longer has interval-level properties. But it very closely approximates interval-level characteristics because the difference of $55.1 - 54 = 1.1$ inches in the underlying heights between scores of 5 and 4 is almost equal to the underlying height difference between, say, scores of 2 and 1 ($52 - 51 = 1$).

As we will see in later chapters, the validity of many statistical tests assumes equal-interval measurement. However, if the approximation to interval properties is reasonable (as in the preceding example), these tests can be applied even when this is not the case. In fact, there is evidence that the approximation can, in some instances, be quite crude and still not affect the validity of the test.

1.5 Discrete and Continuous Variables

The Concept of Discrete and Continuous Variables

An important distinction that is made in statistics is between a **discrete variable** and a **continuous variable**. Often, the number of values that a variable can assume is finite. This is true both for variables that can take on a relatively small number of values (such as the number of people in one's family) and for variables that can take on a large number of values (such as the number of inhabitants of a city). Or a variable may have a finite number of values that can occur between any two points. For example, consider the number of people who visit an anxiety clinic. Only one value can occur between the values of 1 person and 3 persons (namely, 2 persons). We do not think of there being 1.5 or 2.7 persons. Variables for which only a finite number of values can occur between any two points are called discrete variables.

In contrast, continuous variables can theoretically assume an infinite number of values between any two points. Reaction time to a stimulus is an example of a continuous variable. Even between the values of 1 and 2 seconds, an infinite number of values could occur (1.001 seconds, 1.002 seconds, 1.003 seconds, and so on).

It should be emphasized that whether a variable is classified as discrete or continuous depends on the nature of the underlying theoretical dimension and not on the scale used to measure that dimension. Tests for measuring intelligence, for example, yield scores that are whole numbers (101, 102, and so on). Nevertheless, intelligence is continuous in nature because an infinite number of values can theoretically occur between any two points on the underlying dimension, even though the available assessment tools are not sensitive enough to make such fine distinctions. A similar situation exists with the measurement of time. For instance, although the measurement of reaction time can be very precise with modern equipment, there is a limit to the precision of any timer. Such limits in the precision of measurement do not make the underlying dimension discrete. Reaction time is continuous in nature.

Real Limits of a Number

If a variable is continuous, it follows that the measurements taken on that variable must be approximate. When we say that a person reacted to a stimulus in 10 seconds, we do not usually mean that the person reacted in *exactly* 10 seconds. Rather, we typically mean that the person reacted in *approximately* 10 seconds because more refined measures (for example, 10.1 seconds, 10.14 seconds, or 10.143 seconds) are always possible. When we say that the reaction took 10 seconds, we actually mean that it took somewhere between 9.5 seconds and 10.5 seconds because any value less than 9.5 would be rounded to 9 and any value greater than 10.5 would be rounded to 11. Thus, it is often inaccurate to talk about a specific value of a particular measurement for a continuous variable. Rather, such measurements are more accurately represented in terms of their **real limits**. *The real limits of a number are those points that fall one-half a measurement unit below that number and one-half a measurement unit above that number.* For instance, the real

FIGURE 1.2   **Real Limits of 10**

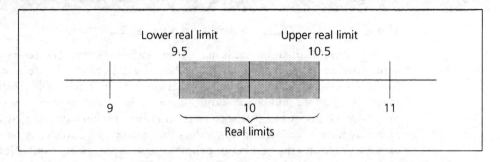

limits of the number 10 are 9.5 and 10.5. The quantity 9.5 is called the *lower real limit,* and the quantity 10.5 is called the *upper real limit.* Figure 1.2 graphically presents the concept of real limits.

Real limits can be stated for numbers that are expressed as decimals as well as for whole numbers. For example, consider the number 10.6. Because it is expressed in tenths, the unit of measurement is one-tenth, or .1. One-half a measurement unit is therefore .1/2 = .05. The lower real limit is thus 10.6 − .05 = 10.55, and the upper real limit is 10.6 + .05 = 10.65. Similarly, the lower and upper real limits of 10.63 are 10.63 − .005 = 10.625 and 10.63 + .005 = 10.635, respectively.

STUDY EXERCISE 1.2

State the real limits of the following numbers, assuming that they are measured in the units reported:

(a) 20
(b) 8.4
(c) 12.23
(d) 16.0478

Answers

(a) 19.5 and 20.5
(b) 8.35 and 8.45
(c) 12.225 and 12.235
(d) 16.04775 and 16.04785

1.6   Populations and Samples

In scientific research, we are often interested in making descriptive statements about a group of individuals, objects, or events. For example, one might state that the average number of times that adult women in the United States go to a psychologist in a given year is 2.1, that the average weight of a certain type of rock is 12.73 ounces, or that the average duration of major league baseball games is 2 hours and 43 minutes. Such statements are made with reference to a **population**. A population is the aggregate of all cases that one wishes to generalize to. In the first example, the population consists of all adult women in the United States. In the second example, the population consists of all rocks of the specified type. In the third example, the population consists of all major league baseball games during a given time span.

It is often not possible to make observations on every member of the population about which one wishes to make a descriptive statement due to the time and the expense that this would entail and the difficulty of identifying all such entities and obtaining a valid score for each. Under this circumstance, an investigator must resort to using a **sample** of the population. A sample is simply a subset of the population. Based on sample observations, it is often possible to generalize to the underlying population.

Throughout this book, we refer to various numerical indexes that are based on data from either populations or from samples. When such indexes are based on data from an entire population, they are referred to as **parameters**. When they are based on data from a sample, they are referred to as **statistics**. An easy way to remember this is that the Ps go together (*p*opulation *p*arameters), as do the Ss (*s*ample *s*tatistics).

When we select a sample in order to make a statement about a population on a given dimension (for example, the average number of children), we want to ensure that we are using a **representative sample** of the population. If the population has 60% men and 40% women, we want our sample to reflect this. We do not want a *biased* sample that will lead us to make erroneous statements about the population. Box 1.1 presents an interesting example of biased sampling as described by Darrell Huff in his book *How to Lie with Statistics* (1954).

BOX 1.1

Biased Sampling

"The average Yaleman, Class of '24," *Time* magazine noted once, commenting on something in the *New York Sun,* "makes $25,111 a year." Well, good for him! But wait a minute. What does this impressive [at the time of the report] figure mean? Is it, as it appears to be, evidence that if you send your boy to Yale, you won't have to work in your old age and neither will he? Two things about the figure stand out at first suspicious glance. It is surprisingly precise. It is quite improbably salubrious. . . .

Let us put our finger on a likely source of error, a source that can produce $25,111 as the "average income" of some men whose actual average may well be nearer half that amount. This is the sampling procedure, which is the heart of the greater part of the statistics you meet on all sorts of subjects. Its basis is simple enough, although its refinements in practice have led into all sorts of byways, some less than respectable. If you have a barrel of beans, some red and some white, there is only one way to find out exactly how many of each color you have: Count 'em. However, you can find out approximately how many are red in much easier fashion by pulling out a handful of beans and counting just those, figuring that the proportion will be the same all through the barrel. If your sample is large enough and selected properly, it will represent the whole well enough for most purposes. If it is not, it may be far less accurate than an intelligent guess and have nothing to recommend it but a spurious air of scientific precision. It is sad truth that conclusions from such samples, biased or too small or both, lie behind much of what we read or think we know.

The report on the Yale men comes from a sample. We can be pretty sure of that because reason tells us that no one can get hold of all the living members of that class of '24. There are bound to be many whose addresses are unknown twenty-five years later. And, of those whose addresses are known, many will not reply to a questionnaire, particularly a rather personal one. With some kinds of mail questionnaire, a five or ten per cent response is quite

(*Continued*)

Box 1.1 *(continued)*

high. This one should have done better than that, but nothing like one hundred per cent. So we find that the income figure is based on a sample composed of all class members whose addresses are known and who replied to the questionnaire. Is this a representative sample? That is, can this group be assumed to be equal in income to the unrepresented group, those who cannot be reached or who do not reply?

Who are the little lost sheep down in the Yale rolls as "address unknown"? Are they the big-income earners—the Wall Street men, the corporation directors, the manufacturing and utility executives? No; the addresses of the rich will not be hard to come by. Many of the most prosperous members of the class can be found through *Who's Who in America* and other reference volumes even if they have neglected to keep in touch with the alumni office. It is a good guess that the lost names are those of the men who, twenty-five years or so after becoming Yale bachelors of arts, have not fulfilled any shining promise. They are clerks, mechanics, tramps, unemployed alcoholics, barely surviving writers and artists . . . people of whom it would take half a dozen or more to add up to an income of $25,111. These men do not so often register at class reunions, if only because they cannot afford the trip.

Who are those who chucked the questionnaire into the nearest wastebasket? We cannot be so sure about these, but it is at least a fair guess that many of them are just not making enough money to brag about.

It becomes pretty clear that the sample has omitted two groups most likely to depress the average. The $25,111 figure is beginning to explain itself. If it is a true figure for anything it is one merely for that special group of the class of '24 whose addresses are known and who are willing to stand up and tell how much they earn. Even that requires an assumption that the gentlemen are telling the truth.

Source: Adapted from *How to Lie with Statistics*, by D. Huff. Copyright © 1954 W. W. Norton & Company, Inc. Adapted with permission.

One procedure for generating representative samples is **random sampling.**[*] The term *random* has a very precise meaning in scientific discourse. As applied to sampling, the essential characteristic of randomness is that every member of the population has an equal chance of being selected for the sample.

Researchers implement random sampling in a variety of ways. For instance, in order to obtain a random sample of a population, a survey researcher might make use of a *random number table*. This is simply a compilation of numbers that have been generated by a computer that has been programmed for this purpose. Computers are used to construct such tables because the typical person is not capable of generating truly random numbers. For example, a given individual might have a tendency to list mostly even numbers or those ending in 5 or 0.

The first step in obtaining a random sample using a random number table involves obtaining a list of all members of the population of interest and then arbitrarily assigning a number to each. For instance, if the population consists of 500 individuals, a list would be made of the names of these people and each name would be represented by a number from 1 to 500. The investigator would then consult a random number table, such as the one in Appendix A. Using the directions

---

[*] There are several types of random sampling. We will focus on the most basic type, known as *simple* random sampling.

provided, the investigator would draw a sample of, say, 50 individuals. The use of a random number table ensures that the selection will be random and not influenced by any unknown selection bias that the investigator may have.

It should be emphasized that random sampling is an ideal that is seldom achieved in practice. This is not surprising given the difficulty, for example, of compiling a complete listing of a population. Furthermore, the use of random sampling procedures does *not* guarantee that a sample will be representative of the population. Random sampling will tend to yield representative samples, but sometimes nonrepresentative samples will result even when random sampling is used. Nevertheless, random sampling is an important concept in statistical theory.

1.7 Descriptive and Inferential Statistics

The discipline of statistical analysis has traditionally been divided into two major subfields: descriptive statistics and inferential statistics. The two are highly related, and in some respects the distinction is arbitrary. **Descriptive statistics** involves the use of numerical indexes to describe either a sample or a population (when measurements have been taken on all members of that population).* In either case, the goal is to *describe* a group of scores in a clear and precise manner. **Inferential statistics**, in contrast, involves taking measurements on a sample and then, from these observations, drawing a conclusion about a population. In this instance, we are again attempting to describe a population. However, we do so not by taking measures on all cases in the population, but rather by selecting a sample, observing scores on the variable of interest for that sample, and then *inferring* something with respect to that variable for the entire population. As we will see, this involves the use of sample statistics to estimate population parameters.

As an example, if we were interested in characterizing the income of all adults in the United States and we were able to obtain a measure of income for every such person, we could calculate the average of the scores to find the average income. Let's say that it was $22,345. This is a descriptive statistical index that describes the average of a set of scores—the income for each adult in the United States. The value of $22,345 is referred to as a population parameter, as defined in the preceding section, because it is computed on a population.

But suppose that our resources were limited so that we could measure the income of only a random sample of 1,000 adults rather than all of them. If we calculate the average of these 1,000 scores, we might find it to be $23,453. We don't know what the average is for the entire adult population of the United States, but we do know that in the sample, the average is $23,453. If all we want to do is describe the average income for the sample of 1,000 adults without any reference to the broader population of adults in the United States, then the average value of $23,453 is descriptive in character. It describes a set of scores—in this case, the

---

* Although numerical indexes based on data from entire populations are called *parameters*, the term "descriptive *statistics*" has historically been used to encompass the description of both sample and population data.

1,000 scores in the sample. However, suppose that we want to make an inference about what the average income is in the broader population of adults in the United States. Given no other information, we might estimate the population average to be the sample average of $23,453. When we use a statistical index in this fashion—namely, to make a "guess" about a broader population——the index represents an *inferential statistic* because it is based on sample data (thus, it is a statistic rather than a parameter) that is being used as the basis for an inference.

1.8 The Concept of Probability

The concept of **probability** is an essential aspect of statistics, especially inferential statistics. For example, when making inferences about a population from a sample, statisticians frequently report probability information to convey the likelihood that the sample results do not accurately represent what is occurring in the population.

All of us are somewhat familiar with the concept of probability in our everyday life: A weather forecaster tells us that the chances of rain tomorrow are 70%. A bettor at the racetrack knows that the odds on a given horse are 3 to 1. A student thinks it is "likely" that he or she will get an A in a course.

In statistics, *probability* has a precise meaning. In a given situation, there may be several different possible outcomes that are equally likely to occur and any one of them can occur at random. If you roll a die, there are six possible outcomes: 1, 2, 3, 4, 5, and 6. If you draw a card from a standard deck of playing cards, there are 52 different possible outcomes. The probability of some event, *A*, can be defined as the ratio

$$p(A) = \frac{\text{number of observations favoring event } A}{\text{total number of possible observations}}$$

where *p* represents a probability. For instance, we can use this ratio to determine the probability of rolling a 2 on a die. On a given roll, the total number of possible observations is six (that is, 1, 2, 3, 4, 5, and 6). There is only one 2 on a die and, hence, only one possible observation favoring the outcome "2." Thus, the probability is 1/6, or .17. If one draws a card at random from a standard deck, there are 52 possible observations, of which 4 favor an ace. Thus, the probability of drawing an ace is 4/52, or .08. We elaborate on this simple portrayal of probability in Chapter 5.

A probability always ranges from 0 to 1.00. It can never be less than 0 or greater than 1.00. The probability of an impossible event is always 0. For example, the probability of rolling an 8 on a single die is 0 because the number of observations favoring the event "8" is 0. It follows that 0/6 = 0. The probability of a certain event is always 1.00. For example, if an individual rolls a die, what is the probability that he or she will roll a 1, 2, 3, 4, 5, or 6? In this case, there are six outcomes, all of which satisfy the event "1, 2, 3, 4, 5, or 6." The probability is therefore 6/6 = 1.00.

Sometimes probabilities are derived on *logical* grounds, as in the preceding examples. At other times, they are estimated *empirically* based on data. For example, a researcher might estimate the probability of a miscarriage during pregnancy based on the number of miscarriages that occur over 100,000 pregnancies that she has studied. If 20,000 miscarriages occur, the probability of a miscarriage is 20,000/100,000 = .20.

The probability of an event can also be conceptualized in terms of a "long-run" perspective. If we flip a coin ten times, it is unlikely that it will come up heads exactly five times and tails exactly five times. As we continue to flip the coin, however, then across a large number of flips (that is, over the long run), the number of heads relative to the total number of flips will approach 1/2, or .50.

1.9   Mathematical Preliminaries: A Review

The purpose of this section is to review several mathematical concepts that you will encounter in this book.

Summation Notation

Suppose that we have a measure of the number of months each of five individuals worked in the past year. The scores on this variable are as follows:

Individual	Number of months worked (X)
1	3
2	2
3	3
4	3
5	2

In statistical notation, the capital letter X is used as a general name for a variable. In this case, X stands for the variable "number of months worked." Sometimes the X has a numerical subscript to indicate that a particular individual's score is being represented. For instance, X_1 is the first individual's score on X, which in this case is 3, X_2 is the second individual's score on X, which is 2, and so on.

Suppose that we want to sum the five scores on variable X to determine the total number of months worked by the five individuals. **Summation notation** is used in statistics as a shorthand way of indicating that a set of scores should be summed. The summation operation in this instance is written as follows:

$$\sum_{i=1}^{5} X_i$$

where Σ (capital Greek S, called "sigma") is the *summation sign*, the notation below the summation sign tells us to start with individual number 1, and the number above the summation sign tells us to add through individual number 5. The X_i to the right of the summation sign is a general term that stands for the individual X scores. In this case,

$$\sum_{i=1}^{5} X_i = X_1 + X_2 + X_3 + X_4 + X_5 = 3 + 2 + 3 + 3 + 2 = 13$$

If the summation were written as

$$\sum_{i=2}^{4} X_i$$

this would mean to sum the scores of individuals 2 through 4 on variable X:

$$\sum_{i=2}^{4} X_i = X_2 + X_3 + X_4 = 2 + 3 + 3 = 8$$

Often we let the capital letter N represent the total number of cases. For instance, you might encounter this summation notation:

$$\sum_{i=1}^{N} X_i \qquad\qquad [1.1]$$

which is the same as having the number that represents the total number of scores above the summation sign. In our example, $N = 5$ because there are five individuals. Thus,

$$\sum_{i=1}^{N} X_i = \sum_{i=1}^{5} X_i = 13$$

as calculated above.

Expression 1.1 represents the simplest possible use of summation notation. Other summation expressions require that mathematical operations be applied to each score before the individual results are added together. One such expression is

$$\sum_{i=1}^{N} (X_i)^2 \qquad\qquad [1.2]$$

This means that each X score should be first squared and then summed:

$$\sum_{i=1}^{N} (X_i)^2 = (X_1)^2 + (X_2)^2 + (X_3)^2 + (X_4)^2 + (X_5)^2$$

$$= 3^2 + 2^2 + 3^2 + 3^2 + 2^2 = 35$$

A third summation expression is

$$\left(\sum_{i=1}^{N} X_i \right)^2 \qquad\qquad [1.3]$$

This is *not* the same as Expression 1.2 because the parentheses signal that the summation operation should be executed first (that is, that the X scores should be summed) and then this sum should be squared:

$$\left(\sum_{i=1}^{5} X_i \right)^2 = (X_1 + X_2 + X_3 + X_4 + X_5)^2$$

$$= (3 + 2 + 3 + 3 + 2)^2 = 169$$

In short, then, *Expression 1.2 means to sum the squared X scores, whereas Expression 1.3 means to square the summed X scores.*

This demonstrates a general rule of summation notation: *Perform any mathematical operations that are within parentheses before performing the operations outside the parentheses.* We will follow this rule with all summation expressions that we encounter in this book.

Frequently, a shorthand version of these expressions is used. For instance, Expression 1.1 may also be written as

$$\sum X$$

Note that there is no subscript for X, no notation below the summation sign, and no symbol above the summation sign. It is understood that X has an i subscript, that $i = 1$ applies below the summation sign, and that N applies above it. Thus,

$$\sum_{i=1}^{N} X_i = \sum X$$

$$\sum_{i=1}^{N} X_i^2 = \sum X^2$$

$$\left(\sum_{i=1}^{N} X_i\right)^2 = \left(\sum X\right)^2$$

We use the shorthand versions of these expressions wherever possible in this book.

We will sometimes want to simultaneously consider two variables. When this is the case, the capital letter Y can be used to represent the second variable. For instance, if we have scores for monthly income as well as for the number of months worked for the five workers from the earlier example, we can represent the scores for the two variables as follows:

Individual	Number of months worked (X)	Monthly income, in dollars (Y)
1	3	200
2	2	300
3	3	200
4	3	300
5	2	300

Of course, everything we have just said applies to variables identified as variable Y as well as to those identified as variable X. For example,

$$\sum_{i=1}^{N} Y_i = \sum_{i=1}^{5} Y_i = Y_1 + Y_2 + Y_3 + Y_4 + Y_5$$
$$= 200 + 300 + 200 + 300 + 200 = 1{,}300$$

If variables X and Y are both included in the same summation expression, the indicated operation(s) should be performed for each pair of scores. We will consider several such expressions in later chapters.

STUDY EXERCISE 1.3

Given the following values for X and Y, complete the requested operations:

Individual	X	Y
1	3	3
2	4	3
3	2	3
4	7	5

(a) ΣX (d) ΣY
(b) ΣX^2 (e) ΣY^2
(c) $\Sigma(X)^2$ (f) $(\Sigma Y)^2$

Answers

(a) $\Sigma X = 3 + 4 + 2 + 7 = 16$
(b) $\Sigma X^2 = 3^2 + 4^2 + 2^2 + 7^2 = 78$
(c) $(\Sigma X)^2 = 16^2 = 256$
(d) $\Sigma Y = 3 + 3 + 3 + 5 = 14$
(e) $\Sigma Y^2 = 3^2 + 3^2 + 3^2 + 5^2 = 52$
(f) $(\Sigma Y)^2 = 14^2 = 196$

Rounding

It is often desirable to round numbers to a certain number of decimal places. For instance, the fraction 7/3 in decimal notation is equivalent to 2 followed by a decimal point and an infinite number of 3s (that is, 2.33333 . . .). In a case like this, we have to round off.

The following commonly accepted rounding rules are adopted in this book:

1. If the remainder to the right of the decimal place that you wish to round to is greater than one-half a measurement unit, increase the last digit kept by 1.

Suppose that we wish to round to two decimal places. In this case, the unit of measurement is one-hundredth, or .01, and one-half a measurement unit is .01/2 = .005. Thus, according to this rule, 5.338 is rounded to 5.34 because the remainder after the second decimal place, .008, is greater than .005. The quantity 5.335001 is also rounded to 5.34 because .005001 is greater than .005.

2. If the remainder to the right of the decimal place that you wish to round to is less than one-half a measurement unit, leave leave the last digit kept as it is.

Thus 7/3 is represented in decimal notation as 2.33 because the remainder after the second decimal place, .00333 . . . , is less than .005. Similarly, 2.3348 is rounded to 2.33.

3. If the remainder to the right of the decimal place that you wish to round to is exactly one-half a measurement unit (that is, if it is a 5 followed by nothing or by nothing but zeros), leave the last digit kept as it is if it is an even number, but increase it by 1 if it is an odd number. *Note that when this rule is used, the last digit of the answer will always be an even number (that is, 0, 2, 4, 6, or 8).*

According to this rule, 10.345 is rounded to 10.34 because the 4 in the hundredths place is an even number, and 10.335 is also rounded to 10.34 because the 3 in the hundredths place is an odd number. The purpose of the rule is to avoid a bias in rounding up or down across a large set of numbers. With the rule, approximately half the time you will round up and half the time you will round down. An analogy can be made to buying a pound of something at the deli counter of a supermarket on a weekly basis. Given the imprecision of scales, it is unlikely that the counter person will always weigh out *exactly* the right amount. However, if she sometimes weighs out slightly more than a pound and sometimes weighs out slightly less, over the course of time you both you and the supermarket will get a fair (unbiased) exchange.

The number of decimal places that are used in reporting a statistic in a research report will differ depending on the nature of the variable that is being reported. The average annual income of a group of individuals might be rounded to the nearest whole number (for example, $10,030), whereas the average number of seconds it takes a group of rats to run a maze might be reported to two decimal places (for example, 5.32 seconds). The number of decimal places that you should report depends on how precise you need to be in order to make your point. In practice, statistics in the behavioral sciences are most commonly reported to two decimal places.

When rounding, do not forget to include ending zeros. For instance, if you are reporting numbers to two decimal places, 12/10 should be reported as 1.20, not 1.2. The key is to treat zeros as you would any other numbers; do not arbitrarily add zeros where they do not belong but make sure to include zeros where you would include nonzero values.

When computing many of the statistics that we will be discussing in this book, it will be necessary to do intermediate calculations before you arrive at a final answer. Again, the exact number of decimal places that you should use in your calculations will depend on the variable that you are studying and the nature of the calculations that are being performed. No hard-and-fast rules can be given to reduce rounding error. *Generally speaking, intermediate calculations should be taken to at least one decimal place beyond the number of decimal places that you plan to report in your final answer.* If you are performing your computations on a calculator, rounding error can be substantially reduced by keeping all digits shown until you round the final result.

In this book, calculations are generally rounded to two decimal places. For clarity of presentation, we follow this strategy even when reporting intermediate values. Your instructor will let you know if he or she wants you to use a different rounding strategy.

STUDY EXERCISE 1.4

Round the following numbers to two decimal places:

(a) 8.337
(b) 7.443
(c) 7.555001
(d) 10.54500
(e) 13.63500

Answers

(a) 8.34
(b) 7.44
(c) 7.56
(d) 10.54
(e) 13.64

1.10   Statistics and Computers

In practice, all but the simplest statistical calculations are done on the computer rather than by hand using statistical software that has been designed for this purpose. Such programs are usually identified by an acronym. The more popular statistical packages in the behavioral sciences are SPSS for Windows, BMDP, SAS, MINITAB, and STATISTICA.

There are two main advantages of doing statistical analyses on the computer. Most importantly, the use of computers frees the analyst from the tedious task of calculating (as opposed to interpreting) statistical measures. In fact, there are many statistical analyses that are so complex and time-consuming that they would be impractical to do by hand. Furthermore, computer analyses are often more precise than those done by hand because mathematical errors are eliminated and statistical programs are designed to round intermediate calculations to a large number of decimal places.

It is important to recognize that there is nothing "magical" about statistical computer programs; they perform the same computations that one would by hand. Furthermore, as with any computer software, the results that are obtained using a statistical program are only as good as the information that the user provides to the computer. Statistical software is only a tool, and if incorrect data are input to the computer, the results of a computer analysis will not accurately reflect what is going on in the original data set.

Because there are so many statistical packages and we do not know which one, if any, your Instructor will be using in your course, it is not possible for us to focus on a specific package in this book. However, where relevant, we will point out things that will help you to link statistical computer results in general to the book content. This information can be found in the "Links Between Computer Results and Book Content" sections that appear at the end of selected chapters.

1.11 The Role of Statistical Formulas

If computers can be used for statistical analyses, then why must students be taught statistical formulas? In fact, we discuss two types of formulas in this book: conceptual formulas that underscore the statistical theory behind a statistic procedure and computational formulas that are used to perform calculations. In our experience, exposure to both types of formulas is important.

Conceptual formulas are, in essence, summary statements of statistical theory, and an understanding of these formulas fosters an understanding of the underlying logic of statistics. However, as we will see, conceptual formulas are often time-consuming and unwieldy because they involve many calculations and instances of rounding, thus the need for more efficient computational formulas when undertaking hand calculations.

Although, as noted above, in practice all but the simplest statistical calculations are done on the computer rather than by hand, we feel that it is important for beginning statistics students to "get down and dirty" with data. Doing so provides a more complete picture of what is involved in statistical analysis in much the same way that a business owner will be more in tune with her company if she spends time in the plants where her products are manufactured as well as in her office. However, we recognize that instructors differ in how much emphasis they place on hand calculations. We suggest, though, that even if your course is structured such that you are not asked to perform any hand analyses, you will find it helpful to follow the computational examples in the book.

1.12 Links Between Computer Results and Book Content

The default for many statistical programs is to report results to two decimal places beyond the number of decimal places in the data. Because of the nature of some statistical indexes, these might be routinely rounded to more decimal places, however. Regardless of the default value, most programs allow users to request that results be reported to a different number of decimal places if they so desire. Of course, consistent with our recommendation in Section 1.9, the computer always rounds intermediate calculations to a large number of places to ensure the accuracy of the reported values.

1.13 Links Between Chapters

As we noted in Section 1.2, the primary purpose of this chapter is to introduce you to some basic concepts that are central to statistical analysis. Thus, it is not surprising that you will encounter the symbols, terms, and concepts from this chapter in many places throughout this book. As necessary, refer back to this chapter to review this information. Where relevant, we will point out links between current chapters and this as well as other earlier chapters in the "Links Between Chapters" sections that appear throughout this book.

Applications to the Analysis of a Social Problem Using SPSS for Windows

Throughout this book, we illustrate the concepts that we develop in the main text using a database that we have collected for analyzing unintended teenage pregnancies. This will allow you to observe firsthand how real data designed to provide insight into this important social problem are analyzed.

We begin by providing some background on the problem of teenage pregnancy. We then discuss the data from the perspective of some of the issues raised in this chapter. In later "Applications to the Analysis of a Social Problem Using SPSS for Windows" sections, we will present and discuss copies of computer printouts produced by SPSS (Statistical Package for the Social Sciences) for Windows statistical software in order to expose you to statistical output. However, consistent with our discussion in Section 1.10, we will not describe the steps that led to the creation of this output, as your instructor might choose to use a different software program in your course.

There are about 1 million teenage pregnancies each year. Among teenagers in 1995, nearly 85% of such pregnancies were unintended. About 40% of all teenage pregnancies are terminated through abortion. Given current rates, it has been estimated that approximately four out of ten girls who are now 14 will get pregnant during their teenage years.

The social and economic implications of childbirth for the teenager are well documented. Early childbirth is linked to lower levels of educational attainment and career preparation. For example, teenage mothers and fathers are less likely to ob-tain high school diplomas than are teenagers who do not have children. With decreased educational opportunities, there is a higher chance of unemployment, lower income, greater reliance on public assistance, and, ultimately, a higher incidence of living in poverty.

Furthermore, if teen mothers marry, they are more likely to separate or divorce than women who postpone childbearing until their 20s. It has been estimated that nearly 45% of women who give birth between the ages of 14 and 17 are separated or divorced within 15 years, a rate that is three times greater than for women who do not begin childbearing until age 20.

Finally, early childbirth has consequences for the subsequent development of the children of teenage mothers. For example, data from the state of New York suggest that babies born to teenage mothers are more than twice as likely to die in the first year of life than are those born to mothers over the age of 20. Similarly, teenage mothers are more likely to have babies who are premature or of low birth weight. The forces that produce this state of affairs are complex and include biological, social, and economic factors.

There have been many broad-based approaches to confronting the problem of unintended pregnancy in adolescents. One approach is sex education in the schools. A second approach is making birth control widely available to teens through the establishment and funding of community family planning clinics. A third approach is making abortion widely available to teens. All of these approaches are controversial.

We have been developing a fourth approach—namely, influencing teen behavior through their parents. Our work has focused on making parents better communicators with their teens with an eye toward preventing unintended pregnancy through more effective communication.

In general, behavioral scientists are skeptical about such an approach. Adolescence is viewed as a period when teens are rejecting their parents and are heavily influenced by peers. In addition, parents tend to have limited knowledge about birth control and sexual behavior. Despite these perceptions, we undertook a study under the premise that parents can indeed influence the behavior of their adolescent children and that this issue needs to be explored in more depth.

The analyses that we discuss in this book are based on data that were collected in the inner city of Philadelphia from a random sample of 751 14-, 15-, 16-, and 17-year-old African American youths and their mothers. Participants were asked a range of questions about general parent–teen relationships, sexual behavior, and birth control. We will provide more details about the study in later chapters. For now, let us consider several issues relevant to the material covered in this chapter.

We restricted the sampling plan to adolescents between the ages of 14 and 17. This was primarily because of cost considerations. Based on census data, we determined that a random sample would yield approximately equal numbers of male and female teens and about equal numbers of 14-, 15-, 16-, and 17-year-olds. The analysis of gender differences and age differences was central to many of our hypotheses, and if we covered a larger age range, it would be difficult to apply many of the statistical tests described in later chapters with any degree of confidence.

The strategy used to obtain the random sample was complex and somewhat different from the random sampling strategy that we described earlier. For example, it is not possible to obtain a list of all African American youths between the ages of 14 and 17 who live in the inner city of Philadelphia for the purpose of selecting a random sample using a random number table like that in Appendix A. Instead, we used a strategy called area sampling, which we describe in the "Polls and Random Samples" box in Chapter 7.

Another set of issues concerns the validity of our measures. We asked a wide range of questions, some of which are highly sensitive. For example, each teen was asked to indicate whether or not he or she had engaged in sexual intercourse and, if so, how often during the past 6 months. One issue is whether such self-reports are valid. Perhaps teens would not tell the truth when asked such questions.

To decrease the likelihood of this occurrence, we implemented the following strategies. First, all of the interviewers were trained in proper interviewing techniques, including how to be objective and nonjudgmental. Second, all interviews were completely confidential and the teens were told that their names would never be associated with their responses. Third, the teens answered the questions in writing so that they would not have to reveal their answers face-to-face to the interviewer. Also, the completed answer sheets were placed in sealed envelopes that were delivered directly to the project director. Fourth, the importance of honest responding for the scientific integrity of the project was stressed. Fifth, sensitive questions were asked only after good rapport had been established between the teen and the interviewer. Finally, we included a set of social *desirability* checks in the broader interview. These are questions that generally are not true of anyone but that might be endorsed by someone who is trying to create a good impression. For example, in the context of a larger battery of questions, teens were asked to indicate if they agreed or disagreed with the statements "I never get sad," "I never criticize other people," and "I never argue with others." If a teen consistently responded to such questions in the affirmative, this indicated that the teen was likely to distort answers to other questions in hopes of creating a favorable impression. Consequently, his or her data was treated as being suspect.

After obtaining the self-reports, we performed several validation checks on the data using community-wide statistics from hospitals on the frequency of sexually transmitted diseases and teen pregnancies. These generally supported the validity of our measures.

Summary

Scientific research can be characterized as a five-step process. The first step is forming a question about some phenomenon, the second step is forming a hypothesis (a statement proposing that something is true) that addresses the question about the phenomenon, the third step is conducting an investigation to test the validity of the hypothesis, the fourth step is analyzing the data collected in the investigation, and the final step is drawing conclusions from the data and thinking about their implications for future research.

Most hypotheses in the behavioral sciences concern relationships between variables. A variable is a characteristic that takes on different values. Variables can differ on several dimensions. One important distinction is between independent variables and dependent variables. An independent variable is any variable that is presumed to influence a second variable, which is known as the dependent variable.

The four types of measurement that are typically used in the behavioral sciences are nominal, ordinal, interval, and ratio. Nominal measurement involves using numbers merely as labels. Ordinal measurement involves classifying individuals into categories that are ordered along a dimension of interest. Interval measurement possesses the same properties as ordinal measurement but is also sensitive to the magnitude of differences along the dimension because numerically equal distances on the scale represent equal distances on the dimension that is being measured. Ratio measurement has all of the properties of interval measurement but, in addition, ratio measures map onto the underlying dimension in such a way that ratios between the numbers represent ratios on the dimension that is being measured.

Variables that are measured on an ordinal, interval, or ratio level are known as quantitative variables, whereas variables that are measured on a nominal level are known as qualitative variables. The majority of the statistical techniques that we consider in this book assume that the dependent variable is measured on a level that at least approximates interval characteristics. This means that these variables must be measured on an ordinal level that approximates interval characteristics, on an interval level, or on a ratio level.

Variables for which only a finite number of values can occur between any two points are called discrete variables. In contrast, continuous variables can theoretically assume an infinite number of values between any two points. If a variable is continuous, it follows that the measurements taken on that variable must be approximate. Thus, it is often inaccurate to talk about a specific value of a particular measurement for a continuous variable. Rather, such measurements are more accurately represented in terms of their real limits. The real limits of a number are those points that fall one-half a measurement unit below that number and one-half a measurement unit above that number.

A population is the aggregate of all cases that one wishes to generalize to, and a subset of a population is known as a sample. Numerical indexes that are based on data from an entire population are referred to as parameters and numerical indexes that are based on data from a sample are referred to as statistics. If we want to generalize from a sample to a population, the sample should be representative of the population from which it was selected. One procedure for generating representative samples is random sampling. With this technique, every member of the population has an equal chance of being selected for the sample.

Descriptive statistics involves the use of numerical indexes to describe either a sample or a population. Inferential statistics, in contrast, involves making inferences about a population from sample observations. This is accomplished by using sample statistics to estimate population parameters.

The concept of probability is an essential aspect of statistics, especially inferential statistics. A probability always ranges from 0 to 1.00. The probability of an impossible event is always 0 and the probability of a certain event is always 1.00. Probabilities can be derived on logical grounds, estimated empirically based on data, or conceptualized in terms of a "long-run" perspective.

Summation notation is used in statistics as a shorthand way of indicating that a set of scores should be summed. A general rule of summation notation is to perform any mathematical operations that are within parentheses before performing the operations outside the *parentheses*.

It is often desirable to round numbers to a certain number of decimal places, and we adopt three commonly accepted rounding rules in this book. Which rule to apply depends on whether the remainder to the right of the decimal place that you wish to round to is greater than one-half a measurement unit, less than one-half a measurement unit, or exactly one-half a measurement unit. In practice, statistics in the behavioral sciences are most commonly reported to two decimal places. When rounding, do not forget to include ending zeros. Generally speaking, intermediate calculations should be taken to at least one decimal place beyond the number of decimal places that you plan to report in your final answer.

Exercises

Answers to asterisked (*) exercises appear at the back of the book.

1. What are the five stages of the scientific research process?
*2. Identify each of the following as a variable or a constant. Explain the reasons for your choices.
   a. the number of hours in a day
   b. people's attitudes toward abortion
   c. the country of birth of presidents of the United States
   d. the value of a number divided by itself
   e. the total number of points scored in a football game
   f. the number of days in a month
*3. Identify each of the following as a qualitative or a quantitative variable:
   a. weight   d. age
   b. religion   e. gender
   c. income   f. eye color

For each of the studies described in Exercises 4–7, identify the independent and the dependent variables and indicate whether each is quantitative or qualitative in nature.

*4. Eron (1963) examined the relationship between the exposure of young children to violent television shows and the amount of aggression they exhibit toward peers by gathering information concerning the aggressive behavior and television-viewing habits of 875 third-grade children. By questioning parents about their child's viewing habits, Eron developed a 4-point scale to measure a child's preference for aggressive TV shows. The scale had the following categories: very low preference for aggressive TV shows, low preference for aggressive TV shows, moderately high preference for aggressive TV shows, and high preference for aggressive TV shows. Aggression was measured by peer ratings of each child by at least two other children. These ratings could range from 0 to 32, with higher scores indicating greater amounts of aggression.

*5. Touhey (1974) studied the relationship between various types of occupations and the prestige people associate with them. Five different occupations were studied: architect, professor, lawyer, physician, and research scientist. A large number of individuals were asked to rate each of these occupations on a 60-point scale measuring perceptions of occupational prestige. Low scores indicated low levels of prestige and higher scores indicated increasingly higher levels of prestige.

6. Steiner (1972) discussed a series of experiments that studied the relationship between group size and how quickly a group could solve problems. In one experiment, six different group sizes were created: two members, three members, four members, five members, six members, and seven members. Each group was then given a series of problems to solve, and the time until solution was measured for each group and compared.

7. Rubovits and Maehr (1973) were interested in the effect of teachers' expectancies on their behavior toward students. Female undergraduates who were enrolled in a teacher training class were asked to prepare a lesson for four seventh- and eighth-grade students. Just before meeting with the students, each teacher was told that two of the students were "gifted" and had high IQs, whereas the other two were "not gifted" and possessed average intelligence. In reality, all children were about equal in ability, and the labels were assigned in an arbitrary manner. The teachers were then observed during a 40-minute period while they interacted with the four students. Rubovits and Maehr measured the numbers of times the teacher interacted with each student. The average number of interactions were then compared for students who were labeled "gifted" versus those who were labeled "not gifted."

8. Indicate whether each measure is a nominal measure, ordinal measure, interval measure, or ratio measure. Explain the reasons for your choices.
   a. inches on a yardstick
   b. Social Security numbers
   c. dollars as a measure of income
   d. order of finish in a car race
   e. intelligence test scores

9. What is the difference between ordinal, interval, and ratio measures? Give an example of each.

*10. Indicate whether each of the following variables is discrete or continuous:
   a. grains of sand on a beach
   b. height

   c. the annual federal budget
   d. shyness

*11. State the real limits of the following numbers, assuming they are measured in the units reported:
   a. 21,384.11
   b. .689
   c. 13
   d. 13.0
   e. 13.00

12. What is the difference between a sample and a population? Give three examples of each.

*13. A newspaper conducted a survey in which readers were asked to indicate their preference for either of two mayoral candidates in an election, John Doe or Jane Smith. People were asked to cut out a ballot provided in the paper that day and send it to the newspaper with their preference indicated. One week later, the newspaper reported it received 1,000 ballots, of which 800 favored Jane Smith. It stated that the "spirit of the community lies with Jane Smith" and predicted her victory in the upcoming election. A total of 100,000 people live in the community. Is the newspaper's sample a representative sample of the community in general? Why or why not? What implication does this have for the newspaper's conclusion about the election?

14. What is the essential characteristic of random sampling?

15. Suppose you have a list of all 1,000 members of a population of interest to you numbered from 1 to 1,000. Using the random number table in Appendix A, select a random sample of 25 individuals.

*16. Repeat the random sampling process described in Exercise 15. How many of the same individuals were selected to participate in *both* samples? What does this indicate about the use of random sampling to approximate representative samples?

17. How are descriptive and inferential statistics different?

18. Compute the probability of each of the following events:
    a. drawing an ace, king, or queen from a standard deck of 52 cards
    b. throwing a 2 or a 3 on a single die
    c. for a pair of dice, rolling a combination that totals 7
    d. drawing a face card from a standard deck of 52 cards
*19. Suppose you are considering whether to have a particular type of operation. A total of 420 procedures of this nature have been performed in the past, of which 21 have been successful. Given only this information, what is the probability of success of the operation?
20. Consider the following data for eight individuals:

Individual	X	Y
1	4	5
2	1	7
3	2	3
4	8	2
5	8	1
6	2	1
7	5	4
8	7	7

Calculate the following sums:
a. ΣX
b. ΣY
c. ΣX^2
d. ΣY^2
e. $(\Sigma X)^2$
f. $(\Sigma Y)^2$

*21. Express the following statements in summation notation for $N = 5$:
a. $X_1 + X_2 + X_3 + X_4 + X_5$
b. $X_3^2 + X_4^2 + X_5^2$
c. $X_1^2 + X_2^2 + X_3^2 + X_4^2 + X_5^2$
d. $(Y_1 + Y_2 + Y_3 + Y_4 + Y_5)^2$
e. $Y_1 + Y_2 + Y_3$

*22. Round each of the following numbers to three decimal places:

a. 4.8932		h. .39572	
b. 8.9749		i. .9999	
c. 1.4153		j. 3.6666	
d. 4.1450		k. 12.2538	
e. 6.245002		l. 9.724001	
f. 2.615501		m. 1.9950	
g. 6.3155		n. 2.0050	

23. Round the numbers in Exercise 22 to two decimal places. Compare your answers with those you derived previously.

*24. Consider the following data for five individuals:

Individual	X
1	3.8753
2	4.2660
3	4.1156
4	3.4954
5	4.2061

Perform the following calculations on the given scores, keeping all digits shown until rounding the final answers to two decimal places. Then repeat the calculations, rounding the scores and all intermediate values to two decimal places. Compare the two sets of results. What accounts for the difference between them?
a. ΣX
b. $(\Sigma X)^2$
c. ΣX^2

25. Consider the following data for five individuals:

Individual	X
1	5.4749
2	4.8348
3	4.2947
4	5.3650
5	4.7749

Perform the following calculations on the given scores, keeping all digits shown until rounding the final answers to two decimal places. Then repeat the calculations, rounding the scores and all intermediate values to two decimal places. Compare the two sets of results. What accounts for the difference between them?

a. ΣX

b. $(\Sigma X)^2$

c. ΣX^2

Multiple-Choice Questions

*26. In an investigation on the effect of religious upbringing on moral development, moral development is

a. the independent variable

b. the dependent variable

c. a constant

d. none of the above

27. Which of the following is *not* a quantitative variable?

a. time

b. number of children in a family

c. religion

d. height of a child

*28. What is the upper real limit of 20?

a. 19

b. 19.5

c. 20.5

d. 21

29. Calculate ΣX^2 for the following scores: 2, 2, 3, 2.

a. 2.25

b. 9

c. 21

d. 81

30. Round 2.34577 to two decimal places.

a. 2.33

b. 2.34

c. 2.35

d. none of the above

*31. Random sampling is a procedure for generating _____ samples.

a. representative

b. nonrepresentative

c. biased

d. discrete

32. Which of the following does *not* constitute a quantitative level of measurement?

a. ordinal

b. ratio

c. nominal

d. interval

*33. The use of numerical information to describe a group of scores in a clear and precise manner is referred to as _____ statistics.

a. descriptive

b. inferential

c. summation

d. quantitative

34. $\Sigma X^2 = (\Sigma X)^2$

a. true

b. false

*35. Numerical indexes derived from population data are _____; numerical indexes derived from sample data are _____.

a. parameters; parameters

b. statistics; statistics

c. statistics; parameters

d. parameters; statistics

36. The process of _____ sampling is one in which every member of the population has an equal chance of being selected for the sample.

a. biased

b. population

c. random

d. none of the above

Frequency and Probability Distributions

Suppose that an educational psychologist asks 1,000 college students how many hours they studied during the past week or whether they are satisfied or dissatisfied with their major. Or suppose that an urban sociologist asks 800 inner-city 13-year-olds whether they have ever used drugs and, if so, how often during the past 6 months. In each of these instances, the behavioral scientist will want to convey a sense of people's responses in the research report. To do so, the statistical techniques discussed in this chapter can be of use.

2.1 Frequency Distributions for Quantitative Variables: Ungrouped Scores

Hyperactivity has been extensively studied by child psychologists. Hyperactive children have inappropriately high activity levels and have difficulty controlling their energy in structured settings. Although hyperactivity is usually first diagnosed when children attend school (because of the structured demands that school places on children and the inability of the hyperactive child to deal with that structure), many hyperactive children show signs of heightened activity, such as irregular biological functions (for instance, eating and sleeping), early in life.

Hyperactive children often do poorly in school and have difficulty forming friendships with other children. Thus, it is important to identify hyperactive children so that steps can be taken to ensure their optimal development before the hyperactivity creates a negative situation.

Suppose that an investigator administers to a class of 15 children a test designed to measure hyperactive tendencies. Scores on this test can range from 0 to 12, with higher values indicating greater activity levels and a score of 10 or higher being indicative of hyperactivity. The scores for the 15 children are as follows:

8	8	10	10	7
4	9	4	7	7
8	8	9	7	9

How can we best describe the scores on this test? One way is to list all 15 scores. By examination, we can then obtain an intuitive feel about what the scores tend to be like. But suppose that instead of 15 scores, there are 500 scores across a large number of classes. It then becomes impractical to list of all the scores individually.

A useful tool for summarizing a large set of data is a **frequency distribution**. This is a compilation of all of the score values in a set of scores and the number of times that each occurs. Frequency distributions are often presented in the form of **frequency tables**. Such tables list the scores on a variable and the number of individuals who obtained each value.

The first step in the creation of a frequency table is to list the obtained score values from highest to lowest in a column that clearly identifies the variable under study. We then derive **absolute frequencies** (commonly referred to simply as *frequencies*) by counting the number of individuals who received each score, and we indicate these frequencies next to the corresponding score values. These steps yield the following frequency table for the 15 scores in our example:

Hyperactivity	f
10	2
9	3
8	4
7	4
4	2

where f is the symbol for an absolute frequency. We can see from the frequency table that two children obtained a score of 10, three children obtained a score of 9, four children obtained a score of 8, and so on. Adding together the frequencies for all the score values, we find that there are a total of 15 cases.

If only a relatively small number of different scores are possible, researchers sometimes include all possible score values, even those that were not actually obtained, in the frequency table. When this is done, a frequency of 0 is indicated where appropriate. If we followed this approach, our frequency table would appear as follows:

Hyperactivity	f
12	0
11	0
10	2
9	3
8	4
7	4
6	0
5	0
4	2
3	0
2	0
1	0
0	0

This illustrates an important point: Unlike most of the other statistical procedures that we discuss, there are few hard-and-fast rules for presenting frequency information. Rather, several approaches are possible. The guidelines that we present here are those that we find most useful. They are, however, only guidelines and, as such, might have to be modified depending on the specific characteristics of the data.

Considered alone, an index of frequency is not easily interpreted. Suppose you are told that the results of a study showed that 200 people in a given town are prejudiced. This tells you little unless you also know the size of the town. With the information that the town population is 400, however, the frequency of 200 takes on more meaning: Half (200/400) of the town is prejudiced! This illustrates a second statistic used by researchers—**relative frequencies**.

A relative frequency indicates the *proportion* of times that a score occurred and is derived by dividing the number of scores of a given value by the total number of scores in the distribution. Thus, the formula for converting an absolute frequency to a relative frequency is

$$rf = f/N \tag{2.1}$$

where rf represents a relative frequency and N is the total number of cases. For instance, 4 of the 15 children in the hyperactivity example obtained a score of 7, so the relative frequency for this score is $4/15 = .267$. The other relative frequencies for this example are obtained in a similar fashion:

Hyperactivity	f	rf
10	2	2/15 = .133
9	3	3/15 = .200
8	4	4/15 = .267
7	4	4/15 = .267
4	2	2/15 = .133

Several aspects of this table should be noted. First, for the sake of precision, the relative frequencies are rounded to three decimal places. We will follow this strategy with all relative frequencies that we will encounter in this book. Second, the relative frequencies sum to 1.000, as is always the case for a set of relative frequencies.

Relative frequencies bear an important relationship to probabilities. Recall from Section 1.8 that the probability of an event is the ratio of the number of observations that favor that event to the total number of possible observations. For example, the probability of randomly selecting a score of 7 from the 15 hyperactivity scores is $4/15 = .267$. Note that this is the same value as was obtained above for the relative frequency for a score of 7. In fact, the probability of randomly selecting a score from a distribution of scores will always be equal to the relative frequency for that score.

When a relative frequency is multiplied by 100, it reflects the **percentage** of times that the score occurred. In our example, 13.3% of the children obtained a score of 10, 20.0% obtained a score of 9, and so on. As shown in the following table, percentages are indicated in a frequency distribution by the symbol %.

In addition to frequencies, relative frequencies, and percentages, we sometimes want to compute **cumulative frequencies** (symbolized as cf) and **cumulative relative frequencies** (symbolized as crf). For the hyperactivity example, these values are as follows:

Hyperactivity	f	rf	%	cf	crf
10	2	.133	13.3	15	1.000
9	3	.200	20.0	13	.867
8	4	.267	26.7	10	.667
7	4	.267	26.7	6	.400
4	2	.133	13.3	2	.133

The entries in the cumulative frequency column are obtained by successive addition of the entries in the frequency column. For any given score (for example, 7), the cumulative frequency is the frequency associated with that score (for the score of 7, the frequency is 4) plus the sum of all frequencies below that score. For the score of 7, the cumulative frequency is $4 + 2 = 6$. For the score of 9, the cumulative frequency is $3 + 4 + 4 + 2 = 13$. Cumulative relative frequencies are computed in the same manner but use the column of relative frequencies instead of the column of frequencies. For the score of 7, the cumulative relative frequency is $.267 + .133 = .400$. For the score of 9, the cumulative relative frequency is $.200 + .267 + .267 + .133 = .867$.

The advantage of cumulative frequencies is that they allow us to tell at a glance the number of scores that are equal to or less than a given score value. We can readily see that 10 children obtained scores of 8 or lower and that 13 children obtained scores of 9 or lower. Looking at the cumulative relative frequency column, we see that the proportion of children who obtained scores of 8 or lower is .667 and that the proportion of children who obtained scores of 9 or lower is .867. If we wished, we could also compute **cumulative percentages** to indicate the percentage of children who obtained scores equal to or lower than a given score value.

When we are dealing with a continuous variable such as hyperactive tendencies, frequencies and relative frequencies should be thought of in terms of the real limits of the scores. In the present example, although 4 children obtained a score of 8, this is more properly conceptualized as 4 individuals having scores that are between 7.5 and 8.5. Similarly, cumulative frequencies and cumulative relative frequencies are conceptualized with respect to the upper real limit of a score. For instance, the cumulative frequency for a hyperactivity score of 8 is 10 in our example. Technically, this means that 10 individuals obtained scores of 8.5 or lower. For discrete variables, the concept of real limits is not applicable.

STUDY EXERCISE 2.1

Construct a frequency table that contains frequencies, relative frequencies, percentages, cumulative frequencies, and cumulative relative frequencies for the following set of test scores:

87	75	87	83	93
72	77	70	91	90
91	83	74	75	74
75	87	91	75	83

Answer

Score	f	rf	%	cf	crf
93	1	.050	5.0	20	1.000
91	3	.150	15.0	19	.950
90	1	.050	5.0	16	.800
87	3	.150	15.0	15	.750
83	3	.150	15.0	12	.600
77	1	.050	5.0	9	.450
75	4	.200	20.0	8	.400
74	2	.100	10.0	4	.200
72	1	.050	5.0	2	.100
70	1	.050	5.0	1	.050

2.2   Frequency Distributions for Quantitative Variables: Grouped Scores

The preceding analysis of frequency distributions examined the case in which a quantitative variable took on relatively few different values: 10, 9, 8, 7, and 4. Often, however, a quantitative variable takes on many different values. For example, suppose that an educational psychologist who is interested in describing the income of teachers in a large city obtains a random sample of 100 teachers and finds that each has a different annual salary. It would be neither practical nor informative to construct a frequency table by listing 100 different values, each with a frequency of 1. Rather, the psychologist would want to group the data into intervals, perhaps as follows:

Income ($)	f	rf	%	cf	crf
40,000–44,999	14	.140	14.0	100	1.000
35,000–39,999	21	.210	21.0	86	.860
30,000–34,999	30	.300	30.0	65	.650
25,000–29,999	19	.190	19.0	35	.350
20,000–24,999	16	.160	16.0	16	.160

Because the scores are grouped together in intervals, tables of this type are referred to as **grouped frequency tables**. Note that as with the *ungrouped* frequency tables that we discussed in Section 2.1, the scores in the preceding table are listed from high to low. Also note that the lower bound for each group of scores appears on the left and the upper bound appears on the right.

An important consideration in presenting grouped data is how to form the groups. Three questions are central: (1) How many groups should be reported? (2) What should the interval size be for each group? (3) What should be the beginning value for the lowest interval? No standard rules govern these issues. In large part, the nature of the grouping will depend on the particular characteristics of the data. Nevertheless, useful guidelines are available for each question.

Number of Groups

In deciding how many groups to report, a researcher must strike a balance between having so many groups that the data are incomprehensible and having so few groups that the table is imprecise. The problem of too many groups would occur in its extreme in the income example if each of the 100 incomes were listed individually. The problem of too few groups is illustrated in the following table, which reports the scores of 65 individuals who completed a measure of how satisfied they are with their jobs. Scores on this measure can range from 0 to 100, with higher values indicating greater satisfaction.

Job satisfaction	f	rf	%	cf	crf
50–100	57	.877	87.7	65	1.000
0–49	8	.123	12.3	8	.123

This table is not very informative; it provides little insight into how the individuals differ in their job satisfaction. Too many of the individuals are grouped into a single category, and we simply do not have much appreciation for how they differ in their job satisfaction.

In general, if the number of possible score values is small, fewer groups can be used, whereas if the number of possible score values is large, more groups are required. Generally speaking, the use of 5 to 15 groups tends to strike the appropriate balance between imprecision and incomprehensibility in most instances.

Size of the Interval

Once we have an idea of how many groups we wish to present, the question of the size of the interval arises (for example, should the interval for the income problem be $10,000, $5,000, or $1,000?). Typically, an interval size of 2, 3, or a multiple of 5 (for instance, 5, 10, or 15) is used. The first step in determining the appropriate interval size for a particular set of data is to subtract the lowest score from the highest score. This difference should then be divided by the desired number of groups and the result rounded to the nearest of the commonly used interval-size values.

In the job satisfaction example, suppose that the lowest obtained score is 47 and the highest obtained score is 99. Further suppose that the decision is made to present the frequency analysis using five groups. In this case, $99 - 47 = 52$ and $52/5 = 10.40$. Because 10 is a multiple of 5, we drop the .40 and use 10 as the interval size.

Beginning of the Lowest Interval

We now know that we will report five groups with an interval of 10 units per group. The final question is where to begin the lowest interval (at 40? at 45? at 47?). The conventional starting point is the closest number that is evenly divisible by the interval size that is equal to or less than the lowest score. In our example, the lowest score is 47 and the interval size is 10. The closest number that is equal to or less than 47 that is evenly divisible by 10 is 40. This should be the starting point for the lowest interval.

The frequency table using the above guidelines appears as follows:

Job satisfaction	f	rf	%	cf	crf
90–99	3	.046	4.6	65	1.000
80–89	6	.092	9.2	62	.954
70–79	15	.231	23.1	56	.862
60–69	21	.323	32.3	41	.631
50–59	12	.185	18.5	20	.308
40–49	8	.123	12.3	8	.123

Note that the lower bound of each interval is a multiple of the interval size of 10. Also note that it is necessary to use six groups instead of five because of the interval size and the starting point that were identified based on the guidelines. Again, these guidelines are only suggestions that might be useful in presenting grouped data.

STUDY EXERCISE 2.2

Construct a grouped frequency table that contains frequencies, relative frequencies, percentages, cumulative frequencies, and cumulative relative frequencies by grouping the following self-esteem scores into ten groups:

9	29	39	5	34	43	39	26	22	4
29	14	28	22	15	26	25	44	24	16
36	8	39	16	21	7	24	17	23	21
15	24	49	23	35	44	19	25	45	34
37	13	27	6	11	49	17	31	27	14
12	6	31	46	32	28	5	42	28	35
38	48	9	38	2	20	33	43	3	13
19	19	26	4	19	41	32	12	18	36
37	2	18	49	29	1	27	3	42	21
47	25	1	39	11	41	23	33	22	46

Answer   The first step is to determine the interval size. The highest score is 49 and the lowest is 1. The difference between these values is $49 - 1 = 48$. Because 48 divided by 10, the number of groups, is 4.80, we define the interval size as 5. The next step is to determine the beginning of the lowest interval. The lowest score is 1. The closest number that is equal to or less than 1 that is evenly divisible by 5 is 0. This will be the starting point for the lowest interval. The frequency table appears as follows:

Self-esteem	f	rf	%	cf	crf
45–49	8	.080	8.0	100	1.000
40–44	8	.080	8.0	92	.920
35–39	12	.120	12.0	84	.840
30–34	8	.080	8.0	72	.720
25–29	15	.150	15.0	64	.640
20–24	13	.130	13.0	49	.490
15–19	12	.120	12.0	36	.360
10–14	8	.080	8.0	24	.240
5–9	8	.080	8.0	16	.160
0–4	8	.080	8.0	8	.080

2.3   Frequency Distributions for Qualitative Variables

Frequency tables for qualitative variables begin with a listing of the variable categories in the first column. This is followed by frequency, relative frequency, and/or percentage columns. The concepts of cumulative frequencies, cumulative relative frequencies, and cumulative percentages are not applicable because the "scores" for qualitative variables are not ordered on any dimension.

As an example of a frequency table for a qualitative variable, consider the following distribution of religious affiliations in a random sample of American citizens:

Religion	f	rf	%
Protestant	590	.590	59.0
Catholic	270	.270	27.0
Jewish	19	.019	1.9
Muslim	9	.009	.9
Eastern Orthodox	9	.009	.9
Other	31	.031	3.1
None	72	.072	7.2

The variable categories are "Protestant," "Catholic," "Jewish," "Muslim," "Eastern Orthodox," "Other," and "None." Adding up the individual frequencies, we find that $N = 1,000$. We also see that the majority of the respondents are either Catholic or Protestant, with Protestant individuals outnumbering Catholic individuals by more than 2 to 1.

2.4   Outliers

Thus far, we have used frequency tables to convey information about a set of scores. Another use of frequency analyses is to identify **outliers**. An outlier is a score that is very extreme relative to the majority of the scores in the data set—so extreme that the score is suspect. Consider the following frequency table for the number of times that college students engage in sexual intercourse during the first 3 months that they are at college:

Incidence of intercourse	f
48	1
5	2
4	3
3	3
2	5
1	10
0	135

The score of 48 is unusually high relative to the other scores. When an outlier occurs, it is important to determine why. Sometimes it may just be a clerical error, as would be the case if a researcher incorrectly calculated or incorrectly copied a person's score from a psychological test or a set of attitude measures.

Alternatively, it may be that the person who gave the response is unique relative to the other people in the study. For example, the individual who indicated 48 instances of sexual intercourse may be an older, married student who is returning to college after many years away from school. In this case, the researcher might decide to exclude the outlying score of 48 from any additional statistical analyses, in which case it is imperative that the research report explicitly state this. When outlying scores are excluded from an analysis, the results of that analysis will apply only to a population that explicitly excludes individuals with the types of unusually low and/or unusually high scores that were excluded. We discuss issues related to outliers further in Chapter 5.

2.5   Frequency Graphs

Frequency Graphs for Quantitative Variables

Because graphs can be easier to follow than tables, investigators sometimes report their data graphically. Generally speaking, a graph should "stand alone" so that anyone who looks at it can readily interpret it. The guidelines that we present here are intended to accomplish this.

Consider the frequencies for the hyperactivity scores from Section 2.1:

Hyperactivity	f
10	2
9	3
8	4
7	4
4	2

These data can also be presented in the form of a **frequency histogram,** such as the one depicted in Figure 2.1. The horizontal dimension of this graph is referred to as

FIGURE 2.1   **Frequency Histogram**

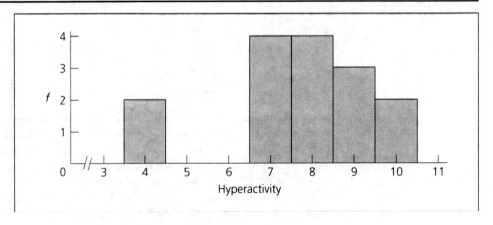

the *X axis* or as the **abscissa,** and the vertical dimension is referred to as the *Y axis* or as the **ordinate.**

The abscissa lists the score values from low to high, extending from 1 unit below the lowest score to 1 unit above the highest score, that is, from 3 to 11. A label that clearly identifies the variable under study is centered beneath the score values.

The ordinate lists frequency values from 0 to the highest frequency that was observed in the study (4). As is the case with a frequency table, the fact that the ordinate represents absolute frequencies is indicated by the symbol *f*, which should be centered to the left of the frequency scores.

The frequency associated with each score value is indicated by a bar that extends to that point on the ordinate. For instance, the bar for a hyperactivity score of 4 goes up 2 units, indicating that two individuals obtained a score of 4; the bar for a hyperactivity score of 7 goes up 4 units, indicating that four individuals obtained a score of 7; and so forth.

If a variable is continuous, the vertical boundaries of the bar for a score represent the real limits of that score. Consider the bar for a score of 4. The leftmost boundary of the bar represents the lower real limit, 3.5, and the rightmost boundary of the bar represents the upper real limit, 4.5. The center of the bar corresponds to the midpoint of the real limits 3.5 to 4.5, or 4. Notice also that the abscissa is broken by a double slash. This should be included anytime the abscissa "jumps" from 0 to a larger number such that it is not drawn to scale. The same principle holds for the ordinate.

A **frequency polygon** is similar to a frequency histogram except that bars are not used to indicate the frequencies associated with the score values. Rather, solid dots that correspond to the appropriate frequencies are placed directly above the score values. The dots are then connected with lines. Frequency polygons are always "closed" with the abscissa in the sense that the abscissa always includes a value that is a unit lower than the lowest observed score and a value that is a unit higher than the highest observed score, with a frequency of 0 denoted for each. This serves to connect the lines to the abscissa and, thus, to form the polygon.

The frequency polygon in Figure 2.2 demonstrates these points as they relate to the hyperactivity data. The similarity of this graph to the frequency histogram in Figure 2.1 can be seen in Figure 2.3, where they are superimposed on one another.

There are no specific rules for when a frequency histogram as opposed to a frequency polygon should be used. Frequency polygons are typically utilized when the variables being reported are continuous in nature, whereas frequency histograms are typically utilized when the variables being reported are discrete. The major reason is that, from a visual perspective, the frequency polygon tends to highlight the "shape" of the entire distribution more than the frequency histogram does. The frequency histogram, in contrast, tends to highlight the frequency of specific scores rather than the entire distribution. The use of a frequency polygon for a continuous variable is thus more consistent with the notion of illustrating a continuum.

A graph that is closely related to the frequency polygon is the **line plot.** A line plot is constructed exactly like a frequency polygon except that it is not "closed."

FIGURE 2.2   **Frequency Polygon**

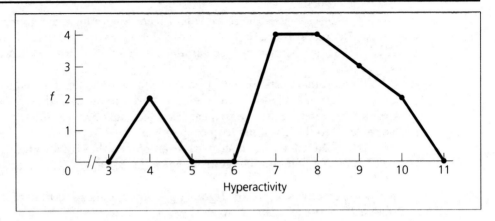

Rather, the left- and rightmost points of the line end at the lowest and the highest obtained score values, respectively. Figure 2.4 presents a line plot for the hyperactivity data.

Line plots are particularly useful when one or more research participants receive the lowest or the highest score possible on a particular measure. For instance, one or more children could have obtained the maximum score of 12 on the hyperactivity test. If this were the case, it would not be meaningful to indicate that a score of 13 occurred with a frequency of 0 because 13 is not a valid score on the hyperactivity measure. Thus, it would not make sense to create a frequency polygon by closing the graph with the abscissa at the upper end. In this case, one might use a line plot instead of a frequency polygon. This would also be true if one or more children obtained the minimum score of 0.

FIGURE 2.3   **Frequency Histogram and Frequency Polygon Superimposed**

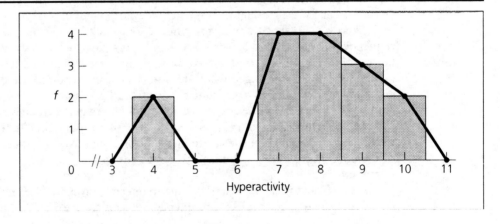

FIGURE 2.4   **Line Plot**

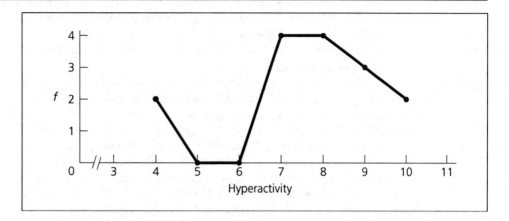

Frequency polygons and line plots are useful when one wants to compare distributions for two or more groups of individuals. Consider data for a group of 115 14-year-olds and an equal-sized group of 17-year-olds who are asked to indicate how satisfied they are with their relationship with their mother on a 1 (*very dissatisfied*) to 5 (*very satisfied*) scale that also includes the response options *moderately dissatisfied, neither satisfied nor dissatisfied*, and *moderately satisfied*. Figure 2.5 represents separate line plots for the samples of 14-year-olds and 17-year-olds on the same graph. A legend in the body of the graph identifies the line for each age

FIGURE 2.5   **Line Plot with Two Groups**

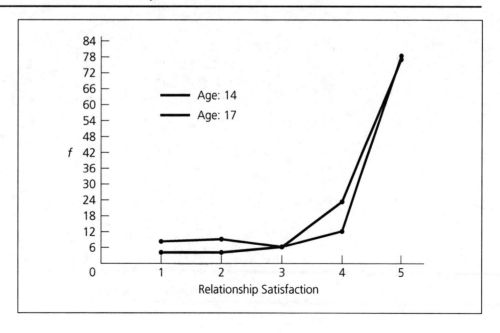

group. The distributions are similar in that the majority of teens are very satisfied with their relationship with their mothers. However, more 17-year-olds are very or moderately dissatisfied with their relationship with their mothers (scores of 1 or 2) and more 14-year-olds are moderately satisfied with their relationship (scores of 4). In later chapters in this book, we discuss ways to examine these differences more formally using inferential statistics.

It is also possible to construct frequency histograms for multiple groups. As an example, the data from Figure 2.5 are regraphed in histogram form in Figure 2.6. In this figure, the bars for the two groups are presented side by side, but with different color "fills" used to distinguish them from one another. Different patterns may also be used. A legend in the body of the graph identifies the groups.

Frequency histograms and frequency polygons can be constructed for grouped as well as ungrouped scores. When the scores are grouped, the abscissa might list the midpoints of the score intervals rather than the individual score values. Alternatively, the score intervals may be presented. The procedure for indicating the frequency associated with each interval then parallels that for ungrouped scores.

An example of a grouped frequency histogram is presented in Figure 2.7. This histogram presents the number of live births that were reported by the 4,040,958 women who participated in a 1989 national survey of fertility behavior. It is meaningful to break this down by age groups because a substantial body of research indicates that children born to both very young (as in the case of adolescents) and to older mothers are at increased risk for a number of physical and developmental problems. Note that eight intervals are represented in this graph and that the interval size is 5. It can be seen that more women in the 25 to 29 age group gave birth

FIGURE 2.6   Histogram with Two Groups

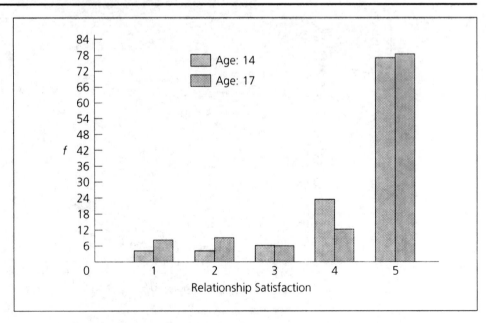

FIGURE 2.7   **Frequency Histogram of Grouped Data**

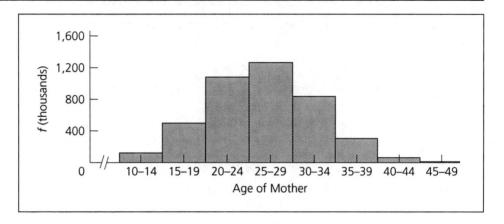

than did any other group. Also of note is the fact that relatively few women gave birth when they were age 40 or older.

Another useful technique for graphing the frequencies of quantitative variables is a **stem and leaf plot**. For instance, suppose that 50 first-year college students are asked to estimate what their scores would be on an intelligence test. They are told that the average score for first-year college students is 100 and that about two-thirds of these students score between 90 and 110. They are also shown a frequency distribution of the scores of 1,000 first-year students from the previous year. This distribution shows that the most frequently occurring score is 100 and that very few students (only about 5%) scored 115 or above. Using this information as a reference point, the 50 students estimate the following scores for themselves:

95	95	100	100	100	100	100	105	105	105
110	110	110	110	110	110	110	110	110	115
115	115	115	115	115	115	115	115	115	115
120	120	120	120	120	120	120	120	125	125
125	125	130	130	130	130	135	135	140	140

A stem and leaf plot of these scores appears in Figure 2.8a. The digits that represent the numbers of "hundreds" and "tens" (for example, the 10 from 105, the 11 from 110, and the 12 from 120) are listed at the far left and are separated from the rest of the table by a vertical line. Those two digits constitute the base, or the "stem," of the stem and leaf plot. The digits that represent the number of "ones" for each base value (for example, the 0 from 130 representing zero "ones" and the 5 from 135 representing five "ones") are listed to the right of the line, one for each score within that group. These digits are the "leaves." Stem and leaf plots are useful as long as the number of scores is not too large and the number of values of the base is more than 1 or but less than 20.

Stem and leaf plots provide a compact way of conveying both individual scores and the general "shape" of a frequency distribution. More specifically, a stem

FIGURE 2.8   **Estimated Intelligence Data Dispalyed in (a) a Stem and Leaf Plot, (b) a Frequency Histogram, and (c) a Rotated Stem and Leaf Plot**

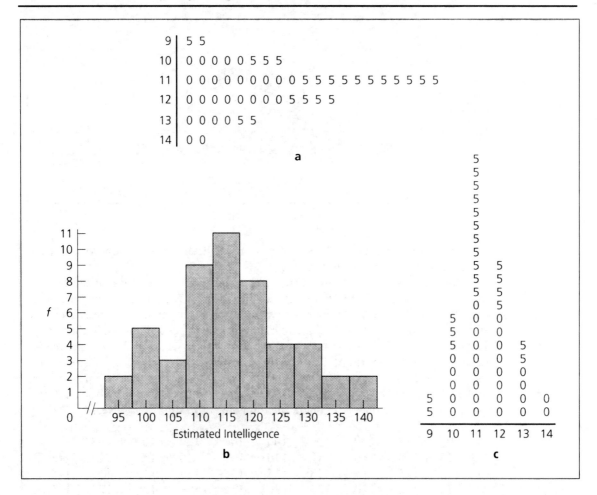

and leaf plot is somewhat like a frequency histogram turned on its side. To illustrate this, Figure 2.8b presents a traditional frequency histogram for the estimated intelligence test scores and Figure 2.8c presents the stem and leaf plot from Figure 2.8a rotated so that the "hundreds" and the "tens" digits appear at the base rather than on the left and the "ones" digits are displayed vertically rather than horizontally. Note the similarity in the relative heights of the columns in the histogram and the rotated stem and leaf plot.

Even though the average intelligence score for first-year students was presented to these students as being 100, most of them felt that they would score well above 100 on the intelligence test. The most frequently estimated intelligence score was 115, which is very high given that they had been informed that only about 5% of last year's first-year students had scores of 115 or above. Apparently, these students have a high opinion of their intellect!

FIGURE 2.9   **Bar Graph**

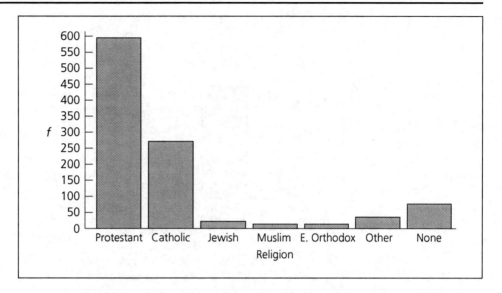

There are many other types of frequency graphs besides those that we describe here. These include pie charts and three-dimensional histograms. Interested readers are referred to Fox and Long (1990).

Frequency Graphs for Qualitative Variables

So far, we have discussed strategies for graphing frequency data for quantitative variables. Frequency graphs can also be constructed for qualitative variables. For instance, Figure 2.9 depicts a **bar graph** of the religious affiliation data from Section 2.3. The basic principles in constructing this graph are the same as those for a frequency histogram except that the bars do not touch one another because each bar in a bar graph represents a distinct category. As before, the values of the variable are listed on the abscissa and the frequencies are listed on the ordinate.

2.6   Misleading Graphs

The presentation of data in graphic form can be highly informative, but it can also be misleading. Consider a consumer psychologist who interviews 100 people to determine their preference for two products, which we will refer to as product A and product B. Suppose that 45 prefer product A over product B and that 55 prefer product B over product A. This information can be depicted graphically as in either of the two frequency histograms in Figure 2.10.

The two graphs make the preferences for the two products appear different, even though they display the identical data. In Figure 2.10b, the difference between the number of people who prefer product B and the number who prefer product A

FIGURE 2.10   **Examples of (a) Properly Formatted and (b) Potentially Misleading Graphs**

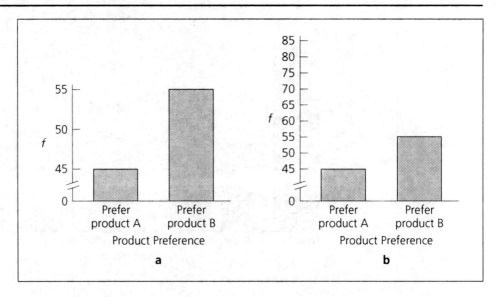

appears smaller than that in Figure 2.10a because the demarcations for the frequencies are closer together. As a result, even though the ordinate for Figure 2.10b is taller than that for Figure 2.10a, a much smaller portion of the ordinate in Figure 2.10b is actually used to represent the observed frequencies.

Because frequency graphs can be misleading depending on how the abscissa and the ordinate are formatted, the ordinate should be drawn such that its height at the demarcation for the highest frequency is approximately two-thirds to three-fourths the length of the abscissa.* In addition, as we discussed earlier, the ordinate should start with a frequency of 0 and end at the highest frequency that was observed in the study, with "jumps" to a larger number indicated by a break in the form of a double slash if the ordinate is not drawn to scale. Also, the demarcation units for the ordinate should be evenly spaced along its length. These guidelines ensure a uniform, clearly interpretable presentation of graphed results.

All of the guidelines are followed in Figure 2.10a, but not in Figure 2.10b. This explains why Figure 2.10b makes it appear that product B is less preferred over product A than it actually is. Can you identify two ways that Figure 2.10b violates the format guidelines?

2.7 Graphs of Relative Frequencies, Percentages, Cumulative Frequencies, and Cumulative Relative Frequencies

Relative frequencies can also be depicted in graph form. For instance, a polygon of the relative frequencies for the hyperactivity data from Section 2.1 appears in Figure 2.11. Notice that the ordinate is labeled *rf* and demarcated with relative frequency values. Also notice that the shape of the polygon is identical to the shape

---

* Due to space considerations, this guideline is not always followed in this book.

FIGURE 2.11   **Graph of Relative Frequencies**

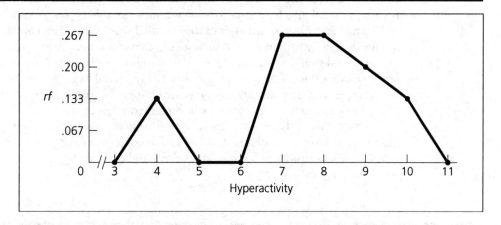

of the frequency polygon in Figure 2.2. Similarly, a relative frequency histogram for these data would take the identical shape as the frequency histogram in Figure 2.1. This should not be surprising, because the relative frequencies for a data set are proportional to the absolute frequencies. Specifically, as we discussed in Section 2.1, a relative frequency is equal to the corresponding absolute frequency divided by N. It follows that graphs of percentages will also take the identical shape as the corresponding frequency graphs. However, the ordinate will be labeled % and demarcated with percentage values.

It is also possible to represent cumulative frequency information graphically. This has been done in Figure 2.12 for the hyperactivity example. The ordinate is labeled cf and demarcated with cumulative frequency values. Solid dots representing the

FIGURE 2.12   **Graph of Cumulative Frequencies**

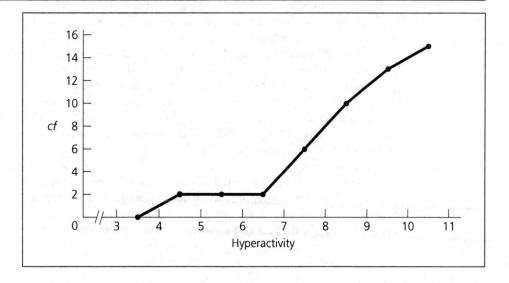

cumulative frequencies are placed above the upper real limit of each score value because a cumulative frequency for a continuous variable encompasses all scores up to and including the upper real limit of the specified score value. This contrasts with placing the dots directly above the score values in frequency and relative frequency graphs.

An additional aspect of Figure 2.12 should also be noted: Because the cumulative frequency for a given score value is always equal to or greater than the cumulative frequency for the preceding score value, the cumulative frequency curve always remains level or increases as it moves from left to right.

Cumulative relative frequencies can also be represented in graph form. Such a graph would take the identical shape as the corresponding cumulative frequency graph, but its ordinate would be labeled *crf* and demarcated with cumulative relative frequency values.

2.8   Probability Distributions

In Section 2.1, we noted that the probability of randomly selecting a score from a distribution of scores will always be equal to the relative frequency for that score. However, there is an important conceptual difference between probabilities and relative frequencies: *Whereas a relative frequency indicates the proportion of times that some score was previously observed, a probability represents the likelihood of observing that score in the future.* This distinction should be kept in mind as you read the following discussion.

Probability Distributions for Qualitative Variables and Discrete Quantitative Variables

Consider the case of a qualitative variable, gender, that takes on two values: male and female. If we have a population of 150 women and 50 men, the relative frequency for women is 150/200 = .75 and that for men is 50/200 = .25. Therefore, the probability of randomly selecting a woman from this population is .75, and the probability of randomly selecting a man is .25.

When the values for a qualitative variable are such that a person can have one and only one score (for example, it is impossible for the person to be both male and female—he or she must be one or the other), the score values are said to be *mutually exclusive.* When the values are also *exhaustive* (that is, when they include all possible values that could occur), the probabilities associated with the individual score values represent a **probability distribution** with respect to that variable. This also holds for discrete quantitative variables.

Probability distributions are most commonly represented in graph form. In fact, graphs of probability distributions for qualitative and discrete variables are created in a manner similar to relative frequency graphs and take the identical shape as the corresponding frequency graphs. However, the ordinate in this instance is labeled p to indicate that probabilities are being depicted. An example of such a

FIGURE 2.13   **Graph of a Probability Distribution for a Qualitative Variable**

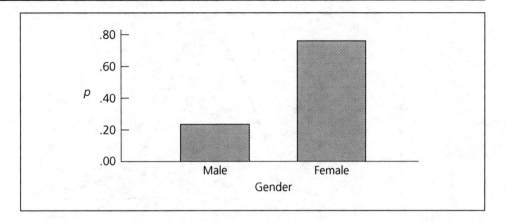

graph appears in Figure 2.13, which presents the probability distribution for gender for the population of 150 women and 50 men referred to above.

Probability Distributions for Continuous Variables

Recall from Section 1.5 that a score on a continuous variable is properly considered as falling within the real limits of the number that was recorded for a measurement. When we say that a person solved a problem in 30 seconds, we do not usually mean that the person solved the problem in *exactly* 30 seconds but, rather, that he solved it in somewhere between 29.5 and 30.5 seconds. Because it is always possible, in principle, to have a measuring device that is more accurate than the one we used, we cannot meaningfully talk about the probability of obtaining a score equal to an *exact* value for a continuous variable. Rather, a probability is better conceptualized as being associated with a range of values, such as between 29.5 and 30.5.

Because the number of values that a continuous variable can have is, in principle, infinite, it is not possible to specify a probability distribution for a continuous variable by listing all possible values of the variable and their corresponding probabilities. Statisticians therefore conceptualize probability distributions for continuous variables somewhat differently than they conceptualize probability distributions for qualitative or discrete variables. Specifically, probability distributions for continuous variables are conceptualized in terms of **probability density functions**.

For instance, Figure 2.14 presents a graph of a probability density function for the continuous variable of shyness for a hypothetical population. As illustrated in this figure, a continuous probability distribution is always represented by a smooth curve over the abscissa. Although it is not formally demarcated, the abscissa represents all possible shyness values, with increasingly greater shyness implied as the abscissa moves from left to right. The ordinate, though also not formally demarcated, is used to determine the probability of observing a specified range of score

FIGURE 2.14   **Graph of a Probability Distribution for a Continuous Variable**

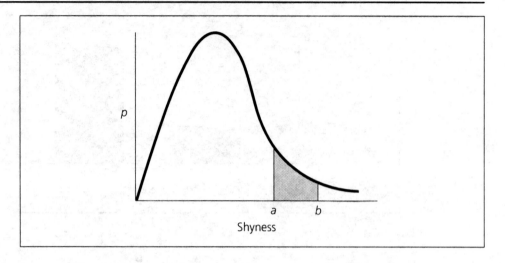

values. The higher the curve is between two points, the more "dense" the corresponding scores are and the more likely they are to occur. Thus, statisticians refer to
the probability associated with a specified range of score values as a *density*.

The key to understanding a probability density function is to think of the
probability of a continuous variable as being equivalent to an *area* under the curve
or, as it is more formally called, the **density curve**. The total area under the curve
represents 1.00, or the probability that everybody in the relevant sample or population has *some* value on the dimension in question. Using the appropriate mathematical procedures, we can compute the size of a given area and, in this way, specify the
probability of obtaining a score that falls within the corresponding interval. Specifically, the probability of obtaining a score within a given interval equals the area
under the density curve that corresponds to that interval.

In Figure 2.14, points *a* and *b* have been marked on the abscissa to represent the
limits of an interval. The portion of the curve that is shaded represents the area bounded
by the two points. Based on the total area under the curve being 1.00, this area is .11.
Thus, the probability of obtaining a score between point *a* and point *b* is .11.

2.9   Empirical and Theoretical Distributions

An important distinction in statistics is between **empirical distributions** and **theoretical distributions**. Empirical distributions are based on measurements that are actually taken on a variable. In contrast, theoretical distributions are not constructed by
formally taking measurements but, rather, by making assumptions and representing
these assumptions mathematically.

One very important type of theoretical distribution that has been studied
extensively by statisticians is the **normal distribution**. The normal distribution was

so named in the early 19th century by a French mathematician named Quetelet, who believed that it characterized the shape of a large number of phenomena, including height, weight, intelligence, and many psychological variables. Indeed, even today the normal distribution is used to represent a wide range of human characteristics.

There is actually a family of normal distributions, each member of which is precisely defined by the mathematical formula given in Appendix 4.1. Figure 2.15 presents some examples of normal distributions. As can be seen, all distributions in this family are symmetrical and are characterized by a "bell shape."

Theoretical distributions are sometimes used to represent real-world occurrences when practical limitations make it impossible to construct empirical distributions. For instance, a distribution of the intelligence test scores of *all* adults in the United States could not be constructed empirically. However, if we are willing to make the assumption that the distribution of intelligence test scores is approximately normal, then our knowledge of the normal distribution can be used to help us gain insight into the nature of intelligence test scores in the real world. As we will see in later chapters, inferential statistics makes extensive use of theoretical distributions.

The usefulness of the normal distribution for representing real-world data is demonstrated in Figure 2.16 on the next page, where Figure 2.16a presents a relative frequency histogram for an empirical distribution of intelligence test scores for the population of students in a particular high school and Figure 2.16b presents a theoretical distribution of intelligence test scores for this same group. The latter distribution is normal in shape and closely corresponds to the empirical distribution in Figure 2.16a.

FIGURE 2.15   **Examples of Normal Distributions**

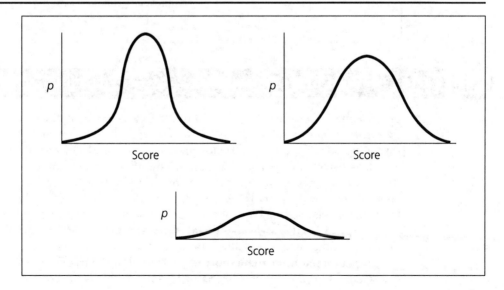

FIGURE 2.16   **(a) Empirical and (b) Theoretical Distributions of Intelligence Test Scores**

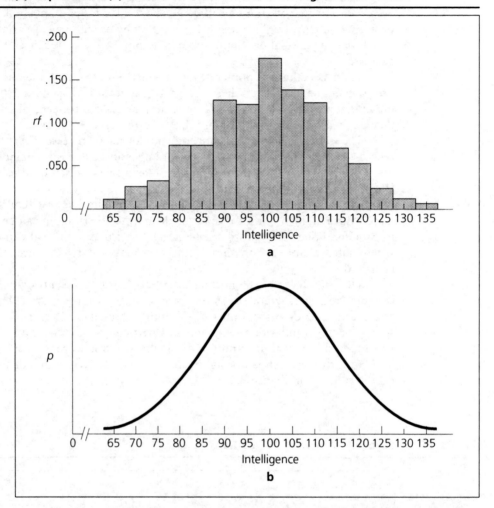

2.10 Method of Presentation

Because many behavioral science journals follow the guidelines presented in the *Publication Manual of the American Psychological Association* (APA) (American Psychological Association, 2001) for presenting the results of statistical analyses, we will demonstrate the format that authors should use according to APA style when submitting manuscripts to journals for publication. One important issue is how to present statistical symbols. According to APA (2001) style, the symbols for frequencies, relative frequencies, and so on should be "expressed by italicized Latin letters" (p. 139). APA style also dictates the way that tables and graphs should be formatted and provides guidelines for giving them informative titles.

It is rare for a research report to present all of the frequency information that is discussed in this chapter. The major reason for this is the cost of journal space.

However, it is up to the investigator to decide how results can be most meaningfully represented. Most research reports present absolute frequencies and percentages. As we will see, this format allows interested readers to derive all of the other frequency measures that we have discussed, should they for some reason desire to do so.

As an example of a table that might be presented, consider the following:*

Percentage of Individuals Who Approve or
Disapprove of Nuclear Power Plants

Response category	f	%
Strongly approve	53	24.7
Moderately approve	42	19.5
Neither approve nor disapprove	18	8.4
Moderately disapprove	44	20.5
Strongly disapprove	58	27.0

This table reports responses to a question asked of 215 college students concerning their approval or disapproval of nuclear power plants. Note that the percentages add to 100.1% rather than 100.0% because of the rounding error that resulted when each frequency was divided by the sample size and rounded to one decimal place.

Based on this information, readers can derive relative frequencies, cumulative frequencies, and cumulative relative frequencies if they so desire. The relative frequencies are determined by dividing each percentage by 100. Specifically, 24.6/100 = .246, 19.5/100 = .195, 8.4/100 = .084, 20.5/100 = .205, and 27.0/100 = .270. The cumulative frequencies and the cumulative relative frequencies are determined by successive addition of the entries in the frequencies and the cumulative frequencies columns, respectively.

Because of cost and space considerations, frequency graphs are typically used only when they are necessary to illustrate major trends in the data that might otherwise be difficult to convey. However, given an appropriately presented frequency table, readers can, if they wish, construct a graph from the table. When frequency graphs are used, it is important that the guidelines presented earlier in this chapter be followed.

2.11 Examples from the Literature

The concept of intelligence is of major interest to behavioral scientists, and many attempts, some controversial, have been made to measure this construct. One of the most widely used intelligence tests for adults is the Wechsler Adult Intelligence Scale (WAIS). This test has been extensively studied with many different groups, and it has even been applied to several national samples in the United States.

---

* Although American Psychological Association (2001) format requires that all text and tables be double spaced, for the sake of brevity single spacing is used throughout this book.

One such application is reported in Wechsler (1958), who found the following frequency breakdown for IQ (intelligence quotient) scores on the WAIS for a sample of 2,052 individuals:

Intelligence	f	rf	%	cf	crf	Verbal description
Above 129	29	.014	1.4	2,052	1.000	Very superior
120–129	150	.073	7.3	2,023	.986	Superior
110–119	349	.170	17.0	1,873	.913	Bright normal
100–109	525	.256	25.6	1,524	.743	Average
90–99	504	.246	24.6	999	.487	Average
80–89	299	.146	14.6	495	.241	Dull normal
70–79	132	.064	6.4	196	.095	Borderline
Below 70	64	.031	3.1	64	.031	Mentally retarded

The verbal descriptions on the extreme right of this table are labels that once were used by psychologists to describe the ranges of scores on the far left. However, the American Psychological Association (2001) now strongly discourages the use of labels of this type.

Notice that scores in the range of 90 to 109 (*average*) are the most common. Also, the proportion of individuals with scores above 129 (*very superior*) is quite small. This is also true for individuals with scores below 70 (*mentally retarded*). Only 1.4% of the sample had scores above 129, and 3.1% had scores below 70.

In 1926, a behavioral scientist named Cox published an extensive study of eminent men in history in which she attempted to estimate the IQ scores that these individuals would have achieved had they lived in a time when this could be assessed. Based on an extensive analysis of case records, Cox derived the following estimates, among others:

Francis Galton, English scientist: 200
John Stuart Mill, English philosopher: 190
Johann Wolfgang von Goethe, German writer and philosopher: 185
Gottfried Wilhelm Leibniz, German philosopher and mathematician: 185
Samuel Taylor Coleridge, English writer and poet: 175
John Quincy Adams, American statesman and president: 165
David Hume, English philosopher: 155
Alfred Tennyson, English poet: 155
René Descartes, French philosopher and mathematician: 150
Wolfgang Amadeus Mozart, Austrian composer: 150
William Wordsworth, English poet and writer: 150
Francis Bacon, English philosopher and scientist: 145

Charles Dickens, English writer: 145
Benjamin Franklin, American inventor and statesman: 145
George Frideric Handel, German composer: 145
Thomas Jefferson, American statesman and president: 145
John Milton, English poet: 145
Daniel Webster, American statesman and senator: 145

The magnitude of these estimates is impressive, especially in light of the previous frequency analysis. However, it is difficult to extrapolate IQ scores from archival data such as that used by Cox, and numerous scholars (for example, Fancher, 1985) have questioned the accuracy of Cox's estimates.

2.12   Links Between Computer Analysis and Book Content

The data that the user provides to the computer for analysis are known as **input**. When a statistical program is properly executed, **output** in the form of the requested analyses will be produced. If so desired, the user can request that the input and/or the output be printed out to produce a **printout**.

Graphs that are generated by statistical programs will invariably look different from what we advocate in this chapter. For instance, depending on the statistical package, labels may not be centered on the axes and symbols other than solid dots may be used to indicate frequencies in frequency polygons. Also, some programs routinely order the scores in frequency tables from low to high rather than high to low and label the various types of frequencies differently from what we recommend. However, if one understands the concepts introduced herein, these differences should not interfere with the ability to read and interpret frequency output.

2.13   Links Between Chapters

You probably noticed that much of what we discussed in this chapter relates to the basic concepts that we introduced in Chapter 1. Indeed, we have seen that the nature of both frequency tables and frequency graphs differs depending on whether variables are qualitative or quantitative, and we also noted the role of real limits in creating frequency histograms and graphs of cumulative frequencies. We also expanded our knowledge of probability by learning how to depict probability information in graph form and how the area under the density curve can be used to determine the probability of obtaining a score within the corresponding interval. In turn, the concepts from this chapter will be invoked repeatedly as we progress through this book.

Applications to the Analysis of a Social Problem Using SPSS for Windows

Three questions of interest that can be addressed by analyzing the parent–teen communication data described in Chapter 1 are how sexually active teenagers are, how sexually active their mothers believe that they are, and when they begin to engage in sexual intercourse. Table 2.1 presents the computer output for three frequency analyses that address these issues.

The first frequency table in Table 2.1 contains the results for a self-report measure of whether each 14-year-old has ever experienced sexual intercourse. A score of 0 was assigned to each teen who reported never having engaged in sexual intercourse and a score of 1 was assigned to those who reported that they had. The name that we assigned to this variable (HADSEX) appears at the top of the table, and this is followed by a more complete *variable label* that we also specified.

The output is organized into five columns. The first column contains the *value labels* that we specified for each level of the variable and the second column presents the corresponding absolute frequencies. This is followed by two columns that contain different types of percentage information. The percentages in the "Percent" column correspond to the absolute frequencies in the "Frequency" column, whereas the percentages in the "Valid percent" column are based on only those cases for which there are valid scores, which, in this instance, is all of them. Thus, the percentages in this column are identical to those in the "Percent" column. However, this will not always be the case, as we will see shortly. The final column presents the cumulative percentages based on the "Valid percent" values. Almost 36% of the teens reported that they have engaged in sexual intercourse. This is a high incidence of sexual activity for 14-year-olds.

The second frequency table in Table 2.1 relates to the mothers' perceptions of whether their 14-year-olds had ever engaged in sexual intercourse. As is indicated at the top of the table, we

named this variable "MSEX." The frequency of 5 to the right of the label "Missing system" indicates that data is missing for 5 of the 115 mothers because they did not answer the question. Note that these cases are included in the frequency counts in the second column. The percentages in the "Percent" column are also based on *all* of the mothers. As can be seen, missing data constituted 4.3% of all responses. This column also shows that 81.7% of the mothers did not think their teen had ever engaged in sexual intercourse. The "Valid percent" column gives the percentage of mothers who have a given score, *excluding* those mothers with missing data. For example, 85.5% of the mothers who responded to the question thought that their teen had never engaged in sexual intercourse. Note that this value is somewhat higher than that in the "Percent" column because it is calculated based on a total of 110 rather than 115 scores.

The values in the "Valid percent" column are often more meaningful than those in the "Percent" column because missing data are excluded. However, this is not always the case. There are many situations where both the "Percent" and the "Valid percent" values are of theoretical interest, with each providing a slightly different perspective on the data. Any time "Valid percent" values are discussed in a research report, it is imperative that the researcher qualifies the findings by explicitly stating the number and nature of those individuals who did not answer each question.

It is evident from these analyses that the mothers underestimated the sexual activity of their teens: Although almost 36% of the teens reported having engaged in sexual intercourse, only about 14% of the mothers thought their teen had done so. These results are consistent with numerous interviews that we have conducted with parents

(continued)

TABLE 2.1   Computer Output for Frequency Distributions for Parent–Teen Sexual Communication Variables

HADSEX Whether teen has ever had sexual intercourse

		Frequency	Percent	Valid percent	Cumulative percent
Valid	0 No sexual intercourse	74	64.3	64.3	64.3
	1 Had sexual intercourse	41	35.7	35.7	100.0
	Total	115	100.0	100.0	

MSEX Whether mother thinks teen has had sexual intercourse

		Frequency	Percent	Valid percent	Cumulative percent
Valid	0 Thinks has not had sex	94	81.7	85.5	85.5
	1 Thinks has had sex	16	13.9	14.5	100.0
	Total	110	95.7	100.0	
Missing system		5	4.3		
Total		115	100.0		

AGEFIRST Age at first intercourse

		Frequency	Percent	Valid percent	Cumulative per-cent
Valid	6.00	4	.5	1.0	1.0
	7.00	9	1.2	2.2	3.2
	8.00	6	.8	1.5	4.7
	9.00	13	1.7	3.2	7.9
	10.00	23	3.1	5.7	13.6
	11.00	27	3.6	6.7	20.3
	12.00	62	8.3	15.3	35.6
	13.00	101	13.4	25.0	60.6
	14.00	109	14.5	27.0	87.6
	15.00	43	5.7	10.6	98.3
	16.00	7	.9	1.7	100.0
	Total	404	53.8		
Missing	System	347	46.2		
Total		751	100.0		

(continued)

that suggest that parents are reluctant to acknowledge their child's sexual tendencies, especially during younger adolescence. Instead, many parents insist on viewing their young adolescents as children rather than as emerging adults. Not surprisingly, this perspective gets in the way of effective parent–teen communication about premarital pregnancy because many parents will delay communicating about this important topic if they do not think that their child is sexual—yet. Clearly, parents need to be educated that young teens are more sexually active than they think they are.

The third frequency table in Table 2.1 addresses the self-reports of how old the entire sample of 751 teens were the first time that they had sexual intercourse. Thus, this table includes scores for the 15-, 16-, and 17-year-olds as well as the 14-year-olds. The variable in this instance is named "AGEFIRST." The 347 cases of missing data represent those teens who have not yet engaged in intercourse. Of those teens who reported being sexually active, the most common ages for the first experience of intercourse were 13 and 14. Looking at the "Valid percent" column, we see that 25.0%

of the sexually active teens had their first intercourse at age 13 and 27.0% of them had their first intercourse at age 14.

The teens who reported first intercourse at very young ages (ages 6 to 9) most certainly reflect instances of sexual abuse. If we eliminate these teens as being "atypical," the "Percent" column shows that 3.1% of the entire sample (that is, including those teens who have not yet engaged in sexual intercourse) had their first intercourse at age 10, 3.6% had their first intercourse at age 11, and 8.3% had their first intercourse at age 12, for a total of 15.0% who reported experiencing intercourse by the age of 12. When ages 13 and 14 are also considered, this percentage increases to 42.9%.

Overall, the data suggest that a substantial number of adolescents are sexually active at relatively young ages, thereby increasing the risk of unintended pregnancy. Technically, this conclusion applies only to the population of teens that is represented by our sample, but other data shows that adolescent sexuality and teenage pregnancy are more general problems in our society.

Summary

A frequency distribution is a compilation of all of the score values in a set of scores and the number of times that each occurs. Frequency distributions are often presented in the form of frequency tables. Such tables can also be used to convey relative frequency, percentage, cumulative frequency, and cumulative relative frequency information for a set of scores.

When a quantitative variable takes on many different values, it is advantageous to group the data into intervals. To do so, we must first decide how many groups to report, what the interval size should be for each group, and the beginning value for the lowest interval.

Frequency tables are useful for identifying outliers—scores that are very extreme relative to the majority of the scores in the data set. When outlying scores are excluded from a statistical analysis, the results of that analysis will apply only to a population that explicitly excludes individuals with the types of unusually low and/or unusually high scores that were excluded.

Because graphs can be easier to follow than tables, investigators sometimes report their data graphically. Frequency graphs for quantitative variables include frequency histograms, frequency polygons, line plots, and stem and leaf plots. Frequency information for qualitative variables can be depicted using bar graphs. Because frequency graphs can be misleading depending on how they are formatted, it is important that the guidelines that we present in the text for ensuring a uniform, clearly interpretable presentation of graphed results be followed.

Graphs of relative frequencies and percentages take the identical shape as the corresponding frequency graphs. It is also possible to represent cumulative frequency and cumulative relative frequency information in graph form.

Whereas a relative frequency indicates the proportion of times that some score was previously observed, a probability represents the likelihood of observing that score in the future. When the values for a qualitative variable or a discrete quantitative variable are mutually exclusive (that is, when a person can have one and only one score for that variable) and exhaustive (that is, when they include all possible values that could occur), the probabilities associated with the individual score values represent a probability distribution with respect to that variable.

Probability distributions are most commonly represented in graph form. Graphs of probability distributions for qualitative variables and discrete quantitative variables take the identical shape as the corresponding frequency graphs.

Probability distributions for continuous variables are conceptualized in terms of probability density functions. Such distributions are represented graphically by a smooth curve over the abscissa. Using the appropriate mathematical procedures, we can compute the size of a given area under the curve and, in this way, specify the probability of obtaining a score that falls within the corresponding interval. Specifically, the probability of obtaining a score within a given interval equals the area under the density curve that corresponds to that interval.

An important distinction can be made between empirical distributions and theoretical distributions. Empirical distributions are based on measurements that are actually taken on a variable, whereas theoretical distributions are derived by making assumptions and representing these assumptions mathematically. One very important type of theoretical distribution is the normal distribution. This is a family of symmetrical and bell-shaped distributions that are used to represent a wide range of human characteristics. Theoretical distributions such as the normal distribution are sometimes used to represent real-world occurrences when practical limitations make it impossible to construct empirical distributions.

Exercises

Answers to asterisked (*) exercises appear at the back of the book.

Use the following information to complete Exercises 1–11:

An employer kept records of how many days her 20 employees reported in sick during the previous year. The scores on this variable were as follows:

8 7 6 4 3
6 3 7 6 6
4 6 6 6 7
6 6 8 7 6

*1. Construct a frequency table that contains absolute frequencies.

*2. Compute the relative frequencies, percentages, cumulative frequencies, and cumulative relative frequencies.

*3. What proportion of employees were sick for 8 days? What proportion were sick for 8 or fewer days? What proportion were sick for fewer than 8 days?

*4. What proportion of employees were sick for 7 days? What proportion were sick for 7 or more days? What proportion were sick for more than 7 days?

5. What proportion of employees were sick for 4 days? What proportion were sick for 4 or more days? What proportion were sick for more than 4 days?

*6. Suppose you randomly selected a score from the 20 scores. What is the probability the selected score would be an 8? What is the probability the selected score would be a 6 or an 8? What is the probability the selected score would be 7 or less?

*7. Draw a frequency histogram for the set of scores.

8. Draw a frequency polygon for the set of scores.

9. Draw a line plot for the set of scores.

*10. Draw a polygon of the relative frequencies. Compare the shape of this graph with that of the frequency polygon from Exercise 8.

11. Draw a graph of the cumulative frequencies.

*12. How does a grouped frequency table differ from an ungrouped frequency table?

13. What are the three questions that must be considered when deciding how to group data?

Use the following information to complete Exercises 14–23:

A principal in a small school measured the intelligence of fifth-grade students in her school. The intelligence test scores for these students were as follows:

129	99	98	113	103	128	102	110	80	105
93	98	109	109	100	111	106	96	108	90
104	94	92	119	127	89	95	92	105	108
83	100	107	106	101	118	84	119	105	111
118	106	122	120	102	117	103	117	103	88

14. Draw a frequency histogram for the set of scores.

15. Draw a stem and leaf plot for the set of scores. Rotate the plot so that the tens and hundreds digits appear at the base rather than on the right. Compare the relative heights of the columns in this graph with those in the histogram from Exercise 14.

*16. Construct a grouped frequency table that contains absolute frequencies by grouping the scores into five groups.

17. Compute the relative frequencies, percentages, cumulative frequencies, and cumulative relative frequencies for the grouped scores.

*18. What proportion of students had scores of 109 or lower? What proportion had scores of 99 or lower? What proportion had scores of 110 or higher?

19. Draw a frequency histogram of the grouped data for the set of scores.

*20. Draw a frequency polygon of the grouped data for the set of scores.

21. Draw a histogram of the relative frequencies for the grouped data. Compare the shape of this graph with that of the frequency histogram from Exercise 19.

*22. Draw a graph of the cumulative frequencies for the grouped data. Compare the general shape of this graph with the cumulative frequency graph for the data on sick days from Exercise 11. What accounts for the similarity in their shapes?

23. Suppose that you want to compute a frequency table for the data by grouping the scores into ten groups. What size interval should you use? With what value should the lowest interval begin?

Use the following information to complete Exercises 24–26.

Suppose that you were commissioned to survey a small community to determine the marital status of all adults over 18 years of age. You select a random sample of 50 individuals and ask them if they are married (M), divorced (D), widowed (W), or single (S). The data for these individuals are as follows:

M M M M M S M W M S D S M M D W M
M S M W M M S M M M M M S M S D M
M S S D M M M D W M M M W M M S

24. Construct a frequency table that contains absolute frequencies, relative frequencies, and percentages.

25. Draw a bar graph for the set of scores.
26. Draw a bar graph of the relative frequencies. Compare the shape of this graph with that of the bar graph from Exercise 25.
27. What does a break in the ordinate or abscissa of a frequency graph indicate?
*28. How tall should the ordinate of a frequency graph be relative to the abscissa? Why is this important?
29. Redraw the frequency histogram from Exercise 7 so that the height of the ordinate at the demarcation for the highest frequency is visually more than three-fourths the length of the abscissa. Now redraw it so that the height of the ordinate at the demarcation for the highest frequency is visually less than two-thirds the length of the abscissa. Compare the three graphs in terms of what they seem to suggest about employee sick days.
*30 What is a probability distribution? Why is the nature of probability distributions for qualitative and discrete variables different from that for continuous variables?
31. What is the difference between an empirical distribution and a theoretical distribution?
*32. A researcher surveyed 1,850 people on their attitudes toward capital punishment. One question asked respondents to indicate whether they thought the death penalty should be legal. Responses to this question could range from 1 ("definitely should not be legal") to 5 ("definitely should be legal"), where 3 represented a neutral stance. Compute the absolute frequencies, relative frequencies, cumulative frequencies, and cumulative relative frequencies for the set of responses based on the following percentage results:

Attitude	%
5	20.0
4	30.0
3	10.0
2	22.0
1	18.0

Multiple-Choice Questions

Refer to the following frequency distribution of the number of hours students studied for a test to do Exercises 33–36.

Study hours	f
8	20
7	30
6	30
5	10
4	10

*33. What proportion of students studied for 7 hours or longer?
   a. .300
   b. .500
   c. .800
   d. none of the above
34. The cumulative frequency for a score of 6 is
   a. 20
   b. 30
   c. 50
   d. 80
*35. What percentage of students studied for 5 hours?
   a. 10.0
   b. 20.0
   c. 30.0
   d. 90.0
36. A bar graph is a more appropriate way of graphing the data than is a frequency histogram.
   a. true
   b. false
37. Suppose that you are constructing a grouped frequency table and you decide to use ten groups. If the highest score is 100 and the lowest score is 50, what interval size should you use?
   a. 2   c. 5
   b. 3   d. 10
38. A normal distribution is always bell-shaped.
   a. true
   b. false
*39. The frequency of a score in comparison to the total number of scores in the group is called a

a. cumulative frequency
b. absolute frequency
c. relative frequency
d. cumulative relative frequency

*40. A probability density function
a. can be graphically represented as a bar graph
b. can be used only to represent variables that are measured on a ratio level
c. is a smooth curve including all possible values of a continuous variable
d. is always bell-shaped

*41. A stem and leaf plot is similar to a
a. frequency histogram turned on its side
b. frequency polygon
c. bar graph
d. line plot

42. A line plot is always closed with the abscissa.
a. true
b. false

*43. A case that shows a very extreme score relative to the majority of cases in the data set is known as a(n)
a. descriptive statistic
b. extremist
c. outlier
d. none of the above

Measures of Central Tendency and Variability

Describing a set of scores in terms of frequencies can be a highly informative way of presenting information about a variable. However, we often want to communicate information about data in a more succinct fashion. Towards this end, statisticians have developed more concise statistical measures for characterizing scores for quantitative variables. The present chapter introduces you to these important indexes, which are commonly referred to as **descriptive statistics**.

In the first section of this chapter, we focus on two types of measures. The first type is measures of central tendency. *Central tendency* refers to the "average" score in a set of scores. When we specify a central tendency, we are, in essence, trying to specify a "representative" value of a set of scores. The second type is measures of variability. These measures indicate the extent to which scores within a set differ from one another.

As an example, suppose that a researcher interviews a group of 100 14-year-olds who smoke and asks them how many cigarettes they smoke in a typical day. The average number of cigarettes is 13.27, which conveys a sense of how much these youths smoke. However, do all of these teens smoke about 13 cigarettes a day, or is there variability about this average, with some of the smokers consuming only a few cigarettes a day and others consuming a large number of cigarettes? The heavy and light smokers might "average each other out," yielding a central tendency that is between the two extremes.

All of the measures discussed in this chapter can be applied to both samples and populations. The rationale and calculations are identical in both cases. However, some of the statistics that we introduce are symbolized differently depending on whether a sample or a population is being described. In instances where the notation differs, we will use the sample notation. We point out differences between sample notation and population notation in Section 3.9.

3.1   Measures of Central Tendency for Quantitative Variables

One piece of information that is useful when describing a set of scores is where the scores tend to fall on the numerical scale, or their **central tendency**. A central tendency refers to an *average*, or a score around which other scores tend to cluster. There are many indexes of central tendency. We consider three of them: the mode, the median, and the mean.

Mode

The **mode** of a distribution of scores is the most easily computed index of central tendency. It is simply the score that occurs most frequently. For the set of scores 6, 8, 8, 8, 10, 10, the mode is 8 because 8 occurs more frequently (three times) than any other score in the data set. When the mode is used as the index of central tendency, we are using the most common score as the "representative" value for the set of scores. If we were to randomly select one score from a set of scores, that score would be more likely to be equal to the mode than to any other value because the mode occurs more frequently than any other score. In a graph of a distribution of scores, the modal score has the highest "peak" in the graph.

Although the mode is a relatively straightforward index of central tendency, it has some disadvantages. The major problem is that there can be more than one modal score. For example, consider the following scores: 6, 6, 6, 8, 8, 10, 10, 10. Both 6 and 10 occur with the same highest frequency. In this case, there is ambiguity about which score is *the* mode because both 6 and 10 occur with equal frequency. This set of scores is *multimodal* because it has more than one mode. More specifically, it is said to be *bimodal* because it has two modes. When the mode is not equal to one unique value, it loses some of its effectiveness in characterizing the central tendency of a distribution of scores.

Median

Another measure of central tendency is the median. The **median** is the point in the distribution of scores that divides the distribution into two equal parts. In other words, 50% of the scores occur below the median and 50% of the scores occur above the median. If the median is used as the index of central tendency, then we are using the "middlemost" score as the "representative" value for the set of scores.

There are three different approaches to computing the median of scores for a continuous variable. The first approach applies when there is an even number of scores, the second when there is an odd number of scores, and the third when there are duplications of the middle score(s), regardless of whether the number of scores is even or odd. These are reviewed in turn.

1. *Computation of the median when there is an even number of scores:* Suppose that we measure how long it takes six students to complete a test and find that their times are 20, 16, 25, 22, 27, and 18 minutes. To compute the median, we first order the scores from lowest to highest:

      16   18   20   22   25   27

The median is the arithmetic average of the two middle scores, or $(20 + 22)/2 = 21$. Figure 3.1a presents this case graphically on a frequency histogram that also shows the real limits of each score value. Note that 50% of the scores occur below 21 and 50% of the scores occur above 21.

2. *Computation of the median when there is an odd number of scores:* Suppose that we measure the test-taking times of seven students and find that their scores are 6, 16, 12, 8, 16, 6, and 14 minutes. To compute the median, we order the scores from lowest to highest:

      6   6   8   12   14   16   16

The median is simply the middle score, 12. Figure 3.1b presents this case graphically. It also highlights the importance of considering the median in the context of the real limits of score values. An examination of the scores 6, 6, 8, 12, 14, 16, and 16 shows that 50% of these are *not* less than 12. Only three of the seven scores are less than 12, and three are greater than 12. With an odd number of scores, the problem is what to do with the middle score. The answer lies in the concept of real limits. The individual who obtained the

FIGURE 3.1   **Illustration of the Median (a) When There is an Even Number of Scores, (b) When There Is an Odd Number of Scores, and (c) When There Are Duplications of the Middle Score(s)**

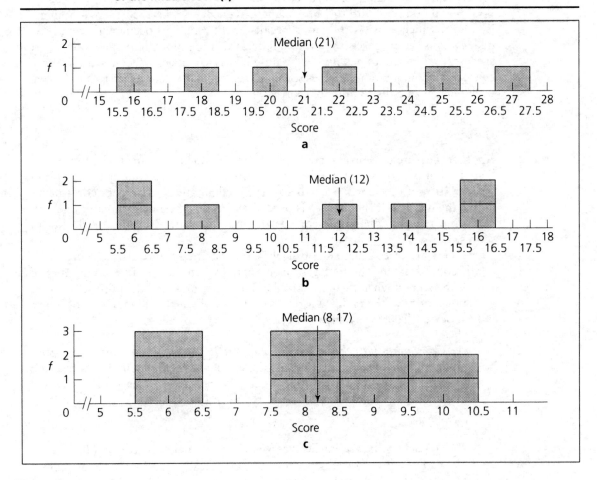

middle score of 12 minutes scored somewhere between 11.5 and 12.5 minutes. We do not know exactly where in the interval, so the most logical thing to do is to divide the interval in half to define the median. This yields a value of 12, which is the same value as we reported above. Note that, consistent with this result, there are $3\frac{1}{2}$ frequency boxes below 12 and $3\frac{1}{2}$ frequency boxes above 12 in Figure 3.1b.

3. *Computation of the median when there are duplications of the middle score(s):* This is the most common occurrence in the behavioral sciences. Suppose that we measure the test-taking times of ten students and find that their scores are 8, 6, 9, 6, 10, 8, 6, 9, 10, and 8 minutes. We order the scores from lowest to highest:

6   6   6   8   8   8   9   9   10   10

Applying the approach for when there is an even number of scores, we get 8 as the arithmetic average of the two middle scores. However, this is not the median—only three of the ten scores are less than 8.

Statisticians have developed a formula for computing the median in situations of this type where there are duplications of the middle score(s). This formula is based on the assumption that the median occurs within the real limits of the middle score(s), and it is applicable regardless of whether there is an even or an odd number of scores.

To gain a conceptual understanding of this formula, consider the example in Figure 3.1c, in which there are ten scores and 8 is the middle score. The median occurs somewhere between 7.5 and 8.5 and represents the point that five scores are less than and five scores are greater than. There are already three scores less than 8 because three individuals have a score of 6. The median must therefore be defined so that two more scores are less than it. Individuals with a score of 8 technically have scores between the real limits 7.5 and 8.5. Because three individuals have a score of 8 and we want to define the median so that two of these three individuals score less than the median, we specify a score two-thirds (or .67) greater than the lower real limit, or 7.5 + .67 = 8.17. Implicit in this approach is the assumption that the actual scores obtained by the three individuals are equally spaced from one another within the real limits of 7.5 and 8.5.*

The formula for computing the median under the assumption that scores are evenly distributed between the real limits of the interval that contains the median (for instance, between 7.5 and 8.5 in our example) is

$$Mdn = L + \left[\frac{(N)(.50) - n_L}{n_w} \right] i \qquad [3.1]$$

where Mdn represents the median, L is the lower real limit of the category that contains the median, N is the total number of scores in the distribution, n_L is the number of scores that are less than L, n_w is the number of scores that are within the category that contains the median, and i is the size of the interval of the category that contains the median (that is, the difference between the upper real limit and the lower real limit of the category that contains the median). The .50 reflects the fact that we are seeking the point that divides the scores such that 50% of them fall below that point and 50% of them fall above that point. This formula can be applied to either grouped or ungrouped scores.

To calculate a median using Equation 3.1, we must first derive the cumulative relative frequencies for the variable of interest. For the present set of test-taking times, these are as follows:

---

* There are alternative ways of calculating a median that make different assumptions, but these approaches are complicated. Interested readers can consult Wilcox (1997).

Time	f	rf	crf
10	2	.200	1.000
9	2	.200	.800
8	3	.300	.600
6	3	.300	.300

Starting from the bottom of the cumulative relative frequencies column, we move up until we find the first cumulative relative frequency that is greater than or equal to .500. The value of this cumulative relative frequency is .600, and this corresponds to a score of 8. The lower real limit of 8 is 7.5, so this is L. The total number of scores, N, is 10. The number of scores that are *less than* 7.5 is 3, so this is n_l, and the number of scores that are between 7.5 and 8.5 is 3, so this is n_w. Last, the interval size, i, is $8.5 - 7.5 = 1.0$. Thus,

$$Mdn = 7.5 + \left[\frac{(10)(.50) - 3}{3}\right](1.0)$$

$$= 7.5 + \left[\frac{2.00}{3}\right](1.0)$$

$$= 7.5 + .67 = 8.17$$

which is the same value of the median as we reported earlier.

In practice, researchers often forgo Equation 3.1 when there are duplications of the middle score(s) in favor of a quick approximation of the median that is precise enough for most applications. This approximation involves following the first approach above when there is an even number of scores and the second approach when there is an odd number of scores. In our example, $N = 10$, so we apply the approach for an even number of scores. This involves taking the arithmetic average of the two middle scores, which in this case is $(8 + 8)/2 = 8$. This value is similar to the value of the median (8.17) that we calculated using Equation 3.1. When the median is approximated, it should be reported as such. For instance, it would be misleading in our example to report the median as being 8. Rather, it should be reported as being *approximately* 8.

In summary, when there are no duplications of the middle score(s), the median is equal to the arithmetic average of the two middle scores when N is even, and equal to the middle score when N is odd. When there are duplications of the middle score(s), Equation 3.1 yields the value of the point that equally divides the scores in half, taking into consideration the real limits of the scores. It is also possible to approximate the median when there are duplications of the middle score(s) by following the procedures for when there are no duplications.

The median has an important statistical property that underscores its role as a measure of central tendency. To understand this property, we must first introduce the concept of **deviation scores**. Such scores are calculated by subtracting some constant from each score in a set of scores. These deviations are said to be *unsigned* when their absolute values are taken.

Consider the following five scores, which have a median of 3: 1, 2, 3, 7, 8. If we subtract the median from each score and take the absolute values of the resulting differences, we get a set of unsigned deviations from the median. In our example, the absolute values of how far each score is from the median are:

$$|1 - 3| = 2$$
$$|2 - 3| = 1$$
$$|3 - 3| = 0$$
$$|7 - 3| = 4$$
$$|8 - 3| = 5$$

If we add these deviation scores, we obtain a sum of 12. If any value other than the median were subtracted from the set of scores, the sum of the unsigned deviation scores would be greater than 12. In fact, across all scores in the data set, a set of scores will always be closer, in an absolute sense, to the median than to any other value. It is this property—the fact that the median minimizes the absolute difference between it and the scores in the distribution—that qualifies the median as a measure of central tendency. In this sense, an analogy can be made to a technician who sometimes sets a certain control too low and who sometimes sets the control too high but who overall sets the control as close to the optimal setting as is humanly possible.

STUDY EXERCISE 3.1

An organizational psychologist who is interested in the median number of years that the 200 current employees have been working for a company determines the tenure for each by examining their personnel records. The obtained frequency distribution is as follows:

Years with company	f	rf	crf
6	20	.100	1.000
5	20	.100	.900
4	30	.150	.800
3	50	.250	.650
2	50	.250	.400
1	10	.050	.150
0	20	.100	.100

Compute the median number of years that employees have worked for the company.

Answer Using Equation 3.1, we find that

$$Mdn = L + \left[\frac{(N)(.50) - n_L}{n_w} \right] i$$

$$= 2.5 + \left[\frac{(200)(.50) - 80}{50} \right] (1.0)$$

$$= 2.5 + \left[\frac{20.00}{50} \right] (1.0)$$

$$= 2.5 + .40 = 2.90$$

Thus, the median number of years with the company is 2.90.

Alternatively, because there is an even number of scores, the median can be approximated by taking the arithmetic average of the two middle scores: $(3 + 3)/2 = 3$. If this approach is followed, the median should be reported as being *approximately* 3.

Mean

The **mean** of a set of scores is familiar to all of us. It is simply the arithmetic average of the scores, that is, the sum of all of the scores in the data set divided by the total number of scores. Symbolically,

$$\overline{X} = \frac{\sum X}{N} \tag{3.2}$$

where $\overline{X}$ represents the mean of a set of scores on variable X. For instance, the sum of the scores 5, 2, 8, 5, 3, 9, 6, 3, 5, and 4 is

$$\sum X = 5 + 2 + 8 + 5 + 3 + 9 + 6 + 3 + 5 + 4 = 50$$

Hence, the mean is

$$\overline{X} = \frac{\sum X}{N} = \frac{50}{10} = 5.00$$

The mean has an important statistical property that underscores its role as a measure of central tendency. Consider the following five scores, which have a mean of 3.00: 1, 3, 6, 1, 4. If we subtract the mean from each score and retain the signs of the resulting differences, we get a set of *signed* deviation scores:

$$1 - 3.00 = -2.00$$
$$3 - 3.00 = .00$$
$$6 - 3.00 = 3.00$$
$$1 - 3.00 = -2.00$$
$$4 - 3.00 = 1.00$$

These deviation scores sum to 0. If any value other than the mean were subtracted from the set of scores, the sum of the signed deviation scores would be greater than 0 in absolute value. This is true for any set of scores: The sum of signed deviations

FIGURE 3.2   **The Mean as a Balance Point**

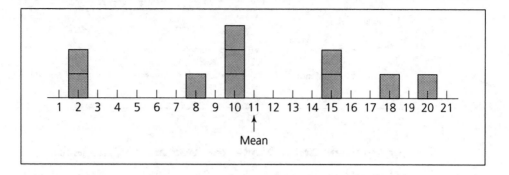

from the mean will always equal 0. It is this property—the fact that the mean balances the deviations of scores above it with the deviations of scores below it—that qualifies the mean as an index of central tendency. Note that this is different from the median. The mean is the value that minimizes the sum of *signed* deviations, whereas the median is the value that minimizes the sum of *unsigned* deviations.

The mean parallels the idea of a center of gravity or a balance point in physics (Hays, 1994). Imagine a long board on which ten small blocks are stacked. Each block weighs the same amount. Twenty-one positions are marked off on the board, as in Figure 3.2. Each block is placed in one of these positions, with some blocks stacked on top of one another. Now suppose that we want to place a fulcrum beneath the board that will perfectly balance it. At what position should we place the fulcrum? It turns out that the point where the fulcrum would perfectly balance the board is the location on the board that corresponds to the mean of the positions of the different blocks. For the example in Figure 3.2, this point is $(2 + 2 + 8 + 10 + 10 + 10 + 15 + 15 + 18 + 20)/10 = 11.00$.

In this analogy, the position of a block is analogous to the score of an individual within a set of scores, and each score is conceptualized as having equal "weight." The mean is like a balance point and, thus, is a measure of central tendency.

STUDY EXERCISE 3.2

Suppose that a researcher is trying to develop a test of reading ability for use in placing students in the appropriate class. A major concern is how long it takes students to complete the test because it has to be administered during a short testing period. For a class of 12 students, the following completion times (in minutes) are recorded:

12	13	11	12	11	13
13	11	12	12	12	12

Compute the mean amount of time that it took the class to complete the test.

Answer   We will compute the mean using Equation 3.2. The first step is to sum the 12 scores:

$$\sum X = 12 + 13 + 11 + 12 + 11 + 13 + 13 + 11 + 12 + 12 + 12 + 12 = 144$$

The mean is thus

$$\overline{X} = \frac{\sum X}{N} = \frac{144}{12} = 12.00$$

Thus, the average amount of time that it took the class to complete the test, as defined by the mean, is 12.00 minutes.

Comparison of the Mode, the Median, and the Mean

The mode, the median, and the mean are all indexes of central tendency. The mode is the most frequently occurring score in a distribution, the median is the point that divides the distribution into halves, and the mean is the arithmetic average of the scores. The mode qualifies as a measure of central tendency because it represents the typical case, the median qualifies because it is closer to the scores in a distribution than any other value in an absolute sense, and the mean qualifies because it represents a balance point.

Which is the best index of central tendency? Ideally, it is useful to characterize a set of scores with all three measures. Each represents something slightly different about the "average" score, and the more information that we have about a data set, the better our understanding of its central tendency will be. However, in practice, most research reports represent central tendency with only one index, with the choice among the three measures depending on what one is trying to communicate.

One way of comparing the mode, the median, and the mean is in terms of a "best guess" interpretation of each. Suppose that all you know about a large set of scores is the values of these three measures. Each score is randomly selected in succession, and after each selection you are to guess the value of the score. What is your best guess? It depends. First, suppose that you want the highest probability of being *exactly* correct. In this case, your best guess is the value of the mode because it is the most frequently occurring score and has the highest probability of predicting each score exactly. Second, suppose that you are not interested in being exactly correct most often but, rather, in making the smallest amount of *absolute* error across all scores. In this case, the *sign* of the error is not important (that is, whether you overpredict or underpredict the value of the score is not critical), but the *size* of the error is. Here, your best guess is the value of the median because it minimizes the absolute (unsigned) error across all scores. Finally, if your goal is to make the *signed* error be as close as possible to 0, then your best guess is the mean. As we noted earlier, this is because across all scores, the sum of signed error from the mean will always equal 0.

The mode, the median, and the mean of a set of scores will sometimes all have the same value. For instance, as illustrated in Figure 3.3, this is always true for normal distributions. But more often than not, the three measures of central tendency will take on different values.

FIGURE 3.3   **Illustration of the Equivalence of the Mode, Median, and Mean in a Normal Distribution**

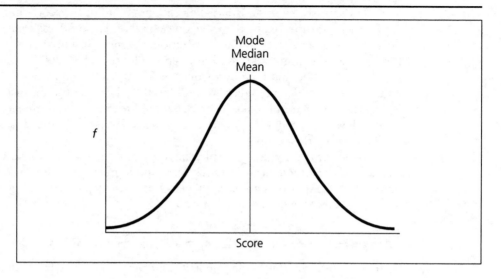

We now consider an example where the mode, the median, and the mean yield very different characterizations of a set of scores. Suppose that you own a business that has seven employees, including yourself. The annual salaries are as follows:

Employee	Salary ($)
1	13,000
2	13,000
3	14,000
4	15,000
5	16,000
6	17,000
You	185,000

For the set of seven scores, the mode is 13,000, the median is 15,000, and the mean is 39,000.00. In characterizing the "average" score, one could portray the company differently depending on the measure of central tendency that is used. (For example, "Look how generous I am—the average salary is $39,000.00" as opposed to "Look how small my business is—the average salary is only $13,000.")

In general, when a distribution has one or more extreme scores (in our example, the salary of $185,000), the information conveyed by the mean can be distorted and lose its ability to "represent" the set of scores. The mode and the median may provide better insight into the central tendency of the data in this instance. Note that in our example, these latter measures are not affected by the extremity of the last score; they would be the same if your salary were $185,000, $17,500, or $250,000.

In contrast, the mean is based on the sum of all of the scores in a distribution and is therefore affected by the value of each score. The more extreme a score is relative to the other scores in the distribution, the more it will alter the mean. Thus, for instance, the mean salary for the seven employees is $39,000.00 when your own salary is $185,000, but the mean would be $15,071.00 if your salary were $17,500 and $48,286.00 if your salary were $250,000. Because the mean is sensitive to extreme scores, variables like income that tend to include a meaningful percentage of very low or very high scores are often reported in terms of modes and, especially, medians rather than means.

As illustrated by this example, the mode and the median are very useful measures of central tendency for purely descriptive purposes. However, most of the inferential statistics that are used by behavioral scientists make use of the mean for the reasons that we discuss in Chapter 7.

Measures of Central Tendency for Discrete Variables

Our discussion of the mode, median, and mean has thus far assumed that the underlying variable being measured is continuous. However, these concepts also apply to discrete variables. For example, suppose that we measure the number of children in each of several families. Although this is a discrete variable, we might calculate the mean number of children and find it to be 2.07. It may seem awkward to think of families as having, on average, 2.07 children because a family cannot have .07 of a child. However, rounding a mean to two (or more) decimal places provides a better measure of where scores for a discrete variable tend to cluster and is more useful than a crude index that rounds the mean to the nearest integer.

For example, a mean number of children of 2.07 and a mean number of children of 2.49 would both be rounded to 2. However, the use of a mean of 2.07 versus a mean of 2.49 to characterize the number of children in families in the United States would translate into a difference of hundreds of thousands of children. This sensitivity is lost when means are rounded to the nearest integer. For this reason, means for discrete variables are typically rounded to two decimal places using the rounding rules that we discussed in Section 1.9.

Use of the Mode, the Median, and the Mean

Now that we are familiar with the mode, the median, and the mean, it is meaningful to examine the types of measures that each can be applied to. When a quantitative variable is measured on a level that at least approximates interval characteristics, all three measures of central tendency are meaningful. When a quantitative variable is measured on an ordinal level that departs markedly from interval characteristics, the mean is not an appropriate index of central tendency and the mode or median should be used instead. This is because the mean relies on calculating a sum, and sums are meaningful only when the intervals between successive categories are approximately equal.

3.2   Measures of Variability for Quantitative Variables

Measures of central tendency indicate where scores tend to cluster in a distribution. A second important characteristic in analyzing quantitative variables is the extent to which scores are alike or different. Consider the following two sets of scores:

Set A: 2 3 3 5 7 7 8
Set B: 4 5 5 5 5 5 6

In both cases, the mean is 5.00. However, the **variability** of the scores, or the extent to which they differ from one another, is quite different. Whereas the scores in Set A tend to be alike, the scores in Set B tend to differ from one another. Statisticians have developed indexes to measure such variability.

Range

The simplest index of variability is the **range**, which is the highest score minus the lowest score in a distribution. In Set A the range is $8 - 2 = 6$, whereas in Set B it is $6 - 4 = 2$. The range is not a very good index of variability because it can be misleading. Consider the extreme case of 900 scores, of which 899 are equal to 100 and one is equal to 10. The range is large, $100 - 10 = 90$, even though almost all of the scores are identical.

Interquartile Range

A second index of variability is the **interquartile range**, which is frequently abbreviated as IQR. The interquartile range is the difference between the highest and the lowest scores (hence, it is a range) *after* the top 25% of the scores and the bottom 25% of the scores have been *trimmed*, or eliminated, from the data set. Stated another way, the interquartile range is the range of the middle 50% of the scores. As an example, consider the following 12 scores: 10, 13, 11, 6, 12, 9, 10, 14, 8, 12, 10, 13. If we order the scores from lowest to highest, we can divide them into four *quartiles* of three scores each:

6 8 9   10 10 10   11 12 12   13 13 14

If we eliminate the bottom and top groups, we have the middle 50% of the scores (10, 10, 10, 11, 12, 12). The range of these scores is $12 - 10 = 2$, which is the interquartile range for this problem.

Some researchers prefer to use the interquartile range rather than the range because the interquartile range is not as sensitive to distortions from extreme cases. For instance, the interquartile range for the example of 900 scores, of which 899 are equal to 100 and one is equal to 10, is $100 - 100 = 0$. Unlike the range, this result is not biased by the one extreme score.

The calculation of the interquartile range was straightforward in the examples above. However, the computation of the interquartile range can get complicated when there are duplicated scores (as is also true for the median) and when the number of scores is not evenly divisible by 4. For these reasons, we will defer a consideration of the formal procedure for calculating the interquartile range to our discussion of two related concepts (percentiles and percentile ranks) in Chapter 4.

Although the interquartile range can be useful, it has been criticized because it does not take into account all of the scores in a distribution. Consider the following sets of scores:

| Set I: | 1 4 5 | 9 9 9 | 11 11 13 | 24 29 33 |
| Set II: | 7 8 8 | 9 9 10 | 11 11 13 | 14 14 14 |

In both cases, the interquartile range is $13 - 9 = 4$, but the sets can hardly be thought of as having the same variability. The scores in Set I are much more diverse, taken as a whole, than the scores in Set II. Because of this, statisticians have developed measures of variability that consider *all* of the scores in a distribution. We now discuss three of these.

Sum of Squares

One index of variability that considers all of the scores in a data set is the **sum of squares**. We develop this measure using the scores from Sets A and B from above, which have been reproduced in Table 3.1.

We begin by asking how far these scores tend to vary from the "typical" score. If we let the "typical" score be represented by the mean, then we are concerned with how much each score deviates from the mean. Columns 2 and 5 of Table 3.1 present deviation scores in which the mean of each data set (5.00 in both cases) has been subtracted from each score in that set. If the scores in the distribution are similar, as in Set B, each will be near the mean and the deviation scores will therefore be close to 0. In contrast, if, as in Set A, the scores tend to differ from one another, the deviation scores will be relatively large.

TABLE 3.1   **Two Sets of Scores with Different Variability**

	Set A			Set B	
X	$X - \overline{X}$	$(X - \overline{X})^2$	X	$X - \overline{X}$	$(X - \overline{X})^2$
2	−3.00	9.00	4	−1.00	1.00
3	−2.00	4.00	5	0.00	0.00
3	−2.00	4.00	5	0.00	0.00
5	0.00	0.00	5	0.00	0.00
7	2.00	4.00	5	0.00	0.00
7	2.00	4.00	5	0.00	0.00
8	3.00	9.00	6	1.00	1.00
$\Sigma X = 35$		$SS = 34.00$	$\Sigma X = 35$		$SS = 2.00$
$\overline{X} = 5.00$			$\overline{X} = 5.00$		

We now want to combine the deviation scores in each data set in some way to derive a single numerical index of overall variability for each one. We cannot use the sum of the deviation scores because, as we noted in Section 3.1, the sum of the signed deviations about the mean will always equal 0. However, statisticians have developed a solution that is very desirable from a statistical perspective. This approach involves first squaring each deviation score and then summing the squares. This has been done in columns 3 and 6 of Table 3.1. Note that the sum of squares for Set A is 34.00 and the sum of squares for Set B is 2.00. This reflects the greater variability in the Set A scores than in the Set B scores.

The sum of squares gets its name from the operations performed: It is short-hand for the *sum of the squared deviations from the mean*. This quantity can be represented symbolically as

$$SS = \sum (X - \overline{X})^2 \tag{3.3}$$

where *SS* is the abbreviation for *sum of squares*.

Students frequently ask why the mean and not the median is used as the mea-sure of central tendency in defining the sum of squares. One reason is that when the mean and the median are different, the sum of the *squared* deviations from the mean will always be less than the sum of the *squared* deviations from the median. In fact, it turns out that the sum of the squared deviations from the mean will always be less than the sum of the squared deviations around any other value. In other words, the mean minimizes the squared error. A second reason for preferring the mean concerns the important role that means and their sums of squares play in making inferences about populations from sample data. We discuss this in depth in Chapter 7.

STUDY EXERCISE 3.3

Suppose that a researcher administers a hyperactivity test to five children and finds them to have scores of 6, 8, 4, 10, and 2. Compute the sum of squares for this set of scores.

Answer   We apply Equation 3.3 as follows:

X	$X - \overline{X}$	$(X - \overline{X})^2$
6	.00	.00
8	2.00	4.00
4	−2.00	4.00
10	4.00	16.00
2	−4.00	16.00
$\sum X = 30$		$SS = 40.00$
$\overline{X} = 6.00$		

Thus, the sum of squares is equal to 40.00.

Variance

One problem with the sum of squares as an index of variability is that its size depends not only on the amount of variability among scores but also on the *number* of scores (N). Consider two sets of data, where the scores in Set I are 2, 4, and 6 and the scores in Set II are 4, 4, 4, 4, 4, 6, 6, 6, 6, and 6. We can readily see that the scores in Set I tend to differ from one another more than do the scores in Set II. Nevertheless, the sum of squares for Set I is 8.00 and the sum of squares for Set II is 10.00. Thus, although there appears to be greater variability in Set I than in Set II, the sum of squares for Set II is larger than the sum of squares for Set I. This is because the sum of squares for Set II is based on ten scores, whereas the sum of squares for Set I is based on only three scores.

To avoid inconsistencies of this type, measures of variability should take into account the number of cases in the data set. One possibility is to divide the sum of squares by N—that is, to compute an average squared deviation from the mean. This index is called the **variance** and is defined by the formula

$$s^2 = \frac{SS}{N} \qquad\qquad [3.4]$$

where s^2 represents the variance. Using this equation, we find that the variance for Set I is 8/3 = 2.67 and the variance for Set II is 10/10 = 1.00. Consistent with our eyeball interpretation, the mean squared deviation score (the variance) is greater in Set I than in Set II.

For the data in Table 3.1, the variance for Set A is

$$s^2 = \frac{34}{7} = 4.86$$

and the variance for Set B is

$$s^2 = \frac{2}{7} = .29$$

The finding of greater variability in Set A than in Set B is consistent with our earlier results for the sums of squares.

Standard Deviation

A fifth index of variability among scores is the **standard deviation**. The standard deviation is the positive square root of the variance and is denoted by the lowercase letter *s*:

$$s = \sqrt{s^2} \qquad\qquad [3.5]$$

For instance, the standard deviation for Set A in Table 3.1 is $s = \sqrt{4.86} = 2.20$ and the standard deviation for Set B is $s = \sqrt{.29} = .54$.

The standard deviation is the most easily interpreted measure of variability among a set of scores. Recall that the variance is the mean squared deviation score.

However, it is difficult to fully comprehend what is being related by squared devia-tion scores, and, by taking the square root of the variance, we are, in essence, elimi-nating the square and returning to the original unit of measurement. *The standard deviation thus represents an average deviation from the mean.** On average, the Set A scores in Table 3.1 deviate 2.20 units from the mean and the Set B scores deviate .54 unit from the mean. Again, more variability is indicated in Set A than in Set B.

Students who are learning about the standard deviation frequently ask what value indicates a large standard deviation. The answer is that it depends on what is being measured. For example, suppose that the mean number of children for fami-lies in a given country is 4.20 with a standard deviation of 3.00. This standard devi-ation represents considerable variability because, on average, scores deviate three "children" from the mean. In contrast, suppose that we measure the annual income for people who live in a particular neighborhood and find a mean of $28,760.40 and a standard deviation of $3.00. In this case, there is very little variability because scores deviate from the mean by an average of only $3.00. When the units are dol-lars and the concern is annual income, a standard deviation of 3.00 is trivial, but when the units are children and the concern is family size, a standard deviation of 3.00 is substantial.

STUDY EXERCISE 3.4

Compute the variance and the standard deviation for the scores in Study Exercise 3.3.

Answer   Because the sum of squares was previously found to equal 40.00 and there are five scores, the variance is equal to

$$s^2 = \frac{SS}{N}$$

$$= \frac{40}{5} = 8.00$$

The standard deviation is found by taking the positive square root of the variance:

$$s = \sqrt{8.00} = 2.83$$

Characteristics of the Sum of Squares, the Variance, and the Standard Deviation

The sum of squares, the variance, and the standard deviation are all useful indexes of variability for quantitative variables, and we will make extensive use of all three in this book. Although, as we will see, the three measures are used in different contexts, they also share some important characteristics: *The sum of squares, the variance, and the standard deviation will always be greater than or equal to 0.* These

---

* Specifically, the standard deviation is the positive square root of the arithmetic average of the squared deviations from the mean. As such, the standard deviation is a type of average.

statistics can never be negative because they are all based on squared deviation scores and any number squared must be nonnegative. When the sum of squares equals 0, the variance and standard deviation will also equal 0. A value of 0 for these statistics means that there is no variability in the scores; they are all the same. As the values of the three statistics become increasingly greater than 0, more variability among the scores is indicated, other things being equal.

Use of the Sum of Squares, the Variance, and the Standard Deviation

When variables are measured on a level that at least approximates interval characteristics, the sum of squares, the variance, and the standard deviation are all appropriate indexes of variability. When variables are measured on an ordinal level that departs markedly from interval characteristics, these indexes are less applicable. Consider the standard deviation. If we want to, we can calculate the standard deviation for any set of scores and the result will reflect how much those particular scores tend to vary. But usually we are not interested in how the scores themselves vary but, rather, in how the phenomenon that the scores supposedly represent varies.

Suppose that we have an ordinal measure of height for three individuals: One individual has a score of 5, another has a score of 7, and a third individual has a score of 9. We know that the third individual is taller than the second individual who, in turn, is taller than the first individual. If we calculate the standard deviation of these three scores, it is 1.63. This value tells us that the scores, on average, deviate 1.63 units from the mean. But this index gives us no sense of how much variability there is on the underlying dimension of height. For example, the individual with a score of 5 might be 62 inches tall, the individual with a score of 7 might be 63 inches tall, and the individual with a score of 9 might be 77 inches tall. Or the individual with a score of 5 might be 60 inches tall, the individual with a score of 7 might be 70 inches tall, and the individual with a score of 9 might be 79 inches tall. Because the measure is only ordinal, the standard deviation of those scores does not help us appreciate how much variability there is on the underlying dimension.

3.3   Computational Formula for the Sum of Squares

The determination of a sum of squares using Equation 3.3 involves computing a deviation score and a squared deviation score for each individual. Each time one of these scores is calculated, the opportunity exists for rounding error. However, there is an alternative formula for computing the sum of squares that does not require the computation of deviation scores. This formula is both more efficient and more precise because it requires fewer steps and presents fewer opportunities for rounding error. The formula is

$$SS = \sum X^2 - \frac{(\sum X)^2}{N} \qquad [3.6]$$

where $\sum X^2$ is the *sum of the squared X scores* and $(\sum X)^2$ is the *square of the summed X scores*. As we demonstrate below, this formula is mathematically equivalent to Equation 3.3.

Consider the seven scores from Set A of Table 3.1. Application of Equation 3.6 requires that we first calculate the sum of the X scores. Next, we square each X score and add the squared scores to get a sum:

X	X^2
2	4
3	9
3	9
5	25
7	49
7	49
8	64
$\sum X = 35$	$\sum X^2 = 209$

Finally, we substitute these values, along with N, into Equation 3.6:

$$SS = 209 - \frac{35^2}{7}$$
$$= 209 - 175.00 = 34.00$$

which is identical to the value that we obtained in Table 3.1 using Equation 3.3.

Given its greater computational ease, we will use Equation 3.6 rather than Equation 3.3 when calculating sums of squares in the remainder of this book.

STUDY EXERCISE 3.5

Compute the sum of squares for the scores in Study Exercise 3.3 using Equation 3.6. Compare your result with the result that you obtained in Study Exercise 3.3 using Equation 3.3.

Answer   We must first determine the sum of the X scores and the sum of the squared X scores:

X	X^2
6	36
8	64
4	16
10	100
2	4
$\sum X = 30$	$\sum X^2 = 220$

Thus,

$$SS = \sum X^2 - \frac{\left(\sum X\right)^2}{N}$$

$$= 220 - \frac{30^2}{5}$$

$$= 220 - 180.00 = 40.00$$

This result agrees with that obtained in Study Exercise 3.3.

3.4 Conceptual Explanation of Variability

Theoretically, each member of a group—be it a sample or a population—should have the same score on a given variable by virtue of the fact that he or she *is* a member of that group. Clearly, however, this is not the case. The fact that members of a given group have different standing on a particular dimension is due to *disturbance variables*. We give a formal definition of such variables in Section 9.3. For now, we merely demonstrate the concept through an example.

Consider whether a random sample of all human beings or a random sample of 20-year-old American male college students should show greater variability on such diverse dimensions as eating habits, athletic ability, income, television viewing, writing skills, and aggressiveness. Clearly, there will typically be much greater variability in the first group because the individuals who comprise this group are much more diverse on characteristics such as age, nationality, gender, and education that should influence many different types of attitudes and behavior. In fact, *individual differences* of this type are an important type of disturbance variable.

If there were no disturbance variables, the scores within a given group would all be the same. The greater the role of disturbance variables, the more variability there will be, and this will be reflected in such things as a larger variance and standard deviation. Thus, measures of variability reflect the influence of disturbance variables. We will return to this and related issues in Chapter 9.

3.5 Relationship Between Central Tendency and Variability

Central tendency and variability represent different characteristics of a distribution. For the purpose of illustration, we will focus on the mean and the standard deviation.

Suppose that we assess the depression levels of a large sample of "typical" adults and find that their mean depression score on some measure is 16.00 and that the standard deviation is 2.00. A frequency graph for this data might look like curve A of Figure 3.4a. Furthermore, suppose that we perform the same assessment on a large sample of individuals who are diagnosed as being clinically depressed and that

FIGURE 3.4   **Illustration of Distributions That Have (a) Identical Standard Deviations but Different Means, and (b) Identical Means but Different Standard Deviations**

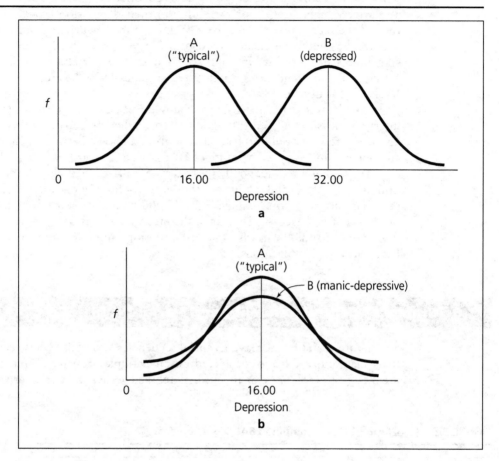

we observe the frequency distribution depicted in curve B of Figure 3.4a. This distribution has the same shape and the same standard deviation as curve A, but the mean is equal to 32.00 rather than 16.00, indicating a higher overall level of depression. This illustrates an important point: Distributions of scores can have identical variability (in this case, standard deviations) but very different central tendencies (in this case, means).

Distributions can also have identical central tendencies but very different variability. For instance, curves A and B in Figure 3.4b present frequency distributions for the depression scores of a large sample of "typical" adults and a large sample of adults who are diagnosed as being prone to manic depression, respectively. This is a psychological condition in which cycles of extreme euphoria, sociability, and hyperactivity (mania) alternate with cycles of extreme despair and social withdrawal (depression). Although the mean depression score is 16.00 for each group, the "typical" sample has a relatively small standard deviation of 2.00, indicating that the depression scores for people in this group tend to be close to 16, whereas the manic-depressive sample has a standard deviation of 5.00, indicating a relatively higher degree of variability in their depression levels. This probably reflects the fact that some members of this group are currently in the manic stage and are thus not experiencing any depression, whereas others are in the depression stage and still others are in remission. The greater variability of the group with manic-depressive tendencies is illustrated graphically by the greater spread of curve B relative to curve A.

As illustrated by this second example, measures of variability can help to interpret measures of central tendency. To further demonstrate this point, think about where you would prefer to live if given a choice between a climate that has an annual daily mean temperature of 70°F with a standard deviation of 10°F and a climate that has an annual daily mean temperature of 70°F with a standard deviation of 25°F. Also, think about whether you would prefer a salaried job for which the mean income across employees is $40,000 with a standard deviation of $6,000 or an incentive-based job for which the mean income is $40,000 with a standard deviation of $14,000. Clearly, standard deviations and other measures of variability have real-world implications.

3.6   Graphs of Central Tendency and Variability

Graphs are useful for displaying central tendencies, especially when scores for more than one group are being considered. As an example of such a graph, consider Figure 3.5. This graph presents the mean combined verbal and quantitative SAT scores

FIGURE 3.5   **Graph of Mean Combined SAT Scores by Year**

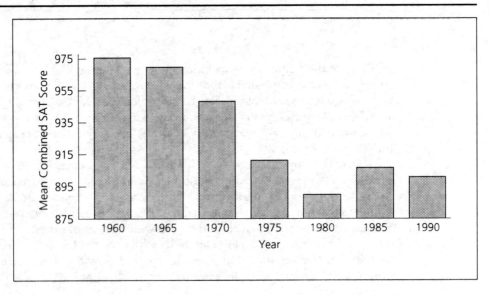

for students in the United States for 1960 to 1990 in 5-year increments. The names of the levels of the independent variable (the year of assessment) appear on the abscissa, and each of the seven levels of this variable (1960, 1965, 1970, etc.) is represented by a bar that extends to the height on the ordinate that corresponds to the mean score on the dependent variable (the combined SAT score). Unlike frequency graphs, it is not necessary for the ordinate for this type of graph to start at 0.

In 1960, the mean combined SAT score was 975, so the corresponding bar reaches to 975 on the ordinate. In 1965, the mean SAT score was 969; in 1970, the mean SAT score was 948; and so on. It can be seen that the combined SAT scores declined rather dramatically from 1960 to 1990—a decline of about 75 points, on average. Mean differences between three or more groups can be formally analyzed using the statistical procedures that we discuss in Chapter 12.

Usually the bars for the different groups do not touch one another, to indicate that the means are from different sets of scores. However, investigators sometimes permit the bars to touch if the independent variable is quantitative (as it is in this case) but they keep the bars from touching if the independent variable is qualitative. However, in the case of mean plots, there is no set rule in this regard.

Another way of graphically presenting the same information is with a line plot. Figure 3.6 presents such a plot, with a vertical line that conveys information about the standard deviation associated with a given mean also included for each group. In this instance, these lines extend one-half a standard deviation below the mean and one-half a standard deviation above the mean. However, line plots are sometimes structured so that each vertical line encompasses a full standard deviation. The choice is arbitrary. The ordinate of Figure 3.6 is different than that of Figure 3.5 because of the rescaling necessary to accommodate the standard deviations.

FIGURE 3.6   **Line Plot of Mean Combined SAT Scores by Year**

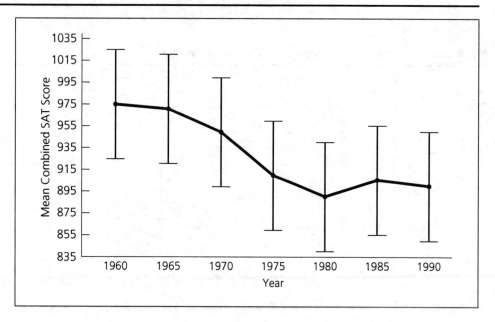

Another type of graph for displaying information about central tendency and variability is the **boxplot**, which is also known as a *box and whisker plot*. For instance, Figure 3.7 presents a boxplot for the hours of weekly exercise over a 3-month period for a random sample of 100 adults from a small rural community. As indicated in the legend, the small square in the middle of the rectangular box represents the mean, which is 7.04 hours. The top of the box represents one standard deviation above the mean, and the bottom of the box represents one standard deviation below the mean. Because the standard deviation for the exercise scores is 2.01, the top of the box is at $7.04 + 2.01 = 9.05$ and the bottom of the box is at $7.04 - 2.01 = 5.03$.

The "Ts" extending away from the box, which are referred to as *whiskers*, are the criteria that are used to define outliers. Suppose, for example, that an investigator decides that any value above 13 or below 1 is an outlier. This is reflected in Figure 3.7. The solid dots above and below the whiskers reflect outlying scores. Two scores are greater than 13 (hence, the two dots above the upper whisker), reflecting the fact that one individual exercised 15 hours a week and a second individual exercised 17 hours a week. Also, one score is less than 1 (hence, the one dot below the lower whisker) because one individual only exercised a half-hour per week.

Boxplots can also be used to present medians and interquartile ranges rather than means and standard deviations. In fact, boxplots were originally designed using the median and the interquartile range. When boxplots are used for this purpose, the median is represented by a small square in the middle of the box in a similar fashion as is done with the mean, the top of the box represents the upper bound of the interquartile range, and the bottom of the box represents the lower bound of the interquartile range. Hence, the interquartile range is reflected in the height of the box.

Figure 3.8 presents boxplots of medians and interquartile ranges for the amount of time that individuals who were convicted of three types of crimes in

FIGURE 3.7 Boxplot with Mean and Standard Deviation

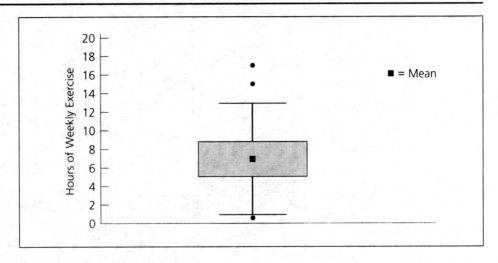

FIGURE 3.8   **Boxplots with Medians and Interquartile Ranges**

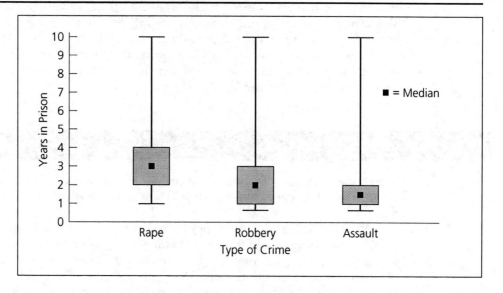

1992 served in prison. The first boxplot depicts these measures for 200 individuals who were convicted of rape, the second boxplot depicts these measures for 200 individuals who were convicted of robbery, and the third boxplot depicts these measures for 200 individuals who were convicted of assault. Any outliers would be indicated by dots above and below the whiskers, as is done with boxplots of means and standard deviations. As can be seen, there were no outlying scores for any of the crimes.

3.7   Measures of Central Tendency and Variability for Qualitative Variables

To this point, all of the measures of central tendency and variability that we have discussed apply to quantitative variables. These indexes are not appropriate for qualitative variables. For example, it makes no sense to talk about a mean or a median political party affiliation (for instance, a mean party affiliation of *Democrat* or a median party affiliation of *Republican*). The closest concept to central tendency for a qualitative variable is the modal category, that is, the category that occurs most frequently. For example, the political party that most people in the United States identify with is the Democratic party, which is the modal value for this qualitative variable.

In terms of variability, we cannot meaningfully define a range for qualitative variables because the categories cannot be ordered to define a low and a high score. The other measures of variability discussed above are also not applicable. Probably the best way to characterize the variability of a qualitative variable is in terms of the entire frequency distribution or in terms of the frequencies (or the percentages) for the categories that are of theoretical interest for the questions being addressed.* If all individuals fall into a single category, then there is no variability. For example, if everyone were a Democrat, there would be no variability in political party affiliation. Maximum variability occurs when the number of individuals is evenly divided among the possible categories (for example, when there are equal numbers of Democrats, Republicans, and Independents).

3.8   Skewness and Kurtosis

Thus far, we have considered two dimensions on which distributions of scores can differ—central tendency and variability. Two other dimensions are *skewness* and *kurtosis*.

Skewness refers to the tendency for scores to cluster on one side of the mean. Stated another way, one of the "tails" of the distribution relative to the central section is disproportionate compared to the other tail. Figure 3.9 presents two graphs of scores that illustrate this concept. The graph in Figure 3.9a is said to be *positively skewed* because the "tail" is toward the right, or positive, end of the abscissa. In positively skewed distributions, most scores occur below the mean and only a relatively few extreme scores occur above it. Thus, the mean will always be larger than the median in a positively skewed distribution. The graph in Figure 3.9b represents a distribution that is *negatively skewed* because the "tail" is toward the left, or

FIGURE 3.9   **Frequency Graphs of (a) Positively Skewed and (b) Negatively Skewed Distributions**

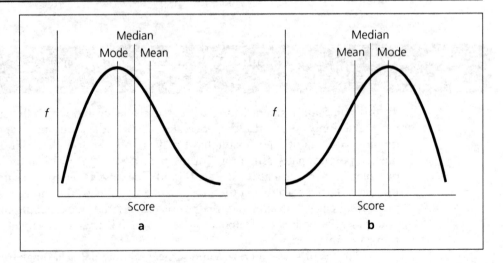

---

* For an attempt to define a formal measure of variability for qualitative variables, see Kirk (1978, pp. 73–75).

FIGURE 3.10   **Frequency Graphs of (a) Leptokurtic, (b) Platykurtic, and (c) Normal Distributions**

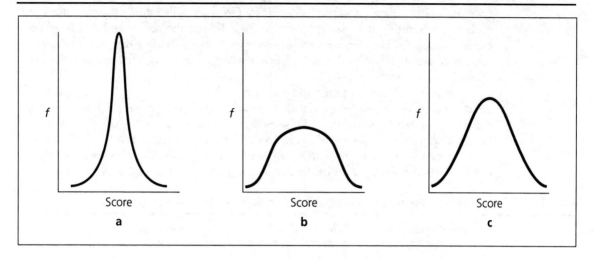

negative, end of the abscissa. Most scores in negatively skewed distributions occur above the mean and only a relatively few extreme scores occur below it. This is reflected in the fact that the mean of a negatively skewed distribution will always be smaller than the median.

Normal distributions, such as that depicted in Figure 3.3, are not skewed because an equal number of scores occur above and below the mean, which is also the median (and the mode). As shown in Figure 3.9, these three measures of central tendency all take on different values in skewed distributions.

A more technical concept is **kurtosis**, which reflects both how flat the peak of a distribution is and how long and flat the tails of the distribution are. Distributions are often said to be *leptokurtic* or *platykurtic* relative to a normal distribution. A leptokurtic distribution has a sharp peak and long, flat tails compared to a normal distribution. A platykurtic distribution has a flat peak and short, steep tails relative to a normal distribution. Figure 3.10 presents graphs of leptokurtic, platykurtic, and normal distributions.

Statisticians have derived numerical indexes of skewness and kurtosis. These are rarely used in the behavioral sciences and, hence, are not described here. Interested readers are referred to Ferguson (1976).

3.9 Sample Versus Population Notation and Formulas

The most frequently used descriptive statistics are the mean, the variance, and the standard deviation. As we proceed through this book, reference will be made to these indexes for both samples and populations. As we stated at the beginning of this chapter, the rationale and calculations are identical in both cases. However, it is traditional to denote indexes derived from populations with Greek letters.

As we have seen, the symbol $\overline{X}$ is typically used to represent a sample mean. The symbol for a population mean is μ (lowercase Greek *m*, called *mu*). Of course, the formula for computing the two indexes is identical: Sum the scores and divide by the number of scores. The Greek notation, however, makes it explicit that we are describing a population, whereas the $\overline{X}$ notation makes it explicit that we are describing a sample.

The symbols for a population variance and a population standard deviation are σ^2 and σ (lowercase Greek *s*, called *sigma*), respectively, paralleling the symbols s^2 and s for a sample variance and a sample standard deviation. Again, the formulas for the population values are identical to those for the sample values.

These indexes are summarized in Table 3.2. In this table, N represents either the number of sample scores or the number of population scores, as relevant.

TABLE 3.2   **Sample and Population Notation and Formulas for Descriptive Statistics**

Statistical term	Sample value	Population value
Mean	$\overline{X} = (\Sigma X)/N$	$\mu = (\Sigma X)/N$
Variance	$s^2 = SS/N$	$\sigma^2 = SS/N$
Standard deviation	$s = \sqrt{s^2}$	$\sigma = \sqrt{\sigma^2}$

3.10 Method of Presentation

Most researchers report means and standard deviations when presenting measures of central tendency and variability.* Occasionally, reports of the mean are supplemented with reports of the median, especially when the mean can be a misleading index of central tendency (for example, when there are extreme scores).

A common format in behavioral science journals presents means and standard deviation measures in a table like the following:

<u>Means and Standard Deviations for Intelligence Scores of Men and Women</u>

Gender	<u>M</u>	<u>SD</u>	<u>n</u>
Men	101.31	10.62	120
Women	102.48	10.31	115

---

* The standard deviations that are presented in research reports are somewhat different than the standard deviations that we discuss in this chapter and are formally known as *standard deviation estimates*. We introduce this measure in Section 3.12 and discuss it at length in Chapter 7.

In this table, M represents the mean and SD represents the standard deviation, consistent with American Psychological Association (APA)(2001) format.[5] It is also common to report the sizes of the samples. This is indicated by n because N is reserved to designate the size of the overall data set when there is more than one group. In this example, $N = 120 + 115 = 235$.

Note that it is possible to compute the variances and the sums of squares from the information provided. For instance, the variance for men is the square of the standard deviation of 10.62, that is, $10.62^2 = 112.78$. The sum of squares can then be computed by multiplying the variance by n: $(112.78)(120) = 13{,}533.60$.

Measures of central tendency and variability can also be presented in the text of a Results section rather than in a table. The decision to present descriptive statistics in tabular or in textual form depends on several factors, most notably, on how many variables there are. According to APA (2001) style, tables should be reserved for "simplifying text that otherwise would be dense with numbers" (p. 147).

As an example of how the information about male and female intelligence scores might appear in textual form, consider the following:[6]

Results

The mean intelligence score for men was 101.31 (SD = 10.62), and that for women was 102.48 (SD = 10.31).

Even though the statement refers only to mean scores, the text follows the APA practice of also reporting standard deviations to help us interpret the mean. Supplemental information of this type is often presented in parentheses so that it will not interfere with the flow of the main text.

Note that the sample size information is not given. Usually the sample sizes are identified in the section of the report that provides details about how the study was conducted, known as the Method section. However, if the sample sizes are not presented in the Method section, they should be included as parenthetical material (for example, $n = 120$) or otherwise integrated into the text of the Results section.

Sample size information should also be reported in the Results section if the sample sizes differ from one variable to the next due to missing data, which is often the case in research. This situation can arise for several reasons. For instance, as noted in Section 2.4, a researcher might exclude outlying scores from the analyses. Another common cause of missing data is that participants fail to properly complete a research task or to otherwise provide a viable score for a particular variable.

---

[5] Technically, SD is the symbol for the standard deviation estimate.

[6] Per the footnote Section 2.10, although American Psychological Association (2001) format requires that all text be double spaced, for the sake of brevity single spacing is used throughout this book.

3.11 Example from the Literature

Psychologists have extensively studied how people form impressions of others and how we perceive various traits and characteristics. For example, Anderson (1968) asked 100 individuals to rate a number of traits in terms of how favorable or desirable each is in forming an impression of another person. The ratings were made on a 0 (least favorable or desirable) to 6 (most favorable or desirable) scale, where 3 represented a neutral evaluation. The means and standard deviations for six of the traits are as follows:

Trait	$\overline{X}$	s
Sincere	5.73	.55
Honest	5.55	.69
Narrow-minded	.80	.76
Selfish	.82	.81
Cunning	2.62	1.48
Inexperienced	2.62	.81

The means for the first two traits are very large (5.73 and 5.55), thus indicating that these traits were rated very positively, and the standard deviations are relatively small, thus indicating that most individuals rated the traits using the upper points of the scale. The traits *narrow-minded* and *selfish* were similarly rated, but in a negative fashion. The traits *cunning* and *inexperienced* both have relatively neutral mean scores (2.62). However, notice the large difference between the standard deviations. The small standard deviation for *inexperienced* indicates that people consistently tended to rate this trait near the neutral point, whereas the large standard deviation for *cunning* indicates that there was considerable variability in these ratings, with many individuals perceiving *cunning* as being a positive trait and many perceiving *cunning* as being a negative trait. When averaged, the mean is near the neutral point. By showing that the perceptions of *cunning* were not really all that neutral but rather exhibited considerable variability across individuals, the standard deviation helps us to interpret the mean.

3.12 Links Between Computer Results and Book Content

Depending on what statistical program is used, there might be some differences between what we have discussed in this chapter and the nature of the descriptive statistics that will be provided as statistical output. For instance, some programs report only the lowest mode when there is more than one modal score. However, all modes for a given variable can be identified by examining the frequency distribution for that variable for all score values that share the highest absolute frequency. Also, some programs report the approximation of the median rather than the actual median when there are duplications of the middle score(s). This is likely the case if the decimal portion for the median is reported to be all zeros when a middle score occurs more than once.

The most important difference between what we have discussed in this chapter and statistical computer results relates to what is represented by the quantities that are standardly labeled as *variance* and *standard deviation* in the output. In actuality, these are usually neither sample values nor population values. Rather, they are the sample e*stimates* of the corresponding population values, commonly referred to as the *variance estimate* and the *standard deviation estimate*, respectively.

Although we will defer an in-depth discussion of this issue until Chapter 7, you should be aware that these are not the same values as would be obtained by using the formulas from this chapter. Rather, the variance estimate is calculated as $SS/(N-1)$ rather than SS/N and the standard deviation estimate is calculated as the positive square root of the variance estimate rather than the positive square root of the variance. Thus, one can convert a "variance" result provided by the computer (which is actually the variance estimate) into the type of variance that we discuss in this chapter by multiplying the "variance" from the computer output by $(N-1)/N$. Once this is done, the square root of this result will yield the standard deviation.

3.13   Links Between Chapters

Data are typically summarized *either* in terms of frequency information, as discussed in Chapter 2, *or* in terms of descriptive statistics. Only rarely will both types of information be presented for a set of scores. For reasons that will become apparent in later chapters, most applications focus on the latter. In fact, measures of central tendency and variability can be viewed as the "building blocks" of statistics. As such, it is very important that you understand the concepts from this chapter. If not, we strongly suggest that you go back and review the information that is giving you difficulty.

Applications to the Analysis of a Social Problem Using SPSS for Windows

Many variables in the parent–teen database described in Chapter 1 can be explored using the descriptive statistics from this chapter. We highlight two of these here: the mother's age and the teen's self-report of whether or not he or she used birth control at first intercourse.

A major purpose of the parent–teen study was to examine communication between teens and their mothers. Past research suggests that the nature of this communication differs as a function of the mother's age. Thus, it was important to document the ages of the mothers who participated in our study. Among other things, this would allow us to use the information that we collected to develop different types of educational materials for fostering mother–teen communication based on how old the mother is.

(continued)

One issue that arose in the planning of the research was how to define who the teen's mother is. The traditional approach is to use the teen's biological mother. However, the teen's primary mother figure is not always the biological mother. For inner-city African American teens, it is not uncommon for the primary female caretaker to be a stepmother, a grandmother, an aunt, or even an older sister. Ultimately, we interviewed the person who the teen identified (based on a series of questions) as the primary female caretaker in the household. This "mother" was not always the biological mother of the teen.

The computer printout in Table 3.3 summarizes the basic descriptive statistics for maternal age (MOTHAGE). The labels "Valid" and "Missing" indicate the number of cases ("N") that were included in the analysis and the number of cases for which no responses were provided, respectively. As can be seen, the mean age for the 634 valid cases is 40.76, and the

modal age is 38.* Although the median age is reported as 39.00, it is probably not exactly 39.00 because SPSS for Windows reports approximate medians rather than exact medians, as we discussed in Section 3.12. The youngest mother figure was 19 years old (indicated by "Minimum"), and the oldest was 81 (indicated by "Maximum"), which yields a range of 62. The standard deviation is 8.23, indicating that, on average, the ages of the mother figures tended to deviate about 8 years from the mean age of 40.76.**

The fact that the mean is greater than the median suggests that the distribution of maternal age is positively skewed. This is confirmed by an examination of Figure 3.11, which presents a grouped frequency histogram for maternal age with a normal distribution superimposed. Note how the upper end of the histogram forms a "tail" relative to the normal distribution, which, it will be remembered, has no skewness.

TABLE 3.3 Computer Output for Descriptive Statistics for Mother's Age and Use of Birth Control

STATISTICS

		MOTHAGE Mother's age	BCFIRST Used birth control at first intercourse
N	Valid	634	425
	Missing	15	326
Mean		40.7590	.4160
Median		39.0000	.0000
Mode		38.00	.00
Std. Deviation		8.2340	.4940
Variance		67.8010	.2440
Range		62.00	1.00
Minimum		19.00	.00
Maximum		81.00	1.00

* As with all statistical computer programs, SPSS for Windows is programmed to report output to a certain number of decimal places, including zeros as decimal portions for integer values. However, for the sake of readability we exclude the ending zeros when discussing integer values in the text. For the same reason, we round other decimal portions to two decimal places.
** Technically, 8.23 is the standard deviation estimate for maternal age. Similarly, the value of 67.80 from Table 3.3 is the *variance estimate*. Both of these measures are discussed briefly in Section 3.12 and at length in Chapter 7.

FIGURE 3.11   Grouped Frequency Histogram for Maternal Age

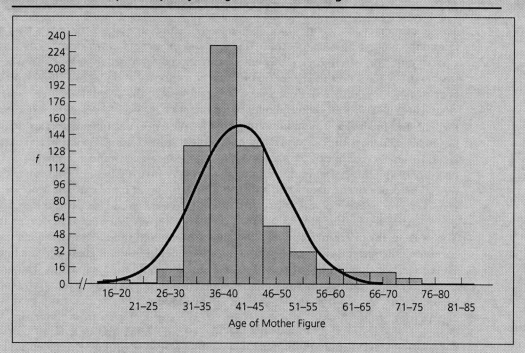

We also calculated descriptive statistics for a self-report of whether or not the teen used birth control at the first instance of sexual intercourse. This is an important variable because teens who engage in unprotected intercourse are at risk of unintended pregnancy. In fact, statistics indicate that an unusually large proportion of unintended pregnancies in teenagers occurs within the first 6 months of sexual initiation.

The birth control variable (BCFIRST) was scored as 0 if the teen reported not using birth control at first intercourse and as 1 if the teen reported using birth control at first intercourse. Variables of this type that have only two values are known as *dichotomous* variables. The descriptive statistics were derived for only the 425 teens who indicated that they had engaged in sexual intercourse, with the other 326 teens being treated as having missing data.

It turns out that the mean of a dichotomous variable that is scored 0 and 1 is equivalent to the pro-

portion of people who have a score of 1. Multiplying the mean by 100 yields a percentage. The mean for this sample is .416, which yields a percentage of 41.6%. Thus, just over 40% of the teens reported using some form of birth control at first intercourse, and 100.0% − 41.6% = 58.4% reported that they engaged in unprotected intercourse (and were thus at risk for an unintended pregnancy). For dichotomous variables, the other descriptive statistics from Table 3.3 either are not applicable or are not informative for our purposes and, hence, we do not consider them here.

It is important to note that self-reports of birth control use must be treated with caution because the teen may not accurately recall this information. In addition, social desirability tendencies may cause teens to overreport birth control use. However, we did not find any relationship between self-reported birth control use and our measures of social desirability tendencies.

Summary

Two important characteristics of a distribution of scores are where the scores tend to fall on the numerical scale (central tendency) and the extent to which the scores are alike or different (variability). Distributions can also be described in terms of skewness (the tendency for scores to cluster on one side of the mean) and kurtosis (how flat the peak of a distribution is and how long and flat the tails of the distribution are).

Three measures of central tendency for quantitative variables are the mode, the median, and the mean. The mode is the most frequently occurring score in a distribution, the median is the point that divides the distribution into halves, and the mean is the arithmetic average of the scores. Although the mean is the most frequently used measure of the three, the mode and the median may provide better insight into the central tendency of the data when a distribution has one or more extreme scores.

Five measures of variability for quantitative variables are the range, the interquartile range, the sum of squares, the variance, and the standard deviation. The range is the difference between the highest score and the lowest score in a distribution. The interquartile range is the difference between the highest and the lowest scores after eliminating the top 25% and the bottom 25% of the scores. The sum of squares is the sum of the squared deviations from the mean. By dividing the sum of squares by N, we obtain the variance. The standard deviation is the positive square root of the variance and represents an average deviation from the mean. As such, it is the most easily interpreted measure of variability among a set of scores. Conceptually, measures of variability reflect the influence of disturbance variables such as individual differences.

The sum of squares, the variance, and the standard deviation will always be greater than or equal to 0. A value of 0 for these statistics means that there is no variability in the scores; they are all the same. As the values of the three statistics become increasingly greater than 0, more variability among the scores is indicated, other things being equal.

Central tendency and variability represent different characteristics of a distribution. Distributions of scores can have identical variability but very different central tendencies. Distributions can also have identical central tendencies but very different variability.

Several methods are available for graphing information about central tendency and variability. These include the use of vertical bars or line plots to indicate the means for the various levels of the independent variable, and boxplots. When line plots are used to display means, they also provide information about the corresponding standard deviations. Boxplots can be used to present means and standard deviations, or medians and interquartile ranges. In either instance, boxplots also provide information about outliers.

None of the measures of central tendency and variability for quantitative variables apply to qualitative variables. The closest concept to central tendency for variables of this type is the modal category, that is, the category that occurs most frequently. Probably the best way to characterize the variability of a qualitative variable is in terms of the entire frequency distribution or in terms of the frequencies (or the percentages) for the categories that are of theoretical interest for the questions being addressed.

The rationale and calculations for the mean, the variance, and the standard deviation are identical for both samples and populations. However, whereas the sample values are symbolized as $\overline{X}$, s^2, and s, respectively, the corresponding population values are μ, σ^2, and σ.

Exercises

Answers to asterisked (*) exercises appear at the back of the book.

1. Identify and define the three measures of central tendency.

2. What are the three approaches to computing the median? When is each appropriate?

*3. Compute the median for the following scores: 6, 4, 9, 4, 4.

4. Compute the median for the following scores: 5, 2, 7, 3, 12, 5.

5. Given the impact of television on children's attitudes and behavior, an important concern of behavioral scientists is the amount of time children of various ages spend watching television. The following data are the weekly viewing times (in hours) of 12-year-olds. Compute the mode, the median, and the mean for these scores.

18	17	22	20	25	20	16
19	18	22	26	23	23	23
24	24	22	21	19	20	20

*6. Compute the mode, the median, and the mean for the following scores: 1, −2, 3, 2, −3, −1, 0, −1 −2, 1, 2, 0, 2, −3, −1, 0, 3, −2, 1, 0.

7. What are unsigned deviation scores? What are signed deviation scores?

*8. Compute the mean for the following five scores: 10, 14, 12, 11, 13. Now, generate a new set of five scores by adding a constant of 3 to each original score. Compute the mean for the new scores. Do the same for another set of five scores generated by subtracting a constant of 10 from each original score. What are the effects on the mean of adding a constant to or subtracting a constant from each score in a set of scores?

9. Suppose you measured the mean amount of time it took ten children to solve a problem and found it to be 35.31 seconds. You later discovered, however, that your timing device (a watch) was 2 seconds too slow for each child. What was the real mean score?

*10. Compute the mean for the following five scores: 20, 50, 30, 10, 40. Now, generate a new set of five scores by multiplying each original score by a constant of 3. Compute the mean for the new scores. Do the same for another set of five scores generated by dividing each original score by a constant of 10. What are the effects on the mean of multiplying or dividing each score in a set of scores by a constant?

*11. Repeat the procedures outlined in Exercises 8 and 10, but compute the median rather than the mean. What are the effects on the median of adding a constant to or subtracting a constant from each score in a set of scores? What are the effects on the median of multiplying or dividing each score in a set of scores by a constant? What effects do you think these operations would have on the mode?

12. What are the advantages and disadvantages of using the mean as a measure of central tendency? The median? The mode?

*13. Consider these two sets of data:

Set A		Set B	
20	21	53	55
20	10	54	54
19	21	54	53
21	300	55	54

For which set is the mean a poorer descriptor of central tendency? Why?

14. Identify and define three measures of variability.

*15. Under what condition is the range a misleading index of variability?

16. Define the interquartile range.

17. What is the problem with the sum of squares as a measure of variability?

*18. If the variance of a set of scores is 100.00, what is the standard deviation?

19. If the standard deviation of a set of scores is 7.00, what is the variance?

*20. Without actually calculating it, what must the standard deviation of the following scores equal: 6, 6, 6, 6, 6? What must the variance equal? What must the sum of squares equal? Why?

*21. Why is the standard deviation more "interpretable" than the variance? That is, what is the advantage of reporting statistics in terms of the standard deviation as opposed to the variance?

22. Compute ΣX^2 and $(\Sigma X)^2$ for the following scores: 3, 6, 12, 5, 9, 2, 3, 6, 11.

*23. For the data in Exercise 22, compute the sum of squares using the defining formula (Equation 3.3). Recalculate the sum of squares using the computational formula (Equation 3.6). Compare the two results. Which approach did you find more efficient?

*24. Compute the range, the sum of squares, the variance, and the standard deviation for the data in Exercise 5.

25. Compute the range, the sum of squares, the variance, and the standard deviation for each of the two sets of data in Exercise 13.

*26. Compute the variance and the standard deviation for the following five scores: 5, 3, 1, 4, 2. Now, generate a new set of five scores by adding a constant of 3 to each original score. Compute the variance and standard deviation for the new scores. Do the same for another set of five scores generated by subtracting a constant of 2 from each original score. What are the effects on the variance of adding a constant to or subtracting a constant from each score in a set of scores? What are the effects on the standard deviation?

27. Suppose that you measured the weights of 100 people and found a mean of 180.29 and a standard deviation of 10.36. Then you learned that your scale was 1 pound too heavy. What were the correct mean and standard deviation?

*28. Compute the variance and the standard deviation for the following eight scores: 6, 10, 8, 8, 10, 8, 6, 8. Now, generate a new set of eight scores by multiplying each original score by a constant of 3. Compute the variance and the standard deviation for the new scores. Do the same for another set of eight scores generated by dividing each original score by a constant of 2. What are the effects on the variance of multiplying or dividing each score in a set of scores by a constant? What are the effects on the standard deviation?

*29. Generate two sets of scores with equal means but unequal standard deviations.

30. Generate two sets of scores with unequal means but equal standard deviations.

*31. How accurate are eyewitness reports of accidents? Behavioral scientists have studied this question in some detail. In one experiment, people viewed a film of an accident in which a car ran through a stop sign and hit a parked car. The speed of the car was 30 miles per hour. After viewing the film, the people were asked to estimate the speed of the car. Fifteen participants gave the following estimates:

15	18	37	40	25
40	35	35	20	30
30	20	28	32	25

Compute the mean and the standard deviation for these data. How accurate are the estimates considering the mean score across all participants? How does the standard deviation help to interpret the mean?

32. An organizational psychologist studied how satisfied employees were in two different companies. All employees were given a job satisfaction test on which scores could range from 1 to 7, with higher values indicating greater satisfaction. The scores were as follows:

Company A	Company B
4	4
6	4
5	4
4	4
3	4
2	4

Compute the mean and the standard deviation for each company. Based on the results, compare employee satisfaction in the two companies. How do the standard deviations help to interpret the means?

*33. A consultant you hired to assess the public's attitude toward your company told you that the mean evaluation on a 1 (extremely negative) to 7 (extremely positive) scale was 5.16 and the standard deviation was −1.43. What should you conclude?

34. What are the three methods for graphing group means? Which of these is also used to graph medians?

35. Draw a boxplot for the data in Exercise 5.

*36. Given a set of scores for which the mode is 12, the median is 15, and the mean is 20.68, are these scores skewed? If so, how? If the mode were 33, the median were 25, and the mean were 20.17, would the scores be skewed? If so, how? If the mode were 20, the median were 20, and the mean were 20.00, would the scores be skewed? If so, how?

37. What does it mean to say that a distribution of scores is more leptokurtic than another distribution? What does it mean to say that a distribution of scores is more platykurtic than another distribution?

38. Identify each of the following symbols in terms of the index it represents and whether it is a sample or a population value:
   a. σ^2 d. σ
   b. $\overline{X}$ e. μ
   c. s f. s^2

Multiple-Choice Questions

*39. Which of the following measures is appropriate for use with qualitative variables?
   a. range
   b. modal category
   c. median
   d. sum of squares

40. μ is the symbol for a
   a. population mean
   b. sample mean
   c. population standard deviation
   d. sample standard deviation

*41. Which measure of central tendency is most influenced by extreme scores?
   a. mean
   b. median
   c. mode
   d. The mean, the median, and the mode are equally influenced by extreme scores.

42. Which of the following is *not* an index of variability?
   a. standard deviation
   b. range
   c. sum of squares
   d. skewness

*43. The vertical lines on a line plot convey information about the _____ associated with each mean.
   a. sample size
   b. sum of squares
   c. variance
   d. standard deviation

44. Which measure of variability is the most easily interpreted?
   a. interquartile range
   b. sum of squares
   c. standard deviation
   d. variance

45. If a set of scores is negatively skewed, this means that it is less peaked than the normal distribution.
    a. true
    b. false

*46. The sum of a set of signed deviations around the mean will always equal 1.00.
    a. true
    b. false

47. What is the interquartile range for the following scores: 8, 1, 7, 4, 1, 9, 3, 6?
    a. 3   c. 7
    b. 4   d. 8

*48. When boxplots are used to display means, they also provide information about the interquartile range and outliers.
    a. true
    b. false

49. Measures of variability reflect the role of _____ variables.
    a. independent
    b. dependent
    c. conceptual
    d. disturbance

CHAPTER **4**

Percentiles, Percentile Ranks, Standard Scores, and the Normal Distribution

Suppose that we tell you that we have developed a measure of dominance and that we administered it to a group of 75 college students, one of whom, Mary, obtained a score of 50. This information is relatively useless when it stands alone. However, suppose that we also tell you that the highest possible score is 100. Now you might infer that Mary is not very dominant. But suppose that you also learn that the mean dominance score for the 75 college students is 30.00. Mary is beginning to look a little more dominant. Now we tell you that the standard deviation for the group of students is 5.00. This is even more enlightening. The mean score is 30.00 and, on average, scores deviate from the mean by 5.00 units. Mary's score is $50 - 30.00 = 20$ units *above* the mean, or 4.00 standard deviations above the mean, indicating that, relative to the rest of the students, her score is very high.

The point to be made is that, in general, observations are meaningful only in relation to other observations. When you are told that a person is 7 feet tall, this is meaningful because you have an intuitive grasp of the distribution of heights in human beings. You know that most people are between 5 and 6 feet tall and that someone who is 7 feet tall is unusually tall. In essence, you are intuitively using information about the mean and the standard deviation of height. In this chapter, we consider several measures that are used to identify the location of a specified score within a set of scores.

4.1   Percentiles and Percentile Ranks

One approach for expressing the relative standing of a score in a distribution is based on percentages. The percentage of scores in a distribution that occur at or below a given value, X, is the **percentile rank** of that value.*

Consider a national survey of 2,000 adults in the United States who respond to the question "Approximately how many hours per week do you watch television?" If 60% of the responses are at or below a score of 30 hours, then the percentile rank of 30 hours is 60. Thus, one way to convey the relative position of a score is in terms of its percentile rank.

On the other hand, we might want to know the reverse—namely, what is the value that a certain percentage of scores are at or below? For instance, we might want to know the number of hours of television viewing that defines the point at which 60% of the reported viewing times are at or below. The value that corresponds to a given percentile rank is called a **percentile**. For instance, the value that corresponds to a percentile rank of 60 is referred to as the 60th percentile. In our example, the 60th percentile is 30.

---

* A percentile rank is different from a *cumulative percentage*, which, following the logic outlined in Section 2.2, is found by adding the percentage of all scores that are equal to X to the percentage of scores that are less than X. As we will see shortly, when determining a percentile rank, half of the scores that have a value of X are considered to be less than X and half are considered to be greater than X. Consequently, the percentile rank and the cumulative percentage for a given score value will differ.

In practice, percentiles and percentile ranks are most commonly determined using statistical computer programs that are available for this purpose. Nevertheless, an understanding of how percentiles and percentile ranks are calculated helps to clarify the underlying concepts, so we examine this and related issues before proceeding to the discussion of an alternative, and, in some ways, more informative, measure of relative standing in Section 4.2.

Percentiles

Suppose that we administer a test designed to measure intelligence to 200 children. A frequency analysis of the children's scores is presented in Table 4.1. Our task is to specify the value that corresponds to a given percentile, P. For instance, if P is 70, then we want to specify the value that defines the 70th percentile.

Actually, we have already considered a special case of the formula for solving this problem in Equation 3.1 for calculating the median. Recall that the median is the score that 50% of the scores in a distribution are greater than and 50% of the scores are less than. The median thus corresponds to the 50th percentile. Accordingly, the procedure for calculating the 50th percentile is the same as that for calculating the median.

The formula for calculating the median for a continuous variable, as presented in Equation 3.1, is

$$Mdn = L + \left[\frac{(N)(.50) - n_L}{n_W} \right] i$$

where Mdn represents the median, L is the lower real limit of the category that contains the median, N is the total number of scores in the distribution, n_L is the number of scores that are less than L, n_W is the number of scores that are within the category that contains the median, and i is the size of the interval of the category that contains the median. The .50 in the numerator is the percentile of interest (the 50th) expressed in the form of a proportion.

TABLE 4.1   **Frequency Analysis of Intelligence Test Scores for 200 Children**

Intelligence	f	rf	cf	crf
105	9	.045	200	1.000
104	16	.080	191	.955
103	20	.100	175	.875
102	26	.130	155	.775
101	29	.145	129	.645
100	30	.150	100	.500
99	25	.125	70	.350
98	21	.105	45	.225
97	14	.070	24	.120
96	10	.050	10	.050

This equation suggests the following general formula for determining the value that defines a given percentile:

$$X_P = L + \left[\frac{(N)(P) - n_L}{n_W} \right] i \qquad [4.1]$$

where X_p represents the value that defines the percentile of interest (that is, the Pth percentile), L is the lower real limit of the category that contains the Pth percentile, N is the total number of scores in the distribution, P is the Pth percentile expressed in the form of a proportion, n_L is the number of scores that are less than L, n_W is the number of scores that are within the category that contains the Pth percentile, and i is the size of the interval of the category that contains the Pth percentile.

For instance, if we were interested in determining the 70th percentile, we would proceed as follows:

$$X_{70} = L + \left[\frac{(N)(.70) - n_L}{n_W} \right] i$$

where X_{70} denotes the value that defines the 70th percentile, L is the lower real limit of the category that contains the 70th percentile, n_W is the number of scores that are within the category that contains the 70th percentile, i is the size of the interval of the category that contains the 70th percentile, and N and n_L are as defined above.

The method of computation is then analogous to that used in computing the median. We start at the bottom of the column of cumulative relative frequencies in Table 4.1 and move up until we find the first cumulative relative frequency that is greater than or equal to .70 (the percentile of interest, expressed in the form of a proportion). The value of this cumulative relative frequency is .775, and this corresponds to a score of 102. The lower real limit of 102 is 101.5, so this is L. The total number of scores, N, is 200. The number of scores that are less than 101.5 is 129, so this is n_L, and the number of scores that are between 101.5 and 102.5 is 26, so this is n_W. Last, the interval size, i, is $102.5 - 101.5 = 1.0$. Thus,

$$X_{70} = 101.5 + \left[\frac{(200)(.70) - 129}{26} \right] (1.0)$$

$$= 101.5 + \left[\frac{11.00}{26} \right] (1.0)$$

$$= 101.5 + .42 = 101.92$$

This constitutes the 70th percentile.

Note that 101.92 is not included in the scores in Table 4.1. This is because the real limits of the score values were considered when determining the percentile rank. Technically, 101.92 should *not* be rounded up to 102 because doing so undermines the idea that the actual scores obtained by the individuals who have recorded scores of 102 are evenly distributed between the real limits of 101.5 and 102.5. The percentile rank for the "rounded-up" value of 102 is actually slightly greater than 70.

Nevertheless, some researchers round percentile calculations to units of the original scale, trading off technical precision for ease of presentation. Indeed, some investigators are uncomfortable with the assumption of scores being evenly dispersed across the real limits of a score value, noting that this may not be true (which would undermine the logic of the approach described here). These individuals also contend that carrying calculations to one or more decimal places beyond the original units implies a level of precision that is not justified. If one took this position, the 70th percentile would be reported as 102, that is, 101.92 rounded to the nearest integer.

We believe that both positions have merit (that is, rounding to units of the original scale and carrying calculations to additional decimal places), and we do not take a formal position on which one should be followed. In either case, it is important to recognize that both approaches yield only an approximation to the true percentile of interest.* For the sake of consistency, we follow the strategy of carrying percentile calculations to two additional decimal places throughout this book.

Before ending our discussion of percentiles, we should note that Equation 4.1 can be used to calculate the interquartile range. As we discussed in Section 3.2, this is the difference between the highest and the lowest scores in a distribution after the top 25% of the scores and the bottom 25% of the scores have been eliminated. In the present context, this is equivalent to the 75th percentile minus the 25th percentile. Applying Equation 4.1 to the data in Table 4.1 yields a 75th percentile of 102.31 and a 25th percentile of 98.70. The interquartile range is therefore $102.31 - 98.70 = 3.61$.

STUDY EXERCISE 4.1

A researcher who is interested in the size of babies at birth measures the birth lengths of 1,000 newborn infants. The distribution of lengths (measured to the nearest inch) is as follows:

Length	f	rf	cf	crf
24	27	.027	1,000	1.000
23	48	.048	973	.973
22	77	.077	925	.925
21	125	.125	848	.848
20	226	.226	723	.723
19	225	.225	497	.497
18	124	.124	272	.272
17	73	.073	148	.148
16	52	.052	75	.075
15	23	.023	23	.023

Compute the value that defines the 90th percentile.

---

* Other methods for estimating percentiles are discussed in Wilcox (1997). These methods tend to be more accurate than the approaches that we present in the text but are more computationally complex.

Answer   Using Equation 4.1, we find that

$$X_{90} = 21.5 + \left[\frac{(1,000)(.90) - 848}{77} \right](1.0)$$

$$= 21.5 + \left[\frac{52.00}{77} \right](1.0)$$

$$= 21.5 + .68 = 22.18$$

Thus, the 90th percentile is 22.18.

Percentile Ranks

Just as Equation 4.1 can be used to determine the value that defines a given percentile, it is also possible to specify a formula for determining the percentile rank for any given score. This formula is

$$PR_X = \left[\frac{(.5)(n_W) + n_L}{N} \right](100) \qquad [4.2]$$

where PR_X represents the percentile rank of a given X score (that is, the percentage of scores in a distribution that are at or below X), n_W is the number of scores that are equal to X, n_L is the number of scores that are less than X, and N is the total number of scores in the distribution.

For example, the percentile rank for a score of 101 from Table 4.1 is

$$PR_{101} = \left[\frac{(.5)(29) + 100}{200} \right](100)$$

$$= \left[\frac{114.50}{200} \right](100)$$

$$= (.572)(100) = 57.20$$

For this distribution, a score of 101 reflects a percentile rank of 57.20. In other words, 57.20% of the 200 children who were studied obtained an intelligence test score of 101 or less.

STUDY EXERCISE 4.2

For the data in Study Exercise 4.1, compute the percentile rank for 20 inches.

Answer   Using Equation 4.2, we get

$$PR_{20} = \left[\frac{(.5)(226) + 497}{1,000} \right](100)$$

$$= \left[\frac{610.00}{1,000} \right](100)$$

$$= (.610)(100) = 61.00$$

Thus, the percentile rank for a length of 20 inches is 61.00. That is, 61.00% of the infants who were studied were 20 inches long or less.

4.2   Standard Scores

A percentile rank is one index of the relative position of a score in a set of scores. However, percentile ranks reflect only an *ordinal* measure of relative standing. To say that a score has a percentile rank of 80 indicates only that 80% of the scores in a distribution are at or below that score. But *how much* lower are these other scores? Consider the following scores on two tests:

Test 1	Test 2
100	100
99	44
98	43
96	40
96	40
95	39

In both cases, a score of 100 reflects the same percentile rank. However, the score of 100 on Test 2 is certainly more distinctive than the score of 100 on Test 1. An index of relative standing that reflects this difference is **standard scores**.

The Concept of Standard Scores

Recall the example at the beginning of this chapter where Mary obtained a score of 50 out of 100 on a dominance measure. When you learned that the average score was 30.00, a score of 50 took on more meaning: Mary scored 20.00 units above the mean. With the additional information that the standard deviation was 5.00, the significance of Mary's score was even clearer. By comparing Mary's score to the mean and standard deviation, we gained considerable insight into its relative position. A standard score does just this: It converts a score from its original, or *raw*, form to a form that takes into consideration its standing relative to the mean and standard deviation of the entire distribution of scores.

Columns 1 and 5 of Table 4.2 present two sets of scores that we will use for illustration. If the data in Table 4.2 represent *sample* information, then the raw scores in each set can be converted to standard scores using the following formula:

$$\text{Standard score} = \frac{X - \overline{X}}{s} \qquad [4.3]$$

The standard score formula for *population* data is

$$\text{Standard score} = \frac{X - \mu}{\sigma} \qquad [4.4]$$

Note that the only difference between these two formulas is the notation that is used for the mean and the standard deviation of the distribution. In both instances, a standard score is the difference between the original score and the mean

TABLE 4.2   **Raw Scores and Standard Scores for Two Sets of Scores**

Set A				Set B			
X	X^2	$X - \overline{X}$	$\dfrac{X - \overline{X}}{s}$	X	X^2	$X - \overline{X}$	$\dfrac{X - \overline{X}}{s}$
1	1	−2.00	−1.49	1	1	−2.00	−2.25
3	9	0.00	.00	3	9	0.00	.00
5	25	2.00	1.49	3	9	0.00	.00
2	4	−1.00	.75	3	9	0.00	.00
3	9	0.00	.00	5	25	2.00	2.25
4	16	1.00	.75	3	9	0.00	.00
1	1	−2.00	−1.49	3	9	0.00	.00
3	9	0.00	.00	3	9	0.00	.00
5	25	2.00	1.49	3	9	0.00	.00
3	9	0.00	.00	3	9	0.00	.00
$\Sigma X = 3.00$	$\Sigma X^2 = 108$	Sum = 0		$\Sigma X = 30$	$\Sigma X^2 = 98$	Sum = 0	
$\overline{X} = 3.00$		Mean = 0		$\overline{X} = 3.00$		Mean = 0	

$$SS = \Sigma X^2 - \frac{(\Sigma X)^2}{N}$$

$$= 108 - \frac{30^2}{10} = 18.00$$

$$s^2 = \frac{SS}{N} = \frac{18.00}{10} = 1.80$$

$$s = \sqrt{s^2} = \sqrt{1.80} = 1.34$$

$$SS = \Sigma X^2 - \frac{(\Sigma X)^2}{N}$$

$$= 98 - \frac{30^2}{10} = 8.00$$

$$s^2 = \frac{SS}{N} = \frac{8.00}{10} = .80$$

$$s = \sqrt{s^2} = \sqrt{.80} = .89$$

of the distribution, divided by the distribution's standard deviation. For purposes of demonstration, unless stated otherwise, we will assume that we are dealing with sample data for all problems in this chapter.

The numerator of the standard score formula reflects the number of units that a score is above or below the mean of its distribution. When the numerator is divided by the standard deviation, the result expresses the number of *standard deviations* the score is above or below its mean. For instance, Mary's score of 50 is $50 - 30.00 = 20.00$ units above its mean. The standard deviation is 5.00 and, hence, Mary's score is $20.00/5.00 = 4.00$ standard deviations above the mean. In other words, her raw score corresponds to a standard score of 4.00. Suppose that John obtained a dominance score of 25. This score differs from its mean by $25 - 30.00 = -5.00$. That is, it is 5.00 units below the mean. John's standard score is thus $-5.00/5.00 = -1.00$, reflecting the fact that his raw score is 1.00 standard deviation below the mean.

Now that we have looked at some examples of how to calculate standard scores, we can state a formal definition: *A standard score represents the number of standard deviation units that a score falls above or below its mean.* In this way, a standard score summarizes an individual's relative standing, taking into consideration the mean and standard deviation of the distribution.

The standard score equivalents of the raw scores in columns 1 and 5 of Table 4.2 can be found, respectively, in columns 4 and 8. To obtain these values, we first computed the mean for each data set. Next, we used the computational formula for the sum of squares to calculate the sum of squares for Set A and the sum of squares for Set B. The sums of squares were then used to calculate the standard deviations. Finally, we subtracted the mean for each data set from the constituent scores in columns 3 and 6 and divided the resulting values by the appropriate standard deviation.

If we compare the standard score for the first raw score in Set A with the standard score for the first raw score in Set B, we find that although the raw scores are the same (both have a value of 1), the standard scores are different, -1.49 as compared to -2.25. The negative signs indicate that in both cases the raw score is below the mean of its distribution. For Set A, a score of 1 is only 1.49 standard deviation units below the mean of its distribution, whereas for Set B, it is 2.25 standard deviation units below the mean of its distribution. Thus, as reflected by the standard scores, a score of 1 is more distinctive in the context of Set B scores than in the context of Set A scores.

STUDY EXERCISE 4.3

For a set of scores with a mean of 20.00 and a standard deviation of 2.00, what standard score corresponds to a raw score of 17?

Answer   Using Equation 4.3, we find that

$$\text{Standard score} = \frac{X - \overline{X}}{s}$$

$$= \frac{17 - 20.00}{2.00} = -1.50$$

Thus, that a score of 17 is 1.50 standard deviations below the mean of its distribution.

Properties of Standard Scores

Standard scores have several important properties: A positive standard score indicates that the original score is greater than the mean, and a negative standard score indicates that the original score is less than the mean. A standard score of 0 indicates that the original score is equal to the mean.

Column 4 of Table 4.2 shows that the sum of the standard scores for Set A is 0, and column 8 shows the same result for Set B. In fact, the sum of a set of standard scores will always be 0. This is because standard scores reflect signed deviation scores and, as we discussed in Section 3.1, the sum of signed deviations about the mean always equals 0. It follows that if the sum of a set of standard scores is always equal to 0, *the mean of a set of standard scores is also always equal to 0.*

Also, if we were to compute the standard deviation for either set of standard scores, the result would be 1.00. In fact, *the standard deviation (and the variance) of a set of standard scores is always equal to 1.00.*

Use of Standard Scores

An important use of standard scores is to compare scores on distributions that have different means and standard deviations. For instance, suppose that you are contemplating employment in one of two fields (management or advertising). Unable to make a decision between the two, you decide to enter the field for which you have the greater aptitude. As assessed by the most widely accepted aptitude tests in the respective fields, your management aptitude score turns out to be 73 (out of 100) and your advertising aptitude score turns out to be 82 (out of 100). At first glance, it appears that your advertising aptitude is substantially greater than your management aptitude. However, before rushing off in search of an advertising position, you should examine the two scores in the context of their respective distributions.

Suppose, for instance, that the mean aptitude score for the population of individuals who have previously taken the management test is 62.00 and that the standard deviation is 4.00. Furthermore, suppose that the mean aptitude score for the population of individuals who have previously taken the advertising test is 78.00 and that the standard deviation is 6.00. Now it is not quite so clear that your advertising aptitude is superior to your management aptitude.

Because the mean and the standard deviation of a set of standard scores always take on the same values (0 and 1.00, respectively), it is possible to compare raw scores from different distributions by converting them to standard scores. In our example, your standard score for management aptitude is

$$\text{Standard score} = \frac{73 - 62.00}{4.00} = 2.75$$

and your standard score for advertising aptitude is

$$\text{Standard score} = \frac{82 - 78.00}{6.00} = .67$$

Thus, compared with other individuals who have taken the two aptitude tests, a management aptitude score of 73 represents relatively greater aptitude than an advertising aptitude score of 82, other things being equal. In the first instance, the aptitude score is 2.75 standard deviation units above the mean of its distribution, whereas in the second instance, the aptitude score is only .67 standard deviation unit above the mean of its distribution.

4.3 The Effects of Standardizing Scores on the Characteristics of a Distribution

The process of *standardizing* scores does not change the fundamental shape of a distribution. A set of scores that are positively skewed will remain positively skewed after having been converted to standard scores. A set of scores that are platykurtic will still be platykurtic after having been converted to standard scores. And a set of scores that are normally distributed will still be normally distributed after having been converted to standard scores.*

Although standardization does not change the skewness or kurtosis of a distribution, it affects its central tendency and variability: As we noted above, a set of standard scores will always have a mean of 0 and a standard deviation of 1.00 regardless of what the original mean and standard deviation were.

4.4   Standard Scores and the Normal Distribution

A standard score yields considerable information about the relative position of a score in a distribution. Such scores are even more meaningful when they occur in a normal distribution.

In Section 2.9, we noted that there is a family of normal distributions, each member of which is precisely defined by a mathematical formula. Although this formula is somewhat complex, it is important to realize that there is a different normal distribution for every unique combination of values of a distribution's mean and standard deviation.[†] It is also important to realize that all normal distributions share similar characteristics. For instance, as we noted in Section 2.9, all normal distributions are symmetrical and are characterized by a "bell shape." We further learned in Section 3.1 that the mode, the median, and the mean of a normal distribution all have the same value. In fact, this value defines the point that a normal distribution is symmetrical about. Another important feature of normal distributions is that they are theoretical in nature.

If we are able to assume that a set of scores approximates a normal distribution, then we can invoke certain statistical properties of normal distributions to aid in interpreting our data. One such property is that the proportion of scores that occur at or below or at or above a given standard score is the same in all normal distributions, as is the proportion of scores that occur between two specified standard scores. It is always the case, for example, that .50 of the scores in a normal distribution occur at or below the mean and that .50 of the scores in a normal distribution occur at or above the mean. This is not surprising when it is remembered that the mean of a normal distribution is also its median. Thus, knowing that a set of scores approximates a normal distribution allows us to make probability statements with respect to those scores.

Figure 4.1 presents a normal distribution and the proportions of scores that occur between selected standard scores. The proportion of scores that fall between standard scores of 0 and 1 is .3413, the proportion of scores that fall between standard scores of 1 and 2 is .1359, and the proportion of scores that fall between standard scores of 2 and 3 is .0215. The proportion of scores that are greater than or equal to a standard score of 3 is .0013.

Note that these same proportions also apply below the mean, which, as stated above, always equals 0 for a set of standard scores. For instance, the proportion of

---

* Many methods are available for transforming scores besides standardizing them. As discussed in Gulliksen (1960), most of these affect the shape of the distribution.

† The normal distribution formula is discussed in detail in Appendix 4.1.

FIGURE 4.1   **Proportion of Scores Between Selected Standard Scores in a Normal Distribution**

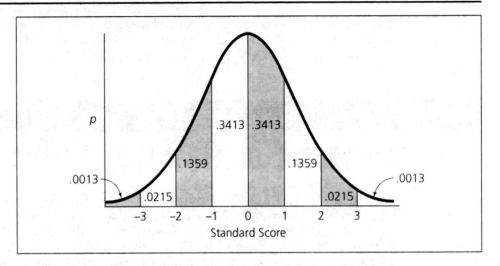

scores that occur between standard scores of 0 and −1 is the same as the proportion of scores that occur between standard scores of 0 and +1. This directly follows from the fact that all normal distributions are symmetrical about the mean.

Thus, in a normal distribution, .6826, or approximately 68%, of all scores fall between standard scores of −1 and +1; .9544, or approximately 95%, of all scores fall between standard scores of −2 and +2; and .9974, or over 99%, of all scores fall between standard scores of −3 and +3. Before proceeding further, take a moment to verify these proportions using the information presented in Figure 4.1.

A standard score in a normal distribution is referred to as a *z* score. Some texts refer to any standard score as a *z* score. However, in traditional statistics, a *z* score is used only to represent a standard score *in a normal distribution*. We will maintain this distinction throughout this book.

The *z* score table in Appendix B indicates the proportions of scores in a normal distribution that occur beyond selected *z* scores (for example, the proportion that are greater than or equal to 1.28). This table also reports the proportions of scores in a normal distribution that occur between selected points. Instructions for using the table are presented in Appendix B and should be read at this time.

You might be wondering where these proportions come from. Normal distributions can be conceptualized as probability density functions. As such, if we let the total area under the normal curve represent 1.00, the probability of obtaining a *z* score between two specified *z* scores or beyond a given *z* score equals the area under the normal curve that corresponds to that interval, as we discussed in Section 2.8. This area also defines the proportion of *z* scores that occur in that interval.*

---

* This directly follows from the fact that the relative frequency for a range of scores will always be equal to the probability associated with that range of scores, consistent with our discussion in Section 2.1 of the correspondence between probabilities and relative frequencies for specific scores.

The proportions in Appendix B have been derived mathematically by statisticians and are valid for any normal distribution.

Determining the Proportion of Raw Scores that Occur Beyond or Between Specified z Scores

Let us now explore how the z score table in Appendix B, coupled with our knowledge of the normal distribution, can give us insight into scores that approximate a normal distribution. For the sake of illustration, try to estimate how many hours per week you spend watching television. This might be easiest to do if you think of each day of the week (Sunday through Saturday) individually and estimate how many hours you typically watch television on those days. Then sum across the seven days to obtain an estimate of how much you tend to watch per week. For us, the estimate is 14 hours per week. How does this compare with others? Let us compare our score with the findings from a national survey of adults in the United States.

Suppose that this survey shows that the mean number of hours of television watched per week by adults in the United States is 25.40 and that the standard deviation is 6.10. Suppose also that the scores in this distribution closely approximate a normal distribution. How does a score of 14 hours per week compare with the other scores from the survey?

If we substitute the more specific z notation for *Standard score* in Equation 4.3, we obtain the following formula for converting a score in a sample to a z score:

$$z = \frac{X - \overline{X}}{s}$$ [4.5]

Similarly, the formula for converting a score in a population to a z score is

$$z = \frac{X - \mu}{\sigma}$$ [4.6]

In our example,

$$z = \frac{14 - 25.40}{6.10} = -1.87$$

A weekly television viewing time of 14 hours is 1.87 standard deviations *below* the national average. From column 3 of Appendix B, we find that the proportion of scores that are less than or equal to a z score of −1.87 is .0307. Thus, 14 hours defines the 3.07th percentile. Stated another way, 3.07% of adults in the United States watch 14 hours or less of television per week. Approximately 1.0000 (the total proportion of all scores) − .0307 = .9693, or 96.93%, of adults in the United States must therefore watch 14 hours or more of television per week. Relative to most American adults, the amount of time we spend watching television is quite low. Do a similar analysis for your own estimated viewing behavior.

Suppose that we want to know what percentage of American adults watch between 30 and 40 hours of television per week. We can use our knowledge of the normal distribution to estimate this. First, we convert the scores of 30 and 40 into z scores:

$$z = \frac{30 - 25.40}{6.10} = .75$$

and

$$z = \frac{40 - 25.40}{6.10} = 2.39$$

Examining Appendix B, we find that .7734 of the scores in a normal distribution are less than or equal to a z score of .75. This is illustrated in Figure 4.2. There are several ways that this value can be obtained. For instance, we could refer to column 3, where we find that .2266 of the scores are greater than or equal to a z score of .75. Thus, $1.0000 - .2266 = .7734$ of the scores must be .75 or less. Alternatively, realizing that .5000 of the scores occur below the mean (a z score of 0), we could refer to column 5, where we find that an additional .2734 of the scores fall between a z score of 0 and a z score of .75. The sum of these figures $(.5000 + .2734)$ is .7734. Appendix B also indicates that .0084 of the scores are greater than or equal to a z score of 2.39. The most direct way to obtain this value is to refer to column 3.

The proportion of scores that occur between .75 and 2.39 is therefore 1.0000 minus the .0084 of the scores that are equal to or greater than a z score of 2.39 and minus the .7734 of the scores that are equal to or less than a z score of .75, or $1.0000 - .0084 - .7734 = .2182$. Thus, approximately 21.82% of American adults watch between 30 and 40 hours of television per week.

FIGURE 4.2   **Proportion of Scores Between z Scores of .75 and 2.39**

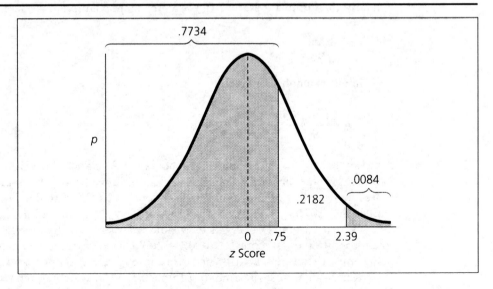

STUDY EXERCISE 4.4

Given a set of scores that are normally distributed with a mean of 100.00 and a standard deviation of 10.00, what proportion of scores is greater than or equal to 120? Less than or equal to 90?

Answer We begin by converting the raw score of interest into a z score. For the proportion of scores greater than or equal to 120,

$$z = \frac{120 - 100.00}{10.00} = 2.00$$

Using column 3 of Appendix B, we find that the proportion of scores that are greater than or equal to a z score of 2.00 is .0228. Thus, the proportion of scores that are greater than or equal to 120 is .0228.

For the proportion of scores that are less than or equal to 90,

$$z = \frac{90 - 100.00}{10.00} = -1.00$$

Again using column 3 of Appendix B, we find that the proportion of scores that are less than or equal to a z score of -1.00 is .1587. Thus, the proportion of scores that are less than or equal to 90 is .1587.

Determining the Raw Scores that Define Specified Areas of an Approximately Normal Distribution

It is possible to reverse the above procedures and determine the raw scores that define specified areas of an approximately normal distribution. This is accomplished by rearranging Equations 4.5 and 4.6 as follows, substituting the values of the distribution mean and standard deviation along with the relevant value of z into one of the revised equations, and solving for X. If we are dealing with sample data, the revised equation is

$$X = \overline{X} + (z)(s) \qquad [4.7]$$

and if we are dealing with population data, the revised equation is

$$X = \mu + (z)(\sigma) \qquad [4.8]$$

where z is the value of z that cuts off the specified proportion of the distribution.

For instance, in the television-viewing example, we might want to determine the number of hours of television viewing at or above which 5% of all weekly viewing times fall. From column 3 of Appendix B, we find that .0505 of all scores in a normal distribution are greater than or equal to a z score of 1.64 and that .0495 of all scores in a normal distribution are greater than or equal to a z score of 1.65. Thus, the value of z that defines the upper .05, or 5%, of scores in a normal distribution is approximately halfway between these two values, or 1.645. Because the mean in our example is 25.40 and the standard deviation is 6.10, the number of hours of television viewing at or above which 5% of all weekly viewing times fall is

$$X = 25.40 + (1.645)(6.10) = 35.43$$

In practice, standard scores are rarely used to determine raw score values in this manner. However, the general logic that we present here is important for understanding certain applications of related concepts that we will encounter in later chapters.

4.5 Method of Presentation

Percentiles and percentile ranks are most commonly encountered in manuals that are available to educators and other professionals for interpreting scores on educational and psychological tests. Such manuals generally list selected percentile ranks and the corresponding raw score values.

For instance, the Miller Analogies Test is designed to measure the general aptitude of applicants for graduate and professional study. The test consists of a series of items that take the following basic form:

A *book* is to *trees* as a *skirt* is to _____ .

(a) shoes   (b) sheep   (c) dresses   (d) women

The task of the test-taker is to select the answer that makes the two comparisons analogous to one another.

Scores on the Miller Analogies Test can range from 0 to 100. A list of the raw score equivalents of selected percentile ranks for various groups of graduate applicants might appear in the test manual as follows:

Percentile Rank	Physical Sciences	Medical Science	Social Sciences	English	Law	Social Work
99	93	92	90	87	84	81
90	88	78	82	80	73	67
80	82	74	76	74	63	61
70	78	67	69	68	58	58
60	74	60	64	65	53	54
50	68	57	61	59	49	50
40	63	53	56	53	45	46
30	58	47	51	46	40	41
20	51	43	46	41	35	37
10	43	34	39	35	30	27
1	28	24	18	7	18	9

Although not all possible values are included in this table, the relative standing of selected test scores can be determined. Focusing on law school applicants, for instance, we find that a score of 49 has a percentile rank of 50, a score of 58 has a percentile rank of 70, and so forth.

Percentile ranks must always be interpreted relative to the group upon which the scores are based. Someone who scores at the 95th percentile on the Miller Analogies Test, for instance, probably has greater general aptitude than someone who scores at the 95th percentile on the SAT (an aptitude test for applicants for undergraduate study). This is because only the brighter students who have done well in college tend to take the Miller Analogies Test, whereas the SAT is taken by a more general population.

It might be interesting to contrast your own major with those of others in terms of which scores define various percentiles in the table above. For example, the 50th percentile is 68 for graduate applicants in the physical sciences, 61 for graduate applicants in the social sciences, 59 for graduate applicants in English (literature and language), 57 for medical applicants, 50 for graduate applicants in social work, and 49 for law applicants.

As an aid to interpreting test scores, most educational and psychological test manuals report the standard score equivalents of raw scores in addition to percentile tables. To avoid any confusion that may be associated with decimals and negative values, standard scores are frequently further transformed into *T scores*.

T scores are directly analogous to standard scores, but instead of having a mean of 0 and a standard deviation of 1.00, they have a mean of 50.00 and a standard deviation of 10.00. The transformation is accomplished using the following formula:

$$T = 50 + 10(\text{standard score}) \tag{4.9}$$

The resulting value of T is usually rounded to the nearest whole number. For instance, a standard score of $-.53$ is equivalent to a T score of $50 + (10)(-.53) = 44.7$, which will typically be reported as 45.

A test manual report of raw scores and their standard score and T score equivalents might use the following format:

Raw score	Standard score	T score
100	2.90	79
99	2.70	77
98	2.50	75
97	2.30	73
96	2.10	71

In practice, all possible raw score values and the corresponding standard and T scores would be included in this listing.

4.6   Links Between Computer Results and Book Content

Statistical computer programs differ in how they report percentiles: Some round percentiles to units of the original scale and some carry percentile calculations to one or more decimal places beyond the original scale. In practice, it usually makes little difference which strategy is used, as the reported values will tend to be very similar. Of course, if a given program utilizes the latter approach, the user can round the reported values to a smaller number of decimal places (for example, to the nearest whole number).

4.7 Links Between Chapters

An understanding of z scores requires an understanding of several concepts that were introduced in earlier chapters. Most notably, it is very important that you understand the rationale for the mean and the standard deviation, as we discussed in Chapter 3, as these are the basis for the standard score and the z score formulas represented by Equations 4.3 to 4.8. Also, our discussion of how to use the area under the density curve to determine the probability of obtaining a score within a given interval from Section 2.8 directly relates to what we said about determining the proportion of scores that occur beyond or between specified z scores in Section 4.4. Several additional links between this and other chapters are made in the Applications to the Analysis of a Social Problem Using SPSS for Windows section.

Applications to the Analysis of a Social Problem Using SPSS for Windows

An important variable in the parent–teen communication study described in Chapter 1 is the amount of adolescents' sexual activity. This was measured by asking them a series of questions about their sexual behavior. One such question asked the teens to indicate the number of times that they had engaged in sexual intercourse during the past 6 months.

The responses to this question should not be interpreted too literally. For example, a teen who reported 12 instances of sexual intercourse probably did not engage in *exactly* 12 instances of intercourse. Rather, this response probably represents an approximate number of instances of sexual intercourse based on some cognitive heuristic that the teen used for answering the question. It would be a serious error to think of these data as having ratio-level properties. As an indicator of sexual activity, our measure probably reasonably approximates interval-level properties, although some researchers might contend that even this is questionable.

Figure 4.3 presents a grouped frequency histogram of the number of instances of sexual intercourse for the total sample, and Table 4.3 presents computer output for many of the basic descriptive statistics that we discussed in Chapter 3 for this same data set. This table also reports the 10th through 90th percentiles for the sexual intercourse variable in 10-unit increments.

Forty-nine teens chose not to respond to the question and, hence, were treated as having missing data. The mean number of times that the teens engaged in sexual intercourse during the past 6 months is 4.38, the median is 0, and the mode is 0. In terms of variability, the lowest score is 0 and the highest is 90, yielding a range of 90 and a standard deviation of 9.82.* The frequency histogram reveals that the distribution is highly positively skewed, and this is reflected in the fact that the mean is greater than the median.

*Technically, 9.82 is the standard deviation *estimate* for the number of instances of sexual intercourse. Similarly, the value of 96.35 that is labeled "Variance" in Table 4.3 is the variance *estimate*. Both of these measures were discussed briefly in Section 3.12 and will be discussed at length in Chapter 7.

FIGURE 4.3   Grouped Frequency Histogram of Instances of Sexual Intercourse for Total Sample

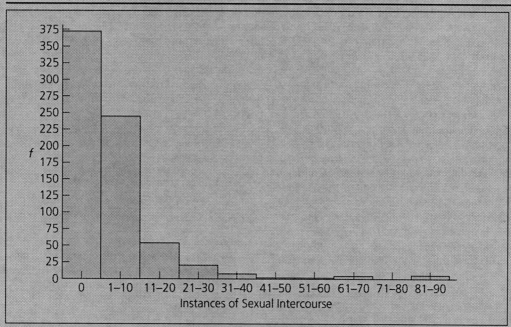

TABLE 4.3   Computer Output for Descriptive Statistics for the Number of Instances of Sexual Intercourse for the Total Sample

```
STATISTICS  Instances of Sexual Intercourse
```

N	Valid	698
	Missing	49
Mean		4.384
Median		.000
Mode		.000
Std. Deviation		9.816
Variance		96.349
Range		90.000
Minimum		.000
Maximum		90.000
Percentiles	10	.000
	20	.000
	30	.000
	40	.000
	50	.000
	60	2.000
	70	3.000
	80	6.000
	90	12.000

(continued)

SPSS for Windows rounds percentiles to units of the original scale and, hence, the percentiles in Table 4.3 are all whole numbers. For these data, the 10th percentile is 0, as are the 20th, 30th, 40th, and 50th percentiles. The 60th percentile is 2, the 70th percentile is 3, the 80th percentile is 6, and the 90th percentile is 12. Thus, only 10% of the adolescents had sexual intercourse more than 12 times in the past 6 months.

Recall from Chapter 3 that the mean is influenced by extreme scores and may not be the most "representative" value for a set of scores when one or more extreme scores exist. In the present instance, the data are positively skewed with multiple extreme scores at the upper end of the distribution. Although the mean is near 4, the frequency histogram and the median and mode (as well as the percentiles) make it clear that many adolescents have not been sexually active during the past 6 months. Thus, the median and modal values of 0 probably best characterize a "representative" value for the data.

If we wish, we can convert the raw scores to standard scores. For example, a single instance of sexual intercourse translates into a standard score of $(1 - 4.38)/9.82 = -.34$, which is about a third of a standard deviation below the mean. Ten instances of sexual intercourse represent a standard score of $(10 - 4.38)/9.82 = .57$, which is just over half a standard deviation above the mean.

However, because standard scores use the mean as the basis for describing how extreme a given score is, standard scores must be interpreted cautiously if the mean is a poor "representative" value, as is the case in our example. In fact, because the original scores are highly positively skewed, the standard scores for the sexual intercourse variable are also highly positively skewed. Therefore, we cannot use the normal distribution to help us interpret what these standard scores mean. Rather, we must rely on percentage and cumulative percentage information, which we can obtain by requesting a frequency breakdown for the data set.

Given the substantial positive skew in the data, some investigators might question whether standard scores are meaningful at all in the present

instance. However, we believe that standard scores (and the mean) are informative for any distribution as long as the researcher keeps in mind their fundamental statistical properties and how they are affected by skewed data and extreme scores. Nevertheless, when data are highly skewed, some investigators prefer to use a variant of standard scores that is based on the median and an index of variability that does not rely on the mean. Let us briefly develop this concept.

The general formula for describing the uniqueness of a given individual's raw score relative to the other scores in a distribution is

$$u = \frac{\text{score for an individual} - \text{measure of central tendency}}{\text{measure of variability}} \quad [4.10]$$

For instance, this represents the formula for a standard score, where the measure of central tendency is the mean and the measure of variability is the standard deviation, per Equations 4.3 and 4.4. An alternative index of uniqueness for skewed data uses the median as the measure of central tendency and either the interquartile range (*IQR*) or a measure called the *median of absolute deviations* (abbreviated as *MAD*) as the measure of variability.

The median of absolute deviations is calculated by first computing for each individual the absolute value of the individual's score minus the median. The median of absolute deviations is the median of these absolute values. The *MAD* index thus reflects how far, on average, a set of scores deviate from its median.*

When Equation 4.10 is applied using the median and the interquartile range, the resulting *u* score is the number of *IQR* units that an individual's score is below or above the median. For the sexual intercourse data, the median value is 0 and the interquartile range is 4. A single instance of sexual intercourse therefore translates into a *u* score of $(1 - 0)/4 = .25$. In other words, one act of sexual intercourse is one-fourth of an interquartile range above the median.

Note how this contrasts with the standard score for one instance of sexual intercourse $(-.34)$.

---

*See Hoaglin, Mosteller, and Tukey (1983) for further discussion of the median of absolute deviations.

When the median and interquartile range are used in Equation 4.10, a single instance of sexual intercourse is somewhat higher than the "central tendency" of the data, whereas when the mean and standard deviation are used, a single instance of sexual intercourse is somewhat lower than the central tendency of the data. Which index do you think is a better descriptor of what a score of 1 on this variable reflects?

Many problem behaviors in adolescence have frequency distributions that are similar to Figure 4.3—namely, highly positively skewed. For example, most teens do not use hard drugs, drink excessively, attempt suicide, run away from home, or drive drunk. However, a significant minority of teens tends to do these things, sometimes excessively so, which yields distributions that are shaped similarly to the one we observe here.

Our analysis has focused on the total sample. Now we briefly examine the data for each age (14 to17) separately. Table 4.4 presents computer output for basic descriptive statistics and selected percentiles for each group. In terms of central tendency, the mode is 0 for all age groups. The median is 0 for 14- and 15-year-olds but shifts to 2 for 16- and 17-year-olds. The mean increases with increasing age and is 1.91 for 14-year-olds, 2.80 for 15-year-olds, 5.84 for 16-year-olds, and 7.66 for 17-year-olds. Chapter 12 discusses formal procedures for comparing multiple means in the context of inferential statistics. Consistent with the differences in central tendency, many of the percentiles also differ as a function of age. For example, the 80th percentile is 3 for 14-year-olds, 4 for 15-year-olds, 9 for 16-year-olds, and 13 for 17-year-olds. Also of note is the fact that the standard deviations are lower for the 14- and 15-year-olds (4.94 and 6.58, respectively) than for the 16- and 17-year-olds (12.28 and 12.71, respectively), which suggests that there is more variability in sexual activity for older as opposed to younger adolescents.

As we discussed in Section 4.5, percentile ranks must always be interpreted relative to the

TABLE 4.4   Computer Output for Descriptive Statistics for the Number of Instances of Sexual Intercourse for the Four Age Groups

AGE 14 Instances of Sexual Intercourse

N	Valid	112
	Missing	3
Mean		1.911
Median		.000
Mode		.000
Std. Deviation		4.935
Variance		24.350
Range		30.000
Minimum		.000
Maximum		30.000
Percentiles	10	.000
	20	.000
	30	.000
	40	.000
	50	.000
	60	.000
	70	.000
	80	3.000
	90	7.000

(continued)

TABLE 4.4   (continued)

AGE 15 Instances of Sexual Intercourse

N	Valid	256
	Missing	17
Mean		2.797
Median		.000
Mode		.000
Std. Deviation		6.581
Variance		43.315
Range		70.000
Minimum		.000
Maximum		70.000
Percentiles	10	.000
	20	.000
	30	.000
	40	.000
	50	.000
	60	1.000
	70	2.000
	80	4.000
	90	9.000

AGE 16 Instances of Sexual Intercourse

N	Valid	256
	Missing	17
Mean		2.797
Median		.000
Mode		.000
Std. Deviation		6.581
Variance		43.315
Range		70.000
Minimum		.000
Maximum		70.000
Percentiles	10	.000
	20	.000
	30	.000
	40	.000
	50	.000
	60	1.000
	70	2.000
	80	4.000
	90	9.000

TABLE 4.4   (continued)

AGE 17 Instances of Sexual Intercourse

N	Valid	118
	Missing	16
Mean		7.661
Median		2.000
Mode		.000
Std. Deviation		12.706
Variance		161.440
Range		90.000
Minimum		.000
Maximum		90.000
Percentiles	10	.000
	20	.000
	30	.000
	40	.000
	50	2.000
	60	5.000
	70	7.000
	80	13.000
	90	25.000

group upon which the scores are based, and the same is true for standard scores. That is, both indexes represent an individual's performance on some variable *relative to some group of individuals*. They do not convey performance in an absolute sense. What is "above-average" sexual activity in one group may be "below-average" sexual activity in another group. For example, three instances of sexual intercourse translates into standard scores of .22 for 14-year-olds, .03 for 15-year-olds, −.23 for 16-year-olds, and −.37 for 17-year-olds, and percentile ranks of approximately 80 for 14-year-olds, approximately 75 for 15-year-olds, approximately 60 for 16-year-olds, and approximately 53 for 17-year-olds. Thus, the same raw score can have different meanings in the context of different reference groups. It follows that the identical standard score or the identical percentile rank can represent very different levels of behavior across groups. For instance, a percentile rank of 60 in the parent–teen communication study represents 0 instances of sexual intercourse for 14-year-olds, 1 instance for 15-year-olds, 3 instances for 16-year-olds, and 5 instances for 17-year-olds. This relative nature of standard scores and percentile ranks is important to keep in mind when interpreting these measures.

Summary

In general, observations are meaningful only in relation to other observations. One approach for identifying the location of a specified score within a set of scores is based on percentages. The percentage of scores in a distribution that occur at or below a given value is the percentile rank of that value. The value that corresponds to a given percentile rank is called a percentile.

Whereas percentile ranks reflect only an *ordinal* measure of relative standing, a standard score converts a score from its original, or *raw*, form to a form that takes into consideration its standing relative to the mean and standard deviation of the entire distribution of scores. Specifically, a standard score is the difference between a score in a distribution and the mean of the distribution, divided by the distribution's standard deviation. A standard score thus represents the number of standard deviation units that a score falls above or below its mean.

Standard scores have several important properties: A positive standard score indicates that the original score is greater than the mean, and a negative standard score indicates that the original score is less than the mean. A standard score of 0 indicates that the original score is equal to the mean. Also, the mean of a set of standard scores is always equal to 0, and the standard deviation (and the variance) of a set of standard scores is always equal to 1.00.

The process of standardizing scores does not change the fundamental shape of a distribution. For instance, a set of scores that are normally distributed will still be normally distributed after having been converted to standard scores.

Standard scores are particularly meaningful when they occur in a normal distribution. Although there is a different normal distribution for every unique combination of values of a distribution's mean and standard deviation, all normal distributions share important characteristics: All normal distributions are symmetrical and are characterized by a "bell shape"; the mode, the median, and the mean of a normal distribution all have the same value, and this value defines the point that the distribution is symmetrical about; and normal distributions are theoretical in nature.

A standard score in a normal distribution is referred to as a *z* score. If we are able to assume that a set of scores approximates a normal distribution, we can use the *z* score table in Appendix B to determine the proportions of scores that occur beyond selected *z* scores and the proportions of scores that occur between selected points. We can also reverse these procedures and determine the raw scores that define specified areas of an approximately normal distribution.

Appendix 4.1   The Normal Distribution Formula

The formula for a normal distribution is

$$d(X) = \frac{e^k}{\sqrt{2\pi\sigma^2}} \qquad [4.11]$$

where $d(X)$ is the probability density function associated with variable X, e is a constant that is approximately equal to 2.7183, $k = -(X - \mu)^2/2\sigma^2$, μ is the mean of the distribution, π (lowercase Greek p, called *pi*) is a constant

that is approximately equal to 3.1416, and σ^2 is the variance of the distribution.

When the values of μ and σ^2 are specified, various values of X can be substituted into the equation to yield the corresponding values of $d(X)$. If all paired values of X and $d(X)$ are plotted graphically, they will form a normal curve. Thus, there is a different normal curve for every unique combination of μ and σ^2.

Exercises

Answers to asterisked (*) exercises appear at the back of the book.

1. What is the relationship between percentile ranks and percentiles?

Use the following information to complete Exercises 2–4:

A researcher administered a questionnaire to 500 people that was designed to measure knowledge of the positions that two presidential candidates held on major issues. Scores on the test could range from 0 to 10, with higher scores indicating more knowledge. The following frequency analysis resulted:

Score	f	rf	cf	crf
8	6	.012	500	1.000
7	44	.088	494	.988
6	51	.102	450	.900
5	49	.098	399	.798
4	200	.400	350	.700
3	98	.196	150	.300
2	52	.104	52	.104

*2. Compute the values that define the following percentiles:
   a. 20th   d. 60th
   b. 40th   e. 80th
   c. 50th   f. 99th

3. Compute the interquartile range.

*4. Compute the percentile ranks that correspond to the following scores:
   a. 2   b. 3   c. 5   d. 7

5. For the following set of data, compute the score that defines the 50th percentile: 94, 95, 96, 97, 97, 98, 99, 99, 100, 100.

6. Compute the interquartile range for the data in Exercise 5.

7. What are the two approaches to reporting percentiles? What rationale underlies each position?

8. What is the advantage of standard scores as compared with percentile ranks as an index of relative standing?

*9. Given a distribution with a mean of 20.00 and a standard deviation of 3.00, compute the standard score equivalents of the following scores:
   a. 21.87   c. 18.91   e. 15.63
   b. 23.00   d. 20.08   f. 24.30

10. Given a distribution with a mean of −4.00 and a standard deviation of 2.50, compute the standard score equivalents of the following scores:
   a. −6.83   c. 2.84   e. 1.00
   b. 0   d. −6.50   f. .87

*11. For the following distribution, convert a score of 50 to a standard score: 60, 55, 50, 50, 55, 60.

12. For the following distribution, convert a score of 6 to a standard score: 14, 6, 13, 17, 11, 13, 14, 9.

*13. What does a positive standard score indicate about the original score's position relative to the mean? What does a negative standard score indicate about the original score's position relative to the mean?

*14. What are the values of the mean and the standard deviation for any set of standard scores?

15. How does standardizing a set of scores affect the shape of a distribution?

*16. John received 90 out of 100 points on an English exam and 60 out of 100 points on a math exam. The overall class performance yielded a mean of 70.00 and a standard deviation of 20.00 on the English exam, and a mean of 40.00 and a standard deviation of 3.00 on the math exam. On which exam was John's performance better (relative to his classmates')?

17. If a person got a score of 80 on a test, which one of the following distributions allows for the most favorable interpretation of that score (assuming that higher values are more favorable)?

a. $\overline{X} = 60.00, s = 5.00$
b. $\overline{X} = 60.00, s = 10.00$
c. $\overline{X} = 60.00, s = 1.00$
d. $\overline{X} = 60.00, s = 20.00$

*18. Describe a situation in which it would be useful to convert scores from two different distributions to standard scores before comparing them.

19. What are the major characteristics of a normal distribution?

20. What is a z score?

21. Given a normal distribution with a mean of 24.87 and a standard deviation of 6.00, compute the z score equivalents of the following scores:

a. 13.78   c. 26.81   e. 37.90
b. 29.42   d. 12.87   f. 33.35

*22. What proportion of z scores in a normal distribution are
a. 2.38 or less
b. 1.17 or greater
c. −1.17 or less
d. between 0 and 2.05
e. between −2.05 and 0
f. between .37 and 3.19
g. between −3.19 and −.37
h. between −1.24 and +1.24

*23. Given a set of normally distributed scores with a mean of 20.00 and a standard deviation of 5.00, what proportion of scores is
a. 25 or higher
b. 15 or less
c. between 15 and 28
d. between 8 and 32
e. 20 or higher
f. 23 or less

24. Suppose that IQ scores in a population are approximately normally distributed with $\mu = 100.00$ and $\sigma = 10.00$. What proportion of individuals has IQ scores of
a. 100 or higher
b. 100 or less
c. between 105 and 112
d. 103 or less
e. 95 or higher
f. 95 or less

*25. People who take lie detector tests are typically asked to answer a series of neutral questions (for example, "What is your name?", "Where do you work?") among which some critical questions regarding the issue of importance are embedded. It is believed that involuntary changes in the autonomic nervous system will occur when people do not tell the truth and, consequently, that a comparison of the physiological reactions that accompany an individual's answers to the critical versus the neutral questions can be used to make inferences about the veridicality of his or her answers.

Consider a situation where physiological measurements in the form of galvanic skin responses are taken as a person answers a long series of questions, including one about the critical issue. The galvanic skin response scores for the set of questions approximate a normal distribution and have a mean of 49.40 and a standard deviation of 3.00. For the critical question, the score is 61.40. Convert this to a standard score and draw a conclusion.

26. A major form of identification in criminal investigations is fingerprints. Fingerprints vary on many different dimensions, one of which is called the *ridgecount*. Suppose that you know that the ridgecounts of human beings follow a normal distribution with a mean of 165.00 and a standard deviation of 10.00. Suppose furthermore that a set of fingerprints was found at the scene of a crime and it was determined that the ridgecount was at least 200 (the exact value being in question because of smudging). Finally, suppose that a particular suspect has a ridgecount of 225. What should you conclude and why?

*27. Given a set of normally distributed scores with a mean of 100.00 and a standard deviation of 10.00, what score corresponds to a z score of
a. 2.86   c. 0   e. 1.59
b. −2.44 d. −1.50 f. .75

*28. Given a normal distribution with a mean of 100.00 and a standard deviation of 5.00, what score would
   a. 33% of the cases be greater than or equal to
   b. 5% of the cases be greater than or equal to
   c. 50% of the cases be less than or equal to
   d. 2.50% of the cases be greater than or equal to
   e. 2.50% of the cases be less than or equal to

29. Suppose that income in a sample is approximately normally distributed with a mean of $20,000.00 and a standard deviation of $2,000.00. What income level defines the
   a. top 2.5% of salaries
   b. bottom 2.5% of salaries
   c. top 5% of salaries
   d. bottom 5% of salaries
   e. top 33% of salaries
   f. bottom 50% of salaries

*30. Convert each of the following standard scores to a T score:
   a. .87   c. 1.56   e. 0
   b. 2.00   d. −1.56   f. 4.04

Multiple-Choice Questions

*31. John received a standard score of −2.37 on an exam. This means that John
   a. did better than the class average
   b. did worse than the class average
   c. received a score equal to the class average
   d. received a raw score of −2.37

32. If a set of scores is normally distributed with a mean of 50.00 and a standard deviation of 10.00, what standard score corresponds to a raw score of 60?
   a. −1.00   c. 1.00
   b. −2.00   d. 2.00

33. If a set of scores has a mean of 100.00 and a standard deviation of 5.00, what is the variance of the standard scores?
   a. 1.00
   b. 5.00
   c. 25.00
   d. this cannot be determined

34. A normal distribution is always bell-shaped.
   a. true
   b. false

*35. On average, it takes a person 5.00 hours to clean a house, with a standard deviation of 1.00. If Bill has a standard score of −2.00, how many hours does it take him to clean his house?
   a. 2.00   c. 5.00
   b. 3.00   d. 7.00

36. In a normal distribution
   a. the mean is usually greater than the mode
   b. the mode is usually greater than the median
   c. the mode, the median, and the mean are always equal to one another
   d. the mode and the median are always equal to one another and are usually greater than the mean

*37. The percentile rank that corresponds to Chester's score on a class test is 30. This means that
   a. Chester answered 30% of the questions on the test correctly
   b. 30% of the obtained scores were greater than or equal to Chester's
   c. 30 students obtained scores that were less than or equal to Chester's
   d. 30% of the obtained scores were less than or equal to Chester's

*38. Which of the following is a problem with percentile ranks as an index of relative standing?
   a. They cannot be precisely calculated.
   b. They can be used only with samples of at least size 30.
   c. They do not tell us anything about the *magnitude* of the score of interest relative to the other scores in the distribution.
   d. They can be used only with ratio data.

39. A negative standard score indicates that its corresponding raw score is
   a. below the mean of the distribution
   b. above the mean of the distribution
   c. negative in value
   d. more than one standard deviation from the mean (in either direction)

*40. Standard scores provide information about a score's location relative to the mean in _____ units of the distribution.
 a. cumulative frequency
 b. variance
 c. raw score
 d. standard deviation

*41. What proportion of scores in a normal distribution lie between z scores of -3.12 and $+3.12$?
 a. .0009   c. .9982
 b. .5018   d. .9991

42. What proportion of scores in a normal distribution lie between the mean and a z score of .44?
 a. .1700
 b. .3300
 c. .3400
 d. .6700

43. What proportion of scores in a normal distribution are less than or equal to a z score of 1.86?
 a. .0314   c. .9372
 b. .4686   d. .9686

*44. Given a set of normally distributed scores with a mean of 12.00 and a standard deviation of 4.00, what proportion of scores are greater than or equal to 14?
 a. .3085   c. .6170
 b. .3830   d. .6915

*45. The median of the absolute values of the difference between each score in a data set and the median is referred to as the
 a. IQR
 b. u score
 c. MAD
 d. none of the above

CHAPTER 5

Pearson Correlation and Regression: Descriptive Aspects

To this point, we have emphasized ways of summarizing and describing scores on a single variable. Research in the behavioral sciences, however, often involves the measurement of two variables for the same individuals. A common question in this situation concerns the way in which scores on the first variable are related to scores on the second variable. For instance, an investigator who is interested in the relationship between women's traditionalism and their ideal family size might conduct a study in which each participant is asked to indicate her ideal number of children and to respond to a traditionalism questionnaire. The question of interest is whether there is a relationship between women's traditionalism scores and their ideal family sizes.

Actually, there are many different ways in which two variables might be related. However, research in the behavioral sciences is often concerned with *linear* relationships. When both variables under study are quantitative, have many values, and are measured on a level that at least approximates interval characteristics, the statistical technique of *Pearson product-moment correlation*, known more simply as **Pearson correlation,** can be used to determine the extent to which they approximate a linear relationship.* Also, a closely related technique known as **regression** can be used to identify the line that, though imperfect, best describes this relationship as determined by a statistical criterion known as *least squares.*

To lay the groundwork for an in-depth discussion of Pearson correlation and regression, we now review the basic characteristics of linear relationships.[†]

5.1 The Linear Model

Consider two variables: the number of hours that one works (X) and the amount of money that one is paid (Y). Each of four individuals works at a rate of \$1 per hour. Their scores on X and Y are as follows:

Individual	X (hours worked)	Y (amount paid, \$)
1	1	1
2	4	4
3	3	3
4	2	2

---

* The condition that both variables be measured on a level that at least approximates interval characteristics means that they must be measured on an ordinal level that approximates interval characteristics, on an interval level, or on a ratio level.

[†] This chapter is concerned with descriptive aspects of Pearson correlation and regression. We discuss inferential aspects of these techniques in Chapter 14.

FIGURE 5.1   **Example of a Scatterplot**

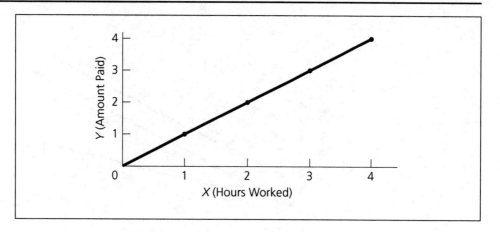

The relationship between variables X and Y is illustrated in the **scatterplot** in Figure 5.1. A scatterplot is a graph that represents the values of variable X on the abscissa, the values of variable Y on the ordinate, and the scores for each individual in the body of the graph. For instance, individual 1 has a score of 1 on X and a score of 1 on Y. We therefore find the value on the X axis that corresponds to her score on X and the value on the Y axis that corresponds to her score on Y, and we place a solid dot where the two values intersect, that is, at the intersection of $X = 1$ and $Y = 1$. The same procedure is repeated for each individual. If we connect the resulting dots, we obtain the straight line depicted in Figure 5.1. Thus, there is a linear relationship between X and Y in this example. This relationship can be stated as $Y = X$. In other words, the amount of money paid equals the number of hours worked.

  Suppose that the four individuals are not paid \$1 per hour, but instead are paid \$2 per hour. The scores on variables X and Y would be as follows:

Individual	X (hours worked)	Y (amount paid, \$)
1	1	2
2	4	8
3	3	6
4	2	4

In this case, the relationship between X and Y can be stated as $Y = 2.00X$. In other words, the number of dollars paid equals 2 times the number of hours worked. Line A of Figure 5.2 presents a scatterplot of these data, and line B reproduces the scatterplot for when $Y = X$ from Figure 5.1. Notice that we still have a straight line (and, hence, a linear relationship) but, in the case of \$2 per hour, the line rises much faster than with \$1 per hour; that is, the **slope** of the line is greater.

FIGURE 5.2 **Three Examples of a Linear Relationship**

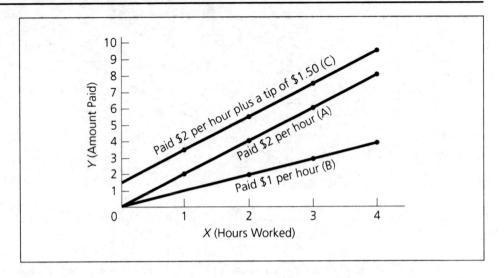

Technically, the slope of a line indicates the number of units that variable Y changes as variable X changes by one unit. When people are paid $2 per hour, an individual who works 1 hour is paid $2, one who works 2 hours is paid $4, and so forth. When X goes up by one unit (for instance, from 1 to 2 hours), Y goes up by two units (for instance, from $2 to $4). The slope that describes this linear relationship is therefore 2. In contrast, the slope that describes the linear relationship Y = X is 1, reflecting that as X changes by one unit, so does Y. Thus, linear relationships can differ in terms of the slopes that describe them.

The slope that describes a linear relationship can be determined from a simple algebraic formula. This formula involves first selecting the X and Y scores of any two individuals. The slope is computed by dividing the difference between the two Y scores by the difference between the two X scores. In other words, the change in Y scores is divided by the change in X scores. Symbolically,

$$b = \frac{Y_1 - Y_2}{X_1 - X_2} \qquad [5.1]$$

where b represents the slope, X_1 and Y_1 are the X and Y scores for any one individual, and X_2 and Y_2 are the X and Y scores for any other individual.

Inserting the scores for individuals 1 ($X = 1$, $Y = 2$) and 2 ($X = 4$, $Y = 8$), we find that the slope for line A is

$$b = \frac{2 - 8}{1 - 4} = 2.00$$

This is consistent with what we stated above.

The value of a slope can be positive, negative, or 0. Consider the following scores:

Individual	X	Y
1	2	3
2	1	4
3	4	1
4	3	2

Inserting the scores for individuals 2 and 4 into Equation 5.1, we find that the slope is

$$b = \frac{4 - 2}{1 - 3} = -1.00$$

Figure 5.3 presents a scatterplot of this relationship. The relationship is still linear, but now the line moves downward as we move from left to right on the X axis. This downward direction characterizes a negative slope, whereas an upward direction characterizes a positive slope. A slope of 0 is represented by a horizontal line because the value of Y is constant for all values of X.

A positive slope indicates a **positive relationship** (also known as a *direct* relationship) between variables X and Y, whereas a negative slope indicates a **negative relationship** (also known as an *inverse* relationship) between variables X and Y. In the case of a positive relationship, as scores on X *increase*, scores on Y also *increase*. In the case of a negative relationship, as scores on X *increase*, scores on Y *decrease*. For instance, the slope in the present example is −1.00, meaning that for every unit that X increases, Y decreases by one unit.

Let us return to the example where individuals are paid $2 per hour worked. Suppose that in addition to this wage, each individual is given a tip of $1.50. Now the relationship between X and Y is

$$Y = 1.50 + 2.00X$$

FIGURE 5.3   **Example of a Linear Relationship with a Negative Slope**

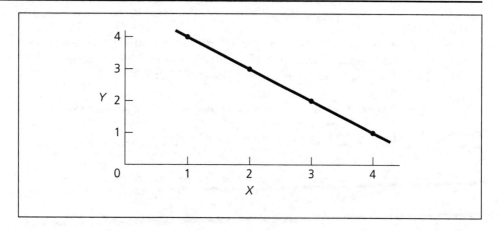

Line C of Figure 5.2 plots this relationship for the four individuals. If we compute the slope of this line, we find it to be 2.00, as before. Notice that lines C and B are parallel but that line C is higher than line B. The amount of separation between these two lines can be measured at the Y axis, where $X = 0$. When $X = 0$, the Y value is 1.50 for line C and 0 for line B. Thus, line C is raised 1.50 units above line B.

The point at which a line intersects the Y axis when $X = 0$ is called the **intercept**, and its value is denoted by the letter a. Linear relationships can differ in the values of their intercepts as well as the values of their slopes, as indicated in the previous problem in which the intercept of line C is 1.50 and the intercept of line B is 0. The general form of the **linear model** is thus

$$Y = a + bX \qquad\qquad [5.2]$$

Any line can be represented by Equation 5.2. A slope and an intercept will always describe the linear relationship between two variables. Given these values, we can substitute scores on X into the **linear equation** to determine the corresponding scores on Y. For example, the linear equation $Y = 1.50 + 2.00X$ tells us that an individual who worked for 2 hours was paid \$5.50 because the Y score associated with an X score of 2 is

$$Y = 1.50 + 2.00X$$
$$= 1.50 + (2.00)(2) = 5.50$$

Similarly, an individual who worked for 3 hours was paid $Y = 1.50 + (2.00)(3) = \$7.50$, and an individual who worked for 4 hours was paid $Y = 1.50 + (2.00)(4) = \$9.50$.

STUDY EXERCISE 5.1

Suppose that you are told that for a group of 20 students, there is a perfect linear relationship between their grade point averages (Y) and their scores on an intelligence test (X). Suppose that you are also told that the equation that describes the relationship is

$$Y = 1.00 + .025X$$

If a student obtained a score of 100 on the intelligence test, what must his or her grade point average be? What must a student's grade point average be if he or she obtained an intelligence test score of 97? Of 108?

Answer   The grade point average associated with an intelligence test score of 100 is

$$Y = 1.00 + (.025)(100) = 3.50$$

The grade point average associated with an intelligence test score of 97 is

$$Y = 1.00 + (.025)(97) = 3.42$$

Last, the grade point average associated with an intelligence test score of 108 is

$$Y = 1.00 + (.025)(108) = 3.70$$

5.2   The Pearson Correlation Coefficient

Characteristics of the Pearson Correlation Coefficient

It is rare in the behavioral sciences to observe a perfect linear relationship between two variables. Far more common is for the relationship between two variables to *approximate* a linear one. The extent of linear relationship between two variables is indexed by a statistic known as the **Pearson correlation coefficient.**

The *correlation coefficient* can range from -1.00 through 0 to $+1.00$ and is traditionally represented as *r*. The *magnitude* of the correlation coefficient, as indexed by its absolute value, indicates the *degree to which a linear relationship is approximated*: The further *r* is in either a positive or a negative direction from 0, the better is the approximation.

The *sign* of the correlation coefficient indicates the *direction* of the linear approximation. A correlation coefficient of $+1.00$ means that the two variables form a perfect linear relationship that is positive, or *direct*, in nature (that is, the higher the score an individual obtains on X, the higher the score that individual obtains on Y). A correlation coefficient of -1.00 also means that the two variables form a perfect linear relationship, but it is negative, or *inverse*, in nature (that is, the higher the score an individual obtains on X, the lower the score that individual obtains on Y). A correlation coefficient of 0 means that there is no linear relationship between the two variables.

Figure 5.4 presents some scatterplots for correlation coefficients of different magnitudes. As can be seen, the more strongly the two variables are correlated, the more closely the data points form a line. In fact, when $r = +1.00$ or -1.00, the relationship between X and Y is perfectly linear so all of the data points fall exactly on a straight line. As we discussed in Section 5.1, this line can be represented by an equation of the form $Y = a + bX$.*

Rationale for the Pearson Correlation Coefficient

To further understand the nature of Pearson correlation, consider Table 5.1 on page 142, which presents data that illustrates (a) a perfect positive linear relationship, (b) a perfect negative linear relationship, and (c) a complete lack of linear relationship between two variables, X and Y. For each example, we have converted the raw scores on X and Y to z scores, which we represent as z_X and z_Y, respectively.

When a linear relationship is positive, the z scores on variable X will tend to be similar to the z scores on variable Y and they will also tend to be alike in sign. In fact, when a positive linear relationship is perfect, the z scores on X and Y will be identical, as is illustrated in columns 4 and 5 of Table 5.1a. This means, for example, that an individual who has a score 1 standard deviation above the mean on

---

* When the correlation between two variables is not perfect, regression can be used to identify a line that, although imperfect, will fit the data points better than any other line that we could try to fit to them, as determined by the least squares criterion. We discuss regression and the least squares criterion in detail in Section 5.5.

FIGURE 5.4   **Scatterplots for (a) a Perfect Positive Relationship, (b) a Perfect Negative Relationship, (c) No Relationship, (d) a Strong Positive Relationship, and (e) a Strong Negative Relationship (Adapted from Johnson & Liebert, 1977)**

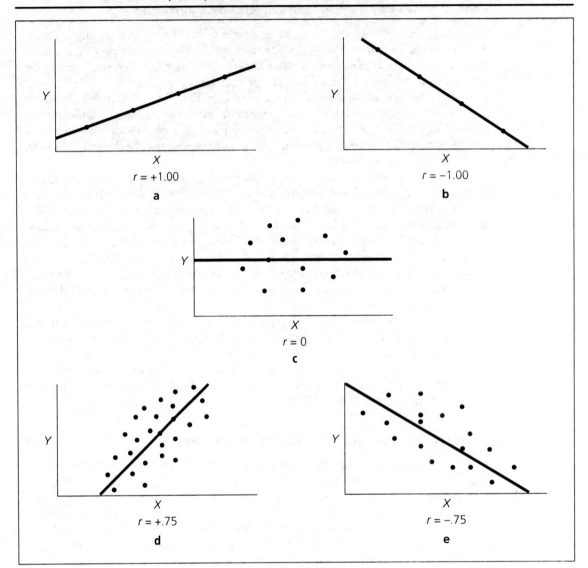

X (that is, a z_X score of 1.00) will also have a score 1 standard deviation above the mean on Y (that is, a z_Y score of 1.00). Similarly, an individual who has a score 1 standard deviation below the mean on X (that is, a z_X score of −1.00) will also have a score 1 standard deviation below the mean on Y (that is, a z_Y score of −1.00).

When the z scores for a given individual are multiplied by each other, the product $(z_X z_Y)$ will be positive because a positive number times a positive number is

TABLE 5.1 **Examples of (a) a Perfect Positive Linear Relationship, (b) a Perfect Negative Linear Relationship, and (c) No Linear Relationship**

(a) Perfect Positive Linear Relationship

Individual	X	Y	z_X	z_Y	$z_X z_Y$	
1	8	10	1.41	1.41	2.00	
2	7	9	.71	.71	.50	
3	6	8	.00	.00	.00	$r = \dfrac{5.00}{5} = +1.00$
4	5	7	−.71	−.71	.50	
5	4	6	−1.41	−1.41	2.00	
					$\Sigma z_X z_Y = 5.00$	

(b) Perfect Negative Linear Relationship

Individual	X	Y	z_X	z_Y	$z_X z_Y$	
1	8	6	1.41	−1.41	−2.00	
2	7	7	.71	−.71	2.50	
3	6	8	.00	.00	.00	$r = \dfrac{-5.00}{5} = -1.00$
4	5	9	−.71	.71	−.50	
5	4	10	−1.41	1.41	−2.00	
					$\Sigma z_X z_Y = -5.00$	

(c) No Linear Relationship

Individual	X	Y	z_X	z_Y	$z_X z_Y$	
1	8	7	1.41	−.27	−.38	
2	7	10	.71	.1.07	.76	
3	6	4	.00	−1.60	.00	$r = \dfrac{.00}{5} = .00$
4	5	10	−.71	.1.07	−.76	
5	4	7	−1.41	−.27	.38	
					$\Sigma z_X z_Y = .00$	

positive and a negative number times a negative number is also positive (unless $z_X = z_Y = 0$, in which case $z_X z_Y$ will also equal 0). When these products are summed across individuals, a relatively large positive value of $\Sigma z_X z_Y$ results. For instance, the sum of the $z_X z_Y$ scores in column 6 of Table 5.1a is 5.00. Positive, though less extreme, values of $\Sigma z_X z_Y$ will similarly result for a nonperfect positive linear relationship between two variables.

When a linear relationship is negative, the z scores on variable X will also tend to be similar to the z scores on variable Y, but they will generally be opposite in sign. For instance, large positive z scores on X will tend to be associated with large negative z scores on Y. For a perfect negative linear relationship, the z scores on X and Y will have different signs but will be identical in size, as is illustrated in columns 4 and 5 of Table 5.1b. For example, an individual who has a score 1 standard deviation *above* the mean on X (that is, a z_X score of 1.00) will have a score 1 standard deviation *below* the mean on Y (that is, a z_Y score of -1.00).

When the z scores for a given individual are multiplied, the product will be negative because a positive number times a negative number is negative (unless $z_X = z_Y = 0$), and when these products are summed across individuals, a relatively large negative value of $\Sigma z_X z_Y$ results. For instance, the sum of the $z_X z_Y$ scores in column 6 of Table 5.1b is -5.00. Negative, though less extreme, values of $\Sigma z_X z_Y$ will similarly result for a nonperfect negative linear relationship between two variables.

Finally, when there is *no* linear relationship, the z scores on variable X will bear no consistent relationship to the z scores on variable Y, in either size or sign. The product of the z scores will be positive for some individuals and negative for others (and, for still others, equal to 0) and, when summed, the positive and the negative $z_X z_Y$ values will cancel each other out, yielding a $\Sigma z_X z_Y$ value of 0. For instance, this is true of the $z_X z_Y$ scores in column 6 of Table 5.1c.

To summarize, when a linear relationship is positive, the sum of the products of z scores will also be positive; when a linear relationship is negative, the sum of the products of z scores will also be negative; and when there is a complete lack of a linear relationship, the sum of the products of z scores will be 0. This finding is consistent with the nature of the correlation coefficient, as we described earlier. We can therefore use the sum of the products of z scores as an index of the relationship between two variables. There is, however, one complication: When the correlation between two variables is nonzero, the value of the sum of z score products is influenced not only by the size of the correlation but also by the sample size (N). For a positive correlation, for example, the larger the number of observations, the greater is the sum of the products, other things being equal. Because we want an index of correlation that is independent of N, we can divide $\Sigma z_X z_Y$ by N.

Dividing by N is also advantageous because of a certain property of z scores. Recall that when the relationship between two variables is positive and perfect, z_X and z_Y for a given individual will be equal. In this case, $\Sigma z_X z_Y = \Sigma z_X^2 = \Sigma z_Y^2$ because $z_X = z_Y$. It turns out that the sum of a set of squared z scores will always equal N. Thus, when the correlation is positive and perfect, $\Sigma z_X z_Y$ will always equal N, and dividing $\Sigma z_X z_Y$ by N will always yield a value of N/N = 1.00. For a perfect negative relationship, $\Sigma z_X z_Y$ will always equal $-N$ such that a perfect negative correlation will always yield a $\Sigma z_X z_Y/N$ value of $-N/N = -1.00$. Nonperfect linear relationships will yield $\Sigma z_X z_Y/N$ values somewhere between the two extremes of -1.00 and $+1.00$.

These properties suggest the following formula for the Pearson correlation coefficient:

$$r = \frac{\sum z_X z_Y}{N} \qquad [5.3]$$

Although Equation 5.3 provides insight into the nature of the correlation coefficient, it is not necessary to convert raw scores to z scores in order to derive r. Alternatively, the Pearson correlation coefficient can be represented in terms of raw scores using the general expression

$$r = \frac{SCP}{\sqrt{SS_X SS_Y}} \qquad [5.4]$$

where SS_X is the sum of squares for variable X, SS_Y is the sum of squares for variable Y, and SCP is the **sum of cross-products**.

Recall that the defining formula for the sum of squares for variable X is $\Sigma(X - X)^2$. This can also be written as

$$\sum(X - \overline{X})(X - \overline{X})$$

In other words, we simply multiply each individual's deviation score by itself and then sum these products across individuals. Similarly, the sum of squares for variable Y can be represented as

$$\sum(Y - \overline{Y})(Y - \overline{Y})$$

A sum of cross-products is similar to a sum of squares but, rather than indicating the extent to which a set of scores varies from its mean, a sum of cross-products indicates the extent to which two sets of scores vary from each other, that is, the extent to which they *covary*. The sum of cross-products is defined as

$$SCP = \sum(X - \overline{X})(Y - \overline{Y}) \qquad [5.5]$$

In other words, we multiply an individual's deviation score for variable X by that individual's deviation score for variable Y and then sum these *cross-products* across individuals.* Unlike a sum of squares, a sum of cross-products can be negative because scores are not squared in its calculation.

Phrased in terms of the defining formulas for its components, Equation 5.4 is thus equivalent to

$$r = \frac{\sum(X - \overline{X})(Y - \overline{Y})}{\sqrt{\sum(X - \overline{X})^2 \sum(Y - \overline{Y})^2}} \qquad [5.6]$$

As we will see shortly, the rationale for this formula closely parallels that for Equation 5.3.

---

* Dividing the sum of cross-products by N yields a statistic known as the *covariance*.

Consider a group of ten women. Two variables have been measured for each: traditionalism as assessed by responses to a ten-item questionnaire concerning general life values (X) and their ideal family size (Y). Scores on the traditionalism questionnaire can range from 0 to 10, with higher values indicating a more traditional orientation. The scores for variables X and Y are presented in columns 2 and 5, respectively, of Table 5.2.

The first step in computing the correlation coefficient is to calculate the sum of squares for the X scores and the sum of squares for the Y scores. This has been done in columns 4 and 7 of Table 5.2, where it can be seen that $SS_X = 80.00$ and $SS_Y = 60.00$. The sum of cross-products is computed in column 8 of Table 5.2. For instance, the first individual's deviation score on X is 4.00 (column 3) and her deviation score on Y is 5.00 (column 6). Her cross-product score is thus $(4.00)(5.00) = 20.00$. Summing the cross-product scores for the entire data set, we find that $SCP = 46.00$.

The correlation coefficient can now be calculated using Equation 5.6:

$$r = \frac{46.00}{\sqrt{(80.00)(60.00)}} = .66$$

A correlation coefficient of .66 indicates that there is some degree of a direct linear relationship between the two variables. The linear trend can be seen in the scatterplot of the two variables in Figure 5.5.

When two variables approximate a positive linear relationship, as in the present case, low scores on one variable will tend to be associated with low scores on the other variable, and high scores will also tend to go together. Consequently, $X - \overline{X}$ and $Y - \overline{Y}$ for a given individual will tend to both be positive (if the

TABLE 5.2   **Data and Calculation of SS_X, SS_Y, and SCP for Traditionalism and Ideal Family Size Study**

Individual	X	$(X - \overline{X})$	$(X - \overline{X})^2$	Y	$(Y - \overline{Y})$	$(Y - \overline{Y})^2$	$(X - \overline{X})(Y - \overline{Y})$
1	9	4.00	16.00	10	5.00	25.00	20.00
2	7	2.00	4.00	6	1.00	1.00	2.00
3	5	.00	.00	3	−2.00	4.00	.00
4	3	−2.00	4.00	6	1.00	1.00	−2.00
5	1	−4.00	16.00	3	−2.00	4.00	8.00
6	1	−4.00	16.00	3	−2.00	4.00	8.00
7	3	−2.00	4.00	5	.00	.00	.00
8	7	2.00	4.00	6	1.00	1.00	2.00
9	5	.00	.00	1	−4.00	16.00	.00
10	9	4.00	16.00	7	2.00	4.00	8.00
	$\Sigma X = 50$		$SS_X = 80.00$	$\Sigma Y = 50$		$SS_Y = 60.00$	$SCP = 46.00$
	$\overline{X} = 5.00$			$\overline{Y} = 5.00$			

FIGURE 5.5   **Scatterplot for Traditionalism and Ideal Family Size Study**

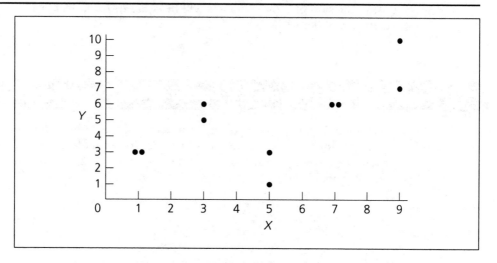

individual scores high on both X and Y, such as individuals 1 and 10) or to both be negative (if the individual scores low on both X and Y, such as individuals 5 and 6). Because a positive number times a positive number is positive and a negative number times a negative number is also positive, most cross-products scores will be positive and the sum of cross-products that constitutes the numerator of Equation 5.6 will also be positive. When divided by $\sqrt{SS_X SS_Y}$, this will yield a positive correlation coefficient. Other things being equal, the greater the approximation to a linear relationship, the greater the sum of cross-products will be and, thus, the greater the correlation coefficient will be in a positive direction.

   When two variables approximate a negative linear relationship, low scores on one variable will tend to be associated with high scores on the other variable, and high scores will tend to be associated with low scores. Thus, either $X - \overline{X}$ or $Y - \overline{Y}$ will tend to be positive and the other will tend to be negative. Because a positive number times a negative number is negative, most cross-products scores will be negative and the sum of cross-products will also be negative. When divided by $\sqrt{SS_X SS_Y}$, this will yield a negative correlation coefficient. Other things being equal, the greater the approximation to a linear relationship, the greater the sum of cross-products will be and, thus, the greater the correlation coefficient will be in a negative direction.

   When two variables are not linearly related, scores on one variable will not be consistently associated with any particular scores on the other variable. Consequently, various combinations of $X - \overline{X}$ and $Y - \overline{Y}$ (that is, positive-positive, positive-negative, negative-negative, and negative-positive) will result. Thus, $(X - \overline{X})(Y - \overline{Y})$ will sometimes be positive and will sometimes be negative [unless an X or Y score is equal to its mean, in which case $(X - \overline{X})(Y - \overline{Y})$ will be equal to 0]. When summed, the positive and the negative values will cancel each other out, so the sum of cross-products will be equal to zero, thus yielding a correlation coefficient of 0.

5.3 Computational Formula for the Pearson Correlation Coefficient

Equation 5.6 expresses Equation 5.4 in terms of the defining formulas for the sum of squares for variable X, the sum of squares for variable Y, and the sum of cross-products. However, the sum of squares for variable X can also be derived using the computational formula

$$SS_X = \sum X^2 - \frac{(\sum X)^2}{N}$$

and the sum of squares for variable Y can be derived using the computational formula

$$SS_Y = \sum Y^2 - \frac{(\sum Y)^2}{N}$$

Analogous to the computational formulas for the sums of squares, the computational formula for the sum of cross-products is

$$SCP = \sum XY - \frac{(\sum X)(\sum Y)}{N} \qquad [5.7]$$

where $\sum X$ is the sum of individuals' X scores, $\sum Y$ is the sum of individuals' Y scores, and $\sum XY$ is the sum of the products of individuals' X and Y scores.

Substituting the computational formulas for the sum of squares of variable X, the sum of squares of variable Y, and the sum of cross-products into the general expression for a correlation coefficient represented by Equation 5.4 yields the following computational formula for the correlation coefficient:

$$r = \frac{\sum XY - \frac{(\sum X)(\sum Y)}{N}}{\sqrt{\left(\sum X^2 - \frac{(\sum X)^2}{N}\right)\left(\sum Y^2 - \frac{(\sum Y)^2}{N}\right)}} \qquad [5.8]$$

This formula is both more efficient and more precise than Equation 5.6 because it requires fewer steps and presents fewer opportunities for rounding error.

The calculation of the intermediate statistics for Equation 5.8 is demonstrated in Table 5.3 for the traditionalism and ideal family size data from Table 5.2. As can be seen, $\sum X^2 = 330$, $\sum Y^2 = 310$, and $\sum XY = 296$. Thus,

TABLE 5.3   **Calculation of Intermediate Statistics for the Correlation Coefficient for Traditionalism and Ideal Family Size Study**

Individual	X	Y	X^2	Y^2	XY
1	9	10	81	100	90
2	7	6	49	36	42
3	5	3	25	9	15
4	3	6	9	36	18
5	1	3	1	9	3
6	1	3	1	9	3
7	3	5	9	25	15
8	7	6	49	36	42
9	5	1	25	1	5
10	9	7	81	49	63
	$\Sigma X = 50$	$\Sigma Y = 50$	$\Sigma X^2 = 330$	$\Sigma Y^2 = 310$	$\Sigma XY = 296$

$$r = \frac{296 - \dfrac{(50)(50)}{10}}{\sqrt{\left(330 - \dfrac{50^2}{10}\right)\left(310 - \dfrac{50^2}{10}\right)}} = \frac{46.00}{\sqrt{(80.00)(60.00)}} = .66$$

This is the same value of r as was calculated using Equation 5.6.

STUDY EXERCISE 5.2

A political psychologist who is interested in the relationship between voters' perceptions that a candidate supports labor unions (X) and their willingness to vote for that candidate (Y) asked nine individuals to indicate on a 10-point scale the extent to which they thought the candidate supported labor unions, with higher scores indicating greater perceived support. They also indicated on a similar 10-point scale their willingness to vote for the candidate. The scores on these variables are presented in the following table. Compute the Pearson correlation coefficient for these data.

Individual	X	Y
1	6	5
2	7	4
3	8	4
4	8	5
5	8	3
6	9	6
7	9	7
8	7	5
9	10	6

Answer   The correlation coefficient is most readily calculated using Equation 5.8. The intermediate statistics necessary for the application of this equation are computed as follows:

Individual	X	Y	X^2	Y^2	XY
1	6	5	36	25	30
2	7	4	49	16	28
3	8	4	64	16	32
4	8	5	64	25	40
5	8	3	64	9	24
6	9	6	81	36	54
7	9	7	81	49	63
8	7	5	49	25	35
9	10	6	100	36	60
	$\sum X = 72$	$\sum Y = 45$	$\sum X^2 = 588$	$\sum Y^2 = 237$	$\sum XY = 366$

Thus,

$$r = \frac{\sum XY - \frac{(\sum X)(\sum Y)}{N}}{\sqrt{\left(\sum X^2 - \frac{(\sum X)^2}{N}\right)\left(\sum Y^2 - \frac{(\sum Y)^2}{N}\right)}}$$

$$= \frac{366 - \frac{(72)(45)}{9}}{\sqrt{\left(588 - \frac{72^2}{9}\right)\left(237 - \frac{45^2}{9}\right)}}$$

$$= \frac{6.00}{\sqrt{(12.00)(12.00)}} = .50$$

A correlation coefficient of .50 indicates that some degree of a direct linear relationship exists between the two variables.

5.4   Correlation and Causation

The fact that two variables are correlated does not necessarily imply that one variable *causes* the other to vary as it does. It is entirely possible for two variables to be related to each other but to have no causal relationship. In fact, there are many reasons why two variables, X and Y, might be correlated. Three possibilities are that (1) X causes Y, (2) Y causes X, or (3) one or more additional variables causes both X and Y, thus producing a *spurious* relationship between them.

For instance, although we might find a positive correlation between the number of hours that college students spend working for pay and the number of campus organizations that they belong to, it is very unlikely that working *causes* students to join organizations or that membership in organizations *causes* students to work. Rather, the correlation between these variables is probably attributable to students' desire to achieve and related personality characteristics—as the desire to achieve increases, individuals might work more as they pursue their financial and occupational goals and join more organizations as a means of achieving in the social realm. As this example illustrates, one must be cautious when drawing causal inferences from correlational analyses.

Numerous examples exist in the literature where the causal relationship underlying a correlation is ambiguous. For example, a correlation has been established between the amount of violence that children watch on television and how aggressive they are. Does watching violent programs make children more aggressive? Or do children who are more aggressive (for reasons other than television-viewing habits) prefer to watch violent television shows? Could it be that as children grow older, they tend to both be more aggressive and watch more television, thus producing a spurious correlation between television viewing and aggression?

Spurious relationships sometimes result in surprising correlations between variables. For example, there is a moderate positive correlation in the United States population between individuals' shoe (foot) size and their verbal ability: People with larger feet tend to have more verbal ability. Surely there is not a causal relationship between these variables. As it turns out, the population of Americans includes a sizable number of children. Very young children tend to have small feet and poor verbal ability. As children grow, they acquire more verbal skills and their feet get larger. Age is a "cause" of both verbal ability and foot size, and this common cause produces a spurious correlation between individuals' shoe size and their verbal ability.

The issues that we raise about correlation and causation also relate to the other statistical tests that we consider in this book. We discuss problems with inferring causation further in Section 9.4.

5.5   Interpreting the Magnitude of a Correlation Coefficient

When students first learn about the correlation coefficient, they frequently ask what represents a "large" correlation, a "moderate" correlation, and a "small" correlation and what magnitude of correlations is typical in behavioral science research. These questions are difficult to answer. A correlation of .50 might be considered a "large" correlation in one context but a "small" correlation in another. For example, if we were studying the reliability and validity of an intelligence test, we might administer the test twice to the same individuals with a 3-week interval between the test administrations. Because intelligence should be stable over a 3-week period, we would expect a valid test to yield highly similar results at the two testing times. In this case, we would expect a correlation in the .80 to .90 range. If we found a correlation of .50, we would not trust the test.

In contrast, suppose that we were trying to determine whether there is a relationship between parental income and children's intelligence test scores. We know that intelligence is a complicated construct that is influenced by many variables. It would be rather remarkable if a single variable showed much of a correlation with intelligence, given all of the factors that influence it. A correlation of .50 would be considered substantial when viewed in these terms.

As an interesting example of interpreting the magnitude of a correlation coefficient, when Rosenthal (1995) asked physicians to identify what they considered to be the most important medical breakthroughs of recent times, most mentioned the introduction of a drug known as *cyclosporine*. This drug is given to patients who are to receive organ transplants to reduce the likelihood of organ rejection. An examination of the relationship between patient survival rates and the use of the drug has revealed a correlation of .15. Although the correlation is near 0, it nevertheless indicates that thousands of lives are being saved.

In behavioral science research, where complex behaviors are studied, correlations of .20 to .30 (and −.20 to −.30) are often considered important. The interpretation of a correlation coefficient's magnitude, however, is complicated by inferential considerations that we will not discuss until Chapter 14.

Sometimes one variable in a correlational analysis can be conceptualized as the independent variable and the other variable can be conceptualized as the dependent variable. When this is the case, the square of the correlation coefficient (that is, r^2) provides useful information beyond that provided by the correlation coefficient per se. More specifically, as we explain more fully in Chapter 14, r^2 indicates the proportion of variability in the dependent variable that can be explained by, or that is associated with, the independent variable. It follows that $1 - r^2$ reflects the proportion of variability in the dependent variable that cannot be explained by, or that is not associated with, the dependent variable. The quantity r^2 is formally known as the *coefficient of determination* and $1 - r^2$ is formally known as the *coefficient of alienation*.

If we conceptualize traditionalism as the independent variable and the ideal family size as the dependent variable in the traditionalism and ideal family size study, then the proportion of variability in the ideal family size that is accounted for by traditionalism is $.66^2 = .44$. If we multiply this value by 100, we obtain the percentage of variability that traditionalism accounts for in the ideal family size—namely, 44%.

5.6 Regression

We noted earlier that when two variables are perfectly correlated, all of the data points will fall exactly on a straight line defined by an equation of the form $Y = a + bX$. However, we will almost certainly never encounter such a situation in the behavioral sciences. In fact, correlations for the types of variables that are typically studied by behavioral scientists seldom exceed +.30 or −.30 and are often considerably smaller.

When two variables are not perfectly correlated, the statistical technique of *regression* can be used to identify a line that, although imperfect, fits the data points better than any other line that we could try to fit to them, as determined by the least squares criterion, which we discuss shortly. This line describes the nature of the linear relationship between the two variables.

We begin our discussion of regression by returning to the traditionalism and ideal family size example. The correlation between these two variables was found to be .66, indicating that some degree of a direct linear relationship exists between them. This linear trend is illustrated in Figure 5.5.

The linear relationship between two variables, X and Y, can be formally represented by a **regression line** that takes the general form

$$\hat{Y} = a + bX \tag{5.9}$$

This equation, which is formally known as the **regression equation**, is similar to the linear model, $Y = a + bX$, but because the data points in our example do not form a straight line, different Y scores might be associated with the same X score. For instance, one of the research participants (Individual 7) had a traditionalism (variable X) score of 3 and indicated a preference for five children (variable Y). A second individual (Individual 4) also had a traditionalism score of 3 but perceived six children, rather than five, as being the ideal family size. Because of this and related issues, the symbol $\hat{Y}$ (read *predicted Y*) is used in the framework of regression to indicate the value of Y that is *predicted* to be paired with a specified value of X. This value of Y is the point on the line $a + bX$ that corresponds to a person's score on X.

Calculation of the Slope and the Intercept

The slope and the intercept of a regression line are readily calculated from formulas. We present the formulas and then discuss the logic underlying them. For the slope, the formula is*

$$b = \frac{SCP}{SS_X} \tag{5.10}$$

Turning again to the traditionalism and ideal family size study, we find that

$$b = \frac{46.00}{80.00} = .58$$

because $SCP = 46.00$ and $SS_X = 80.00$ per our calculations in Section 5.2.

The formula for computing the intercept is

$$a = \overline{Y} - b\overline{X} \tag{5.11}$$

Inserting the value of b from above and the values of $\overline{Y}$ and $\overline{X}$ from Table 5.2, we find that

$$a = 5.00 - (.58)(5.00) = 2.10$$

---

* An alternative formula for the slope is $b = r(s_Y/s_X)$.

The regression equation that describes the relationship between traditionalism (X) and ideal family size (Y) is thus

$$\hat{Y} = 2.10 + 58X$$

The regression line described by this equation is displayed in Figure 5.6. Note that this line intersects the Y axis at the value of the intercept (2.10). Furthermore, the slope of this line is such that when X increases by 1 unit, $\hat{Y}$ increases by .58 unit. The lines with the arrowheads illustrate visually the rationale for defining the values of the slope and intercept by highlighting the distance between each data point and the regression line: The slope and the intercept are defined so as to *minimize the squared vertical distances that the data points, considered collectively, are from the regression line.* This is what we mean when we say that the regression line fits the data points better than any other line that we could try to fit to them. This is accomplished in our example by the equation $\hat{Y} = 2.10 + .58X$. Any other linear equation would result in a larger sum of squared distances from the line generated by that equation.

The criterion for deriving the values of the slope and intercept is formally known as the **least squares criterion**. This can be illustrated algebraically as well as visually. Earlier we noted that a regression equation can be used to identify the value of Y that is predicted to be paired with an individual's score on X. This is done by substituting a person's score on X into the regression equation. For the traditionalism and ideal family size study, this equation is

$$\hat{Y} = 2.10 + .58X$$

Let us substitute the X scores of each of the ten research participants into this equation. These scores are listed in column 2 of Table 5.4. The score on X for the first individual is 9. The predicted Y score ($\hat{Y}$) for this individual is therefore 2.10 + (.58)(9) = 7.32. The score on X for the second individual is 7, so the predicted

FIGURE 5.6 **Scatterplot and Regression Line for Traditionalism and Ideal Family Size Study**

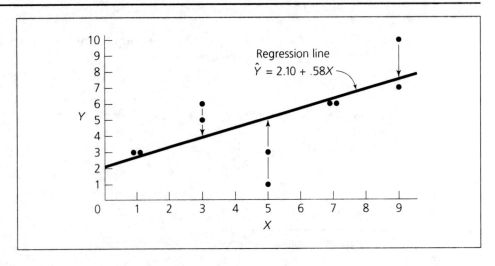

TABLE 5.4   Scores on *X* and *Y*, Predicted Scores, and Discrepancy Scores for Traditionalism and Ideal Family Size Study

Individual	X	Y	$\hat{Y}$	$Y - \hat{Y}$
1	9	10	7.32	2.68
2	7	6	6.16	−.16
3	5	3	5.00	−2.00
4	3	6	3.84	2.16
5	1	3	2.68	.32
6	1	3	2.68	.32
7	3	5	3.84	1.16
8	7	6	6.16	−.16
9	5	1	5.00	−4.00
10	9	7	7.32	−.32

Y score for this person is 2.10 + (.58)(7) = 6.16. The remaining predicted scores are obtained similarly.

Columns 3 and 4 of Table 5.4 present individuals' actual *Y* scores and their predicted *Y* scores based on the regression equation. Inspection of these scores indicates that there are discrepancies between *Y* and $\hat{Y}$. These differences are listed in the last column of Table 5.4. Note that the discrepancies are generally rather small, reflecting the strong approximation to a linear relationship that exists between *X* and *Y* as indicated by the fact that *r* = .66. If the correlation had been smaller, there would be larger discrepancies between the actual and the predicted *Y* scores. The least squares criterion concerns itself with the *squares* of the discrepancy scores and formally defines the values of the slope and intercept so as to minimize the sum of these squares. That is, the least squares criterion defines the regression line such that $\Sigma(Y - \hat{Y})^2$ is minimized.

Standard Error of Estimate

Unless two variables are perfectly correlated, some degree of error will result when scores on *Y* are predicted from scores on *X* using a regression equation. The amount of error for a given individual can be represented by the discrepancy between that person's actual and predicted *Y* scores. However, the usefulness of discrepancy scores as a summary measure of predictive error is limited by the fact that the sum of the discrepancies between actual *Y* scores and *Y* scores predicted from the regression equation will always equal 0. This is demonstrated in column 5 of Table 5.4 for the traditionalism and ideal family size example.

A more useful index of predictive error is provided by the **standard error of estimate**, which is defined as

$$s_{YX} = \sqrt{\frac{\Sigma(Y - \hat{Y})^2}{N}} \qquad\qquad [5.12]$$

where s_{YX} is the standard error of estimate and all other symbols are as defined above. Equation 5.12 is conceptually similar to the defining formula for a standard deviation, which, phrased in terms of variable Y, is

$$s_Y = \sqrt{\frac{\sum(Y - \bar{Y})^2}{N}}$$

The only difference between the two equations is in the numerator. For the standard deviation, the numerator reflects the deviation of the Y scores from their mean. For the standard error of estimate, the numerator reflects the deviation of the Y scores from the predicted Y scores. The standard error of estimate thus represents the average error across individuals when predicting scores on variable Y from the regression equation.

Although Equation 5.12 has the advantage of being conceptually clear, a more efficient computational formula is available for calculating the standard error of estimate:

$$s_{YX} = s_Y\sqrt{1 - r^2} \qquad\qquad [5.13]$$

In this formula, s_Y is the standard deviation for variable Y and $1 - r^2$ is the coefficient of alienation, as discussed above.

Phrased in terms of the sum of squares for variable Y rather than the standard deviation, Equation 5.13 is equivalent to

$$s_{YX} = \sqrt{\frac{SS_Y(1 - r^2)}{N}} \qquad\qquad [5.14]$$

Because $SS_Y = 60.00$ per our calculations in Section 5.2 and $r = .66$, the standard error of estimate for the traditionalism and ideal family size example according to this equation is

$$s_{YX} = \sqrt{\frac{60.00(1 - .66^2)}{10}} = 1.84$$

which indicates that, on average, predicted Y (ideal family size) scores deviate from actual Y scores by 1.84 units.

There are two perspectives in interpreting the standard error of estimate. First, its absolute magnitude is meaningful. In the present example, the average error when predicting scores on variable Y from scores on variable X is 1.84 units. Given the range of possible ideal family sizes, this degree of error is not unreasonable. Second, the standard error of estimate can be compared with the standard deviation of Y. The standard deviation of Y indicates what the average error in prediction would be if one were to predict a Y score equal to the mean of Y for each individual. If variable X helps to predict variable Y, then the standard error of estimate will be smaller than the standard deviation of Y. The better the predictor X is, the smaller the standard error of estimate will be. In the present example, $SS_Y = 60.00$ and $N = 10$, so $S_Y = \sqrt{SS_Y/N} = \sqrt{60.00/10} = 2.45$. The reduction in error from 2.45 (the standard deviation of Y) to 1.84 (the standard error of estimate) when predicting scores on Y when scores on X are considered reflects the strong approximation to a linear relationship that exists between traditionalism and the ideal family size as indicated by the fact that $r = .66$.

STUDY EXERCISE 5.3

Compute the regression equation and the standard error of estimate for the data in Study Exercise 5.2.

Answer   The sum of cross-products and the sum of squares for X were calculated in Study Exercise 5.2 to equal 6.00 and 12.00, respectively. From Equation 5.10, the slope of the regression line is

$$b = \frac{SCP}{SS_X} = \frac{6.00}{12.00} = .50$$

Because $\Sigma X = 72$, $\Sigma Y = 45$, and $N = 9$, the mean of X is $72/9 = 8.00$ and the mean of Y is $45/9 = 5.00$. From Equation 5.11, the intercept of the regression line is

$$a = \overline{Y} - b\overline{X} = 5.00 - (.50)(8.00) = 1.00$$

This yields a regression equation of $\hat{Y} = 1.00 + .50X$.

The standard error of estimate can be calculated using Equation 5.14. For $SS_Y = 12.00$, $r = .50$, and $N = 9$, this is found to equal

$$S_{YX} = \sqrt{\frac{SS_Y (1 - r^2)}{N}}$$

$$= \sqrt{\frac{12.00(1 - .50^2)}{9}} = 1.00$$

This result indicates that, on average, predicted Y (willingness to vote for the candidate of interest) scores deviate from actual Y scores by 1.00 unit.

5.7   Additional Issues Associated with the Use of Correlation and Regression

Nonlinear Relationships

There are many ways in which two variables might be related. Figure 5.7 illustrates a *curvilinear* relationship between two variables. For example, this figure reflects the association between anxiety and test performance: At low levels, increasing amounts of anxiety are associated with better performance (perhaps due to heightened arousal). However, as anxiety becomes more elevated, test performance starts to decrease (perhaps due to the resultant difficulty in concentrating).

Two variables might be related, but if they are related in a fashion that is *nonlinear*, Pearson correlation will not be sensitive to this. For instance, the Pearson correlation coefficient for the data depicted in Figure 5.7 is close to 0 even though there is clearly a strong curvilinear relationship. This is because Pearson correlation assesses only linear relationships. Nonlinearity can be effectively modeled using a technique known as *curvilinear* or *polynomial regression*. This technique is discussed at length in Pedhazur (1997).

FIGURE 5.7   **Scatterplot of a Curvilinear Relationship Between Two Variables**

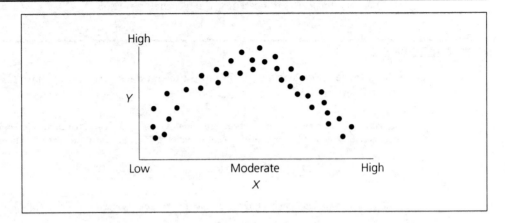

Predicting *X* from *Y*

A second consideration to keep in mind when contemplating the application of regression procedures is that *the* regression *equation for predicting variable X from variable Y is not the same as the regression equation for predicting variable Y from variable X.* An intuitive appreciation for this can be gained from an analogy with foreign-currency exchange rates.

The currency in Mexico is the peso. At present, 1 U.S. dollar is worth 12.138 pesos. The linear equation for converting dollars to pesos is therefore

Pesos = 0 + 12.138 (Dollars)

According to this equation, for every additional dollar that something costs, the number of pesos it costs increases by 12.138. For instance, $1 is worth 12.138 pesos and $2 is worth 24.276 pesos.

If we want to convert pesos to dollars, we must reverse the order of the variables in the linear equation. The equation in this case is

Dollars = 0 + .082 (Pesos)

Note that the conversion rate for this equation is different from that for converting dollars to pesos. In this instance, for every additional peso that something costs, the number of dollars it costs increases by .082. For instance, one peso is worth .082 dollar, or 8.2¢, and two pesos are worth .164 dollar, or 16.4¢.

Just as the conversion rate for dollars and pesos differs depending on which is being exchanged, the slope of a regression equation differs depending on which variable is designated as *X* and which variable is designated as *Y*. For instance, we earlier calculated the following regression equation to describe the relationship between traditionalism (variable *X*) and the ideal family size (variable *Y*):

Ideal family size = 2.10 + .58 (Traditionalism)

If we reverse the variables such that the ideal family size is the *X* variable and traditionalism is the *Y* variable, the regression equation would be

Traditionalism = 1.17 + .77 (Ideal family size)

Using traditionalism to predict how many children a woman thinks is ideal, for every 1 unit that traditionalism increases, we predict the ideal family size to increase by .58 child. In terms of predicting how traditional someone is from the number of children she desires, for every additional child that is desired, traditionalism is predicted to increase .77 unit on the traditionalism scale. In contrast to the slope and intercept, the correlation coefficient is the same in both analyses because it reflects the extent to which the two variables, considered together, approximate a linear relationship.

From a *statistical* perspective, the designation of one variable as X and one variable as Y is arbitrary. It is as easy to derive the line for predicting the first variable from the second as it is to derive the line for predicting the second variable from the first. We merely reverse which variable is labeled X and which variable is labeled Y and apply the usual formulas for the slope and intercept. From a *conceptual* perspective, however, the decision of which variable to designate as X (the variable from which predictions are made) and which variable to designate as Y (the variable that is being predicted) has important implications. A personnel director in a large company would obviously be much more interested in predicting job success from an individual's score on an aptitude test than in the reverse.

The use of regression presupposes an underlying rationale for making predictions about variable Y from variable X. If interest is merely in whether a given variable is linearly *related* to another variable, Pearson correlation can be applied.

Restricted Range

Another issue of note is the effect on the correlation coefficient of examining only a portion of the range of a variable. Depending on the particular circumstances, the magnitude of the correlation when a limited portion of this range is considered might be either less than or greater than if the range had not been so restricted.

Suppose, for instance, that we were interested in the correlation between anxiety and test performance. As we indicated earlier, research has shown that these variables generally tend to have a curvilinear relationship. However, suppose that the sample was selected such that the research participants were all moderately to highly anxious. Figure 5.7 suggests that the linear relationship between anxiety and test performance for this range of anxiety is a strong negative one even though the linear approximation across the whole range of anxiety scores is extremely poor. Consequently, if we were to calculate the correlation coefficient for the restricted sample we would find it to be relatively large (and negative) even though the correlation across the full range of anxiety is close to 0.

On the other hand, if two variables are linearly related, then restricting the range of one variable will often reduce the magnitude of the correlation coefficient. For instance, Figure 5.8 illustrates a strong positive correlation between two variables. However, if only individuals who have moderate to high scores on variable X had been included in the study, the correlation between X and Y would be substantially reduced.

In general, the effect of restricting the range of a variable that is linearly related with another variable is to reduce the magnitude of the correlation coefficient. This might explain the relatively weak correlations that have been reported between Scholastic Aptitude Test (SAT) scores and college grade point averages.

FIGURE 5.8   **The Effect of a Restricted Range on the Correlation Coefficient When Two Variables Are Linearly Related (Based on Howell, 1985)**

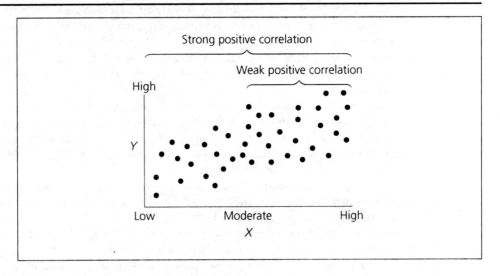

Typically, only students who are interested in pursuing a college education take the SAT. To the extent that this group of students have greater academic aptitude than the general population of high school students (and, thus, are more likely to obtain high SAT scores), the correlations that are observed between SAT scores and grade point averages are based on a restricted range of SAT scores. If all graduating high school students took the SAT, the correlation between SAT scores and grade point averages might reflect a strong positive association.

Because the effect of a restricted range on the Pearson correlation coefficient can never be known with certainty, we must be careful to select our sample such that the entire range of values of interest is studied. We must also be careful not to extend our interpretation of correlational results *outside* the range of the original data set. The conclusions drawn from a correlational analysis apply only to the range of the variables on which the correlation was based. This is because the Pearson correlation coefficient represents the extent to which two variables approximate a linear relationship *for the range of the variables included in its calculation.* For instance, it would be meaningless to try to generalize about the relationship between anxiety and test performance at low to moderate levels of anxiety from the relationship between these variables at moderate to high levels of anxiety.

As you might expect, a similar caution holds for regression analysis: Prediction of Y from X is only meaningful for the range of X values that formed the basis for the calculation of the regression equation. Suppose, for instance, that a researcher is interested in predicting the vividness with which people are able to recall their dreams from the length of time that they sleep. One hundred volunteers spend the night in a sleep laboratory. In the morning, the vividness with which they are able to recall their night's dreams is measured on a scale of 1 to 9, where higher scores indicate more vivid dream recall. The range of sleep duration for the participants in this study is from 5.33 to 8.67 hours, and the regression equation for predicting the vividness of dream recall from the amount of sleep is found to be $\hat{Y} = 8.71 - .68X$. This equation indicates, for example, that the vividness of dream recall for an individual who sleeps 6 hours is predicted to be $8.71 - (.68)(6) = 4.63$, and the vividness of dream recall for an individual who sleeps 8 hours is predicted to be $8.71 - (.68)(8) = 3.27$. This equation also indicates that the vividness of dream recall for an individual who fails to fall asleep is predicted to be a very high $8.71 - (0)(.68) = 8.71$ even though a person cannot dream if he or she is not sleeping! This inconsistency reflects that the regression equation was established on an X value range of 5.33 to 8.67 and does not apply to the relationship between sleep and the vividness of dream recall for an X score of 0.

The Regression Equation for Standard Scores

All of the regression examples that we have considered have focused on raw scores. However, researchers are sometimes interested in the relationship between two sets of *standard* scores. For example, a teacher might want to identify the regression equation that relates the relative performance of students on one test (that is, compared to their classmates' performance) to their relative performance on a second test. In this case, the researcher would first standardize the X and Y scores and would then apply the usual formula (Equation 5.10) to calculate the slope for the regression line based on the standard scores. It is not necessary to calculate the intercept of the regression line when standard scores are analyzed in this manner because this will always equal 0. It is also the case that the slope of the regression line in this instance will always equal the correlation coefficient. Both of these equalities can be proved with simple algebra, although we do not do so here.

The nature of the slope for standard scores provides us with yet another perspective for interpreting the correlation coefficient: A correlation coefficient conveys the number of standard scores that one variable is predicted to change given a change of one standard score in the other variable, other things being equal. Stated another way, a correlation coefficient conveys the number of standard deviations that one variable is predicted to change given a 1 standard deviation change in the other variable. For instance, the correlation of .66 for the traditionalism and ideal family size study tells us that for every standard deviation that traditionalism changes, the ideal family size is predicted to change by .66 standard deviation.

Outliers

The magnitude and even the sign of a correlation coefficient can be influenced by outliers, and it is important for the researcher to consider this possibility. Examine the nine scores in the scatterplot in Figure 5.9a. It is evident that there is no linear trend in these scores, and the correlation coefficient is, in fact, 0. Now suppose that a single outlier is added, as in Figure 5.9b. The correlation between the two variables with this one case added is .84. The addition of a single case changed a correlation of 0 to a correlation of .84! This example is extreme but illustrates that even a single outlier can mask the basic trend in a data set.

Just as outliers can turn a weak correlation into a strong correlation, outliers can also turn a strong correlation into a weak one. It is therefore important for the

FIGURE 5.9   **Scatterplots Illustrating an Outlier Effect**

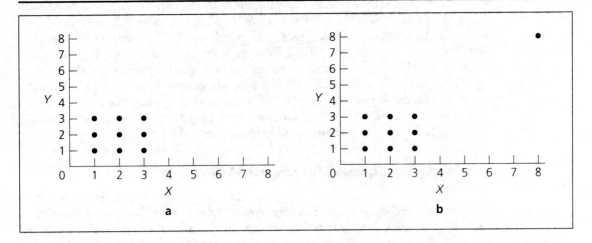

researcher to explore the effect of outliers on the correlation coefficient. Outliers can also have profound effects on regression statistics. Thus, a similar caution holds for regression analysis. Outliers are most likely to complicate interpretation when the sample size is small (which is the case in Figure 5.9).

Statisticians have developed numerous procedures for identifying outliers. One way to determine whether a given case is an outlier is to compute the correlation for the total sample and then compare this with the correlation when the case in question is omitted from the analysis. If the correlation changes relatively little, then the case is not an outlier. However, if the deletion of the case dramatically changes the correlation, then the case *is* deemed an outlier. More sophisticated approaches to outlier identification than the "delete a case" approach described here are discussed in Norusis (1992).

5.8 Links Between Computer Results and Book Content

The statistical computer output for Pearson correlation often takes the form of a correlation **matrix**. In this format, every variable that is specified by the user to be included in the analysis is correlated with every other variable as well as with itself, and the output is organized into rows and columns with the names of the variables listed in the same order as both row and column headings. The correlation coefficients appear in the body of the matrix such that the entry where a row and a column intersect is the coefficient for the correlation between the two corresponding variables. The correlation of a variable with itself is always 1.00. Can you think of why this is the case?

Often, the sample sizes on which the correlation coefficients are based are also included in the computer output. As we discuss in the Links Between Computer Results and Book Content section in Chapter 14, other information might also be presented. We also discuss the nature of the statistical computer output for regression in the same section.

5.9 Links Between Chapters

Whereas this chapter focuses on descriptive aspects of Pearson correlation and regression, Chapter 14 focuses on inferential aspects. Clearly, then, these chapters are highly related. In fact, your instructor might ask you to read these two chapters concurrently.

Applications to the Analysis of a Social Problem Using SPSS for Windows

Our discussion to this point in the book has been on *descriptive* statistics. However, correlation and regression, like all of the other statistics that we have considered so far, are usually pursued in an *inferential* context. We will begin our discussion of inferential statistics in Chapter 7, and we cover inferential aspects of correlation and regression in Chapter 14. It is important to recognize, then, that the conclusions from below are descriptive only of the sample and do not apply to the broader population of individuals that our sample represents.

Based on the analyses that we reported in Chapter 4, we know that many of the teens in the parent–teen communication study are sexually active and that there is variability in the amount of sexual activity: Some teens are more sexually active than others. Another question of interest is whether the amount of sexual activity is associated with how conscientious the teen is about using birth control. Are teens who engage in relatively more sex more careful about not getting (someone) pregnant and therefore using birth control more consistently? Or are teens who engage in relatively little sex just as (un)likely to use birth control as teens who engage in more sexual activity?

Recall that the teens were asked to indicate the number of times that they had engaged in sexual intercourse during the past 6 months. Those teens who reported sexual activity were also asked the following:

When you had intercourse during the past 6 months, how much of the time, if ever, did you or your partner use any birth control (for example, the pill, a condom, etc.) so that you wouldn't get pregnant? Circle the number to the right of the one statement that best describes the use of birth control by you and your partner(s) during the past 6 months.

Always (100% of the time)	6
Most of the time (71% to 99% of the time)	5
Often (51% to 70% of the time)	4
Sometimes (31% to 50% of the time)	3
Occasionally (1% to 30% of the time)	2
Never (0% of the time)	1

Considerable research suggests that this measure is a reasonably valid indicator of the consistency with which an individual uses birth control. For example, the measure has been found to predict unintended pregnancy in both adult and teen populations.

Even though the percentages that accompany the verbal descriptors suggest a scale that is not equal interval, psychometric studies suggest that the heuristics used by teens for generating responses produce measures that reasonably approximate interval-level characteristics. However, psychometric studies have also indicated that teens do not strictly follow the percentages listed in generating responses to the questions, in part because actual use consistency does not map perfectly onto perceived use consistency. For example, a teen who

(continued)

has used birth control 50% of the time might not indicate a response of 3 on the scale.

Frequency histograms for the use consistency measure and the number of instances of sexual intercourse for those teens who reported being sexually active are presented in Figures 5.10 and 5.11, with a normal curve superimposed on each. The use consistency measure shows negative skewness, and the number of instances of sexual intercourse shows positive skewness.

Table 5.5 presents computer output for the correlational analysis between the number of instances of sexual activity (SEXNUM) and the consistency of birth control use (USECONS).* Consistent with our discussion in Section 5.8, the results are organized in the form of a correlation matrix with the names of the two variables appearing as

both row and column headings. Also consistent with our earlier discussion, the number in the matrix where a row intersects a column is the Pearson correlation coefficient between the two corresponding variables. For example, the correlation between the variable in the first row and the variable in the first column is 1.00. This is not surprising because it is the correlation of use consistency with itself, which must be 1.00.

Table 5.5 also reveals that the correlation between the number of instances of sexual intercourse and use consistency is near 0—namely, −.09. Thus, there is very little linear relationship between how sexually active the teens in the sample reported being and how diligent they reported being about protecting themselves from an unintended pregnancy.

FIGURE 5.10   Frequency Histogram of Birth Control Use Consistency

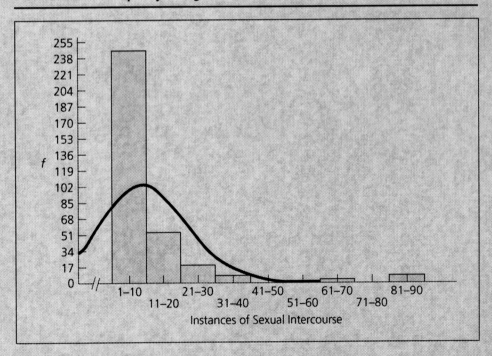

* The association between the two variables can also be examined using other statistical procedures, but consideration of these is beyond the scope of this book.

Figure 5.12 presents a scatterplot for the two variables, with the least squares regression line indicated. Consistent with the very small correlation coefficient, the scatterplot shows minimal linear trend in the data. We also conducted formal analyses to determine whether the correlation coefficient was unduly influenced by any outlying scores. There was no indication that this was the case.

FIGURE 5.11   **Grouped Frequency Histogram of Instances of Sexual Intercourse**

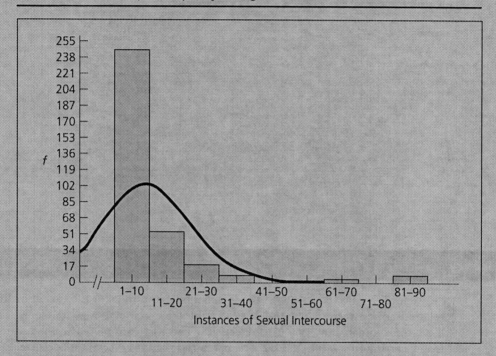

TABLE 5.5   **Computer Output for Pearson Correlation Between Use Consistency and Instances of Sexual Intercourse**

CORRELATIONS

		USECONS	SEXNUM
USECONS	Pearson Correlation	1.000	−.086
SEXNUM	Pearson Correlation	−.086	1.000

(continued)

FIGURE 5.12 Scatterplot for Use Consistency and Instances of Sexual Intercourse

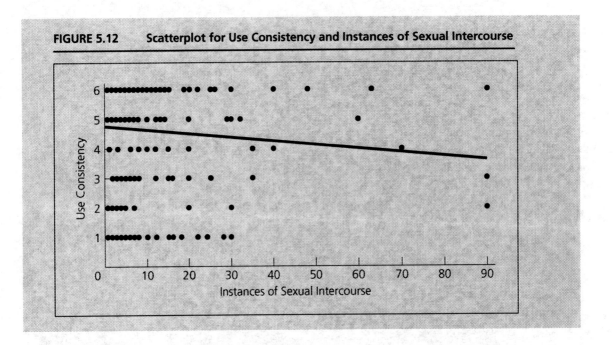

Summary

Pearson correlation is based on the linear model and indexes the extent of linear relationship between two quantitative variables that are measured on a level that at least approximates interval characteristics. The correlation coefficient can range from −1.00 through 0 to +1.00. The magnitude of the correlation coefficient indicates the degree to which the variables approximate a linear relationship, and the sign of the correlation coefficient indicates the direction of the linear approximation. A correlation coefficient of +1.00 means that the two variables form a perfect linear relationship that is direct in nature, a correlation coefficient of −1.00 means that the two variables form a perfect linear relationship that is inverse in nature, and a correlation coefficient of 0 means that there is no linear relationship between the two variables.

The fact that two variables are correlated does not necessarily imply that one variable causes the other to vary as it does. In fact, there are many reasons why two variables, X and Y, might be correlated. For instance, it may be that one or more additional variables causes both X and Y, thus producing a *spurious* relationship between them. Consequently, one must be cautious when drawing causal inferences from correlational analyses.

When one variable in a correlational analysis can be conceptualized as the independent variable and the other variable can be conceptualized as the dependent variable, r^2 indicates the proportion of variability in the dependent variable that can be explained by, or that is associated with, the independent variable, and $1 - r^2$ reflects the proportion of variability in the dependent variable that cannot be explained by, or that is not associated with, the dependent variable. The quantity r^2 is formally known as the coefficient of determination and $1 - r^2$ is formally known as the coefficient of alienation.

The least squares criterion can be used to identify the slope and intercept of the line that fits a set of data points better than any other line that we could try to fit to them. This line, known as the regression line, describes the nature of the linear relationship between the two variables and can be used to identify the value of variable Y that is predicted to be paired with an individual's score on variable X. This is accomplished by substituting a person's score on X into the regression equation. A measure of the average error across individuals when predicting scores on variable Y in this manner is provided by the standard error of estimate.

Several issues are associated with the use of correlation and regression. First, Pearson correlation assesses only linear relationships. If two variables are related in a nonlinear fashion, this will not be reflected in the correlation coefficient. A second consideration is that the regression equation for predicting variable X from variable Y is not the same as the regression equation for predicting variable Y from variable X.

A third issue concerns the effects of examining only a portion of the range of a variable. Depending on the particular circumstances, the magnitude of the correlation coefficient when a limited portion of this range is considered might be either less than or greater than if the range had not been so restricted. Thus, we must be careful to select our sample such that the entire range of values of interest is studied and not to extend our interpretation of correlational results *outside* the range of the original data set, and a similar caution holds for regression analysis: Prediction of Y from X is only meaningful for the range of X values that formed the basis for the calculation of the regression equation.

Fourth, regression can be applied to standard scores rather than raw scores. When this is done, the intercept of the regression line will always equal 0 and the slope will always equal the correlation coefficient. A final issue concerns outlier effects. Outliers are problematic because they can influence the magnitude and even the sign of a correlation coefficient. In fact, even a single outlier can mask the basic trend in a data set by turning a weak correlation into a strong one, or vice versa. Outliers can also have profound effects on regression statistics.

Exercises

Answers to asterisked (*) exercises appear at the back of the book.

1. Draw a scatterplot for the following data:

Individual	X	Y
1	10	9
2	8	7
3	6	5
4	9	8
5	10	8
6	8	8
7	5	6

*2. What information is conveyed by the slope of a line?

3. What information is conveyed by the intercept of a line?

4. What is the general form of the linear model?

*5. Given a perfect linear relationship between two variables, X and Y, and a slope of 3.00, by how many units will Y change if X changes by 1 unit? If X changes by 2 units? If X changes by 7 units?

*6. What information is conveyed by the magnitude of a correlation coefficient?

7. What information is conveyed by the sign of a correlation coefficient?

*8. For each pair of correlation coefficients, indicate which coefficient represents a better approximation to a linear relationship:
   a. +.37 or +.18
   b. −.37 or −.18
   c. +52 or −.76
   d. 0 or +.26
   e. 0 or −.44
   f. +.61 or +1.07

*9. Draw a scatterplot for two variables that are negatively correlated.

10. Draw a scatterplot for two variables that are positively correlated.

*11. Give an example of two variables that are probably positively correlated.

12. Give an example of two variables that are probably negatively correlated.

*13. Compute the Pearson correlation coefficient for the following data:

Individual	X	Y
1	3	7
2	8	9
3	3	3
4	2	8
5	6	8
6	6	9
7	8	6
8	5	4
9	7	2
10	2	4

14. Compute the Pearson correlation coefficient for the following data:

Individual	X	Y
1	9	8
2	7	9
3	9	9
4	7	8
5	6	10
6	8	8
7	10	6
8	7	7
9	9	7
10	8	8

15. Why must one be cautious when drawing causal inferences from correlational analyses?

*16. Give an example of two variables that are probably correlated but not causally related. What additional factor(s) might account for the correlation between these two variables?

17. What is the coefficient of determination? What information does it provide? What is the coefficient of alienation? What information does it provide?

*18. What is the general form of the regression equation? How does this differ from the linear model?

*19. How does the least squares criterion define the values of the slope and the intercept of the regression line?

*20. Compute the regression equation that describes the relationship between X and Y for the data in Exercise 13.

*21. What is the predicted Y score for Individual 1 in Exercise 13? What is the predicted Y score for Individual 5? What is the predicted Y score for Individual 10?

22. Compute the regression equation that describes the relationship between X and Y for the data in Exercise 14.

23. What is the predicted Y score for Individual 2 in Exercise 14? What is the predicted Y score for Individual 4? What is the predicted Y score for Individual 6?

24. What information is conveyed by the standard error of estimate?

*25. Compute the standard error of estimate for the data in Exercise 13.

26. Compute the standard error of estimate for the data in Exercise 14.

*27. What are the effects on the correlation coefficient of restricting the range of one of the variables?

28. When regression is used with standard scores, what will the intercept equal? What will the slope equal? What implication does this have for the interpretation of a correlation coefficient?

29. Why are outliers a problem for correlational analysis?

Multiple-Choice Questions

30. Which of the following correlation coefficients represents the strongest approximation to a linear relationship?
    a. −.60   c. .10
    b. 0   d. .50

*31. The regression equation for predicting X from Y is the same as the regression equation for predicting Y from X.
    a. true   b. false

32. According to the linear equation $Y = 2.16 + 4.37X$, for every 1 unit that X changes, Y will change _____ units.
    a. 2.16   c. 6.53
    b. 4.37   d. cannot be determined

*33. Outliers are most likely to raise interpretational complexities for the correlation coefficient when sample sizes are small.
    a. true   b. false

34. A correlation of .60 between height and weight is an example of a(n) _____ relationship.
    a. direct   c. negative
    b. inverse   d. curvilinear

*35. Given a correlation coefficient of −.83, as scores on variable X increase, scores on variable Y
    a. increase   c. remain the same
    b. decrease   d. cannot be determined

*36. If $SCP = 0$, the correlation coefficient will be
    a. negative   c. 0
    b. positive   d. cannot be determined

37. A graph that represents the linear relationship between two variables is called a
    a. bar graph
    b. boxplot
    c. scatterplot
    d. three-dimensional histogram

*38. Correlations of .20 to .30 (and −.20 to −.30) are often considered important in behavioral science research.
    a. true   b. false

39. Pearson correlation is sensitive to both linear and nonlinear relationships.
    a. true   b. false

Refer to the following data set to do Exercises 40–43.

X	Y
5	4
4	2
3	3

40. What is the sum of cross-products?
   a. 0
   b. 1.00
   c. 2.00
   d. 3.00

*41. What is the correlation between X and Y?
   a. 0
   b. .25
   c. .50
   d. .75

42. What is the slope of the regression line?
   a. 0
   b. .25
   c. .50
   d. .75

*43. What is the intercept of the regression line?
   a. 1.00
   b. 2.50
   c. 5.00
   d. 5.50

Estimation and Sampling Distributions

Suppose that you want to describe the annual income of all married women in the United States. It would be impossible to contact each of these women to determine her income level. Instead, you might decide to select a random sample and then try to make generalizations about the population based on the sample. The use of sample data to make inferences about populations is fundamental to statistical techniques used in the behavioral sciences. This chapter is concerned with estimating population parameters from sample statistics.

7.1   Finite Versus Infinite Populations

Population parameters can be estimated with reference either to small, finite populations or to populations that are so large that for all practical purposes they can be considered infinite. Behavioral science research is typically conducted with the goal of explaining the behavior of large numbers of individuals. For instance, if we were studying the course of a particular brain disease, we might think of the relevant population as all people, whether currently living or not, who have ever had or will have this illness. As such, the statistics that are used in most behavioral science disciplines are applicable to extremely large, if not infinite, populations.

Given that behavioral science research is concerned with very large populations, it is usually impossible for investigators to select truly random samples. Recall from Chapter 1 that a random sample requires listing all members of the population and then using a random number table to select a sample. Because this is not possible for very large populations, behavioral scientists typically select a set of individuals to study and then *assume* that these individuals are randomly drawn from *some* population.

Exactly what population the individuals are assumed to represent depends, in part, on the characteristics of the participants in the study. If a learning experiment was conducted on 200 college students at a midwestern university, the investigator might want to generalize the results to people in general. In this case, the population is conceptualized as consisting of "all people," and the college students are assumed to represent a random sample from this population. Obviously, this is a very questionable assumption. Perhaps the population should be conceptualized as "all college students." Or maybe it should be conceptualized as "all college students at midwestern universities." Maybe it should be conceptualized in even more specific terms.

Behavioral scientists sometimes disagree about what the appropriate population is for the purpose of generalization based on an investigation of a small set of individuals. When interpreting research, you should always keep in mind who the results should generalize to (in other words, exactly what the relevant population is).

For the sake of illustration, the examples in this chapter use small, finite populations. Sampling from a small, finite population *with replacement* (that is, where each sample member is returned to the population before the next sample member is selected) is analogous to sampling from a very large or infinite population *without replacement*, as behavioral science research is conceptualized as doing. Accordingly, when we develop the rationale and procedures for estimating population parameters using finite populations, unless otherwise stated, sampling is done with replacement to mimic the case of very large or infinite populations.*

7.2 Estimation of the Population Mean

Consider the case of 100 families in a small town. An investigator wants to describe the average number of children in each family. Because of practical limitations, the investigator is unable to include all 100 families in her study, so she instead resorts to a sample. Let us assume that the desired sample size is 10. In this case, the *population* is the 100 families in the town and the *sample* is the 10 families who are selected to be interviewed.

Table 7.1 lists the number of children in each family of the population. Although the 100 family sizes are unknown to the investigator, the fact remains that there *are* 100 families in the population and that each one has the indicated number of children. In other words, if the investigator *were* able to interview all 100 families, she would obtain the scores (family sizes) listed in Table 7.1. The true population mean, μ, is 3.50, and the variance, σ^2, is 2.09. Again, the investigator is unaware of the values of μ and σ^2.

Let us randomly select 10 families from this set of 100, and let these represent the 10 families interviewed by the investigator. Suppose that the scores for these families are found to be 3, 4, 4, 5, 2, 4, 1, 1, 4, and 3, which have a mean of 3.10. Note that this value is *not* equal to the true population mean. A sample statistic may differ from the value of its corresponding population parameter because of **sampling error**. Sampling error reflects the fact that sample values are likely to differ from population values because they are based on only a portion of the overall population; it does *not* imply that mistakes have been made in the collection and analysis of the data.

TABLE 7.1   **Numbers of Children in Families for a Hypothetical Population**

3	6	5	4	4	1	3	4	4	5
4	4	6	4	3	3	5	3	4	4
4	3	4	3	5	3	4	3	5	2
2	3	2	5	4	2	3	5	2	3
0	2	4	3	2	4	2	2	1	3
4	3	3	2	4	5	4	4	2	4
3	5	4	5	2	3	5	3	4	3
2	4	3	7	5	1	4	4	5	4
5	2	2	3	7	4	7	3	3	1
2	0	7	4	3	6	5	2	3	1

$$\mu = 3.50$$
$$\sigma^2 = 2.09$$

* For a discussion of statistical applications to finite populations, see Hays (1981).

The amount of sampling error can be represented as the difference between the value of a sample statistic (in the present context, $\overline{X}$) and the value of the corresponding population parameter (in the present context, μ). In our example, the amount of sampling error is $3.10 - 3.50 = -.40$. In practice, an investigator does not know the value of the population parameter, so it is impossible to compute the exact amount of sampling error that occurs.

In the absence of any other information, the sample mean that one observes is the "best estimate" of the value of the population mean. This is because of an important statistical property of the mean. This property can be illustrated with reference to the family size example. Suppose that, in addition to the first sample, we select another random sample of size 10 from the population of 100 families. The scores for this sample are 1, 3, 3, 4, 3, 7, 5, 1, 3, and 4, which have a mean of 3.40. Further suppose that this process is repeated over and over until we have computed the mean score for *every possible random sample of size 10* that could be selected from this population.

Table 7.2 lists 15 of the many sample means that could be observed and the amount of sampling error in each instance (that is, $\overline{X} - \mu$). If we were to compute the average (mean) amount of sampling error that resulted across all possible samples of size 10, it would equal 0. In other words, some of the sample means overestimate the true population mean, whereas others underestimate it. Across all samples of size 10, however, the overestimations cancel the underestimations and the *average* of the many sample means equals the true population mean.

This property of the sample mean makes it a useful estimate of the population mean. In statistical terms, the sample mean is said to be an *unbiased estimator* of the population mean. An **unbiased estimator** of a population parameter is a statistic

TABLE 7.2   **Means for Samples of Size 10 Randomly Selected from the Population in Table 7.1**

Sample scores	$\overline{X}$	$\overline{X} - \mu$
3, 4, 4, 5, 2, 4, 1, 1, 4, 3	3.10	$-.40$
1, 3, 3, 4, 3, 7, 5, 1, 3, 4	3.40	$-.10$
3, 5, 4, 3, 2, 4, 5, 4, 3, 2	3.50	.00
0, 2, 7, 2, 5, 2, 5, 5, 4, 3	3.50	.00
6, 3, 4, 4, 4, 2, 3, 3, 4, 3	3.60	.10
3, 3, 4, 4, 5, 3, 2, 2, 3, 3	3.20	$-.30$
7, 4, 7, 3, 3, 3, 5, 4, 5, 2	4.30	.80
5, 4, 5, 2, 2, 3, 4, 3, 5, 3	3.60	.10
6, 7, 4, 4, 4, 5, 4, 4, 2, 2	4.20	.70
2, 2, 3, 3, 1, 2, 3, 2, 3, 4	2.50	-1.00
3, 4, 3, 4, 3, 4, 3, 4, 3, 4	3.50	.00
1, 3, 3, 2, 4, 3, 4, 3, 2, 0	2.50	-1.00
4, 6, 4, 3, 3, 4, 4, 5, 4, 1	3.80	.30
2, 2, 2, 2, 5, 5, 5, 3, 5, 4	3.50	.00
6, 7, 7, 4, 3, 0, 5, 5, 4, 2	4.30	.80

whose average (mean) across all possible random samples of a given size equals the value of the parameter. It is in this sense that the observed sample mean is the "best estimate" of the population mean.

7.3   Estimation of the Population Variance and Standard Deviation

One of the samples that we selected from the population of 100 families in the previous section had the following family sizes: 3, 4, 4, 5, 2, 4, 1, 1, 4, and 3. If we were to calculate the variance for this set of scores, we would find it to be 1.69. This value is different from the true population variance ($\sigma^2 = 2.09$) and, again, reflects sampling error. Unlike the sample mean, however, the sample variance is not our best estimate of the true population variance. Statisticians have determined that the sample variance is a biased estimator of the population variance because it underestimates (is smaller than) the population variance across all possible samples of a given size.

Equation 3.4 defines the variance of a sample of scores as the sum of squares divided by N:

$$s^2 = \frac{SS}{N}$$

As we just noted this is not our best estimate of the population variance because it is biased. However, an unbiased estimator can be obtained from sample data by dividing the sum of squares by $N - 1$ rather than N. The resulting value constitutes the sample estimate of the population variance, and is formally referred to as the **variance estimate**. Symbolically,

$$\hat{s}^2 = \frac{SS}{N - 1} \tag{7.1}$$

where $\hat{s}^2$ (read *s-hat squared*) represents the variance estimate.

Note that Equation 7.1 is identical to Equation 3.4 except that $N - 1$ is the denominator instead of N. By reducing the size of the denominator, the subtraction of 1 from N makes the variance estimate larger than the sample variance and, hence, corrects for the tendency of the sample variance to underestimate the population variance.

Consider the set of 10 family-size scores from above: 3, 4, 4, 5, 2, 4, 1, 1, 4, and 3. As we stated earlier, the sample variance for these scores is 1.69, reflecting the fact that the sum of squares for the data set is 16.90. Applying Equation 7.1, we find that the variance estimate is

$$\hat{s}^2 = \frac{SS}{N - 1}$$

$$= \frac{16.90}{10 - 1} = 1.88$$

Our best estimate of the value of the population variance, based on these data, is thus 1.88. Again, we recognize that there is sampling error and that the variance estimate will usually not exactly equal the true population variance. On average, though, the variance estimate will be closer to the population variance than will the sample variance. This is, for instance, the case in our example, where $\sigma^2 = 2.09$.

The sample standard deviation is defined as the positive square root of the variance, or $\sqrt{s^2}$. In our example, $s = \sqrt{1.69} = 1.30$. By the same token, the sample estimate of the population standard deviation, which is formally referred to as the **standard deviation estimate**, is the positive square root of $\hat{s}^2$:

$$\hat{s} = \sqrt{\hat{s}^2} \qquad\qquad [7.2]$$

In our example $\hat{s} = \sqrt{1.88} = 1.37$. This is our best estimate of the standard deviation of the population, which in this instance is equal to $\sqrt{2.09} = 1.45$. Paralleling the case for the variance estimate, the standard deviation estimate, on average, will be closer to the population standard deviation than the sample standard deviation will be.*

STUDY EXERCISE 7.1

A sample of 10 individuals took an intelligence test on which scores could range from 0 to 150. This sample yielded a mean score of 100.26 and a sum of squares of 50.00. Compute the variance and the standard deviation for the sample, and estimate the variance and the standard deviation for the population. Compare the two sets of results.

Answer   The sample variance is the sum of squares divided by N, and the sample deviation is the positive square root of the resultant value:

$$s^2 = \frac{50.00}{10} = 5.00$$
$$s = \sqrt{5.00} = 2.24$$

The variance estimate is the sum of squares divided by $N - 1$, and the standard deviation is the positive square root of this value:

$$\hat{s}^2 = \frac{50.00}{9} = 5.56$$
$$\hat{s} = \sqrt{5.56} = 2.36$$

Both estimated values are larger than the corresponding sample values.

---

* Technically, $\hat{s}$ is not an unbiased estimator of σ, and a correction factor is necessary to make it one (Hays, 1981, p. 189). However, if $N > 10$, the amount of bias in $\hat{s}$ tends to be small. Given this and the fact that all of the statistics related to $\hat{s}$ that we consider in later chapters circumvent any problems that are introduced by this bias, we use $\hat{s}$ as the sample estimate of the population standard deviation.

7.4 Summary of Notation and Formulas for the Mean and Measures of Variability

We pointed out in Chapter 3 that different notation is used to represent sample and population values of the mean, the variance, and the standard deviation, and we have made extensive use of this notation since to differentiate sample quantities from population quantities. The notation and formulas for these indexes are summarized in the second and third columns of Table 7.3, which are identical to those in Table 3.2. In this table, N represents either the number of sample scores or the number of population scores, as relevant.

The fourth column of Table 7.3 summarizes the notation and formulas for the *sample estimates* of the population mean, variance, and standard deviation that we just discussed. Because these indexes are based on sample data, their calculations are based on N *sample* scores.

If we had scores for *all* members of a population, we would use the formulas for population values. This situation is extremely rare in the behavioral sciences because we will virtually never know all of the scores in a population. If we had scores for a subset of a population and were interested in describing only that subset *without making inferences to the population,* we would use the formulas for sample values. This situation is also extremely rare in the behavioral sciences because research is seldom concerned with learning only about samples per se. By far the most common focus in behavioral science research is on estimating population parameters from sample data. To do this, we use the formulas for sample estimates of population values.

Some texts do not distinguish between the sample variance and sample standard deviation, on the one hand, and the variance estimate and standard deviation estimate, on the other. Rather, the sample estimates, $\hat{s}$ and $\hat{s}^2$, are introduced as *the* measures of variability for a sample (and usually symbolized as s and s^2). However, the distinction between *sample values* and *sample estimates of population values* is a crucial one for inferential statistics, as will become eminently clear as we proceed through the remaining chapters. Consequently, not making this distinction might lead to confusion in some applications. Hence, we will continue to use different notation to represent sample values and estimated population values of variances and standard deviations throughout this book.

TABLE 7.3 **Notation and Formulas for the Mean and Measures of Variability**

Statistical term	Sample value	Population value	Sample estimate of population value
Mean	$\overline{X} = (\Sigma X)/N$	$\mu = (\Sigma X)/N$	$\overline{X} = (\Sigma X)/N$
Variance	$s^2 = SS/N$	$\sigma^2 = SS/N$	$\hat{s}^2 = SS/(N-1)$
Standard deviation	$s = \sqrt{s^2}$	$\sigma = \sqrt{\sigma^2}$	$\hat{s} = \sqrt{\hat{s}^2}$

An important concept in statistical estimation is *degrees of freedom*. Suppose that you are told that a friend got a score of 95 on a statistics exam. Suppose that you are also told that there were 100 points possible and that your friend missed 5 points. You have been given three pieces of information:

1. Your friend received a score of 95 on a test.

2. The test had 100 points possible.

3. Your friend missed 5 points.

If you had been told any two of these pieces of information, you could have deduced the third (a score of 95 out of 100 means 5 points were missed). Thus, you have actually been given two independent pieces of information and one piece of information that is dependent on (follows from) the other two. Which two of the three are called independent and which of the three is called dependent is arbitrary. The fact of the matter is that only two pieces of information are independent. In statistics, **degrees of freedom** are the number of pieces of information that are "free of each other" in the sense that they cannot be deduced from one another. In the example above, there are two degrees of freedom because there are two pieces of independent information.

Statistical indexes such as the sum of squares and the variance have a certain number of degrees of freedom because they are based on a certain number of pieces of information (specifically, scores on the variable of interest) that are independent of one another. Let us consider the sum of squares. When we compute a sum of squares, it is necessary to derive deviation scores from the mean. Consider the following four scores: 8, 10, 10, 12. The mean of these scores is 10.00, and the signed deviation scores for the first three of them are $8 - 10.00 = -2.00$, $10 - 10.00 = .00$, and $10 - 10.00 = .00$, respectively. Recall from Chapter 3 that the sum of signed deviation scores from the mean will always equal 0. If you know that there are four scores in a distribution and that the deviation scores for three of these are -2.00, $.00$, and $.00$, you also know that the last deviation score must be 2.00. In this sense, the last deviation score to be computed is not *free to vary* but is determined by the other deviation scores. Thus, there are four scores and $4 - 1 = 3$ degrees of freedom in this example. In fact, a sum of squares around a sample mean will always have $N - 1$ degrees of freedom associated with it.

This example leads to a basic principle in estimation techniques: *As the degrees of freedom associated with an estimate increase, the accuracy of the estimate also tends to increase.* Of concern here is the distinction between the number of degrees of freedom and the total number of pieces of information. When an estimate is based on a large number of independent pieces of information, it will tend to be relatively accurate. However, if the pieces of information tend to be dependent on one another, greater error is likely. Technically, the accuracy of a variance estimate (and, thus, a standard deviation estimate) is not a function of the sample size (N) but rather a function of the degrees of freedom ($N - 1$)—that is, the number of independent pieces of information—used in calculating such an estimate.

In later chapters, we will encounter types of sums of squares in which deviations are taken around entities other than the sample mean. The degrees of freedom for these sums of squares will typically not be $N - 1$.

Irrespective of its specific computation, any sum of squares divided by its associated degrees of freedom is referred to as a mean sum of squares, or **mean square**. Symbolically,

$$MS = \frac{SS}{df} \tag{7.3}$$

where MS represents a mean square, SS represents the sum of squared deviations around some entity, and df represents the degrees of freedom.

As we have seen, the mean square derived by dividing the sum of squares around a sample mean by its corresponding degrees of freedom, $N - 1$, is formally known as a variance estimate. That is, $\hat{s}^2 = SS/(N - 1)$ is a type of mean square.

7.6   Summary of Basic Estimation Concepts

To summarize thus far, a sample statistic may differ from the value of its corresponding population parameter because of sampling error. The sample mean is an unbiased estimator of the population mean and the variance and standard deviation estimates are unbiased estimators of the population variance and the standard deviation, respectively. An unbiased estimator is a statistic whose average (mean) across all possible random samples of a given size equals the value of the population parameter. In general, as the degrees of freedom associated with a statistic increase, the more accurate that statistic will be in estimating the corresponding population parameter.

7.7   The Sampling Distribution of the Mean and the Central Limit Theorem

As we have noted, a sample mean will usually differ from the corresponding population mean because of sampling error. For a given population of scores, a useful index of the degree to which sampling error affects the accuracy of the sample mean as an estimator of the population mean is provided by the value that we would obtain if we were to select all possible samples of a specified size, calculate the mean score for each sample, and then compute the standard deviation of the sample means across all samples.

For the sake of illustration, suppose that we are trying to estimate the mean number of children for the population of 100 families referred to in Section 7.2 from a sample of 10 cases. As shown in Table 7.1, the overall population mean is 3.50. If we randomly select a sample of 10 families, we might observe a mean score of, say, 3.10. Although we would not actually do so in practice, suppose that we were to select another random sample of size 10 from the 100 families and find the mean to be 3.70. Furthermore, suppose that we repeated this process over and over until we computed the mean score for all possible random samples of size 10. We would then have a distribution of "scores" composed of the mean scores for all possible samples of size 10.

The distribution of the means for all possible random samples of a given size is referred to as the **sampling distribution of the mean.** The key to understanding the sampling distribution of the mean is to realize that sampling distributions are *theoretical* in nature, in that it is virtually never possible to obtain scores for an entire population given the very large population sizes that behavioral science research is concerned with.* It follows that it is also not possible to actually select all possible random samples of a specified size from that population and thus, that it is not possible to calculate the mean score for each of these samples.

Rather, we select only *one* sample of a given size, as we have done throughout this book, and use this to estimate characteristics of the population. However, it is important to realize that this sample is only one of many different samples of that size that we *could have* obtained when we sampled from the population. At another point in time or space, a researcher using the identical sampling procedure (for instance, random sampling via a random number table) might obtain a totally different sample or one with only minimal overlap in individuals from one sample to the other. It is the distribution of means for all possible samples of a specified size that we *could* obtain that constitutes the sampling distribution of the mean.

If we were able to actually derive a sampling distribution of the mean, we could compute a mean for the scores that make up this distribution (that is, the sample means) just as we could for any other set of scores. We could also compute a standard deviation for these scores. This would constitute our measure of sampling error.

If we assume that the distribution of the sample means is based on random samples of independent observations, insight into the mean and standard deviation of a sampling distribution of the mean, as well as its shape, is provided by an important formulation called the **central limit theorem.** This theorem has been stated in different ways in the statistical literature (for example, see Freund, 1962), but the essence of it is captured by the following statement:

> *Given a population with a mean of μ and a standard deviation of σ, the sampling distribution of the mean has a mean of μ and a standard deviation of $\sigma/\sqrt{N}$ and approaches a normal distribution as the sample size on which it is based, N, approaches infinity.*

Although the central limit theorem may seem abstract, it characterizes several key aspects of how sample means are distributed in sampling distributions. We now develop each of these.

The Mean of the Sampling Distribution of the Mean

As stated in the central limit theorem, *the mean of a sampling distribution of the mean will always be equal to the population mean* (of the raw scores). We laid out

---

* If we were able to obtain scores for all members of a population, we could calculate population parameters directly without having to estimate them from sample statistics.

the rationale for this when we discussed the estimation of the population mean in Section 7.2: When we select samples of a given size, some of the sample means will overestimate the true population mean and others will underestimate it. However, when we average all of these, the underestimations will cancel the overestimations, with the result being the true population mean. If we were, for instance, to compute the mean of all possible sample means in the family size example, it would equal the population mean of 3.50. This characteristic of a sampling distribution of the mean is very important for the statistical concepts that we develop in Chapter 8.

The Standard Deviation of the Sampling Distribution of the Mean

The standard deviation of a sampling distribution of the mean is called the **standard error of the mean.** *The standard error of the mean reflects the accuracy with which sample means estimate a population mean.* Recall from Chapter 3 that a standard deviation represents an average deviation from the mean of a distribution. Because the mean in this case is the true population mean, μ, the standard error of the mean represents an average deviation of the sample means from the *population* mean. If the standard error of the mean is small, then the sample means based on a given sample size (N) will tend to be similar and all will tend to be close to the population mean. If the standard error of the mean is large, then the sample means based on samples of a given size will tend to differ from one another, and only some will be close to the population mean.

If the standard error of the mean for samples of size 10 was 1.30 for the family size example, this would mean that, on average, the sample means differ 1.30 units (that is, 1.30 *children*) from the true population mean. This indicates a sizable amount of error, and one would have to be concerned with how similar the particular observed sample mean is to the actual population mean. If, on the other hand, the standard error of the mean for samples of size 10 was only .10, this would mean that, on average, the sample means deviate only .10 unit from the true population mean. You would now have reason to believe that the sample mean is a fairly accurate estimator of the population mean.

As stated in the central limit theorem, the standard deviation of a sampling distribution of the mean is equal to

$$\sigma_{\overline{X}} = \frac{\sigma}{\sqrt{N}} \qquad\qquad [7.4]$$

where $\sigma_{\overline{X}}$ represents the standard error of the mean, σ is the standard deviation of scores in the population, and N is the sample size. For instance, the standard error of the mean for the family size example is

$$\sigma_{\overline{X}} = \frac{1.45}{\sqrt{10}} = .46$$

Equation 7.4 indicates that two factors influence the size of the standard error of the mean. The first is the sample size. As the sample size increases, the standard error becomes smaller, other things being equal. If, in the example on family sizes, we had used a sample size of 99 instead of 10, it is clear that the sampling distribution would consist of sample means that are very similar to one another because each would be based on 99 of the same 100 scores. Furthermore, because 99 of the 100 cases in the population are being encompassed in each sample, the sample means would also tend to be close to the population mean. This would result in a relatively small value of $\sigma_{\overline{X}}$. However, with smaller sample sizes, there is likely to be greater variability among the sample means because some will be much closer to the population mean than will others. A compelling example of how the sample size can also affect other statistical outcomes is presented in Box 7.1.

The second factor that influences the size of the standard error of the mean is the variability of scores in the population. As σ becomes smaller, so does the standard error, other things being equal. To take an extreme example, if all of the scores in the population were identical (that is, if $\sigma = 0$), then every sample would yield a mean exactly equal to the population mean. For instance, if all the scores were 4, then the mean of any sample would also be 4.00, as would the population mean. This would result in a value of $\sigma_{\overline{X}}$ of 0. However, when there is considerable variability in the population, the mean of a given sample might be influenced by one or more extreme scores. This would result in greater variability among the sample means and, consequently, a larger standard error of the mean.

BOX 7.1

Polls and Random Samples

All of us have encountered political polls in newspapers or other media. However, you may not be aware of how these polls are conducted or of the importance of sampling error in interpreting their results. Thus, a consideration of the sampling procedures used by major polling agencies and how sampling error affects polling results may be useful.

Recall from Chapter 1 that a random sample requires a list of every member of the population. Such a list is often not feasible, or even possible, to construct. For example, no master list of the names of all people in the United States currently exists, and even if it did, such a list would become dated very quickly. Because of this, many polling agencies use a variant of random sampling, called *area sampling*, when doing national polls.

With this method, the United States is first divided into a large number of homogeneous geographic regions. A subset of these regions is then randomly selected using a random number table. Each of these regions is then subdivided into a large number of geographic areas (based on census tracts or districts). A subset of these areas is then randomly selected. Within each area, a list of the city or town streets is compiled. A subset of streets is then randomly selected. Finally, on each of the chosen streets, the house addresses are listed, and a subset of these is, in turn, randomly selected. The interviewer then approaches each house and randomly selects an individual within it. This completes the process. The overall region is selected at random. The tract is selected at random. The streets are selected at random. The houses are selected at random. And the individuals are selected at random. The end result is that every individual ideally has an equal chance of being included in the sample.

(continued)

Box 7.1 *(continued)*

Although this is true in theory, it does not really hold in practice. The chosen dwelling might be vacant. Or the individual within the dwelling may not agree to participate in the poll. No nationwide survey has ever reached every person designated in a random sample and, accordingly, special *correction factors* must be adopted. A detailed consideration of these is presented in Gallup (1976). The process of area sampling is extremely expensive and is usually carried out only by major polling firms. Many smaller companies, newspapers, and magazines obtain samples in ways that call their representativeness into question. The results of public opinion polls must always be interpreted in light of their sampling procedures.

One of the most famous polling errors in presidential elections was the prediction made by the *Literary Digest* in 1936. The polling procedure used by this magazine had accurately predicted previous election results. It consisted of mailing out millions of postcard ballots to individuals who were listed in the phone book or who were on lists of automobile owners. This system was effective as long as the more affluent (people with phones or cars) were as equally likely to vote Democratic or Republican as the less affluent (people without phones and cars). With the advent of the New Deal, however, a shift in the American electorate occurred, with the more affluent tending to vote Republican and the less affluent tending to vote Democratic. The result was that the *Literary Digest* sample overrepresented Republican voters, leading to a prediction that the Republican candidate (Landon) would defeat the Democratic candidate (Roosevelt) by a margin of 57% to 43%. Of course, Landon did not win and was, in fact, defeated by Roosevelt by a margin of 62.5% to 37.5%.

Even when random procedures are used, a sample may not be representative of its population because unrepresentative samples can still occur by chance. What factors influence whether a random sample will truly reflect the population? One factor noted in this chapter is the size of the sample. In general, the larger the sample, the closer a sample estimate will be to the corresponding population parameter. Most reputable polling agencies report *margins of error* (ranges that have a high probability of containing the actual population values) for their polls, and these are directly related to the size of the sample. In most cases, sample sizes of approximately 1,500 have been found to produce acceptable margins of error for political polls in the United States.

An Example of an Empirical Sampling Distribution of the Mean

We can demonstrate the points just made by considering a contrived example with a small population, using sampling with replacement. Consider a population of four individuals who have the following scores: 2, 4, 6, and 8. The mean for this population, μ, is $(2 + 4 + 6 + 8)/4 = 5.00$, and the standard deviation, σ, is 2.24.

We can construct an empirical sampling distribution of the mean for samples of size two by listing all possible samples of this size and their corresponding means. This has been done in columns 1 and 2 of Table 7.4. The mean of the 16 sample means is 5.00. Thus, the mean of the sampling distribution equals μ. The standard deviation of the 16 sample means can be derived using the usual procedures for a standard deviation. As shown in Table 7.4, the standard deviation of the sample

TABLE 7.4   **All Possible Random Samples and Sample Means for Samples of Size 2 (Based on Minium, 1978)**

Population: 2, 4, 6, 8

Sample values	Sample mean	(Sample mean)^2
2, 2	2.00	4.00
2, 4	3.00	9.00
2, 6	4.00	16.00
2, 8	5.00	25.00
4, 2	3.00	9.00
4, 4	4.00	16.00
4, 6	5.00	25.00
4, 8	6.00	36.00
6, 2	4.00	16.00
6, 4	5.00	25.00
6, 6	6.00	36.00
6, 8	7.00	49.00
8, 2	5.00	25.00
8, 4	6.00	36.00
8, 6	7.00	49.00
8, 8	8.00	64.00
	Sum = 80.00	Sum = 440.00

$$\text{Mean} = \frac{80.00}{16} = 5.00$$

$$\text{Sum of squares of sample means} = 440.00 - \frac{80.00^2}{16} = 40.00$$

$$\text{Variance of sample means} = \frac{40.00}{16} = 2.50$$

$$\text{Standard deviation of sample means} = \sqrt{2.50} = 1.58 = \sigma_{\bar{X}}$$

means is 1.58. This is the standard error of the mean, $\sigma_{\bar{X}}$ and indicates how far, on average, the sample means deviate from μ. This same value would result if we computed $\sigma_{\bar{X}}$ using Equation 7.4: $\sigma_{\bar{X}} = \sigma/\sqrt{N} = 2.24/\sqrt{2} = 1.58$.

Suppose that instead of a sample size of two, we construct a sampling distribution for a sample size of three. Table 7.5 lists all possible samples of size three and their corresponding means. The mean of these sample means is, as before, equal to 5.00, the value of μ. Due to space limitations, we have not calculated the standard deviation of the 64 sample means. If we were to do so, we would find that it equals 1.29, the same value we would obtain if we used Equation 7.4: $\sigma_{\bar{X}} = \sigma/\sqrt{N} = 2.24/\sqrt{3} = 1.29$.

Note that the standard error of the mean for samples of size three ($\sigma_{\bar{X}} = 1.29$) is smaller than the standard error of the mean for samples of size two ($\sigma_{\bar{X}} = 1.58$).

This is consistent with what we have stated about the effect of the sample size on the standard error.

The Shape of the Sampling Distribution of the Mean

The third key point of the central limit theorem is that the sampling distribution of the mean increasingly approximates a normal distribution as the sample size on which it is based becomes larger. Of crucial importance is the fact that this holds *regardless of the shape of the underlying population.* When the sample size is greater than around 30, the normal approximation is quite good. For sample sizes of 30 or less, the approximation is less exact, although in many instances, particularly if the population is not highly skewed, the fit will be reasonable. The relationship of the sampling distribution of the mean to the normal distribution is very important and will be referred to extensively in later chapters.

TABLE 7.5   **All Possible Random Samples and Sample Means for Samples of Size 3 (Based on Minium, 1978)**

Population: 2, 4, 6, 8

Sample values	Sample mean	Sample values	Sample mean	Sample values	Sample mean
2, 2, 2	2.00	4, 4, 6	4.67	6, 8, 2	5.33
2, 2, 4	2.67	4, 4, 8	5.33	6, 8, 4	6.00
2, 2, 6	3.33	4, 6, 2	4.00	6, 8, 6	6.67
2, 2, 8	4.00	4, 6, 4	4.67	6, 8, 8	7.33
2, 4, 2	2.67	4, 6, 6	5.33	8, 2, 2	4.00
2, 4, 4	3.33	4, 6, 8	6.00	8, 2, 4	4.67
2, 4, 6	4.00	4, 8, 2	4.67	8, 2, 6	5.33
2, 4, 8	4.67	4, 8, 4	5.33	8, 2, 8	6.00
2, 6, 2	3.33	4, 8, 6	6.00	8, 4, 2	4.67
2, 6, 4	4.00	4, 8, 8	6.67	8, 4, 4	5.33
2, 6, 6	4.67	6, 2, 2	3.33	8, 4, 6	6.00
2, 6, 8	5.33	6, 2, 4	4.00	8, 4, 8	6.67
2, 8, 2	4.00	6, 2, 6	4.67	8, 6, 2	5.33
2, 8, 4	4.67	6, 2, 8	5.33	8, 6, 4	6.00
2, 8, 6	5.33	6, 4, 2	4.00	8, 6, 6	6.67
2, 8, 8	6.00	6, 4, 4	4.67	8, 6, 8	7.33
4, 2, 2	2.67	6, 4, 6	5.33	8, 8, 2	6.00
4, 2, 4	3.33	6, 4, 8	6.00	8, 8, 4	6.67
4, 2, 6	4.00	6, 6, 2	4.67	8, 8, 6	7.33
4, 2, 8	4.67	6, 6, 4	5.33	8, 8, 8	8.00
4, 4, 2	3.33	6, 6, 6	6.00	Sum = 320.00	
4, 4, 4	4.00	6, 6, 8	6.67		

$$\text{Mean} = \frac{320.00}{64} = 5.00$$

The above points are illustrated in Figure 7.1, which presents graphs of frequency distributions for three different populations and the corresponding frequency graphs of sampling distributions of the mean for each of two sample sizes, $N = 10$ and $N = 30$. Note that in all cases, the sampling distribution is bell-shaped and symmetrical. The most frequently occurring sample mean is the true population

FIGURE 7.1   **Frequency Distributions for Three Populations and Corresponding Sampling Distributions for Two Sample Sizes (Adapted from Johnson & Lieber, 1977)**

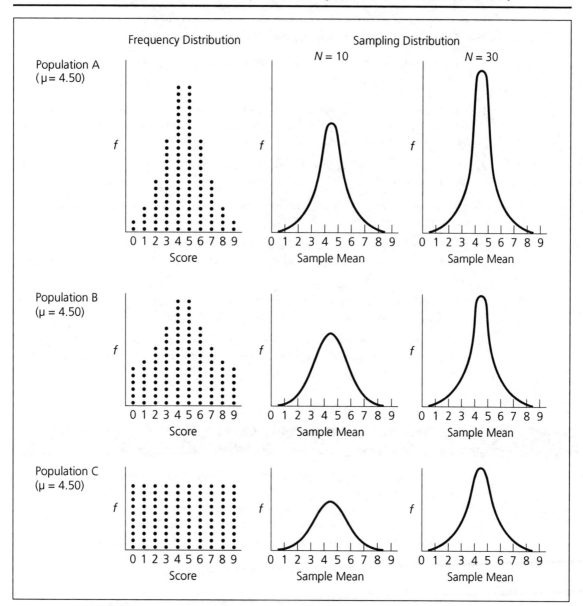

mean, with sample means that are much smaller or much larger than this value being infrequent. This is true even for population C even though all scores in the population occur with equal frequency. Also note that the frequency of highly deviant sample means is much lower when the sample size is larger (for each population, compare the graphs for $N = 10$ and $N = 30$) and when the population variability is lower (for each sample size, compare the graphs for population A, which has a relatively small standard deviation, and population B, which has a relatively large standard deviation). This is consistent with our earlier discussion of the standard error of the mean.

The Sampling Distribution of the Mean Summarized

The major points about the sampling distribution of the mean can be summarized as follows:

1. There is a different sampling distribution for every sample size. For instance, a sampling distribution of the mean for random samples of size 10 is different from a sampling distribution of the mean for random samples of size 90.

2. The mean of a sampling distribution of the mean equals the population mean (of the raw scores).

3. The standard deviation of a sampling distribution of the mean is called the *standard error of the mean*.

4. The sample mean is a more accurate estimator of the population mean when the standard error of the mean is small than when the standard error of the mean is large.

5. The standard error of the mean gets smaller as the sample size increases and as the variability of scores in the population decreases, other things being equal.

6. The sampling distribution of the mean approximates a normal distribution given a sufficiently large sample size. This is true regardless of the shape of the underlying population.

7.8   The Estimated Standard Error of the Mean

In practice, the population standard deviation, σ, is rarely known. Rather, we typically have data based on one sample. We must therefore estimate the standard error of the mean by substituting a sample estimate of the population standard deviation for σ in Equation 7.4. As we have seen, this estimate is $\hat{s}$, the standard deviation estimate. Substituting $\hat{s}$ into Equation 7.4 for σ yields the following formula for the *estimated standard error of the mean*:

$$\hat{s}_{\overline{X}} = \frac{\hat{s}}{\sqrt{N}} \qquad\qquad [7.5]$$

TABLE 7.6   **Numerical Example for Estimating the Standard Error of the Mean**

	Sample A		Sample B	
	X	X^2	X	X^2
	19	361	26	676
	21	441	30	900
	20	400	34	1,156
	19	361	35	1,225
	20	400	25	625
	21	441	30	900
	21	441	24	576
	20	400	30	900
	20	400	30	900
	19	361	36	1,296

$\Sigma X = 200 \qquad \Sigma X^2 = 4,006 \qquad\qquad \Sigma X = 300 \qquad \Sigma X^2 = 9,154$

$\overline{X} = 20.00 \qquad\qquad\qquad\qquad\qquad\qquad \overline{X} = 30.00$

$$SS = \Sigma X^2 - \frac{(\Sigma X)^2}{N} \qquad\qquad SS = \Sigma X^2 - \frac{(\Sigma X)^2}{N}$$

$$= 4,006 - \frac{200^2}{10} = 6.00 \qquad\qquad = 9,154 - \frac{300^2}{10} = 154.00$$

$$\hat{s}^2 = \frac{SS}{N-1} = \frac{6.00}{9} = .67 \qquad\qquad \hat{s}^2 = \frac{SS}{N-1} = \frac{154.00}{9} = 17.11$$

$$\hat{s} = \sqrt{\hat{s}^2} = \sqrt{.67} = .82 \qquad\qquad \hat{s} = \sqrt{\hat{s}^2} = \sqrt{17.11} = 4.14$$

$$\hat{s}_{\overline{X}} = \frac{\hat{s}}{\sqrt{N}} = \frac{.82}{\sqrt{10}} = .26 \qquad\qquad \hat{s}_{\overline{X}} = \frac{\hat{s}}{\sqrt{N}} = \frac{4.14}{\sqrt{10}} = 1.31$$

where $\hat{s}_{\overline{X}}$ represents the estimated standard error of the mean and all other terms are as previously defined. Let us consider two numerical examples.

Suppose that we randomly sample ten individuals from a certain population, which we will refer to as population A. The left half of Table 7.6 reports the ages for the ten individuals who constitute the sample. We begin by calculating the sample mean and the standard deviation estimate based on the sample data. As can be seen in Table 7.6, these values are 20.00 and .82, respectively. We then estimate the standard error of the mean by dividing the standard deviation estimate by the square root of N. This yields a value of .26.

Let us also suppose that we randomly sample ten individuals from a second population, which we will refer to as population B. The right half of Table 7.6 reports the ages for these individuals, and the sample mean and the standard deviation estimate based on the sample data are also presented. These values are 30.00 and 4.14, respectively. Dividing the standard deviation estimate by the square root of N yields an estimated standard error of the mean of 1.31.

Further insight into the estimated standard error of the mean is gained by comparing the two estimated standard errors. The fact that the estimated standard error based on the first sample is smaller than the estimated standard error based on the second sample suggests that the mean for sample A probably estimates the mean of population A better than the mean for sample B estimates the mean of population B. Because the samples are the same size ($N = 10$), the difference in the estimated standard errors of the mean reflects the different sizes of the standard deviation estimates (for sample A, $\hat{s} = .82$; for sample B, $\hat{s} = 4.14$).

STUDY EXERCISE 7.2

Compute the estimated standard error of the mean for the scores in Study Exercise 7.1.

Answer   The estimated standard error of the mean is the standard deviation estimate divided by the square root of the sample size:

$$\hat{s}_{\overline{X}} = \frac{\hat{s}}{\sqrt{N}}$$

$$= \frac{2.36}{\sqrt{10}} = .75$$

7.9   Types of Sampling Distributions

Although we have focused on the sampling distribution of the mean, it is also possible to conceptualize sampling distributions for other statistics, such as the mode, the median, and the variance. In the case of the median, for example, the sampling distribution reflects the medians for all possible random samples of size N that can be drawn from a population.

Given the same population, the sampling distribution of the mean will show less variability (that is, it will have a smaller standard error) than either the sampling distribution of the mode or the sampling distribution of the median. It is for this reason that the mean is usually preferred by statisticians as a measure of central tendency.

7.10   Links Between Computer Results and Book Content

As we noted in Section 3.12, even though they are standardly labeled as *variance* and *standard* deviation in statistical computer output, the measures of variability that are usually provided as statistical computer results are actually the variance *estimate* and the standard deviation *estimate*, respectively. Similarly, the quantity that is labeled as *standard error of the mean* is actually the *estimated* standard error of the mean.

7.11 Links Between Chapters

This chapter extends the concepts of the variance and the standard deviation that we introduced in Chapter 3 from *describing* the variability in a sample or a population to *estimating* the variability in a population based on sample data. From a broader perspective, by introducing such topics as estimation, degrees of freedom, sampling distributions, and standard errors, this chapter also provides a transition from descriptive statistics to inferential statistics, which is the focus of the remainder of this book. We will see, for instance, that the concepts from this chapter are central to our discussion of hypothesis testing in Chapter 8.

Applications to the Analysis of a Social Problem Using SPSS for Windows

We can gain an appreciation for the concepts developed in this chapter by referring to the parent–teen communication study described in Chapter 1. Recall that the study involved the selection of a random sample of 14- to 17-year-old African American youths from inner-city Philadelphia. The population to which we can generalize with a fair degree of confidence is therefore 14- to 17-year-old African American youths who live in the inner city of Philadelphia. To the extent that such teens are representative of inner-city adolescents in other major urban areas, we can also generalize to them.

As part of our study, we asked the teens' mothers how old they thought children should be when their parents start to talk to them about sex and, in a separate question, how old they thought children should be when their parents start to talk to them about birth control. Tables 7.7 and 7.8 present the computer output for the frequency distributions, measures of central tendency, standard deviation estimates, variance estimates, and estimated standard errors of the mean for the two questions.

As can be seen in Table 7.7, the mean age at which the mothers thought that parents should talk with children about sex is 10.46, with an estimated population standard deviation of 2.83. This indicates that the ages suggested by mothers deviate, on average, by about 3 years from the mean

preferred age. The estimated standard error of the mean (indicated by "Std err") of .11 is relatively small and suggests that the sample mean is relatively close to the population mean.

The mean age at which the mothers thought that parents should talk about birth control is higher than that for talking about sex. As shown in Table 7.8, this mean is 12.09, with an estimated population standard deviation of 2.29. The estimated standard error of the mean is .09, which suggests a relatively small amount of sampling error.

If parental communication about sex and birth control is going to be effective, it is best if parents talk to their children before they start to have sex. Our analyses in Chapter 2 indicated that 15.0% of the teens in the sample (excluding instances of sexual abuse) had intercourse by age 12, that another 13.4% had intercourse by age 13, and that another 14.5% had intercourse by age 14. This means that sexual behavior should be discussed long before age 12 if parents are going to effectively discourage sexual intercourse or encourage the use of birth control for protecting against pregnancy at the time of first intercourse. However, a consideration of the means and standard deviation estimates above suggests that parent–teen

(continued)

TABLE 7.7   **Computer Output for Frequency Distribution and Summary Statistics for Age to Talk About Sex**

AGESEX   Age when should talk about sex

Value label	Value	Frequency	Percent	Valid percent	Cum percent
	4	16	2.3	2.3	2.3
	5	30	4.3	4.3	6.5
	6	30	4.3	4.3	10.8
	7	34	4.8	4.8	15.6
	8	51	7.2	7.2	22.8
	9	46	6.5	6.5	29.4
	10	162	23.0	23.0	52.3
	11	45	6.4	6.4	58.7
	12	137	19.4	19.4	78.2
	13	83	11.8	11.8	89.9
	14	23	3.3	3.3	93.2
	15	19	2.7	2.7	95.9
	16	22	3.1	3.1	99.0
	17	1	.1	.1	99.1
	18	5	.7	.7	99.9
	19	1	.1	.1	100.0
Total		705	100.0	100.0	

Mean	10.464	Std err	.107	Median	10.000
Mode	10.000	Std dev	2.829	Variance	8.005
Range	15.000	Minimum	4.000	Maximum	19.000

discussions about sex and birth control will occur too late for a sizeable proportion of teens. A further understanding of this issue can be gained by examining the percentages in Tables 7.7 and 7.8.

Figures 7.2 and 7.3 present frequency histograms for the two age questions, with a normal distribution superimposed on each. There appears to be little skewness in either distribution. However, despite the fact that Tables 7.7 and 7.8 show that the mode, the median, and the mean all have comparable values within each distribution, both distributions are decidedly nonnormal because of the low frequencies for age 11 as compared to ages 10 and 12. It is interesting to note that if the decision had been made to present these distributions using grouped intervals (for example, ages 4 to 6, 7 to 9, 10 to 12, etc.), this nonnormality would be masked.

The concepts developed in this chapter are also applicable to dichotomous variables. For instance, Table 7.9 presents computer output for the mean and the estimated standard error of the mean for an important dichotomous variable that we discussed in the Applications to the Analysis of a Social Problem Using SPSS for Windows section in Chapter 3: whether or not the teen used birth control at the first instance of sexual intercourse. This variable was scored as 0 if the teen reported not using birth control and as 1 if the teen reported using birth control. As can be seen in Table 7.9, the mean for the 425 cases is .42, and the estimated standard error is .02.

We noted in Chapter 3 that when dichotomous variables are scored as 0 or 1, the mean is simply the proportion of individuals who were assigned a score of 1. We also noted that the mean can be multiplied by 100 to yield a percentage. Thus, consistent with our finding in Chapter 3, (.42)(100) = 42% of the teens *in the sample* used birth control at their first intercourse. Because the observed sample mean is also the best estimate of

(continued)

TABLE 7.8	Computer Output for Frequency Distribution and Summary Statistics for Age to Talk About Birth Control

AGESEX   Age when should talk about birth control

Value label	Value	Frequency	Percent	Valid percent	Cum percent
	4	1	.1	.1	.1
	5	3	.4	.4	.6
	6	5	.7	.7	1.3
	7	7	.9	1.0	2.2
	8	23	3.1	3.2	5.4
	9	26	3.5	3.6	9.1
	10	129	17.2	18.0	27.1
	11	41	5.5	5.7	32.8
	12	201	26.8	28.1	60.9
	13	131	17.4	18.3	79.2
	14	48	6.4	6.7	85.9
	15	39	5.2	5.4	91.3
	16	42	5.6	5.9	97.2
	17	6	.8	.8	98.0
	18	12	1.6	1.7	99.7
	19	1	.1	.1	99.9
	20	1	.1	.1	100.0
	.	35	47	Missing	
	Total	751	100.0	100.0	

Mean	12.092	Std err	.086	Median	12.000
Mode	12.000	Std dev	2.293	Variance	5.259
Range	16.000	Minimum	4.000	Maximum	20.000

the value of the population mean, we estimate the *population* proportion of teens who used birth control at their first intercourse to be .42 and the *population* percentage to be 42%.

When data are dichotomous, the estimated standard error of the mean also conveys important information—it estimates the standard deviation of a sampling distribution of a proportion. Thus, it estimates how far, on average, the proportions yielded by samples of a given size (in this case, $N = 425$) deviate from the true population proportion. Given the small estimated standard error (.02) in our example, the estimate of .42 of the population of teens using birth control at their first intercourse is probably reasonably close to the true population proportion.

As with the mean, multiplying the estimated standard error of the mean of a dichotomous variable by 100 converts it to percentage units.[*] For our example, $(.02)(100) = 2\%$.

(continued)

[*] Alternative formulas for estimating the standard errors for proportions or percentages are discussed in Guilford (1965).

FIGURE 7.2   **Frequency Histogram for Age to Talk About Sex**

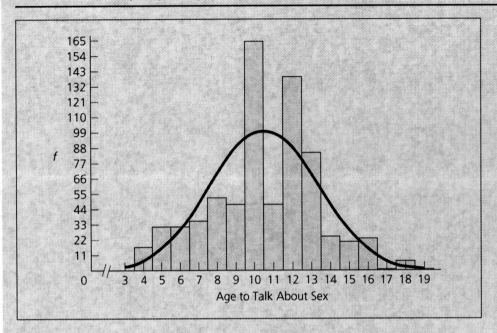

FIGURE 7.3   **Frequency Histogram for Age to Talk About Birth Control**

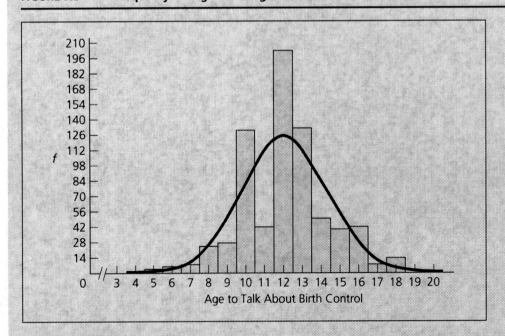

(continued)

TABLE 7.9	**Computer Output for Summary Statistics for Use of Birth Control**

BCFIRST   Whether used birth control at first intercourse

Variable	Mean	S.E. Mean	Std Dev	Variance	Minimum	Maximum	N
BCFIRST	.42	.02	.49	.24	0	1	425

Summary

Whenever behavioral scientists study samples, they must deal with the problem of sampling error, or the fact that a sample statistic might differ from the value of its corresponding population parameter. An unbiased estimator is a statistic whose average (mean) over all possible random samples of a given size equals the value of the population parameter being estimated. The sample mean is an unbiased estimator of the population mean and the variance and standard deviation estimates are unbiased estimators of the population variance and the standard deviation, respectively. In general, as the degrees of freedom associated with a statistic increase, the more accurate that statistic will be in estimating the corresponding population parameter.

A sample mean will usually differ from the corresponding population mean because of sampling error. A key concept for understanding the degree to which sampling error affects the accuracy of the sample mean as an estimator of the population mean is provided by the sampling distribution of the mean. A sampling distribution of the mean is a distribution of the mean scores for all possible random samples of a given size. As stated in the central limit theorem, the mean of a sampling distribution of the mean will always be equal to the population mean (of the raw scores).

The central limit theorem also addresses the standard deviation and the shape of a sampling distribution of the mean. The standard deviation, called the standard error of the mean, indicates the average amount by which the means of random samples of size N deviate from the population mean. The size of the standard error of the mean is influenced by two factors: the sample size (N) and the variability of scores in the population (σ). Specifically, the standard error of the mean gets smaller as the sample size increases and as the variability of scores in the population decreases, other things being equal.

The shape of a sampling distribution of the mean approaches a normal distribution as the sample size on which it is based approaches infinity, regardless of the shape of the underlying population. The fit is particularly good when the sample size is greater than around 30.

In practice, σ is rarely known. Rather, we typically have data based on one sample. We must therefore estimate the standard error of the mean using the sample estimate of the population standard deviation ($\hat{s}$) rather than σ. Consequently, the formula for the estimated standard error of the mean is $\hat{s}_{\overline{X}} = \hat{s} / \sqrt{N}$ rather than $\sigma_{\overline{X}} = \sigma / \sqrt{N}$.

It is possible to conceptualize sampling distributions for statistics other than the mean. Given the same population, the sampling distribution of the mean will show less variability than that for either the mode or the median. It is for this reason that the mean is usually preferred by statisticians as a measure of central tendency.

Exercises

Answers to asterisked (*) exercises appear at the back of the book.

1. Under what circumstance is sampling from a finite population analogous to sampling from an infinite population?

*2. What is sampling error? How can we represent the amount of sampling error that is present in a statistic?

*3. What is an unbiased estimator? What is a biased estimator?

4. Why, in the absence of any other information, is the observed sample mean one's "best estimate" of the value of the population mean?

5. Why is it necessary to divide the sum of squares by $N - 1$ rather than N when computing the variance estimate?

*6. Compute the variance and the standard deviation for the following scores: 6, 5, 3, 7, 4, 8, 4, 2, 5, 6, 3, 6, 5, 4, 7, 5. Estimate the variance and the standard deviation in the population, and compare the two sets of results.

7. Compute the variance and the standard deviation for the following scores: 4, 6, 5, 6, 4, 4, 6, 5, 4, 5, 4, 6, 4, 6, 5, 6. Estimate the variance and the standard deviation in the population, and compare the two sets of results.

*8. What are degrees of freedom? Why are there $N - 1$ degrees of freedom associated with a sum of squares around a sample mean?

9. What is a mean square? What is the relationship between a mean square and a variance estimate?

*10. What is a sampling distribution of the mean? How is a sampling distribution of the mean different from a frequency distribution as discussed in Chapter 2?

*11. What three characteristics of the sampling distribution of the mean are addressed by the central limit theorem?

12. In general terms, what value will the mean of a sampling distribution of the mean always equal? Why?

*13. Given a population with three scores, 2, 4, and 6, specify all possible samples of size two that one could obtain from this population using sampling with replacement. (*Hint:* There are nine of them.) Compute the mean for each sample. Next compute the mean across the nine sample means. How does this result compare with the population mean, μ? What principle does this illustrate?

14. What is a standard error of the mean? What information does it convey?

*15. Distinguish a standard error of the mean from a standard deviation of a set of raw scores.

16. What two factors influence the size of the standard error of the mean?

*17. If a sampling distribution of the mean has an associated standard error of the mean of 0, what does this indicate about the means of the samples drawn from the relevant population?

*18. If a sampling distribution of the mean has an associated standard error of the mean of 0, what does this indicate about the variability of scores in the population (σ)?

*19. A random sample of size 30 is drawn from each of two populations. For population A, $\mu = 10.00$ and $\sigma = 5.00$. For population B, $\mu = 8.00$ and $\sigma = 7.00$. Which sample mean is probably a better estimate of its population mean? Why?

20. For each of two populations, $\mu = 10.00$ and $\sigma = 6.00$. A random sample of size 20 is drawn from population A, and a random sample of size 40 is drawn from population B. Which sample mean is probably a better estimate of its population mean? Why?

*21. Compute the mean and the estimated standard error of the mean for the data in Exercise 6.

22. Compute the mean and the estimated standard error of the mean for the data in Exercise 7.

23. Compare the estimated standard error of the mean calculated in Exercise 21 with that calculated in Exercise 22. Which sample mean is probably a better estimate of its population mean? Why?

24. Match each symbol in the first column with the appropriate term in the second column.

Symbol	Term
1. $\hat{s}_{\bar{X}}$	a. standard error of the mean
2. s	b. standard deviation estimate
3. $\sigma_{\bar{X}}$	c. sample variance
4. σ^2	d. population variance
5. s^2	e. population standard deviation
6. σ	f. variance estimate
7. $\hat{s}^2$	g. estimated standard error of the mean
8. $\hat{s}$	h. sample standard deviation

25. Discuss the relationship between the shape of the sampling distribution of the mean, the sample size, and the shape of the underlying population.

*26. Why do statisticians usually prefer the mean to the mode and the median as a measure of central tendency?

Multiple-Choice Questions

*27. A sampling distribution of the mean is always normal in shape.
   a. true   b. false

28. The sample mean is a biased estimator of the population mean.
   a. true   b. false

29. σ is the symbol for a
   a. sample standard deviation
   b. standard deviation estimate
   c. population standard deviation
   d. population variance

*30. Which of the following is the best measure of the amount of sampling error associated with a sample mean?
   a. population standard deviation
   b. sample standard deviation
   c. standard deviation estimate
   d. standard error of the mean

*31. As the degrees of freedom associated with an estimate of a population value increase, the accuracy of the estimate tends to
   a. decrease
   b. increase
   c. stay the same
   d. sometimes decrease and sometimes increase

32. Sampling error refers to the extent to which mistakes have been made in the collection and analysis of data.
   a. true   b. false

33. The standard deviation of a sampling distribution of the mean is called the
   a. standard deviation estimate
   b. population standard deviation
   c. standard error of the mean
   d. none of the above

*34. The standard error of the mean can never be directly calculated from a set of sample data.
   a. true   b. false

35. The sample variance is a(n) ____ estimator of the population variance because it ____ the population variance across all possible random samples of a given size.
   a. biased; underestimates
   b. biased; overestimates

c. unbiased; equals
d. unbiased; underestimates

*36. Behavioral science research is conceptualized as sampling from ____ populations ____ replacement.
a. finite; with
b. finite; without
c. infinite; with
d. infinite; without

37. $\hat{s}^2$ is the symbol for a(n)
a. population variance
b. sample variance
c. estimated standard error of the mean
d. variance estimate

Use the following information to complete Exercises 38–40:

Suppose that we select a random sample of 100 individuals from a population and find them to have a mean self-esteem score of 82.00. Also suppose that self-esteem scores in the population are slightly negatively skewed, with a mean of 78.00 and a standard deviation of 25.00.

*38. The mean of the sampling distribution of the mean based on $N = 100$ will equal
a. 77.00   c. 80.00
b. 78.00   d. 82.00

*39. The standard deviation of the sampling distribution of the mean based on $N = 100$ will equal
a. .25
b. 2.50
c. 25.00
d. This cannot be determined.

40. The sampling distribution of the mean based on $N = 100$ will approximate a ____ distribution.
a. negatively skewed
b. positively skewed
c. normal
d. leptokurtic

CHAPTER **8**

Hypothesis Testing: Inferences About a Single Mean

In this chapter we consider basic principles of hypothesis testing. This material is central to all of inferential statistics and should be studied carefully. Our discussion relies on the following concepts that were developed in earlier chapters, and you should make sure that you are familiar with these before covering the present material:

probability (Section 1.8 and Chapter 6)
probability distributions (Section 2.8)
the normal distribution (Sections 2.9 and 4.4)
standard and z scores (Sections 4.2 through 4.4)
the sampling distribution of the mean, the central limit theorem, and the
    standard error of the mean (Section 7.7)
the estimated standard error of the mean (Section 7.8)

Of course, many of these concepts are based on simpler concepts, so you should make sure that you are familiar with these too. You may wish to return to previous chapters to review anything that you are unsure about before proceeding.

8.1   A Simple Analogy for Principles of Hypothesis Testing

Some of the basic steps of hypothesis testing in behavioral science research can be characterized by a simple analogy: Suppose that you are given a coin and asked to determine whether it is fair or whether it is biased toward heads or tails. You might respond by conducting a simple experiment. If you assume that the coin is fair, then you would expect that flipping the coin a large number of times would result in heads about one-half the time because the probability of a head is .500. So you flip the coin 100 times and count the number of heads that occur.

Suppose that the tosses result in heads 52 times. This does not correspond *exactly* to what you would expect based on a probability of .500, but it certainly is close (52 out of 100 heads compared with 50 out of 100 heads). Because the result is not very discrepant from the expected result, and because you know that your observed result could have deviated somewhat from the expected result just by chance, you might conclude that the coin is not biased. But suppose that the result of 100 flips had yielded 65 or 95 heads. At some point the discrepancy from the expected result becomes too great to attribute to chance and, at this point, you would reject your original assumption that the coin is fair.

In behavioral science research, the process of **hypothesis testing** is very similar to this experiment. The investigator begins by stating a proposal, or *hypothesis*, that is assumed to be true (in our example, that the coin is fair). Based on this assumption, an expected result is specified (in our example, that we should obtain 50 heads out of 100 flips). The data are collected, and the observed result is compared with the expected result (in our example, 52 heads versus an expectation of 50 heads). If the observed result is so discrepant from the expected result that it is very unlikely that the difference is due to chance, then the original hypothesis is rejected. Otherwise, it is not rejected.

8.2   Statistical Inference and the Normal Distribution: The One-Sample *z* Test

Suppose that an investigator wants to know whether the mean intelligence level of students who attend a college by the name of Victor University differs from the typical intelligence level of college students in general. Also suppose that past research on a particular intelligence test has shown that a score of 100 represents the performance of the typical college student. The question of interest, then, is whether the mean intelligence test score for the population of students who attend Victor University is different from 100.

Competing Hypotheses

We can state this issue more precisely in terms of two competing hypotheses about the population mean. First, the mean intelligence test score for students who attend Victor University may, in fact, equal the value of interest, 100. This possibility is stated in a **null hypothesis**:

$$H_0: \mu = 100$$

where H_0 is the symbol for a null hypothesis and μ represents the actual population mean for the students who attend Victor University. We will provide a technical definition of the null hypothesis shortly. Informally, the null hypothesis can be thought of as the hypothesis of "no difference": If the intelligence of Victor University students does not differ from the national average, then their mean must equal the national average—hence, the null hypothesis that $\mu = 100$.

Second, the actual population mean for these students may not equal 100 but rather may be less than or greater than 100. We state this in an **alternative hypothesis**:

$$H_1: \mu \neq 100$$

where H_1 is the symbol for an alternative hypothesis. The task at hand is to choose between these two competing hypotheses.

The investigator decides to do this by collecting some data. A random sample of 50 students who currently attend Victor University is administered the intelligence test. The mean score for the sample is found to be 105.00. These data would seem to support the second hypothesis stated above because the sample mean is not equal to 100, but rather is equal to 105.00. However, we know from Chapter 7 that a sample mean may not be an accurate descriptor of the population mean because of sampling error. Maybe the actual population mean is 100 and we observed a sample mean of 105.00 because of sampling error. We need to test the viability of this possibility.

Our knowledge of sampling distributions and the normal distribution helps us in this regard. More specifically, when the variable under study is quantitative in nature and measured on a level that at least approximates interval characteristics, hypotheses about the value of a population mean can be tested using the **one-sample *z* test**.

Analysis of Sampling Distributions

In the coin-flipping example, we tested whether the coin was fair by assuming that such was the case and, based on this assumption, specifying an expected result that we then compared with the observed result. We will do the same for the intelligence test example. Assume that the actual population mean for Victor University students is equal to 100. If we select a random sample of 50 students from the population, we would expect the mean of the sample to be near 100. We would not expect it to be exactly 100 because of sampling error (just as we would not expect flipping a fair coin 100 times to yield exactly 50 heads and 50 tails). How much sampling error can we reasonably expect to have if μ equals 100? If the sample mean were equal to 101.00, could this be due to sampling error? What about 110.00?

We can be quite specific on this matter by making reference to a sampling distribution of the mean based on all possible random samples of size 50. Recall from Section 7.7 that the mean of a sampling distribution of the mean equals the actual population mean. We have assumed, for the purpose of our statistical test, that the actual population mean is 100. Also recall that the standard deviation of the sampling distribution of the mean is called the *standard error of the mean* ($\sigma_{\overline{X}}$) and, per Equation 7.4, is equal to the population standard deviation divided by the square root of the sample size. In the present context, $\sigma_{\overline{X}}$ represents how much, on average, sample means based on $N = 50$ deviate from the actual population mean.

Suppose that we know that the value of the population standard deviation is 17.68 and, thus, that the value of the standard error of the mean is*

$$\sigma_{\overline{X}} = \frac{\sigma}{\sqrt{N}}$$
$$= \frac{17.68}{\sqrt{50}} = 2.50$$

This indicates that, on average, sample means based on $N = 50$ deviate 2.50 units from the actual population mean.

If the actual population mean is 100 and the standard error of the mean is 2.50, how much sampling error can we reasonably expect in our data? Recall from our discussion of the central limit theorem in Chapter 7 that a sampling distribution of the mean based on a relatively large sample size is approximately normally distributed. Also recall from Chapter 4 that 68.26% of all scores in a normal distribution occur between one standard deviation below the mean and one standard deviation above the mean. About 68% of all means in a sampling distribution of the mean will therefore occur between one standard error below μ and one standard error above μ.

---

* In practice, the standard error of the mean is usually not known and must be estimated using Equation 7.5. We consider hypothesis testing when an estimate of the standard error is used in Section 8.10.

Between what two scores will 95% of the sample means in a sampling distribution occur? If we consult column 2 of the *z* score table in Appendix B, we find that 95% of all scores in a normal distribution fall between 1.96 standard deviations below the mean and 1.96 standard deviations above the mean. If 95% of all sample means fall within ±1.96 standard errors from the mean, less than 5% of all sample means must fall beyond ±1.96 standard errors from the mean. Thus, the *probability* that we would observe a sample mean *outside* the range of −1.96 to +1.96 standard errors is less than .05. This is a highly unlikely event.

The mean of our sample *is* outside this range. It is $105.00 - 100 = 5.00$ units above the hypothesized population mean. Because the standard error of the mean is equal to 2.50, this is equivalent to $5.00/2.50 = 2.00$ standard errors above the hypothesized population mean. Given this, we might reasonably conclude that it is very unlikely that the observed sample mean being as large as it is is due to sampling error and that the assumption that $\mu = 100$ is therefore untenable. We would therefore reject the null hypothesis and, given that the sample mean is 105.00, conclude that the mean intelligence test score for the population of students who attend Victor University is higher than the typical score of 100 for college students in general.

Steps in Hypothesis Testing

We can formally summarize the steps above as follows:

1. Translate the research question into two competing hypotheses: a null hypothesis and an alternative hypothesis. The null hypothesis is the hypothesis of "no difference." More technically, it is the hypothesis that we assume to be true for the purpose of conducting a statistical test.

> In our example, the null hypothesis is $H_0: \mu = 100$, and the alternative hypothesis is $H_1: \mu \neq 100$.

2. *Assuming that the null hypothesis is true* (that is, that the population mean is, in fact, equal to the value stated in the null hypothesis), state an expected result in the form of a range of values within which the sample mean would be expected to fall. This is expressed in terms of the *z* scores, called **critical values**, that define the endpoints of this range. The set of all *z* scores more extreme than the critical values (that is, less than the negative critical value or greater than the positive critical value) is called a **rejection region** and constitutes an unexpected result.

> In our example, we assume that the population mean is equal to 100 because the null hypothesis states that $\mu = 100$. Under this assumption, the critical values of *z* are −1.96 and +1.96. Thus, an expected result is defined by all *z* scores in the range −1.96 to +1.96, and an unexpected result (the rejection region) is defined by all *z* scores that are less than −1.96 or greater than +1.96.

3. Characterize the mean and the standard deviation of the sampling distribution of the mean, *assuming that the null hypothesis is true*.

If we assume that the null hypothesis is true in our example, then μ equals 100. It follows that the mean of the sampling distribution of the mean also equals 100 because the mean of such distributions is always equal to the population mean.

The standard deviation of the sampling distribution of the mean is the standard error of the mean. This was previously calculated to equal 2.50 in our example.

4. Convert the observed sample mean to a z score to determine how many standard errors it is from μ, *assuming that the null hypothesis is true*. This is accomplished using the following formula for the one-sample z test:

$$z = \frac{\overline{X} - \mu}{\sigma_{\overline{X}}} \tag{8.1}$$

where z is the **test statistic** for the one-sample z test, $\overline{X}$ is the observed sample mean, μ is the population mean assuming that the null hypothesis is true, and $\sigma_{\overline{X}}$ is the standard error of the mean. The value of z that is calculated using this formula is referred to as the *observed* z score to distinguish it from the critical values. Note the similarity of Equation 8.1 to the formula that we introduced in Chapter 4 for converting a score in a sample to a z score:

$$z = \frac{X - \overline{X}}{s}$$

In both cases, we divide the difference between some score and the mean of the corresponding distribution by the standard deviation of that distribution. However, rather than comparing a raw score in a distribution of raw scores with the sample mean, Equation 8.1 compares a sample mean in a distribution of sample means with the hypothesized population mean.

This suggests a general formula for converting any score to a z score:

$$z = \frac{\text{score of interest} - \text{mean of the distribution}}{\text{standard deviation of the distribution}} \tag{8.2}$$

For the one-sample z test, the score of interest is the observed sample mean, we assume that the mean of the distribution is the value of μ from the null hypothesis, and the standard deviation of the distribution is the standard error of the mean.

In our example,

$$z = \frac{105.00 - 100}{2.50} = 2.00$$

5a. Compare the value of z that was calculated using Equation 8.1 with the expected result as defined by all z scores that fall between the critical values of z. If the observed z score exceeds either the positive or the negative critical value, reject the null hypothesis. If the observed z score does not exceed either the positive or the negative critical value, do not reject the null hypothesis.*

If the null hypothesis is rejected, proceed to step 5b. If the null hypothesis is not rejected, do not proceed to step 5b.

In our example, the observed z score of 2.00 exceeds the positive critical value of +1.96. This suggests that the observed difference between the sample mean and the hypothesized population mean is too large to be attributed to sampling error, and the null hypothesis is therefore rejected.

5b. If the null hypothesis is rejected, compare the observed sample mean $(\overline{X})$ with the value of μ stated in the null hypothesis. If the observed sample mean is *greater* than the stated μ, conclude that the actual population mean is *greater* than the stated population mean. If the observed sample mean is *less* than the stated μ, conclude that the actual population mean is *less* than the stated population mean.*

Because the observed sample mean of 105.00 in our example is greater than the stated μ of 100, we conclude that the mean intelligence test score of the population of students who attend Victor University is higher than 100.

8.3 Defining Expected and Unexpected Results

A major step in hypothesis testing is the specification of what constitutes expected and unexpected results under the assumption that the null hypothesis is true. As we have discussed, this is stated in terms of a positive and a negative critical value and a corresponding rejection region. Rejection regions are determined with reference to a probability value known as an **alpha level**. For example, when the alpha level is .05, a result is defined as "unexpected" if the probability of obtaining that result, assuming the null hypothesis is true, is less than .05.

As noted previously, 95% of all sample means in the example pertaining to intelligence test scores at Victor University will fall between −1.96 and +1.96 standard errors of the actual population mean, which, for the purpose of hypothesis

---

* The logic of using an extreme result to reject the null hypothesis has been questioned by Cohen (1994), who argues that the statistical test that we described provides information about the probability of observing the obtained result (or a result more extreme) given that the null hypothesis is true, whereas what behavioral scientists are really interested in is the probability that the null hypothesis is true given the observed result. He correctly notes that these two conditional probabilities may or may not be the same.

Cohen's analysis has sparked considerable debate among behavioral scientists about the best way to conduct statistical analyses. Nevertheless, the dominant practice continues to be the traditional hypothesis testing approach that we describe in this chapter, and we retain this approach throughout this book. In all instances, we assume that the two conditional probabilities of interest are equal. Interested readers are urged to read the Cohen article and the many commentaries that follow it.

* Because the observed value of z will be positive if the sample mean is greater than the stated value of μ and negative if the sample mean is less than the stated value of μ, an alternative approach is to examine the sign of the observed z score.

STUDY EXERCISE 8.1

Suppose that a researcher is interested in whether the mean score on a particular aptitude test for students who attend rural elementary schools differs from the typical score of elementary school students in general, which is known to be 50. To examine this issue, he administers the test to a random sample of 25 rural elementary school students and finds the sample mean to be 56.00. The population standard deviation, σ, is known to equal 10.00. Conduct a one-sample z test to test the viability of the hypothesis that μ = 50.

Answer   *We begin by explicitly stating the null and alternative hypotheses:*

$$H_0: \mu = 50$$
$$H_1: \mu \neq 50$$

Next, we state an expected result under the assumption that the null hypothesis is true. For an alpha level of .05, this includes any z score between +1.96 and −1.96. An unexpected result thus consists of all z scores less than −1.96 or greater than +1.96.

Because σ = 10.00 and N = 25, the standard error of the mean can be calculated using Equation 7.4:

$$\sigma_{\bar{X}} = \frac{\sigma}{\sqrt{N}} = \frac{10.00}{\sqrt{25}} = 2.00$$

According to Equation 8.1, the observed value of z is thus

$$z = \frac{\bar{X} - \mu}{\sigma_{\bar{X}}} = \frac{56.00 - 50}{2.00} = 3.00$$

Because 3.00 exceeds +1.96, we reject the null hypothesis and, based on a comparison of the observed sample mean (56.00) with the value of μ stated in the null hypothesis (50), we conclude that the actual population mean for rural elementary school students is greater than the typical score of 50 for elementary school students in general.

---

testing, is assumed to equal 100. Thus, there is less than a .05 probability of observing a sample mean outside this range. For an alpha level of .05, then, an unexpected result includes any sample mean that is more than 1.96 standard errors below or above the value of μ represented in the null hypothesis.

Although alpha can be set at levels other than .05, it is traditional to adopt an alpha level of .05 in behavioral science research. We discuss the issue of setting the alpha level in more detail shortly.

8.4   Failing to Reject Versus Accepting the Null Hypothesis

In the Victor University example, the observed sample mean was inconsistent with a sampling error interpretation of the data and the null hypothesis was therefore rejected. However, if the observed sample mean had been close to 100, say, 100.50, would we have accepted the null hypothesis? The answer is no.

When researchers obtain a result that is consistent with the null hypothesis (that is, when it falls within the range defined by the critical values rather than in the rejection region), they do not *accept* the null hypothesis as being true. Rather, the researchers *fail to reject* the null hypothesis. There is a subtle distinction here that is very important. In principle, *we can never accept the null hypothesis as being true based on statistical tests; we can only reject it as being untenable.*

Consider the null and alternative hypotheses from the Victor University example:

H_0: $\mu = 100$

H_1: $\mu \neq 100$

Note that the null hypothesis is stated such that the actual population mean must equal one and only one value (100), whereas the alternative hypothesis is stated such that the actual population mean could potentially equal any of an infinite number of values (for example, 100.51, 101.08, 97.63, or 112.30—anything but 100). When we observe a highly discrepant sample mean and reject the null hypothesis, we are saying that it is unlikely that the actual population mean equals 100 and, in this sense, we "accept" the alternative hypothesis.

In contrast, because of sampling error, we can never unambiguously conclude that the actual population mean is equal to any one specific value based on sample data. If the observed sample mean is not extremely discrepant from the hypothesized population value of 100, we can say only that the sample mean is too close for us to confidently conclude that the actual population mean does *not* equal 100. We cannot say that μ is equal to 100, but we also cannot confidently say that it is not. Even an observed sample mean of exactly 100 does not prove that the *population* mean is equal to 100 because sampling error could produce a sample mean of 100 even when the population mean is a much different value. Thus, when the observed value of z falls within the range defined by the critical values, we *fail to reject* the null hypothesis.

8.5 Decisions About the Alternative Hypothesis

Following the preceding logic, if we fail to reject the null hypothesis, we must also fail to reject the alternative hypothesis. Similarly, if we reject the null hypothesis, we must also accept the alternative hypothesis. Because nonrejection of the null hypothesis always implies nonrejection of the alternative hypothesis and rejection of the null hypothesis always implies acceptance of the alternative hypothesis, for the sake of simplicity we do not explicitly refer to the alternative hypothesis when discussing the outcomes of statistical tests in this book.

8.6 Type I and Type II Errors

Because it is based on probability, the nature of hypothesis testing is such that errors will sometimes occur. Thus, when an investigator draws a conclusion with respect to the null hypothesis, that conclusion can be either correct or in error.

Two types of errors are possible, and these are illustrated in Table 8.1. In this table, the columns represent the true state of affairs *in the population*. That is, although we do not know whether or not the actual population mean is equal to the value of μ stated in the null hypothesis, the reality is that the null hypothesis is always either true (if the actual population mean is equal to the stated value of μ) or false (if the actual population mean is not equal to the stated value of μ). The

TABLE 8.1   **Two Types of Errors in Hypothesis Testing**

		True State of Affairs	
		H_0 is true	H_0 is false
Decision on the Basis of a Statistical Test	Reject H_0	Type I error (Probability = α)	Correct decision (Probability = $1 - \beta$ = power)
	Fail to reject H_0	Correct decision (Probability = $1 - \alpha$)	Type II error (Probability = β)

rows of this table represent the decision that we make on the basis of a statistical test, in this instance, the one-sample z test. Of course, this test utilizes *sample* data.

One type of error that we will sometimes make is to reject the null hypothesis when it is true. This is referred to as a Type I error. This type of error is summarized in the upper left quadrant of Table 8.1. The probability of making a Type I error is equal to the alpha level—in most cases, .05—and is referred to as **alpha**. As can be seen, alpha is symbolized as α, the lowercase Greek *a*.

Second, we will sometimes fail to reject the null hypothesis when it is false. This is referred to as a **Type II error**. This type of error is summarized in the lower right quadrant of Table 8.1. The probability of making a Type II error is referred to as **beta** and is symbolized as β, the lowercase Greek *b*.

The nature of decision errors can be explained with reference to Figures 8.1 and 8.2. Let us focus first on the case where the null hypothesis is true. Suppose that we are testing the null hypothesis that $\mu = 100$ and that the population mean is, in fact, 100. Figure 8.1 depicts the sampling distribution of the mean for this population based on $N = 50$. The point marked "$\mu = 100$" represents the population mean. Because the hypothesized population mean is equal to the actual population mean in this instance, a Type I error would occur if we select a sample from the population and conclude, based on the sample mean, that μ does not equal 100.

If the alpha level was .05, this would occur, on the average, only 5 times out of 100 because only 5% of the sample means would occur outside the range -1.96 to $+1.96$ standard errors. Thus, the probability of a Type I error equals the alpha level and is indicated by the shaded areas of Figure 8.1. It follows that the probability, given a true null hypothesis, of *not* making a Type I error—that is, of failing to reject the null hypothesis—must be equal to $1 - \alpha$. This occurrence is summarized in the lower left quadrant of Table 8.1 and is defined by the area labeled $1 - \alpha$ in Figure 8.1.

Let us now consider the case where the null hypothesis is false. Suppose that we are testing the null hypothesis that $\mu_A = 100$, as before, but that the mean of the population that we are studying is actually 105. Distribution A in Figure 8.2 depicts the sampling distribution of the mean for this population based on $N = 50$. The point marked "$\mu_A = 105$" represents the actual population mean. However, we do not know that this is the case. In fact, because we are testing the null hypothesis that $\mu = 100$, we will assume that the population mean is 100, as we did in the previous example.

The sampling distribution of the mean based on $N = 50$ for a population of scores for which $\mu = 100$ is depicted by distribution B in Figure 8.2. This distribution

FIGURE 8.1   **Illustration of Type I Errors**

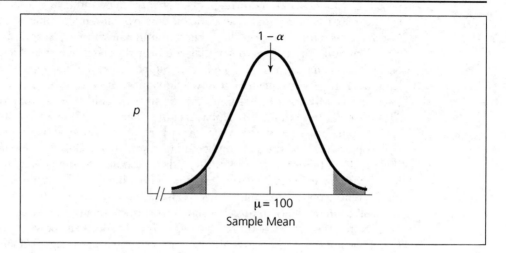

FIGURE 8.2   **Illustration of Type II Errors and Power**

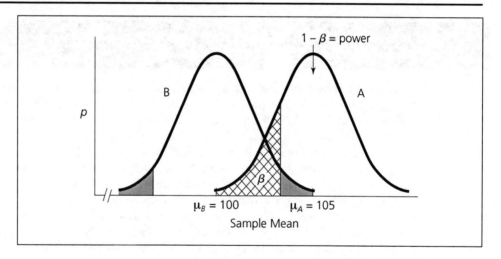

is the same as that in Figure 8.1 except that the point marked "$\mu_B = 100$" now represents the *hypothesized* population mean. Consistent with the usual hypothesis testing procedures that we have been discussing, if the sample mean falls more than ± 1.96 standard errors from 100 (that is, if it falls in the shaded areas), we will reject the null hypothesis. Otherwise, we will fail to reject the null hypothesis.

Note that a sample mean that occurs anywhere within the crosshatched area does *not* fall more than ± 1.96 standard errors from 100. Thus, we will fail to reject the null hypothesis when it is, in fact, false. This crosshatched area represents the probability of a Type II error, or β. It follows that the area labeled $1 - \beta$ defines the probability that an investigator will reject the null hypothesis when it is false, and this probability is called the **power** of the statistical test. This occurrence is summarized in the upper right quadrant of Table 8.1.

These concepts can be illustrated intuitively with an electronics analogy. Suppose that you are listening through a set of earphones and trying to decide whether you hear a particular signal. The static on the earphones makes this difficult for you. You have been told that you should hear the signal within 30 seconds. One type of error that you can make is to say that you hear the signal when, in fact, it does not occur. This is analogous to a Type I error. Suppose that making such an error would lead to negative consequences. You would want to be very sure of yourself. Only if you are virtually certain that you hear the signal would you say that you heard it. This is similar to setting a low alpha level (for example, .05) in an investigation.

On the other hand, there is another type of error that you can make—saying that you do not hear the signal when, in fact, it is there. This corresponds to a Type II error. The ability not to miss the signal corresponds to the power of a statistical test. If you have a very sensitive ear, you will be likely to detect the signal when it occurs (corresponding to high power). However, if you do not have a sensitive ear, you will be more likely to miss the signal (corresponding to low power).

Notice that the value of the alpha level directly affects the power of the statistical test. If you are very conservative about saying that you hear the signal (analogous to setting a very low alpha level), this decreases the likelihood that you will say the signal is there when it is indeed present (analogous to decreasing the power of a statistical test).

8.7 Effects of the Alpha Level and the Sample Size on the Power of Statistical Tests

As noted above, the alpha level in an investigation reflects the probability of making a Type I error. The practice of adopting a low, or *conservative*, alpha level in behavioral science research evolved from experimental settings where it was very important to avoid a certain kind of false conclusion.

An example of such an experiment is testing a new drug with the aim of ensuring that it is safe for the general adult population. In this case, deciding that a drug is safe when, in fact, it tends to produce adverse reactions in a meaningful proportion of adults is an error that is certainly to be avoided. Under these circumstances, a medical researcher would cast the proposal that "the drug is unsafe" as the null hypothesis and the proposal that "the drug is safe" as the alternative hypothesis and would choose a low alpha level to minimize the risk of concluding that the drug is safe when actually it is not.

Several researchers have argued that behavioral scientists have been preoccupied with Type I errors at the expense of Type II errors (Cohen, 1977; Greenwald, 1975). The alpha level directly affects the power of a statistical test (and, hence, the probability of making a Type II error), with more conservative alpha levels yielding less powerful tests, everything else being equal. The argument is that it is hard to justify that a Type I error will have the drastic character implied by a low alpha level in all behavioral science research. It is not necessarily worse, the argument goes, to conclude falsely that there is a difference between a mean and a hypothesized value (that is, to make a Type I error) in many research situations than it is to conclude falsely that there is not a difference (that is, to make a Type II error).

The issue concerns the balance between the risk of placing a false finding in the body of scientific knowledge and the risk of letting an existing difference go undetected and, thus, unreported. By setting alpha at a less conservative level, we reduce the risk of the latter type of error, albeit at the expense of the former, other things being equal. The issue of setting an alpha level enjoys much controversy. Interested readers are referred to Kirk (1972) for a detailed discussion of this issue.

In terms of the power of a statistical test, not only is the alpha level important, but so too is the sample size: The larger the sample size, the more powerful the statistical test will be, other things being equal. This can be seen with reference to the formula for the one-sample z test (Equation 8.1):

$$z = \frac{\overline{X} - \mu}{\sigma_{\overline{X}}}$$

which can also be written as

$$z = \frac{\overline{X} - \mu}{\sigma/\sqrt{N}}$$

In this equation, as N becomes larger, $\sigma_{\overline{X}}$ becomes smaller, so z becomes more extreme, other things being equal. As z becomes more extreme, it is more likely that we will reject the null hypothesis when it is false, thereby increasing the power of the statistical test.

In summary, a researcher typically has control over the alpha level as well as the sample size to be used in the investigation. The power of one's test can be increased by selecting a larger sample size and a higher alpha level. Selecting a larger sample size must be evaluated relative to the increased costs of obtaining more research participants. Research is expensive, and the time and effort involved in collecting data can be extensive. In addition, increasing the alpha level must be evaluated relative to the importance of making a Type I versus a Type II error.

There comes a point when increasing the power of a test is of diminishing value because the test is already sufficiently powerful to draw a conclusion with a suitable degree of confidence and more and more participants are needed to obtain a given increment in power. As a rough guide, investigators generally attempt to achieve statistical power (the probability of correctly rejecting the null hypothesis when it is false) in the range of .80 to .95, depending on the nature of the proposition being investigated.

The power of a statistical test can be estimated from tables developed for this purpose. In future chapters, we will encounter such tables, which are based on the principles of power analysis discussed in Cohen (1977). These tables can also be used to estimate the sample sizes necessary to achieve desired levels of power, given the value of alpha. In most instances, researchers adopt the traditional alpha level of .05. We will follow this convention in the remainder of this book.

8.8   Statistical and Real-World Significance

If the null hypothesis is rejected, the results of a statistical test are commonly said to be *significant*. If the null hypothesis is not rejected, the term *nonsignificant* is often used instead. It is important to realize that these terms are meant to apply only to the *statistical* outcome. We have seen many instances in the popular press where studies are quoted as reporting "significant" findings when the researchers simply intended to convey that the null hypothesis was rejected. A statistically significant result (meaning the null hypothesis was rejected) may or may not have important real-world implications.

Consider the following example. The poverty index in the United States for a family of four was defined in 1991 as an annual income of $14,120. Suppose that a researcher is interested in whether the mean 1991 income of a certain ethnic group differed from the official poverty level. The researcher examines this issue using data from a large national survey of 500,000 individuals from the ethnic group of interest. Suppose that the observed sample mean for the ethnic group is found to be $14,300.23. If the population standard deviation is also known, a one-sample z test can be applied.

Suppose that application of this test leads to rejection of the null hypothesis so the researcher concludes that the mean income for the survey sample "significantly" differs from the official poverty index. Following the preceding logic, the researcher further concludes that the mean for the ethnic population is not the same as the official poverty level and that, in fact, it is greater. These conclusions say nothing about *how* different the mean population income is from the poverty index, nor does it say anything about the practical implications of the discrepancy. This general point is important to keep in mind when interpreting the results of a hypothesis test.

We believe that science would be better served by eliminating the jargon of "significance." However, this language is firmly entrenched in the behavioral sciences at this time. To help avoid possible confusion, we recommend that researchers use the term *statistically significant* in place of *significant* and the term *statistically nonsignificant* in place of *nonsignificant* in order to emphasize the statistical nature of the conclusion.

Why would such a small discrepancy from the poverty index in this example be statistically significant? In this instance, the sample mean is probably a very accurate estimator of the population mean because the sample size is extremely large. Because of this, when we observe a sample mean that differs at all from the poverty index, we can be almost certain that the population mean is different from the poverty index as well. Stated more formally, the one-sample z test in this case has very high statistical power and is capable of detecting even minor departures from the official poverty index.

8.9   Directional Versus Nondirectional Tests

In each of the preceding examples, the alternative hypothesis has been *nondirectional*. It has stated that the actual population mean is *either* higher *or* lower than the value specified in the null hypothesis. A *directional* alternative hypothesis, in contrast, specifies that a population mean is different from a given value and also indicates the direction of that difference. For instance, the alternative hypothesis

$$H_1: \mu > 100$$

states that the actual population mean is *greater* than 100.

A **directional test** is designed to detect differences from a hypothesized population mean (for example, $\mu = 100$) in one direction only. Suppose, for example, that a counselor is concerned with whether freshman students at her college have adequate reading skills. She decides to administer a reading test to a sample of incoming freshmen; if the mean reading score for the sample is statistically significantly lower than the national test average of 112, she will institute a remedial program. In this instance, the null hypothesis would be $H_0: \mu = 112$, and the investigator would state a directional alternative hypothesis regarding the population mean of incoming freshmen:

$H_1: \mu < 112$

That is, the counselor wants the null hypothesis to be rejected only if the mean reading test score for the population of incoming freshmen is less than the national average of 112 because this will indicate a deficiency in reading skills. The concern in this case is only with detecting a population mean that is *lower* than the national average.

Figure 8.3a presents the rejection region for the lower end of a sampling distribution for an alpha level of .05. Referring to column 3 of Appendix B, we find that this region consists of all z scores that are less than -1.645.* Consistent with the prior examples, any score that falls in this region will lead to the rejection of the null hypothesis. Because they focus on only one tail of the distribution, directional tests are often referred to as **one-tailed tests**.

Figure 8.3b presents a rejection region for a **nondirectional test**—one that is designed to detect differences either above or below the hypothesized population mean by considering both alternatives to the null hypothesis (the population mean being less than the value specified in the null hypothesis and the population mean being greater than this value). In this case, the .05 alpha level is "split" such that .025 of the scores occur at the upper end of the distribution and .025 of the scores occur at the lower end of the distribution. Thus, nondirectional tests are also called **two-tailed tests**. As we discussed earlier, the z scores that define the rejection region are now -1.96 and $+1.96$. This can be verified from column 4 of Appendix B.

Note in Figure 8.3 that the directional test is more sensitive than the nondirectional test to freshman scores being lower than the national average: If the null hypothesis is false because scores are lower than the national average, then the observed sample mean is more likely to fall in the rejection region for the directional test (all z scores that are less than -1.645) than in the corresponding rejection region for the nondirectional test (all z scores that are less than -1.96) because it is broader. This reflects the fact that for a given level of alpha, the critical values for a directional test will always be less extreme than the critical values for a nondirectional test. Thus, we will be more likely to correctly reject the null hypothesis with the directional test than with the nondirectional test. In other words, in this example, the directional test is *more powerful* than the nondirectional test.

---

* Specifically, Appendix B indicates that .0505 of scores in a normal distribution are less than or equal to a z score of 21.64 and that .0495 of scores in a normal distribution are less than or equal to a z score of 21.65. Therefore, .05, or 5%, of scores in a normal distribution must be less than or equal to a z score of $[-1.64 + (-1.65)]/2 = -1.645$.

FIGURE 8.3 **Rejection Regions for (a) Directional and (b) Nondirectional Tests (from Witte, 1980)**

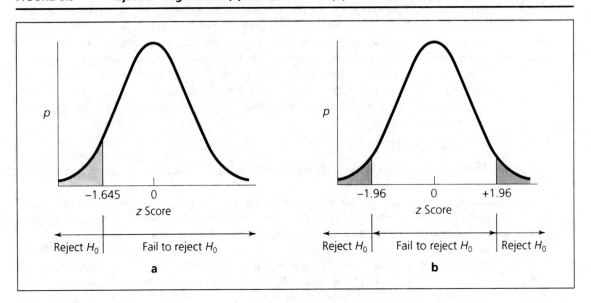

In general, a directional test will be more powerful than a corresponding nondirectional test if the actual population mean and the hypothesized population mean differ in the specified direction. Thus, when there is *exclusive* concern that the population mean differs from a hypothesized value in a specified direction, a directional test should be used. This concern must be stated before the data are analyzed. Never compute a statistical test and then, based on the results, decide that a directional hypothesis should be used. This defeats the logic of hypothesis testing.

However, if the actual population mean differs from the hypothesized population mean in the opposite direction from that stated in the alternative hypothesis, a nondirectional test will be more powerful than its directional counterpart. This is because the null hypothesis cannot be rejected if the observed z score falls in the tail that does not contain the critical value. For instance, if the mean reading test score for the population of freshmen in the present example were greater than 112, perhaps yielding a sample mean corresponding to a z score of 2.36, the null hypothesis would be rejected if a nondirectional test were used (because 2.36 exceeds the critical value of $+1.96$) but not if a directional test were used (because 2.36 does not exceed the critical value of -1.645). Thus, if the concern is not with a specific direction of difference, a nondirectional test should be used. Again, this concern must be stated before the data are analyzed.

Because researchers are often interested in detecting deviations from the null hypothesis regardless of their nature, most research in the behavioral sciences utilizes nondirectional statistical tests. A general guideline is to use a directional test only if there is a compelling reason for doing so based on the existing theory and research.

8.10   Statistical Inference Using the Estimated Standard Error: The One-Sample *t* Test

The Estimated Standard Error of the Mean and the *t* Distribution

An important property of the one-sample z test that we developed in Section 8.2 was that the standard error of the mean, $\sigma_{\overline{X}}$, was known. It is more common that the standard error of the mean is not known and that it must be estimated from sample data.

Suppose that an investigator administers a scale designed to measure attitudes toward living in dormitories to a random sample of 100 college students. Scores on the scale can range from 1 to 7, with higher values representing more favorable attitudes toward living in dormitories. A score of 1 indicates a very unfavorable attitude; a score of 4, a neutral attitude; and a score of 7, a very favorable attitude. The investigator is interested in whether the mean attitude score for the population is different from 4, the score that represents a neutral feeling. The null and alternative hypotheses are

$$H_0: \mu = 4$$
$$H_1: \mu \neq 4$$

Note that the alternative hypothesis is nondirectional because the investigator is interested in whether the mean attitude is either unfavorable (less than 4) or favorable (greater than 4).

The data collected from the sample of 100 students yield a mean of 4.51 with a standard deviation estimate of 1.94. Although the sample mean is consistent with the alternative hypothesis, we must test for the possibility that the null hypothesis is true and that the observed value is due to sampling error.

Unlike the previous problems that we have encountered we do not know the value of the standard error of the mean, $\sigma_{\overline{X}}$. Thus, we are unable to apply a one-sample z test. However, we can estimate $\sigma_{\overline{X}}$ using Equation 7.5:

$$\hat{s}_{\overline{X}} = \frac{\hat{s}}{\sqrt{N}}$$
$$= \frac{1.94}{\sqrt{100}} = .19$$

Given this estimate, you might reason that we can modify Equation 8.1 from $z = (\overline{X} - \mu)/\sigma_{\overline{X}}$ to $z = (\overline{X} - \mu)/\hat{s}_{\overline{X}}$ by simply substituting the estimated standard error of the mean, $\hat{s}_{\overline{X}}$, for the actual standard error, $\sigma_{\overline{X}}$.

Unfortunately, some complications would result from this. Because $\hat{s}_{\overline{X}}$ is calculated from sample data, it is subject to sampling error, whereas $\sigma_{\overline{X}}$ is not. Consequently, the estimate of the standard error will tend to vary from sample to sample; many different values of $\hat{s}_{\overline{X}}$ would be obtained if multiple samples were selected from the same population. This is true even for samples that have the same mean. Because the value yielded by the ratio $(\overline{X} - \mu)/\hat{s}_{\overline{X}}$ is influenced by the size of $\hat{s}_{\overline{X}}$, different z scores might be observed for the same value of $\overline{X}$.

Statisticians have developed a strategy for dealing with this problem. Although the mathematics are complex, the general idea can be stated as follows: When $\sigma_{\bar{X}}$ is known and we convert a sample mean to a z score, we are calculating the *exact* number of standard errors that the sample mean is from the mean of the sampling distribution, μ. If we substitute $\hat{s}_{\bar{X}}$ for $\sigma_{\bar{X}}$ and calculate a z score, we are calculating the *estimated* number of standard errors that the sample mean is from μ. The probability that a sample mean will be a certain number of *actual* standard errors from μ is not the same as the probability that a sample mean will be a certain number of *estimated* standard errors from μ. The sampling distribution in this latter instance does not follow a normal distribution, but, rather, approximates a well-known theoretical distribution called the **t distribution**, given the assumptions that we discuss next. The t distribution can thus be used to determine the probability that a result would occur by chance, given a true null hypothesis.

Actually, as with the normal distribution, there is not a single t distribution but, rather, a family of t distributions. Unlike the normal distribution, the exact shape of the t distribution is influenced by the number of degrees of freedom that are associated with it, which, as we will see shortly, is related to the number of scores in the sample. Thus, there is a different t distribution for every sample size.

All t distributions are similar to the normal distribution in that they are bell-shaped and symmetrical. In addition, as is the case with a distribution of z scores, the mean of a t distribution is always 0.*

Figure 8.4 presents examples of t and normal distributions for the one-sample situation. Note that the two distributions become more similar as the sample size increases from 5 to 15 to 45. This is consistent with the fact that, in general, the normal and t distributions are similar when $N > 40$. In fact, when the sample size is theoretically infinite, the t distribution and the z distribution are identical.

FIGURE 8.4   **Comparisons of t and Normal Distributions for Sample Sizes of 5, 15, and 45**

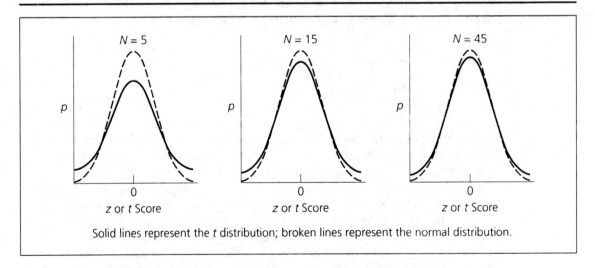

Solid lines represent the t distribution; broken lines represent the normal distribution.

---

* Technically, the mean of the t distribution is 0 only when the associated degrees of freedom are greater than 1.

When the sample size is 40 or less, the shapes of the two distributions can differ somewhat. Roughly speaking, the *t* distribution is a little "fatter" in the extreme regions (tails) and slightly "flatter" in the central region, with these differences becoming more pronounced as *N* decreases. This is clearly illustrated in Figure 8.4.

Thus, given an interval at the end of a distribution, the proportion of scores in that interval will be greater in the *t* distribution than in the normal distribution. Stated in terms of probability, this means that the probability associated with an interval of scores at the end of the distribution will be greater for the *t* distribution than for the normal distribution. The smaller the sample size, the greater this discrepancy will be, other things being equal.

The One-Sample *t* Test

The foregoing suggests the following formula for the **one-sample *t* test**:

$$t = \frac{\overline{X} - \mu}{\hat{s}_{\overline{X}}} \qquad [8.3]$$

which is the same as the formula for calculating a *z* score but with $\hat{s}_{\overline{X}}$ (the estimated standard error of the mean) substituted for $\sigma_{\overline{X}}$ (the actual standard error of the mean) in the denominator. As before, $\overline{X}$ is the observed sample mean and μ is the population mean assuming that the null hypothesis is true. A *t* score, then, is analogous to a *z* score except that it represents the number of *estimated* standard errors that a sample mean is from the hypothesized value of μ.

In fact, with the exceptions that we have already noted or that we note below, everything that we have discussed in relation to the one-sample *z* test also applies to the one-sample *t* test. Thus, for instance, as with the *z* test, a general guideline is to only use a directional *t* test if there is a compelling reason for doing so based on the existing theory and research. Issues relating to Type I and Type II errors and power are also relevant.

Applying Equation 8.3 to the example concerning attitudes toward dormitories, we find

$$t = \frac{4.51 - 4}{.19} = 2.68$$

Just as statisticians have studied the normal distribution extensively, a considerable amount of information is also known about the *t* distribution. For example, it is possible to determine the probability associated with *t* scores that exceed any specified value of *t*. This is done in a similar manner as is done with *z* scores, as we discussed in Section 4.4. This information can then be used to determine the critical values of *t* that define relevant rejection regions.

Because of the complexity of the *t* distribution, Appendix D presents a table of critical *t* values for only selected alpha levels. Instructions for using this table are also presented in Appendix D. As noted earlier, there is a different *t* distribution for every sample size. Technically, there is a different *t* distribution depending on the degrees of freedom that are associated with the *t* statistic, which, in the one-sample case that we are considering, are equal to

$$df = N - 1 \qquad [8.4]$$

As with the one-sample z test, if the observed t score exceeds either the positive or the negative critical value, we will reject the null hypothesis. If the observed t score does not exceed either the positive or the negative critical value, we will fail to reject the null hypothesis.

If the null hypothesis is rejected, we will compare the observed sample mean with the value of μ stated in the null hypothesis. If the observed sample mean is *greater* than the stated μ, we will conclude that the actual population mean is *greater* than the stated population mean. If the observed sample mean is *less* than the stated μ, we will conclude that the actual population mean is *less* than the stated population mean.

In our example, the critical values of t that define the rejection region for an alpha level of .05, nondirectional test, and $N - 1 = 100 - 1 = 99$ degrees of freedom are approximately -1.987 and $+1.987$.* Thus, any observed t score that is less than -1.987 or greater than $+1.987$ will lead us to reject the null hypothesis. The observed value of t for our problem is 2.68, and we therefore reject the null hypothesis. Given that the observed sample mean of 4.51 is greater than the hypothesized population mean of 4, we conclude that attitudes toward living in dormitories, on average, are favorable for the population of college students.

Numerical Example

The legal highway speed limit near populated areas in many parts of the United States is 55 miles per hour. To determine whether people exceed the 55-miles-per-hour limit, suppose that a state monitors the speeds of 25 cars at selected highway locations. The observed speeds are listed in Table 8.2. As can be seen, the mean of the sample is 58.00, with a standard deviation estimate of 3.34.

The population from which this sample is drawn is conceptualized as all people who drive in this particular state. Can we conclude from these data that the average speed of this population is, in fact, higher than the 55-miles-per-hour limit? We begin by specifying a null hypothesis and an alternative hypothesis:

H_0: $\mu = 55$
H_1: $\mu > 55$

The problem dictates a directional test because we are interested only in whether people drive faster, on average, than 55 miles per hour.

For an alpha level of .05, directional test, and $N - 1 = 25 - 1 = 24$ degrees of freedom, the critical t value, taken from Appendix D, is 1.711. If the observed value of t is greater than 1.711, then the null hypothesis will be rejected.

---

* Because there are no entries in Appendix D for $df = 99$, we must interpolate—that is, estimate the relevant critical values from the critical values associated with the next lowest and the next highest degrees of freedom that are listed in the t table. In the present example, the closest listed degrees of freedom below and above 99 are 60 and 120. For an alpha level of .05, nondirectional test, the respective critical values are ± 2.000 and ± 1.980, a difference of .020 unit. Because 99 is $39/60 = .65$ of the way between 60 and 120, the positive critical value for $df = 99$ can be interpolated as $2.000 - (.65)(.020) = +1.987$, thus yielding an estimated negative critical value of -1.987. The same general strategy can be applied whenever the degrees of freedom of interest are not included in a statistical table.

TABLE 8.2   **Data and Calculations for Driving Speed Study**

X	X^2
55	3,025
60	3,600
60	3,600
55	3,025
57	3,249
60	3,600
55	3,025
58	3,364
63	3,969
54	2,916
65	4,225
56	3,136
61	3,721
58	3,364
55	3,025
57	3,249
59	3,481
53	2,809
59	3,481
65	4,225
56	3,136
61	3,721
55	3,025
54	2,916
59	3,481
$\Sigma X = 1,450$	$\Sigma X^2 = 84,368$

$\overline{X} = 58.00$

$$SS = \sum X^2 - \frac{(\sum X)^2}{N}$$

$$= 84,368 - \frac{1,450^2}{25} = 268.00$$

$$\hat{s}^2 = \frac{SS}{N-1} = \frac{268.00}{25-1} = 11.17$$

$$\hat{s} = \sqrt{\hat{s}^2} = \sqrt{11.17} = 3.34$$

Because $\hat{s} = 3.34$ and $N = 25$,

$$\hat{s}_{\overline{X}} = \frac{\hat{s}}{\sqrt{N}}$$

$$= \frac{3.34}{\sqrt{25}} = .67$$

Thus,

$$t = \frac{\overline{X} - \mu}{\hat{s}_{\overline{X}}}$$

$$= \frac{58.00 - 55}{.67} = 4.48$$

Because the observed t score of 4.48 exceeds 1.711, we reject the null hypothesis and conclude that the population of people who drive in this state, on average, drive faster than the 55-miles-per-hour speed limit.

Although the statistical results are consistent with the conclusion that drivers in this particular state drive faster than 55 miles per hour, this conclusion is not definitive. Beyond the statistical analysis, one must consider the research design in order to draw an appropriate conclusion.

For example, if the speeds were measured during one day only, perhaps there was something unique about that day relative to other days that caused drivers to speed. For instance, driving speeds are affected by weather conditions such as temperature and wind currents. Or maybe the measurements were taken during a holiday period so an unusual number of out-of-state drivers were passing through the state.

Appropriate interpretation of one's data requires consideration of both the results of the statistical analysis *and* the research design that was used to collect the data. We consider this issue in detail in the next chapter.

STUDY EXERCISE 8.2

It is generally recommended that adults exercise at least twice a week for a minimum of 15 to 20 minutes. Suppose that a researcher examines whether the mean number of workouts undertaken by 35- to 40-year-olds differs from the two-workouts-a-week recommendation. The mean number of times that a random sample of 30 individuals from this age group exercises in a particular week is found to be 1.84, with a standard deviation estimate of 1.68. Test the viability of the hypothesis that $\mu = 2$ using a one-sample t test.

Answer   The null and alternative hypotheses are

H_0: $\mu = 2$

H_1: $\mu \neq 2$

For an alpha level of .05, nondirectional test, and $N - 1 = 30 - 1 = 29$ degrees of freedom, the critical values of t from Appendix D are ± 2.045. Thus, if the observed t score is less than -2.045 or greater than $+2.045$, we will reject the null hypothesis.

Because $\hat{s} = 1.68$ and $N = 30$,

$$\hat{s}_{\overline{X}} = \frac{\hat{s}}{\sqrt{N}}$$

$$= \frac{1.68}{\sqrt{30}} = .31$$

Using Equation 8.3, we compute the observed *t* value:

$$t = \frac{\overline{X} - \mu}{\hat{s}_{\overline{X}}}$$

$$= \frac{1.84 - 2}{.31} = -.52$$

Because $-.52$ does not exceed the negative critical value of -2.045, we fail to reject the null hypothesis that the mean number of workouts undertaken by the population of 35- to 40-year-olds is two per week.

Assumptions of the One-Sample *t* Test

The one-sample *t* test is appropriate when the variable being studied is quantitative in nature and measured on a level that at least approximates interval characteristics. In addition, the test is based on the following assumptions:

1. The sample is independently and randomly selected from the population of interest. In most applications, independence is achieved by ensuring that the scores on the variable are provided by different individuals.

2. The scores on the variable are normally distributed in the population. This is known as the **normality assumption.**

These assumptions are important because they assure that the sampling distribution of $(\overline{X} - \mu)/\hat{s}_{\overline{X}}$ reasonably approximates the theoretical *t* distribution. This, in turn, assures that the incidence of Type I errors will be equal to alpha and that the incidence of Type II errors will be equal to beta, as previously discussed. This has obvious implications for the accuracy of the inferences to be drawn from the test.

Although it is essential that the assumption of independent and random selection be met for the test to be valid, under some conditions the one-sample *t* test is **robust** to violations of the normality assumption. When we say that a test is *robust* to violations of a distributional assumption, we mean that the frequencies of Type I and Type II errors and, thus, the accuracy of our conclusions, are relatively unaffected compared with when the assumption is met.

As you might expect, the robustness of a test can be influenced by several factors, including the sample size (in general, robustness increases as sample size increases), the *degree* of violation (in general, robustness decreases as violations become more severe), and the *form* of the violation. In the present context, for instance, a population of scores might be positively skewed, negatively skewed, bimodal, leptokurtic, platykurtic, and so forth.

Statisticians have found that, in many instances, even marked violations of the normality assumption will not seriously affect the validity of the one-sample *t* test when the sample size is larger than about 10 (Pearson and Please, 1978). Although the test continues to be robust to various minor to moderate violations when the sample size decreases, marked violations under these circumstances can seriously affect the frequency of both Type I and Type II errors.

When a test is robust to violations of an assumption, it is appropriate to apply that test even when that assumption is violated. The difficulty lies in establishing that the test is indeed robust for the specific circumstances under study. We discuss procedures for assessing violations of distributional assumptions and their inherent problems in Chapter 9.

8.11 Confidence Intervals

Suppose that we are trying to estimate the mean intelligence test score for a population of students at a large university. We do so by selecting a random sample of 100 students and administering the test to them. Suppose the mean score for the sample is 107.00. If we wanted to estimate the actual population mean with one value, our best estimate would be 107.00. But we would also not be very confident that the actual population mean is exactly 107.00 because of sampling error.

Another approach to estimating the population mean would be to specify a range of values that we are relatively confident the population mean falls within (for example, between 100 and 110). The larger the range of values that we specify, the more confident we are that it will contain the actual population mean. Statisticians have developed a procedure for specifying such a range of values based on sampling distributions and probability theory.

The interval to be constructed is called a **confidence interval**. The values that define the boundaries of the interval are called the **confidence limits**. The degree of confidence we have that the population mean is contained within the confidence interval is stated in terms of a probability or a percentage. Researchers in the behavioral sciences most commonly use a 95% *confidence interval*.

The construction of confidence intervals differs somewhat depending on whether the standard error of the mean is known or has to be estimated from sample data. As discussed next, this disparity involves the use of $\sigma_{\bar{X}}$ and z versus $\hat{s}_{\bar{X}}$ and t in the formula for computing confidence intervals depending on whether $\sigma_{\bar{X}}$ is known or unknown.

Confidence Intervals When $\sigma_{\bar{X}}$ Is Known

Confidence intervals are conceptualized with respect to sampling distributions. In the intelligence test example, the relevant sampling distribution is the sampling distribution of the mean for samples of size 100. The central limit theorem tells us that this distribution will be approximately normally distributed. When $\sigma_{\bar{X}}$ is known, we can invoke our knowledge of the area under the normal curve to determine the desired confidence interval. To illustrate the procedure, we continue with the intelligence test example.

Suppose that $\sigma_{\bar{X}}$ is known to equal 2.00. Given that the sampling distribution is approximately normal in shape, we know that 68.26% of all sample means based on $N = 100$ will fall between standard error below μ and one standard error above μ or, in terms of raw score units, between $(1.00)(\sigma_{\bar{X}}) = (1.00)(2.00) = 2.00$ units below μ and 2.00 units above μ. Similarly, we know that 95% of all scores in a normal distribution fall between -1.96 and $+1.96$ standard deviations (in the case of a sampling distribution of the mean, standard errors) from the mean. Thus, 95% of all sample means based on $N = 100$ will fall between $(-1.96)(\sigma_{\bar{X}}) = (-1.96)(2.00) = -3.92$ and $(1.96)(\sigma_{\bar{X}}) = (1.96)(2.00) = 3.92$ raw score units of μ.

In practice, we will not know the value of μ, and, in fact, μ is what we are trying to estimate based on data from our sample. Consequently, confidence intervals are calculated around the observed sample mean, $\overline{X}$, rather than μ. Establishing confidence intervals around $\overline{X}$ as opposed to μ makes sense when it is remembered that in the absence of additional information, $\overline{X}$ is one's "best guess" of the value of μ.

The observed sample mean in our example is 107.00, so the 95% confidence limits are

$$107.00 - (1.96)(2.00) = 107.00 - 3.92 = 103.08$$

and

$$107.00 - (1.96)(2.00) = 107.00 + 3.92 = 110.92$$

The range of 103.08 to 110.92 constitutes the confidence interval.

The preceding calculations reflect the general formula

$$CI = \overline{X} - (z)(\sigma_{\overline{X}}) \quad \text{to} \quad \overline{X} + (z)(\sigma_{\overline{X}}) \qquad [8.5]$$

where *CI* represents the confidence interval, $\overline{X} - (z)(\sigma_{\overline{X}})$ is the *lower confidence limit*, $\overline{X} + (z)(\sigma_{\overline{X}})$ is the *upper confidence limit*, and z is the positive value of z corresponding to 1.00 minus the confidence level. When using Appendix B to find the relevant z value, one should always refer to the nondirectional column (column 4) because the goal is to establish equivalent ranges below and above $\overline{X}$. In our example, we are concerned with the 95% confidence interval, so 1.00 minus the confidence level is $1.00 - .95 = .05$, and the appropriate value of z is thus 1.96.

The use of a single sample mean in the construction of a confidence interval raises an important interpretational issue. Suppose that we draw all possible random samples of size N from a population and for each sample mean we compute the 95% confidence interval using Equation 8.5. We would find that 95% of these confidence intervals would contain the value of μ and 5% of the confidence intervals would not. *A confidence claim reflects the long-term performance of an extended number of confidence intervals across all possible random samples of a given size.*

In practice, only one confidence interval is constructed and that one interval either contains the population mean or does not contain the population mean. We never know for sure whether a particular confidence interval contains μ. However, the percentage associated with the confidence interval (for example, 95%) gives us an appreciation of the degree of confidence we can have that the interval contains μ.

Sometimes investigators construct 99% confidence intervals (in which case $z = 2.575$) rather than 95% confidence intervals. The selection of a confidence level should depend on how important it is not to have a "false" interval (that is, one that does not contain μ). The lower the confidence level (for example, 80% as opposed to 95%), the more likely it is that false intervals will be observed. On the other hand, other things being equal, the higher the degree of confidence (for example, 99% as opposed to 95%), the wider the confidence interval will be and the more likely it is that the interval will contain μ. The problem with wide confidence intervals is that as the width of the confidence interval increases, the larger is the range of values that might contain μ.

At some point, the range of the confidence interval becomes so large that the utility of the confidence interval is diminished. In our intelligence example, the 95% interval is 103.08 to 110.92, whereas the 99% interval is

$$CI = \overline{X} - (z)(\sigma_{\overline{X}}) \quad \text{to} \quad \overline{X} + (z)(\sigma_{\overline{X}})$$
$$= 107.00 - (2.575)(2.00) \quad \text{to} \quad 107.00 + (2.575)(2.00)$$
$$= 101.85 \quad \text{to} \quad 112.15$$

Because the width of a confidence interval is influenced by $\sigma_{\overline{X}}$ in addition to the confidence level, it follows that the population standard deviation, σ, and the sample size will also affect how wide the interval is. As σ becomes larger, so does $\sigma_{\overline{X}}$, so the width of the confidence interval increases, other things being equal. As the sample size becomes larger, $\sigma_{\overline{X}}$ becomes smaller, so the width of the confidence interval decreases, other things being equal.

Confidence Intervals When $\sigma_{\overline{X}}$ Is Unknown

The formula for confidence intervals when $\sigma_{\overline{X}}$ is unknown is the same as when $\sigma_{\overline{X}}$ is known except that the t distribution is used in place of the z distribution and $\hat{s}_{\overline{X}}$ is used in place of $\sigma_{\overline{X}}$. Thus, this formula is

$$CI = \overline{X} - (t)(\hat{s}_{\overline{X}}) \quad \text{to} \quad \overline{X} + (t)(\hat{s}_{\overline{X}}) \qquad [8.6]$$

where t is the positive nondirectional value of t corresponding to 1.00 minus the confidence level and all other terms are as previously defined. When determining the t value to be used in Equation 8.6, the appropriate degrees of freedom are, as usual, $N - 1$.

For the driving speed example presented in Section 8.10, where $N = 25$, $\overline{X} = 58.00$, and $\hat{s}_{\overline{X}} = .67$, the relevant value of t is 2.064 and the 95% confidence interval is

$$CI = 58.00 - (2.064)(.67) \quad \text{to} \quad 58.00 + (2.064)(.67)$$
$$= 56.62 \quad \text{to} \quad 59.38$$

We have a relatively high level of confidence (95%) that the true value of the population mean falls within the range 56.62 to 59.38.

Confidence Intervals and Hypothesis Testing

Confidence intervals bear an important relationship to hypothesis testing: Any null hypothesis that specifies a value of a population mean that falls outside of the corresponding confidence interval will be rejected at the relevant level of alpha, whereas any null hypothesis that specifies a population mean that falls within the interval will not be rejected. Because of this property, confidence intervals provide the researcher with more information than the formal hypothesis testing procedures that we discussed earlier. Specifically, a confidence interval indicates all null hypotheses that would or would not be rejected with a nondirectional test.

For instance, suppose that the following null hypothesis is tested for $N = 18$, $\overline{X} = 110.00$, and $\hat{s}_{\overline{X}} = 2.00$ at an alpha level of .05, nondirectional test:

$$H_0: \mu = 100$$

The observed value of t based on this information is

$$t = \frac{110.00 - 100}{2.00} = 5.00$$

Because this value exceeds the positive critical value of $+2.110$, the appropriate decision in this instance is to reject the null hypothesis.

Applying Equation 8.6, we find that the 95% confidence interval for the mean is

$$CI = 110.00 - (2.110)(2.00) \quad \text{to} \quad 110.00 + (2.110)(2.00)$$
$$= 105.78 \quad \text{to} \quad 114.22$$

Note that the value of μ stated in the null hypothesis (100) is not contained within this interval. Thus, consistent with the decision that we made on the basis of the one-sample t test, this confidence interval leads us to reject the null hypothesis. Similarly, any other null hypothesis that specifies a population mean outside of the range 105.78 to 114.22 will also be rejected, whereas any null hypothesis that specifies a population mean in this range will not be rejected.

Given the wealth of information that they communicate, it is not surprising that some behavioral scientists have advocated reporting confidence intervals rather than the results of formal tests about specific values of μ when providing statistical results. Nevertheless, the large majority of research reports that you will encounter use the formal hypothesis testing procedures presented earlier rather than the present strategy, which is formally known as **interval estimation**. Sometimes these reports provide both hypothesis testing results and confidence interval information.

Before concluding our discussion of confidence intervals, we should note that confidence intervals can be constructed for many parameters other than the mean. We discuss the calculation of such intervals for selected statistical tests in later chapters.

STUDY EXERCISE 8.3

An investigator administered a reading test to a sample of 30 students and found a mean of 83.00 with a standard deviation estimate of 17.35. Calculate the 95% and 99% confidence intervals.

Answer   Because the population standard deviation is unknown, the standard error of the mean must be estimated using Equation 7.5:

$$\hat{s}_{\bar{X}} = \frac{\hat{s}}{\sqrt{N}} = \frac{17.35}{\sqrt{30}} = 3.17$$

Because there are $30 - 1 = 29$ degrees of freedom, the t value used in determining the 95% confidence interval in this case is 2.045. Applying Equation 8.6, we find that the 95% confidence interval is

$$CI = \bar{X} - (t)(\hat{s}_{\bar{X}}) \quad \text{to} \quad \bar{X} + (t)(\hat{s}_{\bar{X}})$$
$$= 83.00 - (2.045)(3.17) \quad \text{to} \quad 83.00 + (2.045)(3.17)$$
$$= 76.52 \quad \text{to} \quad 89.48$$

The *t* value used in determining the 99% confidence interval is 2.756, so the 99% confidence interval is

$$CI = 83.00 - (2.756)(3.17) \quad \text{to} \quad (83.00 + (2.756)(3.17)$$

$$= 74.26 \quad \text{to} \quad 91.94$$

8.12   Method of Presentation

The *Publication Manual of the American Psychological Association* (APA) (American Psychological Association, 2001) states that when presenting the results of a statistical test, "include information about the obtained magnitude or value of the test statistic, the degrees of freedom, the probability of obtaining a value as extreme or more extreme than the one obtained, and the direction of the effect. Be sure to include sufficient descriptive statistics (e.g., per-cell sample sizes, means, correlations, standard deviations) so that the nature of the effect being reported can be understood by the reader" (p. 22). In addition, the alpha level that was used should be explicitly stated either in a general statement or when providing the results of individual tests.

We illustrate the typical method of presentation that you will encounter for the one-sample *t* test by focusing on the driving speed example that we discussed in Section 8.10. The results for this problem might be reported as follows:

Results

A one-sample *t* test using an alpha level of .05 compared the sample mean with the 55-miles-per-hour speed limit. The sample mean of 58.00(*SD* = 3.34) was found to be statistically significantly different from this value, *t*(24) = 4.48, *p* < .01, one-tailed, suggesting that the mean driving speed in the state is greater than 55 miles per hour. The 95% confidence interval for the mean was 56.62 to 59.38.

The heading "Results" identifies this as a Results section. Other sections of a research report are typically headed "Method" and "Discussion." A fourth main section, the introduction, is not formally labeled because it always appears at the beginning of a research article.

The first sentence states the type of test that was conducted, the alpha level that was used, and the value of µ specified in the null hypothesis. As discussed earlier in this chapter, alpha is typically set equal to .05 by convention. If a different value of alpha is used, justification for this should be provided in the report.

It should be noted that the null and alternative hypotheses are not formally written out when reporting the results of a statistical test. This is because the hypothesis testing steps discussed earlier in this chapter are implied whenever a statistical test is reported, so writing out each step would be a poor use of journal space.

The second sentence begins by specifying the values of the sample mean and the standard deviation estimate (symbolized as *SD*, per Section 3.10) and then presents selected aspects of the statistical analysis, per APA (2001) requirements. The symbol *t* indicates that a *t* test was performed. This is followed, in parentheses, by the degrees of freedom associated with the relevant t distribution. Next comes the observed value of t based on Equation 8.3. The statement "$p < .01$" indicates that the probability of obtaining a t score as extreme as the one observed in the study, assuming that the null hypothesis is true, is less than .01. The terminology *one-tailed* is used to indicate that a directional test was used. If this is not explicitly stated, a nondirectional test is assumed.

The value associated with p is referred to as a **significance level**. The p value is also commonly called a *probability level*. A significance level is distinct from the alpha level. An alpha level reflects the researcher's decision about how extreme the results of a statistical test should be before the null hypothesis is rejected, whereas a significance level represents the probability of obtaining a result as extreme as the one that was observed, given a true null hypothesis. Thus, it is not possible to determine a significance level until the sample mean has been converted to a t score.

In the present example, the observed t score of 4.48 not only exceeds the critical value of 1.711 that defines the (directional) .05 rejection region, but it also exceeds the critical values of 2.064 and 2.492 that define the .025 and .01 rejection regions, respectively, as can be seen in Appendix D. In fact, the observed t score of 4.48 also exceeds the critical values (2.797 and 3.745, respectively) that define the .005 and the .0005 rejection regions. However, APA style dictates that significance levels should generally be reported to two decimal places, with "the lowest reported significance probability being $p < .01$" (American Psychological Association, 2001, p. 129). The significance level in this instance is thus reported as being less than .01.

The advantage of reporting significance levels is that readers might have different ideas about where alpha should be set, and if the probability associated with the observed result is specified, readers can immediately determine whether the null hypothesis would have been rejected had a different alpha level been adopted.

Most statistical computer programs provide the exact significance level associated with a statistical result. It is becoming increasingly common to report this exact value in Results sections. For instance, if the probability associated with a particular test result is .037, this can be presented as $p = .037$ rather than $p < .05$. A p value of less than .05 indicates that the null hypothesis should be rejected at a .05 alpha level.

A Results section takes the same general form when the null hypothesis is not rejected as when it is. As before, the alpha level, the observed sample mean, the standard deviation estimate, the degrees of freedom, and the observed t score are reported. However, the statement of the significance level identifies the largest probability value from Appendix D that is exceeded by the test result (for example, $p > .10$). Alternatively, the exact probability associated with the statistical result can be reported (for example, $p = .16$). A p value of .05 or greater indicates that the null hypothesis cannot be rejected at a .05 alpha level.

The third sentence reports the 95% confidence interval for the mean to provide the reader with a sense of the sampling error. Of course, if a different confidence level is used, the confidence interval should be adjusted accordingly. The *Publication Manual of the American Psychological Association* (2001) emphasizes the importance of reporting confidence intervals and, in fact, refers to them as "the best reporting strategy" (p. 22) for communicating statistical results in situations where they are relevant.

8.13 Examples from the Literature

Accuracy of Subjective Life Expectancies

A *subjective life expectancy* is an individual's estimate of what age he or she expects to live to. One interesting question is how subjective life expectancies compare with actual life expectancies as represented by actuarial predictions. In a study of this issue, Robbins (1988) asked 49 female and 27 male college students to indicate their expected age in response to this question: Approximately how long do you expect to live? These estimates were then compared with actuarial predictions from the National Center for Health Statistics. Results showed that the mean subjective life expectancy for women (77.2 years) did not significantly differ from the actuarial prediction of 79.2 years, $t(48) = -.85$, $p > .20$. The mean subjective life expectancy of 77.6 years for men, on the other hand, was significantly greater than the actuarial prediction of 72.4 years, $t(26) = 2.49$, $p < .02$, thus indicating that men tend to overestimate their life spans.

Validation of a Priming Procedure

According to a cognitive principle known as the *availability heuristic,* the more readily instances of a class of objects come to mind, the larger that class of objects is judged to be. For instance, it has been found that people estimate that more words begin with the letter K than have K in the third position when, in actuality, the reverse is true. This bias presumably results from the fact that it is easier to think of words that start with K than words that have K as the third letter.

One factor that has been hypothesized to influence the ease with which instances of a class of objects come to mind and subsequent frequency judgments is the recency with which that class has been cognitively activated, or *primed*, through prior exposure; the more recent the exposure, the more available that information should be in memory and the greater the estimate of the class size should be. According to this perspective, this should be true even if the prior exposure occurs on an unconscious, or *subliminal*, level.

In a test of this proposition, Gabrielcik and Fazio (1984) asked 15 college students to judge the frequency with which the letter T appears in the English language. Participants had previously been assigned to conditions where they were either subliminally exposed to a series of 40 words containing the letter T (the *primed* condition) or subliminally exposed to strings of asterisks (the control condition). If priming has the predicted effect on frequency judgments, students in the primed condition should estimate the letter T to be more common than should students in the control condition.

Crucial to this experiment was the establishment that the presentation of the 40 T words was indeed subliminal. This was accomplished in a preliminary study by asking eight undergraduate students to view a series of 40 words flashed before them for 1/500 second each. Unbeknownst to the students, each of these words contained one or more Ts. After each presentation, students were given a slip of paper that contained four words. They were instructed to circle the word they had just viewed and to make a guess if uncertain. If the presentation of the words was indeed subliminal, students' responses to the recognition test should have been no better than chance. For a 40-item test with four response options, a chance result is $(40)(.25) = 10.00$ correct responses.

The students' actual mean of 9.13 correct responses was compared with this value using a one-sample t test. This test was found to be statistically nonsignificant, $t(7) < 1$ (the specific value of t was not reported), $p > .20$, thus suggesting that word exposure of $1/500$ second might be sufficiently short to be subliminal. With this established, Gabrielcik and Fazio were able to proceed with the main experiment. Consistent with their hypothesis, participants who were primed with the subliminal T words estimated the letter T to appear significantly more frequently than did the control participants.

8.14 Links Between Computer Results and Book Content

As we noted in Section 8.12, most statistical computer programs provide the exact significance level associated with a statistical result. The default for most programs is to report nondirectional p values unless a directional test is explicitly specified. However, it is easy to generate directional significance levels from nondirectional p values, and vice versa: To determine the directional significance level, merely halve the p value that is provided for a nondirectional result. To determine the nondirectional significance level, merely double the p value that is provided for a directional result.

It is not uncommon to see p values that appear as all zeroes. This does not mean that the probability associated with a result is actually 0. Rather, it is a reflection of rounding error. For example, a p value of .000 indicates that the actual p value is .0005 or less and that the computer rounded to three decimal places.

Researchers often conduct a large number of analyses at once. In fact, it is not uncommon for a study to produce dozens of pages of statistical output. When this is the case, it is very tedious to have to examine the p value for each test to identify which results are statistically significant. However, many statistical programs use asterisks or some other method to delineate any test value that has a low significance level. For instance, one asterisk might indicate that a result is statistically significant at an alpha level of .05 and two asterisks might indicate that a result is statistically significant at an alpha level of .01. This format makes it easy for the researcher to differentiate statistically significant from statistically nonsignificant findings. We find it helpful to circle or highlight the statistically significant results to further emphasize them.

8.15 Links Between Chapters

In practice, one-sample tests are seldom used in the behavioral sciences because researchers are generally more interested in studying the relationship between two (or more) variables then they are in single means. The analysis of relationships between variables is, in fact, the focus of the rest of this book. However, because it is the simplest type of mean-based inferential test, the one-sample z test allows us to introduce many important concepts that are much more difficult to demonstrate with more complex procedures.

We will see in later chapters that just as many of the points that we made in relation to the one-sample z test also apply to the one-sample t test, many of the things that we discussed in the context of the one-sample t test also apply to other statistical procedures. In fact, we can conceptualize the one-sample t test as a special case of the equation

$$t = \frac{\text{score of interest} - \text{hypothesized mean of the distribution}}{\text{estimated standard error of the distribution}}$$ [8.7]

in much the same way as the one-sample z test can be viewed as a special case of Equation 8.2, as we saw in Section 8.2. We discuss two other applications of Equation 8.7 in Chapters 10 and 11 when we consider the independent groups and the correlated groups t tests.

Applications to the Analysis of a Social Problem Using SPSS for Windows

There is no conceptual question of interest for the parent–teen communication study described in Chapter 1 that relates to the one-sample z test or the one-sample t test. However, we can use data from that study to demonstrate the application of confidence intervals.

In Chapter 7, we calculated two means that are of practical interest: the mean age at which mothers think parents should talk with children about sex and the mean age at which mothers think parents should talk with children about birth control. We found the former to be 10.46 and the latter to be 12.09. We can form 95% confidence intervals for these means.

Table 8.3 presents the computer output for these intervals along with that for various measures of central tendency and variability. As indicated by the label "95% Confidence Interval for Mean," the lower and upper confidence limits for the mean age to talk about sex (AGESEX) are 10.25 and 10.67, respectively. The lower and upper confidence limits for the mean age to talk about birth control (AGEBC) are 11.92 and 12.26, respectively. The confidence intervals are relatively narrow, which implies that there is little sampling error.

TABLE 8.3   Computer Output for Confidence Intervals for Ages to Talk About Sex and Birth Control

			Statistic	Std. Error
AGESEX	Mean		10.46	.11
	95% Confidence	Lower Bound	10.25	
	Interval for Mean	Upper Bound	10.67	
	N		705	
	Median		10.00	
	Variance		8.00	
	Std Deviation		2.83	
	Minimum		4	
	Maximum		19	
	Range		15	
	Interquartile Range		3.00	

TABLE 8.3   **(Continued)**

			Statistic	Std. Error
AGEBC	Mean		12.09	.09
	95% Confidence	Lower Bound	11.92	
	Interval for Mean	Upper Bound	12.26	
	N		716	
	Median		12.00	
	Variance		5.26	
	Std. Deviation		2.29	
	Minimum		4	
	Maximum		20	
	Range		16	
	Interquartile Range		3.00	

Summary

In this chapter, we considered the basic logic underlying hypothesis testing. In doing so, we introduced two statistical tests for assessing whether or not a population mean differs from some hypothesized value. The one-sample z test is used when the standard error of the mean is known, whereas the one-sample t test is used when the standard error of the mean must be estimated. Both tests require that the variable under study be quantitative in nature and measured on a level that at least approximates interval characteristics.

The logic of hypothesis testing begins with specifying a null hypothesis (a hypothesis that we assume to be true for the purpose of conducting the statistical test) and an alternative hypothesis. The alternative hypothesis can be either directional or nondirectional, depending on the nature of the question being asked, although a general guideline is to only use a directional test if there is a compelling reason for doing so based on the existing theory and research. Next, an alpha level, usually .05, is specified and, based on this (and, in the case of the t test, the degrees of freedom), a rejection region is defined. The data are then analyzed by converting the observed sample mean to a z or t score, as appropriate. If a nondirectional test is used, the observed z or t score is compared with the positive *and* negative critical values that define the nondirectional rejection region, and a conclusion is drawn. If a directional test is used, the observed z or t score is compared with the positive *or* negative critical value, as appropriate, that defines the directional rejection region instead. Based on this comparison, we either reject or we fail to reject the null hypothesis. The null hypothesis can never be accepted.

The nature of hypothesis testing is such that errors will sometimes occur. One type of error that we will sometimes make is to reject the null hypothesis when it is true. This is referred to as a Type I error. The probability of a Type I error is equal to the alpha level. Second, we will sometimes fail to reject the null hypothesis when it is false. This is referred to as a Type II error. The probability of making a Type I error is indicated by alpha (α), and the probability of making a Type II error is indicated by beta (β). The probability that an investigator will reject the null hypothesis when it is false is called the power of the test and is indicated by $1 - \beta$.

The alpha level directly affects the power of a statistical test (and, hence, the probability of making a Type II error), with more conservative alpha levels yielding less powerful tests, everything else being equal. Thus, the power of a statistical test can be increased by selecting a higher alpha level, as well as by selecting a larger sample size. Increasing the alpha level must be evaluated relative to the importance of making a Type I versus a Type II error. In addition, selecting a larger sample size must be evaluated relative to the increased costs of obtaining more research participants.

Confidence intervals can be used to specify a range of values that has a high probability of containing the actual population mean. When the standard error of the mean is known, confidence intervals for the mean can be determined from our knowledge of the area under the normal curve. When the standard error of the mean is estimated from sample data, the t distribution is used instead.

Exercises

Answers to asterisked (*) exercises appear at the back of the book.

Exercises to Review Concepts

1. Define each of the following:
   a. null hypothesis
   b. alternative hypothesis
   c. critical values
   d. rejection region
   e. test statistic
   f. alpha level

*2. Why is it necessary to assume the null hypothesis is true in the context of hypothesis testing?

3. Summarize the five steps involved in hypothesis testing for the one-sample z test.

*4. An economist is interested in whether high school students in a certain geographic area save more or less than $100 per month toward their college education. Translate this question into a null hypothesis and an alternative hypothesis.

*5. Given $H_0: \mu = 4$, $H_1: \mu \neq 4$, $\overline{X} = 7.31$, $\sigma = 14.78$, and $N = 64$, calculate the observed value of z.

*6. Test the viability of the null hypothesis for the problem in Exercise 5, and draw a conclusion about the actual value of μ.

7. Given $H_0: \mu = 10$, $H_1: \mu \neq 10$, $\overline{X} = 3.80$, $\sigma = 2.77$, and $N = 81$, calculate the observed value of z.

8. Test the viability of the null hypothesis for the problem in Exercise 7, and draw a conclusion about the actual value of μ.

*9. Why can we never accept the null hypothesis as being true based on statistical tests?

10. Define each of the following:
    a. Type I error   d. beta
    b. Type II error   e. power
    c. alpha

*11. What is the relationship between alpha and the probability of a Type I error? What is the reason for this relationship?

*12. What is the relationship between power and the probability of a Type II error? What is the reason for this relationship?

*13. What is the relationship between alpha and power? What is the reason for this relationship?

14. What effect does sample size have on the power of a statistical test?

*15. Why is it important to use the terms *statistically significant* and *statistically nonsignificant* rather than the terms *significant* and *nonsignificant* when discussing the results of a statistical test?

16. Under what circumstance should a directional rather than a nondirectional test be

used? Why? Under what circumstance should a nondirectional rather than a directional test be used? Why?

17. When is the t distribution used instead of the normal distribution to test hypotheses about population means?

*18. State the critical value(s) of t for a one-sample t test for an alpha level of .05 under each of the following conditions:

a. $H_0: \mu = 3$, $H_1: \mu \neq 3$, $N = 20$
b. $H_0: \mu = 3$, $H_1: \mu > 3$, $N = 20$
c. $H_0: \mu = 3$, $H_1: \mu < 3$, $N = 20$
d. $H_0: \mu = 3$, $H_1: \mu \neq 3$, $N = 10$
e. $H_0: \mu = 3$, $H_1: \mu > 3$, $N = 10$
f. $H_0: \mu = 3$, $H_1: \mu < 3$, $N = 10$

*19. Test the viability of the hypothesis that $\mu = 100$ using a nondirectional one-sample t test under each of the following conditions:

a. $\overline{X} = 101.00$, $\hat{s} = 10.00$, $N = 10,000$
b. $\overline{X} = 101.00$, $\hat{s} = 10.00$, $N = 100$
c. $\overline{X} = 101.00$, $\hat{s} = 2.00$, $N = 100$

In each of these cases, the difference between the sample mean ($\overline{X} = 101.00$) and the hypothesized population mean ($\mu = 100$) is the same. Why is the result in part (a) different than the result in part (b)? Why is the result in part (c) different than the result in part (b)?

20. A researcher administered a measure of life satisfaction to a sample of 30 individuals and found a mean of 121.00 with a standard deviation estimate of 10.77. Test the viability of the hypothesis that the actual population mean equals 110 using a nondirectional one-sample t test.

21. What are the assumptions underlying the one-sample t test? Why are these assumptions important?

22. What is a confidence interval?

*23. A researcher administered a test of mathematical ability to a sample of 169 students. The mean of the sample was 74.40. The standard deviation for the population, σ, was known to be 13.00. Compute the 95% and 99% confidence intervals.

*24. Assuming the sample size for Exercise 23 was 200 instead of 169, compute the 95% and

99% confidence intervals. What is the effect of increasing N on the width of the intervals?

25. Assuming the population standard deviation for Exercise 23 was 7.00 instead of 13.00, compute the 95% and 99% confidence intervals. What is the effect of decreasing σ on the width of the intervals?

*26. Compute the 95% and 99% confidence intervals for the problem in Exercise 20.

27. Explain the relationship between interval estimation and formal hypothesis testing procedures.

28. What is a significance level? How does it differ from the alpha level?

Multiple-Choice Questions

29. Directional tests are also called two-tailed tests.
a. true
b. false

*30. The alpha level is traditionally set equal to ____ in behavioral science research.
a. .001
b. .01
c. .05
d. .10

*31. Statistical power is the probability of
a. making a Type I error
b. making a Type II error
c. correctly rejecting the null hypothesis
d. none of the above

32. Beta (β) is the probability of
a. making a Type I error
b. making a Type II error
c. correctly rejecting the null hypothesis
d. none of the above

*33. Alpha (α) is the probability of
a. making a Type I error
b. making a Type II error
c. correctly rejecting the null hypothesis
d. none of the above

34. A statistically significant result for a statistical test means that
a. the null hypothesis was not rejected
b. the null hypothesis was rejected
c. a Type I error was made
d. the result has important practical implications

35. The alpha level and the p value represent the same information.
    a. true
    b. false

*36. What is meant by $p < .01$?
    a. The probability of obtaining a statistical result as extreme as the one that was observed, given a true null hypothesis, is less than 1%.
    b. The probability of obtaining a statistical result as extreme as the one that was observed, given a true null hypothesis, is greater than 1%.
    c. Alpha was set equal to .01.
    d. Alpha was set at less than .01.

*37. Which of the following statements regarding confidence intervals is *not* true?
    a. The boundaries of confidence intervals are known as confidence limits.
    b. Any null hypothesis that specifies a population mean outside of the confidence interval will be rejected at a specified level of alpha.
    c. 95% of all 95% confidence intervals will contain the actual population mean.
    d. The greater the probability that a confidence interval contains the actual population mean, the narrower the confidence interval will be.

38. If $N = 26$, $\overline{X} = 16.00$, and $\hat{s}_{\overline{X}} = 1.00$, what is the 95% confidence interval?
    a. 13.94 to 18.06
    b. 14.04 to 17.96
    c. 14.29 to 17.71
    d. 15.60 to 16.40

*39. What are the degrees of freedom for a one-sample t test?
    a. $N + 1$
    b. $N/2$
    c. $N - 1$
    d. $N - 2$

40. When the sample size is greater than 40, the normal and t distributions are quite similar to one another.
    a. true   b. false

*41. When a statistical test is robust to violations of an assumption, it can be appropriately applied even when that assumption is violated.
    a. true
    b. false

42. The one-sample t test tends to be robust to violations of the normality assumption when the sample size is larger than about 10.
    a. true
    b. false

Exercises to Apply Concepts

*43. The overall reproduction rate in the United States is currently below the zero population growth rate of 2.11. That is, if couples have an average of 2.11 children, the size of the population will remain stable. However, substantial variability exists across subgroups in the average number of children that there are in families, and an important task is to identify and educate groups that exceed the 2.11 children average.

Suppose that a researcher who is interested in whether Catholics in the United States are having children at a rate consistent with zero population growth obtains the following data for the numbers of children in a sample of Catholic families. Test the viability of the hypothesis that Catholics are reproducing at a zero population growth rate using a nondirectional one-sample t test, draw a conclusion, and report your results using the principles developed in the Method of Presentation section.

Number of children				
4	6	2	1	2
5	3	4	3	1
2	3	0	4	8
3	2	3	5	2
4	2	3	0	2

44. It is commonly believed by laypersons that marijuana affects human physiological processes. One of the more common beliefs is that smoking marijuana makes one hungry (gives one the "munchies"). Although the precise physiological mechanism that causes hunger is not well understood by psychologists, one factor that is often associated with hunger is blood sugar level. Several theorists have suggested that this mechanism may be the cause of marijuana-induced hunger.

    Weil, Zinberg, and Nelson (1968) examined this issue empirically. Ten 21- to 26-year-old men who smoked tobacco cigarettes regularly but who had never tried marijuana participated in the study. Each received a large dose of marijuana by smoking a potent marijuana cigarette. The level of blood sugar was measured for each man before he smoked marijuana and again 15 minutes after he smoked marijuana. A "change score" was then computed for each man by subtracting the amount of sugar in the blood after smoking marijuana from the amount of sugar in the blood before smoking marijuana.

    Hypothetical data (measured in mg/100 ml) representative of the results of the study are presented in the table. If marijuana has no effect on blood sugar level, the mean change score in the population would be 0. Test the viability of the hypothesis that marijuana has no effect on blood sugar level using a nondirectional one-sample t test, draw a conclusion, and report your results using the principles developed in the Method of Presentation section.

Blood sugar change (before − after)	
14	−2
−2	−6
6	−2
−2	−18
−2	−6

45. One method that researchers use to determine the accuracy with which people perceive the passage of time is *verbal estimation*. With this technique, research participants are asked to estimate how much time has passed during a given time interval. If people accurately perceive the passage of time, the mean time estimate in the population will equal the amount that has actually passed.

    Hypothetical data representative of the estimation of 12 seconds are presented in the table. Test the viability of the hypothesis that people accurately estimate the passage of time using a nondirectional one-sample t test, draw a conclusion, and report your results using the principles developed in the Method of Presentation section.

Estimated times			
12	13	12	16
13	16	11	14
10	16	15	12
15	14	13	14

46. A sports psychologist designed a program to improve the batting averages of major league baseball players. The basis of this program is positive imagery, whereby a player imagines that he can clearly see the rotation of the ball as it approaches home plate and that he displays perfect batting form as he swings at it and gets a clean hit. However, the psychologist also recognized that this technique might encourage some players to "overthink" and thereby decrease their averages.

    Suppose that the following changes in batting averages occurred from one season to the next for players who used the positive imagery program. Test the viability of the hypothesis that positive imagery has no effect on players' batting averages using a nondirectional one-sample t test, draw a conclusion, and report your results using the principles developed in the Method of Presentation section.

Batting average change			
.037	.067	.034	.016
.024	−.019	.045	−.003
.012	.020	.007	.010
−.023	−.006	.028	.022
.011			

PART **2**

THE ANALYSIS OF BIVARIATE RELATIONSHIPS

CHAPTER **9**

Principles of Research Design and Statistical Preliminaries for Analyzing Bivariate Relationships

Part 2 of this book focuses on the analysis of relationships between two variables, or **bivariate relationships**. In this chapter, we review some general issues of research design and test selection. In Chapters 10 to 16, we discuss specific statistical techniques used in the bivariate case. We make extensive use throughout of the basic statistical concepts from Part 1.

The results of a statistical analysis must be interpreted in the context of the research design that is used to generate the data. In order to facilitate an understanding of the use of statistics in interpreting research, we begin by reviewing the general principles that guide research design. As noted in Chapter 1, statistics and research design are highly interwoven, and a consideration of design principles will lead to a better understanding of the statistics considered in later chapters.

9.1 Two Strategies of Research

When studying the relationship between two variables, the researcher is essentially interested in determining how the values of one variable are associated with the values of another variable. For instance, if an investigator studied the relationship between gender and mathematical ability, the concern would be with whether the two values (male and female) for the variable of gender are associated with different values for the variable of mathematical ability (that is, whether men have either more or, alternatively, less mathematical ability than women).

The Experimental Strategy

Behavioral scientists use two general strategies for assessing the relationship between variables. First, they may use an **experimental strategy** whereby a set of manipulations is performed to *create* different values of the independent variable for the research participants. The relationship of the different values of the independent variable to the dependent variable is then examined.

For example, a researcher interested in the affect of test anxiety (the independent variable) on test performance (the dependent variable) might create three different values for test anxiety by telling one-third of the research participants that their performance on a test is very important and will reveal many aspects of their personal competencies (thus creating high test anxiety), telling another third that the test is unimportant and will not reflect on them personally (thus creating low test anxiety), and not addressing the issue of the test's importance with the final third. In this instance, test anxiety has three values, or *levels,* and each research participant can be distinguished in terms of what value describes him or her.

Notice that in this example, the third group of participants was not actually exposed to the independent variable. A group of this type is formally known as a **control group**. The advantage of including a control group when utilizing an experimental strategy is that it provides a *baseline* for evaluating the effect of the experimental manipulation.

Suppose, for instance, that participants in the high test anxiety condition obtain higher test scores than participants in the low test anxiety condition. If a control group were not incorporated into the design, we would be unable to determine whether this was due primarily to high test anxiety *increasing* scores on the dependent variable, low test anxiety *decreasing* scores on the dependent variable, or some combination of the two. However, by including a control group, we can compare the dependent variable scores of each experimental group with those that occur in the absence of the manipulation and thus determine the extent to which each value of the independent variable influences performance on the behavior of interest.

The Observational Strategy

In contrast to an experimental strategy, an **observational strategy** (also called a *nonexperimental strategy*) does not involve creating values on an independent variable but, rather, involves measuring differences in values that naturally exist in the research participants. For instance, a person's gender might be measured based on his or her response to the question "What is your gender?" In this instance, the researcher is not using a set of manipulations to create values of a variable but, rather, is measuring the values that naturally exist.

Experimental and observational strategies are often used concurrently. For example, a study might investigate the effects of a person's gender *and* test anxiety on test performance. Gender would be indexed by an observational strategy and test anxiety could be indexed by the manipulations noted above.

A dependent variable is always measured in the "observational" sense. This is because we are trying to determine how the dependent measure varies with the manipulation of the independent variable or with the naturally existing values of the independent variable. In this context, it is important to note that many of the statistical techniques that we discuss in subsequent chapters are applicable to both experimental and observational situations.

STUDY EXERCISE 9.1

For each of the following studies, identify the independent variable and indicate whether an experimental or an observational research strategy is involved.

Study I

A researcher studied the relationship between television viewing and aggressive behavior in children. Fifty children were identified as characteristically watching television less than 5 hours per week (low viewers), 50 children were identified as characteristically watching television between 5 and 10 hours per week (moderate viewers), and 50 children were identified as characteristically watching television more than 10 hours per week (high viewers). For each child, a measure of aggressiveness was determined by interviewing the child's teacher and classmates. The children were subsequently rated as being low in aggressiveness, moderate in aggressiveness, or high in aggressiveness, and these ratings were compared for the three television-viewing groups.

Answer The independent variable is the amount of television viewing. Because the children characteristically watch low, moderate, or high amounts of television in their daily lives, this study involves an observational research strategy.

Study II

An investigator examined the effect of music on problem-solving performance. Two hypotheses are possible: (1) Music helps to relax people and should therefore facilitate problem-solving performance. (2) Music serves to distract people and, hence, should interfere with problem-solving performance. One hundred individuals each tried to solve ten problems with soft background music playing. Three weeks later, the same individuals returned and tried to solve ten similar problems. This time, however, there was no background music. The number of problems that were correctly solved in each of the two conditions was compared.

Answer The independent variable is the music level. Because the presence or absence of background music was manipulated by the investigator, this study involves an experimental research strategy.

9.2 Controlling for Alternative Explanations

A major goal of research design is to control for alternative explanations. Consider an experiment in which an investigator studies the effect of alcohol on reaction time. Two mixed-gender groups of college students serve as participants. One-half respond to a reaction time task while under the influence of alcohol, and the other half respond to the same reaction task while not under the influence of alcohol. The task involves pressing a button when a certain slide appears in a series of slides. Upon completion of the study, the investigator computes the mean reaction time in each group.

Suppose that the mean reaction time in the alcohol condition is 2.45 seconds, whereas in the no-alcohol condition the mean reaction time is .98 second. It appears that alcohol has had an effect. However, there are alternative explanations. We now consider two of these.

Random Assignment to Experimental Groups

One possibility is that the alcohol did *not* affect reaction time and that the difference between the means is simply the result of students in the alcohol condition having slower reaction times than the students in the no-alcohol condition, independent of the effect of alcohol. If the study had been conducted without giving alcohol to any of the students, perhaps the students in the alcohol condition would still have a higher mean reaction time than the students in the no-alcohol condition.

To control for differences in participants from one condition to another, investigators typically assign individuals to groups using procedures similar to those used for selecting random samples (for instance, random number tables). If the condition that each person participates in is determined on a completely random basis, then it is not more likely that students who are assigned to the alcohol condition will have slower reaction times than those who are assigned to the no-alcohol condition, independent of alcohol. Thus, *random assignment* to conditions helps to control for alternative explanations of results.

Of course, random assignment is feasible only when an experimental strategy is used to create values on an independent variable. If gender is the independent variable, we cannot randomly assign participants to the conditions "male" and "female." By definition, men are male and women are female. Thus, random assignment is not possible with an observational strategy.

It is important to note that random assignment *does not guarantee* that the research groups will not differ beforehand on the dependent variable. Rather, it is *unlikely* that they will. There is always the chance that even with random assignment, the groups will differ on the dependent variable before the study begins.

Reducing Sampling Error

A second approach to controlling for alternative explanations focuses on sampling error. Consider the alcohol and reaction time experiment. The investigator conceptualizes the two groups of participants as random samples from two populations: (1) a population of students who are under the influence of alcohol and (2) a population of similar individuals who are not under the influence of alcohol. The two populations are assumed to be similar in all respects except one—the presence or absence of alcohol.

This is a reasonable assumption if participants are randomly assigned to experimental conditions. If this is the case and if the alcohol has no effect on reaction time, then the two populations are, for all intents and purposes, similar in *all* respects, and we would expect the mean reaction time scores for the two populations to be the same. If the alcohol *does* have an effect on reaction time, then we would expect the population means to differ.

The mean reaction times of 2.45 seconds in the alcohol condition and .98 seconds in the no-alcohol condition in our example appear to be consistent with the notion that the means for the two populations are different. However, we know from Chapter 7 that a sample mean does not usually equal the corresponding population mean because of sampling error. Perhaps the two population means are equal and the difference in the sample means only reflects sampling error. Ideally, we would like to minimize sampling error so that we can rule this out as an alternative explanation for our findings. We now consider ways to accomplish this.

Recall from Chapter 7 that the accuracy of a sample mean as an estimate of the population mean is influenced by the size of the sample and the variability of scores in the population. One way an investigator can reduce sampling error is to increase the sample sizes for the groups being studied. In general, the larger the sample size for each group, the less the sampling error. Obviously, there are practical limitations to the number of participants to include in a research group based on financial, time, and effort considerations. As such, researchers will sometimes have to settle for relatively small sample sizes.

A second way to reduce sampling error is to define the research groups such that the variability of the scores in each population is relatively small. Consider the alcohol and reaction time example. The population of students represented by the alcohol group includes both men and women, as does the population of students represented by the no-alcohol group. However, there is evidence that men generally have slightly faster reaction times than women on tasks similar to that used in our experiment. The presence of both men and women in each population therefore yields more variability in reaction time scores than if either gender were considered separately.

This is illustrated by the following hypothetical population reaction time scores for men only, women only, and men and women combined for students who are not under the influence of alcohol:

Men	Women	Men and women combined	
1.10	1.30	1.10	1.30
1.20	1.40	1.20	1.40
1.30	1.50	1.30	1.50
$\mu = 1.20$	$\mu = 1.40$	$\mu = 1.30$	
$\sigma = .082$	$\sigma = .082$	$\sigma = .129$	

Although we use unrealistically small population sizes for ease of presentation, the logic that we outline applies to any size population.

Note that the reaction time for men is slightly faster, on average, than the reaction time for women. Note also that the variability for the combined groups (a standard deviation of .129) is greater than the variability for either group considered separately (a standard deviation of .082 in both cases).

Sampling error could be reduced by *holding gender constant* by restricting the experiment to only women or to only men. This would yield smaller variability for both the alcohol and the no-alcohol groups relative to a study that includes both men and women. Unfortunately, in reducing the variability, we have restricted the generalizability of the results of the study to one gender only.

Behavioral scientists frequently find themselves in such trade-off situations. Researchers must weigh the benefits of reducing sampling error against the cost of reducing the generalizability of their results.

9.3 Confounding and Disturbance Variables

Much of behavioral science research is designed to study relationships between independent and dependent variables. In order to draw unambiguous inferences about such relationships, it is necessary to control other variables in the research setting. In the previous section, we implicitly considered two basic types of variables that a researcher must control. In this section, we make the nature of these variables explicit.

Confounding Variables

One type of variable that a researcher seeks to control is a *confounding variable*. Suppose that a researcher examines the relationship between the gender of job applicants and the likelihood of their being hired by conducting a study in which the resumes of 25 male and 25 female applicants are selected from personnel files.

A group of personnel directors is then asked to read each resume and rate on a 20-point scale the likelihood that they would hire each applicant.

Suppose that the statistical analysis indicates that there is, in fact, a relationship between the applicants' gender and the likelihood-of-hiring ratings, with men being more likely to be hired than women. Would this be evidence for gender discrimination? Not necessarily. The strongest evidence for gender discrimination would be if men are chosen over women who are equally or more qualified. In this study, the women may be less qualified than the men. Rather than the likelihood-of-hiring ratings being a function of the applicants' gender, they may simply reflect the applicants' qualifications, which happen to be related to their gender. If this were the case, the test for gender discrimination would be ambiguous because the result could be attributed either to gender discrimination *or* to differences in the quality of the applicants.

In this study, the qualifications of the applicants represent a **confounding variable**. This is *a variable that is related to the independent variable (the presumed influence) and that affects the dependent variable (the presumed effect), rendering a relational inference between the independent variable and the dependent variable ambiguous.*

Disturbance Variables

A second type of variable that must be controlled in research aimed at drawing relational inferences is a **disturbance variable**. This is *a variable that is unrelated to the independent variable (and, hence, not confounded with it) but that affects the dependent variable.* We first encountered such variables in Section 3.4 when we noted that they increase the variability within a group. Consequently, disturbance variables also increase sampling error.

Disturbance variables can obscure or even mask a relationship that exists between the independent and dependent variables. To use an electronics analogy, they create "noise" in a system where we are trying to detect a "signal," and the more "noise" there is, the harder it is to detect the "signal."

In the alcohol and reaction time study in Section 9.2, the gender of the participants is a disturbance variable. Other individual differences among participants (for instance, experience with alcohol, body weight, hand-eye coordination) would also qualify as disturbance variables if they meet the above definition.

For a further discussion of confounding and disturbance variables, see Box 9.1.

Controlling for Confounding and Disturbance Variables

Behavioral scientists use several procedures to control for confounding variables. Three of the most common strategies are (1) holding a variable constant, (2) matching, and (3) random assignment to experimental groups. Holding a variable constant can also be used to control for disturbance variables.

Let us demonstrate these strategies by considering the relationship between a woman's religion and how many children she wants to have in her completed family (that is, her ideal family size): Generally speaking, the research in this area shows that Catholic women want more children than Protestant women, who in turn want more children than Jewish women.

BOX 9.1

Confounding and Disturbance Variables

Huck and Sandler (1979) present an interesting collection of 100 studies that appeared in professional forums or that received attention in the popular press. For each one, they elaborate on some confounding and disturbance variables that could affect the interpretation of the results. Indeed, the identification of such variables is critical for evaluating any research design. An example from their book illustrates their approach and underscores the importance of controlling these types of variables.

Problem

The following story appeared about an advertisement in a weekly news magazine as well as in the local newspapers—you may have seen it yourself. It seems that the Pepsi-Cola Company decided that Coke's three-to-one lead in Dallas was no longer acceptable, so they commissioned a taste-preference study. The participants were chosen from Coke drinkers in the Dallas area and asked to express a preference for a glass of Coke or a glass of Pepsi. The glasses were not labeled "Coke" and "Pepsi" because of the obvious bias that might be associated with a cola's brand name. Rather, in an attempt to administer the two treatments (the two beverages) in a blind fashion, the Coke glass was simply marked with a "Q" and the Pepsi glass with an "M." Results indicated that more than half chose Pepsi over Coke. Besides a possible difference in taste, can you think of

any other possible explanation for the observed preference of Pepsi over Coke? (p. 11)

Solution

After seeing the results of the Pepsi experiment, the Coca-Cola Company conducted the same study, except that Coke was put in both glasses. Participants preferred the letter "M" over the letter "Q," thus creating the plausible rival hypothesis that letter preference rather than taste preference could easily have accounted for the original results. [In other words, the type of beverage might have been confounded with the letter used to label the glasses.] Since no statistical tests were given, another plausible rival hypothesis is that of instability; that is, we don't know whether "more than half" means 51 percent or 99 percent or how much confidence we should place in the finding. Flipping a coin 100 times is almost sure to result in either heads or tails occurring more than half the time.

Strangest of all was the fact that the same design error of using one letter exclusively for each brand was repeated in a second study conducted by Pepsi. In a feeble attempt to demonstrate that their initial results were not biased by the use of an "M" or a "Q," Pepsi duplicated their first study, this time using an "L" for Pepsi and an "S" for Coke! Clearly, these three studies indicate that there is sometimes more in advertisements than meets the eye (or the taste buds). (p. 158)

Sociologists have interpreted this in terms of the religious doctrine that these women are exposed to. Another interpretation is possible, however. Catholic women tend to come from larger families than Protestant women, who tend to come from larger families than Jewish women. It may not be religion that influences ideal family size but rather that women who are raised in large families prefer large families and women who are raised in small families prefer small families. Thus, religion and the size of the family one is raised in might be confounded with one another. How might family size background be controlled?

We saw in Section 9.2 how the disturbance variable of gender can be controlled in the alcohol and reaction time study by being held constant. **Holding a variable constant** can also be used to control for a confounding variable, such as family size background. For example, a study might be undertaken with Catholic, Protestant, and Jewish women who all come from families with two children. In this case, family size background and religion are *not* related because family size background has been held constant. Any differences in ideal family size between the three religious groups cannot be attributed to differences in family size background because everyone in the study comes from the same size family. The variables are no longer confounded.

As noted earlier, the major disadvantage of holding a variable constant is that it may restrict the generalizability of a study's results. If the religion and ideal family size study was conducted with only women who come from families with two children, would the results generalize to individuals who come from families with five children? Perhaps religion influences ideal family size when one comes from a relatively small family (two children) but not when one comes from a relatively large family (five children).

When we hold a variable constant, we have no way of knowing the extent to which the results will generalize across other levels of the variable that is held constant. One way to circumvent this problem in the religion and ideal family size study would be to examine the effect of religion at each of several levels of family size background (for example, one child, two children, three children, and so on). A design of this type is called a *factorial design* and will be discussed at length in Chapter 17.

A second strategy that is used to control for confounding variables is **matching**. With this approach, an individual in one research group is "matched" with an individual in each of the other groups such that the matched individuals all have the same value on the confounding variable. This strategy is different from holding a variable constant because the confounding variable can vary considerably within a group. However, for each individual in one group, there is a comparable individual in each of the other groups who has the same value on the confounding variable.

As an example of matching, five Catholic, five Protestant, and five Jewish women having the following family size backgrounds might be selected for inclusion in the religion and ideal family size study:

Catholic	Protestant	Jewish
3	3	3
4	4	4
2	2	2
3	3	3
1	1	1
$\overline{X} = 2.60$	$\overline{X} = 2.60$	$\overline{X} = 2.60$

Note that the average family size background is identical for the three groups. This is not surprising given that the women were explicitly matched on the basis of their family size backgrounds. Thus, any differences between the groups in the mean ideal family size cannot be attributed to differences in family size background. Again, religion and family size background are now unconfounded. Furthermore, the problem of restricted generalizability of results that occurs when holding a variable constant is not an issue because a range of family size backgrounds is included. Unfortunately, however, in practice it is often difficult to identify appropriate variables to serve as a basis for matching and, once identified, to readily complete the matching process.

A final strategy for dealing with confounding variables is **random assignment** to experimental groups. For instance, we saw in the alcohol and reaction time study in Section 9.2 that confounding due to the alcohol and the no-alcohol groups differing in reaction time before the study begins can be avoided by randomly assigning participants to conditions. More generally, random assignment helps to control for confounding variables due to individuals' backgrounds and characteristics. However, because random assignment cannot be done with observational groups, observational independent variables will always be confounded with all other variables that are naturally related to them if these variables cannot be controlled by being held constant or by matching.

An Electronics Analogy

Many concepts related to confounding and disturbance variables can be illustrated using the electronics analogy from Section 8.6. Suppose that you are listening through a set of earphones and trying to decide whether you hear a particular signal. There is a good deal of static on the earphones. In research design, the static corresponds to disturbance variables, and your goal is to eliminate it to the extent that you can.

Suppose that you do some repair work and thereby eliminate a large portion of the static. This is analogous to controlling for disturbance variables. There is still another problem, however: There are two other signals very much like the one that you must detect. If you hear them, you will think that your signal has occurred when, in fact, it has not.

These other signals represent confounding variables. A mechanical device that you hook up completely eliminates one of these signals and turns the other one into static (that is, into a disturbance variable). The additional static is relatively minor, so you decide that you have done everything possible to ensure accurate the identification of the target signal.

However, you are confronted with yet another problem. As we discussed in Section 8.6, two types of error are possible when reporting whether or not you hear the signal: (1) You might say that you hear it when, in fact, it does not occur or (2) you might say that you do not hear it when, in fact, it is there. These correspond to Type I and Type II errors, respectively. Suppose that you decide that falsely saying that the signal is present would be very detrimental and that falsely saying that it does not occur would be of little importance. In this case, you would want to ensure that you minimize the first type of error. This would correspond to setting a low alpha level for an analysis. With this in mind, you adopt a strategy of reporting the signal only if you are certain that you hear it.

9.4   Problems with Inferring Causation

The statistical tests that we consider in this book are designed to indicate whether there is a relationship between variables in the context of a research investigation. It must be emphasized that these statistics say nothing about whether two variables are *causally* related.

It is possible for two variables to be related to each other but for no causal relationship to exist between them. A good example of this is the relationship between hair length and height. A random sample of adults in the United States would typically reveal a moderate negative relationship between the length of one's hair and how tall someone is: People with shorter hair tend to be taller than people with longer hair. Is there a causal relationship between these variables? If you cut your hair, will you grow taller? As you grow taller, does your hair necessarily get shorter? Certainly not. It turns out that this relationship is due to a confounding variable—gender. Women tend to wear their hair longer than men. Women also tend to be shorter than men. These gender differences serve to produce a relationship between hair length and height. If we were to remove the influence of gender, there would be no relationship between these two dimensions.

Most statistics and research design texts emphasize this point about causation only when considering correlational analysis.* However, the issue of causal inference must be considered for *all* statistical tests that assess the relationship between variables. *The ability to make a causal inference between two variables is a function of one's research design, not the statistical technique that is used to analyze the data that are yielded by that research design.*

Because observational independent variables will always be confounded with all other variables that are naturally related to them, causal inferences are typically not possible when an observational research strategy is used. When an experimental research strategy is used, inferences of causation can be made only when confounding variables are controlled. The fact that two variables being related does not necessarily imply causation is important to keep in mind when interpreting statistics in the context of behavioral science research.

9.5   Between- Versus Within-Subjects Designs

Types of Research Designs

Consider an experiment where the investigator wants to know whether two drugs, A and B, differentially affect performance on a learning task. Fifty participants are randomly assigned to one of two conditions. In the first condition, 25 participants are administered drug A and then read a list of 15 words. They are subsequently asked to recall as many of the words as possible. A learning score is derived by counting the number of words correctly recalled (hence, scores can range from 0 to 15).

---

* In fact, we discuss correlation and causation in Section 5.4. The issues that we consider in that section also relate to other statistical tests, so if you have not already read that material, you might want to do so now.

In the second condition, a different set of 25 participants reads the same list of 15 words and responds to the same recall test after being administered drug B. The relative effects of the drugs on learning are determined by comparing the scores of the two groups.

In this experiment, the investigator is studying the relationship between two variables: (1) the type of drug and (2) learning as measured on a recall test. The type of drug is the independent variable, and the learning measure is the dependent variable. For the independent variable, participants who receive drug A do *not* receive drug B, and those who receive drug B do *not* receive drug A; that is, the two groups include different individuals. A variable of this type is known as a *between-subjects* variable because the values of the variable are "split up" between participants. Research designs that utilize between-subjects independent variables are referred to as **between-subjects designs** or *independent groups designs*.

We consider several statistical tests for analyzing between-subjects designs in later chapters. These include the independent groups t test in Chapter 10, one-way between-subjects analysis of variance in Chapter 12, the chi-square test in Chapter 15, Pearson correlation and regression in Chapter 14, and two-way between-subjects analysis of variance in Chapter 17.

Now consider a similar experiment that is conducted in a slightly different fashion. Twenty-five participants are administered drug A and then given the recall test. One month later, the same 25 people return to the experimental laboratory and are given the recall test after being administered drug B. The performance of these participants under the influence of drug B is then compared with their earlier performance under the influence of drug A. Note that in this experiment, the 25 individuals who receive drug A also receive drug B; that is, the same individuals participate in both conditions. A variable of this type is known as a *within-subjects* variable because all values of the variable occur for (within) each participant. Research designs that utilize within-subjects independent variables are referred to as **within-subjects designs,** *correlated groups designs,* or *repeated measures designs*.

We consider several statistical tests for analyzing within-subjects designs in later chapters. These include the correlated groups *t* test in Chapter 11 and one-way repeated measures analysis of variance in Chapter 13.

As illustrated by our examples, between-subjects designs and within-subjects designs are both viable strategies when the independent variable is experimental in nature. For many observational independent variables, only between-subjects designs are applicable. Consider the variable of gender, which has two levels: male and female. This variable is, by definition, between-subjects in nature: Individuals who are in the "male" group cannot also be in the "female" group.

We should note that there is a third class of research designs, known as **matched-subjects designs,** in which different individuals are included in the different conditions but are conceptualized as if a within-subjects design is in force. In these designs, each participant in one condition is "matched" with a participant in each of the other conditions who has similar characteristics. The data are then treated as if the matched participants represent the same individual.

As we noted in Section 9.3, matching is difficult to achieve in practice. For this and other reasons (see Thorndike, 1942), there are serious problems with this strategy, and its use is recommended only under restricted circumstances. Consequently, we do not consider matched-subjects designs in the following discussion.

STUDY EXERCISE 9.2

For each of the studies in Study Exercise 9.1, indicate whether the independent variable is between-subjects or within-subjects in nature.

Answer   The independent variable in Study I, the amount of television viewing, is between-subjects in nature because the 50 children who are low viewers are not the same children as the 50 who are moderate viewers, who, in turn, are not the same children as the 50 who are high viewers. The independent variable in Study II, music status, is within-subjects in nature because the same 100 individuals participated in both the background music and the no-music conditions.

Advantages and Disadvantages of Between- Versus Within-Subjects Designs

The advantages and disadvantages of designing an investigation using a between-subjects versus a within-subjects design can be illustrated in the context of the drug and learning experiment. One advantage of the within-subjects approach is that it is more economical in terms of participants. For instance, in our example, half the number of participants are required to achieve the same per-condition sample size (25) when a within-subjects design is used as when a between-subjects design is used (25 versus 50). Participant economy is particularly important when a large amount of time, effort, or money is necessary to recruit and train research participants.

A second advantage of within-subjects designs is the control of confounding variables that they provide. In the ideal experiment, individuals in the two conditions (drug A versus drug B) would be identical in all respects except one—the type of drug they are given. If the two groups differ in learning, then there would be one and only one logical explanation: The difference in drugs *caused* the difference in learning.

Participants in a between-subjects design can be randomly assigned to one of the two conditions in an attempt to "equalize" the two groups on all variables except the drug. If the participants are randomly assigned, it is unlikely that the individuals in one condition will, for example, be more intelligent (on average) than the individuals in the other condition. But the key word here is *unlikely*. Although it is *unlikely* that a between-group difference in intelligence will occur, it *could* happen due to chance factors. When this does occur, the differential intelligence in the two conditions could make one drug appear superior when it is not. Or, it might offset the effect of the superior drug, making it appear as if there is no difference between the drugs when there actually is.

In contrast, this cannot happen with within-subjects designs. The same individuals who receive drug A also receive drug B. Because the same individuals are involved, intelligence must be the same in both conditions (unless it changed in the month that separated the administration of the drugs). This is true not only of intelligence but also of all other individual differences that might otherwise render the interpretation of the research findings ambiguous. Thus, within-subjects designs can offer considerably more experimental control than between-subjects designs.

This point must be qualified by additional considerations. A potential problem with within-subjects designs is that the treatment in the first condition may have **carry-over effects** that influence performance in the second condition. For example, the effect of drug A may not have worn off completely when drug B is administered. This could make the interpretation of the experiment ambiguous.

Carry-over effects are not necessarily restricted to the independent variable of interest. For instance, performance on the dependent variable during the second condition of the drug and learning experiment might be better than in the first condition. However, instead of reflecting the effects of the drugs, this may simply reflect the fact that the participants are taking the recall test for the second time and are therefore more familiar with it. This increased familiarity rather than the type of drug could produce the difference in learning.

When an investigator is confident that no carry-over effects will occur, a within-subjects design is usually preferable to a between-subjects design. When carry-over effects are possible, a between-subjects design may be more appropriate. We return to the issue of within-subjects versus between-subjects designs in later chapters.

9.6 Parametric and Nonparametric Statistics

Parametric Statistics

Many of the inferential tests that we discuss in this book involve the analysis of means and measures of variability. Such techniques are called **parametric statistics** because they make assumptions about the distribution of scores within the populations of interest, that is, about population parameters. Parametric tests require quantitative dependent variables and are usually applied when these variables are measured on a level that at least approximates interval characteristics.

Distributional assumptions serve several purposes. Sometimes an assumption is used to simplify mathematical derivations so as to make a statistic more *manageable*. Other times an assumption is used because it characterizes what is likely to be the case in the real world; that is, the assumption is *credible*. As an example, a statistical test that assumes that every intelligence test score occurs with equal frequency would have little applicability to most real-world problems. The assumption of a normal distribution, with a large proportion of central scores and few extreme scores, is much more credible.

In fact, the *normality* assumption is one of the most common distributional assumptions that we will encounter in future chapters. As we discussed in Section 8.10, this assumption requires that scores for a variable be normally distributed in the population from which they are drawn. Another common assumption is that of *homogeneity of variance*. This assumption is applicable when two or more groups of scores are considered in the research design. It requires that the variances of the scores be equal, or *homogeneous*, in the populations underlying each of the samples. Note that *these assumptions relate to the populations from which the samples were drawn rather than to the samples themselves*. Thus, determining whether a distributional assumption is violated requires sophisticated statistical procedures.

A number of methods have been proposed for assessing violations of the normality and homogeneity of variance assumptions. Unfortunately, each of these tests has problems associated with it. For instance, the most commonly cited tests for homogeneity of variance (Bartlett's test, Cochran's test, and Hartley's F max test) have been found to be unsatisfactory when the population data are not normally distributed.

Robustness of Parametric Tests

When certain conditions are met, parametric tests are robust to violations of their distributional assumptions. **Robustness** refers to the extent to which conclusions drawn on the basis of a statistical test (for example, that the null hypothesis should be rejected) are unaffected by violations of their underlying assumptions. When a test is robust to violations of an assumption, it is appropriate to apply that test even when that assumption is violated because the frequencies of Type I and Type II errors will be similar to what they would be when no violation occurs. Thus, the accuracy of the test's conclusions will be relatively unaffected compared with conditions under which the assumption is met. The concept of robustness is very important in inferential statistics.

Statisticians determine the effects of violating assumptions in two ways. First, they may be able to determine the consequences of violating an assumption using mathematical logic. If this is not possible, a *Monte Carlo study* is performed instead. This involves a computer simulation in which the statistician generates scores for hypothetical populations that he or she knows violate a distributional assumption in some way. The statistical test in question is then applied thousands of times to random samples selected from these populations, and the number of times that an incorrect conclusion is made is determined. If a test consistently yields the correct conclusion even though its statistical assumptions are violated, then the test is said to be robust.

As you might expect, the results of studies on the robustness of inferential tests are quite complex. This is because, as we noted in Section 8.10, robustness is influenced by several factors, including sample size, the degree of violation, and the form of the violation. For instance, there are many ways in which the homogeneity of variance assumption can be violated in the three-group situation. Focusing on the *form* of the violation, we may find that two of the population variances are the same but are different from the third or that all three population variances differ from one another. In terms of the *degree* of violation, differences in population variances can range in magnitude from slight to large.

Although a given statistical test might be quite robust under one set of conditions, its robustness might substantially decrease under somewhat different conditions. For example, we saw in Chapter 8 that the one-sample t test is more robust to marked violations of the normality assumption when the sample size is larger than about 10 than when the sample is smaller.

Given the numerous ways that factors can combine to influence robustness, it is impossible to discuss robustness with any degree of precision when we consider the robustness of specific inferential tests in future chapters. Our strategy is therefore to provide general characterizations of the robustness of the tests that are

presented and to cite a few articles that consider the relevant issues in more depth.*
If a researcher has reason to believe that a distributional assumption has been violated to the extent that a parametric test is no longer robust, one possible solution
is to use a nonparametric alternative.

The Use of Parametric Versus Nonparametric Statistics

Nonparametric statistics are a class of statistical tests that focus on *distributions of
scores* (rather than means and measures of variability) and that can be used to analyze nominal variables or quantitative variables that are measured on an ordinal
level. In addition, they do not require many of the assumptions about distributional
properties of scores that parametric statistics rely on. We discuss nonparametric statistics in depth in Chapter 16.

There is controversy among behavioral scientists concerning the use of parametric as opposed to nonparametric statistics. Some argue that nonparametric
analyses should be widely used because measures in the behavioral sciences often
depart radically from interval level characteristics. Furthermore, they argue, the
application of parametric analyses is inappropriate when distributional assumptions
are not met. Those who promote the widespread use of parametric analyses emphasize that parametric statistics are more refined and more powerful than the available nonparametric methods. In fact, some statisticians (for example, Bohrnstedt &
Carter, 1971) advocate that "when one has a variable which is measured at the ordinal level, parametric statistics not only can be, but should be, applied" (p. 322).

9.7   Selecting the Appropriate Statistical Test: A Preview

It is impossible to state any precise rules for determining the statistical test to apply
in a given situation because it is always possible to find exceptions where a different
form of analysis might be more appropriate. Nevertheless, it is useful to have guidelines for what tests should typically be used with the most common research designs.

In Chapters 10 to 16, we consider the most common inferential tests for analyzing bivariate relationships and, in each chapter, we specify the issues to be considered in deciding whether to apply that test. As you will see, the essence of our
approach rests on distinguishing between qualitative and quantitative variables and
between between-subjects and within-subjects designs.

The required steps are to (1) identify the independent and dependent variables, (2) classify each variable as being qualitative or quantitative and determine
whether the dependent variable is measured on a level that at least approximates
interval characteristics, (3) classify the independent variable as being between-
subjects or within-subjects in nature, and (4) note the number of levels that characterize the independent variable. A comprehensive framework for selecting a
statistical test to analyze one's data is presented in Chapter 18.

---

* A complete discussion of distributional assumptions and robustness is beyond the scope of
  this book. Interested readers are referred to Bohrnstedt and Carter (1971), Boneau (1960),
  Lord (1953), Stevens (1951), and an excellent collection of readings in Kirk (1972) for further discussion of these issues.

9.8   Organizing Questions

We address many issues besides those associated with deciding when it is appropriate to apply a particular test when we consider inferential procedures for analyzing bivariate relationships in Chapters 10 to 16. Our discussion is consistently organized around three questions:

1. Given sample data, can we infer that a relationship exists between two variables in the population?
2. If so, what is the *strength* of the relationship?
3. If so, what is the *nature* of the relationship?

9.9   Links Between Chapters

As we have now reiterated several times, statistics and research design are strongly interrelated. As such, principles of research design intertwine in numerous ways with statistical analysis. Simply stated, research serves little purpose if we are unable to make sense of our data and statistics cannot be meaningfully applied to poorly done research.

Hopefully, this chapter has given you a sense of some of the relevant issues. We will see many more links between this and later chapters as we progress through the inferential tests that constitute the rest of this book.

Applications to the Analysis of a Social Problem Using SPSS for Windows

Based on the material covered in this chapter, we can discuss several design features of the parent–teen study described in Chapter 1. Because no variables were manipulated, the study used an observational strategy. A major focus of the investigation was to explore adolescent gender and age differences in relation to parent–teen relationships and sexual behavior. As we noted earlier in this chapter, gender is always a between-subjects independent variable. As we discuss below, age is also a between-subjects independent variable in the context of this study.

Numerous hypotheses about gender effects are possible. For example, one theory states that girls tend to be more "other oriented" than boys in their social relationships and therefore may be more influenced by peer pressure. This theory predicts, among other things, that sexually active girls are more likely than their less active peers to have sexually active friends, whereas this may not be true for boys. Although the confirmation of this pattern of results through statistical analysis would be consistent with the theory, other explanations based on the identification of confounding variables could also be invoked. For example, girls might be more likely than boys to seek out friends who are similar to them. If so, the finding that sexually active girls tend to have sexually active friends may have nothing to do with girls succumbing to peer pressure.

Rather, it may reflect unrelated friendship selection processes. In order to differentiate between these two competing explanations, more fine-grained analyses or an additional study would need to be conducted.

In terms of the teens' ages, the study used a *cross-sectional design*. This is a design in which age serves as a between-subjects independent variable. The 14-year-old girls in our study were not the same individuals as the 17-year-old girls. By contrast, in a *longitudinal design*, age serves as a within-subjects independent variable. For example, a group of 14-year-old girls might be interviewed every year for 4 years, yielding data for 14-year-old, 15-year-old, 16-year-old, and 17-year-old teens.

Longitudinal designs are generally more expensive and time-consuming than cross-sectional designs, and it was primarily because of these practical concerns that we decided to use a cross-sectional design. In so doing, we had to forgo the ability to study how specific individuals changed over time and, instead, relied on comparisons of means, medians, and correlations across age groups to make developmental inferences.

Cross-sectional designs are efficient but have the potential problem of *cohort effects*. This refers to variables that are confounded with age and that therefore serve as alternative explanations to developmental processes. Suppose, for example, that we theorized that because teens mature cognitively and morally throughout the adolescent years, they will become increasingly more responsible with age. This might lead us to predict that sexually active 17-year-old girls will be more consistent in their use of birth control than 16-year-old girls, who in turn will be more consistent in their use of birth control than 15-year-old girls, who will be more consistent in their use of birth control than 14-year-old girls. Further suppose that statistical analysis confirmed this age trend in the consistency of birth control use. This result is consistent with our theory. However, it is also consistent with a number of alternative explanations, one of which involves a cohort effect.

During the years surrounding our study, the problem of AIDS was receiving considerable attention in the media. Consequently, at the time of their participation, teens in the 17-year-old group had been exposed to, on average, one more year of AIDS information campaigns than teens in the 16-year-old group, 2 more years of AIDS information than teens in the 15-year-old group, and 3 more years of AIDS information than teens in the 14-year-old group. Thus, any age differences in the consistency of birth control use may have little to do with maturational changes in cognitive and moral processes but, instead, may merely reflect the differential exposure to AIDS information (and its subsequent effect on increased condom use) experienced by this generation. Such confounds must be considered when interpreting data.

Summary

The results of a statistical analysis must be interpreted in the context of the research design used to generate the data. Behavioral scientists use two general types of research design. An experimental strategy involves performing a set of manipulations to create different values of the independent variable for the research participants. In contrast, an observational strategy involves measuring differences in values of the independent variable that naturally exist in the research participants.

A major goal of research is to control for alternative explanations. When an experimental strategy is used, one approach is to randomly assign participants to conditions. A second approach focuses on reducing sampling error by increasing the sample sizes for the groups being studied or by defining the research groups such that the variability of scores in each population is relatively small. Researchers must weigh the benefits of reducing sampling error against the cost of reducing the generalizability of their results.

In order to draw unambiguous inferences about relationships between independent and dependent variables, it is necessary to control confounding and disturbance variables. A confounding variable is a variable that is related to the independent variable and that affects the dependent variable, rendering a relational inference between the independent variable and the dependent variable ambiguous. A disturbance variable is a variable that is unrelated to the independent variable but that affects the dependent variable. Techniques for controlling confounding variables include holding a variable constant, matching, and random assignment to experimental groups. Holding a variable constant can also be used to control for disturbance variables.

The ability to make a causal inference between two variables is a function of one's research design, not the statistical technique that is used to analyze the data. Because observational independent variables will always be confounded with all other variables that are naturally related to them, causal inferences are typically not possible when an observational research strategy is used. When an experimental research strategy is used, inferences of causation can be made only when confounding variables are controlled.

Research designs in which different individuals participate in different research conditions are referred to as *between-subjects designs*. Research designs in which all participants provide scores in all research conditions are referred to as *within-subjects designs*. Between-subjects designs and within-subjects designs are both viable strategies when the independent variable is experimental in nature. For many observational independent variables, only between-subjects designs are applicable. There are serious problems with matched-subjects designs, and their use is recommended only under restricted circumstances.

One advantage of the within-subjects approach is that it is more economical in terms of participants. A second advantage of within-subjects designs is that they can offer considerably more experimental control than between-subjects designs. However, a potential problem with within-subjects designs is that participation in one condition may have carry-over effects that influence performance in another condition.

A distinction can be made between parametric and nonparametric statistics. Parametric statistics require quantitative dependent variables and are usually applied when these variables are measured on a level that at least approximates interval characteristics. In contrast, nonparametric statistics can be used to analyze nominal variables or quantitative variables that are measured on an ordinal level. Another important feature of parametric tests is the assumptions they make about the distribution of scores within the populations of interest.

When certain conditions are met, parametric tests are robust to violations of the distributional assumptions required of them. When a test is robust to violations of an assumption, it is appropriate to apply that test even when that assumption is violated because the accuracy of the test's conclusions will be relatively unaffected compared with conditions under which the assumption is met. The concept of robustness is very important in inferential statistics. We consider the robustness of specific tests in future chapters.

In Chapters 10 to 16, we consider the most common inferential tests for analyzing bivariate relationships and, in each chapter, we specify the issues to be considered in deciding whether to apply that technique. We also address many other issues for each test. Our discussion consistently focuses on whether we can infer that a relationship exists between two variables in the population given sample data and, if so, what the strength and the nature of the relationship are.

Exercises

Answers to asterisked (*) exercises appear at the back of the book.

1. Differentiate between an experimental research strategy and an observational research strategy.

For each of the studies described in Exercises 2–5, identify the independent variable and indicate whether an experimental or an observational research strategy is involved.

*2. Morrow and Davidson (1976) studied the relationship between race and family-size decisions. These investigators interviewed a total of 300 people; 100 were African American, 100 were Hispanic, and 100 were white. The participants were asked the number of children they wanted to have in their completed family. The average numbers of desired children were compared for the three groups.

*3. Harvath (1943) tested the effect of noise on problem-solving performance. One hundred and fifty individuals participated in the study. They were randomly assigned to two conditions. Seventy-five participants tried to solve 30 problems while a steady "buzz" was present in the background. The other 75 tried to solve the same 30 problems with no background noise. The number of correct solutions was computed for each person and the average numbers of correct solutions compared for individuals in the noise versus the no-noise conditions.

4. Steiner (1972) reviews a number of studies on the effects of the presence of others on problem-solving performance. In one study,

100 female volunteers served as participants. At the first session, each woman was seated alone in a room and given a math problem to solve. The amount of time it took to solve the problem was measured. Two weeks later, the woman returned and solved another problem, but this time there was an observer present watching her. The amount of time it took to solve the problem was again measured. For each of the two conditions—observer present versus observer absent—the mean problem-solving time was computed across the 100 women. These means were then compared.

5. Sears (1969) reviews a number of studies on the relationship between gender and political party preference. In one investigation, 75 men and 75 women were interviewed. Respondents were asked whether they considered themselves Democrats, Republicans, or Independents. The frequencies with which men identified with the three classifications were compared with the corresponding frequencies for women.

*6. What is a control group? What is the advantage of including a control group in the research design?

7. For each of the studies described in Exercises 2–5, indicate whether a control group was used and, if so, identify the nature of this group.

8. What is random assignment? Why is it important?

*9. What are the limitations of random assignment?

*10. What procedures are available for reducing sampling error?

11. What are confounding variables? How can they be controlled?

*12. What are disturbance variables? How can they be controlled?

*13. What are the advantages of within-subjects designs compared with between-subjects designs? What is a potential problem?

*14. Indicate whether the independent variables in the studies described in Exercises 2–5 are between-subjects or within-subjects in nature.

15. How do parametric and nonparametric statistics differ?

*16. What is robustness? Why is it important?

17. What is the normality assumption? What is the homogeneity of variance assumption?

18. What are the two ways in which statisticians determine the effects of violating distributional assumptions?

*19. Identify the three factors that influence the robustness of a statistical test.

20. What are the advantages and disadvantages of cross-sectional versus longitudinal designs?

Multiple-Choice Questions

21. A matched-subjects design is one in which
    a. the same individuals are included in all conditions
    b. the same individuals are included in all conditions but are conceptualized as if a between-subjects design is in force
    c. different individuals are included in different conditions
    d. different individuals are included in different conditions but are conceptualized as if a within-subjects design is in force

22. An experimental strategy does not involve the explicit manipulation of an independent variable.
    a. true   b. false

*23. A confounding variable
    a. is related to the independent variable and affects the dependent variable
    b. is related to the independent variable but does not affect the dependent variable
    c. affects the dependent variable but is not related to the independent variable
    d. is not related to either the independent variable or the dependent variable

24. A disturbance variable
    a. is related to the independent variable and affects the dependent variable
    b. is related to the independent variable but does not affect the dependent variable
    c. affects the dependent variable but is not related to the independent variable
    d. is not related to either the independent variable or the dependent variable

25. Whether or not two variables are *causally* related is an issue only when correlational analysis is used.
    a. true   b. false

*26. By definition, ethnic background is a within-subjects variable.
    a. true   b. false

*27. A statistical test that is robust
    a. can be used to analyze both qualitative and quantitative variables
    b. can be used to analyze both between-subjects and within-subjects variables
    c. will yield conclusions that are relatively unaffected by violations of underlying assumptions
    d. all of the above

28. Between-subjects and within-subjects designs are both viable strategies when the independent variable is experimental in nature.
    a. true   b. false

*29. Random assignment to groups guarantees that there will be no confounding variables.
    a. true   b. false

30. Holding a variable constant can be used to control for
    a. confounding variables
    b. disturbance variables

c. both confounding variables and disturbance variables

d. neither confounding variables nor disturbance variables

*31. The ability to make a causal inference between two variables is a function of

a. the research design that is used

b. the statistical techniques used to analyze the data

c. the size of the samples

d. whether parametric or nonparametric statistics are applied

*32. Distributional assumptions relate both to the populations from which samples are drawn and to the samples themselves.

a. true   b. false

33. Which of the following is *not* a step in selecting a statistical test for analyzing bivariate relationships?

a. Determine whether confounding variables or disturbance variables are more problematic.

b. Note the number of levels that characterize the independent variable.

c. Classify both the independent and the dependent variables as being qualitative or quantitative, and determine whether the dependent variable is measured on a level that at least approximates interval characteristics.

d. Classify the independent variable as being between-subjects or within-subjects.

*34. Matching can be used to control for

a. confounding variables

b. disturbance variables

c. both confounding variables and disturbance variables

d. neither confounding variables nor disturbance variables

CHAPTER **10**

Independent Groups *t* Test

10.1   Use of the Independent Groups *t* Test

The independent groups *t* test is typically used to analyze the relationship between two variables under the following conditions:

1. The dependent variable is quantitative in nature and is measured on a level that at least approximates interval characteristics.

2. The independent variable is *between-subjects* in nature (it can be either qualitative or quantitative).*

3. The independent variable has two, and only two, levels.

Let us consider an example of an experiment that meets these conditions. When a friend describes a stranger to you, you may form an impression as to whether you would like that individual. One question of interest to behavioral scientists has been whether the order in which information is provided about a stranger influences the kind of impression that are formed about him or her.

Consider the following procedures: Twenty college students read a verbal description of a stranger and then rate the extent to which they like or dislike that person on a 1 to 7 scale. The higher the score, the more the stranger is liked. For instance, a score of 1 means that the research participant dislikes the stranger very much, a score of 4 means that the participant neither likes nor dislikes the stranger, and a score of 7 means that the research participant likes the stranger very much.

The stranger is described by six adjectives: intelligent, sincere, honest, conceited, rude, and nervous. The first three characteristics are positive, whereas the last three characteristics are negative. Ten of the participants are randomly selected and given the description in the order listed above—that is, first the positive traits and then the negative traits. The other ten participants are given the same description, but in reverse order—that is, first the negative traits and then the positive traits. Thus, we have two groups reflecting different orders of presentation:

Group 1 (pro–con): intelligent, sincere, honest, conceited, rude, nervous
Group 2 (con–pro): nervous, rude, conceited, honest, sincere, intelligent

The likability ratings for the two conditions are presented in columns 1 and 3 of Table 10.1. If the order of information has no effect on the type of impression that is formed, we would expect that, on average, the two sets of ratings will not differ. However, if the order of information does matter, then the average likability rating should differ for the two conditions.

In this experiment, the order in which the trait information is presented is the independent variable and the likability of the stranger is the dependent variable. The independent variable has two levels (pro–con versus con–pro) and is between-subjects in nature. The dependent variable is quantitative in nature and is measured on a level

---

* Matched-subjects designs are analyzed as if the independent variable is within-subjects in nature using the procedures that are described in Chapter 11.

TABLE 10.1   **Data and Calculations for Order of Information and Likability Experiment**

Pro–Con		Con–Pro	
X	X^2	X	X^2
7	49	1	1
4	16	5	25
3	9	2	4
5	25	5	25
5	25	3	9
6	36	3	9
5	25	3	9
5	25	2	4
4	16	4	16
6	36	2	4
$\Sigma X_1 = 50$	$\Sigma X_1^2 = 262$	$\Sigma X_2 = 30$	$\Sigma X_2^2 = 106$
$\overline{X}_1 = 5.00$		$\overline{X}_2 = 3.00$	

$$SS_1 = \sum X_1^2 - \frac{(\sum X_1)^2}{n_1}$$

$$= 262 - \frac{50^2}{10} = 12.00$$

$$\hat{s}_1^2 = \frac{SS_1}{n_1 - 1} = \frac{12.00}{9} = 1.33$$

$$SS_2 = \sum X_2^2 - \frac{(\sum X_2)^2}{n_2}$$

$$= 106 - \frac{30^2}{10} = 16.00$$

$$\hat{s}_2^2 = \frac{SS_2}{n_2 - 1} = \frac{16.00}{9} = 1.78$$

that at least approximates interval characteristics. Given these conditions, the independent groups *t* test would typically be used to analyze the relationship between the variables.

We now turn to the three questions relevant to the analysis of bivariate relationships: (1) Is there a relationship between the variables? (2) If so, what is the strength of the relationship? (3) If so, what is the nature of the relationship?

10.2   Inference of a Relationship Using the Independent Groups *t* Test

Null and Alternative Hypotheses

The first question to be addressed is whether a relationship exists between the independent and the dependent variables. We begin by stating this question in terms of a null and an alternative hypothesis. This is done with reference to population means.

Because we are interested in generalizing the results of our study beyond just those people who participated in it, we think of the participants as representing random samples from very large populations of similar individuals. In the experiment, there are two populations of interest: (1) individuals who read a verbal description of a stranger in which traits are presented in an order from pro to con and (2) individuals who read a verbal description of a stranger in which traits are presented in an order from con to pro.

Given that participants were randomly assigned to groups, and if we assume that the order of information does *not* matter, then we would expect the population means for the two groups to be equal. The null hypothesis thus takes the form

$$H_0: \mu_1 = \mu_2$$

where μ_1 is the population mean for the first group and μ_2 is the population mean for the second group. The null hypothesis posits that there is no relationship between the independent variable (the order of information) and the dependent variable (likability) as measured by mean scores on the dependent variable. According to this hypothesis, the value of the independent variable does not matter because the mean score on the dependent variable is the same at both levels.

The alternative hypothesis posits that there *is* a relationship between the two variables; the value of the independent variable *does* influence the average score on the dependent variable:

$$H_1: \mu_1 \neq \mu_2$$

We have now restated the question in the context of two competing hypotheses: a null hypothesis ("there is no relationship between the variables") and an alternative hypothesis ("there is a relationship between the variables"). The next step is to choose between these two hypotheses.

Examine the sample means in Table 10.1. The mean likability score for the pro–con group is 5.00, and the mean likability score for the con–pro group is 3.00. The two means are not equal, which appears to be consistent with the alternative hypothesis. However, we know from Chapter 7 that a sample mean may not reflect the true value of its population mean due to sampling error. Thus, the observed difference between the two sample means may not reflect the influence of the order of information on likability but, rather, may reflect sampling error. Our task is to determine whether this is a reasonable interpretation of the observed difference between the sample means.

Sampling Distribution of the Difference Between Two Independent Means

In order to test the sampling error interpretation, we use logic directly analogous to that developed in Chapter 8 for the one-sample *t* test. As an initial step, we must develop the concept of a **sampling distribution of the difference between two independent means.**

Consider two large populations whose mean scores on a variable are equal (that is, $\mu_1 = \mu_2$). Now suppose that we select a random sample of size 10 from each population and compute the mean of each sample as well as the difference between the means. We might find a result such as that illustrated in the first row of Table 10.2. In this table, $\overline{X}_1$ represents the sample mean for population 1, $\overline{X}_2$ represents the sample mean for population 2, and $\overline{X}_1 - \overline{X}_2$ represents the difference between them.

TABLE 10.2   **Illustrative Sample Means and Mean Differences from a Sampling Distribution of the Difference Between Two Independent Means**

$\overline{X}_1$	$\overline{X}_2$	$\overline{X}_1 - \overline{X}_2$
5.00	3.00	2.00
4.30	3.60	.70
5.60	6.40	−.80
4.80	5.40	−.60
4.70	4.70	.00
5.20	5.90	−.70
6.00	5.70	.30
4.30	3.90	.40
5.20	6.50	−1.30
6.10	7.50	−1.40
5.00	3.90	1.10
5.20	5.90	−.70
4.70	4.10	.60
4.90	4.40	.50
5.00	5.90	−.90
6.20	6.40	−.20
4.30	2.50	1.80
5.10	6.40	−1.30
5.70	6.60	−.90
5.10	4.10	1.00
4.90	5.40	−.50
4.50	5.00	−.50

Suppose that we repeat this process again to get a second difference between sample means, as shown in the second row of Table 10.2. In principle, we could do this for all possible random samples of size 10, thereby deriving a distribution of mean differences.* Table 10.2 presents 22 differences that might be observed. The distribution of all possible differences between the sample means for two populations represents a sampling distribution of the difference between two independent means. This is conceptually similar to a sampling distribution of the mean. However, now the concern is with a distribution of scores that represent differences between two means.

As we did in Chapter 7, we can compute the mean and standard deviation for this sampling distribution. If we were to do so, we would find that many of the properties of a sampling distribution of the mean also hold for a sampling distribution of the difference between two independent means. For instance, just as the mean of a sampling distribution of the mean is always equal to the population mean, *the mean of a sampling distribution of the difference between two independent means is always equal to the difference between the population means.* Consider the case

---

* In practice, we would never actually do this, just as we do not actually derive sampling distributions of the mean.

where two population means are equal and, hence, their difference is 0 (that is, $\mu_1 - \mu_2 = 0$). If we were to generate a sampling distribution of the difference between two independent means for these populations, the mean of the differences would equal 0.

The underlying principle is much the same as that developed in Chapter 7: When we select all possible samples for each of two populations and compute all possible differences between the two sets of sample means, some of the differences will overestimate the difference between the population means while others will underestimate it. When we average all of the sample mean differences, the underestimations will cancel the overestimations, with the result exactly equaling the difference between the population means.

The standard deviation of the sampling distribution of the difference between two independent means is formally known as the *standard error of the difference between two independent means* or, more simply, the **standard error of the difference**. Like the standard error of the mean, the standard error of the difference indicates how much sampling error occurs, on average.

Statisticians have developed a formula that allows us to compute the standard error of the difference from the population standard deviations:

$$\sigma_{\overline{X}_1 - \overline{X}_2} = \sqrt{\frac{\sigma_1^2}{n_1} + \frac{\sigma_2^2}{n_2}} \qquad [10.1]$$

where $\sigma_{\overline{X}_1 - \overline{X}_2}$ is the standard error of the difference, σ_1^2 is the population variance for group 1, σ_2^2 is the population variance for group 2, n_1 is the sample size for group 1, and n_2 is the sample size for group 2.*

Note the similarity of this formula to the one for the standard error of the mean (Equation 7.4):

$$\sigma_{\overline{X}} = \frac{\sigma}{\sqrt{N}} = \sqrt{\frac{\sigma^2}{N}}$$

Analogous to the standard error of the mean, the size of the standard error of the difference is influenced by two factors: (1) the sample sizes (n_1 and n_2) and (2) the variability of scores in the populations (σ_1^2 and σ_2^2). Consistent with the logic outlined in Section 7.7, the standard error of the difference becomes smaller as the sample sizes increase and as the variability of the scores in the populations decreases.

Pooled Variance Estimate

If we know the values of σ_1^2, σ_2^2, n_1, and n_2, we can compute the value of the standard error using Equation 10.1. In practice, we typically know the values of n_1 and n_2, but we do not know the values of σ_1^2 and σ_2^2. It is therefore necessary to estimate them from sample data.

---

* As we noted in Section 3.10, when more than one group is involved, *n* refers to the sample size for a particular group, whereas *N* refers to the total number of participants in the study. In the case of two groups, $N = n_1 + n_2$. The independent groups *t* test does not require that n_1 equal n_2.

The independent groups *t* test assumes that the two population variances are equal, or *homogeneous*. This assumption, which is known as the assumption of **homogeneity of variance**, redefines the estimation problem. Instead of estimating σ_1^2 and σ_2^2 separately, our goal is to estimate σ^2, the variance of both populations. In other words, it is assumed that $\sigma_1^2 = \sigma_2^2 = \sigma^2$. The quantity σ^2 can best be estimated by combining, or *pooling*, the variance estimates from the two samples to obtain a **pooled variance estimate**. By pooling the variance estimates from two independent samples, we increase the degrees of freedom on which the estimate of σ^2 is based and thereby obtain a better estimate.

The simplest method of pooling the two variance estimates is to compute their (unweighted) mean. This is, in fact, what is done when n_1 and n_2 are equal. However, if one of the groups is based on a larger sample size than the other, then the variance estimate from that group should be given greater "weight" in determining the pooled variance estimate because the larger the sample size, the greater the degrees of freedom and, thus, the better the estimate, as discussed in Chapter 7. This is accomplished by the following equation:

$$\hat{s}_{pooled}^2 = \frac{(n_1 - 1)\hat{s}_1^2 + (n_2 - 1)\hat{s}_2^2}{n_1 + n_2 - 2} \tag{10.2}$$

where $\hat{s}_{pooled}^2$ is the pooled variance estimate (that is, the pooled estimate of σ^2), $\hat{s}_1^2$ is the variance estimate for group 1, $\hat{s}_2^2$ is the variance estimate for group 2, and n_1 and n_2 are the sample sizes.*

Examine the right-hand side of Equation 10.2. This tells us to multiply the variance estimate for each group by its degrees of freedom, sum the products for the two groups, and then divide the resulting quantity by the total degrees of freedom, which is derived by adding the degrees of freedom for the two groups: $(n_1 - 1) + (n_2 - 1) = n_1 + n_2 - 2$.† This assures that the contributions of $\hat{s}_1^2$ and $\hat{s}_2^2$ to $\hat{s}_{pooled}^2$ are proportional to their degrees of freedom. For example, if $\hat{s}_1^2$ has twice as many degrees of freedom as $\hat{s}_2^2$, it will contribute twice as much to $\hat{s}_{pooled}^2$.

The meaning of Equation 10.2 becomes clearer if we rephrase it as follows:

$$\hat{s}_{pooled}^2 = \frac{(df_1)(\hat{s}_1^2) + (df_2)(\hat{s}_2^2)}{df_{TOTAL}} \tag{10.3}$$

where df_1 is the degrees of freedom for the variance estimate for sample 1, df_1 is the degrees of freedom for the variance estimate for sample 2, and df_{TOTAL} is the total degrees of freedom. In short, Equations 10.2 and 10.3 characterize the pooled variance estimate as the mean of $\hat{s}_1^2$ and $\hat{s}_2^2$ after these values have been weighted by their respective degrees of freedom.

---

* When $n_1 = n_2$, Equation 10.2 reduces to $\hat{s}_{pooled}^2 = (\hat{s}_1^2 + \hat{s}_2^2)/2$.
† The same general procedure can be used with more complex designs to pool the variance estimates of more than two groups.

We demonstrate the application of Equation 10.2 by returning to the order of information and likability example from the beginning of this chapter. Looking at Table 10.1, we find that $\hat{s}_1^2 = 1.33$ and $\hat{s}_2^2 = 1.78$. Because $n_1 = n_2 = 10$,

$$\hat{s}^2_{pooled} = \frac{(10 - 1)(1.33) + (10 - 1)(1.78)}{10 + 10 - 2} = 1.56$$

Estimated Standard Error of the Difference

Under the assumption of homogeneity of variance, $\hat{s}^2_{pooled}$ can be substituted for σ_1^2 and σ_2^2 in Equation 10.1 to yield the following formula for estimating the standard error of the difference between two independent means:

$$\hat{s}_{\overline{X}_1 - \overline{X}_2} = \sqrt{\frac{\hat{s}^2_{pooled}}{n_1} + \frac{\hat{s}^2_{pooled}}{n_2}} \qquad [10.4]$$

where $\hat{s}_{\overline{X}_1 - \overline{X}_2}$ is the estimated standard error of the difference and all other terms are as previously defined.

For the order of information and likability experiment,

$$\hat{s}_{\overline{X}_1 - \overline{X}_2} = \sqrt{\frac{1.56}{10} + \frac{1.56}{10}} = .56$$

Thus, the mean differences that constitute the sampling distribution of the difference between two independent means are estimated to deviate an average of .56 unit from the true difference between the two population means.

If we wish, we can combine the two steps above into one. To do this, we first represent Equation 10.4 as

$$\hat{s}_{\overline{X}_1 - \overline{X}_2} = \sqrt{\frac{\hat{s}^2_{pooled}}{n_1} + \frac{\hat{s}^2_{pooled}}{n_2}}$$

$$= \sqrt{\hat{s}^2_{pooled}\left(\frac{1}{n_1} + \frac{1}{n_2}\right)}$$

We then integrate this and Equation 10.2 to yield the following formula:

$$\hat{s}_{\overline{X}_1 - \overline{X}_2} = \sqrt{\left[\frac{(n_1 - 1)\hat{s}_1^2 + (n_2 - 1)\hat{s}_2^2}{n_1 + n_2 - 2}\right]\left(\frac{1}{n_1} + \frac{1}{n_2}\right)} \qquad [10.5]$$

The decision to calculate $\hat{s}_{\overline{X}_1 - \overline{X}_2}$ using Equation 10.5 or Equations 10.2 and 10.4 is merely a matter of preference. The former approach only requires one set of calculations but the latter approach is conceptually clearer because it makes the fact that the variances are being pooled explicit.

Because a variance estimate is equivalent to the corresponding sum of squares divided by the sample size minus 1, Equation 10.5 can also be expressed as

$$\hat{s}_{\overline{X}_1 - \overline{X}_2} = \sqrt{\left[\frac{(n_1 - 1)\left(\frac{SS_1}{n_1 - 1}\right) + (n_2 - 1)\left(\frac{SS_2}{n_2 - 1}\right)}{n_1 + n_2 - 2}\right]\left(\frac{1}{n_1} + \frac{1}{n_2}\right)}$$

which is equivalent to

$$\hat{s}_{\overline{X}_1 - \overline{X}_2} = \sqrt{\left(\frac{SS_1 + SS_2}{n_1 + n_2 - 2} \right) \left(\frac{1}{n_1} + \frac{1}{n_2} \right)} \qquad [10.6]$$

where SS_1 is the sum of squares for the first group and SS_2 is the sum of squares for the second group. The decision to calculate $\hat{s}_{\overline{X}_1 - \overline{X}_2}$ using Equation 10.6 or using one of the approaches above merely depends on whether one is dealing with variance estimates or sums of squares.

The Independent Groups *t* Test

We now have the background to formally test whether the observed difference between the sample likability means (5.00 versus 3.00) can be attributed to sampling error or whether it reflects a true relationship between the order of information and likability. To do so, we adapt the hypothesis testing steps outlined in Chapter 8 as follows:

1. Translate the research question into a null hypothesis and an alternative hypothesis. The null hypothesis states that the two population means are equal. If so, there is no relationship between the independent and the dependent variables. The alternative hypothesis states that the population means differ in some way. If so, the two variables are related.

In our example, the null hypothesis states that there is no relationship between the order of information and likability. The alternative hypothesis states that there is a relationship between the two variables. Expressed in terms of population means, the null and alternative hypotheses are

$H_0: \mu_1 = \mu_2$

$H_1: \mu_1 \neq \mu_2$

Although the alternative hypothesis is nondirectional in this instance, a directional alternative hypothesis is also possible. This would be phrased in terms of the mean for one population being larger than the mean for the other. As with the one-sample *t* test, directional tests should be used only when there is exclusive concern with a specific direction of difference and the researcher is uninterested in the effect if it is in the direction opposite to that stated in the directional alternative hypothesis. This is rarely the case. A general guideline is to only use a directional test if there is a compelling reason for doing so based on the existing theory and research.

Researchers often use subscripts based on the first letter of a condition's name rather than the more general "1" and "2" notation to identify specific conditions. For instance, we could state the null and alternative hypotheses for the order of information and likability experiment as

$H_0: \mu_P = \mu_C$

$H_1: \mu_P \neq \mu_C$

where the subscript "P" denotes the pro–con ordering and the subscript "C" denotes the con–pro ordering. The advantage of this approach is that it makes it easy to identify what condition is being represented. We adopt this more descriptive notational system where appropriate in the remainder of this book.*

2. Assuming that the null hypothesis is true, state an expected result in the form of a range of values within which the difference between the sample means would be expected to fall. This is expressed in terms of the critical values of t that define the endpoints of the range. The set of all t scores more extreme than the critical values constitutes an unexpected result or, more formally, the rejection region.

The critical values of t are determined by reference to the appropriate t distribution in Appendix D. The degrees of freedom to be used in this instance are those for the independent groups t test:

$$df = n_1 + n_2 - 2 \qquad\qquad [10.7]$$

This reflects the fact that the degrees of freedom associated with the first sample are $n_1 - 1$ and the degrees of freedom associated with the second sample are $n_2 - 1$, and $(n_1 - 1) + (n_2 - 1) = n_1 + n_2 - 2$.† Following the logic outlined in Chapter 8, by convention alpha is typically set equal to .05.

The t distribution in our example has $n_1 + n_2 - 2 = 10 + 10 - 2 = 18$ degrees of freedom. For an alpha level of .05, nondirectional test, and 18 degrees of freedom, Appendix D defines the critical values of t as being ± 2.101. An expected result is therefore defined by all t scores in the range -2.101 to $+2.101$, and an unexpected result is defined by all t scores that are less than -2.101 or greater than $+2.101$.

3. Characterize the mean and the standard deviation of the sampling distribution of the difference between two independent means assuming that the null hypothesis is true.

If we assume that the null hypothesis is true in the present example, then μ_1 and μ_2 are equal, so $\mu_1 - \mu_2 = 0$. It follows that the mean of the sampling distribution also equals 0 because, as we discussed above, the mean of a sampling distribution of the difference between two independent means is always equal to the difference between the population means.

The standard deviation of the sampling distribution of the difference between two independent means is merely the standard error of the difference, as we noted above. This was estimated earlier to equal .56 for our example.

---

* So that students can become familiar with the various statistical formulas, these are consistently presented with the more general numerical subscripts.

† It will be remembered that $n_1 + n_2 - 2$ is also the degrees of freedom for the pooled variance estimate. This reflects the fact that, as we will see shortly, the value of the t statistic in the independent groups case depends on the value of $\hat{s}_{\bar{X}_1 - \bar{X}_2}$, which, in turn, is dependent on the value of the pooled variance estimate.

4. Convert the observed difference between sample means to a *t* score to determine how many estimated standard errors it is from $\mu_1 - \mu_2$, *assuming that the null hypothesis is true*. This is accomplished using the formula

$$t = \frac{(\overline{X}_1 - \overline{X}_2) - (\mu_1 - \mu_2)}{\hat{s}_{\overline{X}_1 - \overline{X}_2}} \qquad [10.8]$$

where $\overline{X}_1 - \overline{X}_2$ is the observed difference between the sample means, $\mu_1 - \mu_2$ is the hypothesized difference between the population means, and $\hat{s}_{\overline{X}_1 - \overline{X}_2}$ is the estimated standard error of the difference.

In most instances, the null hypothesis states that the population means are identical, so $\mu_1 - \mu_2$ will equal 0. However, other null hypotheses are also possible. For instance, a given null hypothesis might state that the mean of the first population is 10 units higher than the mean of the second population. This could be tested by setting $\mu_1 - \mu_2$ equal to 10 in Equation 10.8. Any other hypothesized difference between two population means can be similarly assessed.

When we hypothesize that $\mu_1 - \mu_2$ is equal to 0 (that is, when the null hypothesis states that $\mu_1 - \mu_2$), Equation 10.8 reduces to

$$t = \frac{\overline{X}_1 - \overline{X}_2}{\hat{s}_{\overline{X}_1 - \overline{X}_2}} \qquad [10.9]$$

This is the most commonly used version of the independent groups *t* test. However, because it is conceptually clearer, we use the more general formula represented by Equation 10.8 whenever an independent groups *t* test is called for in the remainder of this chapter.

Note that Equation 10.8 is merely a special case of Equation 8.7:

$$t = \frac{\text{score of interest} - \text{hypothesized mean of the distribution}}{\text{estimated standard error of the distribution}}$$

where the score of interest is the observed difference between the sample means, the hypothesized mean of the distribution is the hypothesized difference between the population means, and the estimated standard error of the distribution is the estimated standard error of the difference. Thus, the independent groups *t* test is conceptually similar to the one-sample t test which, as we saw in Section 8.15, can also be conceptualized as a special case of Equation 8.7.

In our example, $\overline{X}_1 - \overline{X}_2 = 5.00 - 3.00 = 2.00$, $\hat{s}_{\overline{X}_1 - \overline{X}_2} = .56$, and $\mu_1 - \mu_2$ is hypothesized to equal 0. Hence,

$$t = \frac{(\overline{X}_1 - \overline{X}_2) - (\mu_1 - \mu_2)}{\hat{s}_{\overline{X}_1 - \overline{X}_2}}$$

$$= \frac{2.00 - 0}{.56} = 3.57$$

5. Compare the value of *t* that was calculated using Equation 10.8 with the expected result as defined by all *t* scores that fall between the critical values of *t*. If the observed t score exceeds either the positive or the negative critical value, reject the null hypothesis.* If the observed *t* score does not exceed either the positive or the negative critical value, do not reject the null hypothesis.

In our example, the observed *t* score of 3.57 exceeds the positive critical value of +2.101. This suggests that the observed difference between sample means is too large to be attributed to sampling error, and the null hypothesis is therefore rejected. The order of information is related to likability, and we have answered the first of the three questions for the analysis of bivariate relationships.

STUDY EXERCISE 10.1

In order to test for gender discrimination by women against other women, a researcher asks 13 women to read an essay that is presented as being written by "John McKay" and then rate the essay for the quality of the writing style. The ratings are made on a scale from 1 to 10, with higher scores indicating greater perceived quality. Another 15 women read and rate the identical essay but are led to believe that the author is "Joan McKay." The following summary data are observed. Test for a relationship between the alleged gender of the author and the perceived quality of the essay using an independent groups *t* test.

Male author	Female author
$n_M = 13$	$n_F = 15$
$\overline{X}_M = 7.20$	$\overline{X}_F = 6.10$
$SS_M = 15.00$	$SS_M = 18.00$

Answer   The null and alternative hypotheses are

$$H_0: \mu_M = \mu_F$$

$$H_1: \mu_M \neq \mu_F$$

where the subscripts "*M*" and "*F*" represent the male author and the female author conditions, respectively.

For an alpha level of .05, nondirectional test, and $n_1 + n_2 - 2 = 13 - 15 - 2 = 26$ degrees of freedom, the critical values of *t* from Appendix D are ±2.056. Thus, if the observed t value is less than −2.056 or greater than +2.056, we will reject the null hypothesis.

---

* If the null hypothesis is rejected, the nature of the relationship between the independent and dependent variables can be determined using the strategy that is presented in Section 10.4.

The standard error of the difference is estimated using Equation 10.6:

$$\hat{s}_{\overline{X}_1 - \overline{X}_2} = \sqrt{\left(\frac{SS_1 + SS_2}{n_1 + n_2 - 2}\right)\left(\frac{1}{n_1} + \frac{1}{n_2}\right)}$$

$$= \sqrt{\left(\frac{15.00 + 18.00}{13 + 15 - 2}\right)\left(\frac{1}{13} + \frac{1}{15}\right)} = .43$$

The observed difference between the sample means is $\overline{X}_1 - \overline{X}_2 = 7.20 - 6.10 = 1.10$, and the hypothesized difference between the population means is $\mu_1 - \mu_2 = 0$.

Using Equation 10.8, we compute the observed value of *t*:

$$t = \frac{(\overline{X}_1 - \overline{X}_2) - (\mu_1 - \mu_2)}{\hat{s}_{\overline{X}_1 - \overline{X}_2}}$$

$$= \frac{1.10 - 0}{.43} = 2.56$$

Because 2.56 exceeds +2.056, we reject the null hypothesis and conclude that there is a relationship between the alleged gender of the author and the perceived quality of the essay.

Assumptions of the Independent Groups *t* Test

As we noted at the beginning of this chapter, the independent groups *t* test is appropriate when the independent variable is between-subjects in nature and the dependent variable is quantitative in nature and measured on a level that at least approximates interval characteristics. Application of the test also requires that the sampling distribution of the *t* statistic approximates a *t* distribution, which it will when the following assumptions are met:

1. The samples are independently and randomly selected from their respective populations.

2. The scores in each population are normally distributed.

3. The scores in the two populations have equal variances; that is, $\sigma_1^2 = \sigma_2^2$. As we discussed earlier, this is called the assumption of *homogeneity of variance*.

For the test to be valid, it is important that the assumption of independent and random selection be met. However, under certain conditions, the independent groups *t* test is robust to violations of the normality and homogeneity of variance assumptions. In fact, if the sample sizes in the two groups are each greater than 40 and roughly comparable, then the test is robust to rather severe departures from the normality assumption. Indeed, the test is fairly robust to normality violations for sample sizes as small as 15 per group, if not somewhat smaller.

When the sample sizes are equal, the independent groups *t* test is quite robust to violations of the assumption of homogeneity of variance (Posten, 1978). For example, when the sample size is 15 in each group, the test performs satisfactorily even when the population variance for one group is four times larger than the population variance for the other group. This trend is also evident for unequal sample sizes in the two groups, as long as they are not too discrepant.

With fairly discrepant sample sizes, there is a tendency for the test to be conservative (that is, for there to be fewer Type I errors than the alpha level dictates) when the group with the larger sample size has the larger variance. Conversely, the independent groups *t* test is liberal (that is, more Type I errors occur than the alpha level dictates) when the larger sample size is paired with the smaller variance (for further discussion of this issue, see Sawilosky and Hillman, 1992).

As we noted in Section 9.6, formal methods are available for assessing the homogeneity of variance assumption. However, we also noted in Section 9.6 that each of these tests has problems associated with it. To illustrate the general approach of these procedures, we will review the important features of the **Levene test**, which evaluates a null hypothesis of equal variances in the populations against an alternative hypothesis of unequal variances in the populations.

If the Levene test yields a statistically significant result, the null hypothesis of equal population variances will be rejected, thus suggesting that the variances are not homogeneous, that is, that they are *heterogeneous*. Even if this is the case, this is not necessarily problematic because the independent groups *t* test is robust to violations of the homogeneity of variance assumption under the conditions that we just outlined. Rejecting the null hypothesis for the Levene test only allows us to conclude that the variances in the populations are not equal. It does not address the magnitude of the discrepancy in the population variances, which must be substantial to undermine the *t* test.

We can never accept the null hypothesis of equal population variances based on the Levene test. If we fail to reject the null hypothesis, we can only conclude that the data are *consistent with* homogeneous population variances (with the sample differences in the variance estimates being due to sampling error), but we cannot conclude that the population variances are homogeneous.

The Levene test is somewhat sensitive to nonnormality in the data. Although it is much better than the alternative test of homogeneity of variance in this regard, it still must be interpreted cautiously given nonnormal population data because the test has a tendency to yield false significance when the population distributions are skewed.

10.3 Relationships and Parameters

We have examined whether a relationship exists between two variables by conducting a test of the null hypothesis that the population means for two groups are equal. It is also possible to test for a relationship between two variables using population parameters other than the mean. For example, the null hypothesis of equal population *medians* can be examined. If the groups defined by the independent variable have different population medians on the dependent variable, one would conclude that a relationship exists between the independent and dependent variables (at least in terms of medians).

The term *relationship* is general and must be qualified by the particular population parameter being examined. Two variables may exhibit a relationship in terms of one parameter (for example, means) but not another (for example, medians).

The parameters used for characterizing relationships in this book are primarily means and correlations, although we also consider other parameters in Chapters 15 and 16. However, it is important to keep in mind that a relationship between two variables can be examined in terms of any of a number of parameters and that the nature of the relationship might differ depending on the parameter under consideration.

10.4 Strength of the Relationship

If we reject the null hypothesis and conclude that a relationship exists between the independent and dependent variables, it becomes meaningful to address the second question relevant to the analysis of bivariate relationships: What is the strength of the relationship? One approach is to simply examine the size of the difference between the two group means. For example, we know that a mean discrepancy of $4,000 in annual starting salaries for white versus African American entry-level secretaries is a sizable difference in income. This conclusion is based on our understanding of how income is distributed and of what $4,000 will buy. However, sometimes we are not as knowledgeable about the dependent variable, as in the experiment on likability. Is a mean difference of 2.00 small or large? What are the implications of such a difference?

To help us gain perspective on the strength of the relationship between two variables, statisticians have developed a wide range of indexes. We develop the general logic of these approaches using an index known as *eta-squared* and then discuss the advantages and disadvantages of different measures. We initially derive eta-squared using procedures that are computationally inefficient but that clearly illustrate the concept. A computational formula is then presented. We use the order of information and likability experiment to illustrate the relevant points.

The second and third columns of Table 10.3 present the condition in which each of the 20 individuals participated and their corresponding scores on the dependent variable. Looking at column 3, we see that there is variability in the likability ratings; some participants said they like the hypothetical stranger more than did others. Our goal is to analyze this variability and determine what proportion of it is associated with the independent variable. Because of a desirable statistical property to be discussed shortly, we use the sum of squares as our measure of variability.

Sum of Squares Total

As a first step, we need to derive a numerical index of the amount of variability in the likability ratings. This involves computing the sum of squares for the dependent variable across all individuals in the experiment, which can be accomplished using the standard formula for a sum of squares. This has been done in Table 10.3. This sum of squares is called the **sum of squares total** (symbolized as SS_{TOTAL}) because it represents the total amount of variability that exists in the data. In this instance, $SS_{TOTAL} = 48.00$.

TABLE 10.3 **Computation of Sum of Squares Total for Order of Information and Likability Experiment**

Participant	Condition	X	X^2
1	Pro–Con	7	49
2	Pro–Con	4	16
3	Pro–Con	3	9
4	Pro–Con	5	25
5	Pro–Con	5	25
6	Pro–Con	6	36
7	Pro–Con	5	25
8	Pro–Con	5	25
9	Pro–Con	4	16
10	Pro–Con	6	36
11	Con–Pro	1	1
12	Con–Pro	5	25
13	Con–Pro	2	4
14	Con–Pro	5	25
15	Con–Pro	3	9
16	Con–Pro	3	9
17	Con–Pro	3	9
18	Con–Pro	2	4
19	Con–Pro	4	16
20	Con–Pro	2	4
		$\Sigma X = 80$	$\Sigma X^2 = 368$

$$SS_{\text{TOTAL}} = \sum X^2 - \frac{(\sum X)^2}{N}$$

$$= 368 - \frac{80^2}{20} = 48.00$$

Treatment Effects and Variance Extraction

The next step is to determine what effect the independent variable had on the dependent variable. This is done by comparing the mean score in each condition with the mean score for both conditions combined. Because it is based on all individuals in the study, the overall mean is known as the *grand mean* (symbolized as G).

As indicated in column 2 of Table 10.4, the grand mean in this instance is 4.00. The mean likability rating for the pro–con condition was previously found to be 5.00. Thus, the effect of having the traits presented in the pro–con order was to raise the likability ratings, on average, 1 unit above the grand mean. For the con–pro condition, the mean likability score was previously found to be 3.00. The effect of having the traits presented in the con–pro order was thus to lower the likability ratings, on average, 1 unit below the grand mean.

These effects are formally called *treatment effects* (symbolized as T) and are defined as the difference between a given group mean and the grand mean. The treatment effect for the pro–con group is $T_1 = \overline{X}_1 - G = 5.00 - 4.00 = 1.00$ and

TABLE 10.4 **Computation of Sum of Squares Error for Order of Information and Likability Experiment**

Participant	Condition	X	T	$X_n = X - T$	X_n^2
1	Pro–Con	7	1	6	36
2	Pro–Con	4	1	3	9
3	Pro–Con	3	1	2	4
4	Pro–Con	5	1	4	16
5	Pro–Con	5	1	4	16
6	Pro–Con	6	1	5	25
7	Pro–Con	5	1	4	16
8	Pro–Con	5	1	4	16
9	Pro–Con	4	1	3	9
10	Pro–Con	6	1	5	25
11	Con–Pro	1	−1	2	4
12	Con–Pro	5	−1	6	36
13	Con–Pro	2	−1	3	9
14	Con–Pro	5	−1	6	36
15	Con–Pro	3	−1	4	16
16	Con–Pro	3	−1	4	16
17	Con–Pro	3	−1	4	16
18	Con–Pro	2	−1	3	9
19	Con–Pro	4	−1	5	25
20	Con–Pro	2	−1	3	9

$$\Sigma X = 80$$
$$\overline{X} = G = 4.00$$
$$\Sigma X_n = 80 \qquad \Sigma X_n^2 = 348$$

$$SS_{\text{ERROR}} = \Sigma X_n^2 - \frac{(\Sigma X_n)^2}{N}$$

$$= 348 - \frac{80^2}{20} = 28.00$$

the treatment effect for the con–pro group is $T_2 = \overline{X}_2 - G = 3.00 - 4.00 = -1.00$. The treatment effects for the two conditions are listed in column 3 of Table 10.4.

We can use the treatment effects to determine the strength of the relationship between the independent and dependent variables. This requires first removing, or *nullifying,* the influence of the independent variable on the dependent variable. For participants in the pro–con condition, the effect of the order of information was to raise scores, on average, 1 unit *above* the grand mean. If we want to nullify this effect, we can *subtract* 1 unit from each of these individuals' original likability scores. Consider the first person depicted in Table 10.4. The likability rating for this individual is 7. To nullify the effect of being in the pro–con condition, we subtract 1 from his score to get a *nullified score* (symbolized as X_n) of 6. This process has been repeated in column 4 of Table 10.4 for each participant in the pro–con condition.

On the other hand, the effect of the order of information for participants in the con–pro condition was to lower scores, on average, 1 unit *below* the grand mean. If we want to nullify this effect, we simply *add* 1 unit (that is, *subtract* 1 *negative* unit) to each of these individuals' original likability scores. The first person depicted in Table 10.4 for the con–pro condition has a likability rating of 1. To nullify the effect of being in the con–pro condition, we add 1 to his score to get a nullified score of 2. This process has been repeated for each participant in the con–pro condition in column 4 of Table 10.4.

When you examine the nullified scores in column 4, note that there is less variability than there is in the original likability ratings in column 2. This is because we have removed the variability that was associated with the independent variable. Note, however, that there is still variability in the X_n scores due to factors other than the order of information. In statistical terminology, the remaining variability is called **unexplained variance** or **error variance** and reflects the influence of disturbance variables such as the ones that we discussed in Chapter 9.

We can derive a numerical index of how much error variance remains after we have removed the influence of the independent variable by computing a sum of squares for the nullified scores. This is accomplished by applying the standard formula for a sum of squares to the X_n scores, as is done in the right-hand side of Table 10.4. This sum of squares is formally called the **sum of squares error** (symbolized as SS_{ERROR}). In this instance, $SS_{ERROR} = 28.00$.

Whereas the sum of squares total indexes the *total* amount of variability in the dependent variable, the sum of squares error indexes the amount of *unexplained* variability in the dependent variable—that is, variability that remains after the effects of the independent variable have been removed. If we subtract the sum of squares error from the sum of squares total, we obtain an index of **explained variance**—that is, variability that is associated with (explained by) the independent variable. This index is called the **sum of squares explained** (symbolized as $SS_{EXPLAINED}$). In our example, $SS_{EXPLAINED} = SS_{TOTAL} - SS_{ERROR} = 48.00 - 28.00 = 20.00$.

Because $SS_{EXPLAINED} = SS_{TOTAL} - SS_{ERROR}$, simple rearrangement of terms shows that it is also the case that

$$SS_{TOTAL} = SS_{EXPLAINED} - SS_{ERROR} \qquad [10.10]$$

In other words, the total variability in the dependent variable, as represented by the sum of squares total, can be split up, or *partitioned,* into two components: one (the sum of squares explained) that reflects the influence of the independent variable and one (the sum of squares error) that reflects the influence of disturbance variables. It is this property of sums of squares—the fact that they can be meaningfully added to and subtracted from one another—that makes the sum of squares the preferred measure of variability when analyzing the strength of the relationship between variables.*

---

* In contrast, neither standard deviation estimates nor variance estimates can be manipulated in this manner. This is because they are averages (of deviation and squared deviation scores, respectively), and averages cannot be meaningfully added to or subtracted from one another.

Eta-Squared

The stronger the influence of the independent variable on the dependent variable, the larger the sum of squares explained should be relative to the sum of squares total. By dividing the former by the latter, we can calculate the proportion of variability in the dependent variable that is explained by the independent variable. This relationship can be represented symbolically as

$$\text{eta}^2 = \frac{SS_{\text{EXPLAINED}}}{SS_{\text{TOTAL}}}$$
[10.11]

where eta-squared represents a statistic known as **eta-squared** and the other terms are as previously defined.*

Eta-squared indexes the strength of the relationship between the independent and dependent variables because it represents the proportion of variability in the dependent variable that is associated with the independent variable. Eta-squared can range from 0 to 1.00. An eta-squared that approaches 1.00 reflects a stronger relationship between the variables, and an eta-squared that approaches 0 reflects a weaker relationship between the variables.

In our example,

$$\text{eta}^2 = \frac{20.00}{48.00} = .42$$

Thus, 42% of the variability in the dependent variable (likability) is explained by the independent variable (order of information).

Because eta-squared represents the proportion of variability in the dependent variable that is associated with the independent variable, 1.00 minus eta-squared must represent the proportion of variability in the dependent variable that is *not* associated with the independent variable—that is, the proportion of variability that is due to disturbance variables. In our example, $1.00 - .42 = .58$, or 58%, of the variability in likability ratings is attributable to disturbance variables.

What constitutes a large value of eta-squared? Standards differ considerably among researchers on the substantive interpretation of eta-squared. Much depends on the specific area of application. One of us (JJ) has studied the relationship between attitudes and behavior. In this area, an eta-squared of less than .20 represents a "weak" relationship between variables, an eta-squared between .20 and .50 represents a "moderate" relationship, and an eta-squared greater than .50 represents a "strong" relationship. In other contexts, different interpretations might apply.

Behavior is complex, and rarely do only a small number of variables determine that behavior. To the extent that a behavior is determined by a multitude of variables, the explanation of as little as 5% of the variability in the dependent measure is, in some respects, a considerable amount.

Typically, research in the behavioral sciences involves relatively small values of eta-squared, but this should not lead one to conclude that such effects are

---

* It should be noted that eta-squared is equivalent to the square of a statistic called the *point-biserial correlation coefficient.*

necessarily trivial. Rosenthal (1995) describes several research situations where eta-squared values of less than .01 have had tremendous practical implications in a medical context, reflecting the saving of thousands of lives.

In the remainder of this book, we consider an eta-squared near .05 to be a weak effect, an eta-squared near .10 to be a moderate effect, and an eta-squared greater than .15 to be a strong effect. However, these conventions are somewhat arbitrary and can be revised upward or downward depending on the research context. Because the data sets that serve as the basis for our examples throughout this book tend to represent artificially strong relationships, the values of eta-squared that we report are generally substantially inflated relative to those that are observed in actual behavioral science research.

Computational Formula for Eta-Squared

Although it is possible to derive eta-squared with Equation 10.11 using the approach described above, a much simpler computational formula for eta-squared is used in practice:

$$\text{eta}^2 = \frac{t^2}{t^2 + df} \qquad [10.12]$$

where t is the observed value of t and df is the corresponding degrees of freedom.

For the order of information and likability experiment,

$$\text{eta}^2 = \frac{3.57^2}{3.57^2 + 18} = .41$$

This value agrees, within rounding error, with our earlier result and represents a strong effect.

STUDY EXERCISE 10.2

Calculate eta-squared for the data in Study Exercise 10.1.

Answer   Eta-squared is most easily calculated using Equation 10.12:

$$\text{eta}^2 = \frac{t^2}{t^2 + df}$$

$$= \frac{2.56^2}{2.56^2 + 26} = .20$$

The proportion of variability in the perceived quality of the essay that is associated with the alleged gender of the author is .20. This represents a strong effect.

Eta-Squared Following a Statistically Nonsignificant Test

The foregoing discussion demonstrates the utility of examining eta-squared following a statistically significant test. Eta-squared is also informative even when a test is statistically nonsignificant. This relates to the fact that, as we discussed in Chapter 8, power increases with sample size. When the sample sizes are small, power will tend to be low and we will be relatively unlikely to reject a false null hypothesis. By examining eta-squared, we can gain additional insight into the situation. If the null hypothesis is not rejected and eta-squared is small, then the statistical decision is reinforced. However, if the null hypothesis is not rejected and eta-squared is relatively large, this is a "flag" for potentially low statistical power. We might want to collect additional data because this is an indication that the two variables may be related but that the sample sizes were not large enough to yield a statistically significant result with the desired degree of consistency. With this in mind, we recommend that eta-squared be calculated following statistically nonsignificant as well as statistically significant statistical tests, and we follow this strategy throughout this book.

Alternative Measures of the Strength of the Relationship

The proportion of explained variability in a sample can be distinguished from the proportion of explained variability in the population from which that sample comes (Kennedy, 1970; Kesselman, 1975). In this regard, it must be emphasized that eta-squared describes the strength of the relationship between two variables in a set of *sample* data and is merely an estimate of the strength of the relationship in the *population*. In fact, *eta-squared is a biased estimator in that it tends to slightly overestimate the strength of the relationship in the population across random samples.*

Any index of the strength of the relationship that is derived from sample data is subject to sampling error and must be interpreted accordingly. An observed sample eta-squared of .50 could result from a population with a value of eta-squared that is quite different. The confidence one has in the accuracy of a sample eta-squared as an estimate of the corresponding population eta-squared is a function, in part, of the total sample size, that is, of $n_1 + n_2$. The larger the total sample size, the better the estimate. In fact, for total sample sizes of less than 30, the amount of sampling error can be rather sizable (Carrol and Nordholm, 1975). For this reason, indexes of the strength of association must be interpreted with caution.

In light of the above, we advocate the use of eta-squared only as a heuristic to help researchers appreciate relationships within sample data. Eta-squared is limited as an estimate of the strength of the relationship in the population because, in our opinion, *point estimation procedures* (that is, procedures that identify one specific value) are not very useful. Instead, an *interval estimation approach* (that is, the identification of a range of values) seems more reasonable.

Analogous to the confidence intervals about the mean that we discussed in Section 8.11, it is possible to construct confidence intervals about eta-squared. These provide the investigator with ranges of values that, with a specified degree of confidence, contain the population value of eta-squared. The mathematics for calculating such intervals are beyond the scope of this book but are discussed in Fleishman (1980).

A number of alternatives to eta-squared have been proposed, the application of which are controversial. One popular index of relationship strength is Cohen's *d*, which is the difference between the two sample means divided by the pooled standard deviation estimate (that is, the square root of the pooled variance estimate). Cohen's *d* expresses the magnitude of the mean difference in standard deviation units, much like a standard score expresses a raw score in standard deviation units. Cohen's d bears a mathematical relationship to eta-squared such that

$$\text{eta}^2 = \frac{d^2}{d^2 + 4}$$

We prefer to use eta-squared because we find it to be more intuitively interpretable.

Hays (1981) argues for an unbiased estimator of relationship strength known as *omega-squared*. Another unbiased estimator of the strength of the relationship between two variables is *epsilon-squared*. However, these measures have some undesirable statistical properties.[*] For instance, epsilon-squared sometimes takes on negative values, which is nonsensical because epsilon-squared estimates the proportion of explained variability in the population and proportions cannot be negative. This is one reason why some statisticians do not recommend this approach, and there is controversy about how to best handle negative values of epsilon-squared. Nevertheless, epsilon-squared is one of the most commonly used unbiased estimators of relationship strength and, for this reason, we provide the formula for epsilon-squared for the independent groups t test situation in Appendix N, which also presents the formulas for epsilon-squared for many of the other parametric statistical tests that we discuss in this book.

Unstandardized Effect Size and Confidence Intervals

Eta-squared represents a *standardized* measure of relationship strength in that it always ranges from 0 to 1.00. Another strategy that researchers use to characterize the *effect size* (that is, the strength of the relationship between the independent and dependent variables) is the use of *unstandardized* measures of relationship strength. For two independent groups, this measure is simply the difference between the sample means. For example, suppose that we want to compare the mean salaries of male and female doctors during their first year of employment. If we are told that the mean difference that results when we subtract the female mean from the male mean is $15,500, then we have a sense of how large the pay differential is. The difference of $15,500 is meaningful because we are knowledgeable about income, what money can buy, and the practical implications of having an additional $15,500. In many respects, this unstandardized measure of effect size is even more meaningful than a standardized effect size measure such as eta-squared.

On the other hand, when the measures that are used to assess the variables of interest are more arbitrary, unstandardized measures of relationship strength do not convey meaning as straightforwardly. This is the case for the order of information and likability experiment, where the unstandardized mean difference is 2.00, with individuals in the pro–con condition rating the stranger, on average, 2.00 units higher than individuals in the con–pro condition did. Just what does a 2-unit discrepancy mean? Recall that the rating scale has seven response options. Specifically,

---

[*] See Carrol and Nordholm (1975), Fisher (1950), Glass and Hakstian (1969), Haggard (1958), and Kesselman (1975) for a discussion of the statistical properties of various indexes of the strength of the relationship between two variables.

a score of 1 means that the research participant disliked the stranger very much, a score of 4 means that the participant neither liked nor disliked the stranger, a score of 7 means that the research participant liked the stranger very much, and so forth. The 2-unit difference between means is more meaningful when one keeps in mind that it refers to a difference of 2 points on this scale. But the measure simply is not grounded in the real world to the extent that a measure of, say, income is. Despite this, it is usually good practice to include information about unstandardized effect sizes in research reports.

It is fairly easy to calculate confidence intervals for an unstandardized effect size measure such as a mean difference. The rationale and calculation for such intervals are similar to those described in Section 8.11 for the one-sample situation. As we discuss below, the use of confidence intervals in this context has several important advantages over the use of point estimation procedures (such as eta-squared) for describing effect sizes.

We illustrate the calculation of a 95% confidence interval using the order of information and likability experiment as an example. To calculate a confidence interval, we need three values. First, we need the value of the mean difference, $\overline{X}_1 - \overline{X}_2$. Second, we need the absolute value of the critical *t* value that was the criterion for deciding to reject the null hypothesis. We refer to this as $|t_{critical}|$. Note that this value of *t* is the value derived from Appendix D, *not* the observed value of *t* that is computed using Equation 10.8. Finally, we need the estimated standard error of the difference between two independent means, $\hat{s}_{\overline{X}_1 - \overline{X}_2}$.

The formula for a confidence interval in the independent groups case is

$$CI = (\overline{X}_1 - \overline{X}_2) - |t_{critical}|(\hat{s}_{\overline{X}_1 - \overline{X}_2}) \text{ to } (\overline{X}_1 - \overline{X}_2) + |t_{critical}|(\hat{s}_{\overline{X}_1 - \overline{X}_2}) \quad [10.13]$$

For the order of information and likability experiment, $\overline{X}_1 - \overline{X}_2$ is equal to 2.00, $|t_{critical}|$ is equal to 2.101, and $\hat{s}_{\overline{X}_1 - \overline{X}_2}$ is equal to .56. Thus, the 95% confidence interval is

$$CI = 2.00 - (2.101)(.56) \text{ to } 2.00 + (2.101)(.56)$$
$$= .82 \text{ to } 3.18$$

We are 95% confident that the interval .82 to 3.18 contains the true population mean difference in likability ratings.

Paralleling the case for the one-sample *t* test as we discussed in Section 8.11, confidence intervals shed light on whether a relationship exists between the independent and the dependent variables. If a null hypothesis states that two population means are equal, then a 95% confidence interval that does *not* contain the value of 0 indicates that the null hypothesis should be rejected at an alpha level of .05. In the present case, the confidence interval of .82 to 3.18 does *not* contain the value of 0, so this indicates that the null hypothesis should indeed be rejected and that there is therefore a relationship between the independent and dependent variables.

Many behavioral scientists use confidence intervals because they are so informative. Not only do they provide information about the effect size but they also indicate whether a null hypothesis should be rejected, making the formal *t* test described earlier in this chapter unnecessary.

Confidence intervals also provide information about sampling error. When there is a great deal of sampling error, the confidence interval is wide, with a sizable difference between the lower limit and the upper limit. When there is little sampling error, the confidence interval is narrow, with a small difference between the lower limit and the upper limit. For example, suppose that the 95% confidence interval for the order of information and likability experiment was 1.99 to 2.01. This would suggest a very small amount of sampling error because we would be 95% confident that the true population mean lies within an interval that is only $2.01 - 1.99 = .02$ unit wide. Such perspective on sampling error represents yet another advantage of reporting confidence intervals.

Some behavioral scientists have mounted an attack on traditional null hypothesis testing and argue that the focus of statistical analysis should be on interval estimation and effect size estimation strategies rather than on the results of hypothesis tests. One argument is that the null hypothesis is never true if we calculate the population means to enough decimal places, so why give so much attention to a null hypothesis that we know is false? The crucial question, according to the critics, is not whether two means differ but, rather, by *how much* they differ. The mean difference might be trivial and the means then can be treated as if they are *functionally* equivalent. Or the difference might be so substantial that the effect of the independent variable is judged to be nontrivial.

It is not surprising that this issue has sparked considerable debate, with numerous staunch defenders of hypothesis testing arguing against the criticisms of those in the effect size camp. Interested readers are referred to Cohen (1994); Dixon (1998); Harlow, Mulaik, and Steiger (1997); and Jaccard (1996) for further discussion of this matter. We believe that both the hypothesis testing and the effect size approaches have value, with the utility of each depending on the context. We adopt the practice in this book of reporting the results of both hypothesis tests and effect size measures.

10.5 Nature of the Relationship

We have now considered the first two questions regarding the analysis of bivariate relationships: (1) Is there a relationship between the independent and dependent variables? (2) If so, what is the strength of the relationship? The final question concerns the nature of the relationship.

As we discussed in Section 8.5, rejection of the null hypothesis also implies acceptance of the alternative hypothesis. Because this states $\mu_1 \neq \mu_2$, this outcome tells us that exposure to the two levels of the independent variable is related to different mean scores on the dependent variable. The nature of this relationship is determined by comparing the two *sample* means to make a decision about how the two *population* means differ. We simply conclude that the condition that has the larger *sample* mean also has the larger *population* mean.

In the order of information and likability experiment, the mean likability scores are 5.00 for the pro–con condition and 3.00 for the con–pro condition. Because the mean for the pro–con condition is greater than the mean for the con–pro condition, we conclude that the nature of the relationship between the order of information and likability is such that when people are presented information that goes from positive to negative, they will find a stranger more likable than when the order of information goes from negative to positive.

10.6   Methodological Considerations

Several methodological features should be noted about the order of information and likability experiment. These will help place the results of the statistical test in the proper context.

First, the investigator attempted to control for confounding variables by randomly assigning participants to the two experimental conditions. Without this random assignment, differences between the two groups could be attributed to individual differences rather than to the experimental treatment. For example, research has shown that some people have a tendency to view others in a positive light, whereas other people tend to view everyone in a negative light. Without random assignment, it is possible that the pro–con condition could have contained more of the former individuals and the con–pro condition more of the latter. With random assignment, this is unlikely.

Another issue concerns the extent to which disturbance variables were controlled. Disturbance variables have the effect of creating sampling error, the amount of which is reflected in the standard error of the difference. In this experiment, the standard error of the difference was estimated to be .56, which suggests that, on average, the difference between any two sample means based on random samples of size 10 will deviate .56 unit from the true difference between the population means. Given a potential range of 6 (because likability ratings were made on a 1 to 7 scale), this value suggests a relatively small amount of sampling error.

A second perspective on sampling error is gained by examining eta-squared. In this study, 42% of the variability in the dependent variable is associated with the independent variable and 58% is due to disturbance variables. The picture that emerges is one of the disturbance variables (and the consequent sampling error) not overwhelming any "signal" produced by the independent variable.

The experiment has limitations from the standpoint of generalizability. First, it included only college students. Would the results generalize to other individuals as well? Second, only one pro–con list and one con–pro list was used. Maybe something about the particular adjectives that were included on the lists produced the experimental outcome. Would similar results occur if different adjectives were used?

These and other questions of generalizability can be addressed through additional experimentation. It is important that one always consider such issues when drawing conclusions from research results. Statistics and research design go hand in hand when interpreting the results of an investigation.

10.7   Numerical Example

Individuals have long sought ways to help them to relax. One such method is transcendental meditation (TM). An individual who practices TM meditates twice a day for 15 to 20 minutes. During meditation, the individual subvocally repeats a mantra, which is a unique two-syllable sound that is assigned to a meditator by a trained teacher of TM. Proponents of TM emphasize the importance of the mantra in the meditation process. However, it has been suggested that the mantra is not essential to achieve optimal levels of relaxation during meditation and that the same results can be achieved by using any number of arbitrary words instead. Let us consider a hypothetical experiment that is designed to test this assertion.

Twenty individuals served as participants. Ten are randomly assigned to a mantra condition and ten are randomly assigned to a condition where they meditate using the word *orange* instead of a mantra. Each person practices meditation using the relevant subvocalization for 2 weeks prior to the test session. During the test session, the participants engage in their regular 15-minute meditation period while a number of physiological indicators of relaxation are measured. Included in these is heart rate. In general, the more relaxed an individual is, the slower his or her heart rate will be. The heart rate measures for the 20 participants are listed in columns 1 and 3 of Table 10.5.

The null hypothesis is that, in the population, individuals who practice traditional TM will not differ in their mean heart rate from individuals who meditate using the word *orange* in place of a mantra. If so, there is no relationship between the type of subvocalization and heart rate. The alternative hypothesis is that the mean heart rates will differ. If so, the type of subvocalization and heart rate are related. These hypotheses are formally stated as

$$H_0: \mu_M = \mu_O$$

$$H_1: \mu_M \neq \mu_O$$

TABLE 10.5   **Data and Calculations for the Type of Subvocalization and Heart Rate Experiment**

	Mantra			"Orange"	
	X	X^2		X	X^2
	58	3,364		62	3,844
	62	3,844		57	3,249
	54	2,916		67	4,489
	52	2,704		66	4,356
	64	4,096		58	3,364
	58	3,364		60	3,600
	52	2,704		64	4,096
	64	4,096		62	3,844
	56	3,136		57	3,249
	60	3,600		67	4,489

$$\Sigma X_M = 580 \qquad \Sigma X_M^2 = 33,824 \qquad \Sigma X_O = 620 \qquad \Sigma X_O^2 = 38,580$$
$$\overline{X}_M = 58.00 \qquad\qquad\qquad\qquad \overline{X}_O = 62.00$$

$$SS_M = \sum X_M^2 - \frac{(\sum X_M)^2}{n_M} \qquad\qquad SS_O = \sum X_O^2 - \frac{(\sum X_O)^2}{n_O}$$

$$= 33,824 - \frac{580^2}{10} = 184.00 \qquad = 38,580 - \frac{620^2}{10} = 140.00$$

where the subscript "*M*" denotes the mantra condition and the subscript "*O*" denotes the "orange" condition. Assuming that the null hypothesis is true, the critical values of *t* for an alpha level of .05, nondirectional test, and $n_1 + n_2 - 2 = 10 + 10 - 2 = 18$ degrees of freedom are ±2.101.

Because the null hypothesis states that the population means are equal, $\mu_1 - \mu_2 = 0$ for the purpose of hypothesis testing. The other values necessary for the calculation of *t* can be derived using the information presented in Table 10.5. First, $\overline{X}_1 - \overline{X}_2 = 58.00 - 62.00 = -4.00$. Also,

$$\hat{s}_{\overline{X}_1 - \overline{X}_2} = \sqrt{\left(\frac{SS_1 + SS_2}{n_1 + n_2 - 2}\right)\left(\frac{1}{n_1} + \frac{1}{n_2}\right)}$$

$$= \sqrt{\left(\frac{184.00 + 140.00}{10 + 10 - 2}\right)\left(\frac{1}{10} + \frac{1}{10}\right)} = 1.90$$

The observed value of *t* is thus

$$t = \frac{(\overline{X}_1 - \overline{X}_2) - (\mu_1 - \mu_2)}{\hat{s}_{\overline{X}_1 - \overline{X}_2}}$$

$$= \frac{-4.00 - 0}{1.90} = -2.11$$

Because the observed *t* value of −2.11 exceeds the negative critical value of −2.101, we might be tempted to reject the null hypothesis and conclude that there is a relationship between the type of subvocalization and heart rate. However, because these two values are so similar, we should first repeat our calculations to three (or more) decimal places to increase the precision of our answer. If we do so, we obtain an observed *t* value of −2.109. Because this exceeds the negative critical value of −2.101, the null hypothesis is indeed rejected.

The strength of the relationship in the sample is indexed by eta-squared. Using Equation 10.12, we find that

$$\text{eta}^2 = \frac{t^2}{t^2 + df}$$

$$= \frac{-2.11^2}{-2.11^2 + 18} = .20$$

Thus, the proportion of variability in heart rate that is associated with the type of subvocalization is .20. This represents a strong effect.

The 95% confidence interval for the mean difference is calculated as follows:

$$CI = (\overline{X}_1 - \overline{X}_2) - |t_{\text{critical}}|\,(\hat{s}_{\overline{X}_1 - \overline{X}_2}) \text{ to } (\overline{X}_1 - \overline{X}_2) + |t_{\text{critical}}|\,(\hat{s}_{\overline{X}_1 - \overline{X}_2})$$

$$= -4.00 - (2.101)(1.90) \text{ to } -4.00 + (2.101)(1.90)$$

$$= -7.99 \text{ to } -.01$$

We are 95% confident that the interval $-.01$ to -7.99 contains the true population mean difference in heart rate.

The nature of the relationship is indicated by the mean scores for the two conditions. Because the mean heart rate for the mantra group (58.00) is lower than the mean heart rate for the "orange" group (62.00), we conclude that the use of a mantra results in a lower heart rate during meditation than does the repetition of the word *orange*.

You should think about these results in terms of the research design issues from the previous section: Are there any confounding variables that have not been controlled? What is the role of disturbance variables? What kinds of procedures could be used to reduce sampling error? What are the limitations of the study in terms of generalizability?

10.8   Planning an Investigation Using the Independent Groups *t* Test

When designing a study involving two independent groups, the investigator is faced with a number of important decisions. One is how to best control for any potential confounding and disturbance variables that may reasonably be expected to occur in the context of the study. Another concerns the number of participants that should be included in each group.

One consideration that influences this latter decision is that a researcher cannot sample more people than resources permit. Practical matters aside, statistical considerations must also be taken into account. One major issue concerns the desired power of the statistical test that will be used to analyze the data. Recall from Chapter 8 that the power of a statistical test refers to the probability of rejecting the null hypothesis when it is false. For instance, when the power of a test is .70, there is a 7 in 10 chance that we will correctly reject the null hypothesis when it is false.

The power of a statistical test is influenced by three major factors: (1) the strength of the relationship between the two variables *in the population*, (2) the sample sizes, and (3) the alpha level. Consider the first factor. With the sample sizes typical in the behavioral sciences, if the strength of the relationship in the population is weak, it is relatively unlikely that this relationship will manifest itself in the sample data over and above the "noise" of sampling error. Hence, it is relatively unlikely that we will correctly reject the null hypothesis; that is, the power of the test will be relatively low, other things being equal. If the strength of the population relationship between the two variables is strong, however, it is more likely that the relationship will manifest itself in the sample data over and above the "noise" of sampling error. Consequently, it is more likely that we will correctly reject the null hypothesis and conclude that a relationship exists between the independent and dependent variables; that is, the power of the test will be relatively high. Thus, as the strength of the relationship in the population increases, the power of the statistical test also increases.

Next, consider the sample sizes. Following the logic that we presented in Section 8.7 for the one-sample situation, it is more likely that we will detect a difference between population means when one exists when the sample sizes are relatively large. Generally speaking, then, larger sample sizes lead to more powerful tests.

Finally, consider the alpha level. When the alpha level is low, the likelihood that we will reject the null hypothesis is also low because we must be very certain that a relationship exists before we are willing to say that it does. Consequently, we will be relatively likely to overlook a relationship that does exist, especially if it is a weak one and we have small sample sizes. As the alpha level is set higher, the power of a statistical test will increase.

If a Type I error is serious, the investigator will want to minimize its chance of occurrence by setting a low alpha level. This means that the major way that the researcher can minimize the likelihood of a Type II error is by increasing the sample sizes. If a Type II error is also serious, then one will want to achieve high power. Large sample sizes can accomplish this.

Statisticians have developed procedures for estimating the sample sizes necessary to obtain a desired level of power given the strength of the relationship in the population and the alpha level. The required sample sizes also differ depending on whether the test is directional or nondirectional. Appendix E.1 contains tables of the per-group sample sizes necessary to achieve various levels of power for the independent groups *t* test.* A portion of this appendix for an alpha level of .05, nondirectional test, is reproduced in Table 10.6.

TABLE 10.6 **Approximate Sample Sizes Necessary to Achieve Selected Levels of Power for Alpha = .05, Nondirectional Test, as a Function of Population Values of Eta-Squared**

	Population Eta-Squared									
Power	.01	.03	.05	.07	.10	.15	.20	.25	.30	.35
.25	84	28	17	12	8	6	5	3	3	3
.50	193	63	38	27	18	12	9	7	5	5
.60	246	80	48	34	23	15	11	8	7	6
.67	287	93	55	39	27	17	12	10	8	6
.70	310	101	60	42	29	18	13	10	8	7
.75	348	113	67	47	32	21	15	11	9	7
.80	393	128	76	53	36	23	17	13	10	8
.85	450	146	86	61	41	26	19	14	11	9
.90	526	171	101	71	48	31	22	17	13	11
.95	651	211	125	87	60	38	27	21	16	13
.99	920	298	176	123	84	53	38	29	22	18

* All of the tables in Appendix E are based on power estimates given by Cohen (1977).

The first column of this table lists selected values of power, and the column headings are selected values of eta-squared in the population. The table entries are the required sample sizes *per group* to achieve the corresponding level of power.* For example, if the researcher suspects (on the basis of the existing theory and research) that the strength of the relationship that he or she is trying to detect in the population is relatively weak, corresponding to an eta-squared of .03, then the sample size necessary to achieve a power of .95 for an alpha level of .05, nondirectional test, is 211 per group. If the researcher suspects that the strength of the relationship is much stronger, corresponding to an eta-squared of .20, then the necessary sample size to achieve a power of .95 is 27 per group.

It is not always practical to obtain high levels of power by adjusting the sample size, especially when the population relationship is judged to be weak. In the example above, the 211 participants per group that are necessary for a power of .95 when eta-squared is .03 could be costly, especially if the study involves extensive procedures or the use of expensive laboratory animals. Nevertheless, if the consequences of making a Type II error are deemed to be serious (for instance, concluding that gender discrimination might not exist when, in fact, it does), then one should insist on high power.

Investigators generally strive to achieve a power of .80 to .95, as a rough guideline. However, the power can be revised upward or downward, depending on the situation.

In addition to providing the sample sizes necessary to obtain a desired level of power, power tables can also be used to determine the power associated with a statistical test given the directionality of the test, the alpha level, the sample size, and the value of eta-squared in the population. For instance, Table 10.6 shows that the power for a nondirectional independent groups t test with $n = 34$ per group is .60 at an alpha level of .05 when the population eta-squared is .07.

Examination of Table 10.6 and Appendix E.1 provides a general appreciation for the relationships among directionality, the alpha level, sample size, the strength of the relationship that one is trying to detect in the population, and power for the independent groups t test. As can be seen, consistent with the above discussion, power becomes greater as the alpha level, the sample size, and the population eta-squared each increases.

10.9 Method of Presentation

When researchers report the results of an independent groups t test, all three questions from Section 10.1 should be addressed (whether there is a relationship between the two variables, the strength of the relationship, and the nature of the

---

* Given the imprecision of the procedures for estimating the necessary sample sizes, the values contained in this and the other power tables in this book are *approximate*.

relationship). Of course, the last question is relevant only if the null hypothesis is rejected. In fact, if the null hypothesis is not rejected, then the strength of the relationship is also typically not discussed.

The results for the order of information and likability experiment that was discussed earlier in this chapter might be presented as follows:

Results

An independent groups *t* test that compared the mean likability ratings for the pro–con (*M* = 5.00, *SD* = 1.15) and con–pro (*M* = 3.00, *SD* = 1.33) conditions was found to be statistically significant at an alpha level of .05, $t(18)$ = 3.57, $p < .01$, indicating that strangers will be evaluated more favorably when positive information about them is followed by negative information than when the reverse is true. The strength of the relationship between the order of information and likability, as indexed by eta-squared, was .41. The 95% confidence interval for the mean difference was .82 to 3.18.

The first sentence states the statistical test that was used to analyze the data. It also conveys the values of the sample means and the standard deviation estimates, using the symbols *M* and *SD*, respectively, per Section 3.10.* The statement that the *t* test was statistically significant signifies that the null hypothesis was rejected at whatever alpha level was used. As is indicated, the alpha level for this analysis was .05. If the null hypothesis had not been rejected, the terminology *statistically nonsignificant* would have been used instead. Paralleling the format for the one-sample *t* test, this is followed by the degrees of freedom associated with the relevant *t* distribution, the observed value of *t*, and the significance level. Because there is nothing to indicate otherwise, a nondirectional test is assumed. The remainder of this sentence specifies the nature of the relationship.

The next sentence reports the value of eta-squared. It is very important that this or some other measure of the relationship strength be provided because investigators sometimes interpret their data as if a strong relationship exists when, in fact, it is so weak as to be almost trivial. It is not surprising, then, that the *Publication Manual of the American Psychological Association* (American Psychological Association, 2001) advises: "For the reader to fully understand the importance of your findings, it is almost always necessary to include some index of effect size or strength of relationship in your Results section" (p. 25). If such a measure is not provided, eta-squared can be derived from the degrees of freedom and the observed value of *t* using Equation 10.12.

The final sentence provides the 95% confidence interval for the mean difference. It will be remembered from Section 8.12 that the American Psychological Association (2001) strongly recommends the use of such intervals.

---

* The variance estimates were calculated in Table 10.1 to be 1.33 for the pro-con condition and 1.78 for the con-pro condition. The square roots of these values are 1.15 and 1.33, respectively.

10.10 **Examples from the Literature**

Monetary Compensation and the Enjoyableness of a Boring Task

Behavioral scientists have devoted considerable effort to identifying psychological factors that influence attitude change. In a classic experiment in this area (Festinger & Carlsmith, 1959), 60 male college students individually worked on two very boring tasks for 1 hour. After completing the tasks, they were informed that the study was over and that its purpose was to determine how expectations about the experiment would affect task performance. Half of the participants had supposedly been led to believe that the tasks would be interesting and enjoyable whereas the other half had not been told anything about them so that the influence of the expectancy manipulation on their task performance could be studied. In actuality, this was not the true purpose of the study, and none of the participants had actually been informed that the tasks would be interesting and enjoyable. Rather, the study was designed to examine the psychological processes discussed below.

The participants were then told that the person who usually informed waiting people that the tasks were interesting and enjoyable was unable to make it in that day and were offered either $1 or $20 to take his place. After complying with this request, they were asked to rate several aspects of their experience, including how interesting and enjoyable they found the tasks that they had worked on earlier on a −5 (*extremely dull and boring*) to 5 (*extremely interesting and enjoyable*) scale.

At least two principles could operate in this situation to influence the participants' ratings of the tasks. The first is a reinforcement principle, which holds that individuals who were paid $20 for telling another person that the tasks were interesting and enjoyable received greater reinforcement for doing so than those who were paid only $1. This greater reinforcement should generalize to their perception of the tasks; thus, participants in the $20 condition should rate the tasks more positively than those in the $1 condition.

An alternative explanation predicts just the opposite. According to this view, the participants had performed a behavior that was contradictory to what they truly believed: They told someone that boring tasks were interesting and enjoyable. Because of this contradiction, they should experience an unpleasant internal state known as *cognitive dissonance,* which they should then be motivated to reduce.

Individuals in the $20 condition could easily justify their counterattitudinal behavior: They did it for the money. This was not the case, however, for those in the $1 condition, where the reward was not very great. These individuals would have to reduce the dissonance in another way, and one possibility would be to conclude that the tasks were really not all that boring. If this dissonance mechanism were operating, participants in the $1 condition should rate the tasks more positively than those in the $20 condition.

The results of the experiment were analyzed using an independent groups *t* test. The independent variable was the amount of money that was received for telling the waiting person about the tasks ($1 or $20) and the dependent variable was the participants' ratings of how interesting and enjoyable the tasks were. The mean rating in the $1 condition was 1.35 and the mean rating in the $20 condition was −.05. Consistent with a dissonance interpretation, these means were found to be statistically significantly different, $t(38) = 2.22$, $p < .05$. The strength of the relationship as indexed by eta-squared was .11, which represents a moderate effect.

Students' Perceptions of Self-Monitoring of Good and Poor Teachers

An interesting question for teachers and students alike concerns the personality characteristics that distinguish good from poor teachers. One potentially relevant characteristic is *self-monitoring*. Among other things, self-monitoring concerns the extent to which individuals are sensitive to the behavior of others and able to modify their own social behavior accordingly. As self-monitoring increases, individuals become relatively more concerned with the situational appropriateness of their behavior and relatively less constrained by their own internal dispositions. Thus, for instance, high self-monitoring teachers might be expected to be more responsive to the needs of their students and more flexible in their classroom approach.

In an attempt to determine students' perception of the role that teacher self-monitoring plays in the teaching process, Larkin (1987) asked 116 college undergraduates to think of either the best or the worst teacher that they had ever had and to rate this teacher on a 13-item self-monitoring scale. A dependent variable score was derived for each student by summing his or her responses across the 13 items. As predicted, an independent groups *t* test showed that the good teachers ($\overline{X} = 49.56$) were rated as significantly higher in self-monitoring than the poor teachers ($\overline{X} = 29.81$), $t(114) = 13.18$, $p < .01$. Is this result consistent with your own educational experience? As indexed by eta-squared, the strength of the relationship was .60. This represents a strong effect.

10.11   Links Between Computer Results and Book Content

In addition to calculating the independent groups *t* test that we describe in this chapter, a number of statistical computer programs also provide output for an alternative *t* test that is designed to be used if the researcher determines that heterogeneity of population variances is a serious problem. This test does not assume that the population variances are heterogeneous and, consequently, it does not utilize a pooled variance estimate. Also, the degrees of freedom for this test are calculated differently than those for the usual independent groups test.

The rationale and computational procedures for the alternative *t* test are described in Hays (1981). However, given the robustness of the independent groups *t* test, it will seldom be necessary for you to use the alternative test.

10.12   Links Between Chapters

We saw in Section 10.2 how the independent groups *t* test relates to the one-sample *t* test. The independent groups *t* test also bears a strong relationship to one-way between-subjects analysis of variance, as we will see in Chapter 12. In fact, as we will discuss, one-way between-subjects analysis of variance can be conceptualized as an extension of the independent groups t test when there are three or more levels of a between-subjects independent variable. Finally, the independent groups t test is also related to the correlated groups t test, which we discuss in Chapter 11.

It is not by coincidence that these tests are related. Rather, this reflects the fact that although they are used in different situations, they are all based on the same basic principles of hypothesis testing.

Applications to the Analysis of a Social Problem Using SPSS for Windows

It is commonly believed that parents want to discourage premarital sexual intercourse by their teens. However, research suggests that this is not necessarily the case. Some parents feel more adamant about sexual abstinence for teens than do others. For example, some parents believe that if it is with someone who is special and whom the teen has known for a long time, then sexual intercourse is permissible, given proper protection against unintended pregnancy and sexually transmitted diseases.

So that we could learn more about parental attitudes toward adolescent sexuality, teens in the parent–teen communication study described in Chapter 1 were asked a series of questions about their mother's position on premarital sexual activity. Specifically, they were asked to indicate their agreement with the following five statements using a 5-point scale having the response options *strongly disagree, moderately disagree, neither agree nor disagree, moderately agree,* and *strongly agree*:

1. My mother would disapprove of my having sex at this time in my life.
2. My mother has specifically told me not to have sex.
3. My mother thinks I definitely should not be sexually active (having sexual intercourse) at this time in my life.
4. If it were with someone who was special to me and whom I knew well, like a steady boyfriend (girlfriend), my mother would not mind if I had sexual intercourse at this time in my life.
5. My mother thinks it is fine for me to be sexually active (having sexual intercourse) at this time in my life.

The questions were "split up" and asked in different sections of the interview. The teens answered the questions anonymously in writing so that they would not have to reveal their answers face-to-face to an interviewer. The responses to the first three statements were scored from 1 (*strongly disagree*) to 5 (*strongly agree*), whereas the responses to the last two items were reverse scored such that 1 represented strong *agreement* and 5 represented strong *disagreement*.

After undertaking analyses to ensure that it was appropriate to do so, we summed the responses to the five statements to yield an overall index of the extent to which a teen perceived his or her mother as disapproving of the teen engaging in sexual intercourse. Scores on this measure could range from 5 to 25, with higher values indicating greater perceived maternal disapproval of engaging in sex.

One question of interest is whether mothers differ in the extent to which they discourage sexual intercourse by adolescent girls as opposed to boys. We felt that there might be a double standard in this regard. Traditionally, pregnancy and birth control have often been framed as "female" issues that adolescent girls must face. However, unintended pregnancy results from the behavior of both the boy and the girl. If parents are going to discourage premarital sexual activity, they should do so equally for their sons and their daughters.

To test whether teens perceive a double standard of this type, we conducted an independent

(continued)

groups *t* test on the perceived maternal disapproval index, using gender as a between-subjects independent variable. The first step of the analysis was to examine summary statistics and frequency distributions for the dependent variable for boys and girls separately. This allowed us to identify outliers and to examine potential problems with variance heterogeneity and nonnormality. Although the assumptions apply to populations, examination of sample data can be informative in this regard.

Table 10.7 presents the computer output for the summary statistics for the perceived maternal attitude variable (MDISSEX) for the two groups, and Figure 10.1 presents a grouped frequency histogram for each group with a normal curve superimposed on each. The sample sizes for the two groups were large and nearly identical (for boys, *n* = 362; for girls, *n* = 360), which suggests that the analysis will be robust to any assumption violations. The variance estimate for girls (19.95) is comparable to that for boys (23.19), which suggests that heterogeneity of variance is not an issue. As can be seen in the frequency histograms, the distributions of scores are not normal. However, the departures from normality are not large enough to suggest that scores in the population are so nonnormal that the *t* test is undermined (Posten, 1978). No outliers were evident in the data.

The computer output for the independent groups *t* test is presented in Table 10.8. The top portion of the output presents the sample size, the sample mean, the standard deviation estimate, and the estimated standard error of the mean for each group. The bottom of the output presents the results for the Levene test for assessing homogeneity of variance and for the independent groups *t* test.

It will be remembered from Section 10.2 that the Levene test evaluates a null hypothesis of equal variances in the populations against an alternative hypothesis of unequal variances in the populations. The test statistic for the Levene test is an *F* ratio. A significance level of less than .05 for the *F* ratio suggests that the variances are not homogeneous.

The results for the Levene test appear on the far left in the first row of the bottom portion of Table 10.8. As can be seen, the *p* value (labeled "Sig.") for the *F* ratio is .59, which is consistent with our observation that the variance estimates are comparable. The other results in this row are for the independent groups *t* test that we describe in this chapter. The bottom row presents the results for the alternative *t* test that we discussed in Section 10.11 for when heterogeneity of population variances is a serious problem. Because the population variances do not appear to be highly

TABLE 10.7   Computer Output for Summary Statistics for Perceived Maternal Attitude Toward Teens Engaging in Sex

Statistics for Boys MDISSEX			Statistics for Girls MDISSEX		
N	Valid	362	N	Valid	360
	Missing	12		Missing	13
Mean		15.829	Mean		19.103
Std. Error of Mean		.253	Std. Error of Mean		.235
Median		15.000	Median		19.000
Mode		15.000	Mode		25.000
Std. Deviation		4.816	Std. Deviation		4.466
Variance		23.189	Variance		19.948
Range		20.000	Range		20.000
Minimum		5.000	Minimum		5.000
Maximum		25.000	Maximum		25.000

**FIGURE 10.1   Grouped Frequency Histograms for Perceived Maternal Attitude Toward
(a) Male and (b) Female Teens Engaging in Sex**

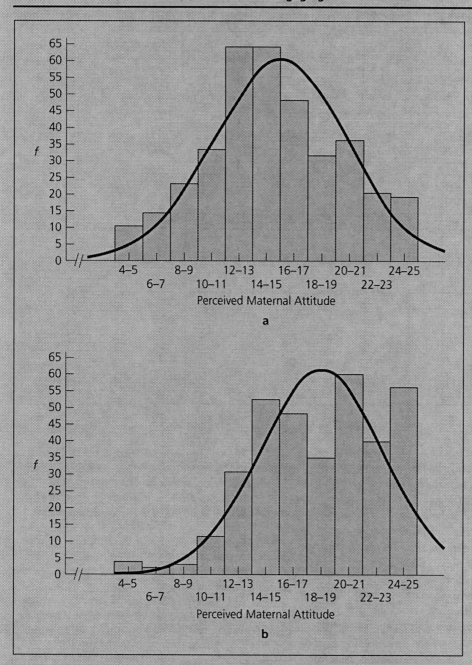

Perceived Maternal Attitude

a

Perceived Maternal Attitude

b

(continued)

TABLE 10.8   Computer Output for Independent Groups *t* Test for Perceived Maternal Attitude Toward Teens Engaging in Sex

Group Statistics

		N	Mean	Std. Deviation	Std.Error Mean
mdissex	Male	362	15.83	4.82	.25
	Female	360	19.10	4.47	.24

Independent Samples Test

	Levene's Test for Equality of Variances		t test for Equality of Means						95% Confidence Interval of the Difference	
	F	Sig.	t	df	Sig. (2-tailed)	Mean Difference	Std. Error Difference		Lower	Upper
mdissex: Equal variances assumed	.291	.590	−9.470	720	.000	−3.27	.35		−3.96	−2.58
Equal variances not assumed			−9.470	716.530	.000	−3.27	.35		−3.96	−2.58

discrepant, our focus in this instance is on the results for the "Equal variances assumed" test.

The observed value of t for this test is −9.47, and there are 720 degrees of freedom. Because the significance level (labeled "Sig. (2-tailed)") is less than .05, the test is statistically significant. The 95% confidence interval (−3.96 to −2.58) is provided at the far right. Examination of the sample means indicates that adolescent girls ($\overline{X}$ = 19.10) perceive their mothers as being more disapproving of sexual activity than adolescent boys do ($\overline{X}$ = 15.83). The strength of the relationship as indexed by eta-squared can be calculated by applying Equation 10.12. The eta-squared value of .11 represents a moderate effect.

The column labeled "Std. Error Difference" presents the estimated standard error of the difference between two independent means. This index is important because it provides a sense of how much sampling error there is. The estimated standard error of .35 in this instance suggests that, on average, random samples of the sizes that we used tend to yield sample mean differences that deviate from the true difference between the population means by about .35 unit.

Although the t test results suggest a double standard on the part of mothers, there is a problem with making such an inference: The data focused on teens' perceptions of maternal attitudes, not maternal attitudes per se. It may be that mothers of adolescent boys are just as disapproving of sexual

FIGURE 10.2   Graph of Means for Perceived and Actual Maternal Attitudes as a Function of Gender

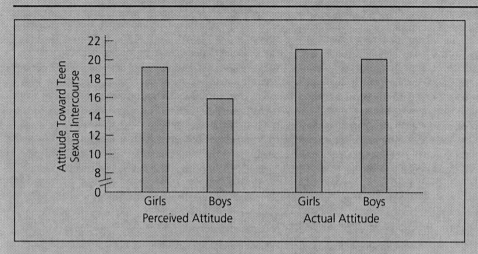

intercourse by their teens as are mothers of adolescent girls, but that adolescent girls are more likely to perceive this disapproval than are boys. Another possibility is that adolescent girls are more likely to have disapproval *conveyed to them* by their mothers than are adolescent boys.

However, we also measured maternal attitudes directly by presenting mothers the five questions from above, but with appropriate wording changes (for example, the statement "My mother would disapprove of my having sex at this time in my life" was phrased "I disapprove of my teen having sex at this time in her/his life"). We summed mothers' responses to the five statements (with reverse scoring for the last two items) to yield an overall index of actual maternal attitudes toward their teen engaging in sex.

Preliminary analyses revealed no outliers, and we found very similar variance estimates for the two groups. We also found that although each distribution of scores is nonnormal, the deviations from normality are not large enough to suggest that nonnormality in the population is great enough to undermine the *t* test.

With this established, we performed an independent groups *t* test on the maternal attitude measure as a function of the gender of the teen. This showed that the mean for mothers of adolescent girls ($\bar{X} = 20.99$) is significantly greater than the

mean for mothers of adolescent boys ($\bar{X} = 19.87$), $t(721) = 3.87$, $p < .01$. Mothers indeed appear to be more disapproving of sexual activity for adolescent girls than for adolescent boys. The strength of the relationship, as indexed by eta-squared, is .02. This represents a weak effect. The 95% confidence interval is -3.96 to -2.58.

Figure 10.2 presents a graph of the means for the maternal attitude variables. Note that the height of the bars is greater for girls than for boys for both variables but that the difference in heights is greater for perceived attitudes than for actual attitudes. This suggests that the mean difference between adolescent girls' and adolescent boys' perceptions of maternal attitudes is greater than the difference for the actual maternal attitudes.

A statistical analysis that we conducted in order to determine whether this is in fact the case was found to be statistically significant and confirmed the fact that the girl-boy difference in perceived maternal attitudes is greater than that for actual maternal attitudes. Thus, even though mothers are more disapproving of sexual activity for adolescent girls than for boys, the teens' perceived attitudes reflect a larger disparity. This probably reflects one or both of the processes proposed above: There may be gender differences in the

(continued)

teens' ability to accurately perceive their mothers' attitudes and/or mothers may communicate their attitudes more clearly or forcefully to their daughters than to their sons.

Before concluding our discussion, we comment on one additional issue—namely, the level of measurement of our dependent variables. These were based on the sums of responses to five questions that were all designed to measure the same construct. Most researchers would argue that the scores for each question and, thus, the resulting "total" scores, are probably ordinal in nature and violate a strict assumption of intervalness. We would not argue with this assessment. However, this does not mean that the data cannot be effectively analyzed using the independent groups *t* test. The crucial issue is not whether a measure is ordinal or interval, but whether the measure approximates interval level characteristics to the degree that an independent groups *t* test can still be appropriately applied.

Several Monte Carlo studies have evaluated how severe the departure from intervalness can be for the independent groups *t* test without affecting the validity of the conclusions of the test. This research has shown the test to be quite robust to rather large departures from intervalness (for example, see the discussion and review by Davison and Sharma, 1988).

Our experience in prior research with the measures of attitudes towards premarital sex suggests that they tend to be reliable, to be unrelated to measures of socially desirable tendencies, and to correlate with other constructs as we theoretically expect. Furthermore, the shapes of the frequency distributions for the attitude scores are consistent with what we might expect on theoretical grounds. When the Monte Carlo studies regarding departures from intervalness are also considered, we are reasonably confident that the psychometric properties of the measures are sufficient to effectively analyze the data using the independent groups *t* test.

Summary

The independent groups *t* test is typically used to analyze the relationship between two variables when (1) the dependent variable is quantitative in nature and is measured on a level that at least approximates interval characteristics, (2) the independent variable is between-subjects in nature, and (3) the independent variable has two and only two levels. The existence of a relationship between the two variables is tested by converting the difference between the sample means to a *t* score that represents the number of estimated standard errors the difference is from the hypothesized difference between the population means. This value of *t* is then compared with the critical value(s) of *t*, and the decision to reject or not to reject the null hypothesis is made accordingly.

The strength of the relationship is measured using eta-squared, which represents the proportion of variability in the dependent variable that is associated with the independent variable. Unstandardized effect sizes and confidence intervals can also be calculated. There are several important advantages associated with the use of these measures. Finally, the nature of the relationship is determined by comparing the two *sample* means to make a decision about how the two *population* means differ. We simply conclude that the condition that has the larger *sample* mean also has the larger *population* mean.

Tables are available for determining the sample sizes necessary for the independent groups *t* test to achieve a desired level of power. The required sample sizes depend on the strength of the relationship between the independent variable and the dependent variable in the population, the alpha level, and whether the test is directional or nondirectional. These tables can also be used to determine the power associated with a test given the directionality of the test, the alpha level, the sample size, and the population value of eta-squared.

Exercises

Answers to asterisked (*) exercises appear at the back of the book.

1. Under what conditions is the independent groups t test typically used to analyze a bivariate relationship?

*2. In general terms, what value will the mean of a sampling distribution of the difference between two independent means always equal?

*3. Explain the rationale that allows us to combine the variance estimates from two samples to obtain a pooled variance estimate.

*4. Compute the pooled variance estimate and the estimated standard error of the difference for $n_1 - 10$, $n_2 - 13$, $\hat{s}_1^2 = 6.48$, and $\hat{s}_2^2 = 4.73$.

*5. Consider the following information for two samples that were randomly selected from their respective populations:

Sample A	Sample B
$n_A = 49$	$n_B = 49$
$\overline{X}_A = 10.00$	$\overline{X}_B = 13.00$
$\hat{s}_A = 1.44$	$\hat{s}_B = 1.58$

a. Compute the estimated standard error of the mean for sample A.

b. Compute the estimated standard error of the mean for sample B.

c. Compute the estimated standard error of the difference between two independent means.

d. Your answer for part (c) should be larger than your answer for parts (a) or (b).

In fact, the estimated standard error of the difference between two independent means will always be larger than the respective estimated standard errors of the mean. Why do you think this is the case?

6. Match each symbol in the first column with the appropriate term in the second column:

Symbol	Term
1. $\hat{s}_{\overline{X}_1 - \overline{X}_2}$	a. variance estimate
2. $\hat{s}_{pooled}^2$	b. null hypothesis
3. $\hat{s}_{\overline{X}}$	c. standard error of the mean
4. $\hat{s}^2$	d. estimated standard error of the mean
5. H_1	e. standard error of the difference between two independent means
6. H_0	f. alternative hypothesis
7. $\sigma_{\overline{X}}$	g. estimated standard error of the difference between two independent means
8. $\sigma_{\overline{X}_1 - \overline{X}_2}$	h. pooled variance estimate

7. Summarize the five steps involved in hypothesis testing for the independent groups t test.

*8. State the critical value(s) of t for an independent groups t test for an alpha level of .05 under each of the following conditions:

a. $H_0: \mu_1 = \mu_2$, $H_1: \mu_1 \neq \mu_2$, $n_1 = 10$, $n_2 = 10$

b. $H_0: \mu_1 = \mu_2$, $H_1: \mu_1 > \mu_2$, $n_1 = 10$, $n_2 = 10$

   c. $H_0: \mu_1 = \mu_2, H_1: \mu_1 \neq \mu_2,$
     $n_1 = 16, n_2 = 14$
   d. $H_0: \mu_1 = \mu_2, H_1: \mu_1 \neq \mu_2,$
     $n_1 = 16, n_2 = 14$
   e. $H_0: \mu_1 = \mu_2, H_1: \mu_1 \neq \mu_2,$
     $n_1 = 23, n_2 = 19$
   f. $H_0: \mu_1 = \mu_2, H_1: \mu_1 \neq \mu_2,$
     $n_1 = 23, n_2 = 19$

9. What are the assumptions underlying the independent groups *t* test?

Use the following information to complete Exercises 10–17.

An investigator tested the relationship between gender and discriminatory attitudes toward women by administering an attitude scale to five men and five women. Scores could range from 1 to 10, with higher values indicating more discriminatory attitudes. The data are presented in the table:

Men	Women
7	4
7	3
8	4
7	5
6	4

*10. Test for a relationship between gender and discriminatory attitudes using a nondirectional independent groups *t* test.

*11. Compute the sum of squares total.

*12. Compute the treatment effect for men and the treatment effect for women.

*13. Based on your answers for Exercise 12, use the variance extraction procedures discussed in this chapter to nullify the effect of gender on discriminatory attitudes (that is, generate a set of scores on the dependent variable with the effect of gender removed).

*14. Compute the sum of squares error and the sum of squares explained for the data derived in Exercise 13.

*15. Based on your answers for Exercises 11 and 14, compute the value of eta-squared

using Equation 10.11. Recalculate this index using Equation 10.12. Compare the two results. (*Note:* In practice, we would use only the approach of Equation 10.12.) Does the observed value represent a weak, moderate, or strong effect?

*16. Compute the 95% confidence interval.

*17. Discern the nature of the relationship between gender and discriminatory attitudes.

Use the following information to complete Exercises 18–25.

A researcher tested the effect of alcohol on reaction time by having five participants consume alcohol until a certain level of intoxication was achieved (as indexed by physiological measures). Another group was not given any alcohol but instead consumed a placebo. All then participated in a reaction-time task. The reaction times (in seconds) for the two groups are presented in the table.

Alcohol	Placebo
2.00	1.00
2.50	.50
2.00	1.00
1.50	1.00
2.00	1.50

18. Test for a relationship between alcohol consumption and reaction time using a nondirectional independent groups *t* test.

19. Compute the sum of squares total.

20. Compute the treatment effect for alcohol and the treatment effect for the placebo.

21. Based on your answers for Exercise 20, use the variance extraction procedures discussed in this chapter to nullify the effect of alcohol consumption on reaction time (that is, generate a set of scores on the dependent variable with the effect of alcohol consumption removed).

22. Compute the sum of squares error and the sum of squares explained for the data derived in Exercise 21.

23. Based on your answers for Exercises 19 and 22, compute the value of eta-squared using Equation 10.11. Recalculate this index using Equation 10.12. Compare the two results. (*Note:* In practice, we would use only the approach of Equation 10.12.) Does the observed value represent a weak, moderate, or strong effect?

24. Compute the 95% confidence interval.

25. Discern the nature of the relationship between alcohol consumption and reaction time.

*26. Explain the interrelationships among the sum of squares total, the sum of squares explained, and the sum of squares error.

27. What would the value of eta-squared be if an independent groups *t* test yielded an observed *t* value of -1.73 for $n_1 = 16$ and $n_2 = 18$? Does this represent a weak, moderate, or strong effect?

*28. Why is it inappropriate to estimate the strength of the relationship between two variables in the population from the sample value of eta-squared?

29. What is the rationale behind calculating eta-squared following statistically non-significant statistical tests?

30. Discuss the means by which confidence intervals provide information about sampling error.

31. What are the three major factors that influence the power of a statistical test?

*32. If a researcher suspects that the strength of the relationship between two variables in the population is .07 as indexed by eta-squared, what sample size should she use per group in a study involving two independent groups and an alpha level of .05, nondirectional test, in order to achieve a power of .95?

33. Suppose that an investigator conducts a study involving two independent groups with $n = 23$ per group. If the value of eta-squared in the population is .10, what would the power of his statistical test be at an alpha level of .05, nondirectional test?

Multiple-Choice Questions

34. The null hypothesis for an independent groups *t* test states that
    a. $\overline{X}_1 = \overline{X}_2$ c. $\mu_1 = \mu_2$
    b. $\overline{X}_1 \neq \overline{X}_2$ d. $\mu_1 \neq \mu_2$

35. If a researcher suspects that the strength of the relationship between two variables in the population is .15 as indexed by eta-squared, what sample size should he use per group in a study involving two independent groups and an alpha level of .05, nondirectional test, in order to achieve a power of .85?
    a. $n = 21$ c. $n = 34$
    b. $n = 26$ d. $n = 38$

*36. A treatment effect is
    a. a nullified score
    b. the difference between the mean for one group and the mean for the second group
    c. the difference between the mean for a given group and the grand mean
    d. the mean score for both groups combined

37. If the mean score for men is 10.00, the mean score for women is 20.00, and the grand mean is 15.00, what is the "effect" of being a man?
    a. -10.00 c. 5.00
    b. -5.00 d. 10.0

38. Eta-squared should be calculated following both statistically significant and statistically nonsignificant statistical tests.
    a. true   b. false

*39. Which measure estimates the average amount by which the mean differences that constitute the sampling distribution of the difference between two independent means deviate from the true difference between the population means?
    a. the pooled variance estimate
    b. *t*
    c. eta-squared
    d. the estimated standard error of the difference

*40. The difference between the sample means is a standardized measure of relationship strength for two independent groups.
    a. true   b. false

41. Unstandardized measures of effect size are always more meaningful than standardized measures.
    a. true
    b. false

*42. If a null hypothesis states that two population means are equal, then a 95% confidence interval that does not contain the value of 0 indicates that the null hypothesis should be rejected (assuming an alpha level of .05, nondirectional test).
    a. true
    b. false

*43. According to critics of traditional null hypothesis testing, the crucial issue is
    a. whether two means differ
    b. by how much two means differ
    c. whether two variance estimates differ
    d. whether directional or nondirectional tests should be used

Use the following information to complete Exercises 44–54.

A researcher examined the effect of studying strategies on test performance. One mixed-gender group of 10 individuals was instructed to study for an exam for 5 hours the night before the exam. A second mixed-gender group of 10 individuals was told to study for 5 hours by studying only 1 hour per night on the 5 nights prior to the exam. Thus, the total amount of study time was the same, but in the first condition the study time was concentrated into 1 night, whereas in the second condition the study time was spread out over 5 nights. The individuals then took an exam on which scores could range from 0 to 100, with higher values indicating better performance. In the "concentrated" group, the mean score on the exam was 65.00; in the "spread-out" group, the mean score was 80.00. The estimated standard error of the difference was 5.00.

*44. If the value of eta-squared in the population is .30, what is the power of the statistical test at an alpha level of .05, nondirectional test?
    a. .30   c. .80
    b. .67   d. .85

*45. The independent variable is
    a. the amount of study time
    b. performance on the exam
    c. gender
    d. the type of studying strategy

46. The dependent variable is
    a. the amount of study time
    b. performance on the exam
    c. gender
    d. the type of studying strategy

*47. The observed value of *t* is
    a. −.60   c. −6.71
    b. −3.00   d. −15.00

*48. Based on this study, we can conclude that the independent variable is related to the dependent variable.
    a. true
    b. false

*49. It is possible that the test results reflect a Type I error.
    a. true
    b. false

50. It is possible that the test results reflect a Type II error.
    a. true
    b. false

51. The strength of the relationship, as indexed by eta-squared, is
    a. .14
    b. .33
    c. .43
    d. .67

*52. The proportion of variability in the dependent variable that is due to disturbance variables is
    a. .45
    b. .67
    c. .82
    d. .86

53. The 95% confidence interval is
    a. −19.70 to −10.30
    b. −23.67 to −6.33
    c. −25.50 to −4.50
    d. −27.76 to −2.24

54. What can we conclude about the effectiveness of the two studying strategies?
    a. The concentrated method is more effective.

b. The spread-out method is more effective.

c. The two strategies are equally effective.

d. The two strategies may or may not differ in their effectiveness.

Exercises to Apply Concepts

*55. Psychologists have studied extensively the effects of early experience on developmental processes. It has long been recognized that a positive, challenging, and diverse environment (sometimes called an *enriched* environment) leads to the acquisition of more positive abilities and personality traits than an environment that is relatively impoverished and isolated.

Bennett, Krech, and Rosenzweig (1964) suggest that the type of environment may even alter the physical characteristics of the brain, and they report a series of studies to investigate this possibility. In one of these, laboratory rats from the same genetic strain were raised in one of two conditions. Half of the rats were raised in an enriched environment, which involved being housed with 10 to 12 other animals in large cages that were equipped with a variety of "toys." Each day these rats were placed in a square field where they were allowed to explore a pattern of barriers that was changed daily. The other half of the rats were raised in an isolated environment in that they were caged singly in a dimly lit room where they could not see or touch another animal (although they could hear and smell them).

All rats in both groups were killed after 80 days so that the structure of the brain could be compared for the animals that were raised in the two environments. One factor that was examined was the weight of the cortex (measured in milligrams). The hypothetical data presented in the table are representative of the results of the study. Analyze these data using a nondirectional test, draw a conclusion, and write up your results using the principles developed in the Method of Presentation section.

Enriched environment	Isolated environment
660	612
630	642
675	592
685	626
645	660
690	610
635	640

56. McConnell (1966) reports a series of experiments on the physiological bases of learning and memory that have been the subject of considerable controversy. The goal of this research was to test the proposal that RNA and DNA protein molecules constitute the physiochemical substrate of learning and that it may be possible to transfer memory biochemically between organisms by transferring the relevant RNA and DNA molecules.

McConnell's initial experiments were conducted with *planaria* (small, wormlike organisms). Classical conditioning procedures were used to teach a group of planaria to contract in size whenever they were exposed to a light. McConnell tried several different methods of transferring the relevant RNA and DNA molecules of these trained planaria to other planaria. The only practical method, however, was cannibalism: The trained planaria were chopped up into small pieces and fed to another group of planaria. This group of *trained cannibals* constituted the experimental group. A control group of *untrained cannibals* was fed chopped planaria that had not been taught to contract when exposed to the light.

McConnell then exposed both the trained and the untrained cannibals to the light 25 times each and counted the number of times that each planarian contracted. If the relevant RNA and DNA molecules had been transferred and had an impact on behavior, the trained cannibals should exhibit a greater number of contractions than the untrained cannibals. Such a demonstration would at least establish the *possibility* of transferring memory from one organism to another via biochemical means.

The hypothetical data listed in the table are representative of the results of the study. Analyze these data using a nondirectional test, draw a conclusion, and write up your results using the principles developed in the Method of Presentation section.

Trained cannibals

14	8	10	13	22	7
6	15	17	10	8	15
21	9	15	4	11	
8	14	12	15	10	

Untrained cannibals

6	4	19	16	10	6
1	7	6	7	10	5
3	6	1	4	4	
11	5	5	7	11	

---

57. One factor that has been proposed to affect creativity is how much choice individuals have in their approach to a task. In a study of this issue, Amabile and Gitomer (1984) varied the amount of choice children between 2 and 6 years of age had in selecting material with which to make collages. Children in the choice condition were presented with ten boxes containing collage materials and told to choose any five of these boxes for making their collages. Children in the no-choice condition had their five boxes selected for them by the experimenter. All sets of material were similar to one another. The children were given approximately 10 minutes to complete their collages, which were subsequently rated in terms of

how creative they were by eight trained artists. Creativity ratings could range from 0 to 320, with higher scores indicating greater creativity.

The hypothetical data presented in the table are representative of the results of the study. Analyze these data using a nondirectional test, draw a conclusion, and write up your results using the principles developed in the Method of Presentation section.

Choice	No choice
207	130
203	142
180	137
167	149
212	146
192	150
172	128
200	154
170	142
164	166
178	145
	133
	161
	156

---

58. Social psychologists have identified many types of love. Perhaps the best known of these is *passionate love*, which is an intense, even overwhelming, emotional response to another person. This is the type of love to which people typically refer when they talk about "falling in love."

One theory of passionate love proposes that the ability to experience this emotion requires that one be exposed to romantic images during one's socialization. To find out whether Eastern and Western cultures differ in the extent to which they contain romantic images and, thus, in the extent to which members of these cultures might experience passionate love, suppose that a researcher examines the romantic content of the ten most popular fairy tales from several cultures. Each fairy tale is classified according to whether or not it contains romantic imagery, and an overall romance index is derived for each culture by determining the total number of romantic fairy tales for that culture. Thus, the romance score for each culture can range from 0 to 10.

Hypothetical data for the study are presented in the table. Analyze these data using a nondirectional test, draw a conclusion, and write up your results using the principles developed in the Method of Presentation section.

Eastern culture		Western culture	
2	3	6	5
3	2	4	7
2	3	5	5
2	1	4	7
4	2	7	6
		6	6

CHAPTER **11**

Correlated Groups *t* Test

11.1 Use of the Correlated Groups *t* Test

The **correlated groups *t* test** is typically used to analyze the relationship between two variables when the following conditions are met:

1. The dependent variable is quantitative in nature and is measured on a level that at least approximates interval characteristics.

2. The independent variable is *within-subjects* in nature (it can be either qualitative or quantitative).

3. The independent variable has two, and only two, levels.

The major difference between the correlated groups *t* test and the independent groups *t* test is that the former is used when the independent variable is within-subjects in nature and the latter is used when the independent variable is between-subjects in nature. The correlated groups *t* test can also be used to analyze matched-subjects designs, although we will not discuss this design further given the problems that we noted with matching in Chapter 9.

An important advantage of the correlated groups *t* test over the independent groups *t* test relates to the control of disturbance variables. As we discussed in Chapter 9, disturbance variables are variables that are unrelated to the independent variable but that influence the dependent variable and that thereby create variability in the dependent variable. In so doing, disturbance variables create "noise" that makes it more difficult to detect a relationship between the independent and dependent variables. As we noted in Section 10.4, this "noise" manifests itself as error variance.

One major source of "noise" is the different backgrounds and personal characteristics of the individuals who participate in an investigation. For example, the fact that some people are more intelligent than others should influence performance on relevant research tasks. If we know the influence of individual differences on the dependent variable, their influence can be separated from the effects of the independent variable. However, if their influence cannot be isolated, these differences in background and personal characteristics remain uncontrolled sources of variability and, thus, increase the error variance.

As we will demonstrate shortly, within-subjects designs allow us to estimate this source of variability and extract it from the dependent variable. In contrast, this cannot be done with between-subjects designs. Consequently, the correlated groups *t* test provides a more sensitive test of the relationship between the independent and dependent variables than does the independent groups *t* test in that it is more likely to detect such a relationship when one exists in the population.

As an example of a study that meets the conditions for the correlated groups *t* test, suppose that an investigator conducts an experiment to examine the relative effects of two drugs, drug A and drug B, on learning. Five individuals are administered drug A and then work on a learning task. One month later, the same five individuals are administered drug B and work on the same type of learning task as before. The number of correct answers on this task following the administration of

TABLE 11.1   **Data and Calculations for Drug and Learning Experiment**

Participant	X for drug A	X for drug B	Difference (D)	D^2
1	3	7	−4	16
2	1	5	−4	16
3	4	4	0	0
4	2	8	−6	36
5	5	6	−1	1

$$\Sigma X_A = \overline{15} \qquad \Sigma X_B = \overline{30} \qquad \Sigma D = \overline{-15} \qquad \Sigma D^2 = \overline{69}$$

$$\overline{X}_A = 3.00 \qquad \overline{X}_B = 6.00 \qquad \overline{D} = -3.00$$

$$SS_D = \Sigma D^2 - \frac{(\Sigma D)^2}{N} = 69 - \frac{(-15)^2}{5} = 24.00$$

$$\hat{s}_D^2 = \frac{SS_D}{N-1} = \frac{24.00}{4} = 6.00$$

$$\hat{s}_D = \sqrt{\hat{s}_D^2} = \sqrt{6.00} = 2.45$$

$$\hat{s}_{\overline{D}} = \frac{\hat{s}_D}{\sqrt{N}} = \frac{2.45}{\sqrt{5}} = 1.10$$

each drug is determined and serves as the dependent variable. These data are presented in the second and third columns of Table 11.1.

The research design involves a within-subjects independent variable with two levels (drug A and drug B) and a quantitative dependent variable that is measured on a level that at least approximates interval characteristics. Hence, the correlated groups *t* test would typically be used to analyze the relationship between the variables.

As was the case with the independent groups *t* test, our discussion of the correlated groups *t* test is organized around the three questions relevant to the analysis of bivariate relationships: (1) Is there a relationship between the variables? (2) If so, what is the strength of the relationship? (3) If so, what is the nature of the relationship?

11.2   Inference of a Relationship Using the Correlated Groups *t* Test

Null and Alternative Hypotheses

The first question to be considered is whether a relationship exists between the type of drug that is administered and learning. We begin by formally phrasing this in terms of a null and an alternative hypothesis:

$$H_0: \mu_A = \mu_B$$

$$H_1: \mu_A \neq \mu_B$$

where the subscripts "*A*" and "*B*," respectively, represent drug A and drug B.

The null hypothesis states that the two population means are equal. If so, there is no relationship between the type of drug and learning. The alternative hypothesis states that the population means differ.* If so, there is a relationship between the type of drug and learning; that is, which drug is administered does matter.

If the null hypothesis is true and the type of drug does not make a difference, performance while under the influence of drug A should be the same as performance while under the influence of drug B. Consequently, the average difference between the scores in condition A and the scores in condition B should be 0.

Column 4 of Table 11.1 reports a difference score (symbolized as D) for each experimental participant. The mean difference score across individuals $(\overline{D})$ is -3.00. Note that this equals the difference between the means for the two conditions $(3.00 - 6.00 = -3.00)$. In fact, the mean of the sample difference scores will always equal the sample mean for the first condition minus the sample mean for the second condition in a correlated groups design (that is, $\overline{D}$ will always equal $\overline{X}_1 - \overline{X}_1$). The question of interest is whether the mean difference of 3.00 is sufficiently different from 0 for us to reject the null hypothesis. To answer this question, it is necessary to specify the nature of the *sampling distribution of the mean of difference scores* based on five difference scores.

The Sampling Distribution of the Mean of Difference Scores

A **sampling distribution of the mean of difference** scores is conceptually similar to a sampling distribution of the mean and a sampling distribution of the difference between two independent means, as we discussed in Chapters 7 and 8, and Chapter 10, respectively. However, now the concern is with a distribution of scores that represent differences across individuals. More specifically, a sampling distribution of the mean of difference scores is a theoretical distribution consisting of the mean difference score across all individuals in a sample for all possible random samples of a given size that can be selected from a population.

A sampling distribution of the mean of difference scores is most readily understood by comparing it with a sampling distribution of the mean. As we discussed in Chapters 7 and 8, this latter distribution provides the basis for testing a sample mean against a hypothesized population mean. The mean of such a distribution is equal to the population mean (μ) and its standard deviation (the standard error of the mean) is equal to $\sigma_{\overline{X}} = \sigma/\sqrt{N}$.

Similarly, the mean of the sampling distribution of the mean of difference scores (symbolized as $\mu_{\overline{D}}$) is equal to the mean of the population difference scores (symbolized as μ_D), that is, to the mean difference score across all individuals in the population. When the population means for the two conditions being studied are identical, μ_D will be equal to 0 because the mean of a population of difference scores is always equal to the difference between the population means for the two conditions (that is, $\mu_D = \mu_1 - \mu_2$), and $\mu_1 - \mu_2 = 0$ when $\mu_1 = \mu_2$.

---

* As with the other tests that we have discussed, the alternative hypothesis can be phrased directionally rather than nondirectionally if there is exclusive concern with a specific direction of mean differences.

The standard deviation of the sampling distribution of the mean of difference scores is formally known as the **standard error of the mean of difference scores** and is symbolized as $\sigma_{\bar{D}}$ and calculated as follows:

$$\sigma_{\bar{D}} = \frac{\sigma_D}{\sqrt{N}}$$ [11.1]

where σ_D is the standard deviation of the population of difference scores and N is the number of difference scores. Note the similarity of this formula to that for the standard error of the mean from above.

Following the logic from earlier chapters, we can obtain an estimate of $\sigma_{\bar{D}}$ by substituting a sample estimate of the standard deviation of the population of difference scores for σ_D in Equation 11.1. This leads to the following formula for estimating the standard error of the mean of difference scores:

$$\hat{s}_{\bar{D}} = \frac{\hat{s}_D}{\sqrt{N}}$$ [11.2]

where $\hat{s}_{\bar{D}}$ is the estimated standard error of the mean of difference scores, $\hat{s}_D$ is the estimated standard deviation for the difference scores in the population as derived from the sample difference scores, and N is the number of difference scores.*

Being a type of standard deviation estimate, $\hat{s}_D$ is calculated by applying the usual procedures for a standard deviation estimate to the difference scores: First the sum of squares for the sample difference scores is determined using the formula $SS_D = \Sigma D^2 - (\Sigma D)^2/N$, which is conceptually identical to the formula for the sum of squares for raw (X) scores. Next, this quantity is divided by $N - 1$ to yield an estimated variance for the population of difference scores. Finally, $\hat{s}_D$ is obtained by taking the square root of the estimated population variance. As shown in Table 11.1, $\hat{s}_D$ in the drug and learning example is equal to 2.45, which yields an estimated standard error of $2.45/\sqrt{5} = 1.10$.

The Correlated Groups *t* Test

The existence of a relationship between an independent variable and a dependent variable in the correlated groups case is tested by converting the mean difference score for the sample to a *t* score that represents the number of estimated standard errors the difference is from the hypothesized mean of the population of difference scores and comparing this with the critical value(s) of *t* that define the rejection region. Specifically, the foregoing suggests the following formula for the correlated groups *t* test:

$$t = \frac{\overline{D} - \mu_D}{\hat{s}_{\bar{D}}}$$ [11.3]

---

* It will always be the case that $n_1 = n_2 = N$ for the type of design that we consider in this chapter.

where $\overline{D}$ is the mean of the sample difference scores (that is, the mean difference score across all individuals in the sample), μ_D is the hypothesized mean of the population difference scores (which will always equal the difference between the hypothesized population means for the two conditions), and $\hat{s}_{\overline{D}}$ is the estimated standard error of the mean of difference scores.

When we hypothesize that the population means for the two conditions are identical, μ_D will equal 0 for the purpose of hypothesis testing. Consequently, Equation 11.3 reduces to

$$t = \frac{\overline{D}}{\hat{s}_{\overline{D}}}$$

[11.4]

This is the most commonly used version of the correlated groups *t* test because the null hypothesis usually states that $\mu_1 = \mu_2$.* However, because it is conceptually clearer, we use the more general formula represented by Equation 11.3 whenever a correlated groups *t* test is called for in the remainder of this chapter.

Note that Equation 11.3 is merely a special case of Equation 8.7:

$$t = \frac{\text{score of interest} - \text{hypothesized mean of the distribution}}{\text{estimated standard error of the distribution}}$$

where the score of interest is the mean of the sample difference scores, the hypothesized mean of the distribution is the hypothesized mean of the population difference scores, and the estimated standard error of the distribution is the estimated standard error of the mean of difference scores. The correlated groups *t* test is thus conceptually similar to the one-sample *t* test, which, as we saw in Section 8.15, can also be conceptualized as a special case of Equation 8.7. In that both tests require two sets of scores, the correlated groups *t* test also shares characteristics with the independent groups *t* test.

Because we are dealing with difference scores, the degrees of freedom for the correlated groups *t* test depend on how many such scores there are in the sample. Specifically, the degrees of freedom for the correlated groups *t* test are equal to

$$df = N - 1$$

[11.5]

There are $N - 1 = 5 - 1 = 4$ degrees of freedom associated with the drug and learning experiment, so the critical values of *t* for an alpha level of .05, nondirectional test, are ± 2.776. Thus, if the observed *t* value is less than -2.776 or greater than $+2.776$, we will reject the null hypothesis.

Because the null hypothesis states that the population means are equal, μ_D can be set equal to 0. Applying Equation 11.3, we find that the observed value of *t* is

$$t = \frac{-3.00 - 0}{1.10} = -2.73$$

Because -2.73 does not exceed the negative critical value of -2.776, we fail to reject the null hypothesis of no relationship between the type of drug and learning.

---

* As with the independent groups *t* test, other null hypotheses are also possible.

STUDY EXERCISE 11.1

Eight individuals indicated their attitudes toward socialized medicine before and after listening to a pro–socialized medicine lecture. Attitudes were assessed on a 1 to 7 scale, with higher scores indicating more positive attitudes. The attitudes before and after listening to the lecture are listed in the table below. Test for a relationship between the time of assessment and attitudes toward socialized medicine using a correlated groups *t* test.

Individual	Before speech	After speech
1	3	6
2	4	6
3	3	3
4	5	7
5	2	4
6	5	6
7	3	7
8	4	6

Answer   The null and alternative hypotheses are

$$H_0: \mu_B = \mu_A$$
$$H_1: \mu_B \neq \mu_A$$

where the subscripts "*B*" and "*A*" represent the before- and after-speech conditions, respectively.

For an alpha level of .05, nondirectional test, and $N - 1 = 8 - 1 = 7$ degrees of freedom, the critical values of *t* are ±2.365. Thus, if the observed *t* value is less than −2.365 or greater than +2.365, we will reject the null hypothesis.

Because the null hypothesis states that the population means are equal, $\mu_D = 0$ for the purpose of hypothesis testing. To obtain the observed value of *t*, we must also calculate $\overline{D}$ and $\hat{s}_{\overline{D}}$ as follows:

Individual	Before speech	After speech	Difference (D)	D^2
1	3	6	−3	9
2	4	6	−2	4
3	3	3	0	0
4	5	7	−2	4
5	2	4	−2	4
6	5	6	−1	1
7	3	7	−4	16
8	4	6	−2	4

$$\Sigma X_B = 29 \qquad \Sigma X_A = 45 \qquad \Sigma D = -16 \qquad \Sigma D^2 = 42$$
$$\overline{X}_B = 3.62 \qquad \overline{X}_A = 5.62 \qquad \overline{D} = -2.00$$

$$SS_D = \Sigma D^2 - \frac{(\Sigma D)^2}{N} = 42 - \frac{-16^2}{8} = 10.00$$

$$\hat{s}_D^2 = \frac{SS_D}{N-1} = \frac{10.00}{7} = 1.43$$

$$\hat{s}_D = \sqrt{\hat{s}_D^2} = \sqrt{1.43} = 1.20$$

We next estimate the standard error of the mean of difference scores using Equation 11.2:

$$\hat{s}_{\overline{D}} = \frac{\hat{s}_D}{\sqrt{N}} = \frac{1.20}{\sqrt{8}} = .42$$

Applying Equation 11.3, we find that the observed value of t is

$$t = \frac{\overline{D} - \mu_D}{\hat{s}_{\overline{D}}}$$

$$= \frac{-2.00 - 0}{.42} = -4.76$$

Because -4.76 exceeds the negative critical value of -2.365, we reject the null hypothesis and conclude that there is a relationship between the time of assessment and attitudes toward socialized medicine.

Assumptions of the Correlated Groups *t* Test

The assumptions underlying the validity of the correlated groups t test parallel those for the one-sample t test, as we discussed in Section 8.10. Specifically, it is assumed that

1. The sample is independently and randomly selected from the population of interest.

2. The population of difference scores is normally distributed.

In addition, the dependent variable should be quantitative in nature and measured on a level that at least approximates interval characteristics.

The assumption of independent and random selection is an important one, as it is for all of the statistical tests that we consider in this book. In contrast, the correlated groups t test is relatively robust to violations of the normality assumption. If the sample size is less than 15, the test may show an increased Type I error rate for data that are markedly skewed (Posten, 1979). However, for sample sizes of 40 or more, the test is remarkably robust, even for distributions that have considerable skewness.

11.3 Strength of the Relationship

The second question to be addressed regarding the analysis of bivariate relationships is how strong the relationship is. We will determine this using eta-squared.* The formula for eta-squared for the correlated groups t test is the same as that for the independent groups t test:

$$\text{eta}^2 = \frac{t^2}{t^2 + df} \tag{11.6}$$

---

* As we discussed in Section 10.4, eta-squared is a biased estimator of the strength of the relationship between two variables. The formula for epsilon-squared, a commonly-used unbiased estimator of relationship strength, is provided in Appendix N for the correlated groups t test situation.

For the drug and learning experiment,

$$\text{eta}^2 = \frac{-2.73^2}{-2.73^2 + 4} = .65$$

However, whereas eta-squared represents the proportion of variability in the dependent variable that is associated with the independent variable in the independent groups case, in the correlated groups case eta-squared represents the proportion of variability in the dependent variable that is associated with the independent variable *after variability due to individual differences has been removed*. It follows that 1.00 minus eta-squared represents the proportion of variability in the dependent variable that is due to disturbance variables other than individual differences.

In our example, the proportion of variability in learning that is associated with the type of drug after the influence of individual differences has been removed is .65, which represents a strong effect. Thus, $1.00 - .65 = .35$, or 35%, of the variability in learning is attributable to disturbance variables other than individual differences. This interpretation of eta-squared can be best demonstrated by using a variance extraction approach similar to that developed in Section 10.4.

STUDY EXERCISE 11.2

Calculate eta-squared for the data in Study Exercise 11.1.

Answer   Eta-squared can be calculated using Equation 11.6:

$$\text{eta}^2 = \frac{t^2}{t^2 + df}$$

$$= \frac{-4.76^2}{-4.76^2 + 7} = .76$$

Thus, the proportion of variability in the time of assessment that is associated with attitudes toward socialized medicine after the influence of individual differences has been removed is .76. This represents a strong effect.

Estimating and Extracting the Influence of Individual Differences

Consider an individual who tries to solve three 5-point math problems on an exam. The individual gets a score of 5 on the first problem, a score of 1 on the second problem, and a score of 3 on the third problem. Another individual works on the same three problems and scores 5 on the first one, 5 on the second, and 2 on the third. Which individual has greater math ability?

In the absence of any other information, the best approach to answering this question is to compare the mean scores of the two individuals. The first individual's mean score is $(5 + 1 + 3)/3 = 3.00$, and the second individual's mean score is $(5 + 5 + 2)/3 = 4.00$. Using the average score across questions as an index of ability, you would conclude that the second individual has greater math ability than the first individual.

In within-subjects designs, estimates of the influence of individual difference variables are derived in a similar fashion. For each individual, the mean score across conditions (symbolized as $\overline{X}_i$) is computed. This has been done for the drug and learning experiment in column 4 of Table 11.2. For instance, the first participant obtained a score of 3 with drug A and a score of 7 with drug B for a mean of $(7 + 3)/2 = 5.00$. Inspection of column 4 shows that some participants have higher average scores than others. These differences reflect variations in the individuals' backgrounds and personal characteristics (for example, intelligence, familiarity with the learning task, and so on).

We now develop the logic for extracting this source of variability. In order to do so, we must first compute a grand mean (symbolized as G). This will serve as a reference point for all participants and is derived by summing *all* of the scores in columns 2 and 3 of Table 11.2 and dividing by the number of summed scores. We find that $G = (3 + 1 + 4 + 2 + 5 + 7 + 5 + 4 + 8 + 6)/10 = 4.50$. Thus, the average score across all participants and across both experimental conditions is 4.50.

Consider the first participant. His mean score across conditions is 5.00. The grand mean is 4.50. Because an individual's average score across conditions reflects the influence of his or her background and personal characteristics, the effect of individual differences in this instance is to raise the individual's score $5.00 - 4.50 = .50$ unit above the grand mean.

Using logic similar to that used to extract variability from scores in Section 10.4, we can nullify this effect by subtracting .50 unit from the scores of this individual. This has been done in columns 5 and 6 of Table 11.2. The score for drug A is 3, and this score is adjusted to $3 - .50 = 2.50$. The score for drug B is 7, and this score is adjusted to $7 - .50 = 6.50$. The new scores have had the effect of the individual's background and personal characteristics removed, or *nullified*. This same approach is taken for each individual. For the second participant, the mean score across conditions is 3.00. This is $3.00 - 4.50 = -1.50$ units below the grand mean. The effect of this individual's background and personal characteristics is to hold performance down 1.50 units from the overall average. To nullify the effect of these factors, we simply add 1.50 to the two scores. The remaining participants' scores are nullified in a similar fashion.

We now have an adjusted data set in which the effects of individual differences in background and personal characteristics have been removed. Compare the nullified data in Table 11.2 with the original data. Note that there is less variability in

TABLE 11.2   Raw and Nullified Scores for Drug and Learning Experiment

Participant	X for drug A	X for drug B	$\overline{X}_i$	Nullified X for drug A	Nullified X for drug B
1	3	7	5.00	2.50	6.50
2	1	5	3.00	2.50	6.50
3	4	4	4.00	4.50	4.50
4	2	8	5.00	1.50	7.50
5	5	6	5.50	4.00	5.00
Mean =	3.00	6.00	4.50	3.00	6.00

the nullified scores because we have removed a source of variability—namely, individuals' backgrounds and personal characteristics. If we were to compute the average nullified score across conditions for each participant, every individual would have the same average score. Again, this is because we have extracted variability due to individual differences.

Because there is a set of nullified scores for drug A and a set of nullified scores for drug B, the adjusted data can be analyzed using the independent groups *t* test.* This test tends to be more sensitive (and, thus, more powerful) than an independent groups *t* test applied to the raw scores because the "noise" created by individual differences has been eliminated. If we were to actually apply an independent groups *t* test to the adjusted data, we would get the same value of *t* (−2.73) as that obtained earlier when the correlated groups *t* test was applied to the difference scores. We demonstrate this in Appendix 11.1.

The equivalence of the two results clarifies the nature of *t* in the correlated groups case: A correlated groups *t* test is analogous to an independent groups *t* test with the effects of individual differences extracted from the dependent variable. It follows that eta-squared in the correlated groups case is analogous to eta-squared in the independent groups case, but with variability due to individual differences removed from the dependent variable.

Unstandardized Effect Size and Confidence Intervals

As with the independent groups *t* test, an unstandardized index of the effect size is provided by the difference between the sample means for the two conditions. For the drug and learning experiment, this is the mean score for drug A minus the mean score for drug B, or $3.00 - 6.00 = -3.00$.

Confidence intervals can be formed for the mean difference using procedures analogous to those presented in Section 10.4. Specifically, the formula for a confidence interval in the correlated groups case is

$$CI = (\overline{X}_1 - \overline{X}_2) - |t_{\text{critical}}| (\hat{s}_{\overline{D}}) \quad \text{to} \quad (\overline{X}_1 - \overline{X}_2) + |t_{\text{critical}}| (\hat{s}_{\overline{D}}) \qquad [11.7]$$

where $\overline{X}_1 - \overline{X}_2$ is the difference between the sample means, t_{critical} is the absolute value of the critical *t* value that was the criterion for deciding to reject the null hypothesis, and, per our discussion above, $\hat{s}_{\overline{D}}$ is the estimated standard error of the mean of difference scores.

For the drug and learning experiment, $\overline{X}_1 - \overline{X}_2$ is equal to −3.00, $|t_{\text{critical}}|$ is equal to 2.776, $\hat{s}_{\overline{D}}$ is equal to 1.10. The 95% confidence interval is thus

$$CI = -3.00 - (2.776)(1.10) \quad \text{to} \quad -3.00 + (2.776)(1.10)$$

$$= -6.05 \quad \text{to} \quad .05$$

We are 95% confident that the interval −6.05 to .05 contains the true population mean difference in the number of correct answers on the learning task.

---

* Technically, a slight modification to the independent groups *t* test formula is required, as we discuss in Appendix 11.1.

11.4   Nature of the Relationship

The third question to be addressed regarding the analysis of bivariate relationships is what the nature of the relationship is. The procedure for determining the nature of the relationship between the independent and the dependent variables for the correlated groups *t* test is identical to that for the independent groups *t* test and involves comparing the two *sample* means to make a decision about how the two *population* means differ. We simply conclude that the condition that has the larger *sample* mean also has the larger *population* mean.

Because we failed to reject the null hypothesis in the drug and learning example, the question of the nature of the relationship is not meaningful. Had we rejected the null hypothesis, the nature of the relationship would be that performance is better following the administration of drug B ($\overline{X}_B = 6.00$) than following the administration of drug A ($\overline{X}_A = 3.00$).

11.5   Methodological Considerations

The drug and learning experiment raises a number of methodological issues. First, consider the potential role of confounding variables. The investigator attempted to control for possible carry-over effects, such as familiarity with the task and the persistence of the effects of drug A into the administration of drug B, by introducing a long time period between the administration of the two drugs.

The presence of the 1-month interval between the two sessions may, in fact, reduce such carry-over effects, but an additional problem arises. Perhaps during the time between the administration of the two drugs, the participants experienced something that improved their performance on the learning task. For instance, if the participants are introductory psychology students, they might have learned about certain memory aids in their course work.

A procedure that circumvents this problem and that could have been used here is **counterbalancing**. With this technique, half of the participants are given drug A first and then, at a later time when carry-over effects should be minimal, they are given drug B. The other half of the participants are given drug B first and then drug A. If this is done, any effects due to familiarity or to intervening events should no longer be related to the administration of the two drugs. Because they are now evenly distributed across conditions, any carry-over effects should influence performance under drug A (for those who were given drug A second) and performance under drug B (for those who were given drug B second) to an equal extent.* In essence, these confounding variables are turned into disturbance

---

* Carry-over effects will generally influence the dependent variable equally in the two conditions when the nature of such effects is the same for the two levels of the independent variable. When the nature of carry-over effects is not the same for the two levels of the independent variable, the dependent variable will generally be affected differently in the two conditions.

variables, which now create "noise" in the experiment. It is possible to remove the disturbance influence of these variables using certain advanced statistical techniques. These are beyond the scope of this book, however, but are discussed in Winer (1971).

Another problem with this experiment is the lack of a control condition in which participants perform the learning task while not under the influence of any drugs. Although the effects of drug A and drug B relative to each other can be determined from the experiment, the effects of the drugs relative to baseline performance cannot. The addition of a control condition would be quite informative. In Chapter 13 we discuss a statistical test that could be used to analyze the study if such a condition were included.

We saw in Chapter 10 that the role of disturbance variables in the between-subjects case can be delineated by examining the magnitude of eta-squared. A similar approach can be taken with within-subjects designs. For instance, the eta-squared of .65 for the drug and learning experiment indicates that, after variability due to individual differences has been removed, 65% of the variability in the dependent variable is associated with the independent variable and 35% is due to disturbance variables other than individual differences. This represents a strong relationship in the sample, yet the *t* test results were such that we could not conclude that a relationship exists in the population.

Although this may appear contradictory, a consideration of the sample size helps to place this in proper perspective. The study was conducted with an extremely small sample size—namely, five individuals. With small sample sizes, very large values of eta-squared are necessary before we can conclude that there is a relationship between the independent and the dependent variables. Although an eta-squared of .65 suggests that the role of disturbance variables is not very great, a sample relationship of this magnitude is still not strong enough for us to be confident that the difference in sample means is not due to sampling error, given the extremely small sample size that this is based on. The implication is that large sample sizes should be used when this is practical. As we have discussed in previous chapters, large sample sizes increase the power of the statistical test and thereby increase the probability of detecting a relationship in the population when one exists.

11.6 Power of the Correlated Groups Versus the Independent Groups *t* Test

Because variability due to individual differences is extracted from the dependent variable as part of the correlated groups *t* test procedure, a correlated groups *t* test will usually be more powerful than a corresponding independent groups *t* test. We can illustrate this by reconsidering the formulas for the two tests.

Suppose that we want to compare the sample means for the two levels of an independent variable. If the two conditions represent a between-subjects variable, then the *t* statistic can be calculated using the usual formula for the independent groups *t* test (Equation 10.8). If we express the denominator of this formula, $\hat{s}_{\overline{X}_1 - \overline{X}_2}$, in terms of Equation 10.4, this can be written as

$$t = \frac{(\overline{X}_1 - \overline{X}_2) - (\mu_1 - \mu_2)}{\sqrt{\dfrac{\hat{s}_{pooled}^2}{n_1} + \dfrac{\hat{s}_{pooled}^2}{n_2}}}$$

For the correlated groups *t* test, the formula is

$$t = \frac{\overline{D} - \mu_D}{\hat{s}_{\overline{D}}}$$

per Equation 11.3. As we noted earlier, it is always the case that $\overline{D} = \overline{X}_1 - \overline{X}_2$ and $\mu_D = \mu_1 - \mu_2$ in a correlated groups design. Thus, the formula for the correlated groups *t* test can be rewritten as:

$$t = \frac{(\overline{X}_1 - \overline{X}_2) - (\mu_1 - \mu_2)}{\hat{s}_{\overline{D}}}$$

Although we are unable to provide the proof for this here, it is also the case that $\hat{s}_{\overline{D}}$ is equal to

$$\hat{s}_{\overline{D}} = \sqrt{\frac{\hat{s}_1^2}{n_1} + \frac{\hat{s}_2^2}{n_2} - \frac{2r\hat{s}_1\hat{s}_2}{N}}$$

where $n_1 = n_2 = N$ and *r* represents the correlation between the scores in the first condition and the scores in the second condition.* We can therefore express the correlated groups *t* test formula as

$$t = \frac{(\overline{X}_1 - \overline{X}_2) - (\mu_1 - \mu_2)}{\sqrt{\dfrac{\hat{s}_1^2}{n_1} + \dfrac{\hat{s}_2^2}{n_2} - \dfrac{2r\hat{s}_1\hat{s}_2}{N}}}$$

When *r* equals 0, the rightmost term in the denominator also equals 0 and this formula reduces to

$$t = \frac{(\overline{X}_1 - \overline{X}_2) - (\mu_1 - \mu_2)}{\sqrt{\dfrac{\hat{s}_1^2}{n_1} + \dfrac{\hat{s}_2^2}{n_2}}}$$

---

* If you have not yet read Chapter 5, you may not be familiar with *r* or the concept of *Pearson correlation*. Simply put, correlation is the extent to which two variables approximate a linear relationship as indexed by the *correlation coefficient, r*. The correlation coefficient can range from −1.00 through 0 to +1.00 where the magnitude of the coefficient indicates the extent of linear relationship, and the sign of the coefficient indicates the direction of the linear approximation. A correlation coefficient of +1.00 means that the two variables form a perfect linear relationship that is direct in nature, a correlation coefficient of −1.00 means that the two variables form a perfect linear relationship that is inverse in nature, and a correlation coefficient of 0 means that there is no linear relationship between the two variables.

which is strikingly similar to the formula for the independent groups *t* test from the beginning of this section. In fact, the only difference is the use of the pooled variance estimate in the independent groups *t* test as opposed to the individual variance estimates here.

When the correlation between scores in the two conditions is positive, as is the case in most behavioral science research, the estimated standard error for the correlated groups *t* test will be smaller than $\sqrt{\hat{s}_1^2/n_1 + \hat{s}_2^2/n_2}$ because $2r\hat{s}_1\hat{s}_2/N$ will be nonzero. As a result, the estimated standard error for the correlated groups *t* test will be smaller than the estimated standard error for the independent groups *t* test. This, in turn, can yield a more powerful statistical test.

However, an exception occurs when *r* is so close to 0 that the magnitude of the estimated standard errors is comparable for the two tests. This relates to the fact that the degrees of freedom for the correlated groups *t* test $(N - 1)$ are smaller than the degrees of freedom for the independent groups *t* test $(n_1 + n_2 - 2)$ when there are the same number of raw scores for the two designs. For example, if there are two sets of 10 scores, $df = 10 - 1 = 9$ for the correlated groups test and $df = 10 + 10 - 2 = 18$ for the independent groups test. Because the *t* distribution requires more extreme values of *t* in order to reject the null hypothesis as the degrees of freedom decrease, the statistical advantage of the correlated groups *t* test having the smaller estimated standard error may be offset by the smaller degrees of freedom. In fact, under this circumstance, a correlated groups test might actually be *less* powerful than an independent groups test. Thus, it is important that a researcher who is considering a within-subjects design accurately anticipate the role of individual differences.

In practice, we would never use a correlated groups *t* test to analyze a between-subjects design or an independent groups *t* test to analyze a within-subjects design. As we stress throughout this book, the statistical technique to be applied to one's data must correspond to the research design that is utilized.

11.7 Numerical Example

Developmental psychologists have attempted to specify the age period when infants begin to show signs of fearing strangers. At very early ages (1 to 2 months), infants generally will show positive reactions when approached or held by any adult. At some point, however, they begin to discriminate among adults and exhibit fear responses in the presence of a stranger (as opposed to a familiar person such as the mother or father).

In order to study this issue further, suppose that a researcher compares the fear responses of eight infants at ages 3 and 6 months. A stranger individually interacts with each infant for 10 minutes, during which time she attempts to engage them in playful behavior. The interactions are standardized as much as possible, and the number of minutes that the infants cry for is used as the measure of fear. The scores on the dependent variable are presented in the second and third columns of Table 11.3.

The null hypothesis posits that the two population means are equal and, therefore, that there is no relationship between infants' ages and the amount of time that

TABLE 11.3   **Data and Calculations for Age and Response to a Stranger Study**

Individual	X for 3 months	X for 6 months	Difference (D)	D^2
1	0	3	-3	9
2	1	2	-1	1
3	2	4	-2	4
4	2	4	-2	4
5	2	4	-2	4
6	1	2	-1	1
7	0	3	-3	9
8	0	2	-2	4
	$\Sigma X_T = 8$	$\Sigma X_S = 24$	$\Sigma D = -16$	$\Sigma D^2 = 36$
	$\overline{X}_T = 1.00$	$\overline{X}_S = 3.00$	$\overline{D} = -2.00$	

$$SS_D = \sum D^2 - \frac{(\sum D)^2}{N} = 36 - \frac{-16^2}{8} = 4.00$$

$$\hat{s}_D^2 = \frac{SS_D}{N-1} = \frac{4.00}{7} = .57$$

$$\hat{s}_D = \sqrt{\hat{s}_D} = \sqrt{.57} = .75$$

$$\hat{s}_{\overline{D}} = \frac{\hat{s}_D}{\sqrt{N}} = \frac{.75}{\sqrt{8}} = .27$$

they cry in response to a stranger. The alternative hypothesis posits that the population means differ and that these two variables are therefore related. These hypotheses can be formally stated as

$$H_0: \mu_T = \mu_S$$

$$H_1: \mu_T \neq \mu_S$$

where the subscripts "T" and "S" denote the ages 3 months and 6 months, respectively. Assuming that the null hypothesis is true, the critical values of t for an alpha level of .05, nondirectional test, and $N - 1 = 8 - 1 = 7$ degrees of freedom are ± 2.365.

    Because the null hypothesis states that the population means are equal, $\mu_D = 0$ for the purpose of hypothesis testing. The other values necessary for the calculation of t are derived in Table 11.3. Applying Equation 11.3, the observed value of t is found to equal

$$t = \frac{\overline{D} - \mu_D}{\hat{s}_{\overline{D}}}$$

$$= \frac{-2.00 - 0}{.27} = -7.41$$

Because -7.41 exceeds -2.365, we reject the null hypothesis and conclude that a relationship exists between infants' ages and the amount of time that they cry in response to a stranger.

The strength of the relationship, as indexed by eta-squared, is

$$\text{eta}^2 = \frac{t^2}{t^2 + df}$$

$$= \frac{-7.41^2}{-7.41^2 + 7} = .89$$

Thus, the proportion of variability in crying time that is associated with age after the influence of individual differences has been removed is .89. This represents a strong effect.

The 95% confidence interval is

$$CI = (\overline{X}_1 - \overline{X}_2) - |t_{\text{critical}}|\,(\hat{s}_{\overline{D}}) \quad \text{to} \quad (\overline{X}_1 - \overline{X}_2) + |t_{\text{critical}}|\,(\hat{s}_{\overline{D}})$$

$$= (1.00 - 3.00) - (2.365)(.27) \quad \text{to} \quad (1.00 - 3.00) + (2.365)(.27)$$

$$= -2.64 \quad \text{to} \quad -1.36$$

We are 95% confident that the interval -2.64 to -1.36 contains the true population mean difference in crying time.

The nature of the relationship is determined by comparing the two *sample* means to make a decision about how the two *population* means differ. The mean crying times in the 3-month and the 6-month conditions are 1.00 and 3.00 minutes, respectively. Therefore, we conclude that infants will cry more in response to a stranger when they are 6 months old than when they are 3 months old.

You should think about these results in terms of basic research design issues: Are there any confounding variables that have not been controlled? What is the role of disturbance variables? What kind of procedures could be used to reduce sampling error? What are the limitations of the study in terms of generalizability?

11.8   Planning an Investigation Using the Correlated Groups *t* Test

Appendix E.1 contains tables of the sample sizes necessary to achieve various levels of power for the correlated groups *t* test. Table 11.4 reproduces a portion of this appendix for an alpha level of .05, nondirectional test. As in Chapter 10, selected values of power are listed in the first column, and various population values of eta-squared serve as column headings. Consistent with the interpretation of sample values of eta-squared, these values of eta-squared are conceptualized as the proportion of variability in the dependent variable that is associated with the independent variable *after the effects of individual differences have been removed*. Thus, to the extent that the dependent variable is influenced by individuals' backgrounds and personal characteristics, the population eta-squared will be greater in the correlated groups case than in the independent groups case, other things being equal.

TABLE 11.4   **Approximate Sample Sizes Necessary to Achieve Selected Levels of Power for Alpha = .05, Nondirectional Test, as a Function of Population Values of Eta-Squared**

Power	.01	.03	.05	.07	.10	.15	.20	.25	.30	.35
					Population Eta-Squared					
.25	84	28	17	12	8	6	5	3	3	3
.50	193	63	38	27	18	12	9	7	5	5
.60	246	80	48	34	23	15	11	8	7	6
.67	287	93	55	39	27	17	12	10	8	6
.70	310	101	60	42	29	18	13	10	8	7
.75	348	113	67	47	32	21	15	11	9	7
.80	393	128	76	53	36	23	17	13	10	8
.85	450	146	86	61	41	26	19	14	11	9
.90	526	171	101	71	48	31	22	17	13	11
.95	651	211	125	87	60	38	27	21	16	13
.99	920	298	176	123	84	53	38	29	22	18

To illustrate the use of the table, if the desired power is .80 and the investigator suspects that the strength of the relationship in the population corresponds to an eta-squared of .07, then the number of participants that should be sampled for an alpha level of .05, nondirectional test, is 53. The power that an investigator requires will, of course, depend on the seriousness of committing a Type II error.

In addition to providing the sample size necessary to obtain a desired level of power, power tables can also be used to determine the power associated with the correlated groups *t* test given the directionality of the test, the alpha level, the sample size, and the value of eta-squared in the population. For instance, Table 11.4 shows that the power for a nondirectional correlated groups *t* test with $N = 21$ is .75 at an alpha level of .05 when the population eta-squared is .15.

Examination of Table 11.4 and Appendix E.1 provides a general appreciation for the relationships among directionality, the alpha level, sample size, the strength of the relationship that one is trying to detect in the population, and power for the correlated groups *t* test. As can be seen, power becomes greater as the alpha level, the sample size, and the population eta-squared each increases.

11.9 Method of Presentation

The method of presentation for the correlated groups *t* test is identical to that for the independent groups *t* test. This should include statements of the alpha level that was used, the degrees of freedom, the observed value of *t*, the significance level, the sample means, the standard deviation estimates, the confidence interval for the mean difference, and, if the analysis is statistically significant, the strength and nature of the relationship between the independent and dependent variables.

The results for the age and crying time study that was discussed in Section 11.7 might be reported as follows:*

Results

A correlated groups *t* test that compared the mean crying time for the infants when they were 3 months of age with the mean crying time when they were 6 months of age was found to be statistically significant at an alpha level of .05, $t(7) = -7.41$, $p < .01$, suggesting that infants are more fearful of strangers when they are 6 months old ($M = 3.00$, $SD = .93$) than when they are 3 months old ($M = 1.00$, $SD = .93$). The strength of the relationship between age and the crying time was .89, as indexed by eta-squared. The 95% confidence interval for the mean difference was -2.64 to -1.36.

11.10   Examples from the Literature

Number of Social Contacts with Same- Versus Opposite-Gender Individuals

Psychologists have studied interpersonal relationships and friendship patterns in many contexts. One approach has been to document daily patterns of social behavior through the use of diaries. For instance, 63 participants in a study by Nezlek (1978) were asked to keep daily diaries of the social contact they had with other people over four 2-week periods. One question of interest was the number of same-gender versus the number of opposite-gender contacts that people make.

An analysis of the diaries indicated that the participants had met, on average, 1.54 same-gender individuals per day and 1.01 opposite-gender individuals per day. A correlated groups *t* test showed that this difference was statistically significant, $t(62) = 2.10$, $p < .05$, such that people tend to make more same-gender than opposite-gender contacts. The strength of the relationship, as indexed by eta-squared, was .07. This represents a weak effect and indicates, as one would expect, that many factors other than a person's gender influence social contact.

Self-Schema Similarity Before and After Discussion of a Hypothetical Person

The term *self-schema* refers to an individual's conception of who and what one is. According to a model of self-schema development proposed by Deutsch and

---

* The standard deviation estimates were calculated by applying the usual formulas for the sum of squares, the variance estimate, and the standard deviation estimate to each of the age conditions in Table 11.3.

Mackesy (1985), during the course of conversation about other people individuals become aware of the person-description dimensions used by the other discussants and come to adopt these dimensions in their descriptions of others and, subsequently, of themselves. According to this model, as reflected in their self-descriptions, individuals' self-schemas should become more similar after they have had the opportunity to share their opinions of another person with one another.

In a test of this hypothesis, Deutsch and Mackesy first instructed their experimental participants to list 10 self-descriptive traits. The participants then individually read a description of a hypothetical person, following which they discussed their impressions of this person with a randomly assigned partner. In a final phase, participants were again instructed to list 10 self-descriptive traits.

The dependent variable was the number of overlapping self-traits reported by partners before versus after discussing the hypothetical person. Consistent with Deutsch and Mackesy's model, a correlated groups t test indicated that there was significantly more self-schema overlap after discussion ($\overline{X} = 2.05$) than there was before discussion ($\overline{X} = 1.30$), $t(19) = 3.29$, $p < .01$. As indexed by eta-squared, the strength of the relationship was .36. This represents a strong effect.

11.11 Links Between Computer Results and Book Content

There are many names for what we have referred to as the *correlated groups t test*. Among these are the *correlated samples t test*, the *paired groups t test*, the *paired measures t test*, the *matched pairs t* test, the *matched samples t* test, the *dependent samples t test*, the *related samples t test*, and the *repeated measures t test*. Not surprisingly, then, the test is referred to differently by different statistical computer programs. For instance, SPSS for Windows refers to it as a *paired samples t test*.

If you are seeking to analyze data from a two-group within-subjects design and you do not see any of these tests listed as an option for your statistical package, it is important that you look carefully at the list of available tests to try to identify one that corresponds to the correlated groups t test. Note that all of the names above capture the within-subjects nature of the correlated group t test and that they all also include the *t test* phraseology.

11.12 Links Between Chapters

We have seen how the correlated groups t test relates to the one-sample t test and to the independent groups t test. The correlated groups t test also bears a strong relationship to one-way repeated measures analysis of variance, as we will see in Chapter 13. In fact, as we will discuss, one-way repeated measures analysis of variance can be conceptualized as an extension of the correlated groups t test when there are three or more levels of a within-subjects independent variable.

Applications to the Analysis of a Social Problem Using SPSS for Windows

Past research suggests that the relationship between parent and teen is an important predictor of many teen problem behaviors: Teens who have relatively poor relationships with their parents are more likely to exhibit problem behavior, other things being equal.

In the parent–teen communication study described in Chapter 1, we obtained ratings of how satisfied the teens were with their relationship with their mother and, using a separate item, how satisfied they were with their relationship with their father. One question of interest was whether teens are more satisfied with their relationship with their mother or their father.

We are developing interventions to help teach parents to communicate more effectively with their teens about such issues as premarital pregnancy, sexually transmitted diseases, and birth control. Financial constraints are such that it is possible to engage only one parent in the intervention effort. If teens, on average, have a better relationship with one parent than the other, then this would be a consideration when deciding whether to develop the interventions around mothers or fathers because our previous research suggests that information about adolescent problem behaviors is more likely to be exchanged between parent and child when a good relationship exists between them. If, for instance, teens tend to be more satisfied with their relationship with their mothers, then it is probably more likely that the premarital pregnancy, sexually transmitted diseases, and birth control information that is an important part of our intervention effort will be passed on to the teen if we provide it to mothers than if we provide it to fathers.

The satisfaction information was obtained by asking teens to indicate how much they agreed or disagreed with the statements "I am satisfied with my relationship with my mother" and "I am satisfied with my relationship with my father." Ratings were made on a 1 (*strongly disagree*) to 5 (*strongly agree*) scale that also included the response options *moderately disagree, neither agree nor disagree*, and *moderately agree*. Although we relied on only a single item to measure overall satisfaction with each parent, prior research has shown that responses to the single item are highly correlated with more complex, multi-item measures of overall relationship satisfaction.* In addition, although our measures are probably not strictly interval, our prior research suggests that they probably approximate interval level characteristics to the extent that we can use the correlated groups *t* test.

Figure 11.1 presents a histogram of difference scores that were created by subtracting the ratings of the mother from the ratings of the father. A score of −4 indicates strong agreement with the mother statement coupled with strong disagreement with the father statement. A score of +4 indicates the reverse. A score of 0 means that the ratings for the mother and the father are identical.

Superimposed on the histogram of differences scores is a normal distribution. Although the distribution of difference scores is nonnormal, the deviation from normality is not large enough to suggest that nonnormality in the population is great enough to undermine the correlated groups *t* test, given the sample size that we used (Posten, 1979).

With this established, we tested whether teens' satisfaction with their maternal and paternal relationships differs by comparing the mean satisfaction rating for mothers with the mean satisfaction rating for fathers using a correlated groups *t* test. The computer output for this analysis is presented in Table 11.5.

The top portion of the output contains the mean, the standard deviation estimate, and the estimated standard error of the mean for each level of the independent variable. The teen's satisfaction with the relationship with the father is designated as SFather and the teen's satisfaction with the

*We discuss a measure of this type in the Applications to the Analysis of a Social Problem Using SPSS for Windows section in Chapter 12.

FIGURE 11.1   Frequency Histogram for Satisfaction with Paternal Relationship Minus Satisfaction with Maternal Relationship Difference Scores

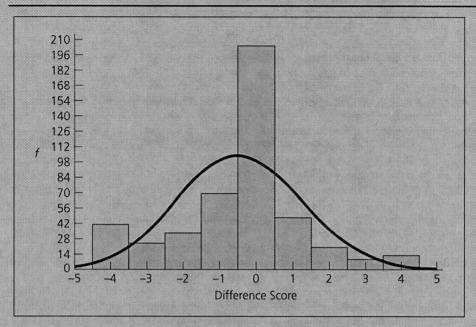

TABLE 11.5   Computer Output for Correlated Groups *t* Test for Satisfaction with Paternal Versus Maternal Relationship

Paired Samples Statistics

	Mean	N	Std. Deviation	Std. Error Mean
SFather	3.90	446	1.38	.065
SMother	4.37	446	1.05	.050

Paired Samples Test

	Paired Differences							
				95% Confidence Interval of the Difference				
	Mean	Std. Deviation	Std. Error Mean	Lower	Upper	t	df	Sig. (2-tailed)
SFather-SMother	−.48	1.70	.081	−.64	−.32	−5.900	445	.000

(continued)

relationship with the mother is designated as SMother. It also contains the sample size. This was much smaller ($N = 446$) than the total sample of 751 adolescents who were interviewed because more than 300 adolescents did not have a "father figure" currently living in their household (due to divorce, single parenthood, widowhood, and the like). This suggests that our intervention should be directed at mothers because they are more likely than fathers to be a member of the teen's household.

The estimated standard errors of the means are quite small, reflecting about .06 of one rating scale unit on a 5-point scale. This suggests that we can be reasonably confident in the accuracy of the sample means as estimators of the population means.

The bottom portion of Table 11.5 presents the difference between the two means (labeled "Mean"), the estimated standard deviation for the population of difference scores (labeled "Std. Deviation"), the estimated standard error of the mean of difference scores (labeled "Std. Error Mean"), the 95% confidence interval, the observed value of *t*, the degrees of freedom, and the significance level [labeled "Sig. (2-tailed)"] for a nondirectional correlated groups *t* test. The mean difference is $-.48$, which corresponds to about half of a rating scale unit, and the estimated standard error of the mean of difference scores is small (only .08).

Because the significance level is less than .05, the *t* test is statistically significant. Examination of the sample means indicates that teens tend to be more satisfied with their relationship with their mothers ($\bar{X} = 4.37$) than with their fathers ($\bar{X} = 3.90$). The strength of the relationship as indexed by eta-squared can be calculated by applying Equation 11.6. The eta-squared value of .07 represents a weak to moderate effect. The 95% confidence interval is $-.64$ to $-.32$.

We also compared the mean satisfaction rating for mothers with the mean satisfaction rating for fathers for adolescent boys and girls separately. According to a formulation known as *identification theory*, children tend to identify more strongly with their same-gender parent and this stronger identification leads to a more satisfying relationship. It is therefore possible that adolescent girls will be more satisfied with their relationship with their mothers but that adolescent boys will be more satisfied with their relationship with their fathers.

Although we do not report the specifics of the analyses here, we found that this was not the case. For each gender, the mean rating for mothers was about half a scale point higher than the mean rating for fathers, and this difference was statistically significant in both cases.

Overall, these findings suggest that our intervention efforts should be focused on the mother. However, issues beyond those considered here must also be taken into account before we make a decision on this matter.

Summary

The correlated groups *t* test is typically used to analyze the relationship between two variables when (1) the dependent variable is quantitative in nature and is measured at a level that at least approximates interval characteristics, (2) the independent variable is within-subjects in nature, and (3) the independent variable has two, and only two, levels. The existence of a relationship between the two variables is tested by converting the mean difference score for the sample to a *t* score that represents the number of estimated standard errors the difference is from the hypothesized mean of the population of difference scores. This value of *t* is then compared with the critical value(s) of *t*, and the decision to reject or not to reject the null hypothesis is made accordingly.

An important advantage of the correlated groups *t* test over the independent groups *t* test is that it extracts the influence of individual differences from the dependent variable, thereby providing a more sensitive test of the relationship between the independent and dependent variables.

The strength of the relationship is measured using eta-squared, which in this case represents the proportion of variability in the dependent variable that is associated with the independent variable after variability due to individual differences has been removed. Unstandardized effect sizes and confidence intervals can also be calculated. Finally, the nature of the relationship is determined by comparing the two *sample* means to make a decision about how the two *population* means differ.

Appendix 11.1   The Equivalence of the Correlated Groups *t* Test and an Independent Groups *t* Test Applied to Nullified Scores

We noted in Section 11.3 that a correlated groups *t* test is analogous to an independent groups *t* test with the effects of individual differences extracted from the dependent variable. We now demonstrate the equivalence of the two approaches.

The logic and computational procedure for the application of an independent groups *t* test to nullified scores in the context of a correlated groups design is identical to that developed in Section 10.4 for the independent groups *t* test, with one exception: The relevant t distribution has $N - 1$ rather than $n_1 + n_2 - 2$ degrees of freedom associated with it. This has implications not only for the critical values of *t* that are used in hypothesis testing but also for the calculation of the estimated standard error of the difference.

We demonstrate the relevant procedures by referring to the drug and learning experiment from earlier in this chapter. The nullified scores for this study from columns 5 and 6 of Table 11.2 are reproduced in the table below. Also appearing in this table are the calculations for the means and sums of squares for the two conditions.

Per Equation 10.8, the formula for the independent groups *t* test is

$$t = \frac{(\overline{X}_1 - \overline{X}_2) - (\mu_1 - \mu_2)}{\hat{s}_{\overline{X}_1 - \overline{X}_2}}$$

For the drug and learning example, $\overline{X}_1 - \overline{X}_2 = 3.00 - 6.00 = -3.00$ and $\mu_1 - \mu_2$ is set equal to 0 because we are testing the null hypothesis that $\mu_1 = \mu_2$. The standard error of the difference can be estimated by the formula

$$\hat{s}_{\overline{X}_1 - \overline{X}_2} = \sqrt{\left(\frac{SS_1 + SS_2}{N - 1}\right)\left(\frac{1}{n_1} + \frac{1}{n_2}\right)}$$

which is identical to Equation 10.6 except that $N - 1$ (the degrees of freedom for the correlated groups case) replaces $n_1 + n_2 - 2$ (the degrees of freedom for the independent groups case). In this equation, N is the number of pairs of scores, and n_1 and n_2 are the sample sizes in condition 1 and condition 2, respectively, such that $n_1 = n_2 = N$.

In our example,

$$\hat{s}_{\overline{X}_1 - \overline{X}_2} = \sqrt{\left(\frac{6.00 + 6.00}{5 - 1}\right)\left(\frac{1}{5} + \frac{1}{5}\right)} = 1.10$$

The observed value of *t* is thus

$$t = \frac{-3.00 - 0}{1.10} = -2.73$$

This is the same value as we obtained in Section 11.2 using the difference score approach.

Nullified Data for Drug A		Nullified Data for Drug B	
X	X^2	X	X^2
2.50	6.25	6.50	42.25
2.50	6.25	6.50	42.25
4.50	20.25	4.50	20.25
1.50	2.25	7.50	56.25
4.00	16.00	5.00	25.00
$\Sigma X_A = 15.00$	$\Sigma X_A^2 = 51.00$	$\Sigma X_B = 30.00$	$\Sigma X_B^2 = 186.00$
$\overline{X}_A = 3.00$		$\overline{X}_B = 6.00$	

$$SS_A = \Sigma X_A^2 - \frac{(\Sigma X_A)^2}{N}$$

$$= 51.00 - \frac{15.00^2}{5} = 6.00$$

$$SS_B = \Sigma X_B^2 - \frac{(\Sigma X_B)^2}{N}$$

$$= 186.00 - \frac{30.00^2}{5} = 6.00$$

Exercises

Answers to asterisked (*) exercises appear at the back of the book.

1. Under what conditions is the correlated groups *t* test typically used to analyze a bivariate relationship?

2. In general terms, what value will the mean of a sampling distribution of the mean of difference scores always equal?

*3. State the critical value(s) of *t* for a correlated groups *t* test for an alpha level of .05 under each of the following conditions:
   a. $H_0: \mu_1 = \mu_2$, $H_1: \mu_1 \neq \mu_2$, $N = 27$
   b. $H_0: \mu_1 = \mu_2$, $H_1: \mu_1 > \mu_2$, $N = 27$
   c. $H_0: \mu_1 = \mu_2$, $H_1: \mu_1 \neq \mu_2$, $N = 14$
   d. $H_0: \mu_1 = \mu_2$, $H_1: \mu_1 < \mu_2$, $N = 14$

4. What are the assumptions underlying the correlated groups *t* test?

5. What interpretation does eta-squared have in the context of the correlated groups *t* test? How does this interpretation differ from that for the independent groups *t* test?

*6. What is the rationale behind counterbalancing the sequence of conditions across participants in within-subjects designs?

*7. Why is a correlated groups *t* test usually more powerful than a corresponding independent groups *t* test? When will this not be the case? Why?

Use the following information to complete Exercises 8–12.

The following scores resulted on a learning test that was administered to five participants under quiet and noisy conditions:

Participant	Quiet	Noisy
1	16	10
2	5	3
3	12	10
4	9	5
5	23	15

*8. Test for a relationship between the amount of noise one is exposed to and learning scores using a nondirectional correlated groups *t* test.

*9. Compute the value of eta-squared. Does the observed value represent a weak, moderate, or strong effect?

*10. Compute the 95% confidence interval.

*11. Discern the nature of the relationship between the amount of noise one is exposed to and learning scores.

*12. Analyze the data as if the independent variable were between-subjects in nature. That is, conduct a nondirectional independent groups *t* test, compute the value of eta-squared and the 95% confidence interval, and determine the nature of the relationship between the experimental condition one is exposed to and learning scores using the procedures developed in Chapter 10. Compare your findings with those for Exercises 8–11. How does this illustrate the advantage of within-subjects research designs?

Use the following information to complete Exercises 13–18.

The following self-esteem scores were provided by five individuals at two different times:

Individual	Time 1	Time 2
1	10	12
2	13	17
3	12	14
4	11	13
5	14	14

13. Test for a relationship between the time of assessment and self-esteem using a nondirectional correlated groups *t* test.

14. Compute the value of eta-squared. Does the observed value represent a weak, moderate, or strong effect?

15. Compute the 95% confidence interval.

16. Discern the nature of the relationship between the time of assessment and self-esteem.

*17. Extract the effects of individual differences (that is, generate a set of nullified scores). Compute the mean for time 1 and the mean for time 2 for the nullified scores. The respective mean values should be the same as for the original scores (for exam-

ple, the mean for time 1 in the adjusted data set should equal the mean for time 1 in the original data set). Why do you think this is the case? (*Hint:* Remember that the individual differences whose effects have been extracted from the dependent variable serve as disturbance variables, as discussed in Chapter 9.)

*18. Using the procedures from Appendix 11.1, conduct a nondirectional independent groups *t* test on the nullified scores from Exercise 17. Compare the observed value of t with that obtained in Exercise 13.

For each of the studies described in Exercises 19–23, indicate whether an independent groups t *test or a correlated groups* t *test should be used to analyze the relationship between the independent and dependent variables. Assume that the underlying assumptions of the tests have been satisfied.*

*19. Frieze, Parsons, Johnson, Ruble, and Zellman (1978) examined the relationship between gender and mathematical ability as measured by the Graduate Record Exam. The mean scores on the quantitative test were compared for men and women who took the exam during 1972.

*20. Based on previous research that showed similar EEG patterns for children who have learning problems and children who have a mild form of epilepsy known as *petit mal*, Smith, Phillipus, and Guard (1968) speculated that because it effectively treats petit mal, a drug known as *ethosuximide* might also serve as a "learning facilitator" for children with learning problems.

In a test of this proposition, these researchers conducted a 6-week study on the effect of ethosuximide on the verbal skills of children who had a history of learning problems. During the first 3 weeks, some of the children were injected with ethosuximide and others were given a placebo. During the second 3 weeks, the procedures were reversed (that is, children who had previously been given a placebo were given ethosuximide, and vice versa).

Each child was given a verbal skills test after the first 3-week period and again after 6 weeks. For all children, the mean score on this test after they received the placebo was compared with the mean score after they received the ethosuximide.

21. A consumer psychologist studied consumers' preference for two types of headache remedies. Five hundred individuals were surveyed and rated each brand on a 10-point scale. The mean ratings for the two brands were compared.

22. Jensen (1973) reviewed research on the relationship between race and intelligence test scores. In one study, the mean scores of African Americans and whites were compared.

23. Gallup (1976) studied attitudes toward nuclear energy over a period of 10 years. The same individuals were interviewed in both 1965 and 1975, and during each interview, the respondents indicated their attitudes toward nuclear energy on a 5-point scale. The mean attitude scores were compared across interviews.

24. If a researcher suspects that the strength of the relationship between two variables in the population is .25 as indexed by eta-squared, what sample size should he use in a study involving two correlated groups and an alpha level of .05, directional test, in order to achieve a power of .90?

*25. Suppose that an investigator conducts a study involving two correlated groups with N = 7. If the value of eta-squared in the population is .30, what would the power of her statistical test be at an alpha level of .05, nondirectional test?

Multiple-Choice Questions

26. In the context of a within-subjects design, an individual obtains scores of 5 in one condition and 7 in a second condition. If the grand mean is 5.00, what are the individual's scores with the effect of her background and personal characteristics removed?
    a. 4.00 and 6.00
    b. 5.00 and 5.00
    c. 5.00 and 7.00
    d. 6.00 and 8.00

27. The correlated groups *t* test provides a less sensitive test of the relationship between the independent and dependent variables than does the independent groups *t* test.
    a. true
    b. false

*28. In most behavioral science research, the correlation between individuals' scores in one condition of a study and the same individuals' scores in a second condition will be
    a. negative
    b. positive
    c. close to 0
    d. none of the above

*29. With small sample sizes, very large values of eta-squared are necessary before statistical tests allow us to conclude that there is a relationship between the independent and the dependent variables.
    a. true
    b. false

Use the following information to complete Exercises 30–40.

A researcher tested the effect of the Three Mile Island nuclear accident on attitudes toward nuclear energy. As part of a larger survey, 48 individuals who lived near Three Mile Island were administered a scale to measure their attitudes toward nuclear energy 6 months before the accident occurred. Scores on this scale could range from 0 to 50, with higher values indicating a more favorable attitude. Three months after the accident, the attitude scale was administered to the 48 people for a second time. The mean attitude score was 45.26 prior to the accident and 35.71 after the accident. The estimated standard error of the mean of difference scores was 2.35.

30. If the value of eta-squared in the population is .10, what is the power of the statistical test at an alpha level of .05, nondirectional test?
    a. .10
    b. .60
    c. .85
    d. .90
31. The independent variable is
    a. the occurrence of the accident
    b. attitudes toward nuclear energy
    c. the time of attitude assessment
    d. the place of residence of the respondents
*32. The dependent variable is
    a. the occurrence of the accident
    b. attitudes toward nuclear energy
    c. the time of attitude assessment
    d. the place of residence of the respondents
*33. The observed value of t is
    a. 1.73   c. 4.06
    b. 2.02   d. 6.23
34. Based on this study, we can conclude that the independent variable is related to the dependent variable.
    a. true   b. false
35. It is possible that the test results reflect a Type I error.
    a. true   b. false
*36. It is possible that the test results reflect a Type II error.
    a. true   b. false
37. The strength of the relationship, as indexed by eta-squared, is
    a. .09   c. .26
    b. .12   d. .54
*38. The proportion of variability in the dependent variable that is due to disturbance variables other than individual differences is
    a. .74
    b. .86
    c. .93
    d. This cannot be determined.
*39. The 95% confidence interval is
    a. −1.61 to 20.71
    b. 4.80 to 14.30
    c. 5.59 to 13.51
    d. 6.45 to 12.65

*40. What can we conclude about the effect of the accident on attitudes toward nuclear energy?
    a. Attitudes became more positive.
    b. Attitudes became more negative.
    c. Attitudes stayed the same.
    d. The accident may or may not have affected attitudes toward nuclear energy.

Exercises to Apply Concepts

*41. The process of decision making has been studied extensively by psychologists. One area of inquiry has been the effect of making a decision on the subsequent evaluation of the decision alternatives. According to Brehm (1956), when individuals are forced to choose between two equally attractive alternatives, they might justify their decision after the choice has been made by downgrading the unchosen alternative and upgrading the chosen one.

In a test of this proposition, participants rated the desirability of two household products. The products had been tested to ensure that they were approximately equally desirable. Participants then read marketing reports on each product and were asked to choose one as payment for participation in the study. Finally, participants were told that their first rating should be considered a first impression and that the researchers wanted to get a second rating because the participant now had more time to think about the products. The ratings were made on an 8-point scale, where 1 indicated low desirability and 8 indicated high desirability.

The hypothetical data presented in the table are representative of the results for the unchosen product. Analyze these data using a nondirectional test, draw a conclusion, and write up your results using the principles developed in the Method of Presentation section.

Participant	Before choice	After choice
1	8	4
2	7	3
3	7	5
4	4	6
5	8	4
6	6	4
7	6	2
8	5	5
9	5	3
10	4	4

42. A common belief held by laypersons is that smoking marijuana affects a person's pupil size. To study this issue, Weil, Zinberg, and Nelson (1968) administered a high dose of marijuana to 10 men by having them smoke a potent marijuana cigarette. These men were all 21 to 26 years of age and all of them smoked tobacco cigarettes regularly but had never tried marijuana.

    The pupil size for each man was measured with a millimeter ruler under conditions of constant illumination with the man's eyes focused on an object at a constant distance. Measurements were taken both before and after the participants smoked their marijuana cigarette.

    The experimental data are presented in the table. Analyze these data using a nondirectional test, draw a conclusion, and write up your results using the principles developed in the Method of Presentation section.

Participant	Before marijuana	After marijuana
1	5	7
2	7	5
3	6	8
4	7	5
5	6	6
6	5	7
7	3	9
8	3	5
9	5	9
10	3	9

43. Kleinke, Meeker, and Staneski (1986) identify several categories of "opening lines" that people use when approaching individuals of the opposite gender. Two such categories are direct and cute–flippant. The direct approach involves an overt statement of interest, such as "I hope you don't mind, but I'd really like to talk to you." The cute–flippant approach involves the use of humor, such as "Did anybody ever tell you that you look like a movie star?"

    In order to study the effectiveness of the two types of lines, suppose that a researcher asks nine women to imagine that they are approached in a singles bar by an attractive man who uses one or the other of the two deliveries. Each woman rates her anticipated reaction to each of the two types of lines on a 7-point scale, where 1 indicates a very negative response and 7 indicates a very positive response.

    Hypothetical data for the study are presented in the table. Analyze these data using a nondirectional test, draw a conclusion, and write up your results using the principles developed in the Method of Presentation section.

Participant	Direct approach	Cute–flippant approach
1	5	4
2	6	3
3	6	4
4	4	5
5	5	3
6	6	5
7	5	4
8	6	3
9	6	4

44. A common belief in our culture is that the full moon exerts a powerful influence on behavior. In fact, the *full-moon effect* has been studied by a number of researchers. One focus is on whether the full moon influences psychological functioning.

To study this issue, suppose that a researcher analyzes the number of emergency admissions to psychiatric hospitals during nights when the moon is full as opposed to when it is not full. Hypothetical data for the study are presented in the table. These scores represent the total number of admissions to each hospital on 10 randomly selected nights of each type over the course of a year. Analyze these data using a nondirectional test, draw a conclusion, and write up your results using the principles developed in the Method of Presentation section.

Hospital	Moon full	Moon not full
1	6	5
2	4	3
3	7	6
4	12	14
5	3	5
6	8	6
7	9	13
8	5	5
9	5	8
10	10	7
11	4	2
12	7	6

CHAPTER **12**

One-Way
Between-Subjects
Analysis of Variance

12.1   Use of One-Way Between-Subjects Analysis of Variance

One-way between-subjects analysis of variance, more simply known as *one-way analysis of variance* (abbreviated as *one-way ANOVA*), is typically used to analyze the relationship between two variables under the following conditions:

1. The dependent variable is quantitative in nature and is measured on a level that at least approximates interval characteristics.

2. The independent variable is *between-subjects* in nature (it can be either qualitative or quantitative).

3. The independent variable has three or more levels.

In short, one-way analysis of variance is used under the same circumstances as the independent groups *t* test except that the independent variable has more than two levels. In fact, one-way analysis of variance can be conceptualized as an extension of the independent groups *t* test for instances where there are three or more levels of a between-subjects independent variable.

   Let us consider an example of an investigation that meets the conditions for this technique. Suppose that an investigator examines the relationship between individuals' religion and what they consider the ideal family size to be by asking seven Catholic, seven Protestant, and seven Jewish individuals what they consider to be the ideal number of children to have in a family.* Their responses are presented in Table 12.1.

TABLE 12.1   **Data for Religion and Ideal Family Size Study**

Catholic	Protestant	Jewish
4	1	1
3	2	1
2	0	2
3	2	0
3	4	2
4	3	0
2	2	1
$\Sigma X_C = 21$	$\Sigma X_P = 14$	$\Sigma X_J = 7$
$\overline{X}_C = \ 3.00$	$\overline{X}_P = \ 2.00$	$\overline{X}_J = 1.00$

---

* For ease of presentation, we restrict our discussion of one-way analysis of variance to the situation where the sample sizes for the groups under study are all equal. Although the same general logic can be extended to unequal sample sizes, some of the computational procedures that we present would have to be modified.

In this investigation, religion is the independent variable. It is between-subjects in nature and has three levels. The ideal family size is the dependent variable. It is quantitative in nature and is measured on a ratio level. Given these conditions, one-way between-subjects analysis of variance would typically be used to analyze the relationship between the variables.*

12.2 Inference of a Relationship Using One-Way Between-Subjects Analysis of Variance

Null and Alternative Hypotheses

The first of the three questions to be addressed regarding the analysis of bivariate relationships is whether a relationship exists between religion and the ideal family size. The null hypothesis states that the population means for the three religious groups are equal. If so, there is no relationship between religion and the ideal number of children. This is expressed similarly to what we have done in previous chapters:

$$H_0: \quad \mu_C = \mu_P = \mu_J$$

where the subscript "C" represents the Catholic religion, the subscript "P" represents the Protestant religion, and the subscript "J" represents the Jewish religion.

Unlike the previous tests that we have considered, the alternative hypothesis for one-way analysis of variance cannot be summarized in a single mathematical statement. This is because there are four ways in which the three population means can pattern themselves so that they are not all equal:

$$\mu_C = \mu_P \neq \mu_J$$

$$\mu_C = \mu_J \neq \mu_P$$

$$\mu_P = \mu_J \neq \mu_C$$

$$\mu_C \neq \mu_P \neq \mu_J$$

The alternative hypothesis does not distinguish between these different possibilities. It simply states that the three population means are *not* all equal to one another. If so, there is a relationship between religion and the ideal family size. The question of the exact patterning of means is addressed in the context of the nature of the relationship. Thus, the alternative hypothesis is

$$H_1: \quad \text{The three population means are not all equal}$$

The task is to choose between the null and alternative hypotheses. If we look at the mean scores for the samples, we find that they are all different. The mean for the Catholic group is 3.00, the mean for the Protestant group is 2.00, and the mean

---

* Our discussion of analysis of variance in this and subsequent chapters will deal with only the type that is most commonly encountered in the behavioral sciences—*fixed-effects analysis*. For a discussion of other approaches to analysis of variance, see Hays (1981).

for the Jewish group is 1.00. This seems to support the alternative hypothesis. However, we know that the nonequivalence of sample means could just reflect sampling error. We therefore want to test the viability of a sampling error interpretation.

The logic for testing this interpretation is similar to the logic that we discussed in previous chapters. First, we assume that the null hypothesis is true. We then state an expected result based on this assumption. Next, we compute a sample statistic. In the case of one-way analysis of variance, this statistic is the *variance ratio*. The sample variance ratio is treated as a score in a sampling distribution of variance ratios based on when the null hypothesis is true. If the score falls within the rejection region, we reject the null hypothesis and conclude that there is a relationship between the two variables. Otherwise, we fail to reject the null hypothesis.

Between- and Within-Group Variability

We can distinguish between two types of variability for the data in Table 12.1. The first relates to differences between the mean scores for the three groups or, in more formal terms, **between-group variability**. If the mean scores for the three groups were all equal, then there would be no between-group variability. The more different the three means are from one another, the more between-group variability there is.

Why do mean differences exist? Two factors contribute to between-group variability. The first is sampling error: Even if the population means were, in fact, equal, we might observe between-group variability in the sample data because of sampling error. A second factor that contributes to between-group variability is the effect of the independent variable on the dependent variable. For instance, if religion influences the ideal number of children, then this will tend to make the sample means different from one another. Thus, between-group variability as reflected in the mean scores on the dependent variable represents two things: (1) sampling error and (2) the effect of the independent variable on the dependent variable.

The second type of variability is that of scores *within* each of the three groups, that is, **within-group variability**. Examine the seven scores for the Catholic group in Table 12.1. Note that there is variability in the scores; some Catholic individuals have a higher ideal number of children than others. The same is true for both the Protestant and the Jewish groups. Because religion is held constant for each group, the variability in the scores cannot be attributed to religious affiliation. Disturbance variables, such as how religious a person is, are operating to cause the variability within each group.

The fact that scores vary within a group suggests that there is also variability in the scores in the *population* represented by that group. Recall from our discussions in earlier chapters that when the variability of scores in a population is large, we expect more sampling error than when the population variability is small. As such, greater variability of scores within a group is indicative of greater variability of scores within the corresponding population and, thus, a greater amount of sampling error. In short, then, within-group variability reflects sampling error.

Note that within-group variability is *not* influenced by the effect of the independent variable on the dependent variable. Because the variability of scores is considered within each group *separately,* the independent variable is held constant within each group and cannot be a source of within-group variability.

Because between-group variability reflects both sampling error *and* the effect of the independent variable, and within-group variability reflects just sampling error, the ratio of these two sources of variability can be used to test the sampling error interpretation discussed above. This ratio, which is referred to as the **variance ratio**, can be represented as

$$\frac{\text{between-group variability}}{\text{within-group variability}} = \frac{\text{sampling error} + \text{effect of the independent variable}}{\text{sampling error}} \quad [12.1]$$

Consider the case where the null hypothesis is true. Under this circumstance, the independent variable has no effect on the dependent variable, so between-group variability reflects only sampling error. Because within-group variability also reflects sampling error, the variance ratio is simply the ratio of one estimate of sampling error divided by another estimate of sampling error. Because of the different ways in which they are derived, these two estimates are independent of each other. The result is a value that, over the long run, will approach 1.00 (because any number divided by itself is 1.00).

In contrast, if the null hypothesis is not true, then between-group variability reflects both sampling error and the effect of the independent variable. In this case, we would expect the variance ratio, over the long run, to be greater than 1.00.

Partitioning of Variability

To compute the variance ratio, it is necessary to first derive numerical estimates of between- and within-group variability. Although this is most readily done with the computational formulas that are presented later in this chapter, it is important to have a conceptual understanding of what these formulas represent. We demonstrate this by drawing a parallel between the way in which we can split up, or *partition*, an individual's score on the dependent variable into the mean score of the group of which he or she is a member and how far his or her score deviates from this mean, and the way in which we can partition the total variability in a set of scores into two similar components.

Consider the first individual in the Catholic group. Her score of 4 deviates $4 - 3.00 = 1$ unit from the group mean of 3.00. Her score can thus be represented as

$$4 = 3.00 + 1$$

We can write a general equation to reflect this relationship:

$$X = \overline{X}_j + d \quad [12.2]$$

where X represents an individual's score, $\overline{X}_j$ is the mean for the group of which the individual is a member (group j), and d is the signed deviation of the individual's score from the group mean such that $d = X - \overline{X}_j$. It is possible to express the score of every participant in the study in this manner, as is demonstrated in Table 12.2.

The column labeled X contains each individual's score on the dependent variable. We can compute an index of how much variability there is in these scores by computing a sum of squares for this column of numbers using the standard formula

TABLE 12.2   Breakdown of Scores on the Dependent Variable for Religion and Ideal Family Size Study

Participant	Religion	X	=	$\overline{X}_j$	+	d^a
1	Catholic	4	=	3.00	+	1
2	Catholic	3	=	3.00	+	0
3	Catholic	2	=	3.00	+	−1
4	Catholic	3	=	3.00	+	0
5	Catholic	3	=	3.00	+	0
6	Catholic	4	=	3.00	+	1
7	Catholic	2	=	3.00	+	−1
8	Protestant	1	=	2.00	+	−1
9	Protestant	2	=	2.00	+	0
10	Protestant	0	=	2.00	+	−2
11	Protestant	2	=	2.00	+	0
12	Protestant	4	=	2.00	+	2
13	Protestant	3	=	2.00	+	1
14	Protestant	2	=	2.00	+	0
15	Jewish	1	=	1.00	+	0
16	Jewish	1	=	1.00	+	0
17	Jewish	2	=	1.00	+	1
18	Jewish	0	=	1.00	+	−1
19	Jewish	2	=	1.00	+	1
20	Jewish	0	=	1.00	+	−1
21	Jewish	1	=	1.00	+	0

$^a d = X - \overline{X}_j$

for a sum of squares. This sum of squares is called the **sum of squares total** (symbolized as SS_{TOTAL}) because it reflects the total variability in the dependent variable across all individuals. As such, it is identical to the sum of squares total that we discussed in Section 10.4. If we were to perform the required calculations, we would find that $SS_{TOTAL} = 32.00$ in this instance.

Examine the scores in the column labeled $\overline{X}_j$ in Table 12.2. The source of variability in these scores is the differences between the group means. If the means of all three groups were equal, every score in this column would be the same. The more the three means differ, the more dissimilar these scores will be from one another. The sum of squares for this column therefore reflects between-group variability. This sum of squares, which is referred to as the **sum of squares between** (symbolized as $SS_{BETWEEN}$), is identical to the sum of squares explained in Section 10.4 and can be calculated by applying the standard formula for a sum of squares to the $\overline{X}_j$ scores. In this instance, $SS_{BETWEEN} = 14.00$.

Examine the scores in the column labeled d. Each of these scores represents a deviation from the group mean, or how far an individual's score deviates from the average score *within the group*. If there were little variability within the groups, all of these scores would tend to be close to 0 and to be very similar to one another. If there were considerable variability within the groups, there would be considerable variability in these scores. The sum of squares for this column therefore reflects how much within-group variability there is. This sum of squares is called the **sum of squares within** (symbolized as SS_{WITHIN}) and can be calculated by applying the standard formula for a sum of squares to the d scores. If we were to do so in the present instance, we would find that $SS_{WITHIN} = 18.00$.

Another name for the sum of squares within is the *sum of squares error*, because it reflects the effects of disturbance variables and, hence, sampling error. This is the term we used when we introduced this concept in Section 10.4.

In Section 10.4 we also noted that the total variability in the dependent variable can be partitioned into two components: one reflecting the influence of the independent variable and one reflecting the influence of disturbance variables. In the present context, the partitioning of variability can be represented as

$$SS_{TOTAL} = SS_{BETWEEN} + SS_{WITHIN} \qquad [12.3]$$

This partitioning is consistent with the idea of expressing each individual's score in terms of the group mean and the score's deviation from the group mean, as we did in Table 12.2. Thus, just as each score can be expressed in terms of these two components, the total *variability* in a set of scores can be expressed in terms of the *variability* between the group means (that is, between-group variability) and the *variability* of deviations from the group means (that is, within-group variability). This is clearly demonstrated in our example (where $SS_{TOTAL} = 32.00$, $SS_{BETWEEN} = 14.00$, and $SS_{WITHIN} = 18.00$), as $32.00 = 14.00 + 18.00$.

Mean Squares and the *F* Ratio

The variance ratio of between-group variability divided by within-group variability that is computed to test the null hypothesis does not utilize sums of squares. Rather, the variance ratio is based on measures of variance, or *mean squares*. As we noted in Section 7.5, a mean square is simply a sum of squares divided by its corresponding degrees of freedom. The reason for using measures of mean squares rather than measures of sums of squares will be made explicit shortly. First, though, we consider the computation of the relevant quantities.

The mean square for between-group variability is formally known as the **mean square between** (symbolized as $MS_{BETWEEN}$) and is derived by dividing the sum of squares between by its degrees of freedom. Symbolically,

$$MS_{BETWEEN} = \frac{SS_{BETWEEN}}{df_{BETWEEN}} \qquad [12.4]$$

where $df_{BETWEEN}$ is the degrees of freedom associated with the sum of squares between.

The sum of squares between is based on deviations of the group means from the grand mean. Because the sum of signed deviations about a mean (in this case, the grand mean) will always equal 0 (see Section 3.1 for the logic underlying this property), if all but one of the group means are known, then the last one is not free to vary. Thus,

$$df_{BETWEEN} = k - 1 \qquad [12.5]$$

where k is the number of groups in the study (that is, the number of levels of the independent variable).

The mean square for within-group variability is formally known as the **mean square within** (symbolized as MS_{WITHIN}) and is derived by dividing the sum of squares within by its degrees of freedom. Symbolically,

$$MS_{\text{WITHIN}} = \frac{SS_{\text{WITHIN}}}{df_{\text{WITHIN}}}$$ [12.6]

where df_{WITHIN} is the degrees of freedom associated with the sum of squares within.

The sum of squares within is based on the deviation of scores about their respective group means. If we use n to represent the per-group sample size, there are $n - 1$ degrees of freedom for each group. Given k groups, this yields $k(n - 1) = kn - k$ degrees of freedom within. Because kn is equivalent to the total number of participants in the study,

$$df_{\text{WITHIN}} = N - k$$ [12.7]

where N is the total sample size (that is, the total number of participants in the study).

As with the sums of squares, the degrees of freedom are additive. If we sum the degrees of freedom between and the degrees of freedom within, we get the degrees of freedom associated with the sum of squares total:

$$df_{\text{TOTAL}} = df_{\text{BETWEEN}} + df_{\text{WITHIN}}$$ [12.8]

Because $df_{\text{BETWEEN}} = k - 1$ and $df_{\text{WITHIN}} = N - k$, $df_{\text{TOTAL}} = (k - 1) + (N - k)$. Because this reduces to $N - 1$, the degrees of freedom total can be calculated directly as

$$df_{\text{TOTAL}} = N - 1$$ [12.9]

In our example, $k = 3$ and $N = 21$, so

$$df_{\text{BETWEEN}} = 3 - 1 = 2$$
$$df_{\text{WITHIN}} = 21 - 3 = 18$$
$$df_{\text{TOTAL}} = 21 - 1 = 20$$

Using Equations 12.4 and 12.6, we obtain the mean squares:

$$MS_{\text{BETWEEN}} = \frac{14.00}{2} = 7.00$$
$$MS_{\text{WITHIN}} = \frac{18.00}{18} = 1.00$$

The mean square between reflects the variability between group means. As such, it bears a mathematical relationship to the quantity we would obtain if we treated the sample means like any other set of scores and applied the usual computations for a variance estimate. In fact, when the sample sizes are all the same, the mean square between is equal to the variance estimate for the sample means multiplied by n to reflect the number of scores on which each mean is based.

Recall that the formula for a variance estimate is $SS/(N - 1)$. In our example, the sample means are 3.00, 2.00, and 1.00. The sum of squares for these three "scores" is 2.00, so the variance estimate is $2.00/(3 - 1) = 1.00$. Multiplying this by 7, the per-group sample size, we obtain a value of 7.00, the same quantity that we obtained using Equation 12.4.

Mean square within is merely another name for the pooled variance estimate that we discussed in Chapter 10. It will be remembered that a pooled variance estimate is derived by multiplying the variance estimate for each group by its degrees of freedom, summing the products across groups, and then dividing the resulting quantity by the total number of degrees of freedom.

In our example, there are three groups: Catholic, Protestant, and Jewish. If we were to compute the variance estimate for each, we would find that the estimated variance is .67 for the Catholic group, 1.67 for the Protestant group, and .67 for the Jewish group. Because each sample consists of seven people, each variance estimate has $n - 1 = 7 - 1 = 6$ degrees of freedom associated with it, and the total degrees of freedom are $6 + 6 + 6 = 18$. The pooled variance estimate is thus

$$\hat{s}^2_{pooled} = \frac{(6)(.67) + (6)(1.67) + (6)(.67)}{18} = 1.00$$

This is the same quantity that we obtained using Equation 12.6.

The variance ratio, which is formally referred to as the **F ratio** (in honor of the statistician Sir Ronald Fisher, who developed this approach), can be represented as

$$F = \frac{MS_{BETWEEN}}{MS_{WITHIN}} \qquad [12.10]$$

In our example,

$$F = \frac{7.00}{1.00} = 7.00$$

To recapitulate, the F ratio in the context of one-way analysis of variance is a ratio of two measures of variance: the mean square between (an index of between-group variability) and the mean square within (an index of within-group variability). These mean squares are derived by computing the sum of squares between and the sum of squares within, respectively, and dividing each by its corresponding degrees of freedom. Dividing the mean square between by the mean square within then yields the F ratio. If the null hypothesis is true, we would expect this ratio, over the long run, to approach 1.00 because the mean square between and the mean square within are independent estimates of sampling error. If the null hypothesis is not true, we would expect the F ratio, over the long run, to be greater than 1.00. Let us now consider this issue in more detail.

Sampling Distribution of the F Ratio

Consider three populations, A, B, and C, where $\mu_A = \mu_B = \mu_C$. Suppose that we select a random sample of 30 individuals from population A, a random sample of 30 individuals from population B, and a random sample of 30 individuals from population C. Using the procedures from above, we could compute an F ratio. Although we would expect the value of this ratio to be near 1.00 (because the null hypothesis is true), it might not equal exactly 1.00 because the mean square between and the mean square within are *independent* estimates of sampling error.

Suppose that the F ratio were found to equal 1.52. Furthermore, suppose that we repeat this procedure by randomly selecting new samples of the same sizes from the same populations and this time we obtain an F ratio of 1.32. If we repeat this procedure for all possible random samples of size 30 for each population, the result would be a large number of F ratios. These F ratios can be treated as "scores" in a distribution and constitute a **sampling distribution of the F ratio**, analogous to the sampling distributions that we have discussed previously.

Under certain conditions that we will describe shortly, a sampling distribution of the F ratio is very similar to an important theoretical distribution known as the **F distribution**. The reason for using measures of mean squares rather than measures of sums of squares to define the F ratio is that when the necessary conditions are met, the former measures yield F ratios that have a sampling distribution that closely approximates an F distribution, whereas the latter measures do not.

As illustrated in Figure 12.1, the F distribution takes on different shapes depending on how many degrees of freedom between and how many degrees of freedom within are associated with it. In all of the distributions, the lowest possible value for F is 0. Also, the median value for F in all of the distributions is 1.00. This is not surprising, as the F ratios are calculated under conditions where the null hypothesis is true. Values of F become increasingly less frequent as they become increasingly greater than 1.00, and large values of F are highly unlikely. The question then becomes similar to the one that we posed in earlier chapters: How large must the F ratio computed from the sample information be before we reject the null hypothesis of no relationship between the independent and the dependent variables?

Just as probability statements can be made with respect to scores in the normal and t distributions, so can probability statements be made with respect to scores in the F distribution. It is therefore possible to set an alpha level and define a critical value such that if the null hypothesis is true, the probability of obtaining an F ratio larger than that critical value is less than alpha. Because all departures from the null hypothesis are reflected in the upper tail of the F distribution (as defined by the critical value), the **F test** is, by its nature, nondirectional.

Before conducting the F test, we summarize all of our previous calculations in a **summary table**:

Source	SS	df	MS	F
Between	14.00	2	7.00	7.00
Within	18.00	18	1.00	
Total	32.00	20		

The first column of this table indicates the sources of variability for the one-way between-subjects situation. The second column reports the sums of squares

FIGURE 12.1   *F* **Distributions for Various Degrees of Freedom**

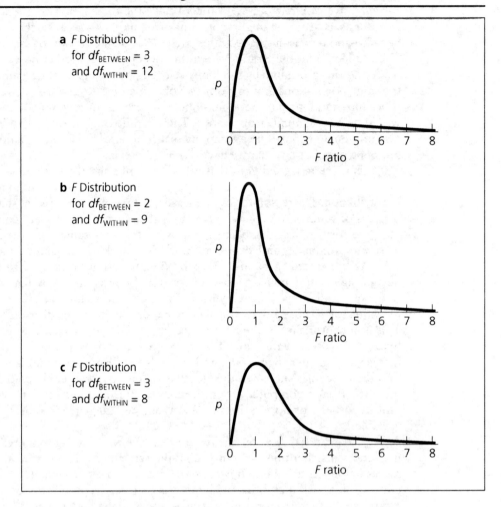

a *F* Distribution
for $df_{\text{BETWEEN}} = 3$
and $df_{\text{WITHIN}} = 12$

b *F* Distribution
for $df_{\text{BETWEEN}} = 2$
and $df_{\text{WITHIN}} = 9$

c *F* Distribution
for $df_{\text{BETWEEN}} = 3$
and $df_{\text{WITHIN}} = 8$

between, within, and total. The next column provides the associated degrees of freedom for each sum of squares, and column 4 presents the mean squares for between-group and within-group variability. The last column contains the *F* ratio.

The test of the null hypothesis involves comparing the observed value of *F* with the appropriate critical value of *F* from Appendix F. Instructions for using this table are contained in the appendix. In order to be statistically significant, the observed value of *F* must exceed the critical value of *F*.

When reporting an *F* value for one-way between-subjects analysis of variance, it is conventional to present the degrees of freedom between followed by the degrees of freedom within. For an alpha level of .05 and $df_{\text{BETWEEN}} = 2$ and $df_{\text{WITHIN}} = 18$, the critical value of *F* is 3.55. Because the observed *F* value of 7.00 exceeds the critical value, we reject the null hypothesis and conclude that a relationship exists between religion and the ideal family size. We have answered the first of the three questions for the analysis of bivariate relationships.

Computational Formulas

There are several ways to derive the information necessary for the calculation of the F ratio. We have already seen how the sum of squares between and the sum of squares within can be determined by computing the variability between the group means and the variability of the deviations from the group means, respectively. We have also seen the equivalence between the mean square between and the variance estimate for the sample means scaled by the per-group sample size, as well as the equivalence between the mean square within and the pooled variance estimate.

Although both of these approaches help to clarify the conceptual foundation of one-way analysis of variance, they are computationally inefficient. In practice, the F ratio is most commonly obtained by calculating the sum of squares between and the sum of squares within with the computationally efficient formulas that are available for this purpose and then dividing these sums of squares by their corresponding degrees of freedom. We now consider these formulas.

We begin by examining the computational formula for the sum of squares total. This is simply the standard computational formula for a sum of squares applied to the entire data set. More specifically, the sum of squares total using the computational formula is obtained by squaring each score in the data set, adding these squared scores, and subtracting the square of the sum of the scores divided by the total sample size. Symbolically,

$$SS_{TOTAL} = \sum X^2 - \frac{(\sum X)^2}{N} \qquad [12.11]$$

where $\sum X^2$ is the *sum of the squared scores*, $(\sum X^2)$ is the *square of the summed scores*, and N is the total sample size.

The data for the religion and ideal family size study are reproduced in Table 12.3. To obtain $\sum X^2$ we must first square each score in the data set and then add these squared scores. For each group, the scores have been squared in the column labeled X^2. Adding all 21 of these squared scores together, we find that

$$\sum X^2 = 16 + 9 + \cdots + 0 + 1 = 116$$

The notation "$\cdots$" is used to indicate that not all of the X^2 scores contributing to the observed sum of 116 are physically represented. Rather, as a means of saving space, we have provided only the first two and the last two X^2 scores. When the "$\cdots$" notation is used, the inclusion in the summation of *all* relevant scores falling between the written values is implicit.

The sum of the X scores is

$$\sum X = 4 + 3 + \cdots + 0 + 1 = 42$$

where the "$\cdots$" notation again indicates that *all* relevant scores (in this case, X scores) are included in the summation. Squaring the observed sum of 42 and dividing by N, we obtain

$$\frac{(\sum X)^2}{N} = \frac{42^2}{21} = 84.00$$

TABLE 12.3   **Data and Computation of the Sums of Squares for Religion and Ideal Family Size Study**

Catholic		Protestant		Jewish	
X	X²	X	X²	X	X²
4	16	1	1	1	1
3	9	2	4	1	1
2	4	0	0	2	4
3	9	2	4	0	0
3	9	4	16	2	4
4	16	3	9	0	0
2	4	2	4	1	1

$$T_C = \sum X_C = 21 \qquad \sum X_C^2 = 67 \qquad T_P = \sum X_P = 14 \qquad \sum X_P^2 = 38 \qquad T_J = \sum X_J = 7 \qquad \sum X_J^2 = 11$$

$$T_C^2 = 441 \qquad\qquad\qquad\qquad\qquad T_P^2 = 196 \qquad\qquad\qquad\qquad\qquad T_J^2 = 49$$

$$\sum X^2 = 16 + 9 + \cdots + 0 + 1 = 116$$

$$\sum X = 4 + 3 + \cdots + 0 + 1 = 42$$

$$\frac{(\sum X)^2}{N} = \frac{42^2}{21} = 84.00$$

$$\frac{\sum T_i^2}{n} = \frac{441 + 196 + 49}{7} = 98.00$$

Thus, the sum of squares total in this example is

$$SS_{TOTAL} = \sum X^2 - \frac{(\sum X)^2}{N}$$
$$= 116 - 84.00 = 32.00$$

which is the same value as we reported previously.

    The computational formula for the sum of squares within is based on the sums of squares for the individual groups. For a given group, this is equal to the sum of that group's squared scores minus that group's squared sum after it has been divided by the relevant sample size, as is demonstrated in Table 12.3 for the religion and ideal family size study. Adding the sums of squares for the individual groups together yields the sum of squares within: $SS_{WITHIN} = SS_C + SS_P + SS_J = 4.00 + 10.00 + 4.00 = 18.00$. This suggests the following computational formula for the sum of squares within:

$$SS_{WITHIN} = \sum X^2 - \frac{\sum T_i^2}{n} \qquad\qquad [12.12]$$

where $\sum X^2$ is as defined above, T_j^2 is the square of the sum of the scores in group j [in other words, $T_j = \sum X$ and $T_j^2 = (\sum X)^2$ for a given group], and n is the per-group sample size.

In our example, T_j^2 equals 441 for the Catholic group, 196 for the Protestant group, and 49 for the Jewish group, per Table 12.3. Thus,

$$\frac{\sum T_j^2}{n} = \frac{441 + 196 + 49}{7} = 98.00$$

so

$$SS_{\text{WITHIN}} = \sum X^2 - \frac{\sum T_j^2}{n}$$

$$= 116 - 98.00 = 18.00$$

This is the same value that we reported previously for the sum of squares within and is also equal to the total of the individual groups' sums of squares from above.

The computational formula for the sum of squares between is

$$SS_{\text{BETWEEN}} = \frac{\sum T_j^2}{n} - \frac{(\sum X)^2}{N} \qquad [12.13]$$

where all terms are as defined above. In our example,

$$SS_{\text{BETWEEN}} = 98.00 - 84.00 = 14.00$$

as we previously reported.

Of course, given that the sum of squares total is equal to the sum of squares between plus the sum of squares within, if two of these quantities have already been calculated, the third can be determined through simple algebraic manipulation. For instance, we could have obtained the sum of squares between as follows:

$$SS_{\text{BETWEEN}} = SS_{\text{TOTAL}} - SS_{\text{WITHIN}}$$

$$= 32.00 - 18.00 = 14.00$$

However, it usually is a good idea to calculate all three sums of squares using the formulas above. This allows us to check for computational errors by determining whether the calculated values of the sum of squares between and the sum of squares within add up to the calculated value of the sum of squares total.

STUDY EXERCISE 12.1

An investigator examined the effects of three types of performance feedback on self-esteem. Five participants were randomly assigned to a positive feedback condition where, irrespective of their actual performance, they were informed that they scored at a very high level on a test of general knowledge. Another five participants were randomly assigned to a negative feedback condition and informed that they performed very poorly. A final five participants—constituting a control group—were not provided with any feedback regarding their test scores. All participants then responded to a measure of self-esteem. Scores on this measure could range from 0 to 10, with higher values indicating greater self-esteem. The self-esteem scores for the three conditions are listed in the table below. Test for a relationship between the type of feedback and self-esteem using a one-way analysis of variance.

Positive feedback	Negative feedback	No feedback
8	5	2
7	6	4
9	7	5
10	4	3
6	3	6

Answer   The null and alternative hypotheses can be stated as follows:

$H_0: \mu_P = \mu_N = \mu_C$

H_1: The three population means are not all equal

where the subscripts "P," "N," and "C" denote the positive feedback, negative feedback, and no feedback (control) conditions, respectively.

Intermediate statistics necessary for calculating the sums of squares are computed as follows:

Positive feedback		Negative feedback		No feedback	
X	X^2	X	X^2	X	X^2
8	64	5	25	2	4
7	49	6	36	4	25
9	81	7	49	5	25
10	100	4	16	3	9
6	36	3	9	6	36
$T_P = 40$		$T_N = 25$		$T_C = 20$	
$\overline{X}_P = 8.00$		$\overline{X}_N = 5.00$		$\overline{X}_C = 4.00$	
$T_P^2 = 1{,}600$		$T_N^2 = 625$		$T_C^2 = 400$	

$$\sum X^2 = 64 + 49 + \cdots + 9 + 36 = 564$$

$$\sum X = 8 + 7 + \cdots + 3 + 6 = 85$$

$$\frac{(\sum X)^2}{N} = \frac{85^2}{15} = 481.67$$

$$\frac{\sum T_i^2}{n} = \frac{1{,}600 + 625 + 400}{5} = 525.00$$

The sum of squares between is computed using Equation 12.13:

$$SS_{\text{BETWEEN}} = \frac{\sum T_i^2}{n} - \frac{(\sum X)^2}{N}$$

$$= 525.00 - 481.67 = 43.33$$

The sum of squares within is computed using Equation 12.12:

$$SS_{\text{WITHIN}} = \sum X^2 - \frac{\sum T_i^2}{n}$$

$$= 564 - 525.00 = 39.00$$

The sum of squares total is computed using Equation 12.11:

$$SS_{TOTAL} = \sum X^2 - \frac{(\sum X)^2}{N}$$

$$= 564 - 481.67 = 82.33$$

The degrees of freedom are computed using Equations 12.6, 12.7, and 12.9:

$$df_{BETWEEN} = k - 1 = 3 - 1 = 2$$

$$df_{WITHIN} = N - k = 15 - 3 = 12$$

$$df_{TOTAL} = N - 1 = 15 - 1 = 14$$

The mean square between and the mean square within are then computed by dividing the corresponding sums of squares by their degrees of freedom:

$$MS_{BETWEEN} = \frac{SS_{BETWEEN}}{df_{BETWEEN}} = \frac{43.33}{2} = 21.67$$

$$MS_{WITHIN} = \frac{SS_{WITHIN}}{df_{WITHIN}} = \frac{39.00}{12} = 3.25$$

Finally, the F ratio is derived by dividing the mean square between by the mean square within:

$$F = \frac{MS_{BETWEEN}}{MS_{WITHIN}} = \frac{21.67}{3.25} = 6.67$$

These calculations yield the following summary table:

Source	SS	df	MS	F
Between	43.33	2	21.67	6.67
Within	39.00	12	3.25	
Total	82.33	14		

The critical value of F from Appendix F for an alpha level of .05 and $df_{BETWEEN} = 2$ and $df_{WITHIN} = 12$ is 3.88. Because the observed F value of 6.67 exceeds the critical value, we reject the null hypothesis and conclude that there is a relationship between the type of feedback and self-esteem.

Assumptions of the F Test

The F test for one-way between-subjects analysis of variance is appropriate when the dependent variable is quantitative in nature and measured on a level that at least approximates interval characteristics. Application of the test also requires that the sampling distribution of the F ratio approximates an F distribution, which it will when the following assumptions are met:

1. The samples are independently and randomly selected from their respective populations.

2. The scores in each population are normally distributed.

3. The scores in each population have equal variances.

Note that these assumptions parallel those for the independent groups t test, as we discussed in Section 10.2.

For the F test to be valid, it is important that the assumption of independent and random selection be met. However, under certain conditions, the F test is robust to violations of the normality assumption. This is particularly true when the sample sizes are moderate (greater than 20) to large and the same for all groups. When this is the case, the F test is quite robust to even marked skewness and kurtosis.

Heterogeneity of population variances can be problematic, more so as the number of groups increases (Wilcox, Charlin, and Thompson, 1986). The F test is relatively robust when the population variance for one condition is as much as 2 to 3 times larger than the population variances for the other conditions (even with somewhat unequal sample sizes). However, the Type I error rate begins to become unacceptable when the population variance for one condition is 4 or more times larger than the population variances for the other conditions.* Just as the Levene test can be used to assess the homogeneity of variance assumption in the context of the independent groups t test, it can also be used to assess this assumption in the context of one-way analysis of variance. All of the issues that we discussed in Section 10.2 regarding the interpretation of this test also apply here.

12.3   Relationship of the F Test to the t Test

The F test for one-way analysis of variance is closely related to the independent groups t test. In fact, for the two-group between-subjects situation that we have been discussing, the F distribution bears a mathematical relationship to the t distribution such that

$$F = t^2 \qquad\qquad [12.14]$$

Thus, if we were to apply the procedures from this chapter to the problems in Chapter 10, the values of F that we would obtain would be equal to the squares of the corresponding t scores and we would draw exactly the same conclusions using the two approaches. However, it is traditional to use the independent groups t test when there are only two levels of the independent variable and to reserve one-way analysis of variance for when there are three or more levels.

12.4   Strength of the Relationship

The second of the three questions to be addressed regarding the analysis of bivariate relationships is how strong the relationship is. We noted in Section 12.2 that the sum of squares between is identical to the sum of squares explained that we discussed in Chapter 10. Accordingly, the strength of the relationship between the independent and dependent variables for one-way analysis of variance can be indexed by substituting

---

* For further discussion of this issue, see Harwell, Rubinstein, and Hayes (1992) and Milligan, Wong, and Thompson (1987).

$SS_{BETWEEN}$ for $SS_{EXPLAINED}$ in Equation 10.11 ($eta^2 = SS_{EXPLAINED}/SS_{TOTAL}$) to yield the following defining formula for eta-squared:*

$$eta^2 = \frac{SS_{BETWEEN}}{SS_{TOTAL}}$$ [12.15]

For the religion and ideal family size study,

$$eta^2 = \frac{14.00}{32.00} = .44$$

In this investigation, 44% of the variability in the ideal family size is associated with religion. This represents a strong effect.

An alternative formula for eta-squared based on the degrees of freedom and the observed value of F is

$$eta^2 = \frac{(df_{BETWEEN})F}{(df_{BETWEEN})F + df_{WITHIN}}$$ [12.16]

For the religion and ideal family size study,

$$eta^2 = \frac{(2)(7.00)}{(2)(7.00) + 18} = .44$$

which is the same result as obtained above.

Equation 12.16 is useful because research reports sometimes present F values and degrees of freedom but not the values of eta-squared. Applying Equation 12.16 will allow you to calculate eta-squared from the information that is provided.

We can also specify the strength of the relationship in unstandardized terms, but because there are more than two groups, the procedure for determining the corresponding confidence intervals requires more background. We will return to this issue after we introduce several relevant concepts in the next section.

STUDY EXERCISE 12.2

Calculate eta-squared for the data in Study Exercise 12.1.

Answer   Eta-squared is most easily calculated using Equation 12.15:

$$eta^2 = \frac{SS_{BETWEEN}}{SS_{TOTAL}} = \frac{43.33}{82.33} = .53$$

This represents a strong effect and indicates that 53% of the variability in self-esteem is associated with the type of feedback.

---

* As we discussed in Section 10.4, eta-squared is a biased estimator of the strength of the relationship between two variables. The formula for epsilon-squared, a commonly-used unbiased estimator of relationship strength, is provided in Appendix N for the one-way between-subjects analysis of variance situation.

12.5 Nature of the Relationship

The third of the three questions to be addressed regarding the analysis of bivariate relationships is what the nature of the relationship is. As we noted at the beginning of this chapter, the F test does not distinguish between the different ways in which the null hypothesis can be false. Rather, it considers the null hypothesis against all possible alternatives. For example, the possible patterns of unequal population means for three groups are $\mu_1 = \mu_2 \neq \mu_3$, $\mu_1 = \mu_3 \neq \mu_2$, $\mu_2 = \mu_3 \neq \mu_1$, and $\mu_1 \neq \mu_2 \neq \mu_3$. If any one of the alternatives holds, the null hypothesis will be rejected, unless a Type II error occurs. However, the alternative hypothesis states only that the population means are not all equal.

Given this state of affairs, it is necessary to conduct additional analyses to determine the exact nature of the relationship between the two variables when three or more groups are included in a study. However, which procedure to use for determining the nature of the relationship after the null hypothesis has been rejected is controversial among statisticians.

Multiple Comparison Procedures

One approach is to use a **multiple comparison procedure**. Among the most common of these procedures are the Scheffé test, the Newman–Keuls test, Duncan's multiple range test, Tukey's honest significant difference (HSD) test, and Fisher's least significant difference (LSD) test. Each of these is discussed in Kirk (1995).

The most general technique is the one proposed by Scheffé. However, the Scheffé procedure tends to produce a high incidence of Type II errors and, for this reason, is often not the test of choice. Because of its ease of presentation and desirable statistical properties (Jaccard, Becker, and Wood, 1984), we focus on the test proposed by Tukey. A competitor to Tukey's test that can be used effectively in a wide range of situations has been proposed by Hayter (1986).*

The **Tukey HSD test** discerns the nature of the relationship by testing a null hypothesis for each possible pair of group means. In the religion and ideal family size study, there are three groups: Catholic, Protestant, and Jewish. The questions of interest for the HSD test are: (1) Is the population mean for individuals who identify themselves as Catholic different than the population mean for individuals who identify themselves as Protestant? (2) Is the population mean for individuals who identify themselves as Catholic different than the population mean for individuals who identify themselves as Jewish? and (3) Is the population mean for individuals who identify themselves as Protestant different than from the population mean for individuals who identify themselves as Jewish? These three questions can be cast in three sets of null and alternative hypotheses.

These hypotheses take the same form as those for the independent groups t test. The first set addresses the means for Catholic and Protestant individuals:

H_0: $\mu_C = \mu_P$

H_1: $\mu_C \neq \mu_P$

---

* Hayter's test has greater statistical power than Tukey's test, but it is not as general.

The second set addresses the means for Catholic and Jewish individuals:

$H_0: \mu_C = \mu_J$

$H_1: \mu_C \neq \mu_J$

The third set addresses the means for Protestant and Jewish individuals:

$H_0: \mu_P = \mu_J$

$H_1: \mu_P \neq \mu_J$

Can we simply compare each pair of group means by conducting three independent groups *t* tests? The answer is *no*. The problem with doing this is that multiple *t* tests increase the probability of making a Type I error for at least one of the tests beyond the probability specified by the alpha level for each individual analysis. Witte (1980) presents a coin-tossing analogy that illustrates the relevant issues:

> When a fair coin is tossed only once, the probability of heads equals .50—just as when a single *t* test is to be conducted at the .05 level of significance, the probability of a Type I error equals .05. When a fair coin is tossed three times, however, heads can appear not only on the first toss but on the second or third toss as well, and hence the probability of heads on at least one of the three tosses exceeds .50. By the same token, when a series of three *t* tests are conducted at the .05 level of significance, a Type I error can be committed not only on the first test but on the second or third test as well, and hence the probability of committing a Type I error on at least one of the three tests exceeds .05.

The Tukey HSD test circumvents this problem by maintaining the probability of making one or more Type I errors in a set of comparisons at the specified alpha level. In most applications, researchers adopt an *overall alpha level* of .05. We will follow this practice in the remainder of this book.

The logic underlying the HSD test is rather complex and is presented in Tukey (1953). We focus here on the mechanics of how to apply it. To facilitate our presentation, the summary table for the religion and ideal family size study is reproduced here:

Source	SS	df	MS	F
Between	14.00	2	7.00	7.00
Within	18.00	18	1.00	
Total	32.00	20		

The HSD test involves the computation of a **critical difference**, which is defined as follows:

$$CD = q\sqrt{\frac{MS_{WITHIN}}{n}} \qquad [12.17]$$

where *CD* represents the critical difference, MS_{WITHIN} is the mean square within from the summary table, *n* is the per-group sample size, and *q* is the **Studentized range value** from Appendix G. The value of *q* is determined with reference to the overall alpha level, the degrees of freedom within from the summary table, and the number of groups in the study, *k*.

In our example, $MS_{\text{WITHIN}} = 1.00$ and $n = 7$. To determine the value of q, we follow the instructions provided in Appendix G. For an overall alpha level of .05, 18 degrees of freedom within, and three groups, we find that q is equal to 3.61. The critical difference is therefore calculated as follows:

$$CD = 3.61\sqrt{\frac{1.00}{7}} = 1.36$$

Consider the first set of hypotheses from above:

$H_0: \mu_C = \mu_P$

$H_1: \mu_C \neq \mu_P$

We want to make a decision with respect to these two competing proposals. The rule for doing so using the HSD test is as follows: If the absolute difference between the sample means for the two groups involved in the comparison exceeds the critical difference, then reject the null hypothesis. Otherwise, fail to reject the null hypothesis. If the null hypothesis is rejected, conclude that the group with the larger sample mean also has a larger mean in the population.

In our example, the absolute difference between the sample means is $|\overline{X}_C - \overline{X}_P| = |3.00 - 2.00| = 1.00$. Because 1.00 does not exceed the critical difference of 1.36, we fail to reject the null hypothesis for the comparison. Thus, we are unable to conclude that Catholic and Protestant individuals differ in their mean ideal family size.

The second set of hypotheses is

$H_0: \mu_C = \mu_J$

$H_1: \mu_C \neq \mu_J$

The absolute difference between the sample means is $|\overline{X}_C - \overline{X}_J| = |3.00 - 1.00| = 2.00$. Because 2.00 is greater than 1.36, we reject the null hypothesis and accept the alternative hypothesis for the comparison. An examination of the sample means indicates that Catholic individuals $(\overline{X}_C = 3.00)$ have a larger ideal family size than Jewish individuals $(\overline{X}_J = 1.00)$.

The third set of hypotheses is

$H_0: \mu_P = \mu_J$

$H_1: \mu_P \neq \mu_J$

The absolute difference between the sample means is $|\overline{X}_P - \overline{X}_J| = |2.00 - 1.00| = 1.00$. Because 1.00 does not exceed 1.36, we fail to reject the null hypothesis for the comparison. Thus, we are unable to conclude that Protestant and Jewish individuals differ in their mean ideal family size.

We can summarize the results of the entire analysis in a table. Note that, for the sake of brevity, this does not explicitly refer to the alternative hypotheses:

Null hypothesis tested	Absolute difference between sample means	Value of CD	Null hypothesis rejected?
$\mu_C = \mu_P$	$\lvert 3.00 - 2.00 \rvert = 1.00$	1.36	No
$\mu_C = \mu_J$	$\lvert 3.00 - 1.00 \rvert = 2.00$	1.36	Yes
$\mu_P = \mu_J$	$\lvert 2.00 - 1.00 \rvert = 1.00$	1.36	No

Placing all of this information in one table allows us to readily discern the nature of the relationship between religion and the ideal family size: Individuals who identify themselves as Catholic ($\overline{X}_C = 3.00$) have a larger ideal family size than individuals who identify themselves as Jewish ($\overline{X}_J = 1.00$). However, we cannot conclude that the ideal family size for either of these groups differs from the ideal family size for individuals who identify themselves as Protestant ($\overline{X}_P = 2.00$). The HSD test clarifies how religion is related to people's beliefs about the ideal number of children to have in a family.

STUDY EXERCISE 12.3

Analyze the nature of the relationship between the type of feedback and self-esteem for the data in Study Exercise 12.1 using the HSD test.

Answer   The first step in applying the HSD test is to phrase the three sets of null and alternative hypotheses. The former are listed in the table below.

We next calculate the critical difference. Referring to Appendix G, we find that for an overall alpha level of .05, $df_{\text{WITHIN}} = 12$, and $k = 3$, q is equal to 3.77. Thus,

$$CD = q\sqrt{\frac{MS_{\text{WITHIN}}}{n}} = 3.77\sqrt{\frac{3.25}{5}} = 3.04$$

The HSD test can now be applied by comparing the absolute difference between the sample means for the two groups involved in a comparison with the critical difference, deciding whether or not the corresponding null hypothesis should be rejected, and, if it is, comparing the two sample means to make a decision about how the two population means differ. However, for the sake of brevity, we do not explicitly show these steps here. We can, however, summarize them in a table as follows:

Null hypothesis tested	Absolute difference between sample means	Value of CD	Null hypothesis rejected?
$\mu_P = \mu_N$	$\lvert 8.00 - 5.00 \rvert = 3.00$	3.04	No
$\mu_P = \mu_C$	$\lvert 8.00 - 4.00 \rvert = 4.00$	3.04	Yes
$\mu_N = \mu_C$	$\lvert 5.00 - 4.00 \rvert = 1.00$	3.04	No

The nature of the relationship is such that self-esteem will be greater when people receive positive feedback ($\overline{X}_P = 8.00$) than when they receive no feedback ($\overline{X}_C = 4.00$). However, we cannot conclude that negative feedback affects self-esteem relative to no feedback, nor can we conclude that positive feedback makes a difference relative to no feedback.

Alternative Procedures

The approach that we have described for determining the nature of the relationship between the independent and dependent variables using analysis of variance can be characterized as (1) using the F test to make an overall, or *omnibus*, test of whether a relationship exists between two variables and (2) analyzing pairwise mean differences using a multiple comparison procedure to discern the nature of the relationship. However, the analysis of variance framework is very flexible, and these steps are sometimes modified.

For example, sometimes investigators are not interested in performing all possible pairwise comparisons when evaluating the nature of the relationship, but instead focus only on one or two contrasts that are of particular theoretical interest. In this case, the Tukey HSD test is not used, and an alternative analytic strategy is pursued instead. For a discussion of the many different approaches for analyzing the nature of the relationship between the two variables within an analysis of variance framework, see Kirk (1995).

12.6 Unstandardized Effect Sizes and Confidence Intervals

Unstandardized effect sizes for the one-way between-subjects case are provided by the difference between each pair of sample means. We can also calculate a 95% confidence interval for each mean difference. However, just as we use the Tukey HSD test to account for the fact that we are conducting multiple comparisons, we must also account for the fact that we are calculating multiple sets of confidence intervals. This allows us to be 95% confident that the intervals contain the true population mean differences when all of the relevant intervals are considered together.

The formula for a 95% confidence interval for a pairwise comparison of means in the one-way between-subjects case is

$$CI = (\overline{X}_i - \overline{X}_j) - CD \quad \text{to} \quad (\overline{X}_i - \overline{X}_j) + CD \qquad [12.18]$$

where $\overline{X}_i$ is the mean for one of the groups being considered, $\overline{X}_j$ is the mean for the other group, and CD is the critical difference for the Tukey HSD test.

The value of the critical difference for the religion and ideal family size study is 1.36. Thus, the 95% Tukey HSD confidence interval for the mean difference between Catholic and Protestant individuals is

$$CI = (3.00 - 2.00) - 1.36 \quad \text{to} \quad (3.00 - 2.00) + 1.36$$
$$= -.36 \quad \text{to} \quad 2.36$$

The 95% HSD confidence interval for the mean difference between Catholic and Jewish individuals is

$$CI = (3.00 - 1.00) - 1.36 \quad \text{to} \quad (3.00 - 1.00) + 1.36$$
$$= .64 \quad \text{to} \quad 3.36$$

Finally, the 95% HSD confidence interval for the mean difference between Protestant and Jewish individuals is

$$CI = (2.00 - 1.00) - 1.36 \quad \text{to} \quad (2.00 - 1.00) + 1.36$$
$$= -.36 \quad \text{to} \quad 2.36$$

We are 95% confident that the true population mean differences fall within these intervals when they are considered simultaneously.

12.7 Methodological Considerations

Although the results for the religion and ideal family size study suggest that a relationship exists between the two variables, the data must be interpreted in light of certain methodological constraints. Consider first the role of confounding variables.

Because religion cannot be manipulated, research participants could not be randomly assigned to groups. Consequently, all variables that are naturally related to religion are possible confounding variables. These include such factors as social class, the size of the family in which one grew up, and education. Therefore, it is impossible to conclude unambiguously that a causal relationship exists between religion and the ideal family size: Religion per se might have no effect on the ideal family size, and the observed relationship might simply be a function of the causal influence of one or more confounding variables.

A large number of disturbance variables were uncontrolled in the study. For instance, research has shown that the ideal family size is influenced by one's religiosity (that is, how religious one is). Individuals within a given religious group in this study almost certainly differed in religiosity, and this would, in turn, create within-group variability. One minus eta-squared provides an index of the extent to which disturbance variables have influenced the dependent measure. Specifically, 1.00 minus eta-squared represents the proportion of variability in the dependent variable that can be attributed to disturbance variables. For the religion and ideal family size data, this equals. Thus, more than half of the variability in the ideal family size is due to disturbance variables. Certainly, this could have been reduced through additional control procedures.

The results of the study must also be considered in terms of their generalizability. For instance, if the participants were all college students, we would have to be very careful about generalizing to younger, older, or less educated groups. Similarly, if the participants were all the same gender, we would be unable to readily generalize to the other gender. In short, the nature of one's samples plays an important role in determining the generalizability of one's findings. For this reason, it is imperative that research reports provide reasonable descriptions of who the participants were.

12.8 Numerical Example

An important issue in court cases is the validity of eyewitness testimony. However, behavioral scientists have suggested that eyewitness accounts can be influenced by many different factors, including the way that questions to eyewitnesses are phrased. If subtle wording can influence the answers given by an eyewitness, such reports must be interpreted with considerable caution. As an example of how this problem can be studied, consider the following experiment:

Twenty individuals watch a film of a car accident in which car A runs through a stop sign and hits car B at a speed of 20 miles per hour. The film depicts the entire incident, including the arrival of a police officer and the citation of the driver of car A. After watching the film, each participant is asked to estimate the speed of car A at the moment of impact.

The question is phrased in four different ways. The first five individuals are asked, "How fast was car A going at the time of the accident with car B?" The second five individuals are asked, "How fast was car A going when it hit car B?" An additional five individuals are asked, "How fast was car A going when it crashed into car B?" Finally, the last five individuals are asked, "How fast was car A going when it smashed into car B?" The issue of interest is whether estimates of the car's speed vary as a function of the wording used in asking about the accident. The speed estimates are provided in Table 12.4.

The null hypothesis is that the four population means are equal. If so, there is no relationship between the way that the question is phrased and the speed estimates. The alternative hypothesis is that the population means are not all equal. If so, there is a relationship between the way that the question is phrased and the speed estimates. These hypotheses can be formally stated as

H_0: $\mu_A = \mu_H = \mu_C = \mu_S$

H_1: The four population means are not all equal

where the subscript "A" represents the *accident* phraseology, the subscript "H" represents the *hit* phraseology, the subscript "C" represents the *crashed* phraseology, and the subscript "S" represents the *smashed* phraseology.

The intermediate statistics necessary for calculating the sums of squares are given in Table 12.4. The sum of squares between is

$$SS_{\text{BETWEEN}} = \frac{\sum T_j^2}{n} - \frac{(\sum X)^2}{N}$$

$$= 11{,}340.00 - 11{,}045.00 = 295.00$$

The sum of squares within is

$$SS_{\text{WITHIN}} = \sum X^2 - \frac{\sum T_j^2}{n}$$

$$= 11{,}380.00 - 11{,}340.00 = 40.00$$

Finally, the sum of squares total is

$$SS_{\text{TOTAL}} = \sum X^2 - \frac{(\sum X)^2}{n}$$

$$= 11{,}380.00 - 11{,}045.00 = 335.00$$

TABLE 12.4   **Data and Computation of the Sums of Squares for Phraseology and Speed Estimation Experiment**

Accident		Hit		Crashed		Smashed	
X	X^2	X	X^2	X	X^2	X	X^2
18	324	23	529	25	625	29	841
20	400	20	400	27	729	28	784
17	289	22	484	26	676	30	900
19	361	19	361	23	529	27	729
21	441	21	441	24	576	31	961

$T_A = 95$ $T_H = 105$ $T_C = 125$ $T_S = 145$

$\overline{X}_A = 19.00$ $\overline{X}_H = 21.00$ $\overline{X}_C = 25.00$ $\overline{X}_S = 29.00$

$T_A^2 = 9{,}025$ $T_H^2 = 11{,}025$ $T_C^2 = 15{,}625$ $T_S^2 = 21{,}025$

$$\sum X^2 = 324 + 400 + \cdots + 729 + 961 = 11{,}380$$

$$\sum X = 18 + 20 + \cdots + 27 + 31 = 470$$

$$\frac{(\sum X)^2}{N} = \frac{470^2}{20} = 11{,}045.00$$

$$\frac{\sum T_j^2}{n} = \frac{9{,}025 + 11{,}025 + 15{,}625 + 21{,}025}{5} = 11{,}340.00$$

The degrees of freedom are

$$df_{\text{BETWEEN}} = k - 1 = 4 - 1 = 3$$
$$df_{\text{WITHIN}} = N - k = 20 - 4 = 16$$
$$df_{\text{TOTAL}} = N - 1 = 20 - 1 = 19$$

The relevant mean squares are

$$MS_{\text{BETWEEN}} = \frac{SS_{\text{BETWEEN}}}{df_{\text{BETWEEN}}} = \frac{295.00}{3} = 98.33$$

$$MS_{\text{WITHIN}} = \frac{SS_{\text{WITHIN}}}{df_{\text{WITHIN}}} = \frac{40.00}{16} = 2.50$$

Thus, the F ratio is

$$F = \frac{MS_{\text{BETWEEN}}}{MS_{\text{WITHIN}}} = \frac{98.33}{2.50} = 39.33$$

These calculations yield the following summary table:

Source	SS	df	MS	F
Between	295.00	3	98.33	39.33
Within	40.00	16	2.50	
Total	335.00	19		

For an alpha level of .05 and $df_{\text{BETWEEN}} = 3$ and $df_{\text{WITHIN}} = 16$, the critical value of F from Appendix F is 3.24. The observed value of F is 39.33. This exceeds the critical value, so we reject the null hypothesis and conclude that the type of phrasing and the speed estimates are related.

As indexed by eta-squared, the strength of the relationship is

$$\text{eta}^2 = \frac{SS_{\text{BETWEEN}}}{SS_{\text{TOTAL}}} = \frac{295.00}{335.00} = .88$$

This represents a strong effect and indicates that 88% of the variability in speed estimates is associated with the way in which the question was phrased.

The nature of the relationship is determined using the Tukey HSD test. This requires that we first phrase the six sets of null and alternative hypotheses. The former are listed in the table below. The critical difference is derived using Equation 12.17. From Appendix G, the value of q for an overall alpha level of .05, $df_{\text{WITHIN}} = 16$ and $k = 4$ is 4.05. Thus,

$$CD = q\sqrt{\frac{MS_{\text{WITHIN}}}{n}} = 4.05\sqrt{\frac{2.50}{5}} = 2.86$$

The HSD test can now be applied by comparing the absolute difference between the sample means for the two groups involved in a comparison with the critical difference, deciding whether or not the corresponding null hypothesis should be rejected, and, if it is, comparing the two sample means to make a decision about how the two population means differ. However, for the sake of brevity, we do not explicitly show these steps here. We can, however, summarize them in a table as follows:

Null hypothesis tested	Absolute difference between sample means	Value of CD	Null hypothesis rejected?
$\mu_A = \mu_H$	$|19.00 - 21.00| = 2.00$	2.86	No
$\mu_A = \mu_C$	$|19.00 - 25.00| = 6.00$	2.86	Yes
$\mu_A = \mu_S$	$|19.00 - 29.00| = 10.00$	2.86	Yes
$\mu_H = \mu_C$	$|21.00 - 25.00| = 4.00$	2.86	Yes
$\mu_H = \mu_S$	$|21.00 - 29.00| = 8.00$	2.86	Yes
$\mu_C = \mu_S$	$|25.00 - 29.00| = 4.00$	2.86	Yes

Inspection of the table suggests the following conclusions: Speed estimates obtained when the question is phrased in terms of car A smashing into car B ($\overline{X}_S = 29.00$) will be higher than speed estimates obtained when the question is phrased in terms of the two cars being involved in an accident ($\overline{X}_A = 19.00$), car A hitting car B ($\overline{X}_H = 21.00$), or car A crashing into car B ($\overline{X}_C = 25.00$). Furthermore, speed estimates obtained using the *crash* phraseology will be higher than the estimates obtained using either the *accident* or the *hit* phraseology. However, we cannot conclude that the *accident* phraseology affects speed estimates relative to the *hit* phraseology.

Finally, we can calculate the 95% Tukey HSD confidence intervals for the pairwise mean contrasts using Equation 12.18. The 95% HSD confidence interval for the mean difference between the *accident* and the *hit* conditions is

$$CI = (19.00 - 21.00) - 2.86 \quad \text{to} \quad (19.00 - 21.00) + 2.86$$
$$= -4.86 \quad \text{to} \quad .86$$

The 95% HSD confidence interval for the mean difference between the *accident* and the *crashed* conditions is

$$CI = (19.00 - 25.00) - 2.86 \quad \text{to} \quad (19.00 - 25.00) + 2.86$$
$$= -8.86 \quad \text{to} \quad -3.14$$

The 95% HSD confidence interval for the mean difference between the *accident* and the *smashed* conditions is

$$CI = (19.00 - 29.00) - 2.86 \quad \text{to} \quad (19.00 - 29.00) + 2.86$$
$$= -12.86 \quad \text{to} \quad -7.14$$

The 95% HSD confidence interval for the mean difference between the *hit* and the *crashed* conditions is

$$CI = (21.00 - 25.00) - 2.86 \quad \text{to} \quad (21.00 - 25.00) + 2.86$$
$$= -6.86 \quad \text{to} \quad -1.14$$

The 95% HSD confidence interval for the mean difference between the *hit* and the *smashed* conditions is

$$CI = (21.00 - 29.00) - 2.86 \quad \text{to} \quad (21.00 - 29.00) + 2.86$$
$$= -10.86 \quad \text{to} \quad -5.14$$

Finally, the 95% HSD confidence interval for the mean difference between the *crashed* and the *smashed* conditions is

$$CI = (25.00 - 29.00) - 2.86 \quad \text{to} \quad (25.00 - 29.00) + 2.86$$
$$= -6.86 \quad \text{to} \quad -1.14$$

You should think about these results in terms of the following research design questions: What confounding variables might be operating? What is the role of disturbance variables? What kind of procedures could be used to reduce sampling error? What are the limitations of the experiment in terms of generalizability? All of these issues are critical for drawing appropriate conclusions from the study.

12.9 Planning an Investigation Using One-Way Between-Subjects Analysis of Variance

Appendix E.2 contains tables of the per-group sample sizes necessary to achieve various levels of power for one-way between-subjects analysis of variance for different numbers of degrees of freedom between. Table 12.5 reproduces a portion of this

TABLE 12.5   **Approximate Sample Sizes Necessary to Achieve Selected Levels of Power for**
df_{BETWEEN} = 2 and Alpha = .05 as a Function of Population Values of Eta-Squared

	Population Eta-Squared									
Power	.01	.03	.05	.07	.10	.15	.20	.25	.30	.35
.10	22	8	5	4	3	2	2	2	—	—
.50	165	55	32	23	16	10	8	6	5	4
.70	255	84	50	35	24	16	11	9	7	6
.80	319	105	62	44	30	19	14	11	9	7
.90	417	137	81	57	39	25	18	14	11	9
.95	511	168	99	69	47	30	22	16	13	11
.99	708	232	137	96	65	41	29	22	18	14

appendix for df_{BETWEEN} = 2 (that is, for three groups) and an alpha level of .05. The first column presents selected values of power, and the column headings are selected values of eta-squared in the population.

To illustrate the use of this table, if the desired power level is .80 and the researcher suspects that the strength of the relationship in the population corresponds to an eta-squared of .15, then the number of participants that should be sampled in *each group* for an alpha level of .05 is 19. The power that an investigator requires will, of course, depend on the seriousness of committing a Type II error.

In addition to providing the sample size necessary to obtain a desired level of power, power tables can also be used to determine the power associated with one-way analysis of variance given the degrees of freedom between, the alpha level, the sample size, and the value of eta-squared in the population. For instance, Table 12.5 shows that the power for a one-way analysis of variance with df_{BETWEEN} = 2 and n = 30 per group is .80 at an alpha level of .05 when the population eta-squared is .10.

Examination of Table 12.5 and Appendix E.2 provides a general appreciation for the relationships among the degrees of freedom between, the alpha level, sample size, the strength of the relationship that one is trying to detect in the population, and power for one-way analysis of variance. As can be seen, power becomes greater as the degrees of freedom between, the alpha level, the sample size, and the population eta-squared each increases.

12.10   Method of Presentation

Reports of a one-way between-subjects analysis of variance should include statements of the alpha level that was used, the degrees of freedom between, the degrees of freedom within, the observed value of F, the significance level, the sample means, the standard deviation estimates, and the confidence intervals for the mean differences. In addition, if the analysis is statistically significant, the strength and nature of the relationship between the independent and dependent variables should be addressed.

The results for the religion and ideal family size study that was discussed earlier in this chapter might be presented as follows:

Results

A one-way analysis of variance that compared the mean ideal family sizes for the three religious groups was found to be statistically significant at an alpha level of .05, $F(2, 18) = 7.00$, $p < .01$. The strength of the relationship, as indexed by eta-squared, was .44.

A Tukey HSD test indicated that the mean for individuals who identified themselves as Catholic $M = 3.00$, $SD = .82$ was significantly greater than the mean for individuals who identified themselves as Jewish $M = 1.00$, $SD = .82$. The mean for Protestant individuals $M = 2.00$, $SD = 1.29$ did not differ significantly from the mean for either of the other groups. Table 1 presents the 95% Tukey HSD confidence intervals for each pairwise comparison of means.

The first sentence identifies the statistical technique that was used to analyze the data. The term *between-subjects* is not used to describe the analysis of variance because, unless stated otherwise, it is assumed that a between-subjects analysis was performed. This sentence also states the alpha level and the results for the test of a relationship. The numbers within the parentheses are the degrees of freedom between and the degrees of freedom within, respectively. This is followed by the observed value of *F* and the significance level.

The second sentence indicates the strength of the relationship. If this is not reported, eta-squared can be derived from the degrees of freedom and the observed value of *F* using Equation 12.16.

The third and fourth sentences present the results of the HSD test, including the sample means, and the standard deviation estimates.* The intermediate statistics that are calculated for the application of a multiple comparison procedure are not reported. The final sentence refers to a table that would present the 95% Tukey HSD confidence intervals.

12.11   Examples from the Literature

The Effectiveness of Different Incentives for Learning

Historically, many educators and parents have assumed that the threat or actual application of punishment is the most effective strategy for motivating children to learn. More recent educational philosophy recognizes the important role of reward as an incentive for learning.

Hurlock (1925) reports a study relevant to this issue in which 106 fourth- and sixth-grade students were randomly divided into four groups. Each group took addition tests in class on five successive days. Students in the first group were separated from the other students and told to work on these tests as they usually do with tests of this type. This constituted the control condition. Students in another group were

---

* The variance estimates were identified in Section 12.2 to be .67 for both Catholic and Jewish individuals and 1.67 for Protestant individuals. The square roots of these values are .82 and 1.29, respectively.

brought to the front of the room each day before the test was given and praised for their good work. Students in the third group were also brought to the front of the room, but these students were reprimanded for their poor work. The students in the fourth group were ignored. Of interest to Hurlock was whether the different strategies had different effects on performance as indicated by scores on the final addition test.

Hurlock's investigation was conducted before the technique of analysis of variance had been developed. However, Kerlinger (1973) analyzed the Hurlock data using a one-way analysis of variance and found that the null hypothesis should be rejected, $F(3, 102) = 10.08$, $p < .01$, thus indicating that the type of strategy is related to performance. The strength of the relationship, as indexed by eta-squared, was .23. This represents a strong effect. An HSD test indicated that the mean for the *praised* group ($\overline{X} = 20.22$) was significantly greater than the mean for each of the other three groups ($\overline{X} = 11.35$ for the control group, 12.38 for the *ignored* group, and 14.19 for the *reprimanded* group). The means for these latter groups, however, did not significantly differ. Thus, consistent with a reward philosophy, the most effective strategy in this experiment was praise.

Body Posture of Message Recipients and Susceptibility to Influence

Research in nonverbal behavior has shown that the body posture of a communicator can affect his or her ability to influence the attitudes of the message recipients. A related issue, but one that has received far less attention, concerns how susceptibility to influence is affected by the recipient's body posture.

In one of the few studies on this topic, Petty, Wells, Heesacker, Brock, and Cacioppo (1983) had 78 college students listen to a persuasive message that advocated a 20% tuition increase at their university while either standing, sitting, reclining on a cushioned table, or reclining on an uncushioned table. Following exposure to this message, the students responded to the question "In general, to what extent do you agree that the tuition should be increased?" Responses were made on a scale of 1 to 12, with higher scores indicating greater agreement.

A one-way analysis of variance applied to these data was statistically significant, $F(3, 74) = 3.33$, $p < .02$. As indexed by eta-squared, the strength of the relationship was .12. This represents a moderate effect. Multiple comparisons showed that students who had heard the persuasive communication while reclining on the cushioned table ($\overline{X} = 7.60$) reported significantly greater positive attitudes than did students who had heard this message while standing ($\overline{X} = 5.63$). The means for the *sitting* ($\overline{X} = 6.00$) and the *uncushioned reclining* ($\overline{X} = 6.95$) conditions did not differ significantly from one another or from the means reported above.

A follow-up study by Petty and colleagues (1983) suggests that "a reclining posture facilitates message-relevant thinking over a standing posture and thereby enhances the importance of message content in producing persuasion" (p. 219). According to this perspective, people are better able to differentiate strong from weak arguments when they are reclining than when they are standing. Consequently, reclining individuals are more susceptible to influence than are standing individuals when persuasive messages are compelling but less susceptible to influence when persuasive messages are specious. The exact reasons for this, however, are unclear.

12.12 Links Between Computer Results and Book Content

Statistical computer programs provide the user with a choice of which of the many available multiple comparison procedures to apply following a statistically significant one-way analysis of variance. For instance, there is a second Tukey multiple comparison test besides the Tukey HSD test that we advocate in this chapter. Thus, be careful to select the procedure that you truly want to use when requesting a multiple comparison procedure for a statistical computer analysis.

Given the many steps involved in the application of a multiple comparison procedure, it is not surprising that the output for these tests can be extensive. However, with a little experience, the interpretation of multiple comparison computer results is straightforward.

12.13 Links Between Chapters

As we have seen, one-way analysis of variance is closely related to the independent groups *t* test. One-way analysis of variance is also closely related to two-way between-subjects analysis of variance, which we discuss in Chapter 17. In fact, the conditions for using two-way between-subjects analysis of variance are identical to those for one-way analysis of variance except that two independent variables rather than one independent variable are studied. To the extent that you understand the rationale and the terminology for the one-way situation, you will be able to seamlessly move to the two-way situation. An understanding of one-way analysis of variance is also helpful for understanding the other advanced analysis of variance techniques that we briefly review in Section 18.6.

Applications to the Analysis of a Social Problem Using SPSS for Windows

As we noted in Chapter 11, an important variable in predicting teen problem behaviors is the quality of the relationship between parent and child: The poorer the teen's relationship with the parent, the more likely the teen is to engage in problem behaviors, other things being equal.

One question of theoretical interest is how the quality of the relationship between parent and teen changes as a function of the adolescent's age. Some theorists argue that this relationship becomes increasingly strained as teens progress from the early to the later stages of adolescence. According to this perspective, with each passing year, the teen is closer to adulthood. This transition to adulthood places strain on parents as children begin to assert their independence and develop their own lifestyles. The quality of the parent–teen relationship is thus negatively influenced by the teen's increasing rejection of the traditional parent–child roles.

An alternative point of view argues just the opposite: The quality of the relationship between parent and teen improves with age. According to this perspective, during the earlier years of adolescence,

(continued)

teens experience stress and strain as they undergo puberty and the tremendous physical and hormonal changes that accompany it. These stresses detract from the quality of the parent–teen relationship as the teen tries to cope with the outside world. In addition, it is during early adolescence when teens typically initiate independence and a "break" from the traditional "parent-as-all-knowing" role that has typified their upbringing. In later adolescence, the teen has already dealt with the harsh stresses of the adolescent growth spurt. In addition, parents and teens have already resolved their differing expectations and have moved from the now inappropriate "parent–child" relationship to the "parent–emerging adult" relationship. Thus, the quality of the parent–teen relationship should improve as a function of age.

We evaluated these opposing predictions by applying a one-way between-subjects analysis of variance to data collected in the parent–teen communication study described in Chapter 1. The independent variable, the age of the teen, had four levels: 14, 15, 16, and 17 years old.

The first step in obtaining scores on the dependent variable was to ask the teens a series of questions that were designed to measure how satisfied they were with their relationship with their mother. Specifically, we asked them to indicate how much they agreed or disagreed with each of 11 statements about different facets of the maternal relationship (for example, "I am satisfied with the way my mother and I communicate with each other," "I am satisfied with the way my mother and I resolve conflicts," "I am satisfied with the respect my mother shows me," "I am satisfied with the emotional support my mother gives me"). Each statement was rated on a 1 (*strongly disagree*) to 5 (*strongly agree*) scale that also included the response options *moderately disagree, neither agree nor disagree,* and *moderately agree.*

After undertaking analyses to ensure that it was appropriate to do so, we summed the responses across the 11 statements to yield an overall index of relationship satisfaction. Scores on this index could range from 11 to 55, with higher values indicating greater satisfaction with the maternal relationship. This constituted our dependent variable. Although the measure may not be strictly interval, our previous research suggests that the approximation is sufficiently close that the use of analysis of variance is appropriate.*

The sample sizes for the four age groups were 114, 270, 220, and 133, respectively. The fact that all four sample sizes are large indicates that the analysis will be relatively robust to any assumption violations that might occur. However, the fact that they are unequal suggests that some caution should be exercised because the robustness of the *F* test can be weakened by unequal sample sizes.

Figure 12.2 presents a grouped frequency histogram for each age group, with a normal curve superimposed on each. In all cases, the satisfaction scores were strongly negatively skewed. Because a few 14-year-olds had abnormally low scores, we double-checked the scores for these individuals as well as their responses to the other questions. This revealed neither coding errors nor anything else unique about these teens relative to their peers. Because they represented only a few cases and because some advanced analyses that we conducted indicated that the results were unaffected by their presence, we included them in the analysis.

Despite the skewness in the sample data, the departures from normality are not so great as to suggest that nonnormality in the population is large enough to undermine the analysis of variance (Harwell, Rubinstein, and Hayes, 1992; Milligan, Wong, and Thompson, 1987). Nevertheless, the strong skewness led us to supplement the present analyses with a nonparametric test. These results are discussed in Chapter 16.

The computer output for the analysis of variance is presented in Table 12.6. The top portion contains the value of the test statistic, the degrees of freedom, and the significance level for the Levene test that we discussed in Section 10.2 for assessing homogeneity of variance. The test is performed by computing a one-way between-subjects analysis of variance on the absolute difference between each individual's score and the mean for that individual's group. Of particular interest is the *p* value yielded by the analysis (labeled "Sig."). In this instance, the *p* value is .36, so we fail to reject the null hypothesis of equal population variances

---

* See Davison and Sharma (1988) for a discussion of how the level of measurement of the dependent variable affects the use of parametric tests.

FIGURE 12.2   Grouped Frequency Histograms for Satisfaction with Maternal Relationship for (a) 14-Year-Olds, (b) 15-Year-Olds, (c) 16-Year-Olds, and (d) 17-Year-Olds

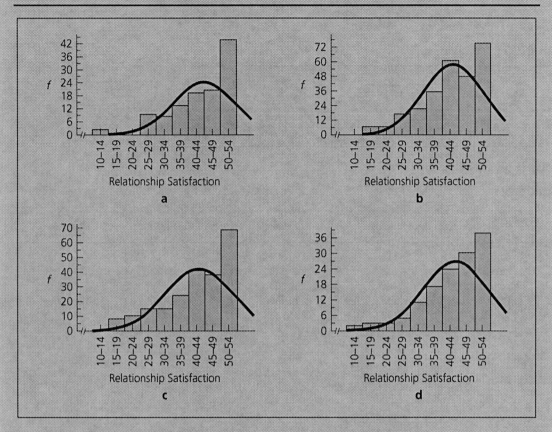

across the age groups. Thus, the data are consistent with homogeneous population variances.

The standard deviation estimates for each of the four age groups are presented in the middle section of Table 12.6, along with the sample sizes, the means, and the estimated standard errors of the mean. The standard deviation estimates (and thus the variance estimates) are fairly homogeneous—the largest standard deviation estimate is only 1.11 times larger than the smallest. Under these circumstances, and given the large sample sizes and the statistically nonsignificant Levene test, heterogeneity of variance is not problematic for the F test (Milligan, Wong, and Thompson, 1987). Also of note is the fact that the estimated standard errors are all relatively small.

The summary table for the analysis of variance is presented at the bottom. Because the p value

(labeled "Sig.") of .37 is greater than the .05 alpha level, we fail to reject the null hypothesis of no age differences in teen satisfaction with the maternal relationship.

As we discussed in Section 10.4, it is worthwhile to calculate eta-squared even when an inferential test is statistically nonsignificant. Application of Equation 12.15 shows that the strength of the relationship in this instance is .004 as indexed by this measure.

Given that we failed to reject the null hypothesis, it is possible that a Type II error may have occurred. To evaluate this possibility, we determined the statistical power for a one-way between-subjects analysis of variance based on four groups, an alpha level of .05, and the sample sizes in our study for

(continued)

TABLE 12.6 **Computer Output for One-Way Between-Subjects Analysis of Variance for Satisfaction with Maternal Relationship**

Test of Homogeneity of Variances

SMOTHER

Levene Statistic	df1	df2	Sig.
1.077	3	733	.358

Descriptives

SMOTHER

	N	Mean	Std. Deviation	Std. Error
Grp14	114	19.0000	9.4651	.8865
Grp15	270	21.0000	9.3370	.5682
Grp16	220	25.0000	10.3949	.7008
Grp17	133	29.0000	9.9285	.8609
Total	737	23.3284	9.7907	.3606

Anova

SMOTHER

	Sum of Squares	df	Mean Square	F	Sig.
Between Groups	300.980	3	100.327	1.047	.371
Within Groups	70250.455	733	95.840		
Total	70551.436	736			

what we considered to be a small population effect size—namely, an eta-squared of .03. Although we accomplished this using the procedure described in Cohen (1988), a rough estimate of power can be obtained from Appendix E.2.* Both approaches yield a statistical power that exceeds .95, which suggests that a Type II error is very unlikely.

There is no evidence that age is related to teen satisfaction with the maternal relationship. Thus, the data are not consistent with the predictions made by either of the theories described earlier. Perhaps the competing processes described by the two theories are both operating and their effects cancel one another out, thus yielding the similar mean scores for the four age groups. Future research or more fine-grained analyses can address this possibility.

* The table in Appendix E.2 for $df_{\text{BETWEEN}} = 3$ and an alpha level of .05 shows that the power for a population eta-squared of .03 will exceed .95 if there are 140 participants in each group. The average sample size in our example is $(114 + 270 + 220 + 133)/4 = 184.25$. This suggests that our power also exceeds .95.

Summary

One-way between-subjects analysis of variance is typically used to analyze the relationship between two variables when (1) the dependent variable is quantitative in nature and is measured on a level that at least approximates interval characteristics, (2) the independent variable is between-subjects in nature, and (3) the independent variable has three or more levels. The rationale for one-way analysis of variance is based on the partitioning of total variability into between-group and within-group components. Between-group variability reflects both sampling error and the effect of the independent variable on the dependent variable. Within-group variability reflects just sampling error. The ratio of variance measures (specifically, the mean square between and the mean square within) based on these sources of variability is called the F ratio. When certain conditions are met, a sampling distribution of the F ratio closely approximates an F distribution. This latter distribution is the basis for the F test used to test for a relationship between the independent and dependent variables.

The strength of the relationship is measured using eta-squared. Unstandardized effect sizes and confidence intervals can also be calculated. The nature of the relationship is analyzed using the Tukey HSD test. The HSD test ensures that the probability of making one or more Type I errors in a set of multiple comparisons will be equal to the specified alpha level.

Exercises

Answers to asterisked (*) exercises appear at the back of the book.

Exercises to Review Concepts

1. Under what conditions is one-way between-subjects analysis of variance typically used to analyze a bivariate relationship?

*2. What general form does the alternative hypothesis take for one-way between-subjects analysis of variance? Why can't it be summarized in a single mathematical statement?

*3. Distinguish between between-group variability and within-group variability.

4. What does between-group variability reflect? Why?

5. What does within-group variability reflect? Why?

*6. Under what circumstance will the F ratio, over the long run, approach 1.00? Under what circumstance will the F ratio, over the long run, be greater than 1.00?

7. Distinguish among the sum of squares total, the sum of squares between, and the sum of squares within. How are they interrelated?

*8. Consider the following scores in an experiment involving three conditions—A, B, and C:

A	B	C
3	5	7
3	5	7
3	5	7
3	5	7
3	5	7

Without actually computing the sum of squares within, what must its value be? Why?

*9. What is the relationship between the mean square between and the sum of squares between? What is the relationship between the mean square within and the sum of squares within?

10. What is the relationship between the mean square within and the pooled variance estimate?

*11. State the critical value of F for a one-way between-subjects analysis of variance for an alpha level of .05 under each of the following conditions:
   a. $k = 3, n = 7$
   b. $k = 4, n = 5$
   c. $k = 3, n = 10$
   d. $k = 5, n = 15$

12. What are the assumptions underlying one-way between-subjects analysis of variance?

*13. Insert the missing entries in the summary table for a one-way analysis of variance having three levels of the independent variable and $n = 20$.

Source	SS	df	MS	F
Between	—	—	—	—
Within	152.00	—	—
Total	182.00	—

14. Insert the missing entries in the summary table for a one-way analysis of variance having four levels of the independent variable.

Source	SS	df	MS	F
Between	—	—	18.00	3.60
Within	—	—	—
Total	—	23

15. What is the advantage, following rejection of the null hypothesis, of determining the nature of the relationship between an independent variable and a dependent variable with the Tukey HSD test rather than with multiple t tests?

*16. An investigator wanted to test the effect of marital status on attitudes toward divorce. A scale measuring attitudes on this issue was administered to 10 single, 10 married, and 10 divorced individuals. Scores could range from 1 to 12, with higher values representing more positive attitudes. The means and summary table are given here:

$$\overline{X}_S = 6.00 \quad \overline{X}_M = 8.00 \quad \overline{X}_D = 10.00$$

Source	SS	df	MS	F
Between	80.00	2	40.00	8.00
Within	135.00	27	5.00	
Total	215.00	29		

Analyze the nature of the relationship between marital status and attitudes toward divorce using the Tukey HSD test.

Use the following information to complete Exercises 17–20.

Suppose that a consumer group was interested in comparing the performance of three models of cars. Random samples of five owners were drawn from the list of owners of each model. These owners were asked how many times their cars had undergone major repairs in the past 2 years. The data follow:

Model 1	Model 2	Model 3
2	5	9
1	4	6
2	3	3
3	4	7
2	4	5

*17. Test for a relationship between the model of car and repair records using a one-way analysis of variance.

*18. Compute the value of eta-squared using Equation 12.15. Recalculate eta-squared using Equation 12.16. Compare the two results. Does the observed value represent a weak, moderate, or strong effect?

*19. Analyze the nature of the relationship between the model of car and repair records using the Tukey HSD test.

*20. Compute the 95% Tukey HSD confidence intervals.

Use the following information to complete Exercises 21–24.

An investigator tested the relationship between the supposed difficulty of a task and task performance. Twenty-four participants worked on the identical spatial ability task, but six of these individuals were led to believe that the task was of low difficulty, six were led to believe that the task was of moderate difficulty, six led to believe that the task was of high difficulty, and six were not given any information about the task's difficulty. Scores could range from 0 to 10, with higher values indicating better task performance. The data follow:

Low	Moderate	High	No information
8	6	4	4
7	7	1	5
5	4	2	5
8	5	4	6
9	4	6	8
7	6	3	6

21. Test for a relationship between the supposed task difficulty and task performance using a one-way analysis of variance.

22. Compute the value of eta-squared. Does the observed value represent a weak, moderate, or strong effect?

23. Analyze the nature of the relationship between the supposed task difficulty and task performance using the Tukey HSD test.

24. Compute the 95% Tukey HSD confidence intervals.

*25. Consider the following scores for two groups of people who were tested under either condition A or condition B:

A	B
6	12
4	10
5	11
3	9
7	13

Test for a relationship between the independent and dependent variables using the one-way analysis of variance procedures developed in this chapter. (*Note:* Even though one-way between-subjects analysis of variance is typically used when there are three or more groups, it can also be applied to the two-group situation.)

*26. Test for a relationship between the independent and dependent variables for the data in Exercise 25 using the procedures developed in Chapter 10 for a nondirectional independent groups t test. Square the observed value of t. Compare this result with the observed value of F from Exercise 25. Square the critical values of t. Compare this result with the critical value of F from Exercise 25. What does this indicate about the relationship between one-way between-subjects analysis of variance and the independent groups t test in the two-group case?

For each of the studies described in Exercises 27–29, indicate the appropriate statistical test for analyzing the relationship between the independent and dependent variables. Assume that the underlying assumptions of the tests have been satisfied.

*27. Barron (1965) administered an intelligence test to creative individuals in four occupations: mathematicians, writers, psychologists, and architects. The mean intelligence scores were compared for the four groups.

28. A researcher studied the ability of people to process information presented to their right

versus their left ear. Twelve individuals participated in the experiment. Headphones were used to present simultaneously one list of 20 words to participants' right ears and a different list of 20 words to participants' left ears. After the lists were presented, the participants were asked to recall as many words from each list as they could. The mean number of words recalled from the list presented to the right ear was compared with the mean number of words recalled from the list presented to the left ear.

29. An investigator examined the effect of practice on problem-solving performance. Study participants were randomly assigned to one of two conditions. Seventy-five individuals tried to solve 30 problems after having a 10-minute practice session on a similar set of problems. A different 75 individuals tried to solve the same 30 problems, but with no practice session. The average number of correct solutions was compared for participants in the practice versus the no-practice conditions.

*30. If a researcher suspects that the strength of the relationship between two variables in the population is .07 as indexed by eta-squared, what sample size should she use per group in a study involving four independent groups and an alpha level of .05 in order to achieve a power of .80?

31. Suppose an investigator conducts a study involving five independent groups with $n = 5$ per group. If the value of eta-squared in the population is .25, what would the power of his statistical test be at an alpha level of .05?

Multiple-Choice Questions

*32. The alternative hypothesis for one-way between-subjects analysis of variance states that
  a. the population means are all equal to one another
  b. specific population means are greater than specific other population means

  c. the sample means are not all equal to one another
  d. the population means are not all equal to one another

33. Researchers most commonly adopt an overall alpha level of .01 when applying the Tukey HSD test.
  a. true
  b. false

34. The F ratio is a ratio of _____ variability divided by _____ variability.
  a. between-group; within-group
  b. within-group; between-group
  c. between-subjects; within-subjects
  d. within-subjects; between-subjects

35. How many comparisons will be included in the set of multiple comparisons if the Tukey HSD test is applied to the five-group situation?
  a. 5
  b. 7
  c. 8
  d. 10

*36. Given a research report that states $F(2, 30) = 5.00$, $p < .05$, what is the strength of the relationship, as indexed by eta-squared?
  a. .06
  b. .25
  c. .50
  d. .96

Use the following information to complete Exercises 37–50.

A researcher examined the effects of three types of presentation formats on the recall of a speech. Ten participants were presented with a tape recording of a speech (the *audio-only* presentation), 10 were presented with a written text of the same speech (the *visual-only* presentation), and 10 were presented with both the tape recording and the written text (the *audio-visual* presentation). All participants then tried to recall the 15 major points that were covered in the speech. The mean number of points recalled was 2.00 in the audio-only condition, 4.00 in the visual-only condition, and 6.00 in the audio and visual condition. The summary table follows:

Source	SS	df	MS	F
Between	80.00	2	40.00	4.00
Within	270.00	27	10.00	
Total	350.00	29		

*37. If the value of eta-squared in the population is .15, what is the power of the statistical test at an alpha level of .05?
   a. .10
   b. .15
   c. .50
   d. .80

*38. The independent variable is
   a. the time interval between the presentation of the speech and trying to recall the major points
   b. the type of presentation format
   c. the number of participants in each condition
   d. the number of points recalled

39. The dependent variable is
   a. the time interval between the presentation of the speech and trying to recall the major points
   b. the type of presentation format
   c. the number of participants in each condition
   d. the number of points recalled

*40. Based on this study, we can conclude that the independent variable is related to the dependent variable.
   a. true
   b. false

*41. It is possible that the test results reflect a Type I error.
   a. true
   b. false

42. It is possible that the test results reflect a Type II error.
   a. true   b. false

*43. The strength of the relationship, as indexed by eta-squared, is
   a. .05
   b. .23
   c. .30
   d. .77

44. The proportion of variability in the dependent variable that is due to disturbance variables is
   a. .70
   b. .77
   c. .93
   d. This cannot be determined.

*45. What can we conclude about recall for the audio-only versus the visual-only presentation formats?
   a. Recall is better with the audio-only presentation.
   b. Recall is better with the visual-only presentation.
   c. Recall is the same for the two presentation formats.
   d. Recall may or may not differ for the two presentation formats.

46. What can we conclude about recall for the audio-only versus the audio-visual presentation formats?
   a. Recall is better with the audio-only presentation.
   b. Recall is better with the audio-visual presentation.
   c. Recall is the same for the two presentation formats.
   d. Recall may or may not differ for the two presentation formats.

47. What can we conclude about recall for the visual-only versus the audio-visual presentation formats?
   a. Recall is better with the visual-only presentation.
   b. Recall is better with the audio-visual presentation.
   c. Recall is the same for the two presentation formats.
   d. Recall may or may not differ for the two presentation formats.

*48. The 95% Tukey HSD confidence interval for the mean difference between the audio-only and the visual-only conditions is
  a. −5.51 to 1.51
  b. −6.50 to 2.50
  c. −6.50 to −.49
  d. −8.50 to .50
*49. The 95% Tukey HSD confidence interval for the mean difference between the audio-only and the audio-visual conditions is
  a. −5.51 to 1.51
  b. −6.50 to 2.50
  c. −7.51 to −.49
  d. −8.50 to .50
50. The 95% Tukey HSD confidence interval for the mean difference between the visual-only and the audio-visual conditions is
  a. −5.51 to 1.51
  b. −6.50 to 2.50
  c. −7.51 to −.49
  d. −8.50 to .50

Exercises to Apply Concepts

*51. One topic of interest to psychologists is jury decision making and the factors that influence jurors' judgments of guilt. One such variable is the defendant's race. Among the many studies in this area is an experiment cited by Stephen (1975) in which participants were presented with a transcript of a trial and asked to indicate the probability that the defendant was guilty. Judgments were made on a 0 to 10 scale, with higher scores representing a greater perceived probability of guilt. All participants read the same transcript. However, one-third of them were told that the defendant was white, another third were told that the defendant was African American, and the last third were told that the defendant was Hispanic.

The hypothetical data presented in the table are representative of the results of the study. Analyze these data, draw a conclusion, and write up your results using the principles developed in the Method of Presentation section.

White defendant	African American defendant	Hispanic defendant
6	10	10
7	10	6
2	9	10
3	4	5
5	4	10
0	10	5
1	10	2
0	10	10
6	3	2
0	10	10

52. Infants who are *securely attached* to their mothers generally seek to be near their mother and to have contact with her. These infants may or may not exhibit distress when separated from their mothers and are generally not anxious about being left alone. Infants who are *avoidant* tend to resist proximity and contact with the mother. Finally, infants who are *ambivalent* display proximity- and contact-seeking behaviors as well as proximity- and contact-avoiding behaviors (hence the term *ambivalent*). When separated from the mother, these infants tend to exhibit anger or become conspicuously passive until the mother returns.

In an attempt to learn more about the relationship between the type of attachment that is exhibited by infants and maternal behavior, Ainsworth, Blehar, Waters, and Wall (1978) conducted a study in which trained observers rated the extent to which the mother was sensitive to her child's signals and communications as the mother and infant interacted. Ratings were made on a 1 to 9 scale, with higher scores indicating greater sensitivity.

Hypothetical data representative of the results of the study are presented in the table.

Analyze these data, draw a conclusion, and write up your results using the principles developed in the Method of Presentation section.

Security	Avoidance	Ambivalence
5	1	3
9	5	3
9	1	1
5	1	1
9	5	3
5	5	1

53. One way in which psychologists study aggression is through the use of the *teacher–learner paradigm*. With this approach, two individuals at a time take part in a study that is presented as an investigation of the effect of punishment on learning. Unbeknownst to the actual participant, the second person in each pair is actually an experimental accomplice. The experimental procedures are such that the participant is always assigned the role of teacher and the accomplice is always assigned the role of learner, whose task is to memorize a list of word pairs. During the test phase, the teacher reads the first word of each pair, along with four response alternatives. Whenever the learner makes a mistake, the teacher is to punish him or her by delivering one or more electric shocks. The total number of shocks that are administered during the course of the experiment constitutes the measure of aggressive behavior. To ensure that all participants have the same opportunity to aggress, the accomplice makes errors in a predetermined sequence. In reality, no shocks are ever actually delivered; the teacher is only led to believe that they are.

As an example of how the teacher–learner paradigm can be used to learn about aggressive behavior, suppose that a researcher examines the effect of verbal provocation on aggression by assigning participants to conditions where the learner acts in a noninsulting, a mildly insulting, a moderately insulting, or a highly insulting manner. Hypothetical data for this study are presented in the table. Analyze these data, draw a conclusion, and write up your results using the principles developed in the Method of Presentation section.

Non-insulting	Mildly insulting	Moderately insulting	Highly insulting
8	12	16	21
8	16	15	16
10	14	23	27
12	10	20	18
8	16	14	32
8	8	21	27
15	10	18	23
8	8	15	24
10	17	18	30
8	15	17	26

54. An important aspect of how we perceive our social world is the causal attributions that we make for our own and other people's behavior. One basic distinction is between internal and external attributions. We make an *internal attribution* when we conclude that an individual's behavior reflects his or her personal characteristics. In contrast, we make an *external attribution* when we conclude that a person's behavior is due to factors that are beyond his or her control.

Many variables have been hypothesized to affect the type of attributions that we make. For instance, according to the *self-serving bias,* we tend to make internal attributions for our own positive outcomes and external attributions for our own negative outcomes. To determine whether a similar bias influences the way we perceive others, suppose that a researcher conducts a study in which some participants are informed that a target person received a very low score on an exam, some participants are informed that this person received an average score, and some participants are informed that this person scored very high. All participants are then asked to make attributions about the target person's performance on a 1 to 7 scale, where a score of 1 indicates that her performance was due entirely to internal factors such as ability and effort, and a score of 7 indicates that it was due entirely to external factors such as luck and the difficulty of the test.

Hypothetical data for this study are presented in the table. Analyze these data, draw a conclusion, and write up your results using the principles developed in the Method of Presentation section.

Very low	Average	Very high
4	5	6
3	3	5
2	4	4
4	3	5
3	5	6
5	2	6
4	5	4
4	4	5
3	3	6

One-Way Repeated Measures Analysis of Variance

13.1   Use of One-Way Repeated Measures Analysis of Variance

One-way repeated measures analysis of variance (abbreviated as *one-way repeated measures ANOVA*) is typically used to analyze the relationship between two variables when the following conditions are met:

1. The dependent variable is quantitative in nature and is measured on a level that at least approximates interval characteristics.

2. The independent variable is *within-subjects* in nature (it can be either qualitative or quantitative).

3. The independent variable has three or more levels.

In short, one-way repeated measures analysis of variance is used under the same circumstances as one-way between-subjects analysis of variance except that the independent variable is within-subjects rather than between-subjects in nature. Just as one-way between-subjects analysis of variance can be conceptualized as an extension of the independent groups *t* test for instances where the independent variable has more than two levels, one-way repeated measures analysis of variance can be conceptualized as an extension of the correlated groups *t* test.

Let us consider an example of an investigation that meets the conditions for this technique. Suppose that a consumer psychologist who is interested in the effect of label information on the perceived quality of wine conducts an experiment in which each participant tastes a wine and then rates its taste in three conditions. The ratings are made on a scale of 1 to 20, with higher scores indicating that the wine tasted better. In all three conditions, the wine is identical; however, in one condition the label indicates that it is a French wine, in a second condition the label indicates that it is an Italian wine, and in a third condition the label indicates that it is an American wine. The experiment is conducted as a within-subjects design in that each of the six participants tastes and rates the wines in the three different conditions. In order to counteract possible confounding variables associated with carry-over effects, the label presented first, second, and third is randomized for each participant.* The taste ratings are presented in Table 13.1.

In this experiment, the independent variable is the type of label, and it has three levels. It is within-subjects in nature because the same individuals participate in all three conditions. The dependent variable is the perceived quality of the wine as reflected in the taste ratings. It is quantitative in nature and is measured on a level that at least approximates interval characteristics. Given these conditions, one-way repeated measures analysis of variance is the statistical technique that would typically be used to analyze the relationship between the variables.

The mean score across conditions for each participant is calculated in column 5 of Table 13.1. Note that there is variability in the mean scores; some participants, on average, rated the wines higher than others. This reflects the influence of an important type of disturbance variable—individual differences. If we could remove

---

* The rationale for randomly ordering the sequence of conditions across participants as a way to deal with confounding variables associated with carry-over effects is discussed in Section 13.6.

TABLE 13.1 **Data for Wine Label and Perceived Quality Experiment**

Participant	French	Italian	American	$\overline{X}_i$
1	14	10	9	11.00
2	16	12	12	13.33
3	17	13	14	14.67
4	16	14	16	15.33
5	15	12	10	12.33
6	12	11	8	10.33
	$\Sigma X_F = 90$	$\Sigma X_I = 72$	$\Sigma X_A = 69$	
	$\overline{X}_F = 15.00$	$\overline{X}_I = 12.00$	$\overline{X}_A = 11.50$	

this influence, we could increase the sensitivity of the statistical test of the relationship between the independent and dependent variables.

When discussing the correlated groups t test in Chapter 11, we noted that an advantage of within-subjects designs is their ability to systematically remove variability due to individual differences from the dependent variable, and we developed the logic of extracting this source of variability in the two-group case. The same procedures can be used to generate a set of nullified scores when a within-subjects independent variable has more than two levels. The nullified data can then be analyzed to determine whether a relationship exists between the independent variable and the dependent variable after the effects of individual differences have been removed.

The results of this analysis would be identical to the results that would be obtained using the more computationally efficient procedures for one-way repeated measures analysis of variance that we describe in the following section. As with the correlated groups t test, the computational approach uses raw rather than nullified scores. For illustration, we return to the wine label and perceived quality experiment.

13.2 Inference of a Relationship Using One-Way Repeated Measures Analysis of Variance

Null and Alternative Hypotheses

The first of the three questions to be considered regarding the analysis of bivariate relationships is whether a relationship exists between the type of label and the perceived quality of the wine. The null hypothesis posits that the population means for the three types of labels are equal. If so, the type of label does not influence the perceived quality of the wine. The alternative hypothesis states that the three population means are not all equal to one another. If so, there is a relationship between the two variables. These hypotheses can be formally phrased as

H_0: $\mu_F = \mu_I = \mu_A$

H_1: The three population means are not all equal

where the subscripts "F," "I," and "A" denote the French, Italian, and American labels, respectively.

Partitioning of Variability

In Section 12.2, we demonstrated that the total variability in the dependent variable in a between-subjects design (the sum of squares total) can be partitioned into two components, one reflecting the influence of the independent variable (the sum of squares between) and one reflecting the influence of disturbance variables (the sum of squares within). We can also identify and partition the total variability when a repeated measures design is used. As before, the total variability in the dependent variable across all individuals and all conditions can be represented by the sum of squares total. This can be partitioned into three components: one reflecting the influence of the independent variable (the **sum of squares IV**), one reflecting the influence of individual differences (the **sum of squares across subjects**), and one reflecting the influence of disturbance variables other than individual differences (the **sum of squares error**).* Symbolically,

$$SS_{\text{TOTAL}} = SS_{\text{IV}} + SS_{\text{ACROSS SUBJECTS}} + SS_{\text{ERROR}} \qquad [13.1]$$

The sum of squares IV is conceptually equivalent to the sum of squares between in the between-subjects design that we discussed in Chapter 12. The sum of squares error and the sum of squares within are also conceptually equivalent because both reflect only the influence of disturbance variables.

The sum of squares across subjects has no counterpart in a between-subjects analysis of variance design. In fact, it is this component that differentiates the two approaches. When a between-subjects design is used, each score is provided by a different participant so it is not possible to estimate the effects of individual differences. Differences in background and personal characteristics (including such things as affinity for wine) thus contribute to sampling error, as reflected in the sum of squares within. However, when a repeated measures design is used, the influence of individual differences can be statistically removed from the dependent variable. This is reflected in the sum of squares across subjects and explains why a repeated measures analysis of variance is often a more sensitive test of the relationship between the independent and dependent variables than is a between-subjects analysis of variance: The sum of squares within in a between-subjects design includes the effects of individual differences, whereas the sum of squares error in a repeated measures design does not.

Thus, given a common data set, the mean square error, which forms the denominator for the F ratio that is used to test for a relationship between the independent and dependent variables in the repeated measures case, will tend to be smaller than the mean square within, which forms the denominator for the F ratio in the between-subjects case. To the extent that the mean square error is in fact smaller than the mean square within, a larger F ratio and a greater likelihood of rejecting the null hypothesis should result.[†]

---

* Some textbooks refer to the sum of squares across subjects as the *sum of squares between subjects*. However, we have found this latter terminology to be confusing to students.

† We return to the issue of the sensitivity of repeated measures versus between-subjects analysis of variance in Section 13.6.

Computation of the Sums of Squares

The formula for the sum of squares total is

$$SS_{TOTAL} = \sum X^2 = \frac{(\sum X)^2}{kN}$$ [13.2]

where $\sum X^2$ is the *sum of the squared scores* in the data set, $(\sum X)^2$ is the *square of the summed scores*, k is the number of conditions in the study (that is, the number of levels of the independent variable), and N is the sample size.

The data for the wine label and perceived quality experiment are reproduced in Table 13.2, where it can be seen that the sum of the 18 X^2 scores is

$$\sum X^2 = 196 + 256 + \cdots + 100 + 64 = 3,081$$

and the sum of the 18 X scores is

$$\sum X = 14 + 16 + \cdots + 10 + 8 = 231$$

Squaring the latter value and dividing by kN, we obtain

$$\frac{(\sum X)^2}{kN} = \frac{231^2}{(3)(6)} = 2,964.50$$

TABLE 13.2 **Data and Computation of the Sums of Squares for Wine Label and Perceived Quality Experiment**

Participant	French X	French X^2	Italian X	Italian X^2	American X	American X^2	s_i	s_i^2
1	14	196	10	100	9	81	33	1,089
2	16	256	12	144	12	144	40	1,600
3	17	289	13	169	14	196	44	1,936
4	16	256	14	196	16	256	46	2,116
5	15	225	12	144	10	100	37	1,369
6	12	144	11	121	8	64	31	961

$$T_F = 90 \qquad T_I = 72 \qquad T_A = 69$$
$$T_F^2 = 8,100 \qquad T_I^2 = 5,184 \qquad T_A^2 = 4,761$$

$$\sum X^2 = 196 + 256 + \cdots + 100 + 64 = 3,081$$

$$\sum X = 14 + 16 + \cdots + 10 + 8 = 231$$

$$\frac{(\sum X)^2}{kN} = \frac{231^2}{(3)(6)} = 2,964.50$$

$$\frac{\sum T_j^2}{k} = \frac{1,089 + 5,184 + 4,761}{6} = 3,007.50$$

$$\frac{\sum s_j^2}{k} = \frac{1,089 + 1,600 + 1,936 + 2,116 + 1,369 + 961}{3} = 3,023.67$$

Thus, the sum of squares total in this example is

$$SS_{TOTAL} = \sum X^2 = \frac{(\sum X)^2}{kN}$$
$$= 3,081 - 2,964.50 = 116.50$$

The formula for the sum of squares IV is

$$SS_{IV} = \frac{\sum T_j^2}{N} = \frac{(\sum X)^2}{kN} \qquad [13.3]$$

where T_j^2 is the square of the sum of the scores in condition j and all other terms are as defined previously. In our example, T_j^2 equals 8,100 for the French label, 5,184 for the Italian label, and 4,761 for the American label. Thus,

$$\frac{\sum T_j^2}{N} = \frac{8,100 + 5,184 + 4,761}{6} = 3,007.50$$

so

$$SS_{IV} = \frac{\sum T_j^2}{N} = \frac{(\sum X)^2}{kN}$$
$$= 3,007.50 - 2,964.50 = 43.00$$

The formula for the sum of squares across subjects is

$$SS_{ACROSS\ SUBJECTS} = \frac{\sum s_i^2}{k} - \frac{(\sum X)^2}{kN} \qquad [13.4]$$

where s_i^2 is the square of the sum of the scores for individual i and all other terms are as defined previously.

For instance, the first participant in Table 13.2 obtained a score of 14 in the French label condition, 10 in the Italian label condition, and 9 in the American label condition. The value of s_i^2 for this individual is thus $(14 + 10 + 9)^2 = 1,089$. The s_i^2 values for the other participants have been calculated in the last column of Table 13.2. We find that s_i^2 equals 1,600 for the second participant, 1,936 for the third, 2,116 for the fourth, 1,369 for the fifth, and 961 for the sixth. Thus,

$$\frac{\sum s_i^2}{k} = \frac{1,089 + 1,600 + 1,936 + 2,116 + 1,369 + 961}{3} = 3,023.67$$

so

$$SS_{ACROSS\ SUBJECTS} = \frac{\sum s_i^2}{k} - \frac{(\sum X)^2}{kN}$$
$$= 3,023.67 - 2,964.50 = 59.17$$

The formula for the sum of squares error is

$$SS_{ERROR} = \sum X^2 + \frac{(\sum X)^2}{kN} - \frac{\sum T_j^2}{N} - \frac{\sum s_i^2}{k} \qquad [13.5]$$

where all terms are as defined above. In our example,

$$SS_{\text{ERROR}} = 3,081 + 2,964.50 - 3,007.50 - 3,023.67 = 14.33$$

Of course, given that the sum of squares total is equal to the sum of squares IV plus the sum of squares across subjects plus the sum of squares error, if three of these quantities have already been calculated, the fourth can be determined through simple algebraic manipulation. For instance, we could have obtained the sum of squares error as follows:

$$SS_{\text{ERROR}} = SS_{\text{TOTAL}} - SS_{\text{IV}} - SS_{\text{ACROSS SUBJECTS}}$$

$$= 116.50 - 43.00 - 59.17 = 14.33$$

This relationship reflects the fact that, as noted above, the sum of squares error represents the influence of disturbance variables other than individual differences—that is, variability in the dependent variable that remains after the effects of the independent variable and individual differences have been partitioned out.

However, it usually is a good idea to calculate all four sums of squares using the formulas above. This allows us to check for computational errors by determining whether the calculated values of the sum of squares IV, the sum of squares across subjects, and the sum of squares error add up to the calculated value of the sum of squares total.

Derivation of the Summary Table

Each of the sums of squares above has a certain number of degrees of freedom associated with it. These are calculated as follows:*

$$df_{\text{IV}} = k - 1 \tag{13.6}$$

$$df_{\text{ACROSS SUBJECTS}} = N - 1 \tag{13.7}$$

$$df_{\text{ERROR}} = (k - 1)(N - 1) \tag{13.8}$$

As with the sums of squares, the degrees of freedom are additive:

$$df_{\text{TOTAL}} = df_{\text{IV}} + df_{\text{ACROSS SUBJECTS}} + df_{\text{ERROR}} \tag{13.9}$$

Because $df_{\text{IV}} = k - 1$, $df_{\text{ACROSS SUBJECTS}} = N - 1$, and $df_{\text{ERROR}} = (k - 1)(N - 1)$, $df_{\text{TOTAL}} = (k - 1) + (N - 1) + [(k - 1)(N - 1)]$. Because this reduces to $k - 1 + N - 1 + N - 1 + (kN - k - N + 1) = kN - 1$, the degrees of freedom total can be calculated directly as

$$df_{\text{TOTAL}} = kN - 1 \tag{13.10}$$

---

* The rationale for the equivalence of the degrees of freedom to the indicated quantities is conceptually similar to that discussed in Section 12.2 for the degrees of freedom in the between-subjects case.

In our example,

$$df_{IV} = 3 - 1 = 2$$

$$df_{ACROSS\ SUBJECTS} = 6 - 1 = 5$$

$$df_{ERROR} = (3 - 1)(6 - 1) = 10$$

$$df_{TOTAL} = (3)(6) - 1 = 17$$

In order to test the null hypothesis of equal population means, it is necessary to calculate mean squares for the independent variable and error components. These are obtained by dividing the relevant sums of squares by their degrees of freedom:

$$MS_{IV} = \frac{SS_{IV}}{df_{IV}} \qquad [13.11]$$

$$= \frac{43.00}{2} = 21.50$$

$$MS_{ERROR} = \frac{SS_{ERROR}}{df_{ERROR}} \qquad [13.12]$$

$$= \frac{14.33}{10} = 1.43$$

The mean square across subjects, on the other hand, does not directly figure in the *F* test that constitutes the test statistic and, thus, is not typically calculated. This is consistent with the fact that the sole function of the sum of squares across subjects is to remove variability due to individual differences from the dependent variable in order to create a more sensitive test of the relationship between the independent and dependent variables.

The *F* test for one-way repeated measures analysis of variance follows the same general logic outlined in Chapter 12 for one-way between-subjects analysis of variance. First, we form an *F* ratio by dividing the mean square IV by the mean square error. If the null hypothesis is true, both of these components reflect only sampling error. Thus, we would expect the *F* ratio, over the long run, to approach 1.00. If the null hypothesis is not true, the mean square error again reflects sampling error but the mean square IV reflects both sampling error and the effect of the independent variable on the dependent variable. We would thus expect the *F* ratio, over the long run, to be greater than 1.00.

Next, we compare the observed value of *F* with the appropriate critical value of *F* from Appendix F. If the observed value of *F* exceeds the critical value of *F*, we reject the null hypothesis and conclude that there is a relationship between the independent and dependent variables. Otherwise, we fail to reject the null hypothesis.

The *F* ratio for one-way repeated measures analysis of variance is*

$$F = \frac{MS_{IV}}{MS_{ERROR}} \qquad [13.13]$$

---

* Analogous to the between-subjects case, the *F* distribution in the two-group within-subjects situation bears a mathematical relationship to the *t* distribution such that the value of *F* obtained using Equation 13.13 will be equal to the square of the *t* score that would be obtained if a correlated groups *t* test were applied to the same data.

which in our example equals

$$F = \frac{21.50}{1.43} = 15.03$$

As we did with one-way between-subjects analysis of variance in Chapter 12, we can summarize our calculations in a summary table:

Source	SS	df	MS	F
IV	43.00	2	21.50	15.03
Error	14.33	10	1.43	
Across subjects	59.17	5		
Total	116.50	17		

When reporting an *F* value for one-way repeated measures analysis of variance it is conventional to present the degrees of freedom IV followed by the degrees of freedom error. For an alpha level of .05 and $df_{IV} = 2$ and $df_{ERROR} = 10$, the critical value of *F* from Appendix F is 4.10. Because the observed *F* value of 15.03 exceeds the critical value we reject the null hypothesis and conclude that there is a relationship between the type of label and the perceived quality of the wine.

STUDY EXERCISE 13.1

An investigator studied the effect of exercise on psychological well-being by placing five volunteers on an aerobic exercise regimen and having them respond to a measure of psychological well-being before beginning the exercise regimen and 2, 4, and 6 weeks later. Scores on this measure could range from 1 to 70, with higher values indicating greater psychological well-being. All participants were of normal weight and health, and none was presently involved in a physical fitness program. The well-being scores for the four assessments are listed in the table below. Test for a relationship between the amount of exercise and psychological well-being using a one-way repeated measures analysis of variance.

Individual	0 weeks	2 weeks	4 weeks	6 weeks
1	60	59	63	68
2	52	53	58	61
3	61	67	69	69
4	44	46	50	50
5	63	62	66	67

Answer   The null and alternative hypotheses can be stated as follows:

$H_0: \mu_Z = \mu_T = \mu_F = \mu_S$

H_1: The four population means are not all equal

where the subscripts "*Z*," "*T*," "*F*," and "*S*" represent 0 (zero), 2, 4, and 6 weeks of exercise, respectively.

The intermediate statistics necessary for calculating the sums of squares are computed as follows:

Individual	0 Weeks		2 Weeks		4 Weeks		6 Weeks		s_i	s_i^2
	X	X^2	X	X^2	X	X^2	X	X^2		
1	60	3,600	59	3,481	63	3,969	68	4,624	250	62,500
2	52	2,704	53	2,809	58	3,364	61	3,721	224	50,176
3	61	3,721	67	4,489	69	4,761	69	4,761	266	70,756
4	44	1,936	46	2,116	50	2,500	50	2,500	190	36,100
5	63	3,969	62	3,844	66	4,356	67	4,489	258	66,564

$$T_Z = 280 \qquad T_T = 287 \qquad T_F = 306 \qquad T_S = 315$$

$$\overline{X}_Z = 56.00 \qquad \overline{X}_T = 57.40 \qquad \overline{X}_F = 61.20 \qquad \overline{X}_S = 63.00$$

$$T_Z^2 = 78,400 \qquad T_T^2 = 82,369 \qquad T_F^2 = 93,636 \qquad T_S^2 = 99,225$$

$$\sum X^2 = 3,600 + 2,704 + \cdots + 2,500 + 4,489 = 71,714$$

$$\sum X = 60 + 52 + \cdots + 50 + 67 = 1,188$$

$$\frac{(\sum X)^2}{kN} = \frac{1,188^2}{(4)(5)} = 70,567.20$$

$$\frac{\sum T_i^2}{N} = \frac{78,400 + 82,369 + 93,636 + 99,225}{5} = 70,726.00$$

$$\frac{\sum s_i^2}{k} = \frac{62,500 + 50,176 + 70,756 + 36,100 + 66,564}{4} = 71,524.00$$

Applying Equations 13.2–13.5, we obtain the following values:

$$SS_{IV} = \frac{\sum T_i^2}{N} - \frac{(\sum X)^2}{kN}$$

$$= 70,726.00 - 70,567.20 = 158.80$$

$$SS_{ACROSS\ SUBJECTS} = \frac{\sum s_i^2}{k} - \frac{(\sum X)^2}{kN}$$

$$= 71,524.00 - 70,567.20 = 956.80$$

$$SS_{ERROR} = \sum X^2 + \frac{(\sum X)^2}{kN} - \frac{\sum T_i^2}{N} - \frac{\sum s_i^2}{k}$$

$$= 71,714 + 70,567.20 - 70,726.00 - 71,524.00 = 31.20$$

$$SS_{TOTAL} = \sum X^2 - \frac{(\sum X)^2}{kN}$$

$$= 71,714 - 70,567.20 = 1,146.80$$

The degrees of freedom are calculated using Equations 13.6, 13.7, 13.8, and 13.10:

$$df_{IV} = k - 1 = 4 - 1 = 3$$

$$df_{ACROSS\ SUBJECTS} = N - 1 = 5 - 1 = 4$$

$$df_{ERROR} = (k - 1)(N - 1) = (4 - 1)(5 - 1) = 12$$

$$df_{TOTAL} = kN - 1 = (4)(5) - 1 = 19$$

The mean square IV and the mean square error are then calculated by dividing the corresponding sums of squares by their degrees of freedom:

$$MS_{IV} = \frac{SS_{IV}}{df_{IV}} = \frac{158.80}{3} = 52.93$$

$$MS_{ERROR} = \frac{SS_{ERROR}}{df_{ERROR}} = \frac{31.20}{12} = 2.60$$

Finally, the F ratio is derived by dividing the mean square IV by the mean square error:

$$F = \frac{MS_{IV}}{MS_{ERROR}} = \frac{52.93}{2.60} = 20.36$$

These calculations yield the following summary table:

Source	SS	df	MS	F
IV	158.80	3	52.93	20.36
Error	31.20	12	2.60	
Across subjects	956.80	4		
Total	1,146.80	19		

The critical value of F from Appendix F for an alpha level of .05 and $df_{IV} = 3$ and $df_{ERROR} = 12$ is 3.49. Because the observed F value of 20.36 exceeds the critical value, we reject the null hypothesis and conclude that a relationship exists between the amount of exercise and psychological well-being.

Assumptions of the *F* Test

The *F* test for one-way repeated measures analysis of variance is appropriate when the dependent variable is quantitative in nature and measured on a level that at least approximates interval characteristics. Its validity rests on the following assumptions:

1. The sample is independently and randomly selected from the population of interest.

2. Each population of scores is normally distributed.

3. The variance of the population difference scores for any two conditions is the same as the variance of the population difference scores for any other two conditions. This is known as the **sphericity** assumption.

As an example of the sphericity assumption, the variance of the scores that we would obtain across the population by subtracting individuals' scores in the Italian label condition and perceived quality experiment from their scores in the French label condition is assumed to be the same as the variance of the scores that we would obtain by subtracting individuals' scores in the American label condition from their scores in the French and the Italian label conditions.

As with one-way between-subjects analysis of variance, the assumption of independent and random sampling is important for the validity of the F test. However, the F test is quite robust to violations of the normality assumption. For sample sizes larger than 30, the Type I error rate remains near the specified alpha level even in the face of marked nonnormality.

In contrast, the F test is not robust to violations of sphericity. This is important because many applications in the behavioral sciences almost certainly violate this assumption, sometimes substantially. Because of this, many statisticians recommend that the traditional F test be modified unless one is confident that sphericity holds. This modification takes the form of multiplying the degrees of freedom IV and the degrees of freedom error by an *adjustment factor* to obtain new degrees of freedom to be used in assessing the significance of the observed F ratio.

Two of the most frequently encountered adjustment factors are the *Huynh–Feldt epsilon* and the *Greenhouse–Geisser epsilon*. Both approaches result in adjusted degrees of freedom that are less than or equal to the usual degrees of freedom of $df_{IV} = k - 1$ and $df_{ERROR} = (k - 1)(N - 1)$. To the extent that the degrees of freedom are reduced, the critical value for F will be larger. This serves to decrease the Type I error rate below what it would otherwise be and, thus, to increase the robustness of the statistical test to violations of the sphericity assumption.

Unfortunately, the formulas for calculating the adjustment factors are complex and difficult to apply by hand. However, most statistical computer programs provide both the Huynh–Feldt epsilon and the Greenhouse–Geisser epsilon as part of the statistical output for repeated measures analysis of variance.

The **Mauchly test** has been proposed as a way to evaluate the probable violation of sphericity in a repeated measures design. Unfortunately, studies have suggested that this test is often of little diagnostic value, in part because it is highly sensitive to nonnormality in the data (Kesselman, Rogan, Mendoza, and Breen, 1980). Thus, unless one is confident on theoretical grounds that sphericity holds, we recommend that an adjustment factor be applied to the degrees of freedom IV and the degrees of freedom error regardless of the results of the Mauchly test.* The Huynh–Feldt procedure is the preferred alternative for most applications in the behavioral sciences, although there are scenarios where other adjustments may be preferred (Maxwell and Delaney, 1990).

---

* All of the examples in this chapter assume that the sphericity assumption is satisfied.

13.3 Strength of the Relationship

The second of the three questions to be addressed regarding the analysis of bivariate relationships is how strong the relationship is. We will determine this using eta-squared.* The formula for computing eta-squared for one-way repeated measures analysis of variance is[†]

$$\text{eta}^2 = \frac{SS_{\text{IV}}}{SS_{\text{IV}} + SS_{\text{ERROR}}} \qquad [13.14]$$

As with the correlated groups *t* test, eta-squared in the context of one-way repeated measures analysis of variance represents the proportion of variability in the dependent variable that is associated with the independent variable *after variability due to individual differences has been removed.*

The strength of the relationship for the wine label and perceived quality experiment is

$$\text{eta}^2 = \frac{43.00}{43.00 + 14.33} = .75$$

In this experiment, 75% of the variability in the dependent variable (the perceived quality of the wine) is associated with the independent variable (the type of label) after the influence of individual differences has been removed. This represents a strong effect.

An alternative formula for eta-squared based on the degrees of freedom and the observed value of *F* is

$$\text{eta}^2 = \frac{(df_{\text{IV}})F}{(df_{\text{IV}})F + df_{\text{ERROR}}} \qquad [13.15]$$

For the wine label and perceived quality experiment,

$$\text{eta}^2 = \frac{(2)(15.03)}{(2)(15.03) + 10} = .75$$

which is the same result as obtained above.

We can also specify the strength of the relationship in unstandardized terms. As we did with one-way between-subjects analysis of variance, we will discuss unstandardized effect sizes and confidence intervals after we learn how to determine the nature of the relationship.

---

* As we discussed in Section 10.4, eta-squared is a biased estimator of the strength of the relationship between two variables. The formula for epsilon-squared, a commonly-used unbiased estimator of relationship strength, is provided in Appendix N for the one-way repeated measures analysis of variance situation.

[†] The denominator of Equation 13.14 is often called the *sum of squares within subjects*; that is, $SS_{\text{WITHIN SUBJECTS}} = SS_{\text{IV}} + SS_{\text{ERROR}}$. This should not be confused with the sum of squares within (SS_{WITHIN}) that represents variability within *groups* in the case of one-way between-subjects analysis of variance.

STUDY EXERCISE 13.2

Calculate eta-squared for the data in Study Exercise 13.1.

Answer   Eta-squared is most easily calculated using Equation 13.14:

$$\text{eta}^2 = \frac{SS_{IV}}{SS_{IV} + SS_{ERROR}}$$

$$= \frac{158.80}{158.80 + 31.20} = .84$$

This represents a strong effect.

13.4 Nature of the Relationship

The third of the three questions to be addressed regarding the analysis of bivariate relationships is what the nature of the relationship is. The procedure for determining this in the case of one-way repeated measures analysis of variance differs depending on whether or not the assumption of sphericity is satisfied. If one is confident that the sphericity assumption is met, then a Tukey HSD test conceptually similar to the one that we discussed in Chapter 12 for one-way between-subjects analysis of variance is applied. The only differences are that N and MS_{ERROR} replace n and MS_{WITHIN} in the formula for the critical difference, and that the value of q is determined with reference to the overall alpha level, the degrees of freedom error, and k (the number of conditions in the study) rather than the overall alpha level, the degrees of freedom within, and k.

Specifically, the critical difference for the Tukey HSD test in the repeated measures case is defined as

$$CD = q\sqrt{\frac{MS_{ERROR}}{N}} \qquad\qquad [13.16]$$

Referring to Appendix G, we find that for an overall alpha level of .05, $df_{ERROR} = 10$, and $k = 3$, q is equal to 3.88. Thus, the critical difference for the wine label and perceived quality experiment is

$$CD = 3.88\sqrt{\frac{1.43}{6}} = 1.89$$

This value will be used to make decisions with respect to the three sets of null and alternative hypotheses that we can phrase for this study. The first set of hypotheses addresses the means for the French and the Italian labels:

$H_0: \ \mu_F = \mu_I$

$H_1: \ \mu_F \neq \mu_I$

The absolute difference between the sample means is $|\overline{X}_F - \overline{X}_I| = |15.00 - 12.00| = 3.00$. Because 3.00 exceeds the critical difference of 1.89, we reject the null hypothesis for the comparison. An examination of the sample means indicates that the wine will be rated as tasting better when it is labeled as French ($\overline{X}_F = 15.00$) than when it is labeled as Italian ($\overline{X}_I = 12.00$).

The second set of hypotheses addresses the means for the French and the American labels:

H_0: $\mu_F = \mu_A$
H_1: $\mu_F \neq \mu_A$

The absolute difference between the sample means is $|\overline{X}_F - \overline{X}_A| = |15.00 - 11.50| = 3.50$. Because 3.50 is greater than 1.89, we reject the null hypothesis and accept the alternative hypothesis for the comparison. An examination of the sample means indicates that the wine will be rated as tasting better when it is labeled as French ($\overline{X}_F = 15.00$) than when it is labeled as American ($\overline{X}_A = 11.50$).

The third set of hypotheses addresses the means for the Italian and the American labels:

H_0: $\mu_I = \mu_A$
H_1: $\mu_I \neq \mu_A$

The absolute difference between the sample means is $|\overline{X}_I - \overline{X}_A| = |12.00 - 11.50| = .50$. Because .50 does not exceed 1.89, we fail to reject the null hypothesis for the comparison. Thus, we are unable to conclude that the wine will be rated differently when it is labeled as Italian than when it is labeled as American.

As we did with one-way between-subjects analysis of variance, we can summarize the results of the entire analysis in a table. As with the between-subjects case, for the sake of brevity, this does not explicitly refer to the alternative hypotheses:

Null hypothesis tested	Absolute difference between sample means	Value of CD	Null hypothesis rejected?
$\mu_F = \mu_I$	$\|15.00 - 12.00\| = 3.00$	1.89	Yes
$\mu_F = \mu_A$	$\|15.00 - 11.50\| = 3.50$	1.89	Yes
$\mu_I = \mu_A$	$\|12.00 - 11.50\| = .50$	1.89	No

This format allows us to readily discern the nature of the relationship between the type of label and the perceived quality of the wine: The wine will be rated as tasting better when it is labeled as French ($\overline{X}_F = 15.00$) than when it is labeled as either Italian ($\overline{X}_I = 12.00$) or American ($\overline{X}_A = 11.50$). However, we cannot conclude that the wine will be rated differently as a function of being labeled as Italian versus American.

If the sphericity assumption is violated, then the HSD test is not appropriate for evaluating the nature of the relationship. Instead, we can use a *modified Bonferroni procedure*, as is described in Appendix 13.1.

STUDY EXERCISE 13.3

Analyze the nature of the relationship between the amount of exercise and psychological well-being for the data in Study Exercise 13.1 using the Tukey HSD test.

Answer   The first step in applying the HSD test is to phrase the six sets of null and alternative hypotheses. The former are listed in the following table.

We next calculate the critical difference. Referring to Appendix G, we find that for an overall alpha level of .05, $df_{ERROR} = 12$, and $k = 4$, q is equal to 4.20. Thus,

$$CD = q\sqrt{\frac{MS_{ERROR}}{N}}$$

$$= 4.20\sqrt{\frac{2.60}{5}} = 3.03$$

The HSD test can now be applied by comparing the absolute difference between the sample means for the two groups involved in a comparison with the critical difference, deciding whether or not the corresponding null hypothesis should be rejected, and, if it is, comparing the two sample means to make a decision about how the two population means differ. However, for the sake of brevity, we do not explicitly show these steps here. We can, however, summarize them in a table as follows:

Null hypothesis tested	Absolute difference between sample means	Value of CD	Null hypothesis rejected?
$\mu_Z = \mu_T$	$\lvert 56.00 - 57.40 \rvert = 1.40$	3.03	No
$\mu_Z = \mu_F$	$\lvert 56.00 - 61.20 \rvert = 5.20$	3.03	Yes
$\mu_Z = \mu_S$	$\lvert 56.00 - 63.00 \rvert = 7.00$	3.03	Yes
$\mu_T = \mu_F$	$\lvert 57.40 - 61.20 \rvert = 3.80$	3.03	Yes
$\mu_T = \mu_S$	$\lvert 57.40 - 63.00 \rvert = 5.60$	3.03	Yes
$\mu_F = \mu_S$	$\lvert 61.20 - 63.00 \rvert = 1.80$	3.03	No

The nature of the relationship is such that psychological well-being will be greater after 4 $(\overline{X}_F = 61.20)$ or 6 $(\overline{X}_S = 63.00)$ weeks of aerobic exercise than before beginning the exercise regimen $(\overline{X}_Z = 56.00)$ or after exercising for only 2 weeks $(\overline{X}_T = 57.40)$. However, we cannot conclude that 2 weeks of exercise affects psychological well-being relative to no exercise or that 6 weeks of exercise affects psychological well-being relative to 4 weeks of exercise.

13.5 Unstandardized Effect Sizes and Confidence Intervals

Unstandardized effect sizes and confidence intervals for the one-way repeated measures case are calculated exactly as they are for the one-way between-subjects case. The unstandardized effect sizes are provided by the difference between each pair of sample means, and a 95% confidence interval can be calculated for each pairwise comparison of means using the formula

$$CI = (\overline{X}_i - \overline{X}_j) - CD \quad \text{to} \quad (\overline{X}_i - \overline{X}_j) + CD \qquad [13.17]$$

where $\overline{X}_i$ is the mean for one of the conditions being considered, $\overline{X}_j$ is the mean for the other condition, and CD is the critical difference for the Tukey HSD test.

The value of the critical difference for the wine label and perceived quality experiment is 1.89. Thus, the 95% Tukey HSD confidence interval for the mean difference between the French and the Italian labels is

$$CI = (15.00 - 12.00) - 1.89 \quad \text{to} \quad (15.00 - 12.00) + 1.89$$

$$= 1.11 \quad \text{to} \quad 4.89$$

The 95% HSD confidence interval for the mean difference between the French and the American labels is

$$CI = (15.00 - 11.50) - 1.89 \quad \text{to} \quad (15.00 - 11.50) + 1.89$$

$$= 1.61 \quad \text{to} \quad 5.39$$

Finally, the 95% HSD confidence interval for the mean difference between the Italian and the American labels is

$$CI = (12.00 - 11.50) - 1.89 \quad \text{to} \quad (12.00 - 11.50) + 1.89$$

$$= -1.39 \quad \text{to} \quad 2.39$$

We are 95% confident that the true population mean differences fall within these intervals when they are considered simultaneously.

13.6 Methodological Considerations

The sum of squares across subjects for the wine label and perceived quality experiment is 59.17. This constitutes a relatively large portion of the total sum of squares (116.50), which indicates that individual differences played an important role in the taste ratings. One way to examine the extent of this influence is to compare the observed F ratio with the F ratio that would have been observed if the experiment had been conducted using a between-subjects rather than a repeated measures design (that is, if each wine had been rated by six *different* individuals) and the same data had been obtained.

As we discussed in Section 13.2, because it is not possible to identify the effects of individual differences in a between-subjects analysis, variability due to individual differences contributes to the sum of squares within along with all of the other disturbance variables that are operating. Not surprisingly, then, the sum of squares within from a one-way between-subjects analysis of variance is mathematically equal to the total of the sum of squares across subjects (which reflects the influence of individual differences) and the sum of squares error (which reflects the influence of disturbance variables other than individual differences) from a one-way repeated measures analysis of variance applied to the same scores. Furthermore, given a common data set, the degrees of freedom within in the between-subjects case is mathematically equal to the total of the degrees of freedom across subjects and the degrees of freedom error in the repeated measures case. Also, the sum of squares and degrees of freedom between are mathematically equal to the sum of squares and degrees of freedom IV, respectively.

Thus, if the wine label and perceived quality data had been obtained using a between-subjects design, the summary table would take the following form:

Source	SS	df	MS	F
Between	43.00	2	21.50	4.39
Within	73.50	15	4.90	
Total	116.50	17		

Note that the F ratio is 4.39, as compared with the F ratio of 15.03 that was obtained when a repeated measures analysis was applied. Because the mean square IV and the mean square between are identical, the difference in F ratios must be due to a difference in the denominator of the F test. Indeed, a comparison of the two summary tables shows that the denominator of the F ratio increased from 1.43 (the mean square error) to 4.90 (the mean square within) when variability due to individual differences was not separately removed from the dependent variable.

Although the F test in this case is still statistically significant (because the critical value of F for an alpha level of .05 and 2 degrees of freedom between and 15 degrees of freedom within is 3.68), there will be instances where the F ratio yielded by a repeated measures analysis of variance will be large enough to lead to rejection of a false null hypothesis, whereas the F ratio yielded by the corresponding between-subjects analysis will not be. It is in this sense that a repeated measures analysis of variance is often a more sensitive test of the relationship between the independent and dependent variables than is a between-subjects analysis of variance.

On the other hand, the degrees of freedom for the denominator of the F test will always be less in the repeated measures case than in the between-subjects case. Because the value of F required to reject the null hypothesis becomes more extreme as the degrees of freedom become smaller, a repeated measures analysis of variance might actually be less powerful than a between-subjects analysis of variance when individual differences have only a minimal influence on the dependent variable. This is parallel to the situation that exists with the independent and correlated groups t tests, as we discussed in Section 11.6. Thus, as we noted in that section, it is important that a researcher who is considering a within-subjects (repeated measures) design accurately anticipate the role of individual differences.

We saw in Section 11.5 that one way to deal with confounding due to carry-over effects is *counterbalancing*. This involves exposing individuals to *predetermined* sequences of the independent variable such that carry-over effects are evenly distributed across conditions. This technique turns any confounding variables that are associated with the treatment order into disturbance variables.

An alternative to counterbalancing as a means for controlling confounding variables is to *randomly* order the conditions for each participant. This is the approach that was taken in the wine label and perceived quality experiment. The rationale is that when the sequence of conditions across participants is randomly determined, chance will ensure that each condition occurs in each position an approximately equal number of times and, thus, that carry-over effects are evenly distributed across conditions. Thus, any carry-over effects should influence the quality ratings in the three label conditions to an equal extent.* In this way, any confounding variables that are associated with the treatment order the are turned into disturbance variables instead.

The eta-squared value of .75 in the present instance indicates that, after variability due to individual differences has been removed, $1 - .75 = .25$ of the variability in the quality ratings is associated with disturbance variables other than individual differences. Included in this figure is any variability that is due to the treatment order.

Randomly ordering the conditions for each participant is particularly useful when the number of conditions is so great that counterbalancing is impractical. For instance, there are 24 ways that four conditions can be ordered and 120 ways that five conditions can be ordered!† Can you think of some potential confounding variables that might have been counteracted in the wine label and perceived quality experiment by using a randomization procedure?

13.7 Numerical Example

One area of interest to cognitive psychologists is memory. To examine the role that the amount of exposure to a stimulus plays in the memory process, suppose that a cognitive psychologist conducts an experiment in which the same list of 10 nonsense syllables (for instance, *blux, gonk,* and *delp*) is presented to participants four different times. The list is presented for 30 seconds on each occasion, and participants are given 60 seconds to recall as many of the syllables as they can after the list is removed. The test sessions are separated by 10 minutes, during which time participants work on a math task designed to occupy their thoughts so that they will not be able to practice the nonsense syllables. Hypothetical data for the seven experimental participants are presented in Table 13.3.

The null hypothesis is that the four population means are equal. If so, there is no relationship between the amount of exposure and recall. The alternative hypothesis is that the population means are not all equal. If so, there is a relationship between the amount of exposure and recall. These hypotheses can be formally stated as

H_0: $\mu_1 = \mu_2 = \mu_3 = \mu_4$

H_1: The four population means are not all equal

where the subscripts "1," "2," "3," and "4" represent the four test sessions.

---

* Consistent with the two-group within-subjects case that we discussed in Section 11.5, carry-over effects will generally influence the dependent variable equally in all conditions when the nature of such effects is the same for all levels of the independent variable. Otherwise, the dependent variable will generally be affected differently across conditions.
† This can be determined using the formula for permutations (Equation 6.10) that was presented in Chapter 6: $_nP_r = n!/(n - r)!$. For instance, the number of permutations of five conditions taken five at a time is $5!/(5 - 5)! = [(5)(4)(3)(2)(1)]/1 = 120$.

The intermediate statistics necessary for calculating the sums of squares are given in Table 13.3. The sum of squares IV is

$$SS_{IV} = \frac{\sum T_j^2}{N} - \frac{(\sum X)^2}{kN}$$

$$= 1{,}306.71 - 1{,}302.89 = 3.82$$

The sum of squares across subjects is

$$SS_{ACROSS\ SUBJECTS} = \frac{\sum s_i^2}{k} - \frac{(\sum X)^2}{kN}$$

$$= 1{,}384.75 - 1{,}302.89 = 81.86$$

TABLE 13.3 **Data and Computation of the Sums of Squares for Amount of Exposure and Recall Experiment**

Participant	Time 1 X	Time 1 X^2	Time 2 X	Time 2 X^2	Time 3 X	Time 3 X^2	Time 4 X	Time 4 X^2	s_i	s_i^2
1	5	25	6	36	6	36	5	25	22	484
2	7	49	6	36	7	49	8	64	28	784
3	8	64	9	81	9	81	10	100	36	1,296
4	3	9	4	16	4	16	6	36	17	289
5	9	81	8	64	9	81	7	49	33	1,089
6	5	25	4	16	6	36	6	36	21	441
7	7	49	10	100	8	64	9	81	34	1,156

$$T_1 = 44 \qquad T_2 = 47 \qquad T_3 = 49 \qquad T_4 = 51$$

$$\overline{X}_1 = 6.29 \qquad \overline{X}_2 = 6.71 \qquad \overline{X}_3 = 7.00 \qquad \overline{X}_4 = 7.29$$

$$T_1^2 = 1{,}936 \qquad T_2^2 = 2{,}209 \qquad T_3^2 = 2{,}401 \qquad T_4^2 = 2{,}601$$

$$\sum X^2 = 25 + 49 + \cdots + 36 + 81 = 1{,}405$$

$$\sum X = 5 + 7 + \cdots + 6 + 9 = 191$$

$$\frac{(\sum X)^2}{kN} = \frac{191^2}{(4)(7)} = 1{,}302.89$$

$$\frac{\sum T_j^2}{N} = \frac{1{,}936 + 2{,}209 + 2{,}401 + 2{,}601}{7} = 1{,}306.71$$

$$\frac{\sum s_i^2}{k} = \frac{484 + 784 + 1{,}296 + 289 + 1{,}089 + 441 + 1{,}156}{4} = 1{,}384.75$$

The sum of squares error is

$$SS_{ERROR} = \sum X^2 + \frac{(\sum X)^2}{kN} - \frac{\sum T_j^2}{N} - \frac{\sum s_i^2}{k}$$

$$= 1{,}405 + 1{,}302.89 - 1{,}306.71 - 1{,}384.75 = 16.43$$

Finally, the sum of squares total is

$$SS_{TOTAL} = \sum X^2 - \frac{(\sum X)^2}{kN}$$

$$= 1{,}405 - 1{,}302.89 = 102.11$$

The degrees of freedom are

$$df_{IV} = k - 1 = 4 - 1 = 3$$

$$df_{ACROSS\ SUBJECTS} = N - 1 = 7 - 1 = 6$$

$$df_{ERROR} = (k - 1)(N - 1) = (4 - 1)(7 - 1) = 18$$

$$df_{TOTAL} = kN - 1 = (4)(7) - 1 = 27$$

The relevant mean squares are

$$MS_{IV} = \frac{SS_{IV}}{df_{IV}} = \frac{3.82}{3} = 1.27$$

$$MS_{ERROR} = \frac{SS_{ERROR}}{df_{ERROR}} = \frac{16.43}{18} = .91$$

Thus, the F ratio is

$$F = \frac{MS_{IV}}{MS_{ERROR}} = \frac{1.27}{.91} = 1.40$$

These calculations yield the following summary table:

Source	SS	df	MS	F
IV	3.82	3	1.27	1.40
Error	16.43	18	.91	
Across subjects	81.86	6		
Total	102.11	27		

The critical value of F from Appendix F for an alpha level of .05 and $df_{IV} = 3$ and $df_{ERROR} = 18$ is 3.16. Because the observed F value of 1.40 does not exceed the critical value, we fail to reject the null hypothesis of equivalent recall during the four test sessions.

As we discussed in Section 10.4, it is worthwhile to calculate eta-squared even when an inferential test is statistically nonsignificant. In our example,

$$eta^2 = \frac{SS_{IV}}{SS_{IV} + SS_{ERROR}}$$

$$= \frac{3.82}{3.82 + 16.43} = .19$$

Thus, the proportion of variability in the recall scores that is associated with the amount of exposure to the nonsense syllables after the effects of individual differences have been removed is .19. Although this indicates a strong relationship between the independent variable and the dependent variable in the sample, we are unable to conclude that the two variables are related in the population.

The large sum of squares across subjects indicates that individual differences were an important source of variability in the recall scores. It is informative to contemplate the role that confounding variables and additional disturbance variables might have played in producing the nonsignificant results. Given that a sample eta-squared of .19 indicates a strong effect, one possibility is that the amount of exposure to nonsense syllables and recall are actually related in the population but that the sample size ($N = 7$) was not large enough to yield a statistically significant result.

Finally, we can calculate the 95% Tukey HSD confidence intervals for the pairwise mean contrasts by first calculating the critical difference and then applying Equation 13.17. If we were to do this, we would find that the interval for the mean difference between Time 1 and Time 2 is −1.86 to 1.02, for the mean difference between Time 1 and Time 3 is −2.15 to .73, for the mean difference between Time 1 and Time 4 is 2.44 to .44, for the mean difference between Time 2 and Time 3 is −1.73 to 1.15, for the mean difference between Time 2 and Time 4 is −2.02 to .86, and for the mean difference between Time 3 and Time 4 is −1.73 to 1.15.

13.8 Planning an Investigation Using One-Way Repeated Measures Analysis of Variance

Appendix E.3 contains tables of the sample sizes necessary to achieve various levels of power for one-way repeated measures analysis of variance for different numbers of degrees of freedom IV. Table 13.4 reproduces a portion of this appendix for $df_{IV} = 2$ (that is, for three conditions) and an alpha level of .05. The first column presents selected values of power, and the column headings are selected values of eta-squared in the population. Consistent with the interpretation of sample values of eta-squared, these values of eta-squared are conceptualized as the proportion of variability in the dependent variable that is associated with the independent variable *after the effects of individual differences have been removed*. Thus, to the extent that the dependent variable is influenced by individuals' backgrounds and personal characteristics, the population eta-squared will be greater in the within-subjects case than in the between-subjects case, other things being equal.

To illustrate the use of the table, if the desired power level is .80 and the researcher suspects that the strength of the relationship in the population corresponds to an eta-squared of .15, then the number of participants that should be sampled for

TABLE 13.4 **Approximate Sample Sizes Necessary to Achieve Selected Levels of Power for $df_{IV} = 2$ and Alpha = .05 as a Function of Population Values of Eta-Squared**

	Population Eta-Squared									
Power	.01	.03	.05	.07	.10	.15	.20	.25	.30	.35
.10	32	11	7	5	4	3	2	2	2	2
.50	247	81	48	34	23	15	11	8	7	6
.70	382	125	74	52	36	23	16	13	10	8
.80	478	157	93	65	44	28	20	15	12	10
.90	627	206	121	85	58	37	26	20	16	13
.95	765	251	148	104	70	45	32	24	19	15
.99	1,060	347	204	143	97	62	44	33	26	21

an alpha level of .05 is 28. The power that an investigator requires will, of course, depend on the seriousness of committing a Type II error.

In addition to providing the sample size necessary to obtain a desired level of power, power tables can also be used to determine the power associated with one-way repeated measures analysis of variance given the degrees of freedom IV, the alpha level, the sample size, and the value of eta-squared in the population. For instance, Table 13.4 shows that the power for a one-way repeated measures analysis of variance with $df_{IV} = 2$ and $N = 37$ is .90 at an alpha level of .05 when the population eta-squared is .15.

Examination of Table 13.4 and Appendix E.3 provides a general appreciation for the relationships among the degrees of freedom IV, the alpha level, sample size, the strength of the relationship that one is trying to detect in the population, and power for one-way repeated measures analysis of variance. As can be seen, power becomes greater as the degrees of freedom IV, the alpha level, the sample size, and the population eta-squared each increases.

13.9 Method of Presentation

The method of presentation for a one-way repeated measures analysis of variance parallels that for a one-way between-subjects analysis of variance, except that the degrees of freedom IV and the degrees of freedom error are reported instead of the degrees of freedom between and the degrees of freedom within. For example, the results for the wine label and perceived quality experiment that was discussed earlier in this chapter might be reported as follows:*

Results

A one-way repeated measures analysis of variance that related the type of label (French, Italian, or American) to the perceived quality of the wine was found to be statistically significant

---

* The standard deviation estimates were calculated by applying the usual formulas for the sum of squares, the variance estimate, and the standard deviation estimate to each of the wine label conditions in Table 13.2.

at an alpha level of .05, $F(2,10) = 15.03$, $p < .01$. The strength of the relationship, as indexed by eta-squared, was .75.

A Tukey HSD test revealed that the wine was rated significantly higher when it was labeled as French ($M = 15.00$, $SD = 1.79$) than when it was labeled as either Italian ($M = 12.00$, $SD = 1.41$) or American ($M = 11.50$, $SD = 3.08$) but that the means for the latter two conditions did not differ significantly. Table 1 presents the 95% Tukey HSD confidence interval for each pairwise comparison of means.

13.10 Examples from the Literature

Age Regression and the Magnitude of the Poggendorff Illusion

The use of hypnosis to "return" individuals to an earlier chronological age is known as *age regression*. The technique is based on the assumption that people who are regressed to a particular age will behave as if they actually were that age.

One type of age-regressed behavior that has been studied is perception. For instance, Parrish, Lundy, and Leibowitz (1969) investigated the effect of age regression on the magnitude of the *Poggendorff illusion*. This illusion refers to the fact that the right half of a diagonal white bar running upward from left to right through a solid black bar appears to be higher than it actually is.

The magnitude of the Poggendorff illusion decreases with age from age 5 to approximately age 10 and then stabilizes. If age regression affects perceptual behavior, this same pattern of results should be observed with age-regressed individuals. In an attempt to determine whether this is indeed the case, Parrish and colleagues exposed ten college students to each of four conditions: no hypnosis, hypnosis but no age regression, hypnosis and regression to age 5, and hypnosis and regression to age 9. The order of these conditions was randomized such that students participated in one condition at a time at weekly intervals.

The experimental task involved adjusting the right half of the diagonal bar on a metal Poggendorff figure to make it line up with the stationary left half. The magnitude of the illusion was measured as the difference in inches between where the students set the right half of the bar and the point at which this portion was actually aligned with the left half. Six trials were undertaken for each participant during each experimental session, with the average of the six responses constituting the dependent variable.

A one-way repeated measures analysis of variance applied to these data yielded statistically significant results, $F(3, 27) = 4.10$, $p < .05$. Multiple comparisons showed that the Poggendorff illusion was stronger for the *hypnosis/regressed-to-age-5 condition* ($\overline{X} = 1.41$ inches) than for either the *no-hypnosis* ($\overline{X} = .96$ inch) or the *hypnosis/no-age regression* ($\overline{X} = 1.03$ inches) condition. None of the comparisons involving the *hypnosis/regressed-to-age-9 condition* ($\overline{X} = 1.26$ inches) was statistically significant, nor were any of the other comparisons. When considered in conjunction with similar findings for a second illusion (the *Ponzo illusion*), these results suggest that age regression affects perceptual behavior in the expected manner. The strength of the relationship, as indexed by eta-squared, was .31. This represents a strong effect.

Sex-Role Orientation and Perceived Sexual Attractiveness

Sex-role orientation has been defined in the psychological literature in terms of two broad classes of traits that an individual may exhibit: instrumental traits (for instance, aggression, risk taking, ambition) and expressive traits (for instance, warmth, sympathy, sensitivity). Psychologists sometimes classify individuals into one of four sex-role groups based on their scores on tests designed to measure these constructs: (1) *masculine* individuals, who score high on instrumental traits but low on expressive traits, (2) *feminine* individuals, who score high on expressive traits but low on instrumental traits, (3) *androgynous* individuals, who score high on both instrumental and expressive traits, and (4) *undifferentiated* individuals, who score low on both instrumental and expressive traits.

Among the findings of research on sex-role orientation is that an individual's sex-role standing affects the ways in which he or she is perceived by others. For instance, Becker and Gaeddert (1988) presented 18 male college students with descriptions of masculine, feminine, androgynous, and undifferentiated female targets. For each of the four descriptions, the students were asked to indicate how sexually attractive they thought the target person was on a 1 to 9 scale ranging from *not at all* to *very much*. The order of presentation was randomized for each participant.

A one-way repeated measures analysis of variance that compared the mean sexual attractiveness ratings for the four targets was found to be statistically significant, $F(3, 51) = 29.42$, $p < .01$. Application of the Tukey HSD test showed that the feminine ($\overline{X} = 5.33$) and the androgynous ($\overline{X} = 6.17$) targets were rated as significantly more sexually attractive than were the masculine ($\overline{X} = 2.78$) and the undifferentiated ($\overline{X} = 2.22$) targets. The means for the feminine versus the androgynous target and the masculine versus the undifferentiated target did not significantly differ. As indexed by eta-squared, the strength of the relationship was .63. This represents a strong effect.

13.11 Links Between Computer Results and Book Content

As we noted in Section 13.2, most statistical computer programs provide both the Huynh–Feldt epsilon and the Greenhouse–Geisser epsilon as part of the statistical output for one-way repeated measures analysis of variance. Moreover, these programs typically also provide the results of the Mauchly test for evaluating the probable violation of sphericity as well as additional information that is irrelevant for our purpose. However, this information—which, depending on the specific statistical program that is used, can be extensive—is important when data from more complex research designs involving one or more within-subjects independent variables are analyzed.

Also of note is the fact that the summary table for one-way repeated measures analysis of variance will not always look as we have depicted. One issue is that statistical programs may not refer to what we call the IV and the error sources of variability by these names. For instance, as we demonstrate in the "Applications to the Analysis of a Social Problem Using SPSS for Windows" section, SPSS for Windows refers to the source of variability due to the independent variable by the name that the user assigns to that variable rather than as IV. Also, the one-way repeated measures analysis of variance summary tables that are provided by many statistical programs often fail to include any information for the across-subjects and the total sources of variability. Again, we demonstrate this for SPSS for Windows in the "Applications" section.

13.12 Links Between Chapters

As we have seen, one-way repeated measures analysis of variance is closely related to the correlated groups t test. One-way repeated measures analysis of variance is also closely related to two-way repeated measures analysis of variance and two-way between-within analysis of variance, which we briefly review in Section 18.6.

Applications to the Analysis of a Social Problem Using SPSS for Windows

It is important that parents take responsibility for ensuring that their teens are well informed about sex and birth control. Nevertheless, many parents do not talk with their teens about these issues. This is unfortunate because research shows that many teens believe that their parents would be a useful source of information about these topics.

Why don't parents talk with their teens about sex and birth control? In an attempt to gain insight into this issue, mothers in the parent–teen communication study described in Chapter 1 were asked to indicate their agreement with the following statements that focus on possible reasons:

It would be difficult for me to explain things if I talked with my daughter (son) about sex and birth control.

It wouldn't do much good if I talked with my daughter (son) about sex and birth control.

My daughter (son) will think I do not trust her (him) if I try to talk to her (him) about sex and birth control.

It would be difficult to find a convenient time and place to talk to my daughter (son) about sex and birth control.

Talking about birth control with my daughter (son) will only encourage her (him) to have sex.

Each statement was rated on a 1 (*strongly disagree*) to 5 (*strongly agree*) scale that also included the response options *moderately disagree, neither agree nor disagree,* and *moderately agree.*

To determine whether mothers differ in the extent to which they endorse each of these reasons, we conducted a one-way repeated measures analysis of variance using the type of reason as the independent variable and the extent of agreement as the dependent variable. The frequency histogram for each level of the independent variable (that is, for each of the five statements) is presented in Figure 13.1, with a normal distribution superimposed on each. All of the distributions are strongly positively skewed, with most mothers indicating that they strongly disagree that the stated reasons are obstacles to discussion. The nonnormality observed in the sample raises questions about the normality of the population scores. However, given the large sample size (732 mothers), the analysis should be robust even to this degree of nonnormality.

Table 13.5 presents the computer output for the analysis of variance. The top portion contains the Mauchly test of the sphericity assumption. The test statistic for the Mauchly test is designated as "Mauchly's W." In this instance, W is equal to .91. If the p value associated with the Mauchly test (labeled "Sig.") is less than .05, as it is in our example, this implies that the sphericity assumption has been violated. However, as we noted in Section 13.2, the Mauchly test is quite sensitive to nonnormality in the data, and this can also produce a significant test result. Consequently, consistent with our recommendation from that same section, we had decided beforehand to apply an adjustment factor to the degrees of freedom IV and the degrees of freedom error regardless of the results of the Mauchly test.

This portion of the output also presents three different adjustments for the degrees of freedom: the Huynh–Feldt and Greenhouse–Geisser epsilons that we discussed in Section 13.2 and a "lower-bound" epsilon that is highly conservative (and, for this reason, that is generally not recommended). We chose to use the Huynh–Feldt adjustment, which equals .97. The degrees of freedom for the F ratio are multiplied by this value when assessing its significance.

The summary table at the bottom of Table 13.5 applies to both the standard repeated measures analysis of variance and the Huynh–Feldt adjusted analysis. The source of variability due to the independent variable is identified as "REASON"

because this is the name that we assigned to this variable. The source of variability due to error is identified as "ERROR (REASON)" to indicate that this is the corresponding error component. SPSS for Windows does not include any information for either the across subjects or the total sources of variability in the summary table.

Note that the sums of squares, the mean squares, and the F ratio are the same for the Huynh–Feldt analysis as for the standard repeated measures analysis of variance. The only difference in the two analyses is the degrees of freedom. The degrees of freedom for the standard F test appear to the right of the "Sphericity assumed" designation and the degrees of freedom for the adjusted analysis appear to the right of the "Huynh-Feldt" designation directly beneath this. In the standard F test, the F ratio of 8.08 is evaluated with 4 degrees of freedom IV and 2,928 degrees of freedom error. In the Huynh–Feldt analysis, this F ratio is evaluated with 3.87 and 2,831.72 degrees of freedom. In both cases, the p value associated with the F ratio is .0005 or less, as indicated by the fact that a significance level of .000 is reported in the summary table. Thus, the F test is statistically significant.

The strength of the relationship as indexed by eta-squared can be calculated by applying Equation 13.14. The eta-squared value of .01 suggests that the relationship between the type of reason and the extent of agreement, though statistically significant, is weak.

We used the modified Bonferroni procedure discussed in Appendix 13.1 to determine the nature of the relationship. The mean scores for the five reasons for not talking about sex and birth control, rank ordered from highest to lowest for ease of comparison, are:

Reason	Mean
Teen will doubt trust	1.72
Will encourage teen to have sex	1.63
Difficult to explain things	1.60
Wouldn't do much good	1.56
Difficult to find time/place	1.50

(continued)

FIGURE 13.1   Frequency Histograms for Maternal Agreement That (a) It Would Be Difficult to Explain Things, (b) It Wouldn't Do Much Good, (c) Teen Will Think I Don't Trust Her/Him, (d) It Would Be Difficult to Find a Time and Place, and (e) It Will Encourage Teen to Have Sex

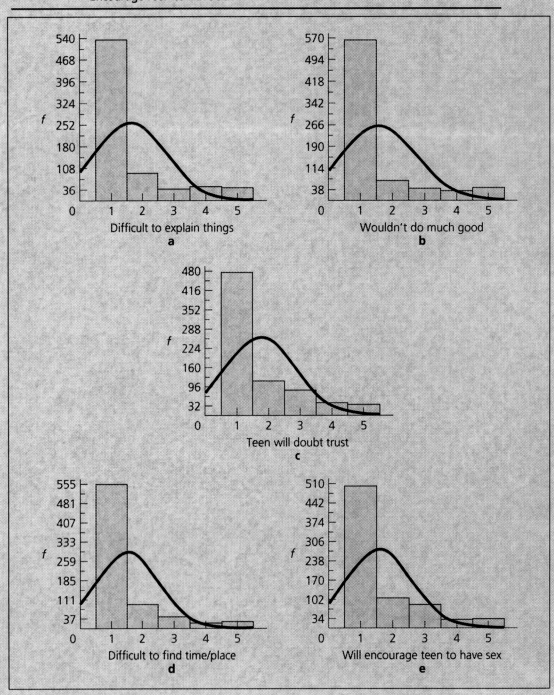

Application of the modified Bonferroni procedure showed that the mean concern about the teen doubting the mother's trust was statistically significantly greater than all of the other means except that for the concern for encouraging the teen to have sex. None of the other pairwise comparisons was statistically significant.

The *statistical* differences between the mean for doubting the mother's trust and some of the other means notwithstanding, one has to question the *practical* significance of these differences given the small effect size that was found, the preponderance of *strongly disagree* responses for all five reasons, and the small absolute differences between the means (a maximum of .22 unit). For all intents and purposes, the mean differences between the five reasons are trivial.

TABLE 13.5 **Computer Output for One-Way Repeated Measures Analysis of Variance for Agreement with Reasons for Not Talking About Sex and Birth Control**

Mauchly's Test of Sphericity
Measure: MEASURE_1

Within-subjects effect	Mauchly's W	Sig.	Epsilon		
			Greenhouse-Geisser	Huynh-Feldt	Lower-bound
REASON	.912	.000	.961	.967	.250

Tests of Within-Subjects Effects
Measure: MEASURE_1

Source		Sum of squares	df	Mean square	F	Sig.
REASON	Sphericity assumed	21.23	4	5.31	8.08	.000
	Huynh-Feldt		3.87		8.08	.000
ERROR(REASON)	Sphericity assumed	1923.57	2928	.66		
	Huynh-Feldt		2831.72			

Summary

One-way repeated measures analysis of variance is typically used to analyze the relationship between two variables when (1) the dependent variable is quantitative in nature and is measured on a level that at least approximates interval characteristics, (2) the independent variable is within-subjects in nature, and (3) the independent variable has three or more levels. One-way repeated measures analysis of variance differs from one-way between-subjects analysis of variance in that it removes the influence of individual differences from the dependent variable. Consequently, a repeated measures analysis of variance is often a more sensitive test of the relationship between the independent and dependent variables than is a between-subjects analysis of variance. Otherwise, the logic underlying the two techniques is identical.

The sphericity assumption requires that the variance of the population difference scores for any two conditions be the same as the variance of the population difference scores for any other two conditions. However, many applications in the behavioral sciences almost certainly violate this assumption, sometimes substantially. Consequently, many statisticians, ourselves included, recommend that the traditional F test be modified unless one is confident on theoretical grounds that sphericity holds. This modification takes the form of multiplying the degrees of freedom IV and the degrees of freedom error by an adjustment factor to obtain new degrees of freedom to be used in assessing the significance of the observed F ratio. The Huynh–Feldt procedure is the preferred alternative for most applications in the behavioral sciences, although there are scenarios where other adjustments may be preferred.

The strength of the relationship is measured using eta-squared. Unstandardized effect sizes and confidence intervals can also be calculated. The nature of the relationship is analyzed using the Tukey HSD test when one is confident that the sphericity assumption is met, or a modified Bonferroni procedure otherwise.

Appendix 13.1   Determining the Nature of the Relationship Under Sphericity Violations

When the sphericity assumption is violated, it is not appropriate to use the mean square error from the overall analysis to calculate a critical difference as is done with the Tukey HSD test. If we are not confident that the sphericity assumption is met, we can use a **modified Bonferroni procedure** instead. This involves performing all possible pairwise comparisons between the group means using the steps outlined next. The rationale for the modified Bonferroni procedure is described in Holland and Copenhaver (1988).

For the wine label and perceived quality experiment, there are three pairwise compar-

isons, also known as *contrasts*. Using the procedures from Chapter 11, we conduct a correlated groups t test for each pair of means involved in a comparison and determine a p value for each of the t values. This usually must be done with the aid of a computer. Next, the absolute t values are ordered in a column from largest to smallest, and the corresponding p values are each compared against a *critical alpha*. If the p value is less than the critical alpha, the null hypothesis in question is rejected. For the sake of precision, both the p values and the critical alphas should be rounded to at least three decimal places.

The value of the critical alpha changes for each successive t value as one proceeds from the top to the bottom of the column. The largest t value must yield a p value that is less than the overall alpha level that we adopt for the set of comparisons divided by the total number of comparisons (in this case, three) for the null hypothesis to be rejected. The next largest t value must yield a p value that is less than the overall alpha level divided by the number of contrasts minus 1 for the null hypothesis to be rejected. The next largest t value must yield a p value that is less than the overall alpha level divided by the number of contrasts minus 2 for the null hypothesis to be rejected. And so on, subtracting an additional unit from the total number of comparisons with each successive contrast.

If a contrast is statistically significant, the nature of the difference between the population means is determined by comparing the mean scores for the two conditions per the usual t test approach. As soon as the first statistically nonsignificant contrast is encountered as one proceeds from the largest to the smallest absolute t value, all remaining comparisons are declared statistically nonsignificant.

The results for the modified Bonferroni procedure for the wine label and perceived quality experiment can be summarized in a table as follows. In deriving this table, we used an overall alpha level of .05.

The decisions for the three null hypotheses in this instance are the same as we made in Section 13.4 using the Tukey HSD test. However, the two approaches will not always yield the same results, so it is important that the modified Bonferroni procedure be applied any time the sphericity assumption is violated.

Null hypothesis tested	Absolute value of t	p value	Critical alpha	Null hypothesis rejected?
$\mu_F = \mu_I$	5.81	.002	.05/3 = .017	Yes
$\mu_F = \mu_A$	4.58	.006	.05/2 = .025	Yes
$\mu_I = \mu_A$	.65	.542	.05/1 = .050	No

Exercises

Answers to asterisked (*) exercises appear at the back of the book.

Exercises to Review Concepts

1. Under what conditions is one-way repeated measures analysis of variance typically used to analyze a bivariate relationship?
2. Distinguish among the sum of squares total, the sum of squares IV, the sum of squares across subjects, and the sum of squares error. How are they interrelated?
*3. Why is a repeated measures analysis of variance usually a more sensitive test of the relationship between the independent and dependent variables than a between-subjects analysis of variance?
*4. Insert the missing entries in the summary table for a one-way repeated measures analysis with five levels of the independent variable and $N = 12$.

Source	SS	df	MS	F
IV	20.00	—	—	—
Error	132.00	—	—	
Across subjects	—	—		
Total	198.00	—		

5. Insert the missing entries in the summary table for a one-way repeated measures analysis of variance with three levels of the independent variable.

Source	SS	df	MS	F
IV	—	—	20.00	10.00
Error	—	18	—	
Across subjects	—	9		
Total	106.00	—		

*6. For a repeated measures analysis of variance with $N = 21$ and five conditions, what would be the values of the degrees of freedom IV, degrees of freedom across subjects, degrees of freedom error, and degrees of freedom total?

*7. State the critical value of F for a one-way repeated measures analysis of variance for an alpha level of .05 under each of the following conditions:
   a. $k = 3, N = 20$ c. $k = 3, N = 15$
   b. $k = 4, N = 21$ d. $k = 5, N = 12$

8. What are the assumptions underlying one-way repeated measures analysis of variance?

*9. How do the Huynh–Feldt epsilon and the Greenhouse–Geisser epsilon increase the robustness of one-way repeated measures analysis of variance to violations of the sphericity assumption?

10. What interpretation does eta-squared have in the context of one-way repeated measures analysis of variance? How does this interpretation differ from that for one-way between-subjects analysis of variance?

*11. Under what circumstance might a one-way repeated measures analysis of variance be less powerful than a corresponding one-way between-subjects analysis of variance? Why?

12. What is the rationale behind randomly ordering the sequence of conditions across participants in repeated measures designs? How does this differ from counterbalancing?

Refer to the following scores on an anxiety test that five individuals completed at three different times to do Exercises 13–17:

Individual	Time 1	Time 2	Time 3
1	2	3	4
2	3	5	8
3	4	5	6
4	5	7	9
5	5	6	4

*13. Test for a relationship between the time of assessment and anxiety using a one-way repeated measures analysis of variance.

*14. Compute the value of eta-squared using Equation 13.14. Recalculate eta-squared using Equation 13.15. Compare the two results. Does the observed value represent a weak, moderate, or strong effect?

*15. Analyze the nature of the relationship between the time of assessment and anxiety using the Tukey HSD test.

*16. Compute the 95% Tukey HSD confidence intervals.

*17. Analyze the data as if the independent variable were between-subjects in nature. That is, conduct a one-way between-subjects analysis of variance, compute the value of eta-squared, use the Tukey HSD test to analyze the nature of the relationship, and compute the 95% Tukey HSD confidence intervals. Compare your findings with those for Exercises 13–16. How does this illustrate the advantage of within-subjects research designs?

Refer to the following numbers of pages that five students read during 6-minute testing sessions under three levels of distraction to do Exercises 18–21.

Student	Low	Moderate	High
1	5	7	2
2	9	7	5
3	8	5	6
4	6	5	4
5	9	6	6

18. Test for a relationship between distraction and the number of pages read using a one-way repeated measures analysis of variance.
19. Compute the value of eta-squared. Does the observed value represent a weak, moderate, or strong effect?
20. Analyze the nature of the relationship between distraction and the number of pages read using the Tukey HSD test.
21. Compute the 95% Tukey HSD confidence intervals.

For each of the studies described in Exercises 22–25, indicate the appropriate statistical test for analyzing the relationship between the independent and dependent variables. Assume that the underlying assumptions of the tests have been satisfied.

*22. Kelman and Hovland (1953) studied the effect of the source of a persuasive communication on attitude change. Three groups of participants listened to a persuasive message on the treatment of juvenile delinquents. For one group, the message was attributed to a trustworthy, well-informed source; for another group, it was attributed to an untrustworthy, poorly informed source; and for the third group, it was attributed to a "neutral" source. The mean amounts of attitude change were compared for the three groups.

*23. A researcher tested the effect of age on infants' memory capacities. Forty infants were given a memory test at the age of 5 months and again at the age of 7 months. Scores on this test could range from 1 to 15. The mean test scores were compared for the two ages.

24. An investigator studied the effects of alcohol and marijuana on driving skills. Thirty participants took part in a driving simulation task under each of three conditions: (1) while under the influence of a small amount of alcohol, (2) while under the influence of a small amount of marijuana, and (3) while not under the influence of either drug. The simulation task yielded "driving scores" that could range from 1 to 100. The mean driving scores were compared for the three conditions.

25. Advertisements for medical products often report the relative number of physicians who give a positive recommendation. A researcher examined whether the context in which such information is presented influences its impact on consumer attitudes. Two groups of individuals were presented with identical descriptions of a brand of aspirin. However, one group was told that "8 out of 10 doctors" recommend the aspirin, whereas the other group was told that "80 out of 100 doctors" recommend the aspirin. Although the *proportion* of doctors who recommended the aspirin was identical for the two groups, the *number* of doctors differed. After reading one of the two descriptions, participants indicated their attitude toward the aspirin on a scale of 1 to 10. The mean attitude scores were compared for the two groups.

26. If a researcher suspects that the strength of the relationship between two variables in the population is .10 as indexed by eta-squared, what sample size should he use in a study involving a within-subjects independent variable with five levels and an alpha level of .05 in order to achieve a power of .80?

*27. Suppose that an investigator conducts a study involving a within-subjects independent variable having four levels with $N = 12$. If the value of eta-squared in the population is .15, what would the power of her statistical test be at an alpha level of .05?

Multiple-Choice Questions

*28. Which sum of squares in a between-subjects design is conceptually equivalent to the sum of squares error in a repeated measures design?
a. sum of squares between
b. sum of squares within
c. sum of squares total
d. none of the above

*29. Which sum of squares in a between-subjects design is conceptually equivalent to the sum of squares across subjects in a repeated measures design?
a. sum of squares between
b. sum of squares within
c. sum of squares total
d. none of the above

30. Which sum of squares in a between-subjects design is conceptually equivalent to the sum of squares IV in a repeated measures design?
a. sum of squares between
b. sum of squares within
c. sum of squares total
d. none of the above

31. The Mauchly test is of great diagnostic value in evaluating the probable violation of the sphericity assumption in practical applications of repeated measures analysis of variance.
a. true   b. false

*32. If a researcher suspects that the strength of the relationship between two variables in the population is .05 as indexed by eta-squared, what sample size should he use in a study involving a within-subjects independent variable with three levels and an alpha level of .05 in order to achieve a power of .80?
a. 62   c. 93
b. 70   d. 133

33. Participants in a repeated measures design are exposed to
a. all levels of the independent variable
b. only one level of the independent variable

c. a varying number of levels of the independent variable, depending on which condition they are assigned to
d. a randomly determined number of levels of the independent variable

*34. The mean square error for a one-way repeated measures analysis of variance will tend to be _____ the mean square within for a one-way between-subjects analysis of variance applied to the same data set.
a. larger than
b. equal to
c. smaller than
d. half the size of

Use the following information to complete Exercises 35–48.

A developmental psychologist studied the number of close friends that a mixed-gender group of 21 children reported having at 8, 10, and 12 years of age. The mean number of friends was 3.48 at 8 years of age, 4.17 at 10 years of age, and 4.35 at 12 years of age. The summary table follows:

Source	SS	df	MS	F
IV	8.86	2	4.43	3.57
Error	49.60	40	1.24	
Across subjects	96.49	20		
Total	154.95	62		

35. If the value of eta-squared in the population is .35, what is the power of the statistical test at an alpha level of .05?
a. .35
b. .80
c. .90
d. .99

36. The independent variable is
a. the gender of the investigator
b. the gender of the children
c. the number of close friends
d. age

*37. The dependent variable is
   a. the gender of the investigator
   b. the gender of the children
   c. the number of close friends
   d. age

38. Based on this study, we can conclude that the independent variable is related to the dependent variable.
   a. true   b. false

39. It is possible that the test results reflect a Type I error.
   a. true   b. false

*40. It is possible that the test results reflect a Type II error.
   a. true   b. false

41. The strength of the relationship, as indexed by eta-squared, is
   a. .02   c. .35
   b. .15   d. .39

*42. The proportion of variability in the dependent variable that is due to disturbance variables other than individual differences is
   a. .61   c. .85
   b. .72   d. .92

*43. What can we conclude about the number of close friends one has at 8 versus 10 years of age?
   a. The number of close friends is greater at age 8.
   b. The number of close friends is greater at age 10.
   c. The number of close friends is the same at the two ages.
   d. The number of close friends may or may not differ at the two ages.

*44. What can we conclude about the number of close friends one has at 8 versus 12 years of age?
   a. The number of close friends is greater at age 8.
   b. The number of close friends is greater at age 12.
   c. The number of close friends is the same at the two ages.
   d. The number of close friends may or may not differ at the two ages.

45. What can we conclude about the number of close friends one has at 10 versus 12 years of age?
   a. The number of close friends is greater at age 10.
   b. The number of close friends is greater at age 12.
   c. The number of close friends is the same at the two ages.
   d. The number of close friends may or may not differ at the two ages.

*46. The 95% Tukey HSD confidence interval for the mean difference between 8 years of age and 10 years of age is
   a. −.87 to −.18
   b. −1.02 to .66
   c. −1.53 to .15
   d. −1.71 to −.03

*47. The 95% Tukey HSD confidence interval for the mean difference between 8 years of age and 12 years of age is
   a. −.87 to −.18
   b. −1.02 to .66
   c. −1.53 to .15
   d. −1.71 to −.03

48. The 95% Tukey HSD confidence interval for the mean difference between 10 years of age and 12 years of age is
   a. −87 to −.18
   b. −1.02 to .66
   c. −1.53 to .15
   d. −1.71 to −.03

Exercises to Apply Concepts

*49. Although numerous studies have examined the factors that women take into consideration when choosing a birth control method, relatively few studies have examined birth control from the standpoint of men. In one of the few investigations that have done so, Jaccard (1980) asked a group of men to indicate how important each of four factors would be to them in deciding whether or not to use an oral contraceptive. Ratings were made on a scale of 1 to 21, with higher scores indicating greater importance.

The hypothetical data presented in the table are representative of those obtained by Jaccard. Analyze these data, draw a conclusion, and write up your results using the principles developed in the Method of Presentation section.

Individual	Health risks	Effectiveness	Cost	Convenience
1	16	16	12	12
2	19	15	11	11
3	18	14	10	10
4	20	12	8	8
5	17	13	9	9

50. Evidence suggests that many rape victims fail to report their victimization to the police or other public authorities. For instance, surveys in large metropolitan areas have found that only about 50% of most crimes—including rape—are ever reported to the police. With this in mind, Feldman-Summers and Ashworth (1980) investigated the extent to which various factors influence women's intentions to report sexual victimization to various agencies and individuals.

As part of this study, each participant was asked to indicate the likelihood that she would report a rape to her husband/boyfriend, the police, her parents, and a female friend. A separate probability judgment was obtained for each source. The judgments were made on a scale of 1 to 7, with higher scores indicating a greater likelihood of reporting the crime.

Hypothetical data representative of the results of Feldman-Summers and Ashworth are presented in the table. Analyze these data, draw a conclusion, and write up your results using the principles developed in the Method of Presentation section.

Individual	Husband/ boyfriend	Police	Parents	Female friend
1	7	6	3	4
2	6	5	4	5
3	7	6	1	2
4	6	5	6	7
5	7	6	3	4
6	6	5	4	5

51. A researcher examined the effectiveness of a particular weight-loss program. Eight subscribers to this program were weighed before beginning the program, at the completion of the program, and, to determine the long-term effect of the program, again 6 months later. The data for the study are presented in the table. Analyze these data, draw a conclusion, and write up your results using the principles developed in the Method of Presentation section.

Individual	Before program	Immediately after program	6 months after program
1	194	186	193
2	246	227	241
3	211	195	209
4	185	172	188
5	207	204	207
6	239	228	236
7	188	175	180
8	226	211	230

52. Although most people know that high levels of stress are associated with such negative life events as losing one's job, the death of a loved one, and serious illness, you might be surprised to learn that positive life events can also be very stressful. In fact, health psychologists have increasingly recognized the role that stress from both negative and positive life events can play in the development of a wide range of physical and psychological problems.

Although most people enjoy vacationing, travel can be stressful. In order to examine the amount of stress that is associated with various aspects of the travel experience, suppose that a researcher asks seven individuals to indicate how stressful they find each of the following to be: planning a vacation, traveling to and from their vacation destination, and getting reorganized once they return. Responses are made on a scale of 1 to 9, with higher scores indicating greater stress.

Hypothetical data for this study are presented in the table. Analyze these data, draw a conclusion, and write up your results using the principles developed in the Method of Presentation section.

Individual	Planning	Traveling	Getting reorganized
1	5	4	6
2	3	3	5
3	5	4	6
4	4	4	7
5	6	5	6
6	4	3	5
7	5	4	6

Pearson Correlation and Regression: Inferential Aspects

14.1 Use of Pearson Correlation

In Chapter 5, we noted the conditions under which Pearson correlation is used to determine the extent of a linear relationship between two variables. We now formalize those conditions. Specifically, Pearson correlation is typically used to analyze the relationship between two variables when

1. Both variables are quantitative in nature and are measured on a level that at least approximates interval characteristics.

2. The two variables have been measured on the same individuals.

3. The observations on each variable are *between-subjects* in nature.

Our discussion of correlation in Chapter 5 focused on the *description* of the relationship between two variables. In practice, however, the most common use of Pearson correlation is to make *inferences* about population correlation coefficients from sample correlation coefficients, and this is the focus of this chapter. For instance, the question of interest for the traditionalism and ideal family size study that we discussed in Chapter 5 is whether we can conclude that a correlation exists between these two variables in the *population* given the correlation of .66 that we observed in the *sample* of ten individuals.

14.2 The Linear Model

To develop the logic of correlational inference and the related technique of regression, we restate the linear model that we developed in Chapter 5, but we now represent the slope and the intercept with Greek letters to indicate that these are the population values:

$$Y = \alpha + \beta X + \varepsilon \qquad [14.1]$$

The model states that a person's score on variable Y is a linear function of variable X, with α representing the intercept and β representing the slope.* However, it is rare in the behavioral sciences to have a perfect linear relationship between two variables, and this is why there is another term, ε (lowercase Greek *e*, called *epsilon*), in Equation 5.1. This term is the **error score** and reflects all factors that are uncorrelated with variable X that influence variable Y.

It is because of these other factors (as well as the fact that relationships are sometimes nonlinear rather than linear) that the absolute correlation between X and Y is not always 1.00. If everyone in the population had an ε score of 0, then the standard deviation of the ε scores across individuals would also be equal to 0,

---

* Note that the use of α and β in this context is different from their earlier use to represent the probability of Type I and Type II errors, respectively.

and Y would be a perfect linear function of X. Thus, the absolute correlation between X and Y would be 1.00. As the ε scores deviate from 0, the Y scores will deviate from the corresponding $\alpha + \beta X$ values, and the relationship between the variables will no longer be perfectly linear.

In this chapter, we discuss procedures for estimating α, β, and the standard deviation of ε, as well as the population correlation between X and Y, ρ (lowercase Greek r, called *rho*). We begin by focusing on Pearson correlation, after which we turn our attention to regression.

14.3   Inference of a Relationship Using Pearson Correlation

As we noted in previous chapters, even if a relationship is observed between two variables in a sample, this does not necessarily mean that a relationship exists between the variables in the corresponding population. Thus, the first question to be addressed regarding the analysis of bivariate relationships in the context of Pearson correlation is whether we can infer that a correlation exists between two variables in the population based on the correlation coefficient that is observed in a set of sample data. We demonstrate the procedure for examining this issue using the traditionalism and ideal family size example from Chapter 5.

Null and Alternative Hypotheses

As with the sample correlation coefficient, r, the population correlation coefficient, ρ, can range from -1.00 to $+1.00$, with a coefficient of 0 indicating that there is no linear relationship between the two variables and a nonzero correlation coefficient indicating that some approximation to a linear relationship. This suggests the following null and alternative hypotheses for the test of Pearson correlation for our example:

$$H_0: \quad \rho = 0$$
$$H_1: \quad \rho \neq 0$$

In other words, the null hypothesis states that the population correlation between traditionalism and the ideal family size is 0 and the alternative hypothesis states that the population correlation between these variables is some value other than 0. If the former is true, there is no linear relationship between how traditional one is and how many children one desires; if the latter is true, some degree of a linear relationship exists between traditionalism and the ideal family size.

The alternative hypothesis above is nondirectional in nature. However, directional alternative hypotheses are also possible. Such hypotheses state either that ρ is greater than 0 (that is, that the two variables are positively correlated in the population) or that ρ is less than 0 (that is, that the two variables are negatively correlated in the population). However, according to the logic that we developed when we discussed the power of nondirectional versus directional t tests, directional alternative hypotheses should be used only when there is a compelling reason for doing so based on the existing theory and research.

Based on the data for the 10 women who comprise our sample, we want to make a decision with respect to the null hypothesis. This is accomplished using hypothesis testing logic analogous to that applied in prior chapters. In the context of Pearson correlation, this involves converting the value of r in the sample to a t score under the assumption that the null hypothesis is true and then determining whether this value of t falls in the rejection region. If it does, then we will reject the null hypothesis and conclude that there is some degree of a linear relationship between traditionalism and the ideal family size. Otherwise, we will fail to reject the null hypothesis.

Sampling Distribution of r

Consider a population in which the correlation coefficient between two variables is 0. From the population, we select a random sample of 10 individuals and compute the correlation coefficient. We might find that $r = .15$. The fact that r does not equal 0 is because of sampling error, as we have discussed in previous chapters. Now suppose that we randomly select another sample of 10 individuals from the population. For this sample, the correlation might be .03. In principle, we could continue this process until we have calculated r for all possible samples of size 10. The resulting distribution of correlation coefficients based on all random samples of size 10 would constitute a **sampling distribution of r** and would have many of the same properties as the sampling distributions that we have discussed in earlier chapters.

The mean of a sampling distribution of r is approximately equal to ρ, the population correlation between the two variables.* When $\rho = 0$ and the assumption of *bivariate normality*, which we will discuss shortly, is met, then as the sample size, N, increases, the distribution of r tends (somewhat slowly) toward a normal distribution. When $\rho \neq 0$, the sampling distribution of r is skewed. Figure 14.1 illustrates sampling distributions of r for $\rho = -.80$, $\rho = 0$, and $\rho = +.80$ for $N = 10$.

Testing the Statistical Significance of a Correlation Coefficient

We can test the null hypothesis that $\rho = 0$ by converting the sample correlation coefficient to the following test statistic:[†]

$$t = \frac{r}{\sqrt{(1 - r^2)/(N - 2)}} \qquad [14.2]$$

The sampling distribution for this statistic closely approximates a t distribution with $N - 2$ degrees of freedom. Thus, the degrees of freedom for a test of Pearson correlation are equal to

$$df = N - 2 \qquad [14.3]$$

---

* When the sample size is larger than 50, the standard error of a sampling distribution of r is approximately equal to $1/\sqrt{N}$.

[†] Null hypotheses other than $\rho = 0$ can be tested using the procedures discussed in Appendix 14.1.

FIGURE 14.1 **Sampling Distributions of *r* for Three Values of ρ for *N* = 10 (From Minium, 1978)**

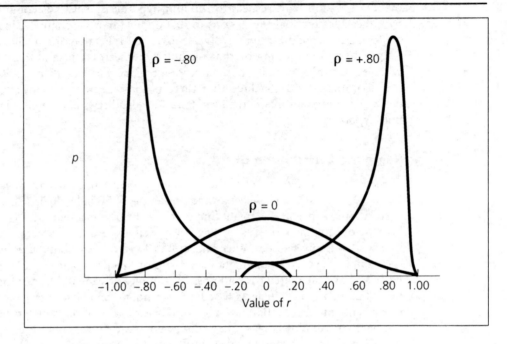

For the traditionalism and ideal family size study,

$$t = \frac{.66}{\sqrt{(1 - .66^2)/(10 - 2)}}$$

$$= \frac{.66}{.27} = 2.44$$

For an alpha level of .05, nondirectional test, and $N - 2 = 10 - 2 = 8$ degrees of freedom, the critical values of *t* from Appendix D are ± 2.306. Because 2.44 exceeds $+2.306$, we reject the null hypothesis. A sample correlation coefficient of .66 based on 8 degrees of freedom is too large to attribute to sampling error, assuming that the null hypothesis is true. We therefore conclude that the population correlation is nonzero—that is, that there is some degree of a linear relationship between traditionalism and the ideal family size.

Tabled Values of *r*

Because the calculation of *t* using Equation 14.2 depends on only the values of *r* and *N*, it is possible, through algebraic manipulation, to determine the values of *r* that will lead to rejection of the null hypothesis that $\rho = 0$ for a given sample size. Following this logic, statisticians have created tables of the critical values of *r* for selected degrees of freedom. One such table appears in Appendix H. If the observed value of *r* is greater than the positive critical value from this table or less than the corresponding negative critical value, we will reject the null hypothesis. Otherwise, we will fail to reject the null hypothesis.

For instance, for an alpha level of .05, nondirectional test, and $N - 2 = 10 - 2 = 8$ degrees of freedom, the critical values of r for the traditionalism and ideal family size example are $\pm.632$. Because the observed correlation coefficient of .66 is greater than $+.632$, we reject the null hypothesis and conclude that there is some degree of a linear relationship between traditionalism and the ideal family size. This is the same conclusion that we reached using the t test procedure. Given its greater computational ease, we follow the strategy of referring to Appendix H when testing the significance of correlation coefficients in the remainder of this chapter.

STUDY EXERCISE 14.1

In Study Exercise 5.2, the correlation between voters' perceptions that a candidate supports labor unions and their willingness to vote for that candidate was calculated to be .50 for a sample of nine individuals. Test the viability of the hypothesis that there is no linear relationship between the two variables in the population.

Answer   The null and alternative hypotheses are

H_0: $\rho = 0$

H_1: $\rho \neq 0$

For an alpha level of .05, nondirectional test, and $N - 2 = 9 - 2 = 7$ degrees of freedom, the critical values of r from Appendix H are $\pm.666$. Because .50 is neither greater than $+.666$ nor less than $-.666$, we fail to reject the null hypothesis of no linear relationship between the two variables.

Assumptions of Pearson Correlation

Pearson correlation is appropriate when both variables are quantitative in nature and measured on a level that at least approximates interval characteristics. The test of the null hypothesis that $\rho = 0$ also assumes that

1. The sample is independently and randomly selected from the population of interest.

2. The population distributions of X and Y are such that their joint distribution (that is, their scatterplot) represents a *bivariate normal distribution*. This is called the assumption of **bivariate normality** and requires that the distribution of Y scores be normal in the population at every value of X.

3. The variances of the Y scores are equal at every value of X in the population.

Although it is important that the first assumption not be violated, Van den Brink (1988) has shown that the t test of the correlation coefficient is robust to large deviations from bivariate normality when the sample size is larger than 15. However, violation of the assumption of equal Y score variances at every value of X

can be problematic.* Tests for evaluating violation of this assumption and procedures for dealing with heterogeneous Y score variances are discussed in Judge, Griffiths, Hill, Lutkephol, and Lee (1985).

14.4 Strength of the Relationship

The second of the three questions to be addressed regarding the analysis of bivariate relationships is how strong the relationship is. Consistent with the other tests that we have discussed, the strength of the relationship between two variables in the case of Pearson correlation can be indexed by eta-squared in the form of the ratio of explained variability to total variability.† This can be represented symbolically using Equation 10.11:

$$\text{eta}^2 = \frac{SS_{\text{EXPLAINED}}}{SS_{\text{TOTAL}}}$$

However, it is not necessary to actually calculate the two sums of squares because eta-squared is mathematically equal to the square of the correlation coefficient. That is,

$$\text{eta}^2 = r^2 \qquad\qquad\qquad [14.4]$$

In the traditionalism and ideal family size study, r was found to equal .66. Thus, r^2, which is formally known as the **coefficient of determination**, is equal to

$$r^2 = .66^2 = .44$$

This represents a strong effect and indicates that the proportion of variability in the ideal family size that is associated with traditionalism is .44, as indexed by a linear model. It follows that $1 - r^2 = 1 - .44 = .56$ reflects the proportion of variability in the ideal family size that is *not* associated with traditionalism. As we noted in Section 5.5., $1 - r^2$ is formally known as the *coefficient of alienation*.

14.5 Confidence Intervals for the Correlation Coefficient

Although confidence intervals can be calculated for the correlation coefficient, the procedure for doing so is complex. Interested readers are referred to Appendix 14.2, where we demonstrate the relevant steps for the traditionalism and ideal family size example. As indicated in the appendix, the 95% confidence interval in this instance is .05 to .91. We are 95% confident that the true population correlation coefficient falls within this interval.

---

* Violation of this assumption can also create problems for regression analysis.
† As we discussed in Section 10.4, eta-squared is a biased estimator of the strength of the relationship between two variables. The formula for epsilon-squared, a commonly-used unbiased estimator of relationship strength, is provided in Appendix N for the Pearson correlation situation.

14.6 Nature of the Relationship

The third of the three questions to be addressed regarding the analysis of bivariate relationships is what the nature of the relationship is. This is determined in the case of Pearson correlation by examining the sign of the correlation that is observed in the sample. If the null hypothesis is rejected and the sample correlation coefficient is positive, then the appropriate conclusion is that the population correlation coefficient is also positive—that is, that the two variables approximate a direct linear relationship. On the other hand, if the null hypothesis is rejected and the sample correlation coefficient is negative, then the appropriate conclusion is that the population correlation coefficient is also negative—that is, that the two variables approximate an inverse linear relationship. Given the observed correlation of .66 in the traditionalism and ideal family size study, we conclude that these variables approximate a direct linear relationship.

By indicating the number of units that variable Y is predicted to change given a 1-unit change in variable X, the slope of the regression line provides additional information about the nature of the relationship. For instance, per our calculations in Section 5.6, the slope of the regression line for predicting the ideal family size from traditionalism is .58. Thus, for every unit that traditionalism increases, the ideal family size is predicted to increase by just over half a child (.58). A larger slope would indicate a greater effect of traditionalism on the ideal family size and, in this sense, the slope of the regression line provides insight into the strength, as well as the nature, of the relationship. For example, a slope of 1.13 would indicate that for every unit that traditionalism increases, the ideal family size is predicted to increase by 1.13 children.

14.7 Planning an Investigation Using Pearson Correlation

Appendix E.4 contains tables of the sample sizes necessary to achieve various levels of power for Pearson correlation for tests of the null hypothesis that $\rho = 0$. Table 14.1 reproduces a portion of this appendix for an alpha level of .05, nondirectional test. The first column presents selected values of power, and the column headings are population values of the correlation coefficient squared (that is, ρ^2).

To illustrate the use of this table, if the desired power is .80 and the researcher suspects that the strength of the relationship in the population corresponds to a ρ^2 of .15, then the number of participants that should be sampled for an alpha level of .05, nondirectional test, is 49. The power that an investigator requires will, of course, depend on the seriousness of committing a Type II error.

In addition to providing the sample size necessary to obtain a desired level of power, power tables can also be used to determine the power associated with Pearson correlation given the directionality of the test, the alpha level, the sample size, and the value of the correlation coefficient squared in the population. For instance, Table 14.1 shows that the power for a nondirectional test of Pearson correlation with $N = 55$ is .67 at an alpha level of .05 when $\rho^2 = .10$.

TABLE 14.1 **Approximate Sample Sizes Necessary to Achieve Selected Levels of Power for Alpha = .05, Nondirectional Test, as a Function of the Population Correlation Coefficient Squared**

Power	Population Correlation Coefficient Squared									
	.01	.03	.05	.07	.10	.15	.20	.25	.30	.35
.25	166	56	34	25	17	12	9	8	6	6
.50	384	127	76	54	38	25	19	15	12	10
.60	489	162	97	69	48	31	23	18	15	13
.67	570	188	112	80	55	36	27	21	17	14
.70	616	203	121	86	59	39	29	23	18	15
.75	692	228	136	96	67	43	32	25	20	17
.80	783	258	153	109	75	49	36	28	23	19
.85	895	294	175	124	85	56	41	32	26	21
.90	1,046	344	204	144	100	65	47	37	30	25
.95	1,308	429	255	180	124	80	58	46	37	30
.99	1,828	599	355	251	172	111	81	63	50	42

Examination of Table 14.1 and Appendix E.4 provides a general appreciation for the relationships among directionality, the alpha level, sample size, the strength of the relationship that one is trying to detect in the population, and power for Pearson correlation. As can be seen, power becomes greater as the alpha level, the sample size, and ρ^2 each increases.

14.8 Method of Presentation for Pearson Correlation

Reports of a correlational analysis should include the alpha level that was used, the degrees of freedom, the observed value of r, and the significance level. It is conventional to also provide the sample mean and the standard deviation estimate for each variable. It is not necessary to explicitly state the strength of the relationship between the variables because this is indicated by the square of the correlation coefficient. However, the confidence interval for the correlation coefficient should be presented. Although the nature of the relationship is indicated by the sign of the correlation coefficient, researchers often choose to state this verbally.

The results for the traditionalism and ideal family size study might be presented as follows:*

Results

A Pearson correlation between traditionalism (M = 5.00, SD = 2.98) and the ideal family size (M = 5.00, SD = 2.98) was found to be statistically significant at an alpha level

---

* The sample means for the two variables were derived in Table 5.2. The standard deviation estimates were calculated by applying the usual procedures for the variance estimate and the standard deviation estimate to the sums of squares for the two variables from the same table.

of .05, $r(8) = .66$, $p < .05$, indicating that the two variables are positively related. The 95% confidence interval for the correlation coefficient was .05 to .91.

14.9 Examples from the Literature

Personality Characteristics and Creativity

Psychologists have studied extensively the process of creativity. For instance, Barron (1965) examined the relationship between creativity and a number of personality dimensions in 44 eminent female mathematicians who were chosen by a panel of mathematics experts to attend a three-day session at the Institute of Personality Assessment and Research (IPAR) at the University of California at Berkeley.

While at IPAR, the mathematicians interacted in both formal and informal settings with the staff of the institute, who subsequently rated each woman on a number of personality characteristics. These ratings were then correlated with ratings of the women's creativity as previously generated by the panel of mathematics experts. The strongest correlations, all of which are statistically significant, are shown in Table 14.2. In each case, these represent strong effects, as indexed by r^2. Barron summarized these findings as suggesting that creativity is related to "genuine unconventionality, high intellectual ability, vividness or even flamboyance of character, moodiness and preoccupation, courage, and self-centeredness."

TABLE 14.2   Correlates of Creativity

Positive Correlations			Negative Correlations		
Personality characteristic	r	r^2	Personality characteristic	r	r^2
Thinks and associates to ideas in unusual ways; has unconventional thought processes	.64	.41	Judges self and others in conventional terms like "popularity," the "correct thing to do," "social pressures," and so forth	−.62	.38
Is an interesting, arresting person	.55	.30			
Tends to be rebellious and nonconforming	.51	.26	Is a genuinely dependable and responsible person	−.45	.20
Genuinely values intellectual and cognitive matters	.49	.24	Behaves in a sympathetic or considerate manner	−.43	.18
Appears to have a high degree of intellectual capacity	.46	.21	Favors conservative values in a variety of areas	−.40	.16
Is self-dramatizing; histrionic	.42	.18	Is moralistic	−.40	.16
Has fluctuating moods	.40	.16			

The Desire to Control Life Events and Gambling Frequency

Among the factors that have been hypothesized to influence gambling behavior is the belief that one can exert control over outcomes that are largely determined by chance. This belief, referred to as the illusion of control, is supposedly induced by elements of gambling situations that hint at the potential for personal control (for instance, observing horses during prerace warm-ups or deciding whether to hold or to draw cards at a poker game).

Burger and Smith (1985) proposed that a person's characteristic desire to control events in his or her life should relate to gambling behavior for games that hold an element of illusion of control but not for games that do not. To test this hypothesis, they asked 18 members of Gamblers Anonymous to complete a desire-to-control scale and to indicate the frequency with which they bet on a number of gambling games. Some of these games (casino games, lotteries) were conceptualized as not inducing an illusion of control, whereas others (card games, horse racing, sports events) were considered capable of inducing such an illusion. For each type of game, a total frequency score was derived for each individual by adding the appropriate frequency ratings. As predicted, desire-to-control scores were found to correlate significantly with gambling frequency for illusion-of-control games, $r(16) = 46$, $p < .05$, but not for the other games, $r(16) = .04, p > .10$. As indexed by r^2, the strengths of the relationships were .21 (representative of a strong effect) and .002 (representative of a weak effect), respectively.

14.10 Regression

In Chapter 5, we noted that a regression equation can be used to identify the value of variable Y that is predicted to be paired with an individual's score on variable X. Our discussion at that time focused on the scores of individuals who were members of the sample on which the regression equation was based. However, an important property of regression is that the ability to predict scores on one variable from scores on another can be extended to individuals who were not included in the original data set.

This is accomplished as follows: Scores on X and Y are determined for a sample of individuals. The procedures from Chapter 5 are then applied to the sample data to derive a regression equation that takes the general form $\hat{Y} = ax + b$. The values of a and b in this equation are estimates of α and β, respectively, in the linear model represented by Equation 14.1. The regression equation can then be applied to individuals outside of the original sample to make predictions about their scores on variable Y from their scores on variable X. This is done by substituting an individual's X score into the regression equation. The resulting value of $\hat{Y}$ is that individual's predicted score on Y.

In the context of regression, prediction merely refers to the fact that we are making inferences about one variable from a second variable. It does not imply that the latter variable precedes the former. For instance, individuals might formulate their beliefs about their ideal family size (variable Y in the traditionalism and ideal family size example) several years before they develop their traditionalism orientation (variable X in the traditionalism and ideal family size example). Nevertheless, we can use regression procedures to get an idea of what a person's ideal family size might be given knowledge of her traditionalism score. The variable that is being predicted, Y, is formally known as the **criterion variable**. The variable from which predictions are made, X, is formally known as the **predictor variable**.* The criterion variable is sometimes also referred to as the *dependent variable* and the predictor variable is sometimes also referred to as the *independent variable* to be consistent with the terminology that is used with other statistical tests.

Consider the following example: The personnel director of an insurance company has rated the performance of every underwriter who has worked for the company during the past 5 years on a scale of 1 to 10, where higher scores indicate greater success. All underwriters also completed an aptitude test designed to measure their work potential as part of the hiring process. Scores on this test could range from 0 to 100, with higher values indicating greater potential.

Suppose that a correlational analysis yields a statistically significant positive correlation between the aptitude test scores (X) and the performance ratings (Y). Given the significance of this relationship, the personnel director might construct a regression equation to help him screen future applicants for underwriting jobs by predicting who is likely to be successful, operationalized as a performance rating of 8 or higher, from aptitude scores.[†] Applicants who meet this criterion will be considered for employment, whereas applicants who do not meet this criterion will not be.

If the regression equation for predicting underwriting performance from aptitude test scores is found to be

$$\hat{Y} = .50 + .10X$$

what should we conclude about an applicant who obtains a test score of 85? Substituting this score into the regression equation, we find a predicted performance rating of

$$\hat{Y} = .50 + (.10)(85) = 9.00$$

A performance rating of 9.00 exceeds the minimum score of 8. Thus, based on this criterion, this applicant remains a viable candidate for employment. On the other hand, the predicted performance rating for an applicant who obtains a test score of 40 is

$$\hat{Y} = .50 + (.10)(40) = 4.50$$

A performance rating of 4.50 is lower than the minimum score of 8, so this individual will not be considered for a position with the company. The performance ratings for other applicants can be similarly estimated by substituting their aptitude test scores into the regression equation.

---

* Although the use of X to represent the independent (predictor) variable in the case of regression differs from the use of X to represent the dependent variable as presented in previous chapters, this notation is consistent with conventional practice in both instances.

† In practice, regression analyses that involve only one predictor variable are rarely encountered in the behavioral sciences. Far more common is the practice of predicting a criterion variable from two or more predictor variables. This technique, which is known as *multiple regression*, is overviewed in Section 18.6.

The Estimated Standard Error of Estimate

Unless the two variables are perfectly correlated, the use of a regression equation to predict scores on variable Y from scores on variable X will have some degree of error associated with it. For instance, the regression equation for predicting the ideal family size from traditionalism was found in Chapter 5 to be $\hat{Y} = 2.10 + .58X$. The predicted ideal family size for a traditionalism score of, for example, 8 according to this equation is $2.10 + (.58)(8) = 6.74$ or, rounded to the nearest whole number, 7. Surely, though, not every woman who obtains a score of 8 on the traditionalism questionnaire desires a family this large. What is needed to gain insight into the predictive utility of a regression equation is an estimate of how much error will occur when predicting scores on Y from scores on X. Such a measure is provided by the *estimated standard error of estimate*.

When we introduced the standard error of estimate in Chapter 5, we defined it in Equation 5.12 as

$$s_{YX} = \sqrt{\frac{\sum(Y - \hat{Y})^2}{N}}$$

where s_{YX} is the standard error of estimate, Y is an individual's actual score on variable Y, $\hat{Y}$ is an individual's predicted score on variable Y based on the regression equation, and N is the sample size. Although this formula represents the average amount of predictive error when predicting scores on Y *across a set of sample data*, it is not an appropriate estimate of how much error will occur when predicting scores on Y *across the population*.

However, the population value of the standard error of estimate (σ_{YX}) can be estimated from sample data by substituting the associated degrees of freedom ($N - 2$) for N in Equation 5.12. These are equal to $N - 2$ because both the slope and the intercept of the regression line must be estimated. This yields the following formula for the **estimated standard error of estimate**:

$$\hat{s}_{YX} = \sqrt{\frac{\sum(Y - \hat{Y})^2}{N - 2}} \qquad\qquad [14.5]$$

where $\hat{s}_{YX}$ is the estimated standard error of estimate and all other terms are as previously defined. This formula estimates the average error that will be made across the population when predicting individuals' scores on variable Y from the regression equation. Indeed, the estimated standard error of estimate represents an estimate of the standard deviation of the ε scores in the linear model represented in Equation 14.1.

Analogous to the computational formulas for the sample standard error of estimate that we presented in Chapter 5 (Equations 5.13 and 5.14), in practice the estimated standard error of estimate is most efficiently calculated using the equation

$$\hat{s}_{YX} = \hat{s}_Y \sqrt{\left(\frac{N - 1}{N - 2}\right)(1 - r^2)} \qquad\qquad [14.6]$$

if one is working with the standard deviation estimate for variable Y and the equation

$$\hat{s}_{YX} = \sqrt{\frac{SS_Y(1 - r^2)}{N - 2}} \qquad [14.7]$$

if one is working with the sum of squares for variable Y.

The interpretation of $\hat{s}_{YX}$ directly follows that for s_{YX}. First, its absolute magnitude provides an estimate of the amount of predictive error that will occur across the population. Second, $\hat{s}_{YX}$ can be compared with the estimated standard deviation of Y. The estimated standard deviation of Y estimates what the average error in prediction would be if one were to predict that everyone in the population has a Y score equal to the mean of Y. If variable X helps to predict variable Y, then the estimated standard error of estimate will be smaller than the estimated standard deviation of Y, and the better the predictor X is, the smaller the estimated standard error of estimate will be.

The estimated standard error of estimate for the traditionalism and ideal family size example is

$$\hat{s}_{YX} = \sqrt{\frac{SS_Y(1 - r^2)}{N - 2}}$$

$$= \sqrt{\frac{60.00(1 - .66^2)}{10 - 2}} = 2.06$$

which indicates that, on average, predicted Y (ideal family size) scores are estimated to deviate from actual Y scores by 2.06 units. Given the range of possible ideal family sizes, this degree of error is not unreasonable.

We can gain further insight into the predictive utility of the regression equation by comparing this value with the estimated standard deviation of Y. Because SS_Y was found in Chapter 5 to be equal to 60.00 and $N = 10$, $\hat{s}_Y = \sqrt{SS_Y/(N - 1)} = \sqrt{60.0/(10 - 1)} = 2.58$. Thus, predicting scores on variable Y from scores on variable X leads to considerably less error (an estimated average prediction error of 2.06 units) than if all Y scores were predicted to be equal to $\overline{Y}$ (an estimated average prediction error of 2.58 units).

14.11   Method of Presentation for Regression

The results of a regression analysis might be presented in several ways. One approach is to include the regression equation and the estimated standard error of estimate along with the information for the correlational analysis. For the traditionalism and ideal family size study, this would require that a statement similar to the following be added to the Results section in Section 14.8: "The regression equation for predicting the ideal family size from traditionalism was found to be $\hat{Y} = 2.10 + .58X$, and the estimated standard error of estimate was found to be 2.06."

On occasion, written reports of regression results are supplemented by scatterplots that show the observed data points and the regression line. By visually depicting this information, such displays can help the reader to more fully appreciate the numerical indices that we discuss in this chapter.

14.12 Numerical Example

A common approach of dating services is matching individuals who indicate similar qualities on questionnaires that they complete as part of the membership process. Underlying this strategy is an important assumption: People will be attracted to others who are similar to themselves.

To test the validity of this assumption, suppose that a researcher randomly matches 15 female members of a dating service with male members who share from one to 10 interests as measured by a ten-item questionnaire. That is, some women are randomly assigned partners who respond the same way as they do on all 10 questions, some are assigned partners who respond the same way as they do on 9 of the questions, and so on, all the way down to 1 similar questionnaire response. Thus, the similarity between partners can range from 1 to 10 shared interests, with higher scores indicating greater similarity. Following their first date with their assigned partner, each woman is asked to rate how attracted she is to this individual on a scale of 1 to 10, where higher ratings indicate greater attraction.

The scores for the two variables are presented in columns 2 and 3, respectively, of Table 14.3. Because the researcher is interested in how partner similarity predicts attraction, the former is conceptualized as variable X and the latter is conceptualized as variably Y.

The null hypothesis of no linear relationship states that the population correlation between these two variables is 0. The alternative hypothesis states that the population correlation is nonzero. These hypotheses can be formally stated as

$$H_0: \ \rho = 0$$

$$H_1: \ \rho \neq 0$$

TABLE 14.3 **Data and Calculation of Intermediate Statistics for Similarity and Attraction Experiment**

Individual	X	Y	X^2	Y^2	XY
1	10	8	100	64	80
2	8	6	64	36	48
3	6	4	36	16	24
4	4	2	16	4	8
5	2	3	4	9	6
6	10	6	100	36	60
7	8	8	64	64	64
8	6	5	36	25	30
9	7	9	49	81	63
10	4	5	16	25	20
11	1	3	1	9	3
12	3	1	9	1	3
13	5	3	25	9	15
14	7	5	49	25	35
15	9	7	81	49	63
	$\Sigma X = 90$	$\Sigma Y = 75$	$\Sigma X^2 = 650$	$\Sigma Y^2 = 453$	$\Sigma XY = 522$
	$\overline{X} = 6.00$	$\overline{Y} = 5.00$			

For an alpha level of .05, nondirectional test, and $N - 2 = 15 - 2 = 13$ degrees of freedom, the critical values of r from Appendix H are $\pm.514$.

Per Equation 5.8, the correlation coefficient can be calculated as

$$r = \frac{\sum XY - \dfrac{(\sum X)(\sum Y)}{N}}{\sqrt{\left[\sum X^2 - \dfrac{(\sum X)^2}{N}\right]\left[\sum Y^2 - \dfrac{(\sum Y)^2}{N}\right]}}$$

The intermediate statistics necessary for the application of this formula are computed in Table 14.3. From these we can derive the correlation coefficient:

$$r = \frac{522 - \dfrac{(90)(75)}{15}}{\sqrt{\left(650 - \dfrac{90^2}{72.00}\right)\left(453 - \dfrac{75^2}{72.00}\right)}}$$

$$= \frac{72.00}{\sqrt{(110.00)(78.00)}} = .78$$

Because .78 is greater than $+.514$, we reject the null hypothesis and conclude that some degree of a linear relationship exists between similarity with one's partner and attraction.

The strength of the relationship is indicated by the square of the correlation coefficient:

$$r^2 = 78^2 = .61$$

Thus, the proportion of variability in the attraction ratings that is associated with partner similarity is .61, as indexed by a linear model. This represents a strong effect.

Applying the procedure described in Appendix 14.2, we find that the 95% confidence interval for the correlation coefficient is .45 to .92. We are 95% confident that the true population correlation coefficient falls within this interval.

The nature of the relationship is indicated by the sign of the correlation coefficient. Because the correlation between partner similarity and attraction is positive, we conclude that these variables approximate a direct linear relationship.

If the researcher was interested in identifying the regression equation for predicting attraction (Y) from partner similarity (X), she would first determine the slope using Equation 5.10:

$$b = \frac{SCP}{SS_X}$$

$$= \frac{72}{110} = .65$$

The obtained value of b can then be substituted into Equation 5.11 along with the means of the two variables to yield the intercept:

$$a = \overline{Y} - b\overline{X}$$

The regression equation is thus

$$\hat{Y} = a + bX$$
$$= 1.10 + .65X$$

This equation can be used to make predictions about how attracted a woman will be to a man following a first date. For instance, a woman is unlikely to be attracted to a man who shares only 3 of 10 interests because the predicted attraction score for a similarity score of 3 is $1.10 + (.65)(3) = 3.05$. In contrast, the predicted attraction score is $1.10 + (.65)(10) = 7.60$ when the two individuals agree on all 10 interests.

These predictions are, of course, subject to error. Specifically, the standard error of estimate in this instance is estimated to be

$$\hat{s}_{YX} = \sqrt{\frac{SS_Y(1 - r^2)}{N - 2}}$$
$$= \sqrt{\frac{78.00(1 - .78^2)}{15 - 2}} = 1.53$$

which indicates that, on average, predicted Y (attraction) scores are estimated to deviate from actual Y scores by 1.53 units. This represents a relatively small degree of error.

To gain further insight into the predictive utility of the regression equation, we can compare the estimated standard error of estimate with the estimated standard deviation of Y. Because $SS_Y = 78.00$ and $N = 15$, $\hat{s}_Y = \sqrt{SS_Y/(N - 1)} = \sqrt{78.00/(15 - 1)} = 2.36$. Thus, predicting scores on variable Y from scores on variable X leads to considerably less error (an estimated average prediction error of 1.53 units) than if all Y scores were predicted to be equal to $\overline{Y}$ (an estimated average prediction error of 2.36 units).

Methodological Considerations

As we noted in Chapter 9, the ability to make a causal inference between two variables is a function of one's research design, not the statistical technique that is used to analyze the data that are yielded by that research design. Thus, as we discussed in Section 5.4, correlation does not necessarily imply causation. Note, however, that the present study used an experimental research strategy: Individuals were *randomly assigned* partners who ranged in similarity from 1 to 10 shared interests. To the extent that confounding variables were controlled, we can thus infer that in this investigation similarity between partners *caused* attraction to vary as it did.

In fact, as with all statistical techniques, causality can be inferred from a statistically significant correlational analysis anytime an experimental, as opposed to an observational, research strategy is used (assuming, of course, that confounding variables are controlled). We should note, however, that in practice most applications of correlation and regression use an observational approach.

Other noteworthy methodological considerations relate to the issues that we addressed in Section 5.7. First, the results above apply only to the linear relationship between the two variables. If we were interested in the nonlinear relationship between similarity and attraction, we could use the curvilinear regression procedures that are described in Pedhazur (1997). Second, the use of regression to predict attraction from partner similarity is predicated on the fact that the researcher explicitly manipulated similarity so that she could determine how it affects attraction. Thus, there would be no justification for deriving the regression equation for predicting partner similarity from attraction. Third, because the sample similarity scores ranged from 1 to 10 similar questionnaire responses, our conclusions apply only across these values. For instance, we are unable to infer the effect of *no* similarity (that is, no similar questionnaire responses) on attraction or what the attraction ratings would be if dating partners shared more than 10 interests.

14.13   Links Between Computer Results and Book Content

As we discussed in Chapter 5, statistical computer output for Pearson correlation often takes the form of a correlation matrix in which every variable that is specified by the user is correlated with every other variable as well as with itself. The coefficients for the individual correlations are usually accompanied by the sample size on which each is based and the corresponding *p* value. Because of differences in the amount of missing data across variables, different coefficients may be based on different numbers of cases.

Given the large number of variables that are often included in correlational studies, correlation matrices are often extensive. For example, if 10 variables are intercorrelated with one another, the matrix will contain 100 correlation coefficients. Fortunately, however, consistent with our discussion in Section 8.14, many statistical programs use asterisks or some other method to delineate any coefficient that has a low significance level. For instance, one asterisk might indicate that a correlation coefficient is statistically significant at an alpha level of .05 and two asterisks might indicate that a coefficient is statistically significant at an alpha level of .01. As we noted in Section 8.14, this format makes it easy for the researcher to differentiate statistically significant from statistically nonsignificant findings, and circling or highlighting the statistically significant coefficients further emphasizes them.

The computer output for a regression analysis is often extensive and typically includes the values of r, r^2, the intercept, the slope, and the estimated standard error of estimate. Tests that the intercept and the slope are equal to 0 in the population are usually also provided along with their corresponding estimated standard errors.

It is also common for regression output to contain terms and symbols other than those that we have discussed. For instance, two types of *regression coefficients*, each of which is mathematically equivalent to a concept from this chapter, are usually reported for a given regression problem: a *standardized coefficient*, which will be equal to the Pearson correlation coefficient for that problem, and an *unstandardized coefficient*, which will be equal to the slope of the regression line. However, a standardized regression coefficient is usually labeled as β or Beta rather than r, and an unstandardized regression coefficient might be labeled as B rather than b depending on the statistical program that is used. Also, r and r^2 are often denoted as R and R^2, respectively.

14.14   Links Between Chapters

In addition to being highly related to Chapter 5, this chapter also has several ties to later chapters. First, Section 16.8 presents a nonparametric alternative to Pearson correlation known as *Spearman rank-order correlation* for when scores on the two variables under study are in the form of ranks. In fact, Chapter 16 also presents nonparametric counterparts for many of the other tests that we have discussed. Second, Section 18.6 provides an overview of a technique known as *multiple regression* that extends the regression procedures that we have discussed to the prediction of a criterion variable from two or more predictor variables.

Applications to the Analysis of a Social Problem Using SPSS for Windows

We noted in both Chapters 11 and 12 that the quality of the relationship between parent and teen is an important predictor of many teen problem behaviors. For example, research indicates that teens who have relatively poor relationships with their parents tend to be more sexually active than other teens.

There are at least two interpretations for this finding. The first posits that teens become sexually active for reasons unrelated to the parental relationship (for example, because of peer pressure or hormonal influences). At some point, the parent finds out about the teen's sexuality and this causes friction between the parent and the teen. Furthermore, the more sexual the teen is, the more friction there is assumed to be. In short, this interpretation holds that increased sexual activity on the part of the teen causes a deterioration of the parent–teen relationship as the parent learns of the extent of the teen's sexual behavior.

A second interpretation reverses the causal direction between the two variables. According to this view, teens reject parental values and seek out risky behaviors to assert their independence because they are unhappy at home. Having distanced themselves from their parents, such teens are more susceptible to peer pressure to engage in sexual behavior, with the result being increased sexual activity. This interpretation, in essence, holds that the poor relationship between the parent and the teen causes increased sexual activity.

We can gain insight into the validity of each of these interpretations by examining the relationship between teens' satisfaction with the maternal relationship and the level of sexual activity for adolescents whose mothers do not think that they are sexual. If the first interpretation is correct (that is, if the quality of the parent–teen relationship deteriorates as the parent learns of the extent of the teen's sexual behavior), this relationship should be statistically nonsignificant because the mothers are not aware of their teens' sexual activity. However, if the second interpretation is correct (that is, if a poor relationship with the parent leads to increased sexual activity on the part of the teen), this relationship should be negative (as it should also be for adolescents whose mothers are aware that they are sexual).

To examine this issue, we tested the Pearson correlation between the teens' satisfaction with the maternal relationship and their sexual frequency for those sexually active teens in the parent–teen communication study described in Chapter 1 whose mothers believed that their child had never engaged in sexual intercourse. Satisfaction with the maternal relationship was assessed using the measure that we describe in Chapter 12, and sexual intercourse frequency was assessed using the measure that we describe in Chapter 4. Recall that the former measure consisted of an overall index of relationship satisfaction that was derived by summing teens' responses to 11 statements about different facets of their maternal relationship. Scores on this index could range from 11 to 55, with higher values indicating greater satisfaction with the maternal relationship. Also recall that the latter measure consisted of the teens' self-reports of the number of times that they had engaged in sexual intercourse during the past 6 months.

Before conducting the correlational analysis, we examined the distributions of the two variables. Figure 14.2 presents a grouped frequency histogram for each, with a normal distribution superimposed in each case. Both variables exhibit marked skewness, suggesting that the assumption of bivariate normality is violated, as normality of each variable is a necessary condition for bivariate normality. However, given our sample size, the test of the correlation coefficient will be robust to any bivariate nonnormality that exists in the population (Van den Brink, 1988).

Consistent with our discussion of the effects of outliers on the correlation coefficient in Section 5.7, the few extreme scores for the sexual intercourse variable raise concerns about outlier effects. Also, an examination of the assumption of equal Y score variances across the values of X using a procedure described by Judge, Griffiths, Hill, Lutkephol, and Lee (1985) indicated sufficient sample heterogeneity to suggest that population heterogeneity might be problematic. Because of these concerns, we supplemented the Pearson correlation with other correlational analyses that are resistant to outliers and that are not adversely affected by heterogeneous Y score variances. One such method is Spearman rank-order correlation, which we discuss in Section 16.8. Another method is based on M estimators (Hamilton, 1992). Both of these analyses yielded results similar to those that we report here based on Pearson correlation.

Table 14.4 presents the computer output for the Pearson correlation analysis. The results are presented in the form of a correlation matrix, as we discussed in Chapter 5. The entries where the variable SMOTHER (which is the relationship satisfaction variable) intersects with the variable SEXNUM (which is the sexual intercourse variable) contain the information for the correlation between these two variables. The first entry is the correlation coefficient, and the second entry is the corresponding nondirectional p value.* Because this is less than .05, the correlation is statistically significant. Even for teens whose mothers believe that their child has never engaged in sexual intercourse, some approximation to a negative linear relationship exists between relationship satisfaction and sexual activity: The poorer the maternal relationship, the more sexually active the teen tends to be. This finding is consistent with the proposal that a poor relationship between the parent and the teen causes increased sexual activity but not with the proposal that teen sexual activity causes a deterioration in the parent–teen relationship as the parent learns of the extent of the teen's sexual behavior. The third entry is the sample size.[†]

Figure 14.3 presents the scatterplot for these variables, with the regression line also indicated. This plot has considerable "noise" in it, and it is difficult to discern any linear trend, which is typical of scatterplots of real data. Neat, easily interpreted scatterplots such as those presented in Chapter 5 are typically found only for hypothetical data in statistics textbooks! Because of this, statisticians have developed *smoothing techniques* that remove much of the "noise" from the scatterplot and thereby provide a better picture of the fundamental trends in the data (Moore and McCabe, 1993).

One smoothing technique is to present a scatterplot for scores on variable X and the mean Y score that corresponds to each X value. Figure 14.4 presents such a graph. The linear trend is more apparent in the smoothed than in the original scatterplot. The smoothed scatterplot also indicates an "outlying mean" (a mean sexual intercourse incidence of 22) at a relationship satisfaction score

(continued)

---

* Following convention, a period rather than a p value is presented for the correlation of a variable with itself. As we noted in Section 5.8, such a correlation will always be equal to 1.00.

† Note that the correlation between the two variables is based on fewer cases ($N = 450$) than is either the correlation of SEXNUM with itself ($N = 452$) or the correlation of SMOTHER with itself ($N = 467$). This reflects the fact that the two variables have missing scores for different individuals, which serves to reduce the sample size for the correlation between two variables relative to the sample size for the correlation between either variable and itself.

FIGURE 14.2   **Grouped Frequency Histograms for (a) Instances of Sexual Intercourse and (b) Relationship Satisfaction**

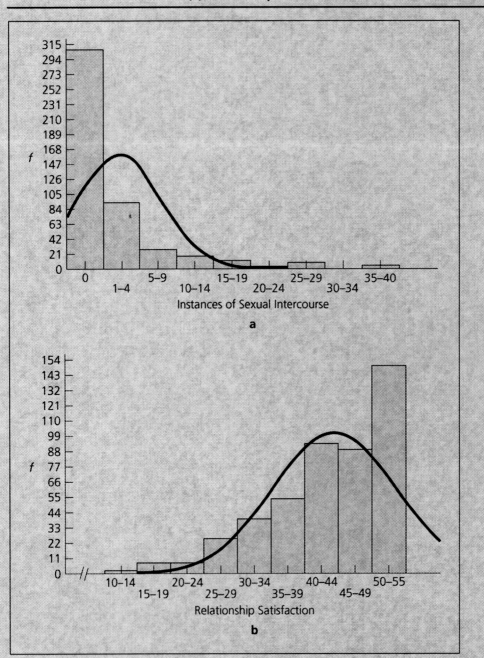

Instances of Sexual Intercourse

a

Relationship Satisfaction

b

TABLE 14.4   Computer Output for Pearson Correlation Between Instances of Sexual Intercourse and Relationship Satisfaction

Correlations

		SEXNUM	SMOTHER
SEXNUM	Pearson Correlation	1.000	−.177
	Sig. (2-tailed)	.	.000
	N	452	450
SMOTHER	Pearson Correlation	−.177	1.000
	Sig. (2-tailed)	.000	.
	N	450	467

of 20. It turns out that this point represents a single individual whose impact on the correlation coefficient is not substantial, given the large sample size.

Although it is inconsistent with the proposal that the quality of the parent–teen relationship deteriorates as the parent learns of the extent of the teen's sexual behavior, the finding of a statistically significant negative correlation between relationship satisfaction and sexual activity for teens whose mothers are unaware of their sexuality does not rule out the possibility that sexual activity causes a deterioration of the parent–teen relationship. It only questions the particular mechanism that was suggested as being the causal factor (that is, that the mother finding out about the extent of the

FIGURE 14.3   Scatterplot and Regression Line for Instances of Sexual Intercourse and Relationship Satisfaction

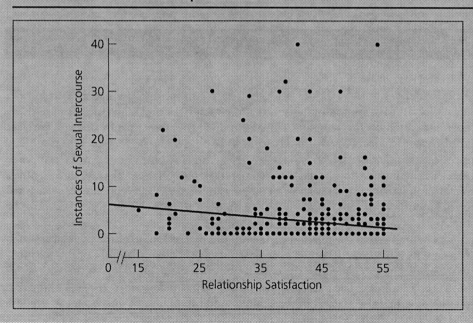

(continued)

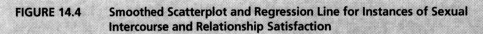

FIGURE 14.4   Smoothed Scatterplot and Regression Line for Instances of Sexual Intercourse and Relationship Satisfaction

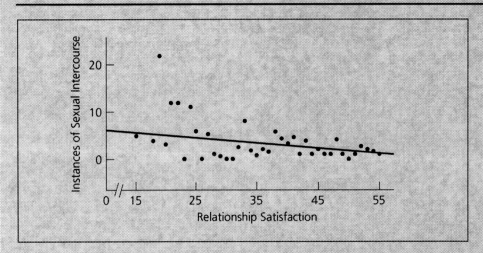

teen's sexual behavior causes the relationship problems). There are other ways in which sexual activity on the part of teens might influence their relationship satisfaction. For example, adolescents who become highly committed to an intense, sexual relationship may spend less time on homework (thereby causing a decline in their school performance) and less time with their parents, and this may cause the parent–teen relationship to deteriorate. These possibilities can be explored in more fine-grained analysis.

Summary

Pearson correlation is typically used to analyze the relationship between two variables when (1) both variables are quantitative in nature and are measured on a level that at least approximates interval characteristics, (2) the two variables have been measured on the same individuals, and (3) the observations on each variable are between-subjects in nature. Hypothesis testing logic analogous to that applied in prior chapters is used to infer whether a correlation exists between two variables in the population based on the correlation coefficient that is observed in a set of sample data. This involves a comparison of the observed value of r with the critical value(s) of r to decide whether the null hypothesis that $\rho = 0$ should be rejected.

The strength of the relationship is indexed by the square of the correlation coefficient, which is formally known as the coefficient of determination. Confidence intervals can also be calculated for the correlation coefficient, although the procedure for doing so is complex. The nature of the relationship is indicated by the sign of the correlation coefficient observed in the sample. Additional insight into both the strength and the nature of the relationship is provided by the slope of the regression line.

Regression equations can be applied to individuals outside of the original sample to make predictions about their scores on variable Y (the criterion variable) from their scores on variable X (the predictor variable). This is done by substituting an individual's X score into the regression equation. The resulting value of $\hat{Y}$ is that individual's predicted score on Y. An estimate of the average error that will be made across the population when making such predictions is provided by the estimated standard error of estimate.

Appendix 14.1   Testing Null Hypotheses Other Than $\rho = 0$

Occasionally, an investigator will want to test a null hypothesis that ρ is equal to a value other than 0. As we noted in Section 14.3, when ρ does not equal 0, the sampling distribution of r is skewed. However, Fisher (1950) derived a logarithmic transformation of r, which we will symbolize r' (read r prime), that has two desirable properties: (1) the sampling distribution of r' is approximately normally distributed irrespective of the value of ρ and (2) the standard error of r' is essentially independent of ρ.* Because of these properties, it is possible to convert a sample correlation coefficient (r) to an r' value and then use the normal distribution to test the null hypothesis that ρ is equal to some value other than 0.

The formula for converting r to r' is

$$r' = .50[\log_e(1 + r) - \log_e(1 - r)] \quad [14.8]$$

where $\log_e$ indicates that the natural logarithms of the quantities that follow it [in the present instance, $(1 + r)$ and $(1 - r)$] are to be calculated. Note that all terms in Equation 14.8 are constants except for r. Thus, r' is simply a rescaling of r. In practice, however, it is not necessary to actually calculate r' because this has been done in Appendix I, which presents a table of values of r' for selected values of r.†

Figure 14.5 presents sampling distributions of r' for $\rho = -.80$, $\rho = 0$, and $\rho = +.80$,

for $N = 10$. Compare these distributions with the comparable sampling distributions of r in Figure 14.1. Unlike the sampling distributions of r, the sampling distributions of r' are similar in shape and variability. This reflects the fact that, as noted above, the standard error of r' is, for all intents and purposes, independent of ρ. Specifically, the standard error of r' (symbolized as $\sigma_{r'}$) is equal to

$$\sigma_{r'} = \frac{1}{\sqrt{N - 3}} \quad [14.9]$$

The above suggests the following equation for testing the null hypothesis that ρ is equal to some value other than 0:

$$z = \frac{r' - \rho'}{\sigma_{r'}} \quad [14.10]$$

where ρ' (read *rho prime*) is the log-transformed value that corresponds to the hypothesized value of ρ, and r' and $\sigma_{r'}$ are as defined above. Substituting these values into Equation 14.10 yields a z score, which is then compared with the appropriate critical value(s) of z from Appendix B. For an alpha level of .05, nondirectional test, these values are ±1.96. As usual, if the observed z score exceeds either the positive or the negative critical value, we will reject the null hypothesis. Otherwise, we will fail to reject the null hypothesis.

---

* Fisher (1950) refers to the r transformation using the symbol Z. Thus, you might see reference in the literature to *Fisher's r to Z transform*. We use the symbol r' to avoid confusing transformed r values with z scores.
† Appendix I can also be used to determine log-transformed values for ρ.

FIGURE 14.5 **Sampling Distribution of r' for Three Values of ρ for $N = 10$**

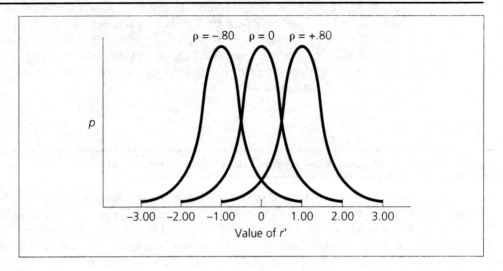

As an example of these procedures, consider the following null and alternative hypotheses:

H_0: $\rho = .25$

H_1: $\rho \neq .25$

Suppose that a correlation of .45 is observed for $N = 100$. From Appendix I, the value of r' that corresponds to a sample correlation coefficient of .45 is .485, and the value of ρ' that corresponds to a population correlation coefficient of .25 is .255.

Applying Equation 14.9, we find that the standard error of r' in this instance equals

$$\sigma_{r'} = \frac{1}{\sqrt{N - 3}}$$

$$= \frac{1}{\sqrt{100 - 3}} = .10$$

The observed value of z is thus

$$z = \frac{r' - \rho'}{\sigma_{r'}}$$

$$= \frac{.485 - .255}{.10} = 2.30$$

This value exceeds the positive critical value of +1.9, so we reject the null hypothesis that the population correlation is .25. Because the sample correlation coefficient of .45 is greater than the hypothesized population correlation coefficient of .25, we conclude that the population correlation between the two variables is greater than .25.

Appendix 14.2   Confidence Intervals for the Correlation Coefficient

The calculation of confidence intervals for the correlation coefficient requires that the observed value of r be converted to an r' value using Appendix I, as we discussed in Appendix 14.1. It also requires that the standard error of r' (that

is, $\sigma_{r'}$) be calculated using Equation 14.9. These values can then be substituted into the following formula to yield a confidence interval for r':

$$CI = r' - (z)(\sigma_{r'}) \quad \text{to} \quad r' + (z)(\sigma_{r'}) \quad [14.11]$$

where z is the positive value of z from Appendix B that corresponds to 1.00 minus the confidence level. The final step is to convert the confidence limits for r' to the confidence limits for r. This can be accomplished using Appendix I.

For the traditionalism and ideal family size study, $r = .66$ and $N = 10$. From Appendix I, the value of r' that corresponds to an r of .66 is .793. Per Equation 14.9, the standard error of r' is

$$\sigma_{r'} = \frac{1}{\sqrt{N-3}}$$

$$= \frac{1}{\sqrt{10-3}} = .38$$

If we are interested in the 95% confidence interval for r, we can calculate the 95% confidence interval for r' as follows:

$$CI = .793 - (1.96)(.38) \quad \text{to}$$

$$.793 + (1.96)(.38)$$

$$= .050 \quad \text{to} \quad 1.54$$

Finally, we convert these confidence limits to confidence limits for r using Appendix I. This yields a confidence interval of .05 to .91. We are 95% confident that the true population correlation coefficient falls within this interval.

Exercises

Answers to asterisked (*) exercises appear at the back of the book.

Exercises to Review Concepts

1. Under what conditions is Pearson correlation typically used to analyze a bivariate relationship?

*2. Explain the equivalence between the t test procedure for testing the significance of a correlation coefficient using Equation 14.2 and the procedure for testing the significance of a correlation coefficient by comparing the observed value of r with critical values of r.

*3. State the critical value(s) of r for Pearson correlation for an alpha level of .05 under each of the following conditions:
   a. $H_0: \rho = 0, H_1: \rho \neq 0, N = 32$
   b. $H_0: \rho = 0, H_1: \rho \neq 0, N = 22$
   c. $H_0: \rho = 0, H_1: \rho > 0, N = 22$
   d. $H_0: \rho = 0, H_1: \rho < 0, N = 15$
   e. $H_0: \rho = 0, H_1: \rho \neq 0, N = 67$

4. What are the assumptions underlying Pearson correlation?

5. What is the relationship between eta-squared and the correlation coefficient?

Use the following data to complete Exercises 6–9.

Individual	X	Y
1	4	9
2	7	11
3	9	14
4	9	10
5	2	8
6	12	14
7	4	8
8	5	9
9	13	10
10	3	7

*6. Compute the Pearson correlation coefficient and test for a relationship between variables X and Y using a nondirectional test.

*7. Compute the value of r^2. Does the observed value represent a weak, moderate, or strong effect?

*8. Compute the 95% confidence interval.

*9. What is the nature of the relationship between the two variables?

Use the following data to complete Exercises 10–13.

Individual	X	Y
1	4	5
2	8	2
3	3	4
4	9	10
5	2	4
6	1	2
7	7	8
8	4	8
9	1	5
10	7	9
11	6	5
12	3	6
13	1	2

10. Compute the Pearson correlation coefficient and test for a relationship between variables X and Y using a nondirectional test.
11. Compute the value of r^2. Does the observed value represent a weak, moderate, or strong effect?
12. Compute the 95% confidence interval.
13. What is the nature of the relationship between the two variables?

For each of the studies described in Exercises 14–18, indicate the appropriate statistical test for analyzing the relationship between the variables. Assume that the underlying assumptions of the tests have been satisfied.

*14. An investigator examined the effects of two drugs on learning. Thirty participants were randomly assigned to take the first drug and a different 30 were randomly assigned to take the second drug. The mean scores on a learning task were compared for the two groups.

*15. A consumer psychologist tested preference for three brands of ice cream. One hundred individuals rated each of the three brands on a scale ranging from 1 to 15. The mean ratings for the three brands were compared.

*16. A sociologist studied the effect of the nuclear accident at Three Mile Island on attitudes toward nuclear energy. One hundred people had been interviewed several months prior to the accident and their attitudes measured on a 10-point scale. Five days after the accident they were reinterviewed and their attitudes measured again. The mean attitude scores were compared across interviews.

17. A researcher tested the relationship between age and blood pressure in a sample of 250 adults.

18. An investigator examined whether different driving conditions require different amounts of gas. Twenty midsize cars were driven 50 miles on smooth roads, 20 were driven 50 miles on hilly roads, and 20 were driven 50 miles on mountainous roads. The mean gas consumption was compared for the three conditions.

*19. If a researcher suspects that the strength of the relationship between two variables in the population is .15 as indexed by the correlation coefficient squared, what sample size should she use in a study involving an alpha level of .05, directional test, to achieve a power of .90?

20. Suppose that an investigator conducts a correlational analysis with $N = 32$. If the value of the correlation coefficient squared in the population is .20, what would the power of his statistical test be at an alpha level of .05, nondirectional test?

21. What is the meaning of prediction in the context of regression?

*22. What information is conveyed by the estimated standard error of estimate?

*23. Compute the regression equation for predicting variable Y from variable X for the data used in Exercises 6–9. What is the predicted Y score for an X score of 3? What is the predicted Y score for an X score of 7? What is the predicted Y score for an X score of 11?

*24. Compute the estimated standard error of estimate for the data used in Exercises 6–9.

25. Compute the regression equation for predicting variable Y from variable X for the data used in Exercises 10–13. What is the predicted Y score for an X score of 2? What is the predicted Y score for an X score of 8? What is the predicted Y score for an X score of 8.50?

26. Compute the estimated standard error of estimate for the data used in Exercises 10–13.

Multiple-Choice Questions

*27. When $\rho = 0$, the sampling distribution of the correlation coefficient will be skewed.
   a. true
   b. false

28. The error score (ε) in the linear model reflects all factors that are uncorrelated with variable X that influence variable Y.
   a. true
   b. false

*29. The estimated standard error of estimate reflects the deviation of
   a. scores on variable X from scores on variable Y
   b. scores on variable X from predicted scores on variable Y
   c. scores on variable Y from predicted scores on variable X
   d. scores on variable Y from predicted scores on variable Y

30. Researchers pursue regression analysis only if a test of Pearson correlation yields statistically nonsignificant results.
   a. true
   b. false

31. If a researcher suspects that the strength of the relationship between two variables in the population is .05 as indexed by the correlation coefficient squared, what sample size should she use in a study involving an alpha level of .05, nondirectional test, to achieve a power of .80?
   a. 121   c. 195
   b. 153   d. 227

*32. The symbol for the coefficient of determination is
   a. r c. b
   b. r^2 d. ρ

*33. Smoothing techniques provide a better sense of the fundamental trends in the data by removing "noise" from a scatterplot.
   a. true
   b. false

34. The slope of the regression line is an index of the strength of the relationship between two variables.
   a. true
   b. false

*35. In the context of regression, the variable from which predictions are made (X) is known as the _____ variable and the variable being predicted (Y) is known as the _____ variable.
   a. independent; predictor
   b. criterion; dependent
   c. criterion; predictor
   d. predictor; criterion

Use the following information to complete Exercises 36–46.

An exercise physiologist studied the relationship between age and the number of sit-ups women that can do. A sample of 21 women aged 18 and older were shown the proper form and asked to do as many sit-ups as possible during a 5-minute period. The mean age of the participants was 36.37 with a sum of squares of 1,446.85, the mean number of sit-ups was 23.21 with a sum of squares of 3,018.96, and the sum of cross-products was −1,247.01.

*36. If the value of the correlation coefficient squared in the population is .35, what is the power of the statistical test at an alpha level of .05, nondirectional test?
   a. .67   c. .85
   b. .75   d. .90

*37. The observed value of r is
   a. −.36   c. −.75
   b. −.60   d. −.77

38. Based on this study, we can conclude that age and the number of sit-ups that women can do are related.
    a. true
    b. false
*39. It is possible that the test results reflect a Type I error.
    a. true
    b. false
40. It is possible that the test results reflect a Type II error.
    a true
    b. false
41. The strength of the relationship, as indexed by r^2, is
    a. −.36   c. .56
    b. .36   d. .59
42. The 95% confidence interval is
    a. −1.16 to −.22
    b. −.82 to −.22
    c. −81 to −.58
    d. −.67 to −.52
*43. What can we conclude about the relationship between age and the number of sit-ups that women can do?
    a. The two variables approximate a direct linear relationship.
    b. The two variables approximate an inverse linear relationship.
    c. There is no linear relationship between the two variables.
    d. There may or may not be some degree of a linear relationship between the two variables.
*44. What is the regression equation for predicting the number of sit-ups that women can do from age?
    a. $\hat{Y} = 38.12 − .41X$
    b. $\hat{Y} = 45.89 − .41X$
    c. $\hat{Y} = 54.49 − .86X$
    d. $\hat{Y} = 56.33 − .86X$
45. What is the estimated standard error of estimate for predicting the number of sit-ups that women can do from age?
    a. 5.24   c. 7.56
    b. 6.98   d. 10.08

46. What is the predicted number of sit-ups for a woman who is 42 years of age?
    a. 18.37   c. 28.67
    b. 20.21   d. none of the above

Exercises to Apply Concepts

*47. Behavioral scientists have extensively studied the factors that determine an effective leader in small-group problem-solving situations. Much of this work has used a scale developed by Fiedler (1967) to measure leadership style. The scale involves having individuals think of all the people with whom they have ever worked and singling out their least preferred coworker (LPC). They then rate this coworker on a series of dimensions, such as the extent to which they believe that the person was pleasant, friendly, and cooperative. A total LPC score is obtained by summing these ratings. According to Fiedler, individuals with high LPC scores tend to see even a poor coworker in a relatively favorable light. These leaders tend to behave in a compliant, nondirective, and generally relaxed manner. In contrast, individuals with low LPC scores tend to be demanding, controlling, and managing in their group interactions.

The hypothetical data presented in the table are representative of the results of a study in which the relationship between the leader's LPC score and group problem-solving performance in the form of how many minutes it took the group to solve a problem was examined. Analyze the data using a nondirectional test, draw a conclusion, and write up your results using the principles developed in the relevant Method of Presentation section. If the correlation is statistically significant, compute the regression equation and the estimated standard error of estimate for predicting minutes until solution from LPC scores and include these in your write-up.

Group	X (leader's LPC score)	Y (minutes until solution)
1	63	11
2	68	12
3	71	15
4	65	10
5	61	6
6	75	19
7	64	9
8	63	7
9	70	13
10	73	7

48. Borden (1978) has hypothesized that one factor that might relate to individuals' concern for the environment is the extent to which they value technology: People who value technological innovation and who believe that technology can solve most world problems should be less likely to perform environment-conserving behaviors than those who question technology as a panacea to environmental problems. To test this hypothesis, Borden administered two scales to a group of individuals. One scale measured their belief in technology, and the other measured the extent to which they tend to engage in environmentally-friendly behavior (for example, saving energy). Scores on each scale could range from 0 to 20, with higher values representing a greater belief in technology and the performance of more environmentally-friendly behavior, respectively.

The hypothetical data presented in the table are representative of the outcome of this investigation. Analyze the data using a nondirectional test, draw a conclusion, and write up your results using the principles developed in the relevant Method of Presentation section. If the correlation is statistically significant, compute the regression equation and the estimated standard error of estimate for predicting environmentally-friendly behavior from one's belief in technology and include these in your write-up.

Individual	X (belief in technology)	Y (environmentally-friendly behavior)
1	12	13
2	17	7
3	13	14
4	15	10
5	10	16
6	14	12
7	16	8
8	19	5
9	16	10
10	7	11
11	16	6
12	8	17

49. One perspective on the relationship between the time that students spend working on an exam and test performance is that performance should be better as test takers spend increasingly more time thinking through their answers and double-checking their responses. A second perspective holds that the most knowledgeable test takers will require less time to complete an exam than will those who are less well prepared. According to the first view, test-completion times and test performance should be positively related; according to the second, they should be negatively related.

In one investigation, Becker and Suls (1982) determined the number of minutes that undergraduate students spent on a course test and their corresponding test scores. The hypothetical data in the table are representative of the results of the study. Analyze the data using a nondirectional test, draw a conclusion, and write up your results using the principles developed in the relevant Method of Presentation section. If the correlation is statistically significant, compute the regression equation and the estimated standard error of estimate for predicting test scores from test-completion times and include these in your write-up.

Student	X (test-completion time)	Y (test score)
1	43	88
2	37	91
3	41	86
4	46	76
5	50	94
6	48	83
7	34	77
8	47	76
9	50	82
10	49	86
11	44	93
12	38	84
13	46	80
14	49	95
15	41	81
16	43	74
17	47	88
18	50	75

*50. Virtually all graduate programs use admission committees to select those applicants with the most promise. In a review of 43 studies, Willingham (1974) identifies the most commonly used criteria for selecting individuals for graduate study as (1) quantitative ability scores (GRE-Q) on the Graduate Record Examination, (2) verbal ability scores (GRE-V) on the Graduate Record Examination, (3) advanced GRE scores (GRE-A) that measure mastery and comprehension of material basic to graduate study in a specific major field, (4) undergraduate grade point average (GPA), and (5) letters of recommendation. Some of these criteria were found to be reasonable discriminators of the performance of graduate students, whereas others were quite poor in their prediction of graduate school success. Nevertheless, all continue to be used to varying degrees by graduate programs when making their admission decisions.

The hypothetical data in Set I below represent the GRE-A scores and the grade point averages after 2 years of graduate study for students in a particular program. Analyze the data using a nondirectional test. If the correlation is statistically significant, compute the regression equation for predicting graduate GPA from GRE-A scores. If only students who are predicted to maintain a 2-year grade point average of 3.00 (B) or better are to be admitted to the program, which of the applicants in Set II are viable candidates for admission?

	Set I	
Student	X (GRE-A)	Y (GPA)
1	533	3.11
2	497	2.89
3	612	3.66
4	564	3.50
5	582	3.29
6	476	3.34
7	607	3.61
8	621	3.74
9	590	3.42
10	512	2.61

	Set II
Applicant	X (GRE-A)
1	532
2	478
3	589
4	483
5	527
6	493
7	546

51. A company that specializes in hand assembly of decorative ornaments needs each assembler to put together a minimum of 40 ornaments a day if it is to make a profit. As part of the hiring process, an industrial-organizational psychologist gives job applicants a test of manual dexterity. Scores on this test can range from 0 to 50, with higher values indicating greater dexterity. The hypothetical data in Set I below represent the manual dexterity and the job productivity (the mean number of ornaments assembled per day) for assemblers who have worked for the company. Analyze the data using a nondirectional test. If the correlation is statistically significant, compute the regression equation for predicting job productivity from manual dexterity scores. If only individuals who are predicted to assemble a minimum of 40 ornaments a day are to be hired, which of the applicants in Set II are viable candidates for employment?

	Set II	
Applicant		X (manual dexterity)
1		38
2		42
3		30
4		34
5		36
6		31
7		44
8		35

	Set I	
Assembler	X (manual dexterity)	Y (job productivity)
1	40	35.21
2	33	37.34
3	30	34.85
4	35	43.02
5	31	42.37
6	38	46.83
7	46	52.28
8	44	48.24
9	34	38.27
10	47	50.56
11	31	34.78
12	42	51.19
13	38	44.76
14	35	40.85

PART 3

ADDITIONAL TOPICS

CHAPTER **17**

Two-Way Between-Subjects Analysis of Variance

Our focus to this point has been on the analysis of the relationship between two variables. For instance, we have seen how one-way between-subjects analysis of variance can be used to examine the relationship between a qualitative or a quantitative independent variable and a quantitative dependent variable. However, it is rare that a given dependent variable is influenced by only one independent variable. For instance, a person's attitude toward abortion might be affected by the religion she was raised in, how religious she is, the type of upbringing she had, and so on. Thus, statistical techniques have been developed to analyze the relationship between a dependent variable and two or more independent variables.

This chapter considers one such technique—that of **two-way between-subjects analysis of variance**. As we will discuss, the term *two-way* indicates that two independent variables are included in the research design and, analogous to the one-way situation, the term *between-subjects* indicates that both of these variables are between-subjects in nature. This technique is also referred to as *two-way analysis of variance* (abbreviated as *two-way ANOVA*) because a between-subjects analysis is assumed unless it is otherwise stated.

For ease of presentation, we will focus on the situation where the sample sizes for the groups under study are all equal. This is the same approach as we took with one-way between-subjects analysis of variance. We consider the case of unequal sample sizes in Section 17.9.

17.1 Factorial Designs

Suppose that an investigator who is interested in the factors that influence the number of children that people want to have in their completed families posits that one important dimension is religious affiliation. To examine this issue, he might conduct a study in which 50 Catholic individuals and 50 Protestant individuals are asked what they consider to be the ideal family size. This is similar to the study that we discussed in Chapter 12, except now we are interested in only two levels of religion rather than three. Further suppose that the data are analyzed using the independent groups *t* test (the independent variable being religion and the dependent variable being the ideal family size) and that the results indicate that Catholic individuals want more children than Protestant individuals.

Also suppose that the same investigator is interested in studying the effect of a second independent variable—how religious an individual is—on the ideal family size. To accomplish this, the investigator will use a measure of religiosity that classifies individuals into one of two categories: religious or nonreligious. Again, a study could be conducted in which 50 religious and 50 nonreligious individuals are asked what they consider to be the ideal number of children in a family. Last, suppose that the data are collected, the independent groups *t* test is applied, and the results indicate that religious individuals want more children than nonreligious individuals.

From the two studies, we would conclude that both religion and religiosity are related to the ideal family size. However, these studies do not tell us anything about how the two variables act *in conjunction with one another* to influence the ideal family size. Fortunately, the joint effects of two independent variables on a dependent variable can be studied using a **factorial design**. Such designs include two or more independent variables in *one* study. For instance, rather than conducting the two studies from above, the investigator can conduct a single study in which the effects of both religion and religiosity on the ideal family size are assessed.

Table 17.1 illustrates a factorial design that is formed by combining the two levels of religion (Catholic and Protestant) with the two levels of religiosity (religious and nonreligious). As can be seen, combining these two dimensions, or **factors**, as independent variables are commonly called in the context of two-way analysis of variance, yields four groups (religious Catholics, nonreligious Catholics, religious Protestants, and nonreligious Protestants), each of which is represented by a unique combination of factors, or **cells**, in Table 17.1.

Because it represents two independent variables, the factorial design in Table 17.1 is more specifically referred to as a *two-way* factorial design. We can also refer to this as a 2 × 2 (read *two by two*) factorial design. More generally, a factorial design that has two factors can be represented by the notation *a* × *b*, where *a* is the number of levels of the first factor and *b* is the number of levels of the second factor.* If the present study had involved three levels of religion instead of two (for instance, Catholic, Protestant, and Jewish), the design would have been a 3 × 2 factorial.

The number of groups in a between-subjects factorial design is simply the product of the number of levels of each factor. For instance, as we demonstrated above for the religion, religiosity, and ideal family size study, the number of groups in a 2 × 2 factorial design is always 2 multiplied by 2, or 4. Similarly, the number of groups in a 3 × 2 factorial design is always 3 multiplied by 2, or 6; the number of groups in a 4 × 2 factorial design is always 4 multiplied by 2, or 8; the number of groups in a 3 × 3 factorial design is always 3 multiplied by 3, or 9; and so on.

This chapter is restricted to the study of the relationship between two independent variables and one dependent variable. However, factorial designs can also be used to examine the relationship between a dependent variable and three or more independent variables. For example, in addition to religion and religiosity, an investigator might study the relationship of gender and the ideal family size. This would require that all three factors be included in a 2 × 2 × 2 factorial design. The

TABLE 17.1 **Example of a Two-Way Factorial Design**

	Religiosity	
Religion	Religious	Nonreligious
Catholic	Religious Catholics	Nonreligious Catholics
Protestant	Religious Protestants	Nonreligious Protestants

* The choice of which independent variable is designated as the first factor and which independent variable is designated as the second factor is arbitrary. For instance, although we have designated religion as the first factor and religiosity as the second factor in the present study, we could have specified the reverse instead.

first factor, consisting of two levels, would be religion; the second factor, also consisting of two levels, would be religiosity; and the third factor, again consisting of two levels, would be gender. This $2 \times 2 \times 2$ factorial design would include $2 \times 2 \times 2 = 8$ groups of individuals.

17.2 Use of Two-Way Between-Subjects Analysis of Variance

The conditions for using two-way between-subjects analysis of variance are similar to those for one-way between-subjects analysis of variance except that two independent variables rather than one independent variable are studied. Specifically, two-way analysis of variance is typically applied when the following conditions are met:

1. The dependent variable is quantitative in nature and is measured on a level that at least approximates interval characteristics.

2. The independent variables are both *between-subjects* in nature (they can be either qualitative or quantitative).

3. The independent variables both have two or more levels.

4. The independent variables are combined to form a factorial design.

Consider the study on the effects of religion and religiosity on the ideal family size. The dependent variable is the ideal family size, and it is quantitative in nature and is measured on a level that at least approximates interval characteristics. Religion is one of the independent variables, and it is between-subjects in nature and has two levels (Catholic and Protestant). Religiosity is the other independent variable, and it is also between-subjects in nature and also has two levels (religious and nonreligious). Finally, religion and religiosity combine to yield a 2×2 factorial design. Given these conditions, two-way between-subjects analysis of variance would typically be used to analyze the relationship between the variables.

17.3 Main Effects and Interactions

As we noted above, a two-way factorial design allows us to study the relationship between a dependent variable and two independent variables. Specifically, such designs allow us to address three questions:

1. Is there a relationship between the first independent variable and the dependent variable?

2. Is there a relationship between the second independent variable and the dependent variable?

3. Is there an interaction between the two independent variables such that the effect of one factor on the dependent variable depends on the other factor?

We will demonstrate the logic underlying the study of the relationship between a dependent variable and two independent variables using the religion, religiosity, and ideal family size study as our example. The three questions of interest in this instance are as follows:

1. Is there a relationship between religion and the ideal family size?

2. Is there a relationship between religiosity and the ideal family size?

3. Is there an interaction between religiosity and religion such that the effect of one of these factors on the ideal family size depends on the other one?

The first two questions are addressed in terms of **main effects**. This refers to the comparison of the means for one independent variable *collapsing across* the levels of the other independent variable. For instance, the main effect for religion is the comparison of the mean ideal family size for Catholic individuals with the mean ideal family size for Protestant individuals, *collapsing across* religiosity. Similarly, the main effect for religiosity is the comparison of the mean ideal family size for religious individuals with the mean ideal family size for nonreligious individuals, *collapsing across* religion.

Collapsing across an independent variable in the context of a two-way factorial design requires that we add *all* of the scores at a given level of that variable, disregarding the level of the other independent variable. Dividing by the total number of scores that contribute to a sum yields the main effect means for that factor.

Let us demonstrate this using the data in Table 17.2 for the 2×2 factorial design that we have been considering. The first factor in Table 17.2 is religion, the second factor is religiosity, and the dependent variable is the ideal family size. This table displays the raw scores for each cell, the cell means, and the means for the two main effects. The main effect mean for Catholics was derived by adding the five scores for religious Catholics and the five scores for nonreligious Catholics and dividing by 10, and the main effect mean for Protestants was derived by adding the five scores for religious Protestants and the five scores for nonreligious Protestants and again dividing by 10. A comparable procedure was used to determine the main effect means for religiosity.

When the cell sizes for a given level of a factor are all equal, an alternative way to calculate the main effect mean for that level of the factor is to add the corresponding cell means and divide by the number of those means. For instance, the main effect mean for Catholic individuals can be determined by taking the average of the cell means for religious (5.00) and nonreligious Catholics (3.00) because there are five scores for each group. Indeed, $(5.00 + 3.00)/2 = 4.00$, which is the same value as was derived by averaging the 10 scores for Catholic individuals.

Each main effect in a two-way analysis of variance has a null hypothesis and an alternative hypothesis associated with it. In each instance, the null hypothesis states that the population means for the groups that constitute an effect are all equal to one another, and the alternative hypothesis states that these means are not all equal. If there are two levels of an independent variable, these hypotheses take the same form as they would for an independent groups *t* test, and if there are three or

TABLE 17.2   **Data for Religion, Religiosity, and Ideal Family Size Study**

| | Religiosity | | |
Religion	Religious X	Nonreligious X	Main effect of religion
Catholic	7	5	Mean = 4.00
	4	2	
	3	1	
	5	3	
	6	4	
	Mean = 5.00	Mean = 3.00	
Protestant	0	2	Mean = 2.00
	4	4	
	2	0	
	2	2	
	2	2	
	Mean = 2.00	Mean = 2.00	
Main effect of religiosity	Mean = 3.50	Mean = 2.50	

more levels of an independent variable, these hypotheses take the same form as they would for a one-way between-subjects analysis of variance.

In our example, the null and alternative hypotheses for the main effect of religion are

$$H_0: \quad \mu_C = \mu_P$$
$$H_1: \quad \mu_C \neq \mu_P$$

where the subscript "C" denotes the Catholic group and the subscript "P" denotes the Protestant group. The null and alternative hypotheses for the main effect of religiosity are

$$H_0: \quad \mu_R = \mu_N$$
$$H_1: \quad \mu_R \neq \mu_N$$

where the subscripts "R" and "N" represent the religious and the nonreligious groups, respectively.

In statistical language, a main effect is said to be present if the null hypothesis concerning that effect is rejected. For instance, if a research report indicates that there is "a main effect for religiosity" but "no main effect for religion," this would mean that the null hypothesis was rejected for the religiosity factor but not for the religion factor. Note that the use of the term *main effect* in this context differs from the more general use of this term to refer to the comparison of the means for one independent variable collapsing across the levels of the other independent variable as we meant previously.

The third question that is addressed by factorial designs concerns **interaction effects.*** This refers to the comparison of the cell means in terms of whether the nature of the relationship between one of the independent variables and the dependent variable differs as a function of the other independent variable. An important feature of factorial designs is that they allow us to test for such effects.

Stated informally, the null hypothesis for an interaction effect is that the differences between the population means for one independent variable are the same at each level of the other independent variable. The alternative hypothesis is that the differences between the population means for one independent variable differ depending on the levels of the other independent variable. We discuss the specification of null and alternative hypotheses for interaction effects in formal statistical terms in Section 17.4.

The perspective from which an interaction effect is stated should be guided by theory and the research questions that are being investigated. In our example, one way to phrase the null hypothesis is that the population difference in the mean ideal family size as a function of religion is the same for religious and nonreligious individuals. The corresponding alternative hypothesis is that the population difference in the mean ideal family size as a function of religion is not the same for religious and nonreligious individuals. Alternatively, we could have phrased the hypotheses in terms of the population difference in the mean ideal family size as a function of religiosity for Catholic versus Protestant individuals instead.

The "presence" of an interaction means that the null hypothesis of no interaction effect was rejected. Thus, the term *interaction* has a much more specific meaning than the term *interaction effect*: Per the above, the latter refers to the comparison of the cell means in terms of whether the two independent variables jointly affect the dependent variable, whereas the former indicates that this effect is statistically significant.

Identifying Main Effects and Interactions with Population Data

In practice, consistent with the approach that we have taken with all of the other statistical tests that we have considered in this book, the identification of main effects and interactions requires that we use *sample* means to make inferences about the nature of differences between population means. However, so that we can develop the relevant concepts without regard to sampling error, the examples in this section utilize *population* means. The appropriate inferential procedures are then developed in Section 17.4.

Table 17.3 presents hypothetical population means for the four combinations of religion and religiosity as well as the corresponding main effect means. Because there are an equal number of individuals in each group, the main effect means are

---

* Our discussion of interaction effects is based on a strategy that is commonly used in the behavioral sciences known as the *moderator approach*. Other approaches to defining and conceptualizing such effects emphasize *residualized means* and treatment effects that reflect the joint influence of the independent variables. For a discussion of the various alternatives, see Jaccard (1996).

TABLE 17.3   **Population Means for the Ideal Family Size as a Function of Religion and Religiosity**

Religion	Religiosity		Main effect of religion
	Religious	Nonreligious	
Catholic	4.00	2.00	3.00
Protestant	2.00	2.00	2.00
Main effect of religiosity	3.00	2.00	

equal to the average of the means for the two cells in a given row or column. In this instance, there is a main effect for religion because $\mu_C \neq \mu_P$. The nature of this effect is such that Catholic individuals ($\mu = 3.00$) want more children than Protestant individuals ($\mu = 2.00$). There is also a main effect for religiosity, as indicated by the fact that $\mu_R \neq \mu_N$. On average, religious individuals ($\mu = 3.00$) want more children than nonreligious individuals ($\mu = 2.00$).

Let us now examine the information in Table 17.3 to determine whether an interaction exists between religion and religiosity. We will accomplish this by focusing on the cell means. We begin by examining the relationship between religion and the ideal family size for just religious individuals. *When we consider only religious individuals,* there is a relationship between religion and the ideal family size: Catholic individuals ($\mu = 4.00$) want more children than Protestant individuals ($\mu = 2.00$). Now examine the same relationship for just nonreligious individuals. For these individuals, religion is unrelated to the ideal family size. On average, Catholic individuals want the same number of children as Protestant individuals (2.00 in each case). Because the nature of the relationship between one of the independent variables and the dependent variable differs as a function of the other independent variable, this illustrates an interaction. Specifically, the relationship between religion and the ideal family size depends on religiosity.

Although we have examined the nature of the relationship between religion and the ideal family size as a function of religiosity, we could have examined the nature of the relationship between religiosity and the ideal family size as a function of religion instead. Consider just Catholic individuals. Inspection of Table 17.3 reveals that religious Catholics ($\mu = 4.00$) want more children than nonreligious Catholics ($\mu = 2.00$). Now consider just Protestant individuals. Table 17.3 shows that religious Protestants want the same number of children as nonreligious Protestants (2.00 in each case). Because the nature of the relationship between religiosity and the ideal family size depends on religion, this again illustrates an interaction.

As with interaction effects, the perspective from which an interaction is stated should be guided by theory and the research questions that are being investigated. The important point for present purposes is that Table 17.3 reflects an interaction between the two independent variables (religion and religiosity) such that they jointly affect the dependent variable (the ideal family size).

Additional Examples of Main Effects and Interactions with Population Data   Let us examine the strategy for identifying main effects and interactions further by referring to the examples of various population means for the four groups defined by the two levels of religion and the two levels of religiosity that are presented in Figure 17.1. The examples are also depicted in graphs. On the abscissas of the graphs are demarcations for the two levels of religion, Catholic and Protestant. On the ordinates of the graphs are demarcations for values of the dependent variable, the ideal family size. Directly above each abscissa demarcation for Catholics is a dot corresponding to the mean ideal family size for religious Catholics and directly above each abscissa demarcation for Protestants is a dot corresponding to the mean ideal family size for religious Protestants.* For each graph, these two points are connected by a line, as are the corresponding points for nonreligious individuals.

Because we are dealing with population values, the most straightforward way to determine whether there is a main effect of religion for a given example is to compare the means for the two columns. If these are the same, there is no main effect; otherwise, a main effect is present. The presence or absence of a main effect of religiosity is similarly determined by comparing the means for the two rows.

When dealing with population means, the simplest way to determine whether an interaction is present is to examine the slopes of the lines in a given graph. One of these lines represents the relationship between religion and the ideal family size for religious individuals, and the other line represents this relationship for nonreligious individuals. If the lines are parallel or the same (as is the case in Figures 17.1a and 17.1b), the nature of the relationship is the same for religious and nonreligious individuals. Thus, there is no interaction. If the lines are not parallel, the nature of the relationship between religion and the ideal family size depends on religiosity, which means that an interaction is present.

Figure 17.1a represents the case where there are neither main effects nor an interaction. In Figure 17.1b, there is a main effect of religion (Protestant individuals, $\mu = 2.00$, want fewer children than Catholic individuals, $\mu = 8.00$) but no main effect of religiosity and no interaction. As indicated by the parallel lines, there are also no interactions in Figures 17.1c and 17.1d. However, there is a main effect of religiosity in Figure 17.1c (religious individuals, $\mu = 7.00$, want more children than nonreligious individuals, $\mu = 3.00$) and main effects of both religion (Protestant individuals, $\mu = 3.50$, want fewer children than Catholic individuals, $\mu = 6.50$) and religiosity (religious individuals, $\mu = 6.50$, want more children than nonreligious individuals, $\mu = 3.50$) in Figure 17.1d.

Figures 17.1e–17.1h contain examples of interactions. Note that in each graph, the lines are nonparallel. This signifies that the nature of the relationship between religion and the ideal family size differs as a function of religiosity. In Figure 17.1e, religious Catholics ($\mu = 7.00$) want more children than religious Protestants ($\mu = 1.00$), but nonreligious Catholics ($\mu = 1.00$) want fewer children than nonreligious Protestants ($\mu = 7.00$). In Figure 17.1f, religious Catholics

---

* The representation of religion on the abscissa and religiosity in the body of the graphs is arbitrary. If we had wished, we could have represented religiosity on the abscissa and religion in the body of the graphs instead.

FIGURE 17.1   **Examples of Main Effects and Interactions for a 2 × 2 Factorial Design (Adapted from Johnson & Liebert, 1977)**

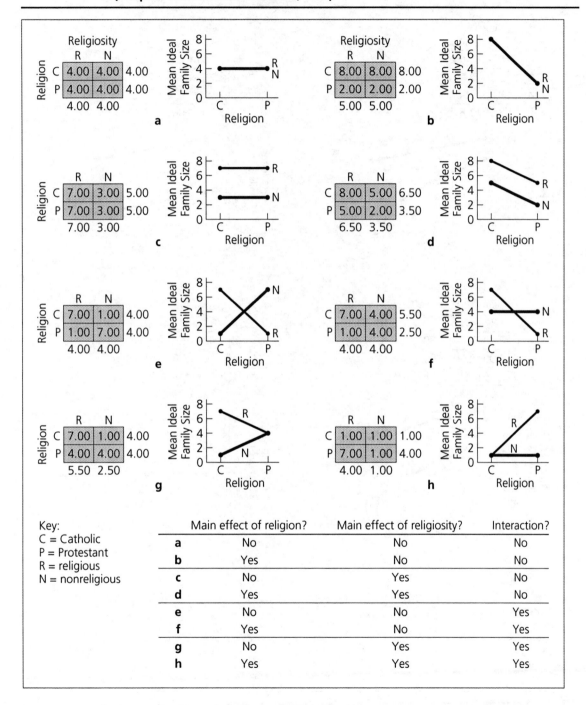

	Main effect of religion?	Main effect of religiosity?	Interaction?
a	No	No	No
b	Yes	No	No
c	No	Yes	No
d	Yes	Yes	No
e	No	No	Yes
f	Yes	No	Yes
g	No	Yes	Yes
h	Yes	Yes	Yes

Key:
C = Catholic
P = Protestant
R = religious
N = nonreligious

FIGURE 17.2   Examples of the Main Effects and Interactions for a 3 × 2 Factorial Design

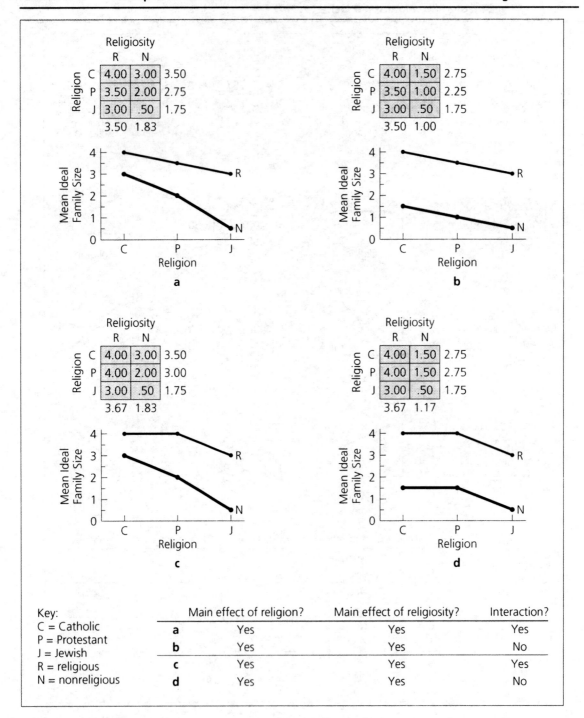

Key:
C = Catholic
P = Protestant
J = Jewish
R = religious
N = nonreligious

	Main effect of religion?	Main effect of religiosity?	Interaction?
a	Yes	Yes	Yes
b	Yes	Yes	No
c	Yes	Yes	Yes
d	Yes	Yes	No

($\mu = 7.00$) again want more children than religious Protestants ($\mu = 1.00$); however, both nonreligious Catholics and nonreligious Protestants have an ideal family size of 4.00. There is also a main effect of religion in Figure 17.1f such that Catholic individuals ($\mu = 5.50$) want more children than Protestant individuals ($\mu = 2.50$). See if you can interpret the nature of the main effects and interactions for Figures 17.1g and 17.1h.

Main Effects and Interactions in Designs with More Than Two Levels for One or Both Factors   The principles for detecting main effects and interactions are readily generalizable from 2×2 designs to designs with more than two levels for one or both factors, as we now demonstrate in terms of Figure 17.2, which presents examples of a 3×2 factorial design that has three levels of religion rather than two: Catholic, Protestant, and Jewish. Whenever the lines are parallel, a lack of interaction is indicated. This is the case in Figures 17.2b and 17.2d. For these examples, the nature of the relationship between one independent variable and the dependent variable is the same irrespective of the level of the other independent variable. When the lines are not parallel, the presence of an interaction is indicated. This is the case in Figures 17.2a and 17.2c. For these examples, the nature of the relationship between religion and the ideal family size differs as a function of religiosity. In all four examples, there are main effects of both religion and religiosity.

Identifying Main Effects and Interactions with Sample Data

In the following section, we examine the inference of main effects and interactions in a population based on sample data. At this point, we wish to emphasize that when dealing with sample data, we *cannot* make these determinations by mere visual inspection of sample means or the slopes of lines in a graph. Rather, the existence of a given population main effect or interaction can be identified only by a statistically significant F ratio. Thus, as with all of the other statistical tests that we have considered in this book, because of the role of sampling error, nonequivalent sample means do not necessarily indicate nonequivalent population means. For the same reason, we cannot assume that an interaction exists in the population just because the lines that connect the sample means are nonparallel. If an interaction effect *is* statistically significant, however, at least some of these lines will have different slopes (unless a Type I error occurs).

17.4 Inference of Relationships Using Two-Way Between-Subjects Analysis of Variance

Null and Alternative Hypotheses

We will demonstrate the inferential procedures for identifying main effects and interactions in a population based on sample information using the data in Table 17.2, which has been reproduced in Table 17.4. Unlike the examples in Figures 17.1 and 17.2, we are now working with sample data, and we will continue to do so for the remainder of the chapter.

TABLE 17.4   Data and Computation of Sums of Squares for Religion, Religiosity, and Ideal Family Size Study

| | Religiosity (B) | | | | |
| | Religious | | Nonreligious | | Main effect |
Religion (A)	X	X^2	X	X^2	of religion
Catholic	7	49	5	25	$T_C = 40$
	4	16	2	4	$\overline{X}_C = 4.00$
	3	9	1	1	$T_C^2 = 1{,}600$
	5	25	3	9	
	6	36	4	16	
	$T_{CR} = 25$		$T_{CN} = 15$		
	$\overline{X}_{CR}^2 = 5.00$		$\overline{X}_{CN}^2 = 3.00$		
	$T_{CR}^2 = 625$		$T_{CN}^2 = 225$		
Protestant	0	0	2	4	$T_P = 20$
	4	16	4	16	$\overline{X}_P = 2.00$
	2	4	0	0	$T_P^2 = 400$
	2	4	2	4	
	2	4	2	4	
	$T_{PR} = 10$		$T_{PN} = 10$		
	$\overline{X}_{PR} = 2.00$		$\overline{X}_{PN} = 2.00$		
	$T_{PR}^2 = 100$		$T_{PN}^2 = 100$		
Main effect of religiosity	$T_R = 35$		$T_N = 25$		
	$\overline{X}_R = 3.50$		$\overline{X}_N = 2.50$		
	$T_R^2 = 1{,}225$		$T_N^2 = 625$		

$$\sum X^2 = 49 + 16 + \cdots + 4 + 4 = 26 \qquad \frac{\sum T_{A_i}^2}{nb} = \frac{1{,}600 + 400}{(5)(2)} = 200.00$$

$$\sum X = 7 + 4 + \cdots + 2 + 2 = 60 \qquad \frac{\sum T_{B_i}^2}{na} = \frac{1{,}225 + 625}{(5)(2)} = 185.00$$

$$\frac{(\sum X)^2}{N} = \frac{60^2}{20} = 180.00 \qquad \frac{\sum T_{A_i B_i}^2}{n} = \frac{625 + 225 + 100 + 100}{5} = 210.00$$

Note that religion is designated as *factor A* and religiosity is designated as *factor B* in this table. As we will see, the differentiation of one independent variable as A and the other as B is necessary for the application of the various formulas that we will be using. Also note that the main effect means for the Catholic and Protestant levels of religion are represented as $\overline{X}_C$ and $\overline{X}_P$, respectively, and that the main effect means for the religious and nonreligious levels of religiosity are represented as $\overline{X}_R$ and $\overline{X}_N$.

The notation for the mean scores for the four groups in the 2×2 design requires two subscripts. The first subscript identifies the level of factor A, and the second subscript identifies the level of factor B. For instance, the cell mean for Catholic individuals who are religious is represented as $\overline{X}_{CR}$ and the cell mean for Protestant individuals who are not religious is represented as $\overline{X}_{PN}$.

Per Section 17.3, the null and alternative hypotheses for the main effect of religion are

$$H_0: \quad \mu_C = \mu_P$$
$$H_1: \quad \mu_C \neq \mu_P$$

and the null and alternative hypotheses for the main effect of religiosity are

$$H_0: \quad \mu_R = \mu_N$$
$$H_1: \quad \mu_R \neq \mu_N$$

The specification of the null and alternative hypotheses for the interaction effect in formal statistical terms is straightforward for 2×2 factorial designs. We will develop these by considering religious and nonreligious individuals separately. The effect of religious affiliation on the ideal family size for the former individuals is reflected in the mean difference $\mu_{CR} - \mu_{PR}$. If the difference between these two means is 0, then religious affiliation has no effect on the ideal family size in the sense that the population mean for Catholics is the same as the population mean for Protestants. If this difference is nonzero, then religious affiliation does have an effect on the ideal family size, and the nature of the effect is indicated by the nature of the mean difference. This is also true for nonreligious individuals. The effect of religious affiliation on the ideal family size in this case is reflected in the mean difference $\mu_{CN} - \mu_{PN}$.

Now suppose that the effect of religious affiliation is exactly the same for religious and nonreligious individuals. This would mean that no interaction is present, as reflected in the fact that $\mu_{CR} - \mu_{PR}$ would equal $\mu_{CN} - \mu_{PN}$. This leads to our null hypothesis for the interaction effect:

$$H_0: \quad \mu_{CR} - \mu_{PR} = \mu_{CN} - \mu_{PN}$$

The alternative hypothesis turns the null hypothesis into an inequality:

$$H_1: \quad \mu_C - \mu_{PR} \neq \mu_{CN} - \mu_{PN}$$

If the alternative hypothesis is true, then there is an interaction because the effect of religious affiliation on the ideal family size is not the same for religious and nonreligious individuals.

Although we have stated the null and alternative hypotheses for the interaction effect in terms of the relationship between religious affiliation and the ideal family size as a function of religiosity, they could have instead been framed in terms of the relationship between religiosity and the ideal family size as a function of religion. If we specified the two hypotheses in this way, they would be

$$H_0: \quad \mu_{CR} - \mu_{CN} = \mu_{PR} - \mu_{PN}$$
$$H_1: \quad \mu_{CR} - \mu_{CN} \neq \mu_{PR} - \mu_{PN}$$

The formal specification of the null and alternative hypotheses for interaction effects for designs that are larger than 2×2 in nature is cumbersome, but these can be stated informally using the approach that we present in Section 17.3.

Partitioning of Variability

In Chapter 12, the relationship between a between-subjects independent variable and a dependent variable was analyzed by defining the total variability in the dependent variable in terms of two components—between-group variability and within-group variability—and then forming a ratio of variance measures based on these sources of variability. Specifically, it will be recalled that the sum of squares total was partitioned into a sum of squares between and a sum of squares within. This was represented symbolically as $SS_{\text{TOTAL}} = SS_{\text{BETWEEN}} + SS_{\text{WITHIN}}$. The sum of squares between and the sum of squares within were then divided by their respective degrees of freedom to obtain a mean square between and a mean square within. An F ratio was then formed by dividing the former by the latter.

The sum of squares total for two-way analysis of variance can be similarly partitioned into a sum of squares between and a sum of squares within:

$$SS_{\text{TOTAL}} = SS_{\text{BETWEEN}} + SS_{\text{WITHIN}} \qquad [17.1]$$

However, the sum of squares between in this instance can be further partitioned into three components: (1) variability due to the first independent variable (factor A), (2) variability due to the second independent variable (factor B), and (3) variability due to the interaction effect. This can be stated symbolically as

$$SS_{\text{BETWEEN}} = SS_A + SS_B + SS_{A \times B} \qquad [17.2]$$

where SS_A is the sum of squares for between-group variability due to factor A, SS_B is the sum of squares for between-group variability due to factor B, and $SS_{A \times B}$ is the sum of squares for between-group variability due to the interaction effect. The sum of squares total for two-way analysis of variance can thus be represented as

$$SS_{\text{TOTAL}} = SS_{\text{BETWEEN}} + SS_{\text{WITHIN}}$$

$$SS_A \qquad SS_B \qquad SS_{A \times B}$$

or, more formally,

$$SS_{\text{TOTAL}} = SS_A + SS_B + SS_{A \times B} + SS_{\text{WITHIN}} \qquad [17.3]$$

Dividing each component of the sum of squares between by its corresponding degrees of freedom yields three mean squares—the mean square for factor A, the mean square for factor B, and the mean square for the interaction effect. These are symbolized as MS_A, MS_B, and $MS_{A \times B}$, respectively. Dividing each of these by the mean square within yields three F ratios. The F ratio formed by $MS_A / MS_{\text{WITHIN}}$ is used to test the null hypothesis for the main effect of factor A. The F ratio formed by $MS_B / MS_{\text{WITHIN}}$ is used to test the null hypothesis for the main effect of factor B. Finally, the F ratio formed by $MS_{A \times B} / MS_{\text{WITHIN}}$ is used to test the null hypothesis for the interaction effect.

We demonstrate these points below for the religion, religiosity, and ideal family size example. First, though, we discuss the computation of each of the sum of squares in Equation 17.3.

Computation of the Sums of Squares

The sum of squares total is calculated by applying the standard computational formula for a sum of squares for a set of scores to the entire data set in the same manner as we did for one-way between-subjects analysis of variance. Specifically,

$$SS_{TOTAL} = \sum X^2 - \frac{(\sum X)^2}{N} \qquad [17.4]$$

where $\sum X^2$ is the *sum of the squared scores* in the data set, $(\sum X)^2$ is the *square of the summed scores*, and N is the total sample size.

The intermediate statistics necessary to calculate this and the other sums of squares for the religion, religiosity, and ideal family size example are presented in Table 17.4. According to this table, the sum of the 20 X^2 scores is

$$\sum X^2 = 49 + 16 + \cdots + 4 + 4 = 246$$

and the sum of the 20 X scores is

$$\sum X = 7 + 4 + \cdots + 2 + 2 = 60$$

Squaring the latter value and dividing by N, we obtain

$$\frac{(\sum X)^2}{N} = \frac{60^2}{20} = 180.00$$

Thus, the sum of squares total in this instance is

$$SS_{TOTAL} = \sum X^2 - \frac{(\sum X)^2}{N}$$
$$= 246.00 - 180.00 = 66.00$$

The formula for calculating the sum of squares for between-group variability due to factor A (in this case, religion) is

$$SS_A = \frac{\sum T_{A_i}^2}{nb} - \frac{(\sum X)^2}{N} \qquad [17.5]$$

where $T_{A_i}^2$ is the square of the sum of the scores at level i of factor A, n is the per-cell sample size (remember that we are focusing on the situation where the sample sizes for the groups under study are all equal), b is the number of levels of factor B, and $(\sum X)^2$ and N are as defined previously.

In our example, $T_{A_i}^2$ equals 1,600 for Catholics and 400 for Protestants. Thus,

$$\frac{\sum T_{A_i}^2}{nb} = \frac{1,6600 + 400}{(5)(2)} = 200.00$$

so

$$SS_A = \frac{\sum T_{A_i}^2}{nb} - \frac{(\sum X)^2}{N}$$

$$= 200.00 - 180.00 = 20.00$$

The formula for calculating the sum of squares for between-group variability due to factor B (in this case, religiosity) is

$$SS_B = \frac{\sum T_{B_i}^2}{na} - \frac{(\sum X)^2}{N} \qquad [17.6]$$

where $T_{B_i}^2$ is the square of the sum of the scores at level j of factor B, a is the number of levels of factor A, and all other terms are as defined above.

In our example, $T_{B_i}^2$ equals 1,225 for religious individuals and 625 for nonreligious individuals. Thus,

$$\frac{\sum T_{B_i}^2}{na} = \frac{1,255 + 625}{(5)(2)} = 185.00$$

so

$$SS_B = \frac{\sum T_{B_i}^2}{na} - \frac{(\sum X)^2}{N}$$

$$= 185.00 - 180.00 = 5.00$$

The formula for calculating the sum of squares for between-group variability due to the interaction effect is

$$SS_{A \times B} = \frac{(\sum X)^2}{N} + \frac{\sum T_{A_iB_i}^2}{n} - \frac{\sum T_{A_i}^2}{nb} - \frac{\sum T_{B_i}^2}{na} \qquad [17.7]$$

where $T_{A_iB_i}^2$ is the square of the sum of the scores in cell A_iB_j and all other terms are as defined above.

In our example, $T_{A_iB_i}^2$ equals 625 for religious Catholics, 225 for nonreligious Catholics, 100 for religious Protestants, and 100 for nonreligious Protestants. Thus,

$$\frac{\sum T_{A_iB_i}^2}{n} = \frac{625 + 225 + 100 + 100}{5} = 210.00$$

so

$$SS_{A \times B} = \frac{(\sum X)^2}{N} + \frac{\sum T_{A_iB_i}^2}{n} - \frac{\sum T_{A_i}^2}{nb} - \frac{\sum T_{B_i}^2}{na}$$

$$= 180.00 + 210.00 - 200.00 - 185.00 = 5.00$$

The formula for calculating the sum of squares within is

$$SS_{\text{WITHIN}} = \sum X^2 - \frac{\sum T_{A_iB_i}^2}{n} \qquad [17.8]$$

where all terms are as defined above.

In our example,

$$SS_{\text{WITHIN}} = 246 - 210.00 = 36.00$$

Of course, given that the sum of squares total is equal to the sum of squares for factor A plus the sum of squares for factor B plus the sum of squares for the interaction effect plus the sum of squares within, if four of these quantities have already been calculated, the fifth can be determined through simple algebraic manipulation. For instance, we could have obtained the sum of squares for the interaction effect as follows:

$$SS_{A \times B} = SS_{\text{TOTAL}} - SS_A - SS_B - SS_{\text{WITHIN}}$$
$$= 66.00 - 20.00 - 5.00 - 36.00 = 5.00$$

However, it is usually a good idea to calculate all five sums of squares using the above formulas. This allows us to check for computational errors by determining whether the calculated values for the other four sums of squares add up to the calculated value for the sum of squares total.

Derivation of the Summary Table

Each of the above sums of squares has a certain number of degrees of freedom associated with it. These are calculated as follows:

$$df_A = a - 1 \qquad\qquad [17.9]$$
$$df_B = b - 1 \qquad\qquad [17.10]$$
$$df_{A \times B} = (a - 1)(b - 1) \qquad\qquad [17.11]$$
$$df_{\text{WITHIN}} = (a)(b)(n - 1) \qquad\qquad [17.12]$$

As with the sums of squares, the degrees of freedom are additive:

$$df_{\text{TOTAL}} = df_A + df_B + df_{A \times B} + df_{\text{WITHIN}} \qquad\qquad [17.13]$$

Because $df_A = a - 1$, $df_B = b - 1$, $df_{A \times B} = (a - 1)(b - 1)$, and $df_{\text{WITHIN}} = (a)(b)(n - 1)$, $df_{\text{TOTAL}} = (a - 1) + (b - 1) + [(a - 1)(b - 1)] + [(a)(b)(n - 1)]$. Because this reduces to $a - 1 + b - 1 + (ab - a - b + 1) + (abn - ab) = abn - 1$ and because abn is equal to N, the degrees of freedom total can be calculated directly as

$$df_{\text{TOTAL}} = N - 1 \qquad\qquad [17.14]$$

In our example,

$$df_A = 2 - 1 = 1$$
$$df_B = 2 - 1 = 1$$
$$df_{A \times B} = (2 - 1)(2 - 1) = 1$$
$$df_{\text{WITHIN}} = (2)(2)(5 - 1) = 16$$
$$df_{\text{TOTAL}} = 20 - 1 = 19$$

The relevant mean squares are obtained by dividing the sum of squares for each source of between-group or within-group variability by its degrees of freedom:

$$MS_A = \frac{SS_A}{df_A} \qquad\qquad [17.15]$$

$$= \frac{20.00}{1.00} = 20.00$$

$$MS_B = \frac{SS_B}{df_B} \qquad\qquad [17.16]$$

$$= \frac{5.00}{1.00} = 5.00$$

$$MS_{A \times B} = \frac{SS_{A \times B}}{df_{A \times B}} \qquad\qquad [17.17]$$

$$= \frac{5.00}{1.00} = 5.00$$

$$MS_{WITHIN} = \frac{SS_{WITHIN}}{df_{WITHIN}} \qquad\qquad [17.18]$$

$$= \frac{36.00}{16} = 2.25$$

The F ratios for testing the null hypotheses for the two main effects and the interaction effect are derived by dividing the corresponding mean squares by the mean square within:

$$F_A = \frac{MS_A}{MS_{WITHIN}} \qquad\qquad [17.19]$$

$$= \frac{20.00}{2.25} = 8.89$$

$$F_B = \frac{MS_B}{MS_{WITHIN}} \qquad\qquad [17.20]$$

$$= \frac{5.00}{2.25} = 2.22$$

$$F_{A \times B} = \frac{MS_{A \times B}}{MS_{WITHIN}} \qquad\qquad [17.21]$$

$$= \frac{5.00}{2.25} = 2.22$$

All of the preceding calculations can be summarized in a summary table:

Source	SS	df	MS	F
A (religion)	20.00	1	20.00	8.89
B (religiosity)	5.00	1	5.00	2.22
A × B	5.00	1	5.00	2.22
Within	36.00	16	2.25	
Total	66.00	19		

This table is similar in many ways to the summary tables that we encountered in Chapter 12 for one-way between-subjects analysis of variance. However, the sum of squares between is now represented by its three components: the main effect for factor A, the main effect for factor B, and the interaction effect.

Tests of the Null Hypotheses

Each of the above F ratios is compared with the appropriate critical value of F from Appendix F to make a decision with respect to the corresponding null hypothesis. Paralleling the format for the one-way situation, when reporting an F value for two-way between-subjects analysis of variance, it is conventional to present the degrees of freedom for the effect followed by the degrees of freedom within. For instance, the test of the null hypothesis for the main effect of religion requires that we compare the F value associated with factor A with the critical value of F for an alpha level of .05 and $df_A = 1$ and $df_{WITHIN} = 16$. From Appendix F, this value is 4.49. Because the observed F value of 8.89 exceeds the critical value, we reject the null hypothesis and conclude that there is a relationship between religion and the ideal family size.

The test of the null hypothesis for the main effect of religiosity requires that we compare the F value associated with factor B with the critical value of F for an alpha level of .05 and $df_B = 1$ and $df_{WITHIN} = 16$. Because these are the same degrees of freedom as for the main effect of religion, the critical value is also the same—namely, 4.49. Because the observed F value of 2.22 does not exceed this value, we fail to reject the null hypothesis of no relationship between religiosity and the ideal family size.

The test of the null hypothesis for the interaction effect requires that we compare the F value associated with the interaction effect with the critical value of F for an alpha level of .05 and $df_{A \times B} = 1$ and $df_{WITHIN} = 16$. Because these are the same degrees of freedom as for the main effect of religion and the interaction effect, the critical value is again 4.49. Because the observed F value of 2.22 does not exceed this value, we fail to reject the null hypothesis of no interaction between religion and religiosity.

Assumptions of the *F* Tests

The *F* tests for two-way between-subjects analysis of variance are based on the same assumptions that underlie one-way between-subjects analysis of variance, as we discussed in Section 12.2. Specifically, it is assumed that

1. The samples are independently and randomly selected from their respective populations.

2. The scores in each population are normally distributed.

3. The scores in each population have equal variances.

In addition, the dependent variable should be quantitative in nature and measured on a level that at least approximates interval characteristics.

For the *F* tests to be valid, it is important that the assumption of independent and random selection be met. However, as with one-way analysis of variance, under certain conditions the *F* tests are robust to violations of the normality assumption. As with the one-way situation, this is particularly true when the sample sizes are moderate (greater than 20) to large and the same for all cells. When this is the case, the *F* tests are quite robust to even marked departures from normality.

Heterogeneity of population variances becomes increasingly problematic as the number of groups in the factorial design increases. Even with a relatively large number of groups, the *F* tests are relatively robust when the population variance for one cell is as much as 2 to 3 times larger than the population variances for the other cells. However, the Type I error rate begins to become unacceptable with an increasing number of groups when the population variance for one cell is 4 or more times larger than the population variances for the other cells.

The robustness of the *F* tests to nonnormality and variance heterogeneity often diminishes, sometimes considerably, when the cell sizes are highly different. For further discussion of this issue, see Harwell, Rubinstein, and Hayes (1992) and Milligan, Wong, and Thompson (1987).

17.5 Strength of the Relationships

The strength of the relationship between the dependent variable and each of the three sources of between-group variability is computed using the following formulas for eta-squared:

$$\text{eta}_A^2 = \frac{SS_A}{SS_{\text{TOTAL}}} \tag{17.22}$$

$$\text{eta}_B^2 = \frac{SS_B}{SS_{\text{TOTAL}}} \tag{17.23}$$

$$\text{eta}_{A \times B}^2 = \frac{SS_{A \times B}}{SS_{\text{TOTAL}}} \tag{17.24}$$

where eta_A^2 represents the proportion of variability in the dependent variable that is associated with the main effect of factor A, eta_B^2 represents the proportion of variability in the dependent variable that is associated with the main effect of factor B, and $\text{eta}_{A \times B}^2$ represents the proportion of variability in the dependent variable that is associated with the interaction effect.

For the religion, religiosity, and ideal family size study,

$$\text{eta}_A^2 = \frac{20.00}{66.00} = .30$$

$$\text{eta}_B^2 = \frac{5.00}{66.00} = .08$$

$$\text{eta}_{A \times B}^2 = \frac{5.00}{66.00} = .08$$

Thus, the proportion of variability in the ideal family size that is associated with the main effect of religion is .30. This represents a strong effect. However, the proportion of variability in the ideal family size that is associated with the main effect of religiosity and with the interaction between religion and religiosity is only .08 in both instances. These represent weak to moderate effects.

Unstandardized effect sizes for the two main effects are provided by the difference between each pair of sample means for a particular effect. Although it is possible to also calculate unstandardized effect sizes for the interaction effect and to calculate confidence intervals for both the main effects and the interaction effect, the procedures for doing so are complex and are beyond the scope of this book. Interested readers are referred to Jaccard (1996).

17.6 Nature of the Relationships

Analysis of Main Effects

When a statistically significant main effect has only two levels, the nature of the relationship for that effect is determined in the same fashion as for the independent groups t test. This involves comparing the two sample means to make a decision about how the two population means differ. In the present example, the nature of the relationship between religion and the ideal family size is such that Catholics ($\overline{X}_C = 4.00$) want more children than Protestants ($\overline{X}_P = 2.00$).

When a statistically significant main effect has three or more levels, the nature of the relationship for that effect is determined by applying a Tukey HSD test in a similar fashion as we did in Chapter 12 for one-way between-subjects analysis of variance. This involves phrasing a null and an alternative hypothesis for each pair of means that make up that effect, computing the absolute difference between each pair of sample means for that effect, comparing each absolute difference against a critical difference, and making a decision with regard to the null and the alternative hypotheses for that comparison.

For the main effect of factor A, the critical difference is defined as

$$CD = q\sqrt{\frac{MS_{WITHIN}}{nb}}$$ [17.25]

where MS_{WITHIN} is the mean square within from the summary table, n is the per-cell sample size, b is the number of levels of factor B, and q is the Studentized range value from Appendix G. The value of q is determined with reference to the overall alpha level for the effect, the degrees of freedom within from the summary table, and the number of levels of *factor A* (symbolized as k in Appendix G).

In order to maintain the probability of making one or more Type I errors in a set of comparisons at the specified alpha level, we will adopt an overall alpha level of .05 for each main effect that we analyze using two-way analysis of variance. This parallels the approach that we took in Chapter 12 with one-way analysis of variance.

For the main effect of factor B, the critical difference is defined as

$$CD = q\sqrt{\frac{MS_{WITHIN}}{na}}$$ [17.26]

where a is the number of levels of factor A and all other terms are as defined previously. In this case, however, q is determined with reference to the overall alpha level for the effect, the degrees of freedom within, and the number of levels of *factor B* (again symbolized as k in Appendix G).

If the absolute difference between a pair of sample means for a given main effect exceeds the critical difference, we reject the null hypothesis for that comparison and conclude that the corresponding population means differ from one another. If the absolute difference between the sample means does not exceed the critical difference, we are unable to draw this conclusion. If the null hypothesis for a given comparison is rejected, we compare the two sample means for that comparison to make a decision about how the two population means differ. We consider a numerical example involving a factor with three levels in Section 17.8.

Analysis of Interactions

When an interaction effect is statistically significant, the nature of the interaction can be determined using a number of different statistical procedures. Two popular approaches are *simple main effects analysis* and **interaction comparisons**. In general, statisticians recommend the latter strategy and, hence, we consider it here.

When the overall design is 2×2 in nature, the nature of the interaction using the interaction comparisons approach is determined by comparing the differences between the cell means for one independent variable at each level of the other independent variable. For example, suppose that the following cell means are obtained in a study of problem-solving performance as a function of experience with a task and gender and that a two-way analysis of variance reveals a statistically significant interaction effect:

	Male	Female
No experience	7.00	2.00
Some experience	5.00	3.00

A comparison of the difference between the means for male and female participants at each level of task experience indicates that men will outperform women both when individuals are inexperienced with the task and when they have some experience with it but that the effect of gender on problem-solving performance will be more pronounced when individuals lack experience with the task (7.00 − 2.00 = 5.00) than when they have some experience (5.00 − 3.00 = 2.00).

For more complex designs, the nature of the interaction is determined by undertaking a series of interaction comparisons coupled with a *modified Bonferroni procedure* to control the Type I error rate across the set of comparisons. The first step in this process is to break the overall factorial design into all possible 2 × 2 subtables and to perform a separate 2 × 2 analysis of variance for each one. For example, the following three 2 × 2 subtables can be formed for a 3 × 2 factorial design that has three levels of task experience (none, some, and much) and two levels of gender (male and female):

	Male	Female
No experience		
Some experience		

	Male	Female
No experience		
Much experience		

	Male	Female
Some experience		
Much experience		

The sum of squares for the interaction effect for each 2 × 2 subtable is equal to

$$SS_{A \times B(k)} = \frac{n(\overline{X}_a + \overline{X}_d - \overline{X}_b - \overline{X}_c)^2}{4} \qquad [17.27]$$

where k represents the particular subtable that is being analyzed and a, b, c, and d represent the four cells for each subtable per the following:

	Variable 2	
	a	b
Variable 1		
	c	d

The mean square for between-group variability due to the interaction effect for a given subtable will always equal the sum of squares for the interaction effect because an interaction effect for a 2 × 2 subtable always has a single degree of freedom associated with it. This relationship is most clearly seen when it is represented symbolically: $MS_{A \times B(k)} = SS_{A \times B(k)}/df_{A \times B(k)} = SS_{A \times B}/1 = SS_{A \times B(k)}$. This mean square is then divided by the mean square within *from the overall summary table* to yield an *F* ratio for the 2 × 2 interaction effect. Symbolically,

$$F_{A \times B(k)} = \frac{MS_{A \times B(k)}}{MS_{\text{WITHIN}}}$$

[17.28]

Using the modified Bonferroni procedure that we discuss in Section 17.8, a decision is made regarding the statistical significance of this *F* ratio based on 1 degree of freedom for the 2 × 2 interaction effect and the degrees of freedom within *from the overall summary table*. If the interaction comparison is statistically significant, we conclude that an interaction exists between the two independent variables for the levels of the factors that are included in that 2 × 2 subtable. The nature of the overall interaction is then determined by comparing the differences between the cell means for one independent variable at each level of the other independent variable for each statistically significant interaction comparison using an analogous procedure as that demonstrated above for the task experience, gender, and problem-solving performance example.

The interactions comparisons/modified Bonferroni procedure strategy is illustrated in Section 17.8 for a 3 × 2 analysis of variance

17.7 Methodological Considerations

Several methodological considerations are worth noting in the context of the religion, religiosity, and ideal family size study. First are the usual issues of uncontrolled disturbance variables and the generalizability of results. There is also the problem of confounding associated with nonrandom assignment to groups when observational independent variables such as religion and religiosity are studied. In addition, this investigation illustrates an important methodological strategy.

It will be remembered that one of the examples that we used to demonstrate one-way between-subjects analysis of variance in Chapter 12 concerned the relationship between religion and the ideal family size. When discussing methodological aspects of this study in Section 12.7, we noted that religiosity was acting as a disturbance variable and thus creating within-group variability. In the present investigation, religiosity was combined with religion to form four groups, and the within-group variability was based on the variability of the scores within each of the four groups separately. As such, the disturbance effects of religiosity did not enter into the computation of within-group variability because, like religion, it was held constant within groups.

This highlights an important advantage of factorial designs: Not only do they allow us to assess the interaction between independent variables but they also remove the individual and joint effects of these variables from the within-group variability. This makes the tests of the main effects more sensitive than if one of the variables was left uncontrolled and took on the role of a disturbance variable. Thus, an addition to the strategies that we discussed in Chapters 9 and 11 for dealing with disturbance variables is to bring a variable into the research design by including it as a factor.

17.8 Numerical Example

Social psychologists have studied extensively the variables that influence the ability of a speaker to persuade an audience. One important factor that has been found to influence the amount of attitude change that a speaker can create is the discrepancy between the position advocated by the speaker and the position of the audience. Up to a point, the more discrepant the speaker's position, the greater the attitude change that will generally occur. However, if the speaker's position becomes too discrepant, the speaker loses credibility and the message is less persuasive.

Some researchers have speculated that the nature of the relationship between message discrepancy and attitude change differs depending on the expertise of the speaker, who is formally referred to as the *source* by behavioral scientists because he or she is providing the persuasive communication. According to this perspective, speakers with high expertise can take much more discrepant positions than speakers with low expertise and still create a large amount of attitude change.

As an example of how this proposition can be tested, consider an experiment in which college students evaluate the quality of a passage of poetry on a 1 (*very poor*) to 21 (*very good*) scale and then listen to a taped message about this passage that is presented as representing the opinion of either an expert (a famous poetry critic) or a nonexpert (an undergraduate student enrolled in a creative writing class). The messages are constructed to be either slightly discrepant, moderately discrepant, or highly discrepant from students' initial ratings of quality, and they are identical for the two sources. For example, if a student in the large-discrepancy condition rates the passage as being relatively high in quality, then the message argues that the passage is low in quality.

After listening to the message, students rerate the poetry. The design is therefore a 3 × 2 factorial with three levels of message discrepancy (small, medium, and large) and two levels of source expertise (high and low). The dependent variable is the amount of attitude change that occurs as reflected in the difference in the quality ratings before and after listening to the message (that is, the difference between the premessage and the postmessage ratings). The higher the score on this dimension, the greater is the attitude change in the direction advocated by the source. Hypothetical data for this study are presented in Table 17.5. In this table, message discrepancy is designated as *factor A* and source expertise is designated as *factor B*.

TABLE 17.5 Data and Computation of Sums of Squares for Message Discrepancy, Source Expertise, and Attitude Change Experiment

Message discrepancy (A)	Source expertise (B)				Main effect of message discrepancy
	High		**Low**		
	X	X^2	X	X^2	
Small	3	9	1	1	$T_S = 20$
	4	16	0	0	$\overline{X}_S = 2.00$
	2	4	2	4	$T_S^2 = 400$
	3	9	1	1	
	3	9	1	1	
	$T_{SH} = 15$		$T_{SL} = 5$		
	$\overline{X}_{SH} = 3.00$		$\overline{X}_{SL} = 1.00$		
	$T_{SH}^2 = 225$		$T_{SL}^2 = 25$		
Medium	8	64	3	9	$T_M = 50$
	7	49	2	4	$\overline{X}_M = 5.00$
	7	49	3	9	$T_M^2 = 2,500$
	7	49	4	16	
	6	36	3	9	
	$T_{MH} = 35$		$T_{ML} = 15$		
	$\overline{X}_{MH} = 7.00$		$\overline{X}_{ML} = 3.00$		
	$T_{MH}^2 = 1,225$		$T^2 = 225$		
Large	9	81	0	0	$T_l = 50$
	8	64	1	1	$\overline{X}_l = 5.00$
	10	100	1	1	$T_{LL}^2 = 2,500$
	9	81	2	4	
	9	81	1	1	
	$T_{LH} = 45$		$T_{LL} = 5$		
	$\overline{X}_{LH} = 9.00$		$\overline{X}_{LL} = 1.00$		
	$T_{LK}^2 = 2,025$		$T_{LL}^2 = 25$		
Main effect of source expertise	$T_H = 95$		$T_L = 25$		
	$\overline{X}_H = 6.33$		$\overline{X}_L = 1.67$		
	$T_H^2 = 9,025$		$T_L^2 = 625$		

$$\frac{(\sum X)^2}{N} = \frac{120^2}{30} = 480.00$$

$$\frac{\sum T_{A_i}^2}{nb} = \frac{400 + 2{,}500 + 2{,}500}{(5)(2)} = 540.00$$

$$\frac{\sum T_{B_i}^2}{na} = \frac{9{,}025 + 625}{(5)(3)} = 643.33$$

$$\frac{\sum T_{A_i B_i}^2}{n} = \frac{225 + 25 + 1{,}225 + 225 + 2{,}025 + 25}{5} = 750.00$$

Null and Alternative Hypotheses

The null and alternative hypotheses for the main effect of message discrepancy are

H_0: $\mu_S = \mu_M = \mu_L$

H_1: The three population means are not all equal

where the subscript "S" represents the small-discrepancy condition, the subscript "M" represents the medium-discrepancy condition, and the subscript "L" represents the large-discrepancy condition.

The null and alternative hypotheses for the main effect of source expertise are

H_0: $\mu_H = \mu_L$

H_1: $\mu_H \neq \mu_L$

where the subscripts "H" and "L," respectively, denote the high-expertise and the low-expertise conditions.

Because the design is larger than 2×2 in nature, the specification of the null and alternative hypotheses for the interaction effect in formal statistical terms is cumbersome and so is not considered here. We can, however, state these informally. Because of the nature of our research question, we will focus on the nature of the relationship between message discrepancy and attitude change at each level of source expertise. The null hypothesis for the interaction effect from this perspective is that the population differences in mean attitude change as a function of message discrepancy are the same for the high-expertise and the low-expertise sources. The corresponding alternative hypothesis is that the population differences in mean attitude change as a function of message discrepancy are not the same for the high-expertise and the low-expertise sources.

Computation of the Sums of Squares

The intermediate statistics necessary for calculating the sums of squares are given in Table 17.5. The sum of squares for message discrepancy is

$$SS_A = \frac{\sum T_{A_i}^2}{nb} - \frac{(\sum X)^2}{N}$$

$$= 540.00 - 480.00 = 60.00$$

The sum of squares for source expertise is

$$SS_B = \frac{\sum T_{B_i}^2}{na} - \frac{(\sum X)^2}{N}$$

$$= 643.33 - 480.00 = 163.33$$

The sum of squares for the interaction effect is

$$SS_{A \times B} = \frac{(\sum X)^2}{N} + \frac{\sum T_{A_i B_j}^2}{n} - \frac{\sum T_{A_i}^2}{nb} - \frac{\sum T_{B_j}^2}{na}$$

$$= 480.00 + 750.00 - 540.00 - 643.33 = 46.67$$

The sum of squares within is

$$SS_{\text{WITHIN}} = \sum X^2 - \frac{\sum T_{A_i B_j}^2}{n}$$

$$= 762 - 750.00 = 12.00$$

Finally, the sum of squares total is

$$SS_{\text{TOTAL}} = \sum X^2 - \frac{(\sum X)^2}{N}$$

$$= 762 - 480.00 = 282.00$$

Derivation of the Summary Table

The degrees of freedom are

$$df_A = a - 1 = 3 - 1 = 2$$
$$df_B = b - 1 = 2 - 1 = 1$$
$$df_{A \times B} = (a - 1)(b - 1) = (3 - 1)(2 - 1) = 2$$
$$df_{\text{WITHIN}} = (a)(b)(n - 1) = (3)(2)(5 - 1) = 24$$
$$df_{\text{TOTAL}} = N - 1 = 30 - 1 = 29$$

The relevant mean squares are

$$MS_A = \frac{SS_A}{df_A} = \frac{60.00}{2} = 30.00$$

$$MS_B = \frac{SS_B}{df_B} = \frac{163.33}{1} = 163.33$$

$$MS_{A \times B} = \frac{SS_{A \times B}}{df_{A \times B}} = \frac{46.67}{2} = 23.34$$

$$MS_{\text{WITHIN}} = \frac{SS_{\text{WITHIN}}}{df_{\text{WITHIN}}} = \frac{12.00}{24} = .50$$

The F ratios are thus

$$F_A = \frac{MS_A}{MS_{\text{WITHIN}}} = \frac{30.00}{.50} = 60.00$$

$$F_B = \frac{MS_B}{MS_{\text{WITHIN}}} = \frac{163.33}{.50} = 326.66$$

$$F_{A \times B} = \frac{MS_{A \times B}}{MS_{\text{WITHIN}}} = \frac{23.34}{.50} = 46.68$$

These calculations yield the following summary table:

Source	SS	df	MS	F
A (message discrepancy)	60.00	2	30.00	60.00
B (source expertise)	163.33	1	163.33	326.66
A × B	46.67	2	23.34	46.68
Within	12.00	24	.50	
Total	282.00	29		

Tests of the Null Hypotheses

The critical value of F from Appendix F for an alpha level of .05 and $df_A = 2$ and $df_{WITHIN} = 24$ is 3.40. Because the observed F value of 60.00 for the main effect of message discrepancy exceeds this value, we reject the null hypothesis and conclude that a relationship exists between message discrepancy and attitude change.

The critical value of F from Appendix F for an alpha level of .05 and $df_B = 1$ and $df_{WITHIN} = 24$ is 4.26. Because the observed F value of 326.66 for the main effect of source expertise exceeds this value, we reject the null hypothesis and conclude that a relationship exists between source expertise and attitude change.

Because the degrees of freedom of $df_{A \times B} = 2$ and $df_{WITHIN} = 24$ for the interaction effect are the same as the degrees of freedom for the main effect of message discrepancy, the critical value of F for an alpha level of .05 is also the same—namely, 3.40. Because the observed F value of 46.68 for the interaction effect exceeds this value, we reject the null hypothesis and conclude that there is an interaction between message discrepancy and source expertise.

Strength of the Relationships

Application of Equations 17.22 to 17.24 shows that the strength of the relationship for each of the three sources of between-group variability is as follows:

$$eta_A^2 = \frac{SS_A}{SS_{TOTAL}} = \frac{60.00}{282.00} = .21$$

$$eta_B^2 = \frac{SS_B}{SS_{TOTAL}} = \frac{163.33}{282.00} = .58$$

$$eta_{A \times B}^2 = \frac{SS_{A \times B}}{SS_{TOTAL}} = \frac{46.67}{282.00} = .17$$

The strongest effect is for the main effect of source expertise. The proportion of variability in attitude change that is associated with this factor is .58. This represents a strong effect. The proportion of variability in attitude change that is associated with message discrepancy is .21. This also represents a strong effect. The interaction between message discrepancy and source expertise accounts for 17% of the variability in attitude change. This again represents a strong effect.

Nature of the Relationships

Analysis of Main Effects   Because it has only two levels, the nature of the relationship for the main effect of source expertise is determined by comparing the two sample means. This comparison shows that messages will produce more attitude change when they are attributed to a high-expertise source ($\overline{X}_H = 6.33$) than when they are attributed to a low-expertise source ($\overline{X}_L = 1.67$).

The main effect of message discrepancy has three levels and, hence, it is necessary to apply the Tukey HSD test to determine the nature of the relationship between this dimension and attitude change. Because message discrepancy is factor A, the value of the critical difference is established using Equation 17.25. From Appendix G, the value of q for an overall alpha level of .05, $df_{\text{WITHIN}} = 24$, and $k = a = 3$ is 3.53. Thus,

$$CD = q\sqrt{\frac{MS_{\text{WITHIN}}}{nb}} = 3.53\sqrt{\frac{.50}{(5)(2)}} = .79$$

This value will be used to make decisions with respect to the three sets of null and alternative hypotheses that we can phrase for this effect. The first set of hypotheses addresses the means for the small- and the medium-discrepancy messages:

H_0: $\mu_S = \mu_M$

H_1: $\mu_S \neq \mu_M$

The absolute difference between the sample means is $|\overline{X}_S - \overline{X}_M| = |2.00 - 5.00| = 3.00$. Because 3.00 exceeds the critical difference of .79, we reject the null hypothesis for the comparison. An examination of the sample means indicates that more attitude change will occur when there is a medium discrepancy in the message content ($\overline{X}_M = 5.00$) than when there is a small discrepancy ($\overline{X}_S = 2.00$).

The second set of hypotheses addresses the means for the small- and the large-discrepancy messages:

H_0: $\mu_S = \mu_L$

H_1: $\mu_S \neq \mu_L$

The absolute difference between the sample means is $|\overline{X}_S - \overline{X}_L| = |2.00 - 5.00| = 3.00$. Because 3.00 exceeds the critical difference of .79, we reject the null hypothesis for the comparison. An examination of the sample means indicates that more attitude change will occur when there is a large discrepancy in the message content ($\overline{X}_L = 5.00$) than when there is a small discrepancy ($\overline{X}_S = 2.00$).

The third set of hypotheses addresses the means for the medium- and the large-discrepancy messages:

H_0: $\mu_M = \mu_L$

H_1: $\mu_M \neq \mu_L$

The absolute difference between the sample means is $|\overline{X}_M - \overline{X}_L| = |5.00 - 5.00| = .00$. Because .00 does not exceed the critical difference of .79, we fail to reject the null hypothesis for the comparison. Thus, we are unable to conclude that attitude change will differ when there is a medium discrepancy in the message content from when there is a large discrepancy.

As we did with one-way between-subjects analysis of variance, we can summarize the results of the entire analysis in a table. As with the earlier case, for the sake of brevity, this does not explicitly refer to the alternative hypotheses:

Null hypothesis tested	Absolute difference between sample means	Value of CD	Null hypothesis rejected?
$\mu_S = \mu_M$	$\|2.00 - 5.00\| = 3.00$	.79	Yes
$\mu_S = \mu_L$	$\|2.00 - 5.00\| = 3.00$	.79	Yes
$\mu_M = \mu_L$	$\|5.00 - 5.00\| = .00$	.79	No

This format allows us to readily discern the nature of the relationship between the amount of message discrepancy and attitude change: Medium- ($\overline{X}_M = 5.00$) and large-discrepancy ($\overline{X}_L = 5.00$) messages will produce more attitude change than small-discrepancy messages ($\overline{X}_S = 2.00$). However, we cannot conclude that the amount of attitude change that is produced by medium- and large-discrepancy messages will differ.

Analysis of the Interaction Because the interaction effect is statistically significant, we will examine the nature of the interaction using interaction comparisons. As a means of controlling the Type I error rate across the set of comparisons, a **modified Bonferroni procedure** will also be utilized. The rationale for this procedure is described in Holland and Copenhaver (1988).

The overall 3 × 2 design can be broken into three 2 × 2 subtables, which we indicate here along with the cell means:

	High expertise	Low expertise
Small discrepancy	3.00	1.00
Medium discrepancy	7.00	3.00

	High expertise	Low expertise
Small discrepancy	3.00	1.00
Large discrepancy	9.00	1.00

	High expertise	Low expertise
Medium discrepancy	7.00	3.00
Large discrepancy	9.00	1.00

The next step in the analysis is to calculate the sum of squares for the interaction effect for each 2×2 subtable using Equation 17.27. For the first subtable, the sum of squares is

$$SS_{A \times B(1)} = \frac{n(\overline{X}_a + \overline{X}_d - \overline{X}_b - \overline{X}_c)^2}{4}$$

$$= \frac{5(3.00 + 3.00 - 1.00 - 7.00)^2}{4} = 5.00$$

For the second subtable, the sum of squares is

$$SS_{A \times B(2)} = \frac{5(3.00 + 1.00 - 1.00 - 9.00)^2}{4} = 45.00$$

and for the third subtable, the sum of squares is

$$SS_{A \times B(3)} = \frac{5(7.00 + 1.00 - 3.00 - 9.00)^2}{4} = 20.00$$

As we noted in Section 17.6, an interaction effect for a 2×2 subtable always has a single degree of freedom associated with it. Consequently, these values also represent the corresponding mean squares for between-group variability due to the interaction effect.

Next, we form an F ratio for each 2×2 interaction effect using these mean squares as the numerator and the mean square within from the overall summary table as the denominator, per Equation 17.28:

$$F_{A \times B(1)} = \frac{5.00}{.50} = 10.00$$

$$F_{A \times B(2)} = \frac{45.00}{.50} = 90.00$$

$$F_{A \times B(3)} = \frac{20.00}{.50} = 40.00$$

To apply the modified Bonferroni procedure, we determine a p value for each of these F ratios based on 1 degree of freedom for the 2×2 interaction effect and 24 degrees of freedom within from the overall summary table. This usually must be done with the aid of a computer. Next, the F ratios are ordered in a column from largest to smallest, and the corresponding p values are each compared against a *critical alpha*. If the p value is less than the critical alpha, the interaction comparison is statistically significant. For the sake of precision, both the p values and the critical alphas should be rounded to at least three decimal places.

The value of the critical alpha changes for each successive F ratio as one proceeds from the top to the bottom of the column. The largest F ratio must yield a p value that is less than the overall alpha level that we adopt for the set of interaction comparisons divided by the total number of comparisons (in this case, three) for the interaction comparison to be statistically significant. The next largest F ratio must yield a p value that is less than the overall alpha level divided by the number of comparisons minus 1 for the interaction comparison to be statistically significant. The next largest F ratio must yield a p value that is less than the overall alpha level divided by the number of comparisons minus 2 for the interaction comparison to be statistically significant. And so on, subtracting an additional unit from the total number of comparisons with each successive interaction comparison.

If a comparison is statistically significant, the nature of the interaction for the corresponding 2×2 subtable is determined by comparing the differences between the cell means for one independent variable at each level of the other independent variable using the procedure that we discussed in Section 17.6. As soon as the first statistically nonsignificant interaction comparison is encountered as one proceeds from the largest to the smallest F ratio, all remaining comparisons are declared statistically nonsignificant.

The results for the modified Bonferroni procedure for the message discrepancy, source expertise, and attitude change experiment can be summarized in a table as follows. In deriving this table, we used an overall alpha level of .05.

Interaction comparison	F ratio	p value	Critical alpha	Interaction comparison significant?
$A \times B_{(2)}$	90.00	.000000001	.05/3 = .017	Yes
$A \times B_{(3)}$	40.00	.000002	.05/2 = .025	Yes
$A \times B_{(1)}$	10.00	.004	.05/1 = .050	Yes

Although all three interaction comparisons in this instance are statistically significant, this will not always be the case.

We will determine the nature of the overall interaction by comparing the differences between the cell means for message discrepancy at each level of source expertise for each comparison. This leads to the following conclusions: Medium-discrepancy messages will produce more attitude change in the advocated direction than small-discrepancy messages when source expertise is high ($7.00 - 3.00 = 4.00$) than when it is low ($3.00 - 1.00 = 2.00$). Similarly, large-discrepancy messages will produce more attitude change in the advocated direction than small-discrepancy messages when source expertise is high ($9.00 - 3.00 = 6.00$) as opposed to low ($1.00 - 1.00 = .00$). Finally, large-discrepancy messages will produce more attitude change in the advocated direction than medium-discrepancy messages when source expertise is high ($9.00 - 7.00 = 2.00$) but less attitude change when source expertise is low ($1.00 - 3.00 = -2.00$).

Figure 17.3 presents the six cell means graphically. The means for the three levels of message discrepancy for students in the high-expertise condition are connected by lines, as are the means for the three levels of message discrepancy for students in the low-expertise condition. These lines have different slopes because the interaction between message discrepancy and source expertise is statistically significant.

FIGURE 17.3 **Mean Attitude Change as a Function of Message Discrepancy and Source Expertise**

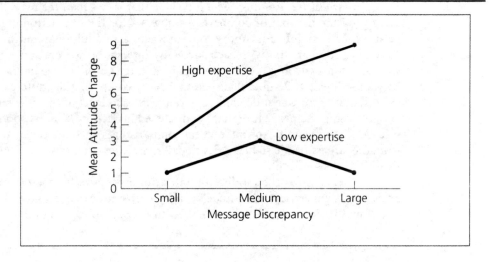

By providing a visual representation of statistically significant interaction effects, graphs help to clarify the nature of the interaction. For this reason, it is often informative to depict interactions in graph form.

17.9 Unequal Sample Sizes

The sample sizes (n) for the two-way analysis of variance examples that we have considered thus far have all been equal. However, this is not always the case in behavioral science research. In fact, there are many reasons why the sample sizes in a study might differ even when the researcher intends to keep them the same. For example, a subject might be lost in animal experimentation because of disease or sickness. Or a person who is scheduled to participate in a particular research condition might not show up or might provide invalid data. When they occur, unequal sample sizes necessitate modifications to the analytical procedures that we discuss in this chapter.

Let us demonstrate this by considering an example where the sample sizes are all equal and a second example where the sample sizes are not all equal. First, consider the following sample sizes for a 2 × 2 factorial design:

	Employment status	
Gender	Employed	Not employed
Male	10	10
Female	10	10

In this study, there are equal sample sizes for all cells, and the two independent variables, *in the context of this data set*, are therefore unrelated to each other. This can be thought of in terms of conditional probabilities: The probability of having a particular employment status given that one is a particular gender is the same as the overall probability for that employment status. Employment status is thus independent of gender. In fact, it is always the case that the two independent variables will be unrelated to each other in the sample when the sample sizes are the same for all cells.

Now consider the case of unequal sample sizes:

	Employment status	
Gender	Employed	Not employed
Male	6	13
Female	13	8

In this instance, a sample relationship exists between gender and employment status. For example, if you know that an individual is male, you also know that it is more likely that he is unemployed than employed. If you know that an individual is female, you also know that it is more likely that she is employed than unemployed. Thus, there is a relationship between the two independent variables.*

The introduction of a relationship between the independent variables creates a number of statistical and conceptual problems for testing the two main effects and the interaction effect. Consider factor A in a design with unequal sample sizes. On the basis of a two-way analysis of variance, we might conclude that factor A is related to the dependent variable in the population and that it therefore accounts for some of the variability on this dimension. However, because factor A is related to factor B due to the unequal sample sizes, some of the variability in the dependent variable that we attribute to factor A may actually be due to factor B.

The problem faced by statisticians is what to do about the between-group variability that is common to both factor A and factor B. One common approach is to apply a technique known as *least squares analysis of* variance. This technique focuses on explained variability that is unique to a given factor and excludes *common explained variability* when calculating the sum of squares associated with that factor. Details of this approach can be found in Kirk (1995).

---

* Another way of thinking about this is that if we were to perform a chi-square analysis on the cell sizes using the procedures that we discussed in Chapter 15, the obtained value of χ^2 would equal 0 in the case of equal *ns* (indicating the absence of a relationship in the sample) but would be greater than 0 in the case of unequal *ns* (indicating the presence of a relationship in the sample). Unequal sample sizes do not introduce a relationship between the two independent variables when the sample sizes for the groups that make up one factor are proportional across levels of the other factor (for example, when the ratio of employed individuals to unemployed individuals is 3 to 1 for both men and women).

17.10 Planning an Investigation Using Two-Way Between-Subjects Analysis of Variance

Appendix E.2 contains tables that are used in determining the per-cell sample sizes necessary to achieve various levels of power for different numbers of degrees of freedom for a given effect for two-way between-subjects analysis of variance. Table 17.6 reproduces a portion of this appendix for $df_{\text{EFFECT}} = 1$ and an alpha level of .05. The first column presents selected values of power, and the column headings are selected values of eta-squared in the population.

Because the cell size necessary to achieve a given level of power is affected by the number of degrees of freedom for an effect, the required sample size must be determined separately for the main effect of factor A, the main effect of factor B, and the interaction effect. We must also adjust the sample sizes in Table 17.5 and Appendix E.2 as follows to take the dimensions of the factorial design (for example, 2 × 3, 3 × 3, or 2 × 4) into account:

$$n' = \frac{(n_T - 1)(df_{\text{EFFECT}} + 1)}{ab}$$ [17.29]

where n' is the adjusted per-cell sample size, n_T is the tabled per-cell sample size, a is the number of levels of factor A, b is the number of levels of factor B, and df_{EFFECT} is the degrees of freedom for the effect in question [that is, $a - 1$, $b - 1$, or $(a - 1)(b - 1)$].

The determination of the per-cell sample size necessary to ensure that the power requirement is met for each effect requires that we calculate the necessary adjusted cell size for each effect individually and then use the *largest* sample size of the three. If this is not a whole number, this value of n' is rounded up to the nearest integer.*

As an example of this strategy, consider a 2 × 2 factorial design for which the investigator suspects that the population value of eta-squared is .15 for factor A,

TABLE 17.6 **Approximate Sample Sizes Necessary to Achieve Selected Levels of Power for $df_{\text{EFFECT}} = 1$ and Alpha = .05 as a Function of Population Values of Eta-Squared**

Power	.01	.03	.05	.07	.10	.15	.20	.25	.30	.35	.40
					Population Eta-Squared						
.10	22	8	5	4	3	2	2	2	—	—	—
.50	193	63	38	27	18	12	9	7	5	5	4
.70	310	101	60	42	29	18	13	10	8	7	6
.80	393	128	76	53	36	23	17	13	10	8	7
.90	526	171	101	71	48	31	22	17	13	11	9
.95	651	211	125	87	60	38	27	21	16	13	11
.99	920	298	176	123	84	53	38	29	22	18	15

* Possible compromises to the strategy that we have described for determining the per-cell sample sizes necessary to achieve various levels of power for two-way analysis of variance are discussed in Cohen (1977).

.25 for factor B, and .10 for the interaction effect and desires a .80 level of power for each effect for an alpha level of .05. Because $df_A = a - 1 = 2 - 1 = 1$, the value of n_T for the main effect of factor A can be obtained from Table 17.5. This is equal to 23. Thus, the adjusted per-cell sample size using Equation 17.29 is

$$n' = \frac{(23 - 1)(1 + 1)}{(2)(2)} = 11.00$$

Because $df_B = b - 1 = 2 - 1 = 1$ and $df_{A \times B} = (a - 1)(b - 1) = (2 - 1)(2 - 1) = 1$, Table 17.5 can also be used to obtain the values of n_T for the main effect of factor B and for the interaction effect. For the main effect of factor B, $n_T = 13$ so

$$n' = \frac{(13 - 1)(1 + 1)}{(2)(2)} = 6.00$$

For the interaction effect, $n_T = 36$ so

$$n' = \frac{(36 - 1)(1 + 1)}{(2)(2)} = 17.50$$

or, rounded up to the nearest integer, 18.

The largest adjusted cell size dictates the number of participants that are required in each group. In this instance, 18 participants should be included in each of the four cells. Note that this will increase the power of the F tests beyond the .80 level for the two main effects.

Examination of Table 17.6 and Appendix E.2 provides a general appreciation for the relationships among the degrees of freedom for an effect, the alpha level, the per-cell sample size, the strength of the relationship that one is trying to detect in the population, and power for two-way analysis of variance. As can be seen, power becomes greater as the degrees of freedom for an effect, the alpha level, the sample size, and the population eta-squared each increases.

17.11 Method of Presentation

The results for a two-way between-subjects analysis of variance are reported in much the same way as those for a one-way between-subjects analysis of variance. As with the one-way case, it is not necessary to use the term *between-subjects* because, unless stated otherwise, it is assumed that a between-subjects analysis was performed.

For each effect, the degrees of freedom for that effect, the degrees of freedom within, the observed value of F, the significance level, the sample means, and the standard deviation estimates should be reported. In addition, a statement should be made of the alpha level that was used for the three F tests.

As a way of avoiding "statistics-laden text that is difficult to read" (American Psychological Association, 2001, p. 160), it is sometimes preferable to present the analysis of variance statistics in a table rather than in the text. When information is presented in tabular form, the guidelines described in Section 15.12 should be followed. American Psychological Association (APA) style also dictates that the format presented on p. 160 of the *Publication Manual of the American Psychological Association* (2001) be used when preparing analysis of variance summary tables. Although the layout of such tables is similar in some ways to the summary tables that we have encountered in this book, it differs in other ways.

If an effect is statistically significant, the strength and nature of the relationship for the effect should also be addressed. Furthermore, the overall alpha level for the modified Bonferroni procedure should be reported if the interaction effect is statistically significant.

It is often more efficient to present the means and standard deviation estimates for the interaction effect in a table rather than in the text. Alternatively, if the interaction effect is statistically significant, the cell means can be depicted in a graph such as that in Figure 17.3. In manuscripts submitted for publication, graphs are placed at the end of the research report and are referred to in the text, where appropriate, by number, starting with Figure 1.

The results for the message discrepancy, source expertise, and attitude change experiment that was discussed earlier in this chapter might be reported as follows:*

Results

Attitude change scores were subjected to a two-way analysis of variance having three levels of message discrepancy (small, medium, and large) and two levels of source expertise (high and low). All effects were found to be statistically significant at an alpha level of .05.

The main effect of message discrepancy yielded an F ratio of $F(2, 24) = 60.00$, $p < .01$. The strength of the relationship, as indexed by eta-squared, was .21. A Tukey HSD test revealed that the means for both the medium-discrepancy ($M = 5.00$, $SD = 2.21$) and the large-discrepancy ($M = 5.00$, $SD = 4.27$) messages were significantly greater than the mean for the small-discrepancy message ($M = 2.00$, $SD = 1.25$). The means for the medium—and large—discrepancy messages did not significantly differ.

The main effect of source expertise was such that the messages from the high-expertise source $M = 6.33$, $SD = 2.26$) produced significantly more attitude change than the messages from the low-expertise source ($M = 1.67$, $SD = 1.18$), $F(1, 24) = 326.66$, $p < .01$. The strength of the relationship, as indexed by eta-squared, was .58.

The interaction effect, $F(2, 24) = 46.68$, $p < .01$, was analyzed using interaction comparisons in conjunction with a modified Bonferroni procedure (Holland & Copenhaver, 1988) based on an overall alpha level of .05. The means and standard deviations for the six cells can be found in Table 1. The interaction comparisons for all three 2×2 subtables were found to be statistically significant and the strength of the overall interaction effect, as indexed by eta-squared, was .17.

A comparison of the differences between the cell means for message discrepancy at each level of source expertise for each subtable revealed the following: The medium-discrepancy messages produced significantly more attitude change in the advocated direction than the small-discrepancy messages when source expertise was high ($7.00 - 3.00 = 4.00$) as opposed to low ($3.00 - 1.00 = 2.00$). Similarly,

---

* The standard deviation estimates were calculated by applying the usual formulas for the sum of squares, the variance estimate, and the standard deviation estimate to each of the effects in Table 17.5.

the large-discrepancy messages produced significantly more attitude change in the advocated direction than the small-discrepancy messages when source expertise was high (9.00 − 3.00 = 6.00) than when it was low (1.00 − 1.00 = .00). Finally, the large-discrepancy messages produced significantly more attitude change in the advocated direction than the medium-discrepancy messages when source expertise was high (9.00 − 7.00 = 2.00) but less attitude change when source expertise was low (1.00 − 3.00 = −2.00).

A reference is given for the modified Bonferroni procedure because many researchers do not incorporate this when conducting interaction comparisons. As we noted in Section 16.6, references should be provided anytime a procedure is not widely used because doing so will allow interested readers to locate information about the technique. The use of an ampersand to connect the names of the two authors in parenthetical material is consistent with APA style.

The table of means and standard deviation estimates for the interaction might appear as follows:

Table 1

Mean Attitude Change as a Function of Message Discrepancy and Source Expertise

| | Message discrepancy | | | | | |
| | Small | | Medium | | Large | |
Source expertise	M	SD	M	SD	M	SD
High	3.00	.71	7.00	.71	9.00	.71
Low	1.00	.71	3.00	.71	1.00	.71

Note. For each cell, $n = 5$.

According to APA (2001) format, general information that relates to the table as a whole is placed below the table and designated by the italicized word "Note" followed by a period. In this instance, the note at the bottom of the table informs the reader that the sample size is 5 for all of the cells of the factorial design.

17.12   Examples from the Literature

Attributions for Success as a Function of the Gender of the Performer and the Type of Task

When someone is successful at a task, we sometimes attribute that success to the person's ability. Alternatively, we may simply think that the person "got lucky" and that the success had little to do with ability. In an attempt to determine whether people apply these two attributions differently when explaining male and female task success, Johnson (1976) conducted a study in which 100 research participants were asked to listen to a tape recording that indicated that either a man or a woman had succeeded at either a traditionally masculine task or a traditionally feminine task. The former involved identifying mechanical objects such as wrenches and screwdrivers, whereas the latter involved identifying household objects such as mops and pots.

Participants were then asked to make attributions about the target person's task performance on a 1 to 13 scale, where a score of 1 indicated that participants thought that the target person's task performance was due entirely to luck and a score of 13 indicated that participants thought that the target person's task performance was due entirely to ability. The design was thus a 2 × 2 factorial, with the gender of the target person and the type of task (masculine or feminine) as the independent variables and the ratings of luck/ability as the dependent variable.

It was hypothesized that for the masculine task, male success would be attributed more to ability than would female success, but the reverse would be true for the feminine task. Thus, Johnson predicted an interaction, with the relationship between the gender of the performer and the ability/luck attributions depending on the type of task.

The main effect for the gender of the performer was statistically significant, $F(1, 96) = 4.38$, $p < .05$, and indicated that successful performance by men ($\overline{X} = 9.24$) will be attributed more to ability than will successful performance by women ($\overline{X} = 8.40$). The strength of the relationship, as indexed by eta-squared, was only .04, however. This represents a weak effect. The main effect for the type of task was not statistically significant, $F(1, 96) = 2.46$, $p < .05$, with the mean for the masculine task being 8.50 and the mean for the feminine task being 9.14. The strength of the relationship, as indexed by eta-squared, was .02. This again represents a weak effect.

Although a statistically significant interaction effect was observed, $F(1, 96) = 9.08$, $p < .01$, the nature of the interaction was somewhat different from what was expected. An analysis of the cell means indicated that for the masculine task, the man's performance ($\overline{X} = 9.53$) was attributed more to ability than was the woman's performance on the same task ($\overline{X} = 7.48$). However, for the feminine task, the mean ratings for the male ($\overline{X} = 8.95$) and the female ($\overline{X} = 9.32$) targets were not significantly different. The strength of the overall interaction effect, as indexed by eta-squared, was .08. This represents a weak to moderate effect. Can you think of an explanation for these findings?

Restaurant Tipping as a Function of Interpersonal Touch and Diners' Gender

Crusco and Wetzel (1984) conducted a field experiment in which restaurant diners were randomly assigned to conditions where, while returning their change, their waitress twice touched their palms with her fingers for .5 second (hand-touch condition), placed her hands on their shoulders for 1 to 1.5 seconds (shoulder-touch condition), or did not touch them (no-touch condition). The researchers predicted that the hand touch would produce positive feelings toward the waitress and thus increase the amount of her tip relative to the no-touch condition. Because a touch on the shoulder can be construed as a sign of dominance, it was felt that this might not be viewed as positively and that tipping might therefore also be greater in the hand-touch condition than in the shoulder-touch condition.

So that possible gender differences in these effects could be determined, separate observations were made for male and female diners. The design was thus a 3×2 factorial, with the type of touch (hand, shoulder, or none) and the gender of the diner as the independent variables. The dependent variable was the percentage of the bill left as a tip.

A two-way analysis of variance yielded a main effect for the gender of the diner, $F(1, 108) = 3.93, p < .05$, such that men $(\overline{X} = 15.3\%)$ tipped more than women $(\overline{X} = 12.6\%)$. The main effect for the type of touch was also statistically significant, $F(2, 108) = 3.45, p < .05$. Analysis of the three touch means showed that tipping was higher in the hand-touch $(\overline{X} = 16.7\%)$ and shoulder-touch $(\overline{X} = 14.4\%)$ conditions than in the no-touch condition $(\overline{X} = 12.2\%)$. The hand-touch and shoulder-touch means did not significantly differ. The interaction effect also failed to attain statistical significance, $F(2, 108) < 1.$* The values of eta-squared were not provided in the research report.

17.13 Links Between Computer Results and Book Content

As we noted in Section 17.9, unequal sample sizes necessitate modifications to the analytical procedures that we discuss in this chapter. As we also noted in that section, a common approach in this situation is to apply a least squares analysis of variance. However, there are also several other ways for dealing with the problem of unequal sample sizes. Consequently, the nature of the summary table that is provided as statistical computer output and the way in which the constituent sums of squares are calculated might differ from what we have discussed. For instance, the sums of squares for factor A, factor B, and the interaction effect will not always add up to the sum of squares between, nor will all of the other sums of squares in the summary table always add up to the sum of squares total.

17.14 Links Between Chapters

As we have seen, the rationale and the analytical procedures for two-way between-subjects analysis of variance are closely related to those for one-way between-subjects analysis of variance. In fact, the conditions for using two-way analysis of variance are identical to those for one-way analysis of variance except that two

---

* It is conventional to use the < 1 notation when the observed value of F is less than 1.00. It is not necessary to report the significance level that is associated with an F value of this magnitude because an F ratio of less than 1.00 can never lead to the rejection of the null hypothesis. Can you think of why this is the case?

independent variables rather than one independent variable are studied. If there are only two levels of one or both factors, two-way analysis of variance is also similar in some important ways to the independent groups t test.

As we will see in Section 18.6, two-way analysis of variance procedures can be extended to analyze the relationship between a dependent variable and three or more independent variables. Two-way analysis of variance is also related to several other advanced analysis of variance techniques that we briefly review in that section, including *two-way repeated measures analysis of variance*, which is used to study the joint influence of two within-subjects independent variables on a dependent variable, and *two-way between-within analysis of variance*, which is used when one independent variable is between-subjects in nature and one is within-subjects in nature.

Applications to the Analysis of a Social Problem Using SPSS for Windows

We noted in the "Applications to the Analysis of a Social Problem Using SPSS for Windows" section in Chapter 10 that not all parents are adamantly opposed to premarital sexual intercourse on the part of their teenage children. For example, some parents believe that if it is with someone who is special and whom the teen has known for a long time, then sexual intercourse is permissible, given proper protection against unintended pregnancy and sexually transmitted diseases.

Interestingly, the results reported in Chapter 10 indicate that adolescent girls perceive their mothers to be more disapproving of sexual activity than adolescent boys do. In this earlier analysis, the age of the teenager was ignored. However, it is possible that boys' and girls' perceptions of maternal disapproval may become either more or, alternatively, less, similar over the adolescent years. For example, mothers might become more accepting of the inevitability of sexual intercourse as the teen ages. This may be especially true in regard to adolescent girls, who, as we reported in Chapter 10, tend to actually experience stronger maternal sanctions against sexual intercourse.

To examine the potential interaction of age and gender in relation to this important predictor of sexual behavior, we conducted a 2 × 4 analysis of variance on perceived maternal disapproval of sexual intercourse using data from the parent–teen communication study described in Chapter 1. The two independent variables were the teens' gender and their age (14, 15, 16, or 17 years old). The dependent variable was the maternal attitude measure described in Chapter 10. Recall that the teens were asked to indicate their agreement with the following five statements:

1. My mother would disapprove of me having sex at this time in my life.
2. My mother has specifically told me not to have sex.
3. My mother thinks I definitely should not be sexually active (having sexual intercourse) at this time in my life.
4. If it were with someone who was special to me and whom I knew well, like a steady boyfriend (girlfriend), my mother would not mind if I had sexual intercourse at this time in my life.
5. My mother thinks it is fine for me to be sexually active (having sexual intercourse) at this time in my life.

Each statement was rated on a 5-point scale having the response options *strongly disagree, moderately disagree, neither agree nor disagree, moderately agree,* and *strongly agree.* The responses to the first three statements were scored from 1 (*strongly disagree*) to 5 (*strongly agree*), whereas the responses to the last two items were reverse scored such that 1 represented strong *agreement* and 5 represented strong *disagreement*. An overall index of the extent to which a teen perceived his or her mother as disapproving of the teen engaging in sexual intercourse was obtained by summing the responses to the five statements. Scores on this measure could range from 5 to 25, with higher values indicating greater perceived maternal disapproval of engaging in sex.

The first step in the analysis was to examine the frequency histograms for each of the eight groups defined by the 2 × 4 design. Figure 17.4 presents the histograms for the 14-year-old boys and the 17-year-old girls, with a normal distribution superimposed on each. These histograms typify the shapes of the other groups, which we omit in the interest of space. Both distributions are nonnormal, with the highest frequency in both instances being for the highest possible perceived maternal disapproval score (25).

Given the relatively large sample sizes in each of our cells, the nonnormality in the samples is not so great as to suggest that nonnormality in the population is large enough to undermine the *F* tests (Milligan, Wong, and Thompson, 1987). However, the histogram for the 17-year-old girls suggests two outliers. We double-checked the coding of the scores for these individuals as well as their responses to the other questions. This revealed neither coding errors nor anything else unique about these teens relative to their peers. Because they represented only two cases and because some advanced analyses that we conducted indicated that the results were unaffected by their presence, we included them in the analysis. Nevertheless, we decided to complement the analysis of variance that is reported here with additional outlier-resistant analyses. These produced comparable conclusions to the results reported below.

Table 17.7 presents the computer output for the analysis of variance. The top portion contains the results for the Levene test for assessing homogeneity of variance that we discussed in Section 10.2. As can be seen, the *p* value (labeled "Sig.") for the *F* ratio that serves as the test statistic for the Levene test is .04, which suggests that the population variances are not homogeneous. However, as we explained in Section 10.2, a statistically significant result may be an artifact of nonnormality in the

data or it may represent a real but trivial difference in population variances.

To gain a further appreciation for whether we should be concerned with the results of the Levene test, we examined the variance estimates for the eight cells of the 2 × 4 design and found that the largest one (27.04) was less than twice as large as the smallest one (13.84). Consistent with our discussion in Section 17.4, the *F* test tends to be robust to such differences for the sample sizes in our study (Milligan, Wong, and Thompson, 1987; Moore and McCabe, 1993).

The middle section of Table 17.7 presents the mean scores for the two main effects, and the summary table appears at the bottom. Because we had unequal sample sizes, we conducted a *least squares analysis of variance* (Kirk, 1995), as is commonly done under this circumstance. Only the main effect of gender was statistically significant, with the *F* value of 84.91 having an associated *p* value of .0005 or less, as indicated by the fact that a significance level of .000 is reported in the summary table. The strength of the relationship, as indexed by eta-squared, is .10, which represents a moderate effect. Examination of the two main effect means indicates that adolescent girls ($\overline{X} = 19.11$) perceive greater maternal disapproval than do adolescent boys ($\overline{X} = 18.81$). Although we cannot accept the null hypothesis, the lack of a significant interaction effect suggests that there is no compelling evidence that the gender effect differs across the age groups.

Given that we failed to reject the null hypotheses for the main effect of age and the interaction effect, it is possible that Type II errors may have occurred. To evaluate this possibility, we determined the statistical power for both the main effect of age and the interaction effect for a 2 × 4 analysis of variance having an alpha level of .05 and the sample sizes in our study for what we considered to be a small effect size—namely, a population eta-squared of .03. Although we accomplished this using the procedure described by Cohen (1988), a rough estimate of power can be obtained using the strategy that we describe in Section 17.10. Both approaches yield a statistical power that exceeds .95 for both effects, which suggests that Type II errors are very unlikely.

(continued)

These results affirm the perceived difference in maternal attitudes toward premarital sexual intercourse for boys versus girls that was found in Chapter 10 and suggest that this difference occurs independent of the age of the adolescent (at least for the age range that we studied).

FIGURE 17.4   Frequency Histograms for Perceived Maternal Attitude Toward (a) 14-Year-Old-Boys and (b) 17-Year-Old Girls Engaging in Sex

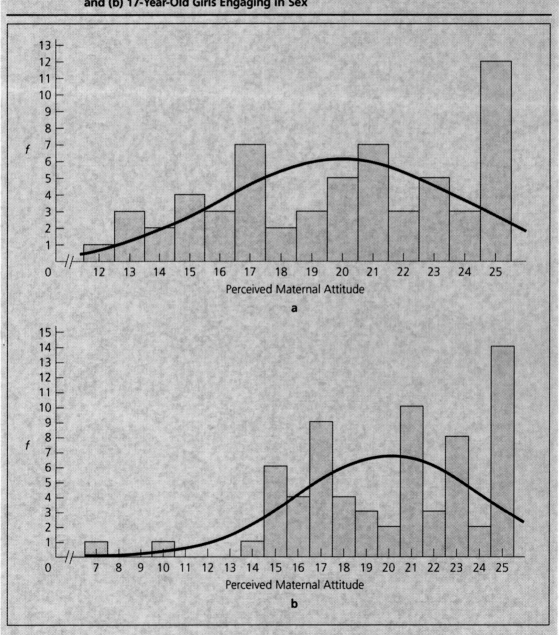

TABLE 17.7   Computer Output for Two-Way Between-Subjects Analysis of Variance for Perceived Maternal Attitude Toward Teens Engaging in Sex

Levene's Test of Equality of Error Variances

Dependent Variable: mdissex

F	df_1	df_2	Sig.
2.811	7	16	.041

Gender

Dependent Variable: mdissex

Gender	Mean
Male	18.814
Female	19.111

Age

Dependent Variable: mdissex

Age	Mean
14	17.745
15	17.796
16	17.244
17	16.901

Tests of Between-Subjects Effects

Dependent Variable: mdissex

Source	Sum of squares	df	Mean square	F	Sig.
Gender	1,830.77	1	1,830.77	84.91	.000
Age	104.09	3	34.70	1.61	.186
Gender*Age	44.13	3	14.71	.68	.563
Within	15,351.85	712	21.56		
Total	17,452.75	719			

Summary

A two-way factorial design is one in which two independent variables are simultaneously studied to determine how they act in conjunction with one another to influence a dependent variable. Such designs are formed by combining the levels of the two independent variables, or factors, to yield a number of groups equal to the product of the number of levels of each factor. Each unique combination of factors that results is referred to as a *cell*.

Two-way factorial designs are analyzed using two-way between-subjects analysis of variance. Two-way analysis of variance is typically applied when (1) the dependent variable is quantitative in nature and is measured on a level that at least approximates interval characteristics, (2) the independent variables are both between-subjects in nature, (3) the independent variables both have two or more levels, and (4) the independent variables are combined to form a factorial design.

Two-way analysis of variance allows us to study the individual and the joint effects of the two independent variables on the dependent variable. This is accomplished by analyzing the two-way factorial design in terms of the main effect for each factor and the interaction effect. The former refers to the comparison of the means for each independent variable collapsing across the levels of the other independent variable. The latter refers to the comparison of the cell means in terms of whether the nature of the relationship between one of the independent variables and the dependent variable differs as a function of the other independent variable.

The rationale for two-way analysis of variance is similar to that for one-way analysis of variance except that the sum of squares between can be partitioned into three components: (1) variability due to the first independent variable, (2) variability due to the second independent variable, and (3) variability due to the interaction effect. Dividing each of these sums of squares by its corresponding degrees of freedom yields mean squares for the two main effects and the interaction effect, and dividing each of these by the mean square within yields F ratios for these same effects. A significant main effect indicates that, collapsing across the levels of the other independent variable, the means for an independent variable are not all equal to one another. A significant interaction effect indicates that the nature of the relationship between one of the independent variables and the dependent variable differs as a function of the other independent variable.

The strength of the relationship between the dependent variable and each of the three sources of between-group variability is computed using eta-squared. Unstandardized effect sizes and confidence intervals for the two main effects and the interaction effect can also be calculated, although the procedures for doing so can be complex.

When a statistically significant main effect has only two levels, the nature of the relationship for that effect is determined in the same fashion as for the independent groups t test. This involves comparing the two sample means to make a decision about how the two population means differ. When a statistically significant main effect has three or more levels, the nature of the relationship for that effect is determined by applying a Tukey HSD test in a similar fashion as we did in Chapter 12 for one-way between-subjects analysis of variance.

When an interaction effect is statistically significant, the nature of the interaction can be determined using interaction comparisons. When the overall design is 2×2 in nature, this involves comparing the differences between the cell means for one independent variable at each level of the other independent variable. For more complex designs, the nature of the interaction is determined by undertaking a series of interaction comparisons coupled with a modified Bonferroni procedure to control the Type I error rate across the set of comparisons. This involves breaking the overall factorial design into all possible 2×2 subtables and performing a separate 2×2 analysis of variance for each one. If an interaction comparison is statistically significant, we conclude that an interaction exists between the two independent variables for the levels of the factors that are included in that 2×2 subtable. The nature of the overall interaction is then determined by comparing the differences between the cell means for one independent variable at each level of the other independent variable for each statistically significant interaction comparison.

There are many reasons why the sample sizes in a study might differ even when the researcher intends to keep them the same. When they occur, unequal sample sizes necessitate modifications to the analytical procedures that we discuss in this chapter. A technique known as *least squares analysis of variance* is often applied in this instance.

Exercises

Answers to asterisked (*) exercises appear at the back of the book.

Exercises to Review Concepts

1. How many groups are required in a 3×3 factorial design? In a 2×5 factorial design? In a 4×3 factorial design?

*2. How many independent variables are in a 3×3 factorial design? In a 2×5 factorial design? In a $2 \times 2 \times 4$ factorial design?

3. Give an example of an investigation that would use a 2×3 factorial design.

4. Under what conditions is two-way between-subjects analysis of variance typically used to analyze the relationship between a dependent variable and two independent variables?

*5. What are the two meanings of the term *main effect*?

*6. What is an interaction effect? An interaction?

*7. For each of the following sets of *population* means, indicate whether there is a main effect of factor A, a main effect of factor B, and/or an interaction effect:

a.

	B_1	B_2
A_1	4.00	5.00
A_2	4.00	5.00

b.

	B_1	B_2
A_1	6.00	6.00
A_2	4.00	4.00
A_3	7.00	7.00

c.

	B_1	B_2	B_3
A_1	1.00	2.00	3.00
A_2	5.00	6.00	7.00
A_3	8.00	9.00	10.00

8. For each of the following sets of *population* means, indicate whether there is a main effect of factor A, a main effect of factor B, and/or an interaction effect:

a.

	B_1	B_2
A_1	5.00	10.00
A_2	10.00	5.00

b.

	B_1	B_2	B_3
A_1	4.00	7.00	9.00
A_2	5.00	6.00	7.00
A_3	6.00	8.00	10.00

c.

	B_1	B_2	B_3	B_4
A_1	5.00	6.00	6.00	7.00
A_2	7.00	8.00	4.00	5.00
A_3	9.00	10.00	2.00	3.00

*9. Generate a set of *population* means for a 2×3 factorial design that reflects a main effect of factor A, no main effect of factor B, and an interaction effect.

10. Generate a set of *population* means for a 2×2 factorial design that reflects no main effect of factor A, no main effect of factor B, and an interaction effect.

*11. What do nonparallel lines indicate in a graph of population means? What do nonparallel lines indicate in a graph of sample means? What accounts for the difference in the two situations?

12. What are the three components of the sum of squares between in two-way between-subjects analysis of variance?

13. Distinguish among the sum of squares total, the sum of squares for factor A, the sum of squares for factor B, the sum of squares for the interaction effect, and the sum of squares within. How are they inter-related?

*14. Insert the missing entries in the summary table for a 3×4 factorial design:

Source	SS	df	MS	F
A	—	—	—	—
B	45.00	—	—	—
A × B	60.00	—	—	—
Within	216.00	—	—	
Total	341.00	119		

15. Insert the missing entries in the summary table for a 3×3 factorial design:

Source	SS	df	MS	F
A	—	—	—	3.50
B	12.00	—	—	—
A × B	40.00	—	—	—
Within	—	27	2.00	
Total	120.00	—		

*16. State the critical values of F for the main effect of factor A, the main effect of factor B, and the interaction effect for a two-way between-subjects analysis of variance for an alpha level of .05 under each of the following conditions:
   a. $a = 2, b = 3, n = 11$
   b. $a = 2, b = 4, n = 7$

   c. $a = 3, b = 3, n = 11$
   d. $a = 4, b = 3, n = 6$

17. What are the assumptions underlying two-way between-subjects analysis of variance?

Refer to the following summary table for a two-way factorial design to do Exercises 18–23.

Source	SS	df	MS	F
A	50.00	1	50.00	10.00
B	40.00	2	20.00	4.00
A × B	40.00	2	20.00	4.00
Within	240.00	48	5.00	
Total	370.00	53		

*18. How many levels of factor A are included in the design? How many levels of factor B? How many groups?

*19. What is the total sample size? Given that there are equal numbers of participants in each group, what is the per-group sample size?

*20. What is the total amount of between-group variability (that is, what is the value of the sum of squares between)?

*21. State the null and alternative hypotheses for the main effect of factor A, the main effect of factor B, and the interaction effect. (The hypotheses for the interaction effect may be stated from either perspective.)

*22. Test the viability of the null hypotheses with respect to the main effect of factor A, the main effect of factor B, and the interaction effect.

*23. Compute the values of eta-squared for the main effect of factor A, the main effect of factor B, and the interaction effect. Indicate whether each value represents a weak, moderate, or strong effect.

*24. How many 2×2 subtables would be included in the set of interaction comparisons for a 2×4 factorial design? For a 2×5 factorial design? For a 3×3 factorial design?

Refer to the following means and summary table for a 2 × 3 factorial design with 11 participants per cell to do Exercises 25–27.

	B_1	B_2	B_3
A_1	10.00	15.00	20.00
A_2	14.00	20.00	24.00

Source	SS	df	MS	F
A	240.00	1	240.00	24.00
B	910.00	2	455.00	45.50
$A \times B$	10.00	2	5.00	.50
Within	600.00	60	10.00	
Total	1,760.00	65		

*25. Test the viability of the null hypothesis with respect to the main effect of factor A. If the null hypothesis is rejected, discern the nature of the relationship between factor A and the dependent variable.

*26. Test the viability of the null hypothesis with respect to the main effect of factor B. If the null hypothesis is rejected, analyze the nature of the relationship between factor B and the dependent variable using the Tukey HSD test.

*27. Test the viability of the null hypothesis with respect to the interaction effect. If the null hypothesis is rejected, analyze the nature of the interaction between factor A and factor B using interaction comparisons coupled with a modified Bonferroni procedure.

Refer to the following means and summary table for a 2 × 3 factorial design with five participants per cell to do Exercises 28–30.

	B_1	B_2	B_3
A_1	10.00	12.00	14.00
A_2	12.00	8.00	4.00

Source	SS	df	MS	F
A	120.00	1	120.00	10.00
B	20.00	2	10.00	.83
$A \times B$	380.00	2	190.00	15.83
Within	288.00	24	12.00	
Total	808.00	29		

28. Test the viability of the null hypothesis with respect to the main effect of factor A. If the null hypothesis is rejected, discern the nature of the relationship between factor A and the dependent variable.

29. Test the viability of the null hypothesis with respect to the main effect of factor B. If the null hypothesis is rejected, analyze the nature of the relationship between factor B and the dependent variable using the Tukey HSD test.

30. Test the viability of the null hypothesis with respect to the interaction effect. If the null hypothesis is rejected, analyze the nature of the interaction between factor A and factor B using interaction comparisons coupled with a modified Bonferroni procedure.

Use the following numbers of job offers received by male and female college seniors in four academic majors to do Exercises 31–35.

Gender	Academic major			
	Computer science	Business	Liberal arts	Behavioral sciences
Male	3	4	2	2
	4	4	2	3
	6	5	1	3
	3	2	3	1
	3	4	2	2
Female	2	1	3	2
	3	2	2	3
	3	2	1	5
	2	3	2	3
	1	1	3	4

31. Test the viability of the null hypotheses with respect to the main effect of gender, the main effect of academic major, and the interaction effect using a two-way analysis of variance.

32. Compute the values of eta-squared for the main effect of gender, the main effect of academic major, and the interaction effect. Indicate whether each value represents a weak, moderate, or strong effect.

33. Discern the nature of the relationship between gender and number of job offers.

34. Analyze the nature of the relationship between academic major and number of job offers using the Tukey HSD test.

35. Analyze the nature of the interaction between gender and academic major using interaction comparisons coupled with a modified Bonferroni procedure.

*36. Why are unequal cell sizes problematic for two-way between-subjects analysis of variance?

*37. If a researcher suspects that the strength of the relationship in the population is .15 for the main effect of factor A, .03 for the main effect of factor B, and .10 for the interaction effect as indexed by eta-squared, what sample size should he use per cell in a study involving three levels of factor A, four levels of factor B, and an alpha level of .05 in order to achieve a power of at least .90 for each effect?

38. If a researcher suspects that the strength of the relationship in the population is .20 for the main effect of factor A, .07 for the main effect of factor B, and .07 for the interaction effect as indexed by eta-squared, what sample size should she use per cell in a study involving two levels of factor A, five levels of factor B, and an alpha level of .05 in order to achieve a power of at least .85 for each effect?

Multiple-Choice Questions

39. As soon as the first statistically nonsignificant comparison is encountered as one proceeds from the largest to the smallest

F ratio for a set of interaction comparisons, all remaining comparisons are declared statistically nonsignificant.
   a. true
   b. false

*40. Suppose that we have a 2×2 factorial design in which the two levels of the first factor, gender, are male (M) and female (F) and the two levels of the second factor, assertiveness, are low (L) and high (H). One way to state the null and alternative hypotheses for the interaction effect is
   a. H_0: $\mu_{ML} - \mu_{FH} = \mu_{MH} - \mu_{FL}$
      H_1: $\mu_{ML} - \mu_{FH} \neq \mu_{MH} - \mu_{FL}$
   b. H_0: $\mu_{ML} - \mu_{FL} = \mu_{FH} - \mu_{MH}$
      H_1: $\mu_{ML} - \mu_{FL} \neq \mu_{FH} - \mu_{MH}$
   c. H_0: $\mu_{ML} - \mu_{MH} = \mu_{FL} - \mu_{FH}$
      H_1: $\mu_{ML} - \mu_{MH} \neq \mu_{FL} - \mu_{FH}$
   d. none of the above

41. Nonparallel lines in a graph of sample means always indicate the existence of an interaction.
   a. true
   b. false

*42. The nature of a statistically significant interaction effect for a 2×2 factorial design is determined using interaction comparisons coupled with a modified Bonferroni procedure.
   a. true
   b. false

43. In a 3×2 factorial design, we can test for ____ main effect(s) and ____ interaction(s).
   a. 1; 2
   b. 2; 1
   c. 3; 2
   d. 6; 1

*44. General information that relates to a table as a whole is placed above the table and designated by the italicized word "Note" followed by a period according to American Psychological Association format.
   a. true
   b. false

*45. Least squares analysis of variance deals with the relationship introduced between the independent variables by unequal cell sizes by focusing on
   a. explained variability that is common to both factors
   b. explained variability that is unique to a given factor
   c. both common and unique explained variability
   d. variability that is unexplained by a given factor

46. A modified Bonferroni procedure is used with interaction comparisons to
   a. simplify the required calculations
   b. control the Type I error rate
   c. control the Type II error rate
   d. determine the nature of statistically significant main effects

47. $SS_{A \times B} = SS_A \times SS_B$
   a. true
   b. false

*48. The values of the critical alpha for the modified Bonferroni procedure
   a. get smaller as the F ratios for the set of interaction comparisons get smaller
   b. get larger as the F ratios for the set of interaction comparisons get smaller
   c. are equal to the overall alpha level
   d. are equal to the overall alpha level divided by the total number of interaction comparisons in the set

49. A possible strategy for dealing with disturbance variables is to bring a variable into the research design by including it as a factor.
   a. true
   b. false

Exercises to Apply Concepts

*50. Psychologists have extensively studied the factors that contribute to weight gain. It is currently believed that individuals use at least two sources of "cues" to decide that they are hungry and should eat. One source is internal cues in the form of changes in one's physiology that create or suggest hunger. A second source is external cues that occur in the environment and suggest to the individual that he or she should be hungry. For example, the approach of 12:00 noon might serve as such a cue by signifying that it is lunch time.

Several researchers have suggested that an important difference between overweight and normal-weight individuals is that normal-weight individuals attend mostly to internal rather than external cues as guidelines for eating, whereas the reverse is true for overweight individuals. Suppose that in an investigation designed to study this issue, 15 overweight and 15 normal-weight individuals are instructed not to eat breakfast on the morning before participating in an experiment. When they arrive at the laboratory, the participants are asked to remove their watches under the pretense that part of the study involves estimating time.

After performing several tasks, one-third of the participants are informed that it is 11:00, another third are informed that it is 12:00 (the actual time), and the final third are informed that it is 1:00. They are then asked to rate how hungry they feel on a 0 to 10 scale, with higher scores indicating greater hunger. The design is thus a 3 × 2 factorial with three levels of supposed time and two levels of weight.

If overweight individuals attend mostly to external cues, we would expect them to report greater hunger the later the supposed time because this implies that they have gone longer without food. If normal-weight individuals attend mostly to internal cues, the time manipulation should not affect their ratings of hunger.

Hypothetical data for this experiment are presented in the table. Analyze these data as completely as possible, draw a conclusion for each effect, and report your results using the principles developed in the Method of Presentation section.

	Overweight	Normal weight
11:00	5	6
	6	6
	7	7
	6	5
	6	6
12:00	9	6
	7	6
	8	5
	9	7
	10	6
1:00	10	7
	10	6
	9	7
	8	8
	9	5

51. Psychologists have extensively studied the factors that influence *social categorization* (that is, the classification of people into such social categories as the "conservative businessperson" and the "typical home-maker") and the effects of such categoriza-tion on behavior. In one study of this issue (Rubovits and Maehr, 1973), white female undergraduates enrolled in a teacher-training course were asked to prepare a lesson for four seventh-grade students. The teachers were then given information about each of the students. For half of the teachers, a par-ticular student was described as being "gifted" (that is, extremely intelligent), whereas for the other half of the teachers, the same student was described as being "nongifted" (that is, of average intelligence). This student was either African American or white, yielding a 2 × 2 factorial design with two levels of race and two levels of attributed intelligence.

Each teacher was observed interact-ing with the target student and the three other students during a 40-minute period.

The number of interactions directed to-ward the target student was recorded, and this served as an index of how much atten-tion the teacher gave the student.

Hypothetical data representative of the results of this experiment are presented in the table. Analyze these data as com-pletely as possible, draw a conclusion for each effect, and report your results using the principles developed in the Method of Presentation section.

	Gifted	Nongifted
African American	30	30
	29	29
	30	28
	30	30
	31	28
White	36	29
	36	32
	36	31
	35	30
	37	33

52. In order to study the effect of video game aggression on affect, Anderson and Ford (1986) conducted an experiment in which male and female college students either did not play a video game or played a mildly or a highly aggressive video game for 20 min-utes. The design was thus a 3 × 2 factorial with three levels of game type and two lev-els of gender.

After playing the assigned game, stu-dents completed the Multiple Affect Adjec-tive Checklist (MAAC). This instrument measures hostility, anxiety, and depression as experienced by respondents at the time of assessment. Students in the no-game condition completed the MAAC with the understanding that they would be playing a video game later. We consider only the hostility ratings.

Hypothetical data representative of the results of this experiment are presented in the table. Analyze these data as completely as possible, draw a conclusion for each effect, and report your results using the principles developed in the Method of Presentation section.

	Male	Female
No game	6	6
	7	7
	7	6
	6	8
	5	6
	5	6
Mildly aggressive game	9	9
	9	9
	8	9
	10	8
	9	10
	10	9
Highly aggressive game	10	10
	10	10
	11	9
	11	11
	9	10
	10	10

53. There are many means by which information can be communicated from one individual to another. Three of the most common are email, texting, and the telephone. In order to determine whether the way in which information is communicated influences its effectiveness, suppose that a communications researcher conducts an experiment in which participants are presented the identical information via an email message, a text message, or a telephone call.

The content of the message is also varied such that one set of messages contains only the relevant information, another set contains both the relevant information and a small number of extraneous details, and the third set contains both the relevant information and a large number of extraneous details. The design is thus a 3×3 factorial with three levels of message format and three levels of message content.

After reading or listening to their assigned message, participants respond to a series of questions about the message content. Hypothetical data for this study in the form of the number of correctly answered questions are presented in the table. Analyze these data as completely as possible, draw a conclusion for each effect, and report your results using the principles developed in the Method of Presentation section.

	Email	Texting	Telephone
No extraneous details	6	5	7
	7	6	6
	7	4	6
	5	4	5
Few extraneous details	5	4	4
	5	3	4
	6	5	6
	4	6	5
	5	5	5
Many extraneous details	4	4	5
	4	5	3
	4	3	4

CHAPTER **18**

Overview and Extension: Selecting the Appropriate Statistical Test for Analyzing Bivariate Relationships and Procedures for More Complex Designs

The focus of this book has been on statistical techniques for analyzing bivariate relationships. We maintain this focus in the first half of this chapter by considering the basic issues involved in selecting the appropriate test for analyzing data in the two-variable case. In the second half, we briefly discuss several commonly used inferential tests for simultaneously analyzing *three or more* variables.

18.1   Selecting the Appropriate Statistical Test for Analyzing Bivariate Relationships

We have considered a total of 12 statistical procedures for studying bivariate relationships.* Except for regression, three questions have guided our analysis in each instance: (1) Given sample data, can we infer that a relationship exists between two variables in the population? (2) If so, what is the strength of the relationship? (3) If so, what is the nature of the relationship? The specific statistics that are used to address each question are summarized in Table 18.1 for each of the relevant inferential tests.

Although a number of techniques are available for analyzing bivariate relationships, the task of selecting a test can be simplified if one adheres to the guidelines that are presented next. It must be emphasized that these are only guidelines, however, and, as such, there are potential exceptions to each one. Nevertheless, they should be of heuristic value in the vast majority of cases. In each instance, the recommendation of a test assumes that the requirements for the application of that test have been met.

The first step in determining the appropriate bivariate test is to note whether each of the two variables is qualitative or quantitative in nature. The four situations that can arise are discussed below. As we review each of these, we consider the relevant test selection issues for that situation.

18.2   Case I: The Relationship Between Two Qualitative Variables

When both of the variables under study are qualitative and between-subjects in nature, the appropriate method of analysis is the chi-square test. This situation would occur, for example, when studying the relationship between gender and political party identification, as we discussed in Chapter 15. If both variables are qualitative but one or both are within-subjects in nature, none of the statistical tests that we have considered can be used. The appropriate statistical procedures in this instance are discussed in McNemar (1962) and Marascuilo and McSweeney (1977).

---

* In reaching this total, we counted the Wilcoxon rank sum test and the Mann-Whitney *U* test as one technique.

TABLE 18.1   **Statistics Used to Address the Three Questions**
                        for the Analysis of Bivariate Relationships for Inferential Tests

Independent Groups t Test

Inference of a relationship:	t statistic
Strength of the relationship:	Eta-squared
Nature of the relationship:	Comparison of group means

Correlated Groups t Test

Inference of a relationship:	t statistic
Strength of the relationship:	Eta-squared
Nature of the relationship:	Comparison of group means

One-Way Between-Subjects Analysis of Variance

Inference of a relationship:	F ratio
Strength of the relationship:	Eta-squared
Nature of the relationship:	Tukey HSD test

One-Way Repeated Measures Analysis of Variance

Inference of a relationship:	F ratio
Strength of the relationship:	Eta-squared
Nature of the relationship:	Tukey HSD test or modified Bonferroni procedure

Pearson Correlation

Inference of a relationship:	r statistic
Strength of the relationship:	r^2
Nature of the relationship:	Sign of r

Chi-Square Test

Inference of a relationship:	χ_r^2 statistic
Strength of the relationship:	Fourfold point correlation coefficient/Cramer's statistic
Nature of the relationship:	Observed - expected frequencies

Wilcoxon Rank Sum Test/ Mann–Whitney U Test

Inference of a relationship:	z statistic/ U statistic
Strength of the relationship:	Glass rank biserial correlation coefficient
Nature of the relationship:	Comparison of mean ranks

Wilcoxon Signed-Rank Test

Inference of a relationship:	T statistic/ z statistic
Strength of the relationship:	Matched-pairs rank biserial correlation coefficient
Nature of the relationship:	Comparison of rank sums

Kruskal–Wallis Test

Inference of a relationship:	H statistic
Strength of the relationship:	Epsilon-squared
Nature of the relationship:	Dunn procedure

Friedman Analysis of Variance by Ranks

Inference of a relationship:	χ^2 statistic
Strength of the relationship:	Concordance coefficient
Nature of the relationship:	Dunn procedure

Spearman Rank-Order Correlation

Inference of a relationship:	r_s statistic
Strength of the relationship:	Magnitude of r_s
Nature of the relationship:	Sign of r_s

18.3 Case II: The Relationship Between a Qualitative Independent Variable and a Quantitative Dependent Variable

Table 18.2 presents a decision tree that can be used to select a statistical test when the independent variable is qualitative and the dependent variable is quantitative. The three decision points represented in Table 18.2 are (1) whether a parametric or a nonparametric test is appropriate, (2) whether the independent variable is between-subjects or within-subjects in nature, and (3) the number of levels that characterize the independent variable.

Use of a Parametric or a Nonparametric Test

An important factor to consider when deciding whether to use a parametric or a nonparametric test in the Case II situation is what aspect of the dependent variable scores one wishes to focus on. This is often dictated by theory or the substantive question of interest. If entire distributions are the focus, then a nonparametric method is appropriate. If the concern is with mean differences, then a parametric test is indicated. However, several additional issues must also be considered before a final decision is made. Specifically, further consideration must be given to (1) the number of values of the dependent variable, (2) the level of measurement of the dependent variable, and (3) the extent to which any distributional assumptions may have been violated.

Let us explore in more depth the issue of the number of values of the dependent variable and how this can influence the choice of an analytic strategy. Consider a study where the independent variable is the geographic location where people live (Northeast, South, Midwest, or West) and the dependent variable is their attitudes toward nuclear energy. The relevant attitude scale could conceivably have anywhere from two to a large number of response options. When the dependent measure has only two or three values, parametric procedures are typically not applicable because an assumption of these tests is that the population scores are normally distributed, and a dependent variable cannot be normally distributed if it has only two or three values. Consequently, this assumption of parametric tests will be violated. Under this circumstance, nonparametric tests are typically used.*

When the dependent measure has only two or three values, the rank tests that we discussed in Chapter 16 might also be of questionable value. This is because with only two or three values of the dependent variable, there will be a large number of ties in ranks and, as we noted in Section 16.1, this can create problems for rank-order approaches. The alternative in this case is to use a correction term for tied ranks or, if the independent variable is between-subjects in nature, to use the chi-square test. When applicable, most researchers choose the chi-square approach or a technique known as *log-linear analysis*, which we describe in Section 18.6.

As an example of a situation where we might apply the chi-square test to a study that has a qualitative independent variable and a quantitative dependent variable with only two values, consider an investigation where the independent variable is

---

* See Hsu and Feldt (1969), Joreskog and Sorbom (1993), and Lunney (1970) for a discussion of some parametric procedures that can be applied in this situation.

TABLE 18.2   Decision Tree for Case II Situations

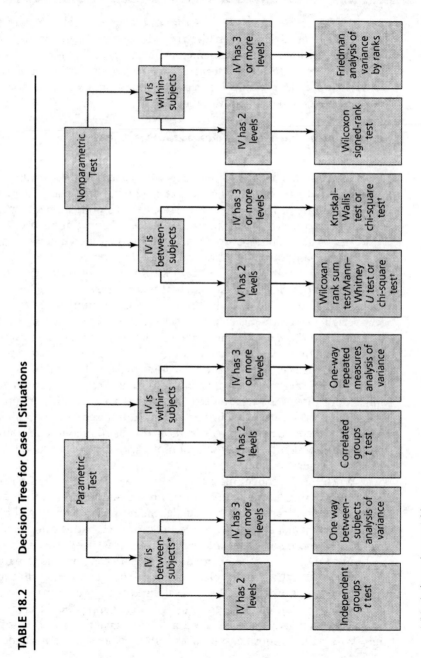

* IV = independent variable.
† The chi-square test is typically used only when the dependent variable has only two or three values.

occupation (blue-collar, white-collar, or clerical) and the dependent variable is the number of hands (one or two) with which one is dexterous. A 3×2 contingency table in which occupation is the row variable and manual dexterity is the column variable can be formed for this problem, and the chi-square procedures developed in Chapter 15 and summarized in Table 18.1 applied to the observed frequencies.

Given a quantitative dependent variable with a sufficient number of values, additional characteristics of the data must be considered when determining whether a parametric test is appropriate. For example, if the dependent variable is measured on an ordinal level that markedly departs from interval level characteristics, then a nonparametric test might be pursued instead of a parametric test. A nonparametric test should also be pursued if there is a reason to believe that the distributional assumptions of the corresponding parametric test have been violated to the extent that the parametric test will not be robust.

Using Table 18.2 to Select the Appropriate Statistical Test

To illustrate the use of Table 18.2, let us consider an investigation where the researcher asks 30 single, 30 married, 30 widowed, and 30 divorced individuals to indicate their life satisfaction on a 7-point scale. We begin by establishing that this is a Case II situation. The independent variable in this instance is marital status, which is qualitative in nature, and the dependent variable is life satisfaction, which is quantitative in nature, so this is indeed the case.

The first step in using Table 18.2 is to decide whether a parametric or a nonparametric test should be applied. The life satisfaction scale has seven values, which is consistent with the use of a parametric test. Next, let us consider the level of measurement for this scale. Measures of this type usually at least approximate interval characteristics, and there is no reason to believe that this is not the case in this instance. Thus, a parametric test is again indicated. Given the equivalence and the magnitude of the sample sizes, a parametric test would also certainly be robust to any violations of distributional assumptions that might occur. Therefore, a parametric test can be meaningfully applied.

The next decision in Table 18.2 is to classify the independent variable as being between-subjects or within-subjects in nature. Because each group includes 30 different individuals, the independent variable in this instance is between-subjects.

Finally, the number of levels of the independent variable has to be considered. In this instance, there are four. This dictates a one-way between-subjects analysis of variance as the analytic technique. Referring to Table 18.1, we would use an F ratio to infer the existence of a relationship between the independent and dependent variables, eta-squared to measure the strength of the relationship, and a Tukey HSD test to determine the nature of the relationship.

18.4   Case III: The Relationship Between a Quantitative Independent Variable and a Qualitative Dependent Variable

Generally speaking, the statistical techniques that we have considered in this book are not conducive to analyzing quantitative independent variables and qualitative dependent variables. However, although it is typically used when both variables are qualitative, the chi-square test can also be applied in Case III situations. When this is done, the values of the quantitative independent variable will either constitute separate levels of the contingency table or be collapsed into a small number of intervals, as we discussed in Section 15.10, depending on how many there are. Other statistical techniques for the Case III situation are *logistic regression* and *multinomial logistic regression*. These procedures are discussed in Koch and Edwards (1988).

18.5   Case IV: The Relationship Between Two Quantitative Variables

Given two between-subjects variables that are measured on a level that at least approximates interval characteristics, the most common method of analysis is Pearson correlation. As we discussed in Chapters 5 and 14, Pearson correlation evaluates a *linear* relationship between variables. If the expected relationship is nonlinear, the procedures for nonlinear relationships discussed in Pedhazur (1997) can be applied. When one or both variables are measured on an ordinal level that markedly departs from interval level characteristics, Spearman rank-order correlation or another rank-order correlation measure known as *Kendall's tau* (see Glass and Stanley, 1970, for a discussion of this technique) is usually the test of choice.

When the independent variable is within-subjects in nature or has fewer than five or so values associated with it, the Case II statistics elaborated in Table 18.2 might also be applicable. As an example, a researcher might investigate the relationship between age and intelligence by administering an intelligence test to 100 5-year-old children, 100 7-year-old children, and 100 9-year-old children. Both of these variables are quantitative in nature, but age has only three values (5, 7, and 9). In fact, the study was explicitly structured to include these three values of the age variable. Under these circumstances, most investigators would use Table 18.2 to choose the appropriate statistical test. Because the independent variable, age, is between-subjects and has three levels, the method of analysis would be one-way between-subjects analysis of variance if a parametric test is appropriate, or the Kruskal-Wallis test if a nonparametric test is indicated.

If the dependent variable has only two or three values, the chi-square test or log-linear analysis can be used. This is true regardless of how many values of the independent variable there are, as the independent variable scores can be collapsed into categories if there are many different values.

18.6   Procedures for More Complex Designs

The focus of the statistical techniques that we have considered to this point has been the analysis of bivariate relationships. However, many research problems require that more than two variables be studied simultaneously, and statistical procedures have been developed to analyze the relationship among three or more variables. Because these procedures consider multiple variables, they are referred to as **multivariate statistics**.

We are already familiar with one multivariate test—that of two-way between-subjects analysis of variance. As we saw in Chapter 17, this technique is a direct extension of one-way between-subjects analysis of variance for when there is one dependent variable and two independent variables. In the sections that follow, we briefly discuss several additional multivariate tests that are commonly used in the behavioral sciences.

Extensions of Analysis of Variance

The basic analysis of variance procedures that we discussed in Chapters 12 and 13 can be extended not only to the two-way between-subjects situation but also to other cases. For instance, just as it is possible to study the joint influence of two between-subjects independent variables on a dependent variable, it is also possible to study the joint influence of two within-subjects independent variables. For example, we can expand the wine label and perceived quality experiment that we discussed in Chapter 13 to include information about when the wine was supposedly produced as well as information about the supposed country of origin. In the simplest case, the wine might be presented as being either an old or a new vintage. Crossing the time of production information with the country of origin information (French, Italian, or American) yields six cells (for instance, old-vintage French wine, new-vintage American wine). Now, instead of having each participant taste a total of three "different" wines, each participant will taste a total of six "different" wines. Because both independent variables are within-subjects in nature, the perceived quality data can be analyzed using a **two-way repeated measures analysis of variance**.

Sometimes research designs involve one between-subjects independent variable and one within-subjects independent variable. For example, another way to conduct the study just outlined would be to use two groups of participants, one of which tastes the supposed French, Italian, and American wines under circumstances where the labels indicate that they are all old vintage, and one of which tastes the wines under circumstances where the labels indicate that they are all new vintage. In this instance, the country of origin variable is within-subjects and the vintage variable is between-subjects, so the appropriate means of analysis is a **two-way between-within analysis of variance**.

All of the procedures that we have referred to for analysis of variance with two independent variables can be extended to analyze the relationship between a dependent variable and three or more independent variables. For instance, the relationship between a dependent variable and three between-subjects independent variables can be examined using a *three-way between-subjects analysis of variance*.

Given the flexibility of analysis of variance, it is not surprising that this is one of the most commonly used multivariate approaches. In fact, analysis of variance is one of the most commonly used statistical approaches in general in the behavioral sciences.

Multivariate Analysis of Variance

A situation that frequently arises in behavioral science research is the analysis of two or more *dependent* variables. For instance, a researcher who is interested in the achievement concerns of high school, junior college, and college graduates might assess each group's concern with social achievement, occupational achievement, and financial achievement. In this design, there is one independent variable (education) and three dependent variables (concern with social achievement, concern with occupational achievement, and concern with financial achievement).

Multivariate analysis of variance (abbreviated as *MANOVA*) tests whether the groups of interest have different population means *on the dependent variables considered jointly*. This is accomplished by calculating a *multivariate F ratio* that is then compared with a critical *F* value. In the present example, the multivariate analysis of variance would enable us to infer whether the three education groups differ in their mean achievement concerns for the three dependent measures considered simultaneously. If the multivariate *F* test is not statistically significant, the null hypothesis of equivalent population means on the dependent variables considered jointly cannot be rejected, so no additional analyses are warranted. However, if the multivariate *F* test is statistically significant, separate follow-up analyses can be applied to the individual dependent variables using procedures that maintain the overall Type I error rate at a specified level.

Multivariate analysis of variance can be used with any number of dependent variables and any number and combination of between-subjects and within-subjects independent variables. When applied to a single between-subjects independent variable that has only two levels, it is called the **Hotelling T^2 test**. When applied to a factorial design, it is called **factorial multivariate analysis of variance**.

Multivariate analysis of variance can also be adapted to analyze within-subject designs. This includes one-way repeated measures designs as well as factorial designs that incorporate repeated measures. An advantage of using this version of repeated measures analysis is that it can produce valid results even when the sphericity assumption is violated. For further discussion of this issue, see Jaccard (1998).

Multiple Regression

In Chapter 14, we saw how a regression equation can be used to predict individuals' scores on one variable (the criterion variable, symbolized as Y) from knowledge of their scores on a second variable (the predictor variable, symbolized as X). **Multiple regression** extends this procedure to the prediction of a criterion variable from two or more predictor variables.

For instance, a common use of multiple regression is to predict educational performance from previous academic achievement. Most college admissions offices have established regression equations for predicting grade point averages at their institution from students' high school grade point average, SAT scores, class rank, teacher ratings, and the like. The rationale for this is that if several of these measures are considered simultaneously, more accurate predictions can be made than if only one predictor variable is used. When this approach is adopted, predicted achievement scores are among the criteria considered when making admission decisions.

Multiple regression is a direct extension of regression with one predictor variable. Per Equation 5.9, the regression equation for the bivariate case is

$$\hat{Y} = a + bX$$

In the case of multiple regression, the right-hand side of this equation is expanded to include more than one predictor variable. For example, if we have two predictors, X_1 and X_2, the **multiple regression equation** would appear as follows:

$$\hat{Y} = a + b_1X_1 + b_2X_2$$

In this equation, a represents the overall intercept and each predictor has a "slope" (b) that is formally referred to as a **regression coefficient** associated with it. These coefficients represent the number of units the criterion variable is predicted to change for each unit change in a given predictor variable *when the other predictor variables are held constant*. For instance, a regression coefficient of .21 for high school grade point average would indicate that, when all of the other predictor variables in the equation are held constant, college grade point average is predicted to increase by .21 unit for each unit increase in high school grade point average.

An index of the strength of the relationship between the criterion variable and the set of predictor variables is provided by the **squared multiple correlation coefficient** (symbolized as R^2). R^2 is analogous to r^2 with one predictor variable and indicates the proportion of variability in the criterion variable that is associated with the predictor variables considered simultaneously.

Factor Analysis

The goal of **factor analysis** is to determine whether the correlations among a set of variables can be accounted for by one or more underlying dimensions, or **factors**, by examining the patterning of correlations among variables and providing information on the type of *factor structure*—that is, the number and makeup of factors—that might underlie the data.

As an example of the use of factor analysis, suppose that an investigator assesses nine different beliefs about abortion. The investigator might hypothesize that individuals' responses to the nine belief statements reflect three underlying dimensions: (1) a concern with the physical effects of abortion, (2) a concern with the emotional effects of abortion, and (3) a concern with moral issues. Factor analysis tests hypotheses of this nature, albeit somewhat indirectly, by analyzing the patterning of correlations between all pairs of variables in the data set.* If the investigator's hypothesis in the abortion-belief study is correct, the correlations among the nine beliefs can be accounted for by the three hypothesized factors, so they should manifest a predictable pattern as reflected in the factor analysis.

Log-Linear Analysis

Sometimes a research question requires that three or more qualitative variables be examined simultaneously. For instance, we might wish to expand the model status and altruism study from Section 15.9 by examining how the likelihood of making a charitable donation is influenced by one's gender in addition to the type of model that one is exposed to. Because the three variables (gender, model status, and outcome) are all qualitative and between-subjects in nature, we could form a three-way

---

* Alternatively, the patterning of *covariances* (that is, SCP/N) can be analyzed.

contingency table of the observed frequencies. Although the chi-square test can be extended to multidimensional tables of this type, a statistical technique known as **log-linear analysis** is usually used instead. Though conceptually similar to chi-square analysis, log-linear analysis possesses statistical properties that make it more suitable for the simultaneous analysis of multiple between-subjects qualitative variables.

18.7   Alternatives to Null Hypothesis Testing

The statistical tests that we describe in this book are firmly entrenched in the behavioral sciences, and you will encounter them frequently in research reports. Nevertheless, as we noted in Section 10.4, criticism has been directed at the *null hypothesis testing* approach that has served as the unifying framework for our approach to statistical analysis.

In an insightful article, Cohen (1994) articulates many of these criticisms, and we highly recommend Cohen's article and the rejoinders to it in the December 1995 issue of *American Psychologist*. He argues that what behavioral scientists typically want to know is "Given these data, what is the probability that the null hypothesis is true?" whereas hypothesis testing tells us "Given that the null hypothesis is true, what is the probability of these (or more extreme) data?" The two issues are quite different, and Cohen develops the implications of approaching science from the two perspectives.

He essentially argues that the first of the three questions relevant to the analysis of bivariate relationships (Is there a relationship between the variables?) is meaningless because (1) the null hypothesis of the means of interest being *exactly* the same or a correlation coefficient being *exactly* 0 is almost always false and (2) formal hypothesis testing procedures address the probability of observing an empirical outcome given that the null hypothesis is true rather than the more relevant question of whether the null hypothesis is true given the data. Instead, Cohen argues, the primary focus should be the second and third questions (What is the strength of the relationship? What is the nature of the relationship?), and he emphasizes the importance of *effect size estimation* (for instance, the use of eta-squared) and *interval estimation* (for instance, the use of confidence intervals) strategies. Where relevant, we have endeavored to incorporate these strategies in this book.

Another approach to bivariate relationships is *Bayesian statistics*. This is a branch of statistics that emphasizes probability and *odds ratios*. The cornerstone of Bayesian statistics is *Bayes' theorem*, which we introduced in Section 6.5. This approach offers many advantages over traditional hypothesis testing frameworks, but it also has some drawbacks. Interested readers are referred to Howson and Urbach (1989).

18.8   Links Between Computer Results and Book Content

All of the multivariate procedures that we discuss in this chapter can be performed using statistical computer programs that have been developed for this purpose. Although the output that is provided by these programs can be very complex, an understanding of this information is facilitated by familiarity with the statistics that we have discussed in this book and with the corresponding issues that we have discussed in previous "Links Between Computer Results and Book Content" sections.

18.9 Links Between Chapters

We have made many references to previous chapters in the foregoing discussion. As necessary, refer back to these or other relevant chapters to review the information of interest.

Summary

Although a number of techniques are available for analyzing bivariate relationships, the task of selecting a test can be simplified if one adheres to the guidelines that are available for this purpose. In each instance, the recommendation of a test assumes that the requirements for the application of that test have been met.

The first step in determining the appropriate bivariate test is to note whether each of the two variables is qualitative or quantitative in nature. Four situations are possible. In the Case I situation, both variables are qualitative; in the Case II situation, the independent variable is qualitative and the dependent variable is quantitative; in the Case III situation, the independent variable is quantitative and the dependent variable is qualitative; and in the Case IV situation, both variables are quantitative.

Given two between-subjects variables, the appropriate method of analysis for Case I situations is the chi-square test. The selection of a statistical test in Case II situations is facilitated by the use of the decision tree in Table 18.2. The three decision points represented in this table are (1) whether a parametric or a nonparametric test is appropriate, (2) whether the independent variable is between-subjects or within-subjects in nature, and (3) the number of levels that characterize the independent variable. Case III situations are analyzed using the chi-square test, logistic regression, or multinomial logistic regression. If both variables are between-subjects in nature, Case IV situations are most commonly analyzed using a correlational procedure. When the independent variable is within-subjects in nature or has fewer than five or so values associated with it, Case II statistics might also be applicable. If the dependent variable has only two or three values, the chi-square test or log-linear analysis can be used.

Statistical techniques that are used to analyze the relationship among three or more variables are referred to as *multivariate statistics*. Among the most commonly used multivariate tests are extensions of basic analysis of variance procedures to between-subjects, repeated measures, between-within, and multiple dependent variable situations.

Other multivariate tests include multiple regression, factor analysis, and log-linear analysis. Multiple regression extends regression with one predictor variable to the prediction of a criterion variable from two or more predictor variables. The goal of factor analysis is to determine whether the correlations among a set of variables can be accounted for by one or more underlying dimensions (factors) by examining the patterning of correlations among variables and providing information on the type of factor structure that might underlie the data. Log-linear analysis is used to simultaneously analyze multiple between-subjects qualitative variables.

Although the statistical tests that we describe in this book are firmly entrenched in the behavioral sciences, criticism has been directed at the null hypothesis testing approach that has served as the unifying framework for our approach to statistical analysis. Cohen (1994) argues that the primary focus for the analysis of bivariate relationships should be the strength and nature of the relationship rather than whether there is a relationship, and he emphasizes the importance of *effect size estimation* (for instance, the use of eta-squared) and *interval estimation* (for instance, the use of confidence intervals) strategies. Another approach to bivariate relationships is Bayesian statistics. This approach offers many advantages over traditional hypothesis testing frameworks, but it also has some drawbacks.

Exercises

Answers to asterisked (*) exercises appear at the back of the book.

*1. What is the appropriate statistical technique to use for analyzing the relationship between two between-subjects qualitative variables?

2. What are the three decision points for selecting a statistical test when the independent variable is qualitative and the dependent variable is quantitative?

3. What factors should be considered in deciding whether to use a parametric or a nonparametric test when the independent variable is qualitative and the dependent variable is quantitative?

*4. What methods are available for analyzing the relationship between two quantitative variables? Identify the conditions under which each of these is used.

Indicate whether each of the studies described in Exercises 5–22 represents a Case I, Case II, Case III, or Case IV situation, and why. For each study, indicate the appropriate statistical test for analyzing the relationship between the variables and state the reasons for your selection. If a parametric technique might be applicable, indicate which test you would use under conditions where (a) the underlying assumptions of the parametric technique have been satisfied and (b) the underlying assumptions of the parametric technique have been violated to the extent that a nonparametric test is required.

*5. A health psychologist who is interested in whether changes in mood are associated with certain times of the year studied whether people tend to be more depressed in the winter or in the spring. One hundred individuals were administered a depression scale in December (winter) and again in May (spring). Scores on this scale can range from 0 to 50.

*6. A consumer psychologist examined the effect of the color of ice cream on taste ratings. Two hundred people tasted each of three "brands" of vanilla ice cream. The ice creams were actually identical to one another except for the shade of yellow used for coloring. The order in which individuals tasted each of the three "brands" was randomized. After tasting a given ice cream, participants rated the quality of its taste on a scale of 1 to 10.

*7. A researcher tested whether the noise level of music affects the growth of houseplants. Forty seeds were randomly assigned to one of two conditions. In one condition, plants were grown with a steady background of music playing at a low volume. In the other condition, plants were grown under identical conditions but with the music playing at a high volume. After 6 months, each plant's growth in inches was measured.

*8. A psychologist examined the relationship between parents' marital status and their children's imagination. For each of 100 first-graders, it was determined whether the parents were married, divorced, separated, widowed, or single and whether or not the child had an imaginary friend.

*9. An investigator tested the relationship between social class and *dogmatism*, that is, the extent to which an individual is closed-minded, inflexible in thought, and intolerant of other viewpoints. Three hundred individuals were administered a dogmatism scale on which scores could range from 1 to 70. The social class of each individual was measured using an occupational index on which scores could range from 1 to 100.

*10. A social psychologist examined the relationship between the number of friends that people have and how much social support they perceive. Forty individuals indicated the number of people that they consider close friends and whether or not they feel that these friends would, in general, "be there" for them in an emergency.

*11. A researcher conducted a study in which 60 participants (20 in each of three conditions) were given a soft drink to consume while waiting for an experiment to supposedly begin. An experimental assistant, posing as another participant, was also given a drink. In one condition, the assistant sipped the drink at a faster rate than the research participant; in another condition, the assistant sipped the drink at the same rate as the participant; and in the last condition, the assistant sipped the drink at a slower rate than the participant. The time it took each participant to consume his or her drink was measured.

*12. A psychologist tested whether hypnosis can influence responses on a biofeedback task. Fifty participants were randomly assigned to one of two conditions. In one condition, participants were hypnotized and then told to try to make one of their hands warmer by just thinking about it. The other group was given the same task but was not placed under hypnosis. The change in hand temperature was measured in centigrade units to the nearest hundredth of a degree using a special temperature gauge.

*13. An investigator studied the relationship between the time between taking an exam and physiological arousal. Thirty individuals scheduled to take an exam on a Thursday were instructed to determine their scores on the Palmer Sweat Index (a measure of physiological arousal on which scores can range from 0 to 100) just before going to bed on Tuesday (2 days before the exam), Wednesday (the day before the exam), Thursday (the day of the exam), and Friday (the day after the exam).

14. A researcher examined the relationship between religious affiliation and the belief in an afterlife. Fifteen Jewish, 15 Catholic, and 15 Protestant individuals were each asked whether or not they believe that there is life after death.

15. In general, we feel weak in the morning when we awaken. A researcher studied whether people are actually weaker when they wake up compared with later in the day. Fifty people were instructed to squeeze a *dynamometer* (a device that measures grip strength) when they woke up in the morning and again 3 hours later. The dynamometer scores could range from 0 to 30.

16. An investigator examined the relationship between gender and marijuana use in college students. Thirty male and 30 female college students were each asked whether or not they had ever used marijuana.

17. An investigator tested for racial discrimination by loan officers at banks. Each of 120 loan officers was given background information on an applicant and asked how much money he or she would be willing to lend the individual. Forty of the loan officers were told that the applicant was African American, 40 were told she was white, and 40 were told she was Hispanic. Aside from this, the descriptions of the applicant were identical.

18. A sociologist studied the relationship between individuals' performance in college and their income 5 years later. Data were obtained on the grade point averages while in college of 250 people and their annual salaries after being out of college for 5 years.

19. A researcher tested the relationship between the number of children in a household and pet ownership. Fifty individuals indicated the number of children aged 18 or younger who were living at home and whether or not they have any pets.

20. A professor examined the relationship between how quickly students finish an exam and how well they perform. As students turned in their tests for a scheduled course examination, the professor kept track of the order in which they were received. The class was then divided into three groups: the first third of the class to turn in the exam, the middle third of the class to turn in the exam, and the last third of the class to turn in the exam. Scores on the exam could range from 0 to 100.

21. A consumer psychologist studied people's impressions of individuals who do and who do not buy generic foods. Ninety participants were presented with a grocery list of a hypothetical shopper. For half of them, the list contained some generic brands, whereas for the other half, the list contained only national brands. All products on the two lists were otherwise identical. After reading the list, each participant indicated how discriminating she thought the shopper was in his food preferences on a scale of 1 to 100.

22. An educational psychologist examined the relationship between psychology departments' national reputations and the number of scientific articles published by their faculties. A national ranking of the top 100 American psychology departments was obtained (where 1 represented the lowest-rated department and 100 represented the highest-rated department), and for each department the number of publications generated by its faculty over the past year was tabulated.

*23. What is the defining characteristic of multivariate statistics?

24. Differentiate among two-way between-subjects analysis of variance, two-way repeated measures analysis of variance, and two-way between-within analysis of variance.

*25. Differentiate between multivariate analysis of variance and the Hotelling T^2 test.

26. What is the rationale behind multiple regression?

*27. What is a regression coefficient? What is a squared multiple correlation coefficient?

*28. What is the goal of factor analysis? How is this accomplished?

29. Under what conditions is log-linear analysis appropriate?

30. What is a criticism of the hypothesis testing approach to data analysis?

Multiple-Choice Questions

31. Multiple regression is used to predict ____ variable(s) from ____ variable(s).
    a. a criterion; two or more predictor
    b. a predictor; two or more criterion
    c. two or more criterion; a predictor
    d. two or more predictor; a criterion

*32. Multivariate analysis of variance is *not* used when there
    a. is only one independent variable
    b. are two or more independent variables
    c. is only one dependent variable
    d. are two or more dependent variables

*33. The relationship between a quantitative independent variable and a qualitative dependent variable can be analyzed using logistic regression or multinomial logistic regression.

a. true   b. false

34. According to Cohen (1994), the primary focus for the analysis of bivariate relationships should be ____ between the variables.

a. whether there is a relationship
b. the strength of the relationship
c. the nature of the relationship
d. the strength and nature of the relationship

35. Given a qualitative independent variable and a quantitative dependent variable that has only two or three values, a parametric test is usually preferred over a nonparametric test.

a. true   b. false

*36. Which of the following is *not* a multivariate statistical test?

a. one-way repeated measures analysis of variance
b. two-way between-subjects analysis of variance
c. log-linear analysis
d. the Hotelling T^2 test

*37. The unifying framework for our approach to statistical analysis is

a. interval estimation
b. null hypothesis testing
c. Bayesian statistics
d. effect size estimation

38. The relationship between a within-subjects qualitative variable and a between-subjects qualitative variable can be analyzed using the chi-square test.

a. true
b. false

*39. The statistics for analyzing the relationship between a qualitative independent variable and a quantitative dependent variable might be applicable to the analysis of two quantitative variables when the independent variable is within-subjects in nature or has fewer than five or so values associated with it.

a. true
b. false

40. In the linear model for multiple regression, *a* represents

a. the squared multiple correlation coefficient
b. a regression coefficient
c. the overall slope
d. the overall intercept

41. If a multivariate *F* test is statistically nonsignificant, separate follow-up analyses can be applied to the individual dependent variables.

a. true
b. false

Proportions of Scores in a Normal Distribution

The following table reports the proportions of scores in a normal distribution that occur within selected ranges of z. A given proportion represents the probability of obtaining scores within the range of interest. Column 1 lists values of z. Column 2 indicates the probability of observing z scores that are greater than or equal to $-z$ and less than or equal to $+z$. Column 3 indicates the probability of obtaining z scores that are greater than or equal to $+z$. This column can also be used to determine the probability of obtaining z scores that are less than or equal to $-z$. Column 4 indicates the probability of obtaining z scores that are less than or equal to $-z$ or greater than or equal to $+z$. Column 5 indicates the probability of obtaining z scores that fall between 0 and the z score of interest.

As an example of the use of this table, consider the z score 1.96. According to Column 2, the probability of obtaining z scores between -1.96 and $+1.96$ is .9500. According to Column 3, the probability of obtaining z scores that are greater than or equal to $+1.96$ is .0250. Because the normal distribution is symmetrical, this column also indicates the probability of obtaining z scores that are less than or equal to -1.96. This probability is also .0250. According to Column 4, the probability of obtaining z scores that are less than or equal to -1.96 or greater than or equal to $+1.96$ is .0500. According to Column 5, the probability of obtaining z scores that fall between 0 and $+1.96$ is .4750. Again, because the normal distribution is symmetrical, this also represents the probability of obtaining z scores that fall between 0 and -1.96.

Adapted from *Fundamental Statistics for Psychology,* by R. B. McCall. Copyright ©1970 Harcourt Brace Jovanovich. Adapted with permission.

Column 1	Column 2	Column 3	Column 4	Column 5
z	$\geq -z$ and $\leq +z$	$\geq +z$ (also use to find $\leq -z$)	$\leq -z$ or $\geq +z$	≥ 0 and $\leq +z$ (also use to find $\geq -z$ and ≤ 0)
.00	.0000	.5000	1.0000	.0000
.01	.0080	.4960	.9920	.0040
.02	.0160	.4920	.9840	.0080
.03	.0240	.4880	.9760	.0120
.04	.0320	.4840	.9680	.0160
.05	.0398	.4801	.9602	.0199
.06	.0478	.4761	.9522	.0239
.07	.0558	.4721	.9442	.0279
.08	.0638	.4681	.9362	.0319
.09	.0718	.4641	.9282	.0359
.10	.0796	.4602	.9204	.0398
.11	.0876	.4562	.9124	.0438
.12	.0956	.4522	.9044	.0478
.13	.1034	.4483	.8966	.0517
.14	.1114	.4443	.8886	.0557
.15	.1192	.4404	.8808	.0596
.16	.1272	.4364	.8728	.0636
.17	.1350	.4325	.8650	.0675
.18	.1428	.4286	.8572	.0714
.19	.1506	.4247	.8494	.0753
.20	.1586	.4207	.8414	.0793
.21	.1664	.4168	.8336	.0832
.22	.1742	.4129	.8258	.0871
.23	.1820	.4090	.8180	.0910
.24	.1896	.4052	.8104	.0948
.25	.1974	.4013	.8026	.0987
.26	.2052	.3974	.7948	.1026
.27	.2128	.3936	.7872	.1064
.28	.2206	.3897	.7794	.1103
.29	.2282	.3859	.7718	.1141
.30	.2358	.3821	.7642	.1179
.31	.2434	.3783	.7566	.1217
.32	.2510	.3745	.7490	.1255
.33	.2586	.3707	.7414	.1293
.34	.2662	.3669	.7338	.1331
.35	.2736	.3632	.7264	.1368
.36	.2812	.3594	.7188	.1406
.37	.2886	.3557	.7114	.1443
.38	.2960	.3520	.7040	.1480

Column 1	Column 2	Column 3	Column 4	Column 5
z	$\geqslant -z$ and $\leqslant +z$	$\geqslant +z$ (also use to find $\leqslant -z$)	$\leqslant -z$ or $\geqslant +z$	$\geqslant 0$ and $\leqslant +z$ (also use to find $\geqslant -z$ and $\leqslant 0$)
.39	.3034	.3483	.6966	.1517
.40	.3108	.3446	.6892	.1554
.41	.3182	.3409	.6818	.1591
.42	.3256	.3372	.6744	.1628
.43	.3328	.3336	.6672	.1664
.44	.3400	.3300	.6600	.1700
.45	.3472	.3264	.6528	.1736
.46	.3544	.3228	.6456	.1772
.47	.3616	.3192	.6384	.1808
.48	.3688	.3156	.6312	.1844
.49	.3758	.3121	.6242	.1879
.50	.3830	.3085	.6170	.1915
.51	.3900	.3050	.6100	.1950
.52	.3970	.3015	.6030	.1985
.53	.4038	.2981	.5962	.2019
.54	.4108	.2946	.5892	.2054
.55	.4176	.2912	.5824	.2088
.56	.4246	.2877	.5754	.2123
.57	.4314	.2843	.5686	.2157
.58	.4380	.2810	.5620	.2190
.59	.4448	.2776	.5552	.2224
.60	.4514	.2743	.5486	.2257
.61	.4582	.2709	.5418	.2291
.62	.4648	.2676	.5352	.2324
.63	.4714	.2643	.5286	.2357
.64	.4778	.2611	.5222	.2389
.65	.4844	.2578	.5156	.2422
.66	.4908	.2546	.5092	.2454
.67	.4972	.2514	.5028	.2486
.68	.5034	.2483	.4966	.2517
.69	.5098	.2451	.4902	.2549
.70	.5160	.2420	.4840	.2580
.71	.5222	.2389	.4778	.2611
.72	.5284	.2358	.4716	.2642
.73	.5346	.2327	.4654	.2673
.74	.5408	.2296	.4592	.2704
.75	.5468	.2266	.4532	.2734
.76	.5528	.2236	.4472	.2764
.77	.5588	.2206	.4412	.2794

	Column 1	Column 2	Column 3	Column 4	Column 5
z	$\geq -z$ and $\leq +z$	$\geq +z$ (also use to find $\leq -z$)	$\leq -z$ or $\geq +z$	≥ 0 and $\leq +z$ (also use to find $\geq -z$ and ≤ 0)
.78	.5646	.2177	.4354	.2823
.79	.5704	.2148	.4296	.2852
.80	.5762	.2119	.4238	.2881
.81	.5820	.2090	.4180	.2910
.82	.5878	.2061	.4132	.2939
.83	.5934	.2033	.4066	.2967
.84	.5990	.2005	.4010	.2995
.85	.6046	.1977	.3954	.3023
.86	.6102	.1949	.3898	.3051
.87	.6156	.1922	.3844	.3078
.88	.6212	.1894	.3788	.3106
.89	.6266	.1867	.3734	.3133
.90	.6318	.1841	.3682	.3159
.91	.6372	.1814	.3628	.3186
.92	.6424	.1788	.3576	.3212
.93	.6476	.1762	.3524	.3238
.94	.6528	.1736	.3472	.3264
.95	.6578	.1711	.3422	.3289
.96	.6630	.1685	.3370	.3315
.97	.6680	.1660	.3320	.3340
.98	.6730	.1635	.3270	.3365
.99	.6778	.1611	.3222	.3389
1.00	.6826	.1587	.3174	.3413
1.01	.6876	.1562	.3124	.3438
1.02	.6922	.1539	.3078	.3461
1.03	.6970	.1515	.3030	.3485
1.04	.7016	.1492	.2984	.3508
1.05	.7062	.1469	.2938	.3531
1.06	.7108	.1446	.2892	.3554
1.07	.7154	.1423	.2846	.3577
1.08	.7198	.1401	.2802	.3599
1.09	.7242	.1379	.2758	.3621
1.10	.7286	.1357	.2714	.3643
1.11	.7330	.1335	.2670	.3665
1.12	.7372	.1314	.2628	.3686
1.13	.7416	.1292	.2584	.3708
1.14	.7458	.1271	.2542	.3729
1.15	.7498	.1251	.2502	.3749
1.16	.7540	.1230	.2460	.3770

Column 1	Column 2	Column 3	Column 4	Column 5
		+z		0 +z
	−z +z	−z	−z +z	−z 0
				≥ 0 and $\leq +z$ (also use to find
		$\geq +z$ (also use to find $\leq -z$)		$\geq -z$ and ≤ 0)
z	$\geq -z$ and $\leq +z$		$\leq -z$ or $\geq +z$	
1.17	.7580	.1210	.2420	.3790
1.18	.7620	.1190	.2380	.3810
1.19	.7660	.1170	.2340	.3830
1.20	.7698	.1151	.2302	.3849
1.21	.7738	.1131	.2262	.3869
1.22	.7776	.1112	.2224	.3888
1.23	.7814	.1093	.2186	.3907
1.24	.7850	.1075	.2150	.3925
1.25	.7888	.1056	.2112	.3944
1.26	.7924	.1038	.2076	.3962
1.27	.7960	.1020	.2040	.3980
1.28	.7994	.1003	.2006	.3997
1.29	.8030	.0985	.1970	.4015
1.30	.8064	.0968	.1936	.4032
1.31	.8098	.0951	.1902	.4049
1.32	.8132	.0934	.1868	.4066
1.33	.8164	.0918	.1836	.4082
1.34	.8198	.0901	.1802	.4099
1.35	.8230	.0885	.1770	.4115
1.36	.8262	.0869	.1738	.4131
1.37	.8294	.0853	.1706	.4147
1.38	.8324	.0838	.1676	.4162
1.39	.8354	.0823	.1646	.4177
1.40	.8384	.0808	.1616	.4192
1.41	.8414	.0793	.1586	.4207
1.42	.8444	.0778	.1556	.4222
1.43	.8472	.0764	.1528	.4236
1.44	.8502	.0749	.1498	.4251
1.45	.8530	.0735	.1470	.4265
1.46	.8558	.0721	.1442	.4279
1.47	.8584	.0708	.1416	.4292
1.48	.8612	.0694	.1388	.4306
1.49	.8638	.0681	.1362	.4319
1.50	.8664	.0668	.1336	.4332
1.51	.8690	.0655	.1310	.4345
1.52	.8714	.0643	.1286	.4357
1.53	.8740	.0630	.1260	.4370
1.54	.8764	.0618	.1236	.4382
1.55	.8788	.0606	.1212	.4394

	Column 1	Column 2	Column 3	Column 4	Column 5
	z	$\geq -z$ and $\leq +z$	$\geq +z$ (also use to find $\leq -z$)	$\leq -z$ or $\geq +z$	≥ 0 and $\leq +z$ (also use to find $\geq -z$ and ≤ 0)
	1.56	.8812	.0594	.1188	.4406
	1.57	.8836	.0582	.1164	.4418
	1.58	.8858	.0571	.1142	.4429
	1.59	.8882	.0559	.1118	.4441
	1.60	.8904	.0548	.1096	.4452
	1.61	.8926	.0537	.1074	.4463
	1.62	.8948	.0526	.1052	.4474
	1.63	.8968	.0516	.1032	.4484
	1.64	.8990	.0505	.1010	.4495
	1.65	.9010	.0495	.0990	.4505
	1.66	.9030	.0485	.0970	.4515
	1.67	.9050	.0475	.0950	.4525
	1.68	.9070	.0465	.0930	.4535
	1.69	.9090	.0455	.0910	.4545
	1.70	.9108	.0446	.0892	.4554
	1.71	.9128	.0436	.0872	.4564
	1.72	.9146	.0427	.0854	.4573
	1.73	.9164	.0418	.0836	.4582
	1.74	.9182	.0409	.0818	.4591
	1.75	.9198	.0401	.0802	.4599
	1.76	.9216	.0392	.0784	.4608
	1.77	.9232	.0384	.0764	.4616
	1.78	.9250	.0375	.0750	.4625
	1.79	.9266	.0367	.0734	.4633
	1.80	.9282	.0359	.0718	.4641
	1.81	.9298	.0351	.0702	.4649
	1.82	.9312	.0344	.0688	.4656
	1.83	.9328	.0336	.0672	.4664
	1.84	.9342	.0329	.0658	.4671
	1.85	.9356	.0322	.0644	.4678
	1.86	.9372	.0314	.0628	.4686
	1.87	.9386	.0307	.0614	.4693
	1.88	.9398	.0301	.0602	.4699
	1.89	.9412	.0294	.0588	.4706
	1.90	.9426	.0287	.0574	.4713
	1.91	.9438	.0281	.0562	.4719
	1.92	.9452	.0274	.0548	.4726
	1.93	.9464	.0268	.0536	.4732
	1.94	.9476	.0262	.0524	.4738

	Column 1	Column 2	Column 3	Column 4	Column 5
z		$\geq -z$ and $\leq +z$	$\geq +z$ (also use to find $\leq -z$)	$\leq -z$ or $\geq +z$	≥ 0 and $\leq +z$ (also use to find $\geq -z$ and ≤ 0)
1.95		.9488	.0256	.0512	.4744
1.96		.9500	.0250	.0500	.4750
1.97		.9512	.0244	.0488	.4756
1.98		.9522	.0239	.0478	.4761
1.99		.9534	.0233	.0466	.4767
2.00		.9544	.0228	.0456	.4772
2.01		.9556	.0222	.0444	.4778
2.02		.9566	.0217	.0434	.4783
2.03		.9576	.0212	.0424	.4788
2.04		.9586	.0207	.0414	.4793
2.05		.9596	.0202	.0404	.4798
2.06		.9606	.0197	.0394	.4803
2.07		.9616	.0192	.0384	.4808
2.08		.9624	.0188	.0376	.4812
2.09		.9634	.0183	.0366	.4817
2.10		.9642	.0179	.0358	.4821
2.11		.9652	.0174	.0348	.4826
2.12		.9660	.0170	.0340	.4830
2.13		.9668	.0166	.0332	.4834
2.14		.9676	.0162	.0324	.4838
2.15		.9684	.0158	.0316	.4842
2.16		.9692	.0154	.0308	.4846
2.17		.9700	.0150	.0300	.4850
2.18		.9708	.0146	.0292	.4854
2.19		.9714	.0143	.0286	.4857
2.20		.9722	.0139	.0278	.4861
2.21		.9728	.0136	.0272	.4864
2.22		.9736	.0132	.0264	.4868
2.23		.9742	.0129	.0258	.4871
2.24		.9750	.0125	.0250	.4875
2.25		.9756	.0122	.0244	.4878
2.26		.9762	.0119	.0238	.4881
2.27		.9768	.0116	.0232	.4884
2.28		.9774	.0113	.0226	.4887
2.29		.9780	.0110	.0220	.4890
2.30		.9786	.0107	.0214	.4893
2.31		.9792	.0104	.0208	.4896
2.32		.9796	.0102	.0204	.4898
2.33		.9802	.0099	.0198	.4901

Column 1	Column 2	Column 3	Column 4	Column 5
z	$\geq -z$ and $\leq +z$	$\geq +z$ (also use to find $\leq -z$)	$\leq -z$ or $\geq +z$	≥ 0 and $\leq +z$ (also use to find $\geq -z$ and ≤ 0)
2.34	.9808	.0096	.0192	.4904
2.35	.9812	.0094	.0188	.4906
2.36	.9818	.0091	.0182	.4909
2.37	.9822	.0089	.0178	.4911
2.38	.9826	.0087	.0174	.4913
2.39	.9832	.0084	.0168	.4916
2.40	.9836	.0082	.0164	.4918
2.41	.9840	.0080	.0160	.4920
2.42	.9844	.0078	.0156	.4922
2.43	.9850	.0075	.0150	.4925
2.44	.9854	.0073	.0146	.4927
2.45	.9858	.0071	.0142	.4929
2.46	.9862	.0069	.0138	.4931
2.47	.9864	.0068	.0136	.4932
2.48	.9868	.0066	.0132	.4934
2.49	.9872	.0064	.0128	.4936
2.50	.9876	.0062	.0124	.4938
2.51	.9880	.0060	.0120	.4940
2.52	.9882	.0059	.0118	.4941
2.53	.9886	.0057	.0114	.4943
2.54	.9890	.0055	.0110	.4945
2.55	.9892	.0054	.0108	.4946
2.56	.9896	.0052	.0104	.4948
2.57	.9898	.0051	.0102	.4949
2.58	.9902	.0049	.0098	.4951
2.59	.9904	.0048	.0096	.4952
2.60	.9906	.0047	.0094	.4953
2.61	.9910	.0045	.0090	.4955
2.62	.9912	.0044	.0088	.4956
2.63	.9914	.0043	.0086	.4957
2.64	.9918	.0041	.0082	.4959
2.65	.9920	.0040	.0080	.4960
2.66	.9922	.0039	.0078	.4961
2.67	.9924	.0038	.0076	.4962
2.68	.9926	.0037	.0074	.4963
2.69	.9928	.0036	.0072	.4964
2.70	.9930	.0035	.0070	.4965
2.71	.9932	.0034	.0068	.4966
2.72	.9934	.0033	.0066	.4967

Column 1	Column 2	Column 3	Column 4	Column 5
		+z		0 +z
	−z +z	−z	−z +z	−z 0
		≥ +z (also use		≥ 0 and ≤ +z (also use to find ≥ −z and ≤ 0)
z	≥ −z and ≤ +z	to find ≤ −z)	≤ −z or ≥ +z	
2.73	.9936	.0032	.0064	.4968
2.74	.9938	.0031	.0062	.4969
2.75	.9940	.0030	.0060	.4970
2.76	.9942	.0029	.0058	.4971
2.77	.9944	.0028	.0056	.4972
2.78	.9946	.0027	.0054	.4973
2.79	.9948	.0026	.0052	.4974
2.80	.9948	.0026	.0052	.4974
2.81	.9950	.0025	.0050	.4975
2.82	.9952	.0024	.0048	.4976
2.83	.9954	.0023	.0046	.4977
2.84	.9954	.0023	.0046	.4977
2.85	.9956	.0022	.0044	.4978
2.86	.9958	.0021	.0042	.4979
2.87	.9958	.0021	.0042	.4979
2.88	.9960	.0020	.0040	.4980
2.89	.9962	.0019	.0038	.4981
2.90	.9962	.0019	.0038	.4981
2.91	.9964	.0018	.0036	.4982
2.92	.9964	.0018	.0036	.4982
2.93	.9966	.0017	.0034	.4983
2.94	.9968	.0016	.0032	.4984
2.95	.9968	.0016	.0032	.4984
2.96	.9970	.0015	.0030	.4985
2.97	.9970	.0015	.0030	.4985
2.98	.9972	.0014	.0028	.4986
2.99	.9972	.0014	.0028	.4986
3.00	.9974	.0013	.0026	.4987
3.01	.9974	.0013	.0026	.4987
3.02	.9974	.0013	.0026	.4987
3.03	.9976	.0012	.0024	.4988
3.04	.9976	.0012	.0024	.4988
3.05	.9978	.0011	.0022	.4989
3.06	.9978	.0011	.0022	.4989
3.07	.9978	.0011	.0022	.4989
3.08	.9980	.0010	.0020	.4990
3.09	.9980	.0010	.0020	.4990
3.10	.9980	.0010	.0020	.4990
3.11	.9982	.0009	.0018	.4991

Column 1	Column 2	Column 3	Column 4	Column 5
				≥ 0 and $\leq +z$
		$\geq +z$ (also use		(also use to find
z	$\geq -z$ and $\leq +z$	to find $\leq -z$)	$\leq -z$ or $\geq +z$	$\geq -z$ and ≤ 0)
3.12	.9982	.0009	.0018	.4991
3.13	.9982	.0009	.0018	.4991
3.14	.9984	.0008	.0016	.4992
3.15	.9984	.0008	.0016	.4992
3.16	.9984	.0008	.0016	.4992
3.17	.9984	.0008	.0016	.4992
3.18	.9986	.0007	.0014	.4993
3.19	.9986	.0007	.0014	.4993
3.20	.9986	.0007	.0014	.4993
3.21	.9986	.0007	.0014	.4993
3.22	.9988	.0006	.0012	.4994
3.23	.9988	.0006	.0012	.4994
3.24	.9988	.0006	.0012	.4994
3.25	.9988	.0006	.0012	.4994
3.30	.9990	.0005	.0010	.4995
3.35	.9992	.0004	.0008	.4996
3.40	.9994	.0003	.0006	.4997
3.45	.9994	.0003	.0006	.4997
3.50	.9996	.0002	.0004	.4998
3.60	.9996	.0002	.0004	.4998
3.70	.9998	.0001	.0002	.4999
3.80	.9998	.0001	.0002	.4999
3.90	.9999	.00005	.00010	.49995
4.00	.99994	.00003	.00006	.49997

Critical Values for the t Distribution

The following table presents critical values of t for directional (one-tailed) and nondirectional (two-tailed) tests. The column headed "df" lists the degrees of freedom for the t distribution of interest. The entries in the table are the t values that define the rejection regions.

The values .10, .05, .025, .01, .005, and .0005 at the top of the table under the heading "Level of Significance for Directional Test" represent alpha levels for directional tests. To find a critical value, follow the row for the degrees of freedom of interest to where it intersects the column for the alpha level of interest. That entry is the critical value for the corresponding degrees of freedom and directional alpha level. For example, the critical value of t for $df = 15$ and an alpha level of .05 for a directional test that focuses on the upper tail of the distribution is 1.753. Because the t distribution is symmetrical, the critical value of t for a directional test that focuses on the lower tail of the distribution is -1.753.

The values .20, .10, .05, .02, .01, and .001 under the heading "Level of Significance for Nondirectional Test" represent alpha levels for nondirectional tests. To find a critical value, we follow the same procedure as before, but now we are interested in where the row for the degrees of freedom of interest intersects the column for the relevant nondirectional alpha level. For example, the positive critical value of t for $df = 15$ and an alpha level of .05 for a nondirectional test is $+2.131$. Because the t distribution is symmetrical, the negative critical value of t is -2.131. The rejection region thus consists of all values of t that are less than -2.131 or greater than $+2.131$.

From Table III in R. A. Fisher and F. Yates, *Statistical Tables for Biological, Agricultural, and Medical Research,* Sixth Edition, published by Addison Wesley Longman Ltd. (1974). Reprinted with permission.

	Level of Significance for Directional Test					
	.10	.05	.025	.01	.005	.0005
	Level of Significance for Nondirectional Test					
df	.20	.10	.05	.02	.01	.001
1	3.078	6.314	12.706	31.821	63.657	636.619
2	1.886	2.920	4.303	6.965	9.925	31.598
3	1.638	2.353	3.182	4.541	5.841	12.941
4	1.533	2.132	2.776	3.747	4.604	8.610
5	1.476	2.015	2.571	3.365	4.032	6.859
6	1.440	1.943	2.447	3.143	3.707	5.959
7	1.415	1.895	2.365	2.998	3.499	5.405
8	1.397	1.860	2.306	2.896	3.355	5.041
9	1.383	1.833	2.262	2.821	3.250	4.781
10	1.372	1.812	2.228	2.764	3.169	4.587
11	1.363	1.796	2.201	2.718	3.106	4.437
12	1.356	1.782	2.179	2.681	3.055	4.318
13	1.350	1.771	2.160	2.650	3.012	4.221
14	1.345	1.761	2.145	2.624	2.977	4.140
15	1.341	1.753	2.131	2.602	2.947	4.073
16	1.337	1.746	2.120	2.583	2.921	4.015
17	1.333	1.740	2.110	2.567	2.898	3.965
18	1.330	1.734	2.101	2.552	2.878	3.922
19	1.328	1.729	2.093	2.539	2.861	3.883
20	1.325	1.725	2.086	2.528	2.845	3.850
21	1.323	1.721	2.080	2.518	2.831	3.819
22	1.321	1.717	2.074	2.508	2.819	3.792
23	1.319	1.714	2.069	2.500	2.807	3.767
24	1.318	1.711	2.064	2.492	2.797	3.745
25	1.316	1.708	2.060	2.485	2.787	3.725
26	1.315	1.706	2.056	2.479	2.779	3.707
27	1.314	1.703	2.052	2.473	2.771	3.690
28	1.313	1.701	2.048	2.467	2.763	3.674
29	1.311	1.699	2.045	2.462	2.756	3.659
30	1.310	1.697	2.042	2.457	2.750	3.646
40	1.303	1.684	2.021	2.423	2.704	3.551
60	1.296	1.671	2.000	2.390	2.660	3.460
120	1.289	1.658	1.980	2.358	2.617	3.373
∞	1.282	1.645	1.960	2.326	2.576	3.291

Critical Values for the *F* Distribution

The following table presents critical values of *F* for alpha levels of .05 and .01. The .05 critical values are in roman type, and the .01 critical values are in **boldface.** The values at the top of the table under the heading "Degrees of Freedom for Numerator" represent the degrees of freedom associated with the numerator of the *F* ratio for the analysis of interest. This is the degrees of freedom between for one-way between-subjects analysis of variance; the degrees of freedom IV for one-way repeated measures analysis of variance; and the degrees of freedom for factor *A*, factor *B*, or the interaction effect for two-way between-subjects analysis of variance.

The values at the left of the table under the heading "Degrees of Freedom for Denominator" represent the degrees of freedom associated with the denominator of the *F* ratio for the analysis of interest. This is the degrees of freedom within for one- and two-way between-subjects analysis of variance, and the degrees of freedom error for one-way repeated measures analysis of variance. For example, the critical value of *F* for a one-way between-subjects analysis of variance for $df_{\text{BETWEEN}} = 2$, $df_{\text{WITHIN}} = 11$, and an alpha level of .05 is 3.98.

Degrees of Freedom for Numerator

DEGREES OF FREEDOM FOR DENOMINATOR

	1	2	3	4	5	6	7	8	9	10	11	12	14	16	20	24	30	40	50	75	100	200	500	∞
1	161 / 4,052	200 / 4,999	216 / 5,403	225 / 5,625	230 / 5,764	234 / 5,859	237 / 5,928	239 / 5,981	241 / 6,022	242 / 6,056	243 / 6,082	244 / 6,106	245 / 6,142	246 / 6,169	248 / 6,208	249 / 6,234	250 / 6,258	251 / 6,286	252 / 6,302	253 / 6,323	253 / 6,334	254 / 6,352	254 / 6,361	254 / 6,366
2	18.51 / 98.49	19.00 / 99.01	19.16 / 99.17	19.25 / 99.25	19.30 / 99.30	19.33 / 99.33	19.36 / 99.34	19.37 / 99.36	19.38 / 99.38	19.39 / 99.40	19.40 / 99.41	19.41 / 99.42	19.42 / 99.43	19.43 / 99.44	19.44 / 99.45	19.45 / 99.46	19.46 / 99.47	19.47 / 99.48	19.47 / 99.48	19.48 / 99.49	19.49 / 99.49	19.49 / 99.49	19.50 / 99.50	19.50 / 99.50
3	10.13 / 34.12	9.55 / 30.81	9.28 / 29.46	9.12 / 28.71	9.01 / 28.24	8.94 / 27.91	8.88 / 27.67	8.84 / 27.49	8.81 / 27.34	8.78 / 27.23	8.76 / 27.13	8.74 / 27.05	8.71 / 26.92	8.69 / 26.83	8.66 / 26.69	8.64 / 26.60	8.62 / 26.50	8.60 / 26.41	8.58 / 26.30	8.57 / 26.27	8.56 / 26.23	8.54 / 26.18	8.54 / 26.14	8.53 / 26.12
4	7.71 / 21.20	6.94 / 18.00	6.59 / 16.69	6.39 / 15.98	6.26 / 15.52	6.16 / 15.21	6.09 / 14.98	6.04 / 14.80	6.00 / 14.66	5.96 / 14.54	5.93 / 14.45	5.91 / 14.37	5.87 / 14.24	5.84 / 14.15	5.80 / 14.02	5.77 / 13.93	5.74 / 13.83	5.71 / 13.74	5.70 / 13.69	5.68 / 13.61	5.66 / 13.57	5.65 / 13.52	5.64 / 13.48	5.63 / 13.46
5	6.61 / 16.26	5.79 / 13.27	5.41 / 12.06	5.19 / 11.39	5.05 / 10.97	4.95 / 10.67	4.88 / 10.45	4.82 / 10.27	4.78 / 10.15	4.74 / 10.05	4.70 / 9.96	4.68 / 9.89	4.64 / 9.77	4.60 / 9.68	4.56 / 9.55	4.53 / 9.47	4.50 / 9.38	4.46 / 9.29	4.44 / 9.24	4.42 / 9.17	4.40 / 9.13	4.38 / 9.07	4.37 / 9.04	4.36 / 9.02
6	5.99 / 13.74	5.14 / 10.92	4.76 / 9.78	4.53 / 9.15	4.39 / 8.75	4.28 / 8.47	4.21 / 8.26	4.15 / 8.10	4.10 / 7.98	4.06 / 7.87	4.03 / 7.79	4.00 / 7.72	3.96 / 7.60	3.92 / 7.52	3.87 / 7.39	3.84 / 7.31	3.81 / 7.23	3.77 / 7.14	3.75 / 7.09	3.72 / 7.02	3.71 / 6.99	3.69 / 6.94	3.68 / 6.90	3.67 / 6.88
7	5.59 / 12.25	4.74 / 9.55	4.35 / 8.45	4.12 / 7.85	3.97 / 7.46	3.87 / 7.19	3.79 / 7.00	3.73 / 6.84	3.68 / 6.71	3.63 / 6.62	3.60 / 6.54	3.57 / 6.47	3.52 / 6.35	3.49 / 6.27	3.44 / 6.15	3.41 / 6.07	3.38 / 5.98	3.34 / 5.90	3.32 / 5.85	3.29 / 5.78	3.28 / 5.75	3.25 / 5.70	3.24 / 5.67	3.23 / 5.65
8	5.32 / 11.26	4.46 / 8.65	4.07 / 7.59	3.84 / 7.01	3.69 / 6.63	3.58 / 6.37	3.50 / 6.19	3.44 / 6.03	3.39 / 5.91	3.34 / 5.82	3.31 / 5.74	3.28 / 5.67	3.23 / 5.56	3.20 / 5.48	3.15 / 5.36	3.12 / 5.28	3.08 / 5.20	3.05 / 5.11	3.03 / 5.06	3.00 / 5.00	2.98 / 4.96	2.96 / 4.91	2.94 / 4.88	2.93 / 4.86
9	5.12 / 10.56	4.26 / 8.02	3.86 / 6.99	3.63 / 6.42	3.48 / 6.06	3.37 / 5.80	3.29 / 5.62	3.23 / 5.47	3.18 / 5.35	3.13 / 5.26	3.10 / 5.18	3.07 / 5.11	3.02 / 5.00	2.98 / 4.92	2.93 / 4.80	2.90 / 4.73	2.86 / 4.64	2.82 / 4.56	2.80 / 4.51	2.77 / 4.45	2.76 / 4.41	2.73 / 4.36	2.72 / 4.33	2.71 / 4.31
10	4.96 / 10.04	4.10 / 7.56	3.71 / 6.55	3.48 / 5.99	3.33 / 5.64	3.22 / 5.39	3.14 / 5.21	3.07 / 5.06	3.02 / 4.95	2.97 / 4.85	2.94 / 4.78	2.91 / 4.71	2.86 / 4.60	2.82 / 4.52	2.77 / 4.41	2.74 / 4.33	2.70 / 4.25	2.67 / 4.17	2.64 / 4.12	2.61 / 4.05	2.59 / 4.01	2.56 / 3.96	2.55 / 3.93	2.54 / 3.91
11	4.84 / 9.65	3.98 / 7.20	3.59 / 6.22	3.36 / 5.67	3.20 / 5.32	3.09 / 5.07	3.01 / 4.88	2.95 / 4.74	2.90 / 4.63	2.86 / 4.54	2.82 / 4.46	2.79 / 4.40	2.74 / 4.29	2.70 / 4.21	2.65 / 4.10	2.61 / 4.02	2.57 / 3.94	2.53 / 3.86	2.50 / 3.80	2.47 / 3.74	2.45 / 3.70	2.42 / 3.66	2.41 / 3.62	2.40 / 3.60
12	4.75 / 9.33	3.88 / 6.93	3.49 / 5.95	3.26 / 5.41	3.11 / 5.06	3.00 / 4.82	2.92 / 4.65	2.85 / 4.50	2.80 / 4.39	2.76 / 4.30	2.72 / 4.22	2.69 / 4.16	2.64 / 4.05	2.60 / 3.98	2.54 / 3.86	2.50 / 3.78	2.46 / 3.70	2.42 / 3.61	2.40 / 3.56	2.36 / 3.49	2.35 / 3.46	2.32 / 3.41	2.31 / 3.38	2.30 / 3.36
13	4.67 / 9.07	3.80 / 6.70	3.41 / 5.74	3.18 / 5.20	3.02 / 4.86	2.92 / 4.62	2.84 / 4.44	2.77 / 4.30	2.72 / 4.19	2.67 / 4.10	2.63 / 4.02	2.60 / 3.96	2.55 / 3.85	2.51 / 3.78	2.46 / 3.67	2.42 / 3.59	2.38 / 3.51	2.34 / 3.42	2.32 / 3.37	2.28 / 3.30	2.26 / 3.27	2.24 / 3.21	2.22 / 3.18	2.21 / 3.16
14	4.60 / 8.86	3.74 / 6.51	3.34 / 5.56	3.11 / 5.03	2.96 / 4.69	2.85 / 4.46	2.77 / 4.28	2.70 / 4.14	2.65 / 4.03	2.60 / 3.94	2.56 / 3.86	2.53 / 3.80	2.48 / 3.70	2.44 / 3.62	2.39 / 3.51	2.35 / 3.43	2.31 / 3.34	2.27 / 3.26	2.24 / 3.21	2.21 / 3.14	2.19 / 3.11	2.16 / 3.06	2.14 / 3.02	2.13 / 3.00
15	4.54 / 8.68	3.68 / 6.36	3.29 / 5.42	3.06 / 4.89	2.90 / 4.56	2.79 / 4.32	2.70 / 4.14	2.64 / 4.00	2.59 / 3.89	2.55 / 3.80	2.51 / 3.73	2.48 / 3.67	2.43 / 3.56	2.39 / 3.48	2.33 / 3.36	2.29 / 3.29	2.25 / 3.20	2.21 / 3.12	2.18 / 3.07	2.15 / 3.00	2.12 / 2.97	2.10 / 2.92	2.08 / 2.89	2.07 / 2.87
16	4.49 / 8.53	3.63 / 6.23	3.24 / 5.29	3.01 / 4.77	2.85 / 4.44	2.74 / 4.20	2.66 / 4.03	2.59 / 3.89	2.54 / 3.78	2.49 / 3.69	2.45 / 3.61	2.42 / 3.55	2.37 / 3.45	2.33 / 3.37	2.28 / 3.25	2.24 / 3.18	2.20 / 3.10	2.16 / 3.01	2.13 / 2.96	2.09 / 2.89	2.07 / 2.86	2.04 / 2.80	2.02 / 2.77	2.01 / 2.75
17	4.45 / 8.40	3.59 / 6.11	3.20 / 5.18	2.96 / 4.67	2.81 / 4.34	2.70 / 4.10	2.62 / 3.93	2.55 / 3.79	2.50 / 3.68	2.45 / 3.59	2.41 / 3.52	2.38 / 3.45	2.33 / 3.35	2.29 / 3.27	2.23 / 3.16	2.19 / 3.08	2.15 / 3.00	2.11 / 2.92	2.08 / 2.86	2.04 / 2.79	2.02 / 2.76	1.99 / 2.70	1.97 / 2.67	1.96 / 2.65
18	4.41 / 8.28	3.55 / 6.01	3.16 / 5.09	2.93 / 4.58	2.77 / 4.25	2.66 / 4.01	2.58 / 3.85	2.51 / 3.71	2.46 / 3.60	2.41 / 3.51	2.37 / 3.44	2.34 / 3.37	2.29 / 3.27	2.25 / 3.19	2.19 / 3.07	2.15 / 3.00	2.11 / 2.91	2.07 / 2.83	2.04 / 2.78	2.00 / 2.71	1.98 / 2.68	1.95 / 2.62	1.93 / 2.59	1.92 / 2.57
19	4.38 / 8.18	3.52 / 5.93	3.13 / 5.01	2.90 / 4.50	2.74 / 4.17	2.63 / 3.94	2.55 / 3.77	2.48 / 3.63	2.43 / 3.52	2.38 / 3.43	2.34 / 3.36	2.31 / 3.30	2.26 / 3.19	2.21 / 3.12	2.15 / 3.00	2.11 / 2.92	2.07 / 2.84	2.02 / 2.76	2.00 / 2.70	1.96 / 2.63	1.94 / 2.60	1.91 / 2.54	1.90 / 2.51	1.88 / 2.49
20	4.35 / 8.10	3.49 / 5.85	3.10 / 4.94	2.87 / 4.43	2.71 / 4.10	2.60 / 3.87	2.52 / 3.71	2.45 / 3.56	2.40 / 3.45	2.35 / 3.37	2.31 / 3.30	2.28 / 3.23	2.23 / 3.13	2.18 / 3.05	2.12 / 2.94	2.08 / 2.86	2.04 / 2.77	1.99 / 2.69	1.96 / 2.63	1.92 / 2.56	1.90 / 2.53	1.87 / 2.47	1.85 / 2.44	1.84 / 2.42

df	1	2	3	4	5	6	7	8	9	10	11	12	14	16	20	24	30	40	50	75	100	200	500	∞
21	4.32 / 8.02	3.47 / 5.78	3.07 / 4.87	2.84 / 4.37	2.68 / 4.04	2.57 / 3.81	2.49 / 3.65	2.42 / 3.51	2.37 / 3.40	2.32 / 3.31	2.28 / 3.24	2.25 / 3.17	2.20 / 3.07	2.15 / 2.99	2.09 / 2.88	2.05 / 2.80	2.00 / 2.72	1.96 / 2.63	1.93 / 2.58	1.89 / 2.51	1.87 / 2.47	1.84 / 2.42	1.82 / 2.38	1.81 / 2.36
22	4.30 / 7.94	3.44 / 5.72	3.05 / 4.82	2.82 / 4.31	2.66 / 3.99	2.55 / 3.76	2.47 / 3.59	2.40 / 3.45	2.35 / 3.35	2.30 / 3.26	2.26 / 3.18	2.23 / 3.12	2.18 / 3.02	2.13 / 2.94	2.07 / 2.83	2.03 / 2.75	1.98 / 2.67	1.93 / 2.58	1.91 / 2.53	1.87 / 2.46	1.84 / 2.42	1.81 / 2.37	1.80 / 2.33	1.78 / 2.31
23	4.28 / 7.88	3.42 / 5.66	3.03 / 4.76	2.80 / 4.26	2.64 / 3.94	2.53 / 3.71	2.45 / 3.54	2.38 / 3.41	2.32 / 3.30	2.28 / 3.21	2.24 / 3.14	2.20 / 3.07	2.14 / 2.97	2.10 / 2.89	2.04 / 2.78	2.00 / 2.70	1.96 / 2.62	1.91 / 2.53	1.88 / 2.48	1.84 / 2.41	1.82 / 2.37	1.79 / 2.32	1.77 / 2.28	1.76 / 2.26
24	4.26 / 7.82	3.40 / 5.61	3.01 / 4.72	2.78 / 4.22	2.62 / 3.90	2.51 / 3.67	2.43 / 3.50	2.36 / 3.36	2.30 / 3.25	2.26 / 3.17	2.22 / 3.09	2.18 / 3.03	2.13 / 2.93	2.09 / 2.85	2.02 / 2.74	1.98 / 2.66	1.94 / 2.58	1.89 / 2.49	1.86 / 2.44	1.82 / 2.36	1.80 / 2.33	1.76 / 2.27	1.74 / 2.23	1.73 / 2.21
25	4.24 / 7.77	3.38 / 5.57	2.99 / 4.68	2.76 / 4.18	2.60 / 3.86	2.49 / 3.63	2.41 / 3.46	2.34 / 3.32	2.28 / 3.21	2.24 / 3.13	2.20 / 3.05	2.16 / 2.99	2.11 / 2.89	2.06 / 2.81	2.00 / 2.70	1.96 / 2.62	1.92 / 2.54	1.87 / 2.45	1.84 / 2.40	1.80 / 2.32	1.77 / 2.29	1.74 / 2.23	1.72 / 2.19	1.71 / 2.17
26	4.22 / 7.72	3.37 / 5.53	2.98 / 4.64	2.74 / 4.14	2.59 / 3.82	2.47 / 3.59	2.39 / 3.42	2.32 / 3.29	2.27 / 3.17	2.22 / 3.09	2.18 / 3.02	2.15 / 2.96	2.10 / 2.86	2.05 / 2.77	1.99 / 2.66	1.95 / 2.58	1.90 / 2.50	1.85 / 2.41	1.82 / 2.36	1.78 / 2.28	1.76 / 2.25	1.72 / 2.19	1.70 / 2.15	1.69 / 2.13
27	4.21 / 7.68	3.35 / 5.49	2.96 / 4.60	2.73 / 4.11	2.57 / 3.79	2.46 / 3.56	2.37 / 3.39	2.30 / 3.26	2.25 / 3.14	2.20 / 3.06	2.16 / 2.98	2.13 / 2.93	2.08 / 2.83	2.03 / 2.74	1.97 / 2.63	1.93 / 2.55	1.88 / 2.47	1.84 / 2.38	1.80 / 2.33	1.76 / 2.25	1.74 / 2.21	1.71 / 2.16	1.68 / 2.12	1.67 / 2.10
28	4.20 / 7.64	3.34 / 5.45	2.95 / 4.57	2.71 / 4.07	2.56 / 3.76	2.44 / 3.53	2.36 / 3.36	2.29 / 3.23	2.24 / 3.11	2.19 / 3.03	2.15 / 2.95	2.12 / 2.90	2.06 / 2.80	2.02 / 2.71	1.95 / 2.60	1.91 / 2.52	1.87 / 2.44	1.81 / 2.35	1.77 / 2.30	1.75 / 2.22	1.72 / 2.18	1.69 / 2.13	1.67 / 2.09	1.65 / 2.06
29	4.18 / 7.60	3.33 / 5.42	2.93 / 4.54	2.70 / 4.04	2.54 / 3.73	2.43 / 3.50	2.35 / 3.33	2.28 / 3.20	2.22 / 3.08	2.18 / 3.00	2.14 / 2.92	2.10 / 2.87	2.05 / 2.77	2.00 / 2.68	1.94 / 2.57	1.90 / 2.49	1.85 / 2.41	1.80 / 2.32	1.77 / 2.27	1.73 / 2.19	1.71 / 2.15	1.68 / 2.10	1.65 / 2.06	1.64 / 2.03
30	4.17 / 7.56	3.32 / 5.39	2.92 / 4.51	2.69 / 4.02	2.53 / 3.70	2.42 / 3.47	2.34 / 3.30	2.27 / 3.17	2.21 / 3.06	2.16 / 2.98	2.12 / 2.90	2.09 / 2.84	2.04 / 2.74	1.99 / 2.66	1.93 / 2.55	1.89 / 2.47	1.84 / 2.38	1.79 / 2.29	1.76 / 2.24	1.72 / 2.16	1.69 / 2.13	1.66 / 2.07	1.64 / 2.03	1.62 / 2.01
32	4.15 / 7.50	3.30 / 5.34	2.90 / 4.46	2.67 / 3.97	2.51 / 3.66	2.40 / 3.42	2.32 / 3.25	2.25 / 3.12	2.19 / 3.01	2.14 / 2.94	2.10 / 2.86	2.07 / 2.80	2.02 / 2.70	1.97 / 2.62	1.91 / 2.51	1.86 / 2.42	1.82 / 2.34	1.76 / 2.25	1.74 / 2.20	1.69 / 2.12	1.67 / 2.08	1.64 / 2.02	1.61 / 1.98	1.59 / 1.96
34	4.13 / 7.44	3.28 / 5.29	2.88 / 4.42	2.65 / 3.93	2.49 / 3.61	2.38 / 3.38	2.30 / 3.21	2.23 / 3.08	2.17 / 2.97	2.12 / 2.89	2.08 / 2.82	2.05 / 2.76	2.00 / 2.66	1.95 / 2.58	1.89 / 2.47	1.84 / 2.38	1.80 / 2.30	1.74 / 2.21	1.71 / 2.15	1.67 / 2.08	1.64 / 2.04	1.61 / 1.98	1.59 / 1.94	1.57 / 1.91
36	4.11 / 7.39	3.26 / 5.25	2.86 / 4.38	2.63 / 3.89	2.48 / 3.58	2.36 / 3.35	2.28 / 3.18	2.21 / 3.04	2.15 / 2.94	2.10 / 2.86	2.06 / 2.78	2.03 / 2.72	1.98 / 2.62	1.93 / 2.54	1.87 / 2.43	1.82 / 2.35	1.78 / 2.26	1.72 / 2.17	1.69 / 2.12	1.65 / 2.04	1.62 / 2.00	1.59 / 1.94	1.56 / 1.90	1.55 / 1.87
38	4.10 / 7.35	3.25 / 5.21	2.85 / 4.34	2.62 / 3.86	2.46 / 3.54	2.35 / 3.32	2.26 / 3.15	2.19 / 3.02	2.14 / 2.91	2.09 / 2.82	2.05 / 2.75	2.02 / 2.69	1.96 / 2.59	1.92 / 2.51	1.85 / 2.40	1.80 / 2.32	1.76 / 2.22	1.71 / 2.14	1.67 / 2.08	1.63 / 2.00	1.60 / 1.97	1.57 / 1.90	1.54 / 1.86	1.53 / 1.84
40	4.08 / 7.31	3.23 / 5.18	2.84 / 4.31	2.61 / 3.83	2.45 / 3.51	2.34 / 3.29	2.25 / 3.12	2.18 / 2.99	2.12 / 2.88	2.07 / 2.80	2.04 / 2.73	2.00 / 2.66	1.95 / 2.56	1.90 / 2.49	1.84 / 2.37	1.79 / 2.29	1.74 / 2.20	1.69 / 2.11	1.66 / 2.05	1.61 / 1.97	1.59 / 1.94	1.55 / 1.88	1.53 / 1.84	1.51 / 1.81
42	4.07 / 7.27	3.22 / 5.15	2.83 / 4.29	2.59 / 3.80	2.44 / 3.49	2.32 / 3.26	2.24 / 3.10	2.17 / 2.96	2.11 / 2.86	2.06 / 2.77	2.02 / 2.70	1.99 / 2.64	1.94 / 2.54	1.89 / 2.46	1.82 / 2.35	1.78 / 2.26	1.73 / 2.17	1.68 / 2.08	1.64 / 2.02	1.60 / 1.94	1.57 / 1.91	1.54 / 1.85	1.51 / 1.80	1.49 / 1.78
44	4.06 / 7.24	3.21 / 5.12	2.82 / 4.26	2.58 / 3.78	2.43 / 3.46	2.31 / 3.24	2.23 / 3.07	2.16 / 2.94	2.10 / 2.84	2.05 / 2.75	2.01 / 2.68	1.98 / 2.62	1.92 / 2.52	1.88 / 2.44	1.81 / 2.32	1.76 / 2.24	1.72 / 2.15	1.66 / 2.06	1.63 / 2.00	1.58 / 1.92	1.56 / 1.88	1.52 / 1.82	1.50 / 1.78	1.48 / 1.75
46	4.05 / 7.21	3.20 / 5.10	2.81 / 4.24	2.57 / 3.76	2.42 / 3.44	2.30 / 3.22	2.22 / 3.05	2.14 / 2.92	2.09 / 2.82	2.04 / 2.73	2.00 / 2.66	1.97 / 2.60	1.91 / 2.50	1.87 / 2.42	1.80 / 2.30	1.75 / 2.22	1.71 / 2.13	1.65 / 2.04	1.62 / 1.98	1.57 / 1.90	1.54 / 1.86	1.51 / 1.80	1.48 / 1.76	1.46 / 1.72
48	4.04 / 7.19	3.19 / 5.08	2.80 / 4.22	2.56 / 3.74	2.41 / 3.42	2.30 / 3.20	2.21 / 3.04	2.14 / 2.90	2.08 / 2.80	2.03 / 2.71	1.99 / 2.64	1.96 / 2.58	1.90 / 2.48	1.86 / 2.40	1.79 / 2.28	1.74 / 2.20	1.70 / 2.11	1.64 / 2.02	1.61 / 1.96	1.56 / 1.88	1.53 / 1.84	1.50 / 1.78	1.47 / 1.73	1.45 / 1.70
50	4.03 / 7.17	3.18 / 5.06	2.79 / 4.20	2.56 / 3.72	2.40 / 3.41	2.29 / 3.18	2.20 / 3.02	2.13 / 2.88	2.07 / 2.78	2.02 / 2.70	1.98 / 2.62	1.95 / 2.56	1.90 / 2.46	1.85 / 2.39	1.78 / 2.26	1.74 / 2.18	1.69 / 2.10	1.63 / 2.00	1.60 / 1.94	1.55 / 1.86	1.52 / 1.82	1.48 / 1.76	1.46 / 1.71	1.44 / 1.68

DEGREES OF FREEDOM FOR DENOMINATOR

df (denom)	1	2	3	4	5	6	7	8	9	10	11	12	14	16	20	24	30	40	50	75	100	200	500	∞
55	4.02 7.12	3.17 5.01	2.78 4.16	2.54 3.68	2.38 3.37	2.27 3.15	2.18 2.98	2.11 2.85	2.05 2.75	2.00 2.66	1.97 2.59	1.93 2.53	1.88 2.43	1.83 2.35	1.76 2.23	1.72 2.15	1.67 2.06	1.61 1.96	1.58 1.90	1.52 1.82	1.50 1.78	1.46 1.71	1.43 1.66	1.41 1.64
60	4.00 7.08	3.15 4.98	2.76 4.13	2.52 3.65	2.37 3.34	2.25 3.12	2.17 2.95	2.10 2.82	2.04 2.72	1.99 2.63	1.95 2.56	1.92 2.50	1.86 2.40	1.81 2.32	1.75 2.20	1.70 2.12	1.65 2.03	1.59 1.93	1.56 1.87	1.50 1.79	1.48 1.74	1.44 1.68	1.41 1.63	1.39 1.60
65	3.99 7.04	3.14 4.95	2.75 4.10	2.51 3.62	2.36 3.31	2.24 3.09	2.15 2.93	2.08 2.79	2.02 2.70	1.98 2.61	1.94 2.54	1.90 2.47	1.85 2.37	1.80 2.30	1.73 2.18	1.68 2.09	1.63 2.00	1.57 1.90	1.54 1.84	1.49 1.76	1.46 1.71	1.42 1.64	1.39 1.60	1.37 1.56
70	3.98 7.01	3.13 4.92	2.74 4.08	2.50 3.60	2.35 3.29	2.23 3.07	2.14 2.91	2.07 2.77	2.01 2.67	1.97 2.59	1.93 2.51	1.89 2.45	1.84 2.35	1.79 2.28	1.72 2.15	1.67 2.07	1.62 1.98	1.56 1.88	1.53 1.82	1.47 1.74	1.45 1.69	1.40 1.62	1.37 1.56	1.35 1.53
80	3.96 6.96	3.11 4.88	2.72 4.04	2.48 3.56	2.33 3.25	2.21 3.04	2.12 2.87	2.05 2.74	1.99 2.64	1.95 2.55	1.91 2.48	1.88 2.41	1.82 2.32	1.77 2.24	1.70 2.11	1.65 2.03	1.60 1.94	1.54 1.84	1.51 1.78	1.45 1.70	1.42 1.65	1.38 1.57	1.35 1.52	1.32 1.49
100	3.94 6.90	3.09 4.82	2.70 3.98	2.46 3.51	2.30 3.20	2.19 2.99	2.10 2.82	2.03 2.69	1.97 2.59	1.92 2.51	1.88 2.43	1.85 2.36	1.79 2.26	1.75 2.19	1.68 2.06	1.63 1.98	1.57 1.89	1.51 1.79	1.48 1.73	1.42 1.64	1.39 1.59	1.34 1.51	1.30 1.46	1.28 1.43
125	3.92 6.84	3.07 4.78	2.68 3.94	2.44 3.47	2.29 3.17	2.17 2.95	2.08 2.79	2.01 2.65	1.95 2.56	1.90 2.47	1.86 2.40	1.83 2.33	1.77 2.23	1.72 2.15	1.65 2.03	1.60 1.94	1.55 1.85	1.49 1.75	1.45 1.68	1.39 1.59	1.36 1.54	1.31 1.46	1.27 1.40	1.25 1.37
150	3.91 6.81	3.06 4.75	2.67 3.91	2.43 3.44	2.27 3.13	2.16 2.92	2.07 2.76	2.00 2.62	1.94 2.53	1.89 2.44	1.85 2.37	1.82 2.30	1.76 2.20	1.71 2.12	1.64 2.00	1.59 1.91	1.54 1.83	1.47 1.72	1.44 1.66	1.37 1.56	1.34 1.51	1.29 1.43	1.25 1.37	1.22 1.33
200	3.89 6.76	3.04 4.71	2.65 3.88	2.41 3.41	2.26 3.11	2.14 2.90	2.05 2.73	1.98 2.60	1.92 2.50	1.87 2.41	1.83 2.34	1.80 2.28	1.74 2.17	1.69 2.09	1.62 1.97	1.57 1.88	1.52 1.79	1.45 1.69	1.42 1.62	1.35 1.53	1.32 1.48	1.26 1.39	1.22 1.33	1.19 1.28
400	3.86 6.70	3.02 4.66	2.62 3.83	2.39 3.36	2.23 3.06	2.12 2.85	2.03 2.69	1.96 2.55	1.90 2.46	1.85 2.37	1.81 2.29	1.78 2.23	1.72 2.12	1.67 2.04	1.60 1.92	1.54 1.84	1.49 1.74	1.42 1.64	1.38 1.57	1.32 1.47	1.28 1.42	1.22 1.32	1.16 1.24	1.13 1.19
1,000	3.85 6.66	3.00 4.62	2.61 3.80	2.38 3.34	2.22 3.04	2.10 2.82	2.02 2.66	1.95 2.53	1.89 2.43	1.84 2.34	1.80 2.26	1.76 2.20	1.70 2.09	1.65 2.01	1.58 1.89	1.53 1.81	1.47 1.71	1.41 1.61	1.36 1.54	1.30 1.44	1.26 1.38	1.19 1.28	1.13 1.19	1.08 1.11
∞	3.84 6.64	2.99 4.60	2.60 3.78	2.37 3.32	2.21 3.02	2.09 2.80	2.01 2.64	1.94 2.51	1.88 2.41	1.83 2.32	1.79 2.24	1.75 2.18	1.69 2.07	1.64 1.99	1.57 1.87	1.52 1.79	1.46 1.69	1.40 1.59	1.35 1.52	1.28 1.41	1.24 1.36	1.17 1.25	1.11 1.15	1.00 1.00

DEGREES OF FREEDOM FOR DENOMINATOR

Studentized Range Values (q)

The following table presents the Studentized range values (q) for overall alpha levels of .05 and .01 for a set of multiple comparisons. The values in the column headed "df for denominator" represent the degrees of freedom within when a between-subjects design is used and the degrees of freedom error when a repeated measures design is used. The values in the column headed "Alpha" represent overall alpha levels of .05 and .01 for each number of degrees of freedom within or degrees of freedom error. The values at the top of the table under the heading "k = Number of Levels of the Independent Variable" represent the number of levels of the independent variable of interest. For example, the Studentized range value (q) for $df_{\text{WITHIN}} = 12$, an overall alpha level of .05, and $k = 3$ (that is, an independent variable that has three levels) is 3.77.

Abridged from Table 29 in E. S. Pearson & H. O. Hartley (Eds.), *Biometrika Tables for Statisticians, vol. 1*, Second Edition. Copyright ©1958 Cambridge University Press. Reproduced with the kind permission of the editors and trustees of *Biometrika*.

df for denominator	Alpha	*k* = Number of Levels of the Independent Variable									
		2	3	4	5	6	7	8	9	10	11
5	.05	3.64	4.60	5.22	5.67	6.03	6.33	6.58	6.80	6.99	7.17
	.01	5.70	6.98	7.80	8.42	8.91	9.32	9.67	9.97	10.24	10.48
6	.05	3.46	4.34	4.90	5.30	5.63	5.90	6.12	6.32	6.49	6.65
	.01	5.24	6.33	7.03	7.56	7.97	8.32	8.61	8.87	9.10	9.30
7	.05	3.34	4.16	4.68	5.06	5.36	5.61	5.82	6.00	6.16	6.30
	.01	4.95	5.92	6.54	7.01	7.37	7.68	7.94	8.17	8.37	8.55
8	.05	3.26	4.04	4.53	4.89	5.17	5.40	5.60	5.77	5.92	6.05
	.01	4.75	5.64	6.20	6.62	6.96	7.24	7.47	7.68	7.86	8.03
9	.05	3.20	3.95	4.41	4.76	5.02	5.24	5.43	5.59	5.74	5.87
	.01	4.60	5.43	5.96	6.35	6.66	6.91	7.13	7.33	7.49	7.65
10	.05	3.15	3.88	4.33	4.65	4.91	5.12	5.30	5.46	5.60	5.72
	.01	4.48	5.27	5.77	6.14	6.43	6.67	6.87	7.05	7.21	7.36
11	.05	3.11	3.82	4.26	4.57	4.82	5.03	5.20	5.35	5.49	5.61
	.01	4.39	5.15	5.62	5.97	6.25	6.48	6.67	6.84	6.99	7.13
12	.05	3.08	3.77	4.20	4.51	4.75	4.95	5.12	5.27	5.39	5.51
	.01	4.32	5.05	5.50	5.84	6.10	6.32	6.51	6.67	6.81	6.94
13	.05	3.06	3.73	4.15	4.45	4.69	4.88	5.05	5.19	5.32	5.43
	.01	4.26	4.96	5.40	5.73	5.98	6.19	6.37	6.53	6.67	6.79
14	.05	3.03	3.70	4.11	4.41	4.64	4.83	4.99	5.13	5.25	5.36
	.01	4.21	4.89	5.32	5.63	5.88	6.08	6.26	6.41	6.54	6.66
15	.05	3.01	3.67	4.08	4.37	4.59	4.78	4.94	5.08	5.20	5.31
	.01	4.17	4.84	5.25	5.56	5.80	5.99	6.16	6.31	6.44	6.55
16	.05	3.00	3.65	4.05	4.33	4.56	4.74	4.90	5.03	5.15	5.26
	.01	4.13	4.79	5.19	5.49	5.72	5.92	6.08	6.22	6.35	6.46
17	.05	2.98	3.63	4.02	4.30	4.52	4.70	4.86	4.99	5.11	5.21
	.01	4.10	4.74	5.14	5.43	5.66	5.85	6.01	6.15	6.27	6.38
18	.05	2.97	3.61	4.00	4.28	4.49	4.67	4.82	4.96	5.07	5.17
	.01	4.07	4.70	5.09	5.38	5.60	5.79	5.94	6.08	6.20	6.31
19	.05	2.96	3.59	3.98	4.25	4.47	4.65	4.79	4.92	5.04	5.14
	.01	4.05	4.67	5.05	5.33	5.55	5.73	5.89	6.02	6.14	6.25
20	.05	2.95	3.58	3.96	4.23	4.45	4.62	4.77	4.90	5.01	5.11
	.01	4.02	4.64	5.02	5.29	5.51	5.69	5.84	5.97	6.09	6.19
24	.05	2.92	3.53	3.90	4.17	4.37	4.54	4.68	4.81	4.92	5.01
	.01	3.96	4.55	4.91	5.17	5.37	5.54	5.69	5.81	5.92	6.02
30	.05	2.89	3.49	3.85	4.10	4.30	4.46	4.60	4.72	4.82	4.92
	.01	3.89	4.45	4.80	5.05	5.24	5.40	5.54	5.65	5.76	5.85
40	.05	2.86	3.44	3.79	4.04	4.23	4.39	4.52	4.63	4.73	4.82
	.01	3.82	4.37	4.70	4.93	5.11	5.26	5.39	5.50	5.60	5.69
60	.05	2.83	3.40	3.74	3.98	4.16	4.31	4.44	4.55	4.65	4.73
	.01	3.76	4.28	4.59	4.82	4.99	5.13	5.25	5.36	5.45	5.53
120	.05	2.80	3.36	3.68	3.92	4.10	4.24	4.36	4.47	4.56	4.64
	.01	3.70	4.20	4.50	4.71	4.87	5.01	5.12	5.21	5.30	5.37
∞	.05	2.77	3.31	3.63	3.86	4.03	4.17	4.29	4.39	4.47	4.55
	.01	3.64	4.12	4.40	4.60	4.76	4.88	4.99	5.08	5.16	5.23

df for denominator	Alpha	k = Number of Levels of the Independent Variable								
		12	13	14	15	16	17	18	19	20
5	.05	7.32	7.47	7.60	7.72	7.83	7.93	8.03	8.12	8.21
	.01	10.70	10.89	11.08	11.24	11.40	11.55	11.68	11.81	11.93
6	.05	6.79	6.92	7.03	7.14	7.24	7.34	7.43	7.51	7.59
	.01	9.48	9.65	9.81	9.95	10.08	10.21	10.32	10.43	10.54
7	.05	6.43	6.55	6.66	6.76	6.85	6.94	7.02	7.10	7.17
	.01	8.71	8.86	9.00	9.12	9.24	9.35	9.46	9.55	9.65
8	.05	6.18	6.29	6.39	6.48	6.57	6.65	6.73	6.80	6.87
	.01	8.18	8.31	8.44	8.55	8.66	8.76	8.85	8.94	9.03
9	.05	5.98	6.09	6.19	6.28	6.36	6.44	6.51	6.58	6.64
	.01	7.78	7.91	8.03	8.13	8.23	8.33	8.41	8.49	8.57
10	.05	5.83	5.93	6.03	6.11	6.19	6.27	6.34	6.40	6.47
	.01	7.49	7.60	7.71	7.81	7.91	7.99	8.08	8.15	8.23
11	.05	5.71	5.81	5.90	5.98	6.06	6.13	6.20	6.27	6.33
	.01	7.25	7.36	7.46	7.56	7.65	7.73	7.81	7.88	7.95
12	.05	5.61	5.71	5.80	5.88	5.95	6.02	6.09	6.15	6.21
	.01	7.06	7.17	7.26	7.36	7.44	7.52	7.59	7.66	7.73
13	.05	5.53	5.63	5.71	5.79	5.86	5.93	5.99	6.05	6.11
	.01	6.90	7.01	7.10	7.19	7.27	7.35	7.42	7.48	7.55
14	.05	5.46	5.55	5.64	5.71	5.79	5.85	5.91	5.97	6.03
	.01	6.77	6.87	6.96	7.05	7.13	7.20	7.27	7.33	7.39
15	.05	5.40	5.49	5.57	5.65	5.72	5.78	5.85	5.90	5.96
	.01	6.66	6.76	6.84	6.93	7.00	7.07	7.14	7.20	7.26
16	.05	5.35	5.44	5.52	5.59	5.66	5.73	5.79	5.84	5.90
	.01	6.56	6.66	6.74	6.82	6.90	6.97	7.03	7.09	7.15
17	.05	5.31	5.39	5.47	5.54	5.61	5.67	5.73	5.79	5.84
	.01	6.48	6.57	6.66	6.73	6.81	6.87	6.94	7.00	7.05
18	.05	5.27	5.35	5.43	5.50	5.57	5.63	5.69	5.74	5.79
	.01	6.41	6.50	6.58	6.65	6.73	6.79	6.85	6.91	6.97
19	.05	5.23	5.31	5.39	5.46	5.53	5.59	5.65	5.70	5.75
	.01	6.34	6.43	6.51	6.58	6.65	6.72	6.78	6.84	6.89
20	.05	5.20	5.28	5.36	5.43	5.49	5.55	5.61	5.66	5.71
	.01	6.28	6.37	6.45	6.52	6.59	6.65	6.71	6.77	6.82
24	.05	5.10	5.18	5.25	5.32	5.38	5.44	5.49	5.55	5.59
	.01	6.11	6.19	6.26	6.33	6.39	6.45	6.51	6.56	6.61
30	.05	5.00	5.08	5.15	5.21	5.27	5.33	5.38	5.43	5.47
	.01	5.93	6.01	6.08	6.14	6.20	6.26	6.31	6.36	6.41
40	.05	4.90	4.98	5.04	5.11	5.16	5.22	5.27	5.31	5.36
	.01	5.76	5.83	5.90	5.96	6.02	6.07	6.12	6.16	6.21
60	.05	4.81	4.88	4.94	5.00	5.06	5.11	5.15	5.20	5.24
	.01	5.60	5.67	5.73	5.78	5.84	5.89	5.93	5.97	6.01
120	.05	4.71	4.78	4.84	4.90	4.95	5.00	5.04	5.09	5.13
	.01	5.44	5.50	5.56	5.61	5.66	5.71	5.75	5.79	5.83
∞	.05	4.62	4.68	4.74	4.80	4.85	4.89	4.93	4.97	5.01
	.01	5.29	5.35	5.40	5.45	5.49	5.54	5.57	5.61	5.65

Critical Values for the Pearson Correlation Coefficient (*r*)

The following table presents critical values for the Pearson correlation coefficient (*r*) for directional (one-tailed) and nondirectional (two-tailed) tests of the null hypothesis that $\rho = 0$. The column headed "*df*" lists the degrees of freedom for the distribution of interest. The entries in the table are the *r* values that define the rejection regions.

The values .05, .025, .01, and .005 at the top of the table under the heading "Level of Significance for Directional Test" represent alpha levels for directional tests. For example, the critical value of *r* for *df* = 25 and an alpha level of .05 for a directional test that focuses on the upper tail of the distribution (that is, for alternative hypotheses of the form $\rho > 0$) is +.323. Since the distribution is symmetrical, the critical value of *r* for a directional test that focuses on the lower tail of the distribution (that is, for null hypotheses of the form $\rho < 0$) is −.323.

The values .10, .05, .02, and .01 under the heading "Level of Significance for Nondirectional Test" represent alpha levels for nondirectional tests. For example, the critical values of *r* for a nondirectional test for *df* = 25 and an alpha level of .05 are ±.381.

---

df	Level of Significance for Directional Test			
	.05	.025	.01	.005
	Level of Significance for Nondirectional Test			
	.10	.05	.02	.01
1	.988	.997	.9995	.9999
2	.900	.950	.980	.990
3	.805	.878	.934	.959
4	.729	.811	.882	.917
5	.669	.754	.833	.874
6	.622	.707	.789	.834
7	.582	.666	.750	.798
8	.549	.632	.716	.765
9	.521	.602	.685	.735
10	.497	.576	.658	.708
11	.476	.553	.634	.684
12	.458	.532	.612	.661
13	.441	.514	.592	.641
14	.426	.497	.574	.623
15	.412	.482	.558	.606
16	.400	.468	.542	.590
17	.389	.456	.528	.575
18	.378	.444	.516	.561
19	.369	.433	.503	.549
20	.360	.423	.492	.537
21	.352	.413	.482	.526
22	.344	.404	.472	.515
23	.337	.396	.462	.505
24	.330	.388	.453	.496
25	.323	.381	.445	.487
26	.317	.374	.437	.479
27	.311	.367	.430	.471
28	.306	.361	.423	.463
29	.301	.355	.416	.456
30	.296	.349	.409	.449
35	.275	.325	.381	.418
40	.257	.304	.358	.393
45	.243	.288	.338	.372
50	.231	.273	.322	.354
60	.211	.250	.295	.325
70	.195	.232	.274	.303
80	.183	.217	.256	.283
90	.173	.205	.242	.267
100	.164	.195	.230	.254

Answers to Selected Exercises

Chapter 1

2. a. a constant because there are always 24 hours in a day
   b. a variable because different people have different attitudes toward abortion
   c. a constant because all presidents of the United States must be born in the United States
   d. a constant because a number divided by itself always equals 1.00
   e. a variable because different total numbers of points are scored in different football games
   f. a variable because different months have different numbers of days

3. a. quantitative   d. quantitative
   b. qualitative   e. qualitative
   c. quantitative   f. qualitative

4. The independent variable is children's preference for aggressive television shows. The dependent variable is the peer ratings of aggression. Both are quantitative.

5. The independent variable is the type of occupation, which is qualitative. The dependent variable is perceptions of occupational prestige, which is quantitative.

10. a. discrete   c. discrete
    b. continuous   d. continuous

11. a. 21,384.105 and 21,384.115   c. 12.5 and 13.5
    b. .6885 and .6895   d. 12.95 and 13.05
                                    e. 12.995 and 13.005

13. The newspaper's sample is probably not a representative sample of the community in general because it represents only those people who read the newspaper and who were willing to take the time and trouble to send in a ballot. This casts doubt on the validity of the newspaper's conclusion about the election.

16. You probably found that only a very small number of individuals were selected to participate in both samples. This suggests that every member of a population has an equal chance of being selected when random sampling is used and, thus, that random sampling will tend to yield representative samples.

19. .05

21. a. ΣX
    b. $\Sigma_{i=3}^{5} X_i^2$
    c. ΣX^2
    d. $(\Sigma Y)^2$
    e. $\Sigma_{i=1}^{3} Y_i$

22. a. 4.893   h. .396
    b. 8.975   i. 1.000
    c. 1.415   j. 3.667
    d. 4.145   k. 12.254
    e. 6.245   l. 9.724
    f. 2.616   m. 1.995
    g. 6.316   n. 2.005

24. Calculations for the original scores:
    a. 19.96
    b. 398.34
    c. 80.06
    Calculations for the rounded scores:
    a. 19.98
    b. 399.20
    c. 80.24
    The difference between the two sets of results is because the original scores were to four decimal places and the rounded scores were to two decimal places. The answers based on the original scores are thus more precise.

26. b   33. a
28. c   35. d
31. a

Chapter 2

1.–2. Sick days	f	rf	%	cf	crf
8	2	.100	10.0	20	1.000
7	4	.200	20.0	18	.900
6	10	.500	50.0	14	.700
4	2	.100	10.0	4	.200
3	2	.100	10.0	2	.100

3. .100; 1.000; .900
4. .200; .300; .100
6. .100; .600; .900

7.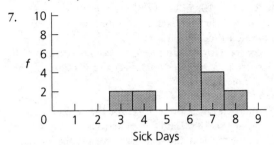

10.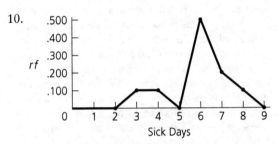

The shape of this graph is identical to the shape of the frequency polygon from Exercise 8.

12. In an ungrouped frequency table, each different score value is listed. In a grouped frequency table, scores are grouped together into intervals.

16.

Intelligence score	f
120–129	5
110–119	10
100–109	20
90–99	10
80–89	5

18. .700; .300; .300

20.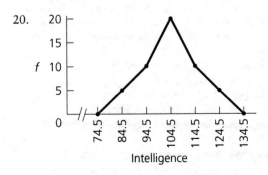

22.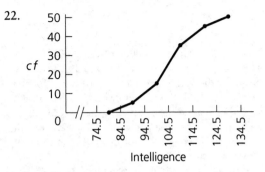

The similarity in shapes is because the cumulative frequency line will always remain level or increase as it moves from left to right.

28. The ordinate of a frequency graph should be presented such that its height at the demarcation for the highest frequency is approximately two-thirds to three-fourths the length of the abscissa. This helps to ensure a uniform, clearly interpretable presentation of graphed results.

30. A probability distribution is a distribution that represents the probabilities associated with all possible score values for a variable. The nature of probability distributions for qualitative variables and discrete quantitative variables is different from that for continuous variables because in the former case it is possible to list all possible values of the variable and their corresponding probabilities. Because the number of values that a continuous variable can have is, in principle, infinite, this is not possible for continuous variables. Instead, probabilities for continuous variables are conceptualized as the areas within the corresponding intervals of the density curve.

32.

Attitude	f	rf	cf	crf
5	370	.200	1,850	1.000
4	555	.300	1,480	.800
3	185	.100	925	.500
2	407	.220	740	.400
1	333	.180	333	.180

33. b   41. a
35. a   43. c
39. c
40. c

Chapter 3

3. 4.33

6. Mode = 0, median = 0.00, mean = 0.00

8. The mean for the first set of scores is 12.00; the mean for the second set is 15.00; the mean for the third set is 2.00. If a constant, k, is added to each score (X) in a set, the mean of the new set of scores will equal $\overline{X} + k$. If a constant is subtracted from each score in a set, the mean of the new set of scores will equal $\overline{X} - k$.

10. The mean for the first set of scores is 30.00; the mean for the second set is 90.00; the mean for the third set is 3.00. If each score (X) in a set is multiplied by a constant, k, the mean of the new set of scores will equal $k\overline{X}$. If each score in a set is divided by a constant, the mean of the new set of scores will equal $\overline{X}/k$.

11. The median for the first set of scores in Exercise 8 is 12; the median for the second set is 15; the median for the third set is 2. Adding a constant to or subtracting a constant from each score in a set has the same effects on the median as on the mean.

    The median for the first set of scores in Exercise 10 is 30; the median for the second set is 90; the median for the third set is 3.00. Multiplying or dividing each score in a set by a constant has the same effects on the median as on the mean.

    The above operations would have the same effects on the mode as on the mean and the median.

13. The mean is a poorer descriptor of central tendency for Set A. This is because the extreme score of 300 in Set A substantially adjusts (increases) the mean and thus leads to a distorted picture of the central tendency of the data.

15. The range is a misleading index of variability when there is an extreme score in a set of scores that are otherwise similar to one another.

18. 10.00

20. All three measures of variability must equal 0 because there is no variability when all of the scores are the same.

21. The standard deviation is more "interpretable" than the variance because it represents an average deviation from the mean in the original unit of measurement. In contrast, the variance is in terms of squared deviation units.

23. The sum of squares equals 104.00 using both approaches. Typically, it is more efficient to apply the computational formula than the defining formula because the computational formula requires fewer steps.

24. Range = 10; SS = 144.95; s^2 = 6.90; s = 2.63

26. The variance for each set of scores is 2.00, and the standard deviation for each set is 1.41. Adding a constant to or subtracting a constant from each score in a set does not affect the variance or the standard deviation.

28. For the first set of scores, the variance is 2.00 and the standard deviation is 1.41; for the second set, the variance is 18.00 and the standard deviation is 4.24; for the third set, the variance is .50 and the standard deviation is .71. If each score in a set is multiplied by a constant, k, the variance of the new set of scores will equal the variance of the old set of scores multiplied by k^2, and the standard deviation will equal the standard deviation of the old set of scores multiplied by k. If each score in a set is divided by a constant, the variance of the new set of scores will equal the variance of the old set of scores divided by k^2, and the standard deviation will equal the standard deviation of the old set of scores divided by k.

29. One example of such scores is:

Set A	Set B
0	9
5	10
10	10
15	10
20	11

Although the mean for both sets of scores is 10.00, the standard deviation is 7.07 for Set A and .63 for Set B.

31. Considering the mean score across all participants, the speed estimates are quite accurate (28.67 compared with the actual speed of 30). However, the relatively large standard deviation (7.74) indicates that the individual estimates are not all that accurate.

33. The consultant should be fired: Standard deviations cannot be negative.

36. The first set of scores is positively skewed, as the three measures of central tendency all take on different values and the mean is greater than the median. The second set of scores is negatively skewed, as the three measures of central tendency all take on different values and the mean is smaller than the

median. The third set of scores is not skewed, as equal numbers of scores occur above and below the mean, as indicated by the fact that the mean is also the median.

39. b   46. b
41. a   48. b
43. d

Chapter 4

2. a. 2.99   d. 4.25
   b. 3.75   e. 5.52
   c. 4.00   f. 7.67
4. a. 5.20   c. 74.90
   b. 20.20   d. 94.40
9. a. .62   d. .03
   b. 1.00   e. −1.46
   c. −.36   f. 1.43
11. −1.23
13. A positive standard score indicates that the original score is greater than the mean. A negative standard score indicates that the original score is less than the mean.
14. 0; 1.00
16. John's performance on the English exam was 1.00 standard deviation above the mean, and his performance on the math exam was 6.67 standard deviations above the mean. Hence, John's performance was better (relative to his classmates') on the math exam.
18. One situation is determining the relative abilities on a given task of people of different ages. For instance, the bowling averages of a child and an adult can be compared in this manner.
22. a. .9913   e. .4798
    b. .1210   f. .3550
    c. .1210   g. .3550
    d. .4798   h. .7850
23. a. .1587   d. .9836
    b. .1587   e. .5000
    c. .7865   f. .7257
25. The standard score that corresponds to a galvanic skin response score of 61.40 is 4.00. Because only .003% of the standard scores in a normal distribution are 4.00 or greater, the person in question displayed an extreme galvanic skin response when asked the question about the critical issue. The implication is that he is lying.
27. a. 128.60 d. 85.00
    b. 75.60   e. 115.90
    c. 100.00 f. 107.50

28. a. 102.20 d. 109.80
    b. 108.22 e. 90.20
    c. 100.00
30. a. 58.7   d. 34.4
    b. 70.0   e. 50
    c. 65.6   f. 90.4
31. b   40. d
35. b   41. c
37. d   44. a
38. c   45. c

Chapter 5

2. The slope indicates the number of units variable Y changes when variable X changes by 1 unit.
5. 3.00 units; 6.00 units; 21.00 units
6. The magnitude of a correlation coefficient indicates the degree to which two variables approximate a linear relationship.
8. a. +.37   d. +.26
   b. −.37   e. −.44
   c. −.76   f. +.61
9. One example of such a scatterplot is:

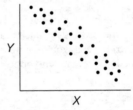

11. Two variables that are probably positively correlated are calorie consumption and weight gain.
13. .18
16. Two variables that are probably (positively) correlated but that are not causally related are the number of automobiles in a household and the number of television sets in a household. The correlation between these two variables is probably attributable to such factors as the number of occupants and their income levels.
18. The general form of the regression equation is $\hat{Y} = a + bX$. This differs from the linear model in that the values yielded by $a + bX$ are predicted Y scores rather than actual Y scores.
19. The values are defined such that the sum of the squared discrepancies between individuals' actual Y scores and their predicted Y scores based on the regression equation is minimized.
20. $\hat{Y} = 5.00 + .20X$
21. 5.60; 6.20; 5.40
25. 2.41

27. If two variables are related in a curvilinear fashion, restricting the range of variable X tends to increase the magnitude of the observed correlation coefficient. If two variables are linearly related, the effect of restricting the range of one of them is often to reduce the magnitude of the observed correlation coefficient.

31. b	38. a
33. a	41. c
35. b	43. a
36. c	

Chapter 6

2. 180
4. 350
5. .514; .486; .500; .500
6. .343; .686; .657; .314
7. Being a man (event A) and favoring the ERA (event B) are not independent because the probability of being a man [p(being a man) = .500] is not the same as the conditional probability of being a man, given that one favors the ERA [p(being a man|favors the ERA) = .333], that is, $p(A) \neq p(A|B)$.
8. .171; .157
9. Four joint probabilities can be calculated: (1) being a man who favors the ERA, (2) being a man who opposes the ERA, (3) being a woman who favors the ERA, and (4) being a woman who opposes the ERA.
10. .843; .829
17. .486
20. .516

23.	a. 60	d. 120
	b. 720	e. 24
	c. 12	

24. 5! equals 120, which is the same answer as for d of Exercise 23. 4! equals 24, which is the same answer as for e of Exercise 23. From this, we can generalize that $_nP_n = n!$.

26.	a. 10	d. 1
	b. 6	e. 1
	c. 6	

28. 216

30.	a. .010	d. .010
	b. .044	e. .044
	c. .172	

33. The correspondence between the binomial and normal distributions is influenced by the number of trials (n) and the probability of success (p). The correspondence improves as n increases and as p becomes closer to .500.

34. $\mu = 90.00; \sigma = 6.00$
36. A score of 30 translates into a z score of 2.50. From Appendix B, the probability of obtaining a z score of 2.50 or greater is .0062. Because .0062 is less than the criterion value of .05, the researcher should conclude that the psychotherapeutic approach is more effective than no treatment in helping individuals to recover from their symptoms.

38. c	47. a
40. c	48. a
42. a	
44. b	

Chapter 7

2. Sampling error refers to the fact that values of sample statistics are likely to differ from values of their corresponding population parameters because they are based on only a portion of the overall population. The amount of sampling error can be represented as the difference between the value of a sample statistic and the value of the corresponding population parameter.
3. An unbiased estimator is a statistic whose average (mean) over all possible random samples of a given size equals the value of the parameter. A biased estimator is a statistic whose average over all possible random samples of a given size does not equal the value of the parameter.
6. The variance and standard deviation estimates (2.67 and 1.63, respectively) are larger than the variance and standard deviation for the sample (2.50 and 1.58, respectively).
8. Degrees of freedom are the number of pieces of statistical information that are independent of one another. There are $N - 1$ degrees of freedom associated with a sum of squares around a sample mean because, given all but one deviation score for a distribution of scores, the last deviation score is determined by the other $N - 1$ deviation scores.
10. A sampling distribution of the mean is a theoretical distribution consisting of the means for all possible random samples of a given size that can be drawn from a population. A frequency distribution, in contrast, is concerned with the frequency with which score values occur within a set of scores.
11. The central limit theorem addresses the mean, the standard deviation, and the shape of a sampling distribution of the mean.

13.

Sample	Sample mean
2, 2	2.00
2, 4	3.00
2, 6	4.00
4, 2	3.00
4, 4	4.00
4, 6	5.00
6, 2	4.00
6, 4	5.00
6, 6	6.00

Sum = 36.00

$$\text{Mean} = \frac{36.00}{9} = 4.00$$

The mean across the sample means is equal to the population mean because $\mu = (2 + 4 + 6)/3 = 4.00$. This illustrates the fact that, as stated in the central limit theorem, the mean of a sampling distribution of the mean is always equal to the population mean.

15. A standard deviation of a set of raw scores represents an average deviation from the mean of the distribution. A standard error of the mean is the standard deviation of a sampling distribution of the mean and represents an average deviation of the sample means from the population mean.

17. A standard error of the mean of 0 indicates that the means of all samples drawn from the relevant population are equal to the population mean.

18. A standard error of the mean of 0 indicates that there is no variability in the scores in the population—that is, that all of the scores are the same and σ therefore equals 0.

19. The sample mean for a random sample of size 30 drawn from population A is probably a better estimator of its population mean than is the sample mean for a random sample of size 30 drawn from population B because, as indexed by its smaller standard deviation, there is less variability in population A than in population B. Consequently, the standard error of the mean for population A (.91) is smaller than the standard error of the mean for population B (1.28), thus indicating that, on average, means for samples of a given size drawn from population A will be closer to the true population mean than will means for samples of the same size drawn from population B.

21. $\overline{X} = 5.00; \hat{s}_{\overline{X}} = .41$

26. The mean is usually preferred to the mode and the median because, given the same population, the sampling distribution of the mean will show less variability (that is, it will have a smaller standard error) than either the sampling distribution of the median or the sampling distribution of the mode.

27. b

30. d

31. b

34. a

36. d

38. b

39. b

Chapter 8

2. Assuming that the null hypothesis is true allows us to compare the observed result of a statistical test with an expected result and, thus, to make inferences about population values from sample values.

4. $H_0: \mu = \$100$
   $H_1: \mu \neq \$100$

5. $z = 1.79$

6. Because the observed z score of 1.79 is neither less than the negative critical value of -1.96 nor greater than the positive critical value of $+1.96$, we fail to reject the null hypothesis. We cannot conclude that the actual value of μ differs from 4.

9. This is because, due to sampling error, we can never unambiguously conclude that the true population mean is equal to any one specific value based on sample data.

11. The probability of a Type I error is equal to alpha because if the null hypothesis is true, the null hypothesis will be incorrectly rejected any time the observed value of the test statistic falls in the rejection region, and the probability of this occurring is equal to alpha.

12. Power is equal to 1 minus the probability of a Type II error because if the probability of making a Type II error by failing to reject a false null hypothesis is equal to β, the probability of making a correct decision by rejecting the null hypothesis under this circumstance (power) must be equal to $1 - \beta$.

13. Power decreases as alpha is set at a lower (more conservative) level because the lower the alpha level, the lower is the probability of rejecting the null hypothesis. Thus, when the null hypothesis is false, the probability of detecting a difference between the hypothesized population mean and the actual population mean (power) decreases as does alpha.

15. The terms *statistically significant* and *statistically nonsignificant* emphasize the statistical nature of a conclusion—that is, whether or not the null hypothesis was rejected. A statistically significant result may or may not have important practical implications.

18. a. ±2.093   d. ±2.262
    b. +1.729   e. +1.833
    c. −1.729   f. −1.833

19. a. The critical values of *t* for an alpha level of .05 and 9,999 degrees of freedom are approximately ±1.960. Because the observed *t* score of 10.00 exceeds the positive critical value, we reject the null hypothesis.

    b. The critical values of *t* for an alpha level of .05 and 99 degrees of freedom are approximately ±1.987, as determined through interpolation. Because the observed *t* score of 1.00 does not exceed the positive critical value, we fail to reject the null hypothesis.

    c. The observed *t* score of 5.00 exceeds the positive critical value of approximately ±1.987 for an alpha level of .05 and 99 degrees of freedom, so we reject the null hypothesis.

    The null hypothesis is rejected in part **a** but not in part **b** because the *t* test in part **a** is based on a larger number of cases. The null hypothesis is rejected in part **c** but not in part **b** because the *t* test in part **c** is based on a smaller standard deviation estimate.

23. The 95% confidence interval is 72.44 to 76.36. The 99% confidence interval is 71.82 to 76.98.

24. The 95% confidence interval is 72.60 to 76.20. The 99% confidence interval is 72.03 to 76.77. The effect of increasing *N* is to decrease the width of the intervals.

26. The 95% confidence interval is 116.98 to 125.02. The 99% confidence interval is 115.58 to 126.42.

30. c   37. d
31. c   39. c
33. a   41. a
36. a

43.   Results
    A one-sample *t* test that compared the mean number of children in the sample (*M* = 2.96, *SD* = 1.81) with a hypothesized reproduction rate of 2.11 was found to be statistically significant at an alpha level of .05, *t*(24) = 2.34, *p* < .05, suggesting that Catholics are reproducing at a greater than zero population growth rate. The 95% confidence interval for the mean was 2.21 to 3.71.

Chapter 9

2. The independent variable is race. This study involves an observational research strategy.

3. The independent variable is the noise level. This study involves an experimental research strategy.

6. A control group is a group in an experiment that is not exposed to the independent variable. The advantage of including a control group is that it provides a baseline for evaluating the effect of the experimental manipulation.

9. One limitation of random assignment is that it is not applicable when an observational research strategy is used. A second limitation is that it does not guarantee that the research groups will not differ beforehand on the dependent variable.

10. Sampling error can be reduced by increasing the sample sizes for the groups being studied or by defining the research groups such that the variability of the scores in each population is relatively small.

12. Disturbance variables are variables that are unrelated to the independent variable but that affect the dependent variable. They can be controlled by holding a variable constant.

13. One advantage of within-subjects designs is that they are more economical in terms of participants. A second advantage is that they offer better control of confounding variables related to individual differences. A potential problem with within-subjects designs is that carry-over effects can occur.

14. The independent variables in the studies described in Exercises 2 (race), 3 (noise level), and 5 (gender) are all between-subjects in nature. The independent variable in the study described in Exercise 4 (observer status) is within-subjects in nature.

16. Robustness is the extent to which conclusions drawn on the basis of a statistical test are unaffected by violations of the assumptions underlying the test. Robustness is important because when a test is robust to violation of an assumption, it is appropriate to apply that test even when that assumption is violated.

19. The three factors that influence the robustness of a statistical test are sample size, the degree of violation of distributional assumptions, and the form of the violation of distributional assumptions.

23. a

26. b

27. c

29. b

31. a

32. b

34. a

Chapter 10

2. The mean of a sampling distribution of the difference between two independent means will always equal the difference between the relevant population means.

3. The independent groups t test assumes that the two population variances are homogeneous. Thus, our goal is to estimate σ^2, the variance of both populations. By pooling the variance estimates from the two samples, we increase the degrees of freedom on which the estimate of σ^2 is based and thereby obtain a better estimate.

4. $\hat{s}^2_{pooled} = 5.48; \hat{s}_{\overline{X}_1 - \overline{X}_2} = .98$

5. a. .21

   b. .23

   c. .31

   d. This is because there is more variability in a sampling distribution of the difference between two independent means than in the corresponding sampling distributions of the mean. For instance, if the smallest sample mean in each of two sampling distributions of the mean were 2.00 and the largest sample mean were 7.00, the range in each case would be $7.00 - 2.00 = 5.00$. However, the smallest mean difference in the sampling distribution of the difference between two independent means based on the two distributions of sample means would be $2.00 - 7.00 = -5.00$, and the largest mean difference would be $7.00 - 2.00 = 5.00$, a range of $5.00 - (-5.00) = 10.00$. Because the estimated standard error of the difference and the estimated standard errors of the mean also reflect variability within the corresponding sampling distributions, it follows that, as with the ranges, the former measure will always be larger than the latter measures.

8. a. ±2.101

   b. +1.734

   c. ±2.048

   d. +1.701

   e. ±2.021

   f. −1.684

10. The critical values of t for an alpha level of .05 and 8 degrees of freedom are ±2.306. Because the observed t score of 6.71 exceeds the positive critical value, we reject the null hypothesis and conclude that there is a relationship between gender and discriminatory attitudes.

11. $SS_{TOTAL} = 26.50$

12. $T_M = 1.50; T_F = -1.50$

13.

Gender	$\overline{X}_n$
Male	6.50
Male	5.50
Male	5.50
Male	5.50
Male	4.50
Female	6.50
Female	5.50
Female	5.50
Female	5.50
Female.	4.50

14. $SS_{ERROR} = 4.00; SS_{EXPLAINED} = 22.50$

15. The value of eta-squared is .85 using both Equation 10.10 and Equation 10.11. This represents a strong effect.

15. The 95% confidence interval is 1.97 to 4.03.

17. Men $(\overline{X} = 7.00)$ are significantly more discriminatory than women $(\overline{X} = 4.00)$.

26. The sum of squares total is equal to the sum of squares explained plus the sum of squares error. In other words, the total variability in the dependent variable, as represented by SS_{TOTAL}, can be partitioned into two components, one $(SS_{EXPLAINED})$ reflecting the influence of the independent variable and one (SS_{ERROR}) reflecting the influence of disturbance variables.

28. It is problematic because eta-squared is a biased estimator. Specifically, eta-squared tends to slightly overestimate the strength of the relationship in the population across random samples.

32. $n = 87$

36. c

39. d

40. b

42. a

43. b

44. c

45. d

47. b

48. a

49. a

52. b

55.
> **Results**
> An independent groups t test using an alpha level of .05 indicated that the cortex weight of rats will be greater when they are raised in an enriched environment $(M = 660.00$ mg, $SD = 24.15$ mg) than when they are raised in an isolated environment $(M = 626.00$ mg, $SD = 23.15$ mg), $t(12) = 2.69, p < .02$. As indexed by eta-squared, the strength of the relationship between the type of environment and cortex weight was .38. The

95% confidence interval for the mean difference was 6.45 to 61.55.

Chapter 11

3. a. ±2.056
   b. +1.706
   c. ±2.160
   d. −1.771

6. The rationale is that potential confounding variables will be evenly distributed across conditions and, thus, turned into disturbance variables.

7. This is because variability due to individual differences is extracted from the dependent variable as part of the correlated groups t test procedure. Because the degrees of freedom for the correlated groups test $(N - 1)$ are less than the degrees of freedom for the independent groups test $(n_1 + n_2 - 2)$, a correlated groups t test will not be more powerful than a corresponding independent groups t test when the correlation between scores in the two conditions is so close to 0 that the magnitude of the estimated standard errors is comparable for the two tests. This reflects the fact that the t distribution requires more extreme values of t in order to reject the null hypothesis as the degrees of freedom become smaller.

8. The critical values of t for an alpha level of .05 and 4 degrees of freedom are ±2.776. Because the observed t score of 3.77 exceeds the positive critical value, we reject the null hypothesis and conclude that there is a relationship between the amount of noise one is exposed to and learning scores.

9. The value of eta-squared is .78. This represents a strong effect.

10. The 95% confidence interval is 1.16 to 7.64.

11. Learning scores are significantly higher under quiet conditions ($\overline{X} = 13.00$) than under noisy conditions ($\overline{X} = 8.60$).

12. Analyzing the data as if the independent variable were between-subjects in nature, we find that the observed t score, $t(8) = 1.18$, does not exceed the positive critical value of +2.306, so we fail to reject the null hypothesis. The value of eta-squared in this instance is .15. This represents a moderate effect. The 95% confidence interval is −4.22 to 13.02.

The fact that eta-squared was .78 in the correlated groups case but only .15 in the independent groups case indicates that individual differences had a sizable effect on the dependent variable. The fact that the null hypothesis was rejected when a correlated groups t test was applied but not when an independent groups t test was applied illustrates the increased power of the statistical analysis when variability due to individual differences is extracted from the dependent variable and, thus, the advantage of within-subjects research designs.

17. See the table at the bottom of the page for the relevant calculations. The respective mean values are the same because we have extracted the effects of individual differences in their role as disturbance variables. Because disturbance variables are unrelated to the independent variable, the means will not be affected.

18. The observed value of t is −3.16. This is the same value obtained in Exercise 12.

19. Independent groups t test

20. Correlated groups t test

25. .60   33. c   40. b
28. b   36. b
29. a   38. a
32. b   39. b

41.   Results

The mean desirability ratings for the unchosen product before versus after choosing between the two options were compared for an alpha level of .05 using a correlated groups t test. This showed

Individual	X for time 1	X for time 2	$\overline{X}_i$	Nullified X for time 1	Nullified X for time 2
1	10	12	11.00	12.00	14.00
2	11	13	12.00	12.00	14.00
3	12	14	13.00	12.00	14.00
4	13	17	15.00	11.00	15.00
5	14	14	14.00	13.00	13.00
Mean	12.00	14.00	13.00	12.00	14.00

that the product in question was rated as significantly more desirable on the first occasion ($M = 6.00$, $SD = 1.49$) than on the second one ($M = 4.00$, $SD = 1.15$), $t(9) = 3.00$, $p < .02$. The strength of the relationship between the time of assessment and the ratings of product desirability was .50, as indexed by eta-squared. The 95% confidence interval was .49 to 3.51.

Chapter 12

2. The alternative hypothesis states that the population means in question are not all equal to one another. It cannot be summarized in a single mathematical statement because there are a number of ways in which three or more population means can pattern themselves so that they are not all equal.
3. Between-group variability concerns the differences between the mean scores in the various groups under study. Within-group variability concerns the variability of scores within each of the groups.
6. The F ratio, over the long run, will approach 1.00 when the null hypothesis is true. The F ratio, over the long run, will be greater than 1.00 when the null hypothesis is not true.
8. The value of the sum of squares within must be 0 because all scores within a given group are the same.
9. The mean square between is the sum of squares between divided by the degrees of freedom between. The mean square within is the sum of squares within divided by the degrees of freedom within.
11. a. 3.55   c. 3.35
    b. 3.24   d. 2.50

13.
Source	SS	df	MS	F
Between	30.00	2	15.00	5.62
Within	152.00	57	2.67	
Total	182.00	59		

16.
Null hypothesis tested	Absolute difference between sample means	Value of CD	Null hypothesis rejected?
$\mu_S = \mu_M$	$\|6.00 - 8.00\| = 2.00$	2.48	No
$\mu_S = \mu_D$	$\|6.00 - 10.00\| = 4.00$	2.48	Yes
$\mu_M = \mu_D$	$\|8.00 - 10.00\| = 2.00$	2.48	No

The nature of the relationship is such that divorced individuals ($\overline{X}_D = 10.00$) have more positive attitudes than single individuals ($\overline{X}_S = 6.00$). However, we cannot conclude that either divorced or single individuals differ in their divorce attitudes from married individuals ($\overline{X}_M = 8.00$).

17.
Source	SS	df	MS	F
Between	40.00	2	20.00	10.00
Within	24.00	12	2.00	
Total	64.00	14		

The critical value of F for an alpha level of .05 and 2 and 12 degrees of freedom is 3.88. Because the observed F value of 10.00 exceeds the critical value, we reject the null hypothesis and conclude that there is a relationship between the model of car and repair records.

18. The value of eta-squared is .62 using both Equations 12.15 and 12.16. This represents a strong effect.

19.
Null hypothesis tested	Absolute difference between sample means	Value of CD	Null hypothesis rejected?
$\mu_X = \mu_Y$	$\|2.00 - 4.00\| = 2.00$	2.38	No
$\mu_X = \mu_Z$	$\|2.00 - 6.00\| = 4.00$	2.38	Yes
$\mu_Y = \mu_Z$	$\|4.00 - 6.00\| = 2.00$	2.38	No

The nature of the relationship is such that Model 1 ($\overline{X}_1 = 2.00$) performs better than Model 3 ($\overline{X}_3 = 6.00$). However, we cannot conclude that either Model 1 or Model 3 differs in performance from Model 2 ($\overline{X}_2 = 4.00$).
20. The 95% Tukey HSD confidence interval for the mean difference between Model 1 and Model 2 is -4.39 to $.39$, for the mean difference between Model 1 and Model 3 is -6.39 to -1.61, and for the mean difference between Model 2 and Model 3 is -4.39 to $.39$.

25.
Source	SS	df	MS	F
Between	90.00	1	90.00	36.00
Within	20.00	8	2.50	
Total	110.00	9		

The critical value of F for an alpha level of .05 and 1 and 8 degrees of freedom is 5.32. Because the observed F value of 36.00 exceeds the critical value, we reject the null hypothesis and conclude that a relationship exists between the independent and dependent variables.

26. The observed value of t is -6.00. The square of this value is 36.00, which is equal to the observed value of F from Exercise 25. The critical values of t for an alpha level of .05 and 8 degrees of freedom are ± 2.306. The square of these values is 5.32, which is equal to the critical value of F from Exercise 25. This indicates that one-way between-subjects analysis of variance bears a mathematical relationship to the independent groups t test in the two-group case such that $F = t^2$.

27. One-way between-subjects analysis of variance
30. $n = 37$
32. d
36. b
37. c
38. b

40. a
41. a
43. b
45. d

48. a
49. c

51.

Source	SS	df	MS	F
Between	140.00	2	70.00	7.38
Within	256.00	27	9.48	
Total	396.00	29		

Null hypothesis tested	Absolute difference between sample means	Value of CD	Null hypothesis rejected?
$\mu_W = \mu_A$	$|3.00 - 8.00| = 5.00$	3.42	Yes
$\mu_W = \mu_H$	$|3.00 - 7.00| = 4.00$	3.42	Yes
$\mu_A = \mu_H$	$|8.00 - 7.00| = 1.00$	3.42	No

Results

A one-way analysis of variance that compared the judgments of the probability of guilt as a function of the defendant's race was found to be statistically significant at an alpha level of .05, $F(2, 27) = 7.38$, $p < .01$. The strength of the relationship was .35, as indexed by eta-squared.

A Tukey HSD test revealed that the mean guilt-probability judgment for the white defendant ($M = 3.00$, $SD = 2.79$) was significantly lower than the mean guilt-probability judgment for both the African American ($M = 8.00$, $SD = 3.02$) and the Hipanic ($M = 7.00$, $SD = 3.40$) defendants. The mean guilt-probability judgments for the African American and the Hispanic defendants did not

significantly differ. Table 1 presents the 95% Tukey HSD confidence interval for each pairwise comparison of means.

(Note: Table 1 would contain the relevant confidence intervals, which are -8.41 to -1.59 for the mean difference between the white defendant and the African American defendant conditions, -7.41 to $-.58$ for the mean difference between the white defendant and the Hispanic defendant conditions, and -2.41 to 4.41 for the mean difference between the African American defendant and the Hispanic defendant conditions.)

Chapter 13

3. This is because variability due to individual differences is removed from the dependent variable in the form of the sum of squares across subjects as part of the repeated measures analysis of variance procedure.

4.

Source	SS	df	MS	F
IV	20.00	4	5.00	1.67
Error	132.00	44	3.00	
Across subjects	46.00	11		
Total	198.00	59		

6. $df_{IV} = 4$; $df_{ACROSS\ SUBJECTS} = 20$; $df_{ERROR} = 80$; $df_{TOTAL} = 104$

7. a. 3.25   c. 3.34
   b. 2.76   d. 2.58

9. The Huynh–Feldt epsilon and the Greenhouse–Geisser epsilon increase the robustness by adjusting the degrees of freedom for the F test so that they are less than or equal to the degrees of freedom IV and the degrees of freedom error usually used in assessing the significance of the observed F ratio. The use of these adjusted degrees of freedom serves to decrease the Type I error rate and, thus, to increase the robustness of the statistical test.

11. A one-way repeated measures analysis of variance might be less powerful than a corresponding one-way between-subjects analysis of variance when the F ratio for the repeated measures test is similar to the F ratio for the between-subjects test because individual differences have only a minimal influence

on the dependent variable. This reflects that the degrees of freedom for the denominator of the F test will always be less in the repeated measures case than in the between-subjects case and that the value of F required to reject the null hypothesis becomes more extreme as the degrees of freedom become smaller.

13.

Source	SS	df	MS	F
IV	14.53	2	7.26	4.78
Error	12.14	8	1.52	
Across subjects	24.26	4		
Total	50.93	14		

The critical value of F for an alpha level of .05 and 2 and 8 degrees of freedom is 4.46. Because the observed F value of 4.78 exceeds the critical value, we reject the null hypothesis and conclude that there is a relationship between the time of assessment and anxiety.

14. The value of eta-squared is .54 using both Equations 13.14 and 13.15. This represents a strong effect.

15.

Null hypothesis tested	Absolute difference between sample means	Value of CD	Null hypothesis rejected?
$\mu_1 = \mu_2$	$|3.80 - 5.20| = 1.40$	2.23	No
$\mu_1 = \mu_3$	$|3.80 - 6.20| = 2.40$	2.23	Yes
$\mu_2 = \mu_3$	$|5.20 - 6.20| = 1.00$	2.23	No

The nature of the relationship is such that anxiety is greater at Time 3 ($\overline{X}_3 = 6.20$) than at Time 1 ($\overline{X}_1 = 3.80$). However, we cannot conclude that anxiety at either Time 1 or Time 3 differs from anxiety at Time 2 ($\overline{X}_2 = 5.20$).

16. The 95% Tukey HSD confidence interval for the mean difference between Time 1 and Time 2 is -3.63 to .83, for the mean difference between Time 1 and Time 3 is -4.63 to $-.17$, and for the mean difference between Time 2 and Time 3 is -3.23 to 1.23.

17.

Source	SS	df	MS	F
Between	14.53	2	7.26	2.40
Within	36.40	12	3.03	
Total	50.93	14		

Analyzing the data as if the independent variable were between-subjects in nature, the observed value of F does not exceed the critical value of 3.88, so we fail to reject the null hypothesis. The value of eta-squared in this instance is .29. This represents a strong effect. The 95% Tukey HSD confidence interval for the mean difference between Time 1 and Time 2 is -4.34 to 1.54, for the mean difference between Time 1 and Time 3 is -5.34 to .54, and for the mean difference between Time 2 and Time 3 is -3.94 to 1.94.

The fact that eta-squared was .54 in the repeated measures case but only .29 in the between-subjects case indicates that individual differences had a sizeable effect on the dependent variable. The fact that the null hypothesis was rejected when a one-way repeated measures analysis of variance was applied but not when a one-way between-subjects analysis of variance was applied illustrates the increased power of the statistical analysis when variability due to individual differences is identified and removed from the dependent variable.

22. One-way between-subjects analysis of variance
23. Correlated groups t test

27. .50	34. c	43. d
28. b	37. c	44. b
29. d	40. b	46. c
32. c	42. c	47. d

49.

Source	SS	df	MS	F
IV	220.00	3	73.33	36.66
Error	24.00	12	2.00	
Across subjects	16.00	4		
Total	260.00	19		

Null hypothesis tested	Absolute difference between sample means	Value of CD	Null hypothesis rejected?
$\mu_H = \mu_E$	$|18.00 - 14.00| = 4.00$	2.66	Yes
$\mu_H = \mu_C$	$|18.00 - 10.00| = 8.00$	2.66	Yes
$\mu_H = \mu_V$	$|18.00 - 10.00| = 8.00$	2.66	Yes
$\mu_E = \mu_C$	$|14.00 - 10.00| = 4.00$	2.66	Yes
$\mu_E = \mu_V$	$|14.00 - 10.00| = 4.00$	2.66	Yes
$\mu_C = \mu_V$	$|10.00 - 10.00| = .00$	2.66	No

Results

A one-way repeated measures analysis of variance that compared the mean ratings of how important the four factors (health risks, effectiveness, cost, and convenience) would be in deciding whether to use a male oral contraceptive was found to be statistically significant at an alpha level of .05, $F(3, 12) = 36.66$, $p < .01$. The strength of the relationship, as indexed by eta-squared, was .90.

A Tukey HSD test indicated that the health risks factor ($M = 18.00$, $SD = 1.58$) was rated as significantly more important than the other three factors and that the effectiveness factor ($M = 14.00$, $SD = 1.58$) was rated as significantly more important than both the cost ($M = 10.00$, $SD = 1.58$) and the convenience $M = 10.00$, $SD = 1.58$) factors. The means for the cost and the convenience factors did not significantly differ. Table 1 presents the 95% confidence interval for each pairwise comparison of means.

(Note: Table 1 would contain the relevant confidence intervals, which are 1.34 to 6.66 for the mean difference between the ratings for the health risks and the effectiveness factors, 5.34 to 10.66 for the mean difference between the ratings for the health risks and the cost factors, 5.34 to 10.66 for the mean difference between the ratings for the health risks and the convenience factors, 1.34 to 6.66 for the mean difference between the ratings for the effectiveness and the cost factors, 1.34 to 6.66 for the mean difference between the ratings for the effectiveness and the convenience factors, and −2.66 to 2.66 for the mean difference between the ratings for the cost and the convenience factors.)

Chapter 14

2. The procedures are equivalent because the critical values of r using the latter approach are the values of r that correspond to the critical values of t using the former approach.
3. a. ±.349   d. −.441
   b. ±.423   e. ±.241
   c. +.360
6. The critical values of r for an alpha level of .05 and 8 degrees of freedom are ±.632. Because the observed r value of +.74 is greater than +.632, we reject the null hypothesis and conclude that there is some degree of a linear relationship between the two variables.
7. The value of r^2 is .55. This represents a strong effect.
8. The 95% confidence interval is 0.21 to 0.93.

9. The two variables approximate a direct linear relationship.
14. Independent groups t test
15. One-way repeated measures analysis of variance
16. Correlated groups t test
19. $N = 54$
22. The estimated standard error of estimate estimates the average error that will be made across the population when predicting scores on Y from the regression equation.
23. $\hat{Y} = 6.87 + .46X$; 8.25; 10.09; 11.93
24. 1.71
27. b   36. c
29. d   37. b
32. b   39. a
33. a   43. b
35. d   44. c
47.   Results
   A Pearson correlation between the leader's LPC score ($M = 67.30$, $SD = 4.79$) and the amount of time that it took each group to solve the problem ($M = 10.90$, $SD = 4.04$) was found to be statistically significant at an alpha level of .05, $r(8) = .67$, $p < .05$. This suggests that these two variables are positively related and, thus, that group problem-solving performance tends to deteriorate as the leader's LPC score increases. The 95% confidence interval for the correlation coefficient was .07 to .91.

   The regression equation for predicting the number of minutes that it will take a group to solve the problem from the leader's LPC score was found to be $\hat{Y} = -27.39 + (.57) X$, and the estimated standard error of estimate was found to be 3.18.
50. The critical values of r for an alpha level of .05 and 8 degrees of freedom are ±.632. Because the observed r value of .75 is greater than +.632, we reject the null hypothesis and conclude that some degree of linear relationship exists between GRE-A scores and graduate GPA. The 95% confidence interval for the correlation coefficient is 0.28 to 0.94.

   The regression equation for predicting graduate GPA from GRE-A scores is $\hat{Y} = .52 + .005X$. Based on this equation, the predicted 2-year grade point averages of Applicants 1, 3, 5, and 7 are all greater than 3.00, so these applicants are viable candidates for admission.

Chapter 15

4. Observed frequencies are the frequencies that are actually observed in an investigation. Expected frequencies are the frequencies that we would expect

to observe if the two variables under study were unrelated in the population.

5. 110

7. 255

8.

Cell	E
Romance—infrequent	10.59
Romance—moderate	15.00
Romance—frequent	19.41
Comedy—infrequent	21.18
Comedy—moderate	30.00
Comedy—frequent	38.82
Drama—infrequent	28.24
Drama—moderate	40.00
Drama—frequent	51.76

9. a. 3.841   c. 5.991
   b. 9.488   d. 16.919

11. The disadvantage is that Yates' correction tends to reduce the power of the chi-square test below what it would otherwise be while adding little control over Type I errors.

13. The critical value of χ^2 for an alpha level of .05 and 1 degree of freedom is 3.841. Because the observed χ^2 value of 7.11 exceeds the critical value, we reject the null hypothesis and conclude that there is a relationship between smoking behavior and cause of death.

14. .22

15. Examination of the $(O - E)^2/E$ and $O - E$ values suggests that smokers are more likely than expected to die of cancer and less likely than expected to die of other causes, whereas the reverse is true of nonsmokers.

16. The observed χ^2 using Equation 15.5 is 7.11. This is the same value as was obtained in Exercise 13 using Equation 15.2.

20. The advantage of analyzing quantitative variables with parametric tests rather than the chi-square test is that parametric tests tend to be more powerful. An advantage of the chi-square approach is that any quantitative variable that must be measured on a level that at least approximates interval characteristics for a parametric test need be measured on only an ordinal level for the χ^2 test.

21. Pearson correlation

22. Chi-square test

27. .85

28. The critical value of χ^2 for an alpha level of .05 and 3 degrees of freedom is 7.815. Because the observed

χ^2 value of 11.37 exceeds the critical value, we reject the null hypothesis and conclude that the distribution of evening news program preference for the population of college students is not the same as national ratings.

29. Examination of the $(O - E)^2/E$ and $O - E$ values suggests that college students are more likely than expected to prefer the CBS and NBC evening news programs, and less likely than expected to prefer the ABC evening news program or to have no evening news program preference.

34. b

36. a   41. b

37. d   43. a

40. b   44. c

46.   Results

    A chi-square test of the relationship between the gender of the central character and the role portrayed by that character was found to be statistically significant at an alpha level of .05, $\chi^2(1, N = 315) = 10.68$, $p < .01$. The observed frequencies for the four cells can be found in Table 1.

    The strength of the relationship, as indexed by the fourfold point correlation coefficient, was .18. This primarily reflects the fact that female central characters are less likely than expected to be portrayed as authorities and more likely than expected to be portrayed as users.

(Note: Table 1 would be similar to the table in the exercise, but it would also include the marginal frequencies.)

Chapter 16

3.

Set I	Set II	Set III	Set IV
5	1.5	1.5	4
2	1.5	6	2
6	6	4.5	2
1	5	1.5	2
3.5	3	4.5	5
3.5	4	3	6

5. The rank transformation approach to nonparametric analysis involves converting a set of scores on a variable to ranks and then analyzing these rank scores using the traditional parametric formulas.

7. The critical values of z for an alpha level of .05 are ±1.96. Because the observed z value of .39 does not exceed the positive critical value, we fail to reject the null hypothesis of no relationship between car ownership and performance in school.

8. .09

9. The critical value of U for an alpha level of .05 and $n_1 = n_2 = 8$ is 13. Because the observed U value of 25 is not equal to or less than 13, we fail to reject the null hypothesis of no relationship between gender and attitudes toward the pill.

10. .22

15. The critical value of χ_r^2 for an alpha level of .05 and 2 degrees of freedom is 5.991. Because the observed χ_r^2 value of 7.20 exceeds the critical value, we reject the null hypothesis and conclude that there is a relationship between the brand of picture tube and quality ratings. (Note: The nature of the relationship can be determined using the Dunn procedure.)

16. .36

17. The critical values of r_s for an alpha level of .05 and N + 18 are ±.475. Because the observed r_s value of +.48 is greater than +.475, we reject the null hypothesis and conclude that there is a relationship between crime rates in cities and the size of a city's police force. The strength of the relationship, as indicated by the magnitude of the correlation coefficient, is .48. The nature of the relationship, as indicated by the sign of the correlation coefficient, is that the two variables approximate a direct linear relationship.

18. d

21. a	31. a
22. b	32. d
24. a	36. d
25. a	37. b
30. a	38. b

42.
Results
A Wilcoxon signed-rank test using an alpha level of .05 compared individuals' self-esteem before versus after participating in the encounter session. The rank sums (22 for the positive differences and 33 for the negative differences) were found to not significantly differ, $N = 10$, $T = 22$, $p < .10$.

43.
Results
A Kruskal–Wallis test compared memory for the positive ($\bar{R} = 8.60$), the negative ($\bar{R} = 5.40$), and the neutral ($\bar{R} = 10.0$) words. The resulting value of H was found to be statistically nonsignificant at an alpha level of .05, $H(2, N = 15) = 2.78$, $p > .30$.

Chapter 17

2. 2; 2; 3

5. The term *main effect* has two related meanings in the context of two-way factorial designs. First, a main effect refers to the comparison of the means for one independent variable collapsing across the levels of the other independent variable. Second, a main effect is said to be present if the null hypothesis concerning that effect is rejected.

6. An interaction effect refers to the comparison of the cell means in terms of whether the nature of the relationship between one of the independent variables and the dependent variable differs as a function of the other independent variable. If the null hypothesis of no interaction effect is rejected, an interaction is said to be present.

7.

	Main effect of factor A?	Main effect of factor B?	Interaction?
a.	No	Yes	No
b.	Yes	No	No
c.	Yes	Yes	No

9.

	B_1	B_2	B_3
A_1	6.00	5.00	4.00
A_2	1.00	2.00	3.00

11. Nonparallel lines in a graph of population means indicate that an interaction is present. Nonparallel lines in a graph of sample means indicate that an interaction *might* be present. The difference in the two situations is due to the fact that, because of the role of sampling error, nonparallel lines in a graph of sample means do not necessarily indicate that an interaction exists in the population.

14.

Source	SS	df	MS	F
A	20.00	2	10.00	5.00
B	45.00	3	15.00	7.50
$A \times B$	60.00	6	10.00	5.00
Within	216.00	108	2.00	
Total	341.00	119		

16. a. 4.00; 3.15; 3.15
    b. 4.04; 2.80; 2.80
    c. 3.10; 3.10; 2.47
    d. 2.76; 3.15; 2.25
18. 2; 3; 6
19. 54; 9
20. 130.00
21. Hypotheses for the main effect of factor A:

H_0: $\mu_{A_1} = \mu_{A_2}$
H_1: $\mu_{A_1} \neq \mu_{A_2}$

Hypotheses for the main effect of factor B:

H_0: $\mu_{B_1} = \mu_{B_2} = \mu_{B_3}$
H_1: The three population means are not all equal

Hypotheses for the interaction effect:

H_0: The difference between the population means for factor A is the same at each level of factor B
H_1: The difference between the population means for factor A differs depending on the levels of factor B

22. The critical value of F for an alpha level of .05 and 1 and 48 degrees of freedom is 4.04. Because the observed F value of 10.00 for the main effect of factor A exceeds the critical value, we reject the null hypothesis and conclude that there is a relationship between this factor and the dependent variable.

The critical value of F for an alpha level of .05 and 2 and 48 degrees of freedom is 3.19. Because the observed F value of 4.00 for the main effect of factor B exceeds the critical value, we reject the null hypothesis and conclude that a relationship exists between this factor and the dependent variable.

The observed F value of 4.00 for the interaction effect exceeds the critical value of 3.19 for an alpha level of .05 and 2 and 48 degrees of freedom, so we reject the null hypothesis and conclude that there is an interaction.

23. The value of eta-squared for the main effect of factor A is .14. This represents a moderate effect. The value of eta-squared for both the main effect of factor B and the interaction effect is .11. These also represent moderate effects.
24. 6; 10; 9
25. The critical value of F for an alpha level of .05 and 1 and 60 degrees of freedom is 4.00. Because the observed F value of 24.00 for the main effect of factor A exceeds the critical value, we reject the null hypothesis and conclude that a relationship exists between this factor and the dependent variable. Scores in

condition A_2 ($\overline{X}_{A_2} = 19.33$) are significantly higher than scores in condition A_1 ($\overline{X}_{A_1} = 15.00$).
26. The critical value of F for an alpha level of .05 and 2 and 60 degrees of freedom is 3.15. Because the observed F value of 45.50 for the main effect of factor B exceeds the critical value, we reject the null hypothesis and conclude that there is a relationship between this factor and the dependent variable.

The HSD test can be applied as follows:

Null hypothesis tested	Absolute difference between sample means	Value of CD	Null hypothesis rejected?
$\mu_{B_1} = \mu_{B_2}$	$\lvert 12.00 - 17.50 \rvert = 5.50$	2.29	Yes
$\mu_{B_1} = \mu_{B_3}$	$\lvert 12.00 - 22.00 \rvert = 10.00$	2.29	Yes
$\mu_{B_2} = \mu_{B_3}$	$\lvert 17.50 - 22.00 \rvert = 4.50$	2.29	Yes

The nature of the relationship is such that the sores in Condition B_3 ($\overline{X}_{B_3} = 22.00$) are significantly higher than the scores in Condition B_2 ($\overline{X}_{B_2} = 17.50$) and Condition B_1 ($\overline{X}_{B_1} = 12.00$). In turn, the scores in Condition B_2 are significantly higher than the scores in Condition B_1.
27. The critical value of F for an alpha level of .05 and 2 and 60 degrees of freedom is 3.15. Because the observed F value of .50 for the interaction effect does not exceed the critical value, we fail to reject the null hypothesis of no interaction between factor A and factor B.
36. Unequal cell sizes are problematic because they introduce a relationship between the two independent variables into the sample. The introduction of such a relationship creates a number of statistical and conceptual issues for testing the two main effects and the interaction effect.
37. $n = 38$
40. c
42. b
44. b
45. b
48. b

50.

Source	SS	df	MS	F
A (supposed time)	18.87	2	9.43	11.79
B (weight)	22.53	1	22.53	28.17
A × B	11.27	2	5.63	7.04
Within	19.20	24	.80	
Total	71.87	29		

HSD test for the main effect of supposed time:

Null hypothesis tested	Absolute difference between sample means	Value of CD	Null hypothesis rejected?
$\mu_F = \mu_T$	$|6.00 - 7.30| = 1.30$	1.00	Yes
$\mu_F = \mu_O$	$|6.00 - 7.90| = 1.90$	1.00	Yes
$\mu_T = \mu_O$	$|7.30 - 7.90| = .60$	1.00	No

Interaction comparisons [Note: When the F ratios for two interaction comparisons are the same, the determination of which is tested against the smaller "critical alpha" should be based on theoretical considerations, when relevant. When theory does not suggest an ordering, as in our example, both F ratios can be tested against the average of the two "critical alphas" that would otherwise be used. Thus, the "critical alpha" is $(.05/3 + .05/2)/2 = (.017 + .025)/2 = .021$ for the first two interaction comparisons.]:

Interaction comparison	F ratio	p value	Critical alpha	Interaction comparison significant?
$A \times B_{(1)}$	10.56	.003	.021	Yes
$A \times B_{(2)}$	10.56	.003	.021	Yes
$A \times B_{(3)}$	0	1.000	$.05/1 = .050$	No

Results

Hunger scores were subjected to a two-way analysis of variance having three levels of supposed time (11:00, 12:00, and 1:00) and two levels of weight (overweight versus normal). All effects were found to be statistically significant at an alpha level of .05.

The main effect of weight was such that overweight individuals ($M = 7.93$, $SD = 1.67$) reported significantly greater hunger than normal-weight individuals ($M = 6.20$, $SD = .86$), $F(1, 24) = 28.17$, $p < .01$. The strength of the relationship, as indexed by eta-squared, was .31.

The nature of the main effect of supposed time, $F(2, 24) = 11.79$, $p = .01$, was determined using a Tukey HSD test. This indicated that hunger was significantly greater at both 12:00 ($M = 7.30$, $SD = 1.64$) and 1:00 ($M = 7.90$, $SD = 1.66$) than at 11:00 ($M = 6.00$, $SD = .67$). The 12:00 and 1:00 means did not significantly differ. As indexed by eta-squared, the strength of the relationship was .26.

The interaction effect, $F(2, 24) = 7.04$, $p < .01$, was analyzed using interaction comparisons in conjunction with a modified Bonferroni procedure (Holland & Copenhaver, 1988) based on an overall alpha level of .05. The means and standard deviations for the six cells can be found in Table 1.

The 2×2 subtables for 11:00 versus 12:00 and 11:00 versus 1:00 yielded statistically significant interaction comparisons. Overweight individuals reported greater hunger at 12:00 than at 11:00 ($8.60 - 6.00 = 2.60$) relative to normal-weight individuals ($6.00 - 6.00 = .00$). The former individuals also reported greater hunger at 1:00 than at 11:00 ($9.20 - 6.00 = 3.20$) relative to the latter ($6.60 - 6.00 = .60$). The change in hunger between 1:00 and 12:00 did not differ for overweight ($9.20 - 8.60 = .60$) versus normal-weight ($6.60 - 6.00 = .60$) participants. The strength of the overall interaction effect, as indexed by eta-squared, was .16.

Table 1

Mean Hunger as a Function of Supposed Time and Weight

	Supposed time		
Weight	11:00	12:00	1:00
Overweight	6.00 (.71)	8.60 (1.14)	9.20 (.84)
Normal	6.00 (.71)	6.00 (.71)	6.60 (1.14)

Note. Standard deviations are in parentheses. For each cell, $n = 5$.

Chapter 18

1. The chi-square test
4. The most common method of analysis for two between-subjects variables that are measured on a level that at least approximates interval characteristics is Pearson correlation. This technique evaluates a *linear* relationship between variables. If the expected relationship is nonlinear, procedures for nonlinear relationships can be applied. When one or both variables are measured on an ordinal level that markedly departs from interval level characteristics, Spearman rank-order correlation or Kendall's tau is usually the test of choice. The Case II statistics elaborated in Table 18.2 might be applicable when the independent variable is within-subjects in nature or has fewer

than five or so values associated with it. If the dependent variable has only two or three values, the chi-square test or log-linear analysis can be used.

5. The independent variable is the time of year. This variable is qualitative in nature. The dependent variable is scores on the depression scale. This variable is quantitative in nature. Hence, this is a Case II situation. Because the independent variable is within-subjects and has two levels, the appropriate parametric and nonparametric tests for analyzing the relationship between the variables are the correlated groups t test and the Wilcoxon signed-rank test, respectively.

6. The independent variable is the color of the ice cream. This variable is qualitative in nature. The dependent variable is the taste ratings. This variable is quantitative in nature. Hence, this is a Case II situation. Because the independent variable is within-subjects and has three levels, the appropriate parametric and nonparametric tests for analyzing the relationship between the variables are one-way repeated measures analysis of variance and Friedman analysis of variance by ranks, respectively.

7. The independent variable is the noise level. This variable is quantitative in nature. The dependent variable is the amount of growth. This variable is also quantitative in nature. Hence, this is a Case IV situation. Because the independent variable is between-subjects and has only two levels, the appropriate parametric and nonparametric tests for analyzing the relationship between the variables are the independent groups t test and the Wilcoxon rank sum test/Mann–Whitney U test, respectively.

8. The independent variable is parents' marital status. This variable is qualitative in nature. The dependent variable is the presence or absence of an imaginary friend. This variable is also qualitative in nature. Hence, this is a Case I situation. Because both variables are between-subjects, the appropriate test for analyzing the relationship between the variables is the chi-square test.

9. The independent variable is social class. This variable is quantitative in nature. The dependent variable is dogmatism. This variable is also quantitative in nature. Hence, this is a Case IV situation. The appropriate parametric and nonparametric tests for analyzing the relationship between the variables are Pearson correlation (assuming that the expected relationship is linear) and Spearman rank-order correlation, respectively.

10. The independent variable is the number of close friends people have. This variable is quantitative in nature. The dependent variable is whether or not people feel that these friends would, in general, "be there" for them in an emergency. This variable is qualitative in nature. Hence, this is a Case III situation. The appropriate test for analyzing the relationship between the variables is the chi-square test, logistic regression, or multinomial logistic regression.

11. The independent variable is the sipping rate of the experimental assistant. This variable is quantitative in nature. The dependent variable is participants' consumption time. This variable is also quantitative in nature. Hence, this is a Case IV situation. Because the independent variable is between-subjects and has only three levels, the appropriate parametric and nonparametric tests for analyzing the relationship between the variables are one-way between-subjects analysis of variance and the Kruskal-Wallis test, respectively.

12. The independent variable is whether or not hypnosis was administered. This variable is qualitative in nature. The dependent variable is the change in hand temperature. This variable is quantitative in nature. Hence, this is a Case II situation. Because the independent variable is between-subjects and has two levels, the appropriate parametric and nonparametric tests for analyzing the relationship between the variables are the independent groups t test and the Wilcoxon rank sum test/Mann–Whitney U test, respectively.

13. The independent variable is the time before taking the exam. This variable is quantitative in nature. The dependent variable is scores on the Palmer Sweat Index. This variable is also quantitative in nature. Hence, this is a Case IV situation. Because the independent variable is within-subjects and has four levels, the appropriate parametric and nonparametric tests for analyzing the relationship between the variables are one-way repeated measures analysis of variance and Friedman analysis of variance by ranks, respectively.

23. The defining characteristic of multivariate statistics is that they analyze the relationship among three or more variables.

25. Multivariate analysis of variance tests whether the groups of interest have different population means on two or more dependent variables considered jointly. When applied to a single between-subjects

independent variable that has only two levels, multivariate analysis of variance is called the Hotelling T^2 test.

27. A regression coefficient (b) indicates the "slope" for a predictor variable in the context of multiple regression and represents the number of units that the criterion variable is predicted to change for each unit change in that variable when the other predictor variables are held constant. A squared multiple correlation coefficient (R^2) indicates the strength of the relationship between the criterion variable and the set of predictor variables. Specifically, it indicates the proportion of variability in the criterion variable that is associated with the predictor variables considered simultaneously.

28. The goal of factor analysis is to determine whether the correlations among a set of variables can be accounted for by one or more underlying dimensions. This is accomplished by analyzing the patterning of correlations (or covariances) between all pairs of variables in the data set in terms of the type of factor structure—that is, the number and makeup of factors—that might underlie the data.

32. c

33. a

36. a

37. b

39. a

Glossary of Major Symbols

Numbers in parentheses indicate the sections where the symbols are first discussed.

A Factor A (17.4)

a Intercept of a line (5.2)/Number of levels of factor A (17.4)

$A \times B$ Interaction of factor A and factor B (17.4)

B Factor B (17.4)

b Slope of a line (5.2)/Number of levels of factor B (17.4)/Regression coefficient (18.6)

C Number of pairs of mean ranks or rank sums to be tested using the Dunn procedure (16.6)

c Number of levels of the column variable in a contingency table (15.4)

$_nC_r$ Number of combinations of n things taken r at a time (6.7)

CD   Critical difference for the Tukey HSD test (12.5)

cf Cumulative frequency (2.1)

CI   Confidence interval (8.11)

CMF_j Column marginal frequency associated with cell j (15.4)

crf Cumulative relative frequency (2.1)

D Difference between raw (11.2) or rank scores (16.8) for an individual

d Signed deviation of an individual's score from the group mean (12.2)

$\bar{D}$ Mean difference score in a sample (11.2)

df Degrees of freedom (*Note:* If df is subscripted, the subscript indicates the source of variability to which the degrees of freedom apply.) (7.5)

E Expected value of the sum of ranks for the Wilcoxon signed-rank test (16.5)

E_j Expected frequency for cell j (15.4) or category j (15.14)/Expected rank sum for group j for the Wilcoxon rank sum test (16.4)

E_R^2 Epsilon-squared (16.6)

eta^2 Eta-squared statistic (10.4)

F F ratio (12.2)

f Frequency of a score (2.1)

G Grand mean (10.3)

H	H statistic in the Kruskal–Wallis test (16.6)
H_0	Null hypothesis (8.2)
H_1	Alternative hypothesis (8.2)
i	Size of the interval of a numerical category (3.1)
IQR	Interquartile range (3.2)
k	Number of levels of a variable (12.2)
L	Lower real limit of a numerical category (3.1)/Number of levels of the variable that has the fewer values in a contingency table (15.6)
$\log_e$	Calculation of the natural logarithm of a number (Appendix 14.1)
M	Sample mean in American Psychological Association format (3.10)
Mdn	Median (3.1)
MS	Mean square (*Note:* If MS is subscripted, the subscript indicates the source of variability to which the mean square applies.) (7.5)
N	Total sample size (1.9)
n	Number of scores in a subgroup (3.9)/Number of trials in the binomial expression (6.8)
n'	Adjusted per-cell sample size necessary to achieve a desired level of power for two-way between-subjects analysis of variance (17.10)
n_L	Number of individuals with scores less than a specified value (3.1)
n_T	Tabled per-cell sample size necessary to achieve a desired level of power for two-way between-subjects analysis of variance (17.10)
n_W	Number of individuals with scores within a numerical category (3.1)
O_j	Observed frequency for cell j (15.4) or category j (15.14)
P	Percentile (4.1)
p	Probability (2.8)/Probability of a "success" in the binomial expression (6.8)/ Significance or probability level (8.12)/Sample proportion (Appendix 15.1)
$_nP_r$	Number of permutations of n things taken r at a time (6.7)
$p(A)$	Probability of event A (1.8)
$p(A\vert B)$	Conditional probability of event A, given event B (6.2)
$p(A, B)$	Joint probability of *both* event A *and* event B (6.3)
$p(A \text{ or } B)$	Probability of *at least one* of event A and event B (6.4)
PR_X	Percentile rank of the score X (4.1)
q	Probability of a "failure" in the binomial expression (6.8)/Studentized range value (12.5)
r	Sample Pearson correlation coefficient (5.3)/Number of "successes" in the binomial expression (6.8)/Number of levels of the row variable in a contingency table (15.4)
R^2	Multiple correlation coefficient (18.6)
r^2	Coefficient of determination (14.4)
r' (r prime)	Fisher's logarithmic transformation of r (Appendix 14.1)

r_C Matched-pairs rank biserial correlation coefficient (16.5)

r_g Glass rank biserial correlation coefficient (16.4)

r_i Number of mutually exclusive and exhaustive events that can occur on trial i (6.7)

R_j R statistic in the Wilcoxon rank sum test (16.4)/Sum of the ranks in condition j for the Kruskal–Wallis test (16.6) and Friedman analysis of variance by ranks (16.7)

R_n Sum of the ranks of the negative differences for the Wilcoxon signed-rank test (16.5)

R_p Sum of the ranks of the positive differences for the Wilcoxon signed-rank test (16.5)

r_s Sample Spearman rank-order correlation coefficient (16.8)

rf Relative frequency (2.1)

rf_j Relative frequency in the population for category j (15.14)

RMF_j Row marginal frequency associated with cell j (15.4)

s Sample standard deviation (3.2)

s^2 Sample variance (3.2)

$\hat{s}$ (s-hat)   Standard deviation estimate (7.3)

$\hat{s}^2$ Variance estimate (7.3)

$\hat{s}_D$ Estimated standard deviation of population difference scores (11.2)

$\hat{s}_{\bar{D}}$ Estimated standard error of the mean of difference scores (11.2)

s_i^2 Square of the sum of the scores of individual i (13.2)

$\hat{s}^2_{pooled}$ Pooled variance estimate (10.2)

$\hat{s}_{\bar{X}}$ Estimated standard error of the mean (7.8)

$\hat{s}_{\bar{X}_1 - \bar{X}_2}$ Estimated standard error of the difference (10.2)

s_{YX} Sample standard error of estimate (5.6)

$\hat{s}_{YX}$ Estimated standard error of estimate (14.10)

SCP Sum of cross-products (5.2)

SD Standard deviation estimate in American Psychological Association format (3.10)

SS Sum of squares (*Note:* If SS is subscripted, the subscript indicates the source of variability to which the sum of squares applies.) (3.2)

T T score (transformed standard score in a distribution that has a mean of 50.00 and a standard deviation of 10.00) (4.5)/Treatment effect (10.4)/T statistic in the Wilcoxon signed-rank test (16.5)

t t statistic (8.10)/Number of scores tied at a particular rank for the Wilcoxon rank sum test and the Kruskal–Wallis test (Appendix 16.1)

T_j^2 Square of the sum of the scores in condition j (12.2)

$T_{A_i}^2$ Square of the sum of the scores at level i of factor A (17.4)

$T_{A_i B_j}^2$ Square of the sum of the scores in cell $A_i B_j$ (17.4)

$T_{B_j}^2$ Square of the sum of the scores at level j of factor B (17.4)

U Mann–Whitney U statistic (16.4)

u Uniqueness of a score (Applications to the Analysis of a Social Problem, Chapter 4)

V Fourfold point correlation coefficient/Cramer's statistic (15.6)

W Concordance coefficient (16.7)

X General name for a variable (1.9)/A predictor variable (14.9)

$\overline{X}$ Sample mean for variable X (3.1)

$\overline{X}_i$ Mean X score for individual i across conditions (11.3)/Mean for one of the groups being considered when calculating a confidence interval when the independent variable has three or more levels (12.6)

$\overline{X}_j$ Mean for one of the groups being considered when calculating a confidence interval when the independent variable has three or more levels (12.6)

X_n Nullified score on variable X (10.4)

X_p Score value defining the Pth percentile (4.1)

Y A criterion variable (14.10)

$\hat{Y}$ (predicted Y)   Predicted score on variable Y (5.6)

z Standard score in a normal distribution (4.4)/z statistic (8.2)

α (alpha)   Probability of a Type I error (8.6)/Intercept of a line for the population (14.2)

β (beta)   Probability of a Type II error (8.6)/Slope of a line for the population (14.2)

χ^2 (chi-square)   Chi-square statistic (15.4)

χ_r^2 Test statistic for Friedman analysis of variance by ranks (16.7)

ε (epsilon)   Error score for an individual in the population (14.2)

μ (mu)   Mean of a population (3.9) and of a sampling distribution of the mean (7.7)

μ_D Mean difference score in a population and in a sampling distribution of the mean of difference scores (11.2)

π (pi)   Population proportion (Appendix 15.1)

ρ (rho)   Population Pearson correlation coefficient (14.2)

ρ' Log-transformed value of ρ (Appendix 14.1)

ρ_s Population Spearman rank-order correlation coefficient (16.8)

Σ (sigma)   Summation sign (1.9)

σ (sigma)   Population standard deviation (3.9)

σ^2 Population variance (3.9)

$\sigma_{\overline{D}}$ Standard error of the mean of difference scores (11.2)

σ_R Standard deviation of the sampling distribution of R for the Wilcoxon rank sum test (16.4)

$\sigma_{r'}$ Standard error of r' (Appendix 14.1)

σ_T Standard deviation of the sampling distribution of T for the Wilcoxon signed-rank test (16.5)

$\sigma_{\bar{X}}$ Population standard error of the mean (7.7)

$\sigma_{\bar{X}_1 - \bar{X}_2}$ Population standard error of the difference (10.2)

! (factorial)   Factorial of a number (6.7)

$1 - \beta$ Power of a statistical test (8.6)

. . .   Indication to include all relevant values that fall between the written values in the algebraic operation (6.7)

Index